Lecture Notes in Computer Science 4153

Nanning Zheng Xiaoyi Jiang
Xuguang Lan (Eds.)

Advances in Machine Vision, Image Processing, and Pattern Analysis

International Workshop on Intelligent Computing in Pattern Analysis/Synthesis, IWICPAS 2006
Xi'an, China, August 26-27, 2006
Proceedings

Springer

Volume Editors

Nanning Zheng
Xi'an Jiaotong University
Institute of Artificial Intelligence and Robotics
Xianning West Road 28, 710049 Xi'an, China
E-mail: nnzheng@mail.xjtu.edu.cn

Xiaoyi Jiang
University of Münster
Department of Mathematics and Computer Science
Einsteinstrasse 62, 48149 Münster, Germany
E-mail: xjiang@math.uni-muenster.de

Xuguang Lan
Xi'an Jiaotong University
Institute of Artificial Intelligence and Robotics
Xianning West Road 28, 710049 Xi'an, China
E-mail: xglan@aiar.xjtu.edu.cn

Library of Congress Control Number: 2006930874

CR Subject Classification (1998): I.4, I.5, I.2.10, I.2.6, I.3.5, F.2.2

LNCS Sublibrary: SL 6 – Image Processing, Computer Vision, Pattern Recognition, and Graphics

ISSN 0302-9743
ISBN-10 3-540-37597-X Springer Berlin Heidelberg New York
ISBN-13 978-3-540-37597-5 Springer Berlin Heidelberg New York

Springer is a part of Springer Science+Business Media

springer.com

Printed in Germany

Typesetting: Camera-ready by author, data conversion by Scientific Publishing Services, Chennai, India
Printed on acid-free paper SPIN: 11821045 06/3142 5 4 3 2 1 0

Preface

This volume contains the papers presented at the International Workshop on Intelligent Computing in Pattern Analysis/Synthesis (IWICPAS 2006), which was organized as a satellite workshop of the 18th International Conference on Pattern Recognition (ICPR 2006) in Hong Kong. This workshop brings together researchers and engineers from the field of pattern analysis/synthesis around the world. It is an international forum for identifying, encouraging and exchanging new ideas on different topics of pattern analysis/synthesis as well as promoting novel applications in an attempt to extend the frontiers of this fascinating research field.

IWICPAS 2006 attracted a record number of 264 paper submissions from 20 different countries. Out of these, 51 papers were accepted by the Program Committee for publication in this volume. The papers in this volume cover topics including: object detection, tracking and recognition, pattern representation and modeling, visual pattern modeling, image processing, compression and coding and texture analysis/synthesis.

The organization of IWICPAS 2006 benefited from the collaboration of many individuals. Foremost, we express our appreciation to the Program Committee members and the additional reviewers who provided thorough and timely reviews. We thank Xuelong Li for his technical assistance with publication of a special issue of the *International Journal of Computer Mathematics* (IJCM, Taylor & Francis). Finally, we thank the members of the IWICPAS 2006 Executive Committee for all their efforts in making IWICPAS 2006 a successful workshop.

It would have been impossible to organize the workshop without the financial support of the National Natural Science Foundation of China. In addition, the technical support of Xi'an Jiaotong University is gratefully acknowledged.

August 2006

Ruwei Dai
Workshop Chair, IWICPAS 2006
Nanning Zheng
Program Chair, IWICPAS 2006
Xiaoyi Jiang
Program Co-chair, IWICPAS 2006

Organization

IWICPAS 2006 was organized by the Institute of Artificial Intelligence and Robotics, Xi'an Jiaotong University, China.

Executive Committee

Workshop Chair:	Ruwei Dai (Institute of Automation, Academia Sinica, China)
Program Chair:	Nanning Zheng (Xi'an Jiaotong University, China)
Program Co-chair:	Xiaoyi Jiang (University of Münster, Germany)
Organizing Chairs:	Yuanyan Tang (Hong Kong Baptist University, Hong Kong, China)
	Yuehu Liu (Xi'an Jiaotong University, China)
Workshop Secretariat:	Xuguang Lan (Xi'an Jiaotong University, China)
	Peilin Jiang (Xi'an Jiaotong University, China)

Program Committee

Narendra Ahuja (USA)
Emin Anarim (Turkey)
Csaba Beleznai (Austria)
Bir Bhanu (USA)
Thomas Breuel (Germany)
Liming Chen (France)
Yung-Fu Chen (Taiwan, China)
Dmitry Chetverikov (Hungary)
Yiuming Cheung (Hong Kong, China)
Da-Chuan Cheng (Germany)
Michal Haindl (Czech Republic)
A.Ben Hamaz (Canada)
Bernd Heisele (USA)
Zhanyi Hu (China)
GuangBin Huang (Singapore)
Xuelong Li (Hong Kong, China)
WenNung Lie (Taiwan, China)
Zhe-Ming Lu (Germany)
Jussi Parkkinen (Finland)
Nicolai Petkov (The Netherlands)
Tomaso Poggio (USA)
Michael Richter (Germany)
Yuanchun Shi (China)
Tieniu Tan (China)
Massimo Tistarelli (Italy)
Klaus Toennies (Germany)
Emanuele Trucco (UK)
Huub van de Wetering (The Netherlands)
Feiyue Wang (USA)
S.Y. Yuen Kelvin (Hong Kong, China)

Additional Referees

Himanshu Arora (USA)
Alexia Briassouli (USA)
Sin-Kuo Chai (Taiwan, China)
Chi Kin Chow (Hong Kong, China)
Markus Clabian (Austria)
Shaoyi Du (China)
Chunyu Gao (USA)
Bernard Ghanem (USA)
Arto Kaarna (Finland)
Lasse Lensu (Finland)
Jianyi Liu (China)
Kai Rothaus (Germany)
Dacheng Tao (UK)
Sinisa Todorovic (USA)
F.Tushabe (Uganda)
Hongcheng Wang (USA)
Sooyeong Yi (USA)
Tianli Yu (USA)
Haotian Wu (Hong Kong, China)
Hong Zeng (Hong Kong, China)

Table of Contents

Object Detection, Tracking and Recognition

Pattern Representation and Modeling

Visual Pattern Modeling

Image Processing

Compression and Coding

Texture Analysis and Synthesis

Robust Tracking with and Beyond Visible Spectrum: A Four-Layer Data Fusion Framework

Jianru Xue and Nanning Zheng

Institute of Artificial Intelligence and Robotics
Xi'an Jiaotong University 710049
Xi'an, Shaanxi, China
{jrxue, nnzheng}@aiar.xjtu.edu.cn

Abstract. Developing robust visual tracking algorithms for real-world applications is still a major challenge today. In this paper,we focus on robust object tracking with multiple spectrum imaging sensors. We propose a four-layer probabilistic fusion framework for visual tracking with and beyond visible spectrum imaging sensors. The framework consists of four different layers of a bottom-up fusion process. These four layers are defined as: visual cues layer fusing visual modalities via an adaptive fusion strategy, models layer fusing prior motion information via interactive multi-model method(IMM), trackers layer fusing results from multiple trackers via adaptive tracking mode switching, and sensors layer fusing multiple sensors in a distributed way. It requires only state distributions in the input and output of each layer to ensure consistency of so many visual modules within the framework. Furthermore, the proposed framework is general and allows augmenting and pruning of fusing layers according to visual environment at hand. We test the proposed framework in various complex scenarios where a single sensor based tracker may fail, and obtain satisfying tracking results.

1 Introduction

Developing robust object tracking algorithms for real world applications remains a major challenge today and will continue to be one in the near future. In recent years, motivated by the ongoing cognitive process used by humans to integrate data continually from their senses to make inference about the external world, data fusion involves combining information from multiple visible spectrum to achieve inferences not possible using a single video camera. Researchers try to build robust object tracking systems with and beyond visible spectrum imaging sensors by using data fusion techniques, data fusion for tracking in computer vision has just become a fertile area for growth in both research analysis and experimentation and includes both civilian and military applications[1,2,3].

Comparing with that most of existing object tracking systems designed for day and night vision in visible infrared- and thermal-spectrum are built upon fundamental building blocks, data fusion for visual tracking is a still a hot research topic at its early stage, it suffers from generality and robustness in real system design. One feasible explanation maybe that data fusion encompasses

N. Zheng, X. Jiang, and X. Lan (Eds.): IWICPAS 2006, LNCS 4153, pp. 1–16, 2006.

many disciplines, including infrared, far infrared, millimeter wave, microwave, radar, synthetic aperture radar, and electro-optical sensors as well as the very dynamic topics of image processing, computer vision and pattern recognition. Within this context, integration of sensor-dependent tracking algorithm is of increasing importance as progress on the individual tracking modules starts approaching performance ceilings. Combining different visual tracking modules requires a common framework which ensures consistency. Only when this framework is available, could it be possible to organize multiple tracking algorithms and search heuristics into a robust tracking system.

We propose a four-layer probabilistic fusion framework for visual tracking with and beyond visible spectrum image sensors. To make a real data fusing tracking system easy to implement, we divide a bottom-up fusion procedure into four different layers with their corresponding fusion algorithms. Layer 1 is the visual cues fusion layer which fuses multiple visual modalities via adaptive fusion strategies. Layer 2 is the models fusion layer which fuses prior motion information via interactive multiple models(IMM)[4]. Layer 3 is the trackers fusion layer whcih fuses results from multiple trackers via adaptive tracking gate adjusting. Layer 4 is the sensors fusion layer which fuses multiple sensors in a distributed way. This framework can be depicted as Fig. 1.

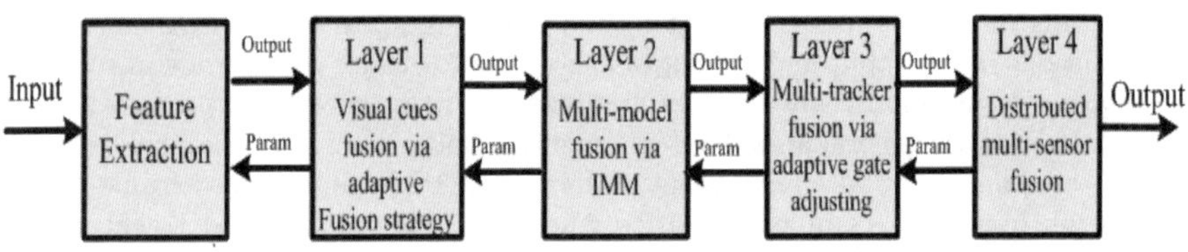

Fig. 1. The four-layer data fusion framework for object tracking

To ensure consistency among these four sequential fusion layers, we define state distributions for input and output of each layer. Sequentially for each input image, each layer provides a probability distribution function(PDF)estimate representation of the tracked object state with different state space. One complete data fusion procedure thus consists of propagation PDF through four stages in correspondence with the four layers defined above. The idea of propagating PDF can find its root in the sequential Monte Carlo techniques framework[5,6]. One important advantage of the sequential Monte Carlo framework is that it allows the information from different measurement sources to be fused in a principled manner. Although this fact has been acknowledged before, it has not been fully exploited within a visual tracking context, where a lot of cues are available to increase the reliability of the tracking algorithm. Data fusion with particle filters has been mostly confined visual cues[7,8]. Another similar idea can be find in [9], it consider combining tracking algorithms in a probabilistic framework, and allows the combinations of any set of sperate tracking algorithms which output either an explicit PDF, or a weighted sample-set. Our work extends this idea and makes it possible to propagate a PDF through all four layers of the fusion process.

There are three contributions in this paper. First, we propose a probabilistic four-layer data fusion framework for visual tracking with and beyond visible spectrum image sensors.Second, we propose a novel adaptive fusion strategy in visual cues fusion layers. At each time instant, the strategy switch to and fro between product fusion rule and weighted sum fusion rule according to the defined reliability of each visual cue. Third, we define a pseudo measurement and adopt it into the IMM in model fusion layers. The pseudo measurement is defined as the fusing result of measurements provided by mean shift procedure [10]which are initialized with predictions from multiple motion models. The fusing coefficient of each model in IMM is given by two likelihood functions: an image-based likelihood and a motion-based association probability.

The rest of the paper is organized as followings. We start by defining the proposed framework in Sect. 2, then we present four fusion layers from Sect. 3 to Sect. 5in details. Finally, the implementation issues and experiment results are given in Sect. 6 and we draw conclusions in Sect. 7.

2 Framework Overview

A typical tracking algorithm consists of two major components. One is target representation and localization,the other is filtering and data association. The former is a bottom-up process which try to cope with the changes in the appearance by exploring and exploiting every visual uniqueness of the target. The later is a top-down process dealing with the dynamics of the tracked object, learning of scene priors, and evaluation of different hypothesizes. Tracking algorithms begin with an a priori estimate of an object's state and update the estimated state to the time of new observation. Similarly, data fusion process for robust visual tracking may be partitioned into four layers: (1) visual cues fusion, (2) models fusion, (3)trackers fusion, and (4)sensors fusion.

Visual cues fusion layer tackles the problem of target representation. It sorts or correlates observations from multiple filters (within the state space defined by a single sensor) or multiple sensors into groups, with each group of representing data related to a single distinct attribute of the target. In the absence of measurement-origin uncertainty, target tracking faces two interrelated main challenges: target motion uncertainty and nonlinearity. Multi-model methods[4] have been generally considered the mainstream approach to maneuvering target tracking under motion (model)uncertainty. Models fusion layer uses multiple motion models simultaneously in order to approximate the dynamics of the target, these models are fused by adopting multiple-model methods(MM).The final two are trackers fusion layer and sensors fusion layers. Both of them aim to increase the robustness of the system. Here we define robustness as the ability of the system to track accurately and precisely during or after visual circumstance that are less ideal. This four-layer structure provides a basic framework for data fusion for visual tracking. It can act as a general guideline in designing data fusion for visual tracking system.

Obviously, the design of data fusion system for visual tracking begins with an inventory of the tracking algorithms that are available for tracking a particular target. The raw material for each fusion layers are tracking algorithms and visual search heuristics. Given a set of visual searching and tracking algorithm, we have to distribute each of them with careful consideration to four layers according to their roles in tracking. To ensure consistency among these sequential four fusion layers, we use a weighted sample set[5]to represent the PDF of the input and output of each layer. Mapping functions are defined for transformations between two state space with different dimensions.

We present in Fig. 2 a typical data fusion for visual tracking system which are with inputs from a CCD Camera, a visible infrared and a thermal-spectrum sensors. For easy to implement, we just consider layer 1-3 within the channel of a single sensor. Layer 4 finally output the final fusion result by the input estimate of these three sensors. In the following sections (Sect. 3 to Sect. 5, more details of each layers are presented.

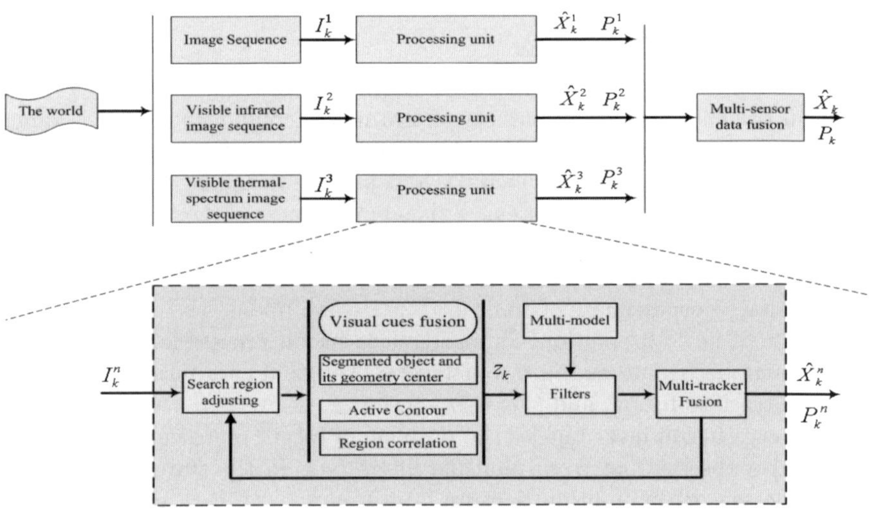

Fig. 2. An overview of the fusion process of a typical tracking system with multiple imaging sensors

3 Layer 1: Visual Cues Fusion

Target representation including geometry , motion, appearance, etc., characterizes the target in a state space either explicitly or implicitly. Since no single cue will be robust and general enough to deal with a wide variety of environmental conditions, their combination promises to increase robustness and generality.

Using multiple cues simultaneously allows not only to use complementary and redundant information at all times but also allows to detect failures more robustly and thus enabling recovery.

Overall system performance may be improved in two main ways, either by enhancing each individual cue, or by improving the scheme for integrating the information from the different modalities. This leads to two main schemes of fusing the output of multiple cues: voting and probabilistic approach. In the first scheme, all visual cues contribute simultaneously to the overall results and none of the cue has an outstanding relevance compared to the others. That is, each cue makes an independent decision before these decisions are combined using a weighted sum. Robustness and generality is a major contribution weighted sum rule, also Jacobs, R.A.[11] convincingly argue for the need for adaptive multi-cue integration and support for their claims with psychophysical experiment. Without ambiguity, we state voting scheme as weighted sum rule since it can be depicted as a mixture distribution density of the form as formula (1).

$$P(\mathbf{y}_1, \cdots \mathbf{y}_n|\mathbf{x}) = \sum_{i=1}^{n} \alpha_i P(\mathbf{y}_i|\mathbf{x}) \tag{1}$$

where $\mathbf{y}_i$ denotes the *ith* visual cues, $\mathbf{x}$ denotes the target state,α_i is the weight of the *ith* visual cue.

Probabilistic methods take more care in designing the model of each so that the different cues combine in the desired manner. However, therein also lies their strength since it forces the user to be explicit in terms of designing the model and specifying what parameters are used and what assumptions are made. In real applications, integrating visual cues with probabilistic methods often ignores correlation among visual cues, and assumes that each visual cue works independent. With this independence assumption, the probabilistic visual cues integration can be stated as product rule, and can be depicted as formula (2).

$$P(\mathbf{y}_1, \cdots \mathbf{y}_n|\mathbf{x}) = \prod_{i=1}^{n} P(\mathbf{y}_i|\mathbf{x}) \tag{2}$$

Even the independence assumption is violated sometimes, it still achieves better tracking performance comparing with that using a single visual cue.

Product rule and weighted sum rule have their own advantages and disadvantages. The product rule has a wide application because of its optimal under the independence assumption. However, it is sensitive to the noise, for example, when the tracked target approaches a similar object, failure occurs when product rule is used. On the other hand, weighted sum rule will not amplify the noise contained in the visual cues, but it cannot increase the belief of the estimate, and cannot be used for a long period. Fig. 3 shows the advantages and disadvantages of the product rule.

We found that weighted sum rule and product rule can be complementary to each other especially when occlusion occurs during tracking. This finding forms the basis of our adaptive fusion strategy: when all cues used are reliable, fusion

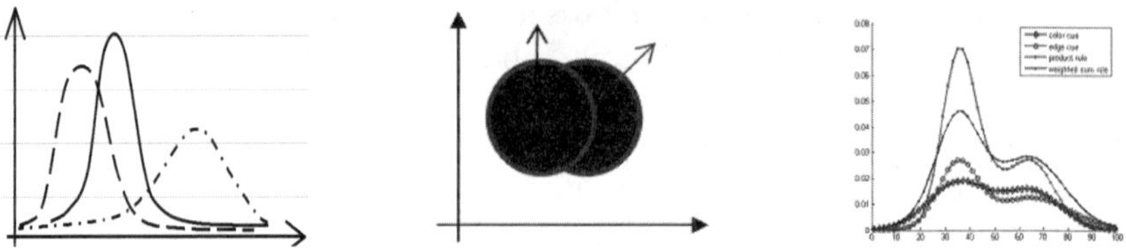

Fig. 3. The left:two dashed curves shows the PDF of the two cues, and the solid-line curve shows the resulted PDF by the product rule. The middle: an occlusion occurs between two similar objects. The right: comparing performances of product rule and weighted sum rule in dealing with occlusion problem. The resulted horizontal direction marginal densities of the tracked object are shown when one applies these two rules in fusing edge cue and color cue.

with product rule can increase the belief of the estimate, when one visual cue degenerates, fusion scheme should switch to weighted sum rule. The uncertainty of the state estimated by the cue can be used to determine whether this cue is degeneration or not. We denote Δ_i as the uncertainty of the ith cues used in fusion, it can be computed as formula (3).

$$\Delta_i = \|Cov(\mathbf{C}_i)\|_F = (\sum_{m=1}^{dim(\mathbf{x})} \sum_{n=1}^{dim(\mathbf{x})} Cov(\mathbf{C}_i)^2_{m,n})^{1/2} \tag{3}$$

where $Cov(C_i)$ is the covariance matrix of the weighted sample set of the ith cue. $\|\cdot\|_F$ denote the Frobenius norm. We define the weighted sample set of the ith cue as $\{\mathbf{x}^{(n)}, \omega_n\}_{n=1}^{M}$. C_i means the ith cue,M is the number of sample, and $\omega_n = p(\mathbf{y}_i|\mathbf{x}^{(n)}, C_i)$ is weight of the ith cue by computing the defined likelihood function. The $Cov(C_i)$ is defined in formula (4).

$$Cov(C_i) = E[(\mathbf{x}-\mathbf{m}_i)\cdot(\mathbf{x}-\mathbf{m}_i)^T|C_i] = \sum_{n=1}^{M} \omega_n \cdot (\mathbf{x}^{(n)} - \mathbf{m}_i)\cdot(\mathbf{x}^{(n)} - \mathbf{m}_i)^T \tag{4}$$

where $\mathbf{m}_i$ is the mean of the sample set of the ith cue. that is $\mathbf{m}_i = \sum_{n=1}^{M} \omega_n \cdot \mathbf{x}^{(n)}$

We define a threshold t_i for each cue to determine whether it is degenerated. The reliability of each cue is defined as $r_i = \Delta_i^{-1}$. Fig. 4 shows an example of the adaptive fusion strategy for two cues. More specific, this strategy employs particle filtering technique, estimating second order moment of the weighted sample set and computing its Frobenius norm to denote how cues are reliable, and then switch between the product rule and weighted sum rule adaptively. The weight α_i in (1) is computed as formula (5)

$$\alpha_i = \Delta_i^{-1} / \sum_{j=1}^{h} \Delta_j^{-1} \tag{5}$$

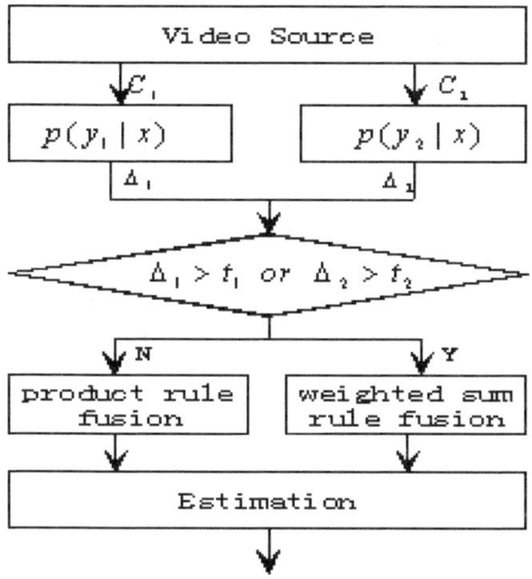

Fig. 4. Adaptive fusion strategy for two cues fusion

4 Layer 2: Models Fusion

A principled choice of dynamics of a tracking system is essential for good results. However, video targets are often highly maneuvering targets, which is the reason that leads to awful track with only one fixed dynamic model. Nowadays, considerable research has been undertaken in the field of hybrid system estimation theory [12] in radar tracking literature. That means several dynamic models can be used simultaneously to characterize motion of agile targets. In models fusion layer, we employ IMM (interacting multiple model) method, one of suboptimal filtering techniques, along with a pseudo measurement to fuse multiple models. IMM has been proven to be one of the best compromises between optimal filtering and computational complexity [12]in radar tracking literature.

We introduce a so-called Pseudo Measurement into multiple-model tracking framework. The pseudo measurement is obtained by combining image based likelihood function and motion based likelihood function together. Fig. 5 demonstrates the structure of the Pseudo Measurement based MM Filtering Framework.

Usually, $n (n \geq 1)$ measurements from several sources are involved in estimating the state of the target. Let $\{z_i(k)\}_{i=1}^{m(k)}$ denote $m(k)$ measurements at time k. The pseudo measurement $\bar{z}(k)$ we defined as formula (6) is used to drive IMM filter.

$$\bar{z}(k) = \sum_{i=1}^{m(k)} \omega_i(k) \cdot z_i(k) \tag{6}$$

$$\omega_i(k) = \frac{p_i(k)}{\sum_i p_i(k)}$$

Here, $m(k)$ is the number of measurement at time k. And $\omega_i(k)$ is the weighting factor determined by the likelihood p_i of each candidate measurement belonging

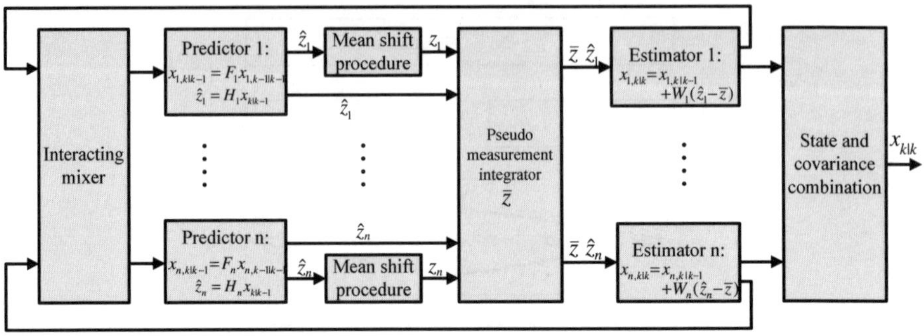

Fig. 5. Pseudo Measurement based MM Filtering Framework

to the real target. (6) indicates that fused pseudo measurement is more accurate than any individual measurement.

When similar targets approach close, it's reasonable that motion information is prior to appearance information for tracking system due to easily confusing the localization of target. So we try to employ the prediction of pseudo measurement to emphasize the motion information from multiple motion models. Let $M_j(k)$ be the jth model at time k, then the model probability conditioned on history measurements is

$$p(M_j(k)|Z^{k-1}) = \sum_{i=1}^{n} p(M_j(k)|M_i(k-1), Z^{k-1}) \cdot p(M_i(k-1)|Z^{k-1}) \tag{7}$$

Where, Z^{k-1} is history measurement up to time $k-1$. $p(M_j(k)|M_i(k-1), Z^{k-1})$ indicates the model transition probability which is preset and $p(M_i(k-1)|Z^{k-1})$ means the previous model probability conditioned on history measurements. For each model, each corresponding filter (such as standard Kalman filter,or Particle filter) can calculate a measurement prediction, denoted by $\hat{Z}_j(k)$. Then we achieve the pseudo measurement prediction by

$$\hat{z}(k) = \sum_{j=1}^{n} p(M_j(k)|Z^{k-1}) \cdot \hat{z}_j(k) \tag{8}$$

This pseudo measurement prediction is crucial in the case of targets' occlusion.

Further, a straightforward likelihood function is built for p_i in (9) using appearance information as well as motion information.

$$p_i = (La_i)^{\alpha} \cdot (Lm_i)^{\beta} \tag{9}$$

Where, La_i and Lm_i denotes image-based likelihood and motion-based likelihood, respectively. α and β are the weights implying the reliabilities of image-based and motion-based information respectively, satisfying $0 \leq \alpha, \beta \leq 1$. (9) indicates the likelihood p_i is more rigorous after considering both points of view in tracking literature: target representation and filtering. In our experiments, we fix α and β for simpleness in spite of their significance for adaptiveness.

There are many choices of the image-based likelihood La_i, such as image based template matching function, feature based template matching function and even statistics based likelihood function. When occlusion occurs, contribution of appearance information of target fades out while the motion information become an important role in the tracker. We assume that the measurement innovation, which is obtained via the pseudo measurement prediction, obeys Gaussian distribution. Similar to IMM's mode likelihood definition[4], we define Lm_i as

$$Lm_i = \frac{1}{\sqrt{2\pi|S_i|}} \exp\left[-\frac{(z_i - \hat{z})^T \cdot S_i^{-1} \cdot (z_i - \hat{z})}{2} \right] \tag{10}$$

where $\hat{z}$ is the predicted pseudo measurement, S_i is the innovation covariance which is calculated with measurement covariance R_i in a standard Kalman filter. The motion-based likelihood function Lm_i indicates that the pseudo measurement is biased to motion prediction, controlled by the parameter α and β.

The detailed steps of pseudo measurement based MM filtering algorithm for models fusion are present in Table 1. Some procedures can be achieved from IMM algorithm (seeing [4]for details).

5 Layer 3-4: Trackers Fusion and Sensors Fusion

This section presents the algorithm we choose for trackers fusion layer and sensors fusion layer.

Trackers fusion layer. the observation of object's appearance in image will vary when it is approaching near to the camera or vice versa. When a target is far away from the camera system, it appears as light spot in the image. When it comes near, the size of the spot becomes bigger and bigger, eventually, its shape feature becomes strong, and finally, texture and geometry of its surface become clear. This causes much difficultics in tracking system using pin-hole camera system. Here we adopt an adaptive window algorithm in [13] to determine the search region. According to the size of the search region, we define four target appearance mode: (1)point target, (2)target with weak-shape, (3) target with salience shape, (4) big target. In each mode, we select a set of specified tracking algorithm for robust tracking. For example, In point target mode, only intensity information is available, only the intensity-based tracker can be used. When the target appears with weak-shape, both intensity-based tracker and correlation-based tracker can be used. With more information coming, more types of tracker are available. In order to make the tracker switch smoothly between different modes, a simple weighted sum fusion rule is adopted.

Sensors fusion layer this framework allows many choices of multiple sensors fusion scheme. We choose a distributes multiple sensors fusion scheme since we have defined the first three fusing layer within a single sensor, so we should

Table 1. Detailed steps of pseudo measurement based MM filtering in one circle

1. Calculate the mixing probabilities: $\mu_{k-1|k-1}(i,j) = \frac{p(i,j)\cdot\mu_{k-1}(i)}{\sum_i p(i,j)\cdot\mu_{k-1}(i)}$
2. Redo the filters' initialization

$$\hat{x}^{(j),0}_{k-1|k-1} = \sum_i \hat{x}^{(i)}_{k-1|k-1}\mu_{k-1|k-1}(i,j)$$
$$\nu_{k-1}(i,j) = \hat{x}^{(i)}_{k-1|k-1} - \hat{x}^{(j),0}_{k-1|k-1}$$
$$P^{(j),0}_{k-1|k-1} = \sum_i \mu_{k-1|k-1}(i,j)\cdot\{P^{(i)}_{k-1|k-1} + \nu_{k-1}(i,j)\cdot\nu^T_{k-1}(i,j)\}$$

3. Filters' prediction: $\hat{z}_j = H_j \cdot \bar{x}^{(j)}_{k|k-1} = H_j \cdot F_j \cdot \hat{x}^{(j),0}_{k-1|k-1}$
4. Calculate pseudo measurement prediction $\hat{z}(k)$ in (8);
5. Mean shift procedure from $\hat{z}_j$ for player localization z_j and SSD for its uncertainty R_j;
6. Get the appearance likelihood La_i via certain localization method;
7. Obtain the motion based likelihood Lm_i by (10);
8. Calculate measurement likelihood p_i in (9);
9. Combine pseudo measurement $\bar{z}$ via (6);
10. All filters run as standard Kalman filter;
11. Update model likelihood and probabilities

$$\Lambda^{(j)}_k = \mathcal{N}(\bar{Z} - h(\hat{x}^{(j),0}_{k|k-1}); 0, S^{(j)}_k);$$
$$\eta^{(j)}_k = \Lambda^{(j)}_k \sum_i p(i,j)\cdot\mu^{(i)}_{k-1}; \quad \mu^{(j)}_k = \frac{\eta^{(j)}_k}{\sum_i \eta^{(i)}_k}$$

12. Estimate and covariance combination

$$\hat{x}_{k|k} = \sum_i \hat{x}^{(i)}_{k|k}\mu^{(i)}_k; \quad P_{k|k} = \sum_i \mu^{(i)}_k\{P^{(i)}_{k|k} + [\hat{x}^{(i)}_{k|k} - \hat{x}_{k|k}]\cdot[\hat{x}^{(i)}_{k|k} - \hat{x}_{k|k}]^T\}$$

pay more attention on fusing decisions from these sensors. Distributed scheme of multi-sensor fusion has a mature theory framework. Since the limitation of page space, please see [14,15] for detail information on distributed scheme of multi-sensor fusion.

6 Implementation Issues and Experiment Results

In this section, we discuss some implementation issues of the system, and some experiment results are also presented. We test the performance of each layer with both visible video sequence and infrared video sequence containing several challenging situations. Since the first three layers of the four-layer fusion framework are performed within a single sensor channel, so only visible video or infrared video are used in the experiments of these three layers. It should be noted experiments in this section just deal with general object tracking without explicit prior knowledge about its type, so no model-based features are involves in visual cues fusion layers.

6.1 Visual Cues Fusion Layer

Two-hand tracking. We test our visual cues fusion algorithm with a video sequence containing two switching hands. We select the occluded hand as the target. Two visual cues are fused, one is color cue and the other is the edge cues. Since particle filer is applied, the likelihood for each cue should be defined. In this experiment, we adopt the similar likelihood function in[16] for color cue. and define a Hausdorff distance-based likelihood in formula (11) for edge cue.

$$p(\mathbf{y}|\mathbf{x}) = p_0 + k_s \exp^{-HD^2(M,P(\mathbf{x}))/2\sigma^2} \tag{11}$$

where HD denotes Hausdorff distance, and M_t is the edge-template,$P(\mathbf{x})$ is edge set the candidate $\mathbf{x}$, $p_0 = 0.1$ is constant to make the likelihood bigger than zero even in the worst case.

Fig. 6 shows some key frames from the tracking result when two hands are switching. Fig. 7 shows the Frobenius norm value of two cues covariance when using three different fusion rules. Experiment results show that adaptive strategy in visual cues fusion layer increases the compactness of the weighted sample efficiently, which also corresponds to the accuracy and robustness of the tracker, comparing with weighted sum rule and product rule.

Fig. 6. Tracking results of visual cues fusion layer. The tracked hand position estimated is marked with a red box attached with particles of each cues. The top row displays tracking result of the product rule. The middle row shows the result of the weighted sum rule. And the result of our method, adaptive strategy, is put in the bottom row, the rule used is shown at the left-bottom of each frame.

6.2 Models Fusion Layer

Tracking football player. We test our algorithm with the video sequence "football.avi", compared with other two common algorithms (one is mean shift

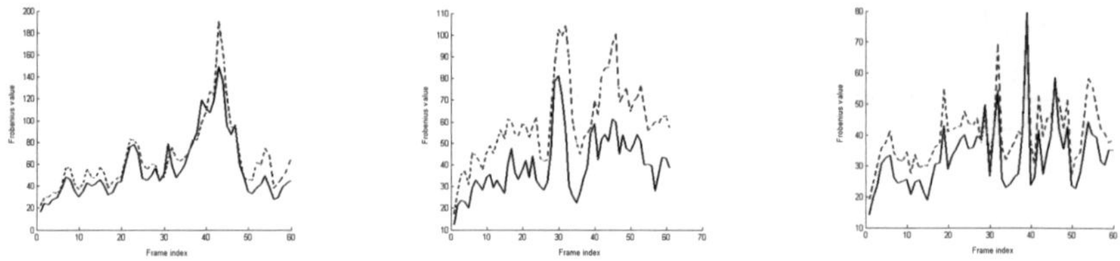

Fig. 7. The Frobenius norm of each cues at each frame,dashed-line curve denotes the color cue, and solid-line curve denotes the edge cue. The left figure shows the results of product rule. The middle one shows the results of the weighted sum rule, and the right shows the results of the adaptive strategy.

procedure only, the other is mean shift with CV model(constant velocity motion model)based Kalman filtering) in several phases. In video "football.avi", a special target with agile motion is selected to be tracked.

Fig. 8presents estimated position marked with a red cross , only frames 6\10\27\28\29 are shown. Obviously, mean shift method failed when two teammates are very close to each other from frame 6 to frame 10, because mean shift can't distinguish them well only by player's appearance. From frame 27 to frame 29 mean shift + Kalman method also failed since the player's position predicted in Kalman filter dropped into the region of another similar player. However, our approach is such a robust tracking method for player tracking that it can succeed in many hard cases. Secondly, the left figure in Fig.9 shows the history of the motion model probabilities for the player selected by our algorithm. Obviously, the motion model probability is not as stable as that in radar literature because the mean shift procedure is not stable for player localization. Thirdly, we redo our method only under the modification of parameter γ, comparing their square root position error with the ground truth marked by hand (the right figure in Fig.9). This experimental result has proven that the image based likelihood did help us to improve the player tracking.

6.3 Trackers Fusion Layer

This section presents experiment results of testing the trackers fusion layer. We choose a peak-based tracker and a correlation-based tracker to fuse in this layer, algorithms in this layer are tested with an infrared video. The test video contains challenging situations that target approaching to and leaving the camera. Fig. 10 presents some tracking results. Experiment result shows that a single tracker cannot track the boat reliably through the test video, while the fused tracker can. It also shows that fusion of multiple tracker increases not only the reliability of tracking, but also its accuracy comparing with using a single tracker.

6.4 System Validation

Finally, we show the tracking results of the system presented in Fig. 2. This system is equipped with a CCD Camera, a visible infrared and a thermal-spectrum

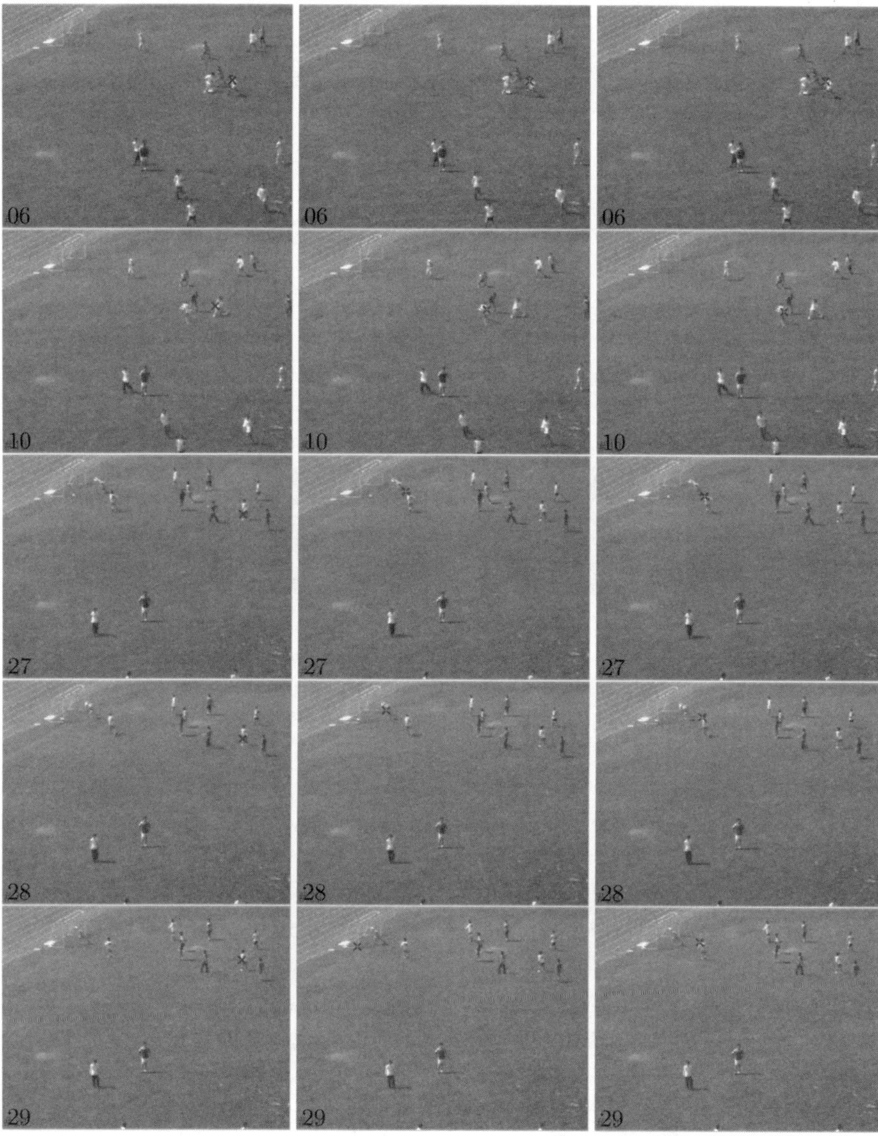

Fig. 8. Tracking results of models fusion layer. The tracked player position estimated is marked with a red cross. The left column displays mean shift only tracking result. The middle column shows the result of Kalman + mean shift method. And the result of our method, pseudo measurement based multiple model approach, is put in the right column.

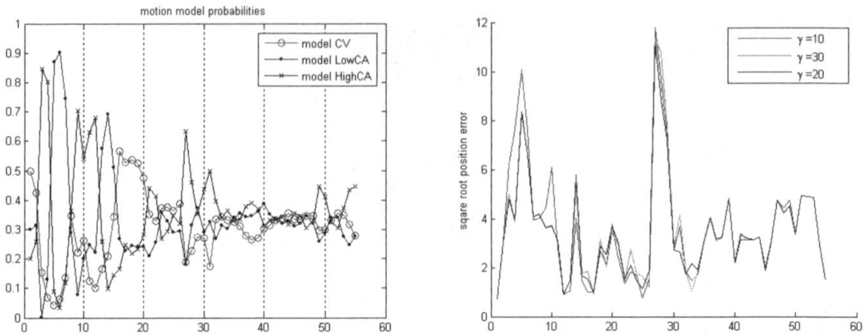

Fig. 9. The left figure is motion model probability of player selected. The right one demonstrates γ adjusting the effectiveness of the image based likelihood.

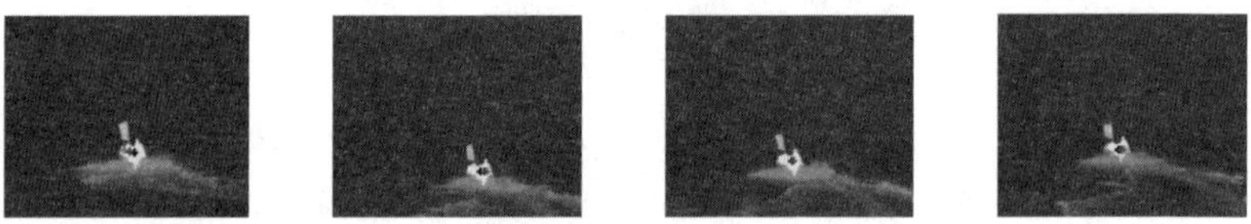

Fig. 10. Tracking results of trackers fusion layer. From left to right, top to bottom, frames 2,15,25,40 of the input video are chosen to present the tracking results. Green,blue and red crosses denote the output of the peak-based tracker, the correlation-based tracker, and the final fusion results, respectively.

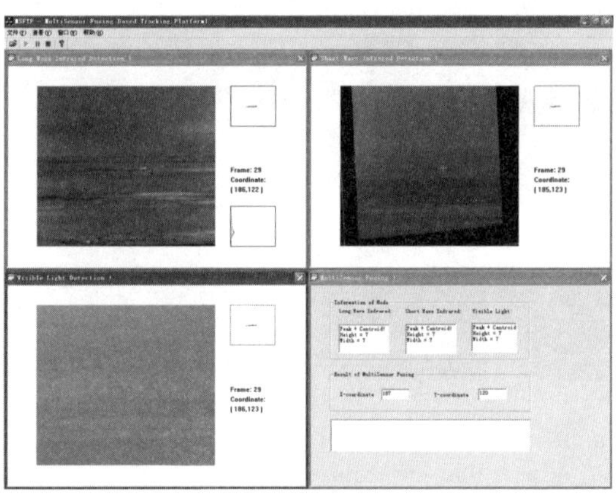

Fig. 11. Data fusion tracking system with three sensors. From left to right, top to bottom, four overlayed views present tracking results of an infrared sensors, a visible thermal-spectrum sensor, a CCD camera and the final fusion results, respectively.

sensors. Secs. 6.1,6.2,6.2,6.3 present experiments results of one layer of the four-layer framework. Fig. 11 presents tracking results of four-layer fusion system with three sensors at a time instant. Extensive experiments shows that fusion of these three sensors not only increases the system performance in the accuracy and robustness, but also extends its applying fields. For more extensive experiments, please visit our webpage(http://www.aiar.xjtu.edu.cn/videocomputing.html).

7 Conclusion

In this paper,we discuss the designing of robust object tracking with multiple spectrum imaging sensors. We propose a four-layer probabilistic fusion framework for visual tracking with and beyond visible spectrum sensors. Four different layers are defined in a bottom-up data fusion process for visual tracking.We show how feature layer fuses multiple visual modalities via adaptive fusion strategies, how models layer fuses prior motion information via interactive multi-model method(IMM), how tracker layer fuses multiple trackers via adaptive tracking mode switching, and how sensors layer fuses multiple sensors in a distributed way. We use state distributions as the interface between each two consequential layers to ensure consistency throughout the framework. Furthermore, the proposed framework is general and allows augmenting and pruning of fusing layers according to visual environment at hand. The proposed framework is tested extensively under various complex scenario where a single sensor based tracker may fail, and obtain satisfying tracking results.

Acknowledgement

This research are supported by NSFC grants 60021302,60405004, by Young Teacher Research Funds from Electronics and Information School of XJTU and XJTU.

References

1. Bhanu, B., Pavlidis, I.: Computer Vision Beyond the Visible Spectrum. Springer (2004)
2. Dai, C., Zheng, Y., Li, X.: Layered Representation for Pedestrian Detection and Tracking in Infrared Imagery. Computer Vision and Pattern Recognition, 2005 IEEE Computer Society Conference on **3** (2005)
3. Perez, P., Vermaak, J., Blake, A.: Data fusion for visual tracking with particles. Proceedings of the IEEE **92**(3) (2004) 495–513
4. Li, X., Jilkov, V.: Survey of Maneuvering Target Tracking. Part V: Multiple-Model Methods. IEEE Transactions on Aerospace and Electronic Systems **41**(4) (2005) 1255
5. Liu, J., Chen, R.: Sequential Monte Carlo Methods for Dynamic Systems. Journal of the American Statistical Association **93**(443) (1998) 1032–1044
6. Isard, M., Blake, A.: CONDENSATIONConditional Density Propagation for Visual Tracking. International Journal of Computer Vision **29**(1) (1998) 5–28

7. Wu, Y., Huang, T.: A co-inference approach to robust visual tracking. Proc. Int. Conf. Computer Vision (2001)
8. Vermaak, J., Perez, P., Gangnet, M., Blake, A.: Towards improved observation models for visual tracking: selective adaptation. European Conference on Computer Vision **1** (2002) 645–660
9. Leichter, I., Lindenbaum, M., Rivlin, E.: A probabilistic framework for combining tracking algorithms. Computer Vision and Pattern Recognition, 2004. CVPR 2004. Proceedings of the 2004 IEEE Computer Society Conference on (**2**)
10. Comaniciu, D., Meer, P.: Mean shift: a robust approach toward feature space analysis. Pattern Analysis and Machine Intelligence, IEEE Transactions on **24**(5) (2002) 603–619
11. Jacobs, R.: What determines visual cue reliability. Trends Cogn. Sci **6** (2002) 345–50
12. Bar-Shalom, Y., Li, X., Kirubarajan, T.: Estimation with applications to tracking and navigation. Wiley New York (2001)
13. Sung, S., Chien, S., Kim, M., Kim, J.: Adaptive window algorithm with four-direction sizing factors for robust correlation-based tracking. Tools with Artificial Intelligence, 1997. Proceedings., Ninth IEEE International Conference on (1997) 208–215
14. Bar-Shalom, Y., Li, X.: Multitarget-multisensor tracking: Principles and techniques. Storrs, CT: University of Connecticut, 1995. (1995)
15. Hall, D., McMullen, S.: Mathematical Techniques in Multisensor Data Fusion. Artech House Publishers (2004)
16. Pérez, P., Hue, C., Vermaak, J., Gangnet, M.: Color-based probabilistic tracking. In: Proceedings of Europe Conference on Computer Vision. (2002) 661–675

Scale Space Based Grammar for Hand Detection

Jan Prokaj[1] and Niels da Vitoria Lobo[2]

[1] University of Central Florida, Orlando, FL 32816, USA
j.prokaj@computer.org
[2] University of Central Florida, Orlando, FL 32816, USA
niels@cs.ucf.edu

Abstract. For detecting difficult objects, like hands, we present an algorithm that uses tokens and a grammar. Tokens are found by employing a new scale space edge detector that finds scale invariant features at object boundaries. We begin by constructing the scale space. Then we find edges at each scale and flatten the scale space to one edge image. To detect a hand we define a hand pattern grammar using curve tokens for finger tips and wedges, and line tokens. We identify a hand pattern by parsing these tokens using a graph based algorithm. We show and discuss the results of this algorithm on a database of hand images.

1 Introduction

Object detection is one of the fundamental problems of computer vision. The most successful technique for detecting objects is to find invariant features, and then match them to a previously defined set. Finding good features, however, is difficult. Lowe [1] has shown that scale space invariance is especially important. SIFT features produce excellent results when detecting rigid objects that are affinely trackable. But these features are less useful for objects that have important information encoded within the shapes of their boundaries. Hands, and other non-rigid objects are a good example of this. Thus, there is a need for different features, which are still scale space invariant, but do not suffer from the lack of affine trackability at boundaries.

Much work has been done on hand tracking [2,3,4], and hand pose estimation [5,6]. But these do not work for the difficult task of hand detection in a single cluttered image.

We cast the problem of finding these features as doing a "lexical analysis" on the input image, producing tokens. In the next section we present a method for finding these scale invariant tokens at boundaries. Then in the following section, we define a grammar using this token alphabet that produces all strings identifying a hand. Subsequently, we present an algorithm that implements the grammar and "parses" these tokens, giving a scale space hand detection algorithm.

2 Finding Tokens

To find tokens at boundaries, it is natural to work with an edge image. A single edge image, however, is computed at only one scale. A common technique is to

N. Zheng, X. Jiang, and X. Lan (Eds.): IWICPAS 2006, LNCS 4153, pp. 17–26, 2006.

smooth the image with a particular σ, calculate its derivative, and use gradients to find local maxima [7]. This can be a problem because if the scale is too large, needed detail may be lost; if the scale is too small, the edges are likely to be disconnected. Motivated by this problem, we offer a scale space edge detector, which avoids these problems. The detected edges then serve as a good source of scale invariant tokens.

For open hand detection we use two kinds of tokens, curves and lines. Curve tokens are used to find finger tip curves, and wedge curves for the region where fingers join. Line tokens are used to find the border of extended fingers. The algorithms are presented in Sect. 2.2 and 2.3.

2.1 Scale Space Edge Detection

A scale invariant, high-fidelity edge image must have at least two properties. It has to have much detail in order to have the best chance of finding a particular shape, as well as have edges that are smooth and connected. These two properties occur at opposite ends of the scale space [8].

By constructing the scale space of an image, we gain access to the result of all possible smoothing operations. This information can be used to calculate one edge image that has a *lot of detail* using data from the bottom of the scale space, and at the same time has *continuous* edges, using data from the top of the scale space.

There are two steps to calculate a scale space edge image. In the first step, a Canny scale space is contructed. In the second step, this scale space is "flattened" to a final edge image.

Step 1: Canny Scale Space. The Canny scale space is derived from the Gaussian scale space. The Gaussian scale space is constructed as a pyramid according to [1], but with a maximum of three octaves. From this scale space, the Canny scale space is derived by applying the Canny edge detection algorithm on every image in the Gaussian scale space. However, the algorithm is modified to compute the gradient without additional blurring in the convolution.

Step 2: Flattening the Space. To convert the Canny scale space into one edge image, it must be flattened without losing too much information. In the first step, the edge images within each octave are combined into one octave edge image; in step two these octave images are then combined into a final edge image.

Combining the images within an octave is straightforward. It begins by unioning the images in each octave. As a result of this operation, an "on" pixel in the union image says that it was "on" in at least one scale in this octave. This union image is then smoothed by setting on any "off" pixels that are surrounded by at least six "on" pixels. To produce thin edges, the smoothed image is skeletonized. See Fig. 1.

Combining the octave edge images is more involved, because the images are different dimensions. The combinations proceed down the scale. Therefore, the

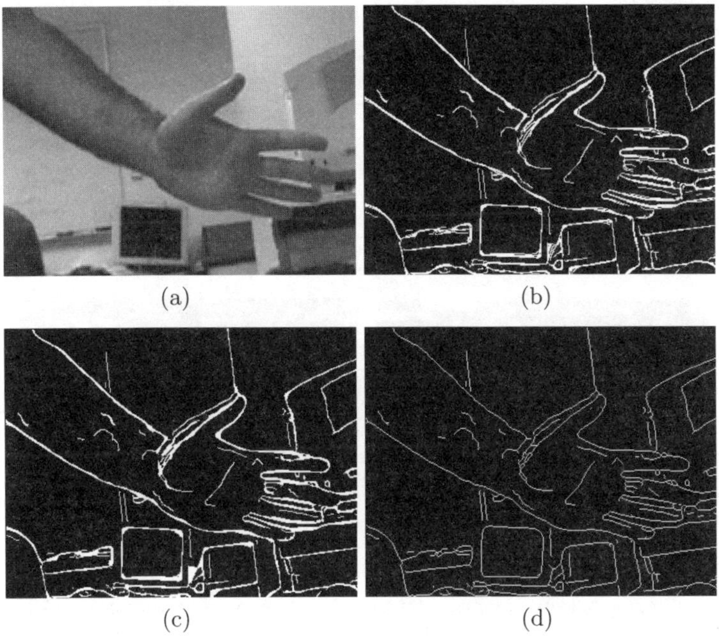

Fig. 1. Combining the images within an octave. (a) The original image. (b) Unioned octave. (c) Smoothed octave. (d) Skeletonized octave.

top two octaves are combined first, followed by a combination with the lowest octave image. The combination algorithm overlaps the lower scale image (larger dimension) with the higher scale image (smaller dimension), thus filling in any gaps in the lower scale image that are connected in the higher scale image. The overlap is done segment by segment, rather than all at once. For each connected segment in the higher scale image, the corresponding points in the lower scale image are traversed until reaching an end point. At this point, the traversal continues on the higher scale segment, marking the edge on the lower scale image, until it is possible to resume again on the lower scale image. See Fig. 2.

After all octave edge images are combined in this manner, the result will be one scale invariant edge image, that is suitable for finding the needed tokens.

2.2 Curve Tokens

A finger tip and a wedge between fingers can both be characterized as curves. They only differ in proportion, one is wider than the other. To find these curves in the edge image, a model-based approach is used. The algorithm is based on [9]. The models used in experiments are shown in Fig. 3.

Curves are found by superimposing a model's edge image to different locations in the scale space edge image, and calculating a similarity score. These

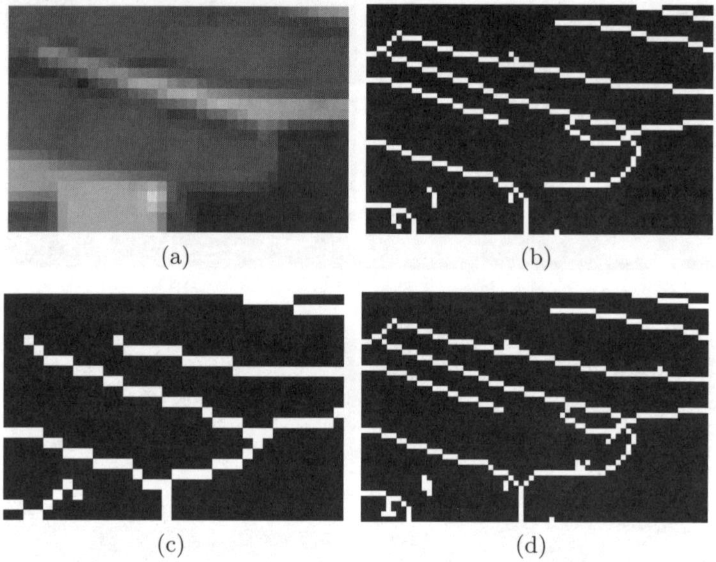

Fig. 2. Combining octave images (detail). (a) The original image. (b) Lower scale image. (c) Higher scale image. (d) Final edge image.

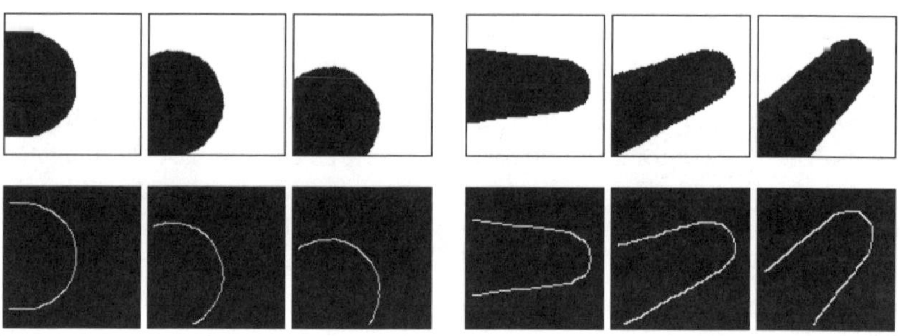

Fig. 3. This figure shows a subset of the finger tip (left) and wedge (right) models, and their edges (bottom), used in the scoring method

"candidate" locations of curves are taken to be the end points and mid points of lines found by a line finder, which is described in Sect. 2.3. To eliminate locations that are not likely to contain curves, mid points of lines are not taken for the the top 25% of longest lines.

To handle multiple orientations of curves, the base model is rotated to give 16 rotated versions of the model. Some of these orientations are shown in Fig. 3. Different curve sizes are handled by precomputing different sized models for each rotated version, keeping the same proportion.

The score for a given candidate location is the maximum of the scores of all sizes of the model with the same orientation as the location. The orientation for any point in the edge image is determined from the gradient of the image at the smallest scale in the Gaussian scale space, because this image has the most accurate orientation data. For each size, actually two opposite orientations are tried, because the gradient can be negative or positive and have the same orientation.

To superimpose a model correctly, the center point of a model's edge curve, which is the top of a curve, is aligned with the candidate location. The score of a model, having a particular size and orientation, is calculated using

$$\frac{\sum_k e^{-0.25\min(D_k)} |\boldsymbol{m}_k \cdot \boldsymbol{v}_k|}{k} , \tag{1}$$

where k is each model edge point, $\min(D_k)$ is the minimum of the five distances to the closest image edge point that would be obtained by shifting the model 0 and ± 1 units in the parallel and perpendicular directions to the model's orientation, $\boldsymbol{m}_k$ is the unit normal vector at the k-th model edge point, and $\boldsymbol{v}_k$ is the unit normal vector at the closest image edge point, given by $\min(D_k)$. In other words, for each model edge point the score is determined by the distance to the closest image edge point and the orientation difference between the two points. The model is shifted one unit in four directions, because this increases its flexibility. The score for a candidate location is compared to a threshold, set to 0.78 in our experiments, and the location is eliminated if the score is less than this.

To eliminate curves that are not likely to be finger tips, we make sure that each curve found is supported by a line token, as found by a modified line finder described in the next section. The line must be parallel, and close to either one of the ends of the curve. This is accomplished by searching for lines in a rectangle 7 pixels wide and $2 * \text{curvesize}$ pixels tall and rotated to be parallel with the curve's orientation. The rectangle is searched twice, the first time when its side is centered on one curve end, and the second time when its side is centered on the other end. The lines must have an orientation within 0.55 rad of the curve's orientation, and their length must be at least $1.1 * \text{curvesize}$.

Since the number of candidate locations is large, especially on curved edges, it is possible that this process produces overlapping curves. These duplicate curves are eliminated by calculating the intersection of the bounding rectangles of two curves. If the intersection is greater than 15% of the area of the smaller curve, the curve with the lower score is eliminated.

This curve detection algorithm is run with finger tip models, as well as with finger wedge models.

2.3 Line Tokens

To find lines on a scale space edge image, we use a modifed Burns line finder [10]. The lines are directly extracted from the edge image, instead of using the raw image as in the original algorithm. As mentioned above, the orientation data for the scale space edge image comes from the gradient of an image with the smallest scale. The Burns algorithm uses two systems of lines to avoid boundary effects of orientation partitioning. These two systems of lines are resolved differently to determine the final set of lines.

The lines from either system are processed in order from the longest to the shortest. For each line, both systems are analyzed for possible merges with other lines. First, a line merges with the corresponding (on the same pixels) lines in the other system. If this causes the line to partially extend over neighboring lines in its own system, then it merges with them as well. The lines in the other system on the same pixels as this new extension are adjusted (shortened), but not merged with. The line lengths are updated as the merging goes on, so that the longest line can be found in the next iteration. This method of resolving the two systems favors long, unbroken lines, which is what is needed to find finger lines.

3 Parsing Tokens

To parse curve and line tokens into strings that identify a hand, a grammar is defined to enforce the detection of the following properties: 1) A finger tip curve has an opposite orientation of a wedge curve. 2) The endpoints of the curves must be closer than the centers of the curves. 3) There is a line token connecting a finger tip curve with a wedge curve. These properties are formally written below, where t is a finger tip curve, w is a wedge curve, and l is a line token.

$$
\begin{aligned}
H &\rightarrow tlwltlwltlwltlwlt \\
H &\rightarrow tlwltlwltlwltlw \mid wltlwltlwltlwlt \\
H &\rightarrow tlwltlwltlwlt \\
H &\rightarrow tlwltlwltlw \mid wltlwltlwlt \\
H &\rightarrow tlwltlwlt \\
H &\rightarrow tlwltlw \mid wltlwlt
\end{aligned}
$$

This grammar eliminates strings with three or less curves. The -t-w-t- sequence produces a “zigzag” pattern across the hand’s fingers. See Fig. 4 for an illustration. Any token can be missing, but as soon as this happens, it is no longer allowed.

3.1 Open Hand Detection (Pattern Parser)

To find the desired pattern, we first construct a complete graph with nodes being all curve tokens, finger tips and wedges. The edges in the graph, termed g-edges, correspond to all possible curve combinations. The weight of each g-edge is a pattern distance [11] between two curves. The pattern distance is defined as a Euclidian pattern distance,

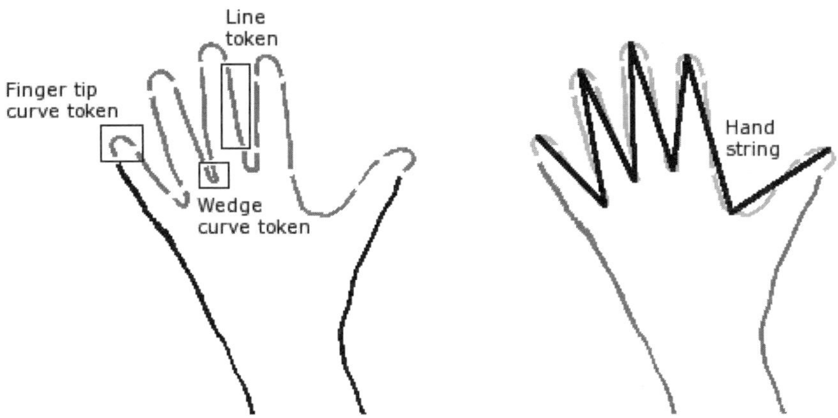

Fig. 4. This figure illustrates the zigzag pattern we are looking for

$$\sqrt{\left(\frac{x_1 - x_2}{xRange}\right)^2 + \left(\frac{y_1 - y_2}{yRange}\right)^2 + \left(\frac{\theta_1 - (\theta_2 + \pi)}{\pi}\right)^2}, \tag{2}$$

where $xRange$ is the maximum distance in the x-dimension and $yRange$ is the maximum distance in the y-dimension. The pattern distance between two curves is the shortest when they are close to each other and have opposite orientations from each other. This ensures a -tip-wedge-tip- sequence.

The next step is to remove those g-edges that cannot possibly make a valid combination. The criteria are determined from the properties above. Using the first property that adjacent curves have to have opposite orientations, g-edges with orientation difference less than $\frac{\pi}{2}$ are removed. The second property says that a g-edge must connect curves back to back, where the back is the two endpoints, not the center of the curve. To enforce the third property that there is a line token connecting the two curves, a rectangular region centered on the g-edge and 7 pixels wide is searched for a line parallel to the g-edge. The orientation difference between the g-edge and line must be less than 0.18 rad, and the length must be between 0.675 and 1.6 times the g-edge length. If no line satisfying this criteria is found, the g-edge is removed.

Once impossible g-edges are removed, the next step is to find a zigzag pattern in this graph. This is done using a back-tracking algorithm. Starting at one node, all possible g-edges connecting it are sorted by the pattern distance above. The g-edge is picked if it satisfies these criteria: the supporting line token has not been used previously in this pattern, the line token is less than 1.6 times the length of the previous line token in the pattern, the angle between this g-edge and the previous g-edge is between 0.12 rad and 1.05 rad, and the g-edge preserves the zigzag – does not cross the previous g-edges. Once the g-edge is picked, the algorithm recursively jumps to that connected node, and looks at all connecting g-edges again. If it is impossible to continue from a node, the algorithm back-tracks to the previous node, and takes the next option. The search stops when we have at least 4 curves, but not more than 9. The pattern parser is run on each node of the graph.

To allow one missing curve token when a particular node has run out of options, we create a virtual curve that is the same size and opposite orientation as the node, and set its location 3∗curvesize in the parallel and opposite direction of the node and 0.5 times the distance to the next curve token in the perpendicular direction. To allow one missing line token, we skip checking for a supporting line when looking at possible curves.

4 Results

On a database of 216 images of open hands against cluttered backgrounds, containing 1087 fingers, the overall rate of finger tip curve detection is 75%. This means that on average, close to 4 finger tips are detected. The rate of wedge curve detection is 65%. The number of false positives, as expected, is high. Figure 5 shows some examples.

To minimize the number of false positives, hand detection was run with the option to allow missing tokens turned off. The hand pattern was successfuly found 73% of the time on a database of 244 images of open hands with cluttered backgrounds. On average, about 4 false positives are found per image, but this largely depends on the image's contents. Anything that has a zigzag pattern will be detected, such as stacked binders. Figure 6 shows some examples.

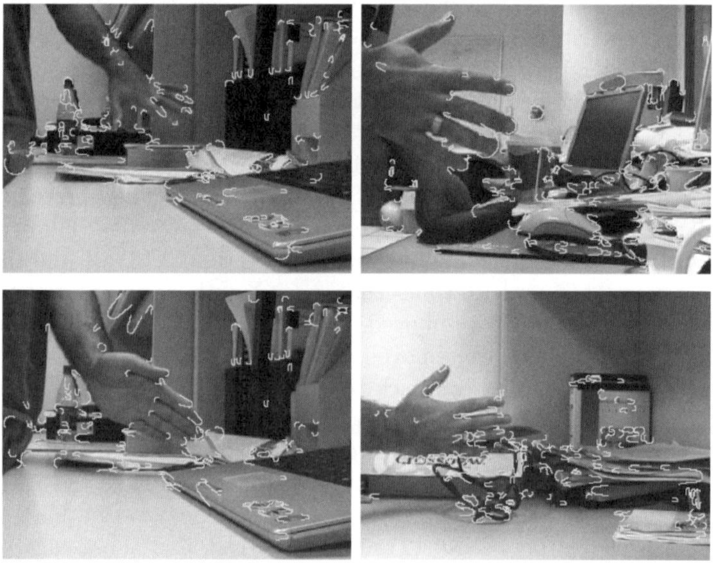

Fig. 5. Examples of detected curve tokens

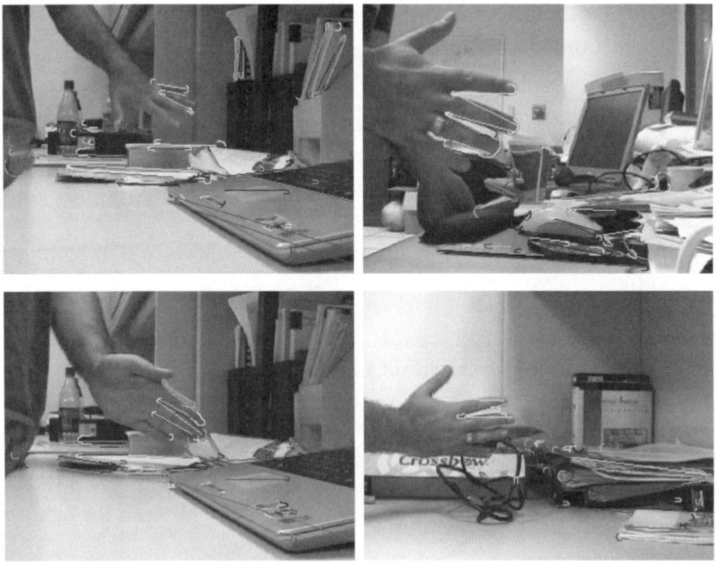

Fig. 6. Examples of detected hand patterns in Fig. 5

5 Discussion, Future Work, and Conclusions

False negatives in curve token detection are caused by the lack of contrast in the input data, which is necessary for edges to be detected in at least one scale. Given the difficulty of the region where fingers are joined, it is encouraging that wedge curves were found. With closed fingers in particular, detection of wedges is difficult. In the future, more curve models with variable widths can be used to increase detection.

The number of false positive curve tokens found is proportional to the number of edge pixels in the edge image. This is because edges are often curve shaped, and thus detectable by the curve finding algorithm. Also, the curve models are not unique in a sense that a finger tip curve model may detect a wedge curve feature, and a wedge curve model may detect a finger tip curve feature. The number of false positives is not critical, however, because the grammar has really helped to eliminate most of them.

False negatives in hand detection are caused by missing curve tokens. Hand detection performed the best when the fingers were spread, but it worked with closed fingers as well. This is because a hand with fingers spread has a higher chance of detecting a wedge curve token, as explained above. The already low false positive rate can be decreased further by considering more features, such as a hand's palm, or an image intensity at the location of the finger tip curve tokens.

In this paper, we presented a new scale space edge detector that enabled us to find scale invariant tokens at object boundaries. This token finding should be useful for any object, where its boundary features are important. We showed its promise for open hand detection.

References

1. Lowe, D.: Distinctive image features from scale-invariant keypoints. International Journal of Computer Vision **60** (2004) 92–110
2. Pavlovic, V.I., Sharma, R., Huang, T.S.: Visual interpretation of hand gestures for human-computer interaction: A review. IEEE Transactions on Pattern Analysis and Machine Intelligence **19** (1997) 677–695
3. Stenger, B., Mendonca, P., Cipolla, R.: Model-based 3d tracking of an articulated hand. In: IEEE Computer Society Conference on Computer Vision and Pattern Recognition. (2001) 310
4. Yuan, Q., Sclaroff, S., Athitsos, V.: Automatic 2d hand tracking in video sequences. In: Seventh IEEE Workshop on Application of Computer Vision. (2005) 250–256
5. Wu, Y., Huang, T.: View-independent recognition of hand postures. In: IEEE Computer Society Conference on Computer Vision and Pattern Recognition. (2000) 2088–2094
6. Athitsos, V., Sclaroff, S.: Estimating 3d hand pose from a cluttered image. In: IEEE Computer Society Conference on Computer Vision and Pattern Recognition. (2003) 432–439
7. Canny, J.: A computational approach to edge detection. IEEE Transactions on Pattern Analysis and Machine Intelligence **8** (1986) 679–698
8. Lindeberg, T.: Scale-space theory in computer vision. Kluwer, Boston, MA (1994)
9. Garcia, J., da Vitoria Lobo, N., Shah, M., Feinstein, J.: Automatic detection of heads in colored images. In: Second Canadian Conference on Computer and Robot Vision. (2005) 276–281
10. Burns, J.B., Hanson, A., Riseman, E.M.: Extracting straight lines. IEEE Transactions on Pattern Analysis and Machine Intelligence **8** (1986) 425–455
11. Jain, A., Dubes, R.: Algorithms for Clustering Data. Prentice Hall, Englewood Cliffs, NJ (1988)

Combined Classifiers for Action Recognition

Arash Mokhber, Catherine Achard, Maurice Milgram, and Xingtai Qu

Laboratoire des Instruments et Systèmes d'Ile de France (LISIF)
Université Pierre et Marie Curie, 4 place Jussieu, Case courrier 252
75252 Paris cedex 05
arash.mokhber@lisif.jussieu.fr, achard@ccr.jussieu.fr,
maum@ccr.jussieu.fr, xingtai.qu@lisif.jussieu.fr

Abstract. In this study, a new method for recognizing everyday life actions is proposed. To enhance robustness, each sequence is characterized globally. Detection of moving areas is first performed on each image. All binary points form a volume in the three-dimensional (3D) space (x,y,t). This volume is characterized by its geometric 3D moments which are used to form a feature vector for the recognition. Action recognition is then carried out by employing two classifiers independently: a) a nearest center classifier, and b) an auto-associative neural network. The performance of these two is examined, separately. Based on this evaluation, these two classifiers are combined. For this purpose, a relevancy matrix is used to select between the results of the two classifiers, on a case by case basis. To validate the suggested approach, results are presented and compared to those obtained by using only one classifier.

1 Introduction

Human activity recognition has received much attention from the computer vision community since it leads to several applications such as video surveillance for security, entertainment systems and monitoring of patients or old people, in hospitals or in their apartments. The activity recognition problem is generally divided in two steps: 1) detecting and tracking the person in motion, and 2) recognition.

The focus of this work is on the second problem which is recognizing actions of everyday life, such as walking, sitting on a chair, jumping, bending or crouching.

Since the human body is not a rigid object and may present a multitude of postures for the same person, a robust modeling is difficult to obtain. Therefore, appearance models are utilized rather than geometric ones.

Among all existing 2D approaches without models, some consider the sequence as a succession of images. Martin and Crowley [1] recognize hand gestures using a finite state machine while in Ref. [2,3], the recognition is then carried out with hidden Markov models.

Recently, Bobick and David [4] have presented a view-based approach to the recognition of human movement. Both characteristics called MEI and MHI, are constructed globally throughout each sequence. Given a set of MEIs and MHIs for each view/movement of aerobic exercises, a statistical description of actions is obtained using the 7 Hu moments.

N. Zheng, X. Jiang, and X. Lan (Eds.): IWICPAS 2006, LNCS 4153, pp. 27 – 34, 2006.

The global study of the sequence can also be conducted by examining the empirical distributions of some characteristics. In Ref. [5], a vector of measurement in each pixel is composed of the exit of a bench of 12 space-time filters. Joint statistics on these vectors represented by a multidimensional histogram make it possible to carry out the recognition of actions. In Ref. [6], actions are characterized on several temporal scales using motion detection. The measurement between two actions is the distance between empirical distributions of these features. Actions can also be considered as 3D volumes. Thus, Schechtman and Irani [7] propose to recognize actions with a correlation between these volumes while Blank et al. [8] characterize them locally using properties of the solution to the Poisson equation.

Action recognition can be carried out by using and combining multiple results provided by several classifiers. The fusion of information, and more precisely the combination of classifiers is used to improve the performance of classification systems.

This combination may be considered for instance, in a sequential way. Viola and Jones [9] combine increasingly more complex AdaBoost classifiers in a “cascade” where a positive response from one classifier triggers the evaluation from the next one. For object detection this allows rejecting as many as possible negative instances (a negative outcome at any point of the cascade leads to immediate rejection) while achieving high true detection rates. The use of AdaBoost method for the training stage implies that each new weak classifier depends on the previous ones via the weighting of training samples.

As presented in this work, the fusion may also be performed in a parallel framework where the outcomes of independent classifiers are combined. This combination can be achieved by different approaches. The fuzzy approach [10] utilizes “fuzzy” fusion rules. The Bayesian approach [11] is based on probability properties; namely the Bayes rule. The neural approach [12] utilizes the outcomes of several classifiers which are combined by a neural network. The combination of classifiers may also be linear or multiplicative. Czyz et al. [13] use a simple summation rule to combine face verification experts which are assumed to be complementary. The result of the combination outperforms the best individual expert. Belaroussi et al. [14] also linearly combine connexionist models, an ellipse model based on the gradient orientation and a skin color model for the purpose of face localization. Tumer and Ghosh [15] provide an analytical framework to quantify the improvement in classification results of linear and order statistics combining.

Based on an earlier study [16], the recognition system developed in this work utilizes an appearance model. Actions are represented by 3D volumes (x,y,t) which are characterized by 3D geometric moments. Invariance to the view point is carried out by multiple views of the same action. In this work, the recognition is based on a modeling of each class. For a large sequence database, this avoids important computing times needed by the nearest neighbor method utilized in Ref. [16]. This recognition process consists of a fusion of two classifiers: a nearest center classifier, and an auto-associative neural network. The classifier combination is achieved by determining which classifier selects the true result for each example of the training database. This allows, when the two experts lead to discordant results, to favor one classifier rather than the other, according to the different cases.

2 Features Extracted from Sequences

The first stage of the activity recognition process consists of detecting moving areas. Therefore, the current image is compared at each instant with a reference image continuously updated. A second stage is also carried out to remove shadows that eventually are present in the scene [16].

The analysis is expanded to represent the 3D volume comprised of all moving points detected (x,y,t). This space-time volume contains information, such as, the silhouette of the person in each image or the action dynamics. To characterize this volume, without extracting (and separating) different information such as posture, movement, etc, 3D geometrical moments are considered. Let $\{x,y,t\}$ be the set of points of the binary volume where x and y represent the space coordinates and t, the temporal coordinate. The moment of order $(p+q+r)$ of this volume is determined by:

$$A_{pqr} = E\{x^p y^q t^r\}. \tag{1}$$

where E$\{x\}$ represents the *expectation* of x. In order to use features invariant to translation, the central moments are considered:

$$Ac_{pqr} = E\{(x - A_{100})^p (y - A_{010})^q (t - A_{001})^r\}. \tag{2}$$

These moments must also be invariant to scale in order to preserve invariance to the size of people or to the distance of the action with respect to the camera. Invariance to the duration of actions is also expected. Thus, for preserving the ratio of width-to-height of the binary silhouettes the following normalization is carried out:

$$M_{pqr} = E\left\{\left(\frac{x - A_{100}}{Ac_{200}{}^{1/4} Ac_{020}{}^{1/4}}\right)^p \left(\frac{y - A_{010}}{Ac_{200}{}^{1/4} Ac_{020}{}^{1/4}}\right)^q \left(\frac{t - A_{001}}{Ac_{002}{}^{1/2}}\right)^r\right\}. \tag{3}$$

For each action, a vector of features O, composed of the 14 moments of 2nd and 3rd order is computed:

$O = \{M_{200}, M_{011}, M_{101}, M_{110}, M_{300}, M_{030}, M_{003}, M_{210}, M_{201}, M_{120}, M_{021}, M_{102}, M_{012}, M_{111}\}$.

3 Presentation of the Sequence Database

A sequence database comprising 8 actions is considered, as follows: (1)"to crouch down", (2)"to stand up", (3) "to sit down", (4) "to sit up", (5) "to walk", (6) "to bend down", (7) "to get up from bending", and (8) "to jump".

As each action is divided into different viewpoints, 37 different classes are considered. The front, 45° and 90° views are captured while others are synthesized from the sequences already recorded (at -45°, at -90°) by symmetry. Each action is executed by 7 people, and repeated 230 times on average. The entire database comprises 1662 sequences. Presented below are some examples of images of the database representing various actions and silhouettes of actors.

Fig. 1. Sample images from the sequence database

For the recognition and training of classifiers, the sequence database is divided into two disjointed sets: 1) a training database, and 2) a test database. To test invariance of the method compared to people morphology, the training database is made up of actions carried out by six people.

4 Recognition with an Auto-associative Neural Network

The first classifier used for the recognition is an auto-associative neural network (AANN). For each of the 37 classes, an AANN is trained, using the training database. It consists of a 2-layer neural network for which the desired output is equal to the input. In this case the number of output cells is 14 (the same number as inputs), and the number of hidden cells is empirically set to 7.

A pre-treatment is achieved independently on each class to set most of the data between –1 and 1. It consists of centering vectors around the mean of their class and normalizing along each dimension by three times the standard deviation of the class.

For the recognition, the vector of features corresponding to the action to recognize is normalized with respect to the parameters of each class and presented as input for each one of the 37 AANNs. The reconstruction error between the input and the output of each AANN is then estimated with the Euclidian distance. Among the 37 classes, the one which results in the lowest distance between the input and the output is then selected to label the action. Table 1 presents the seven recognition rates obtained by placing each of the 7 persons in the test database one by one. These data are average recognition rates on all 8 actions.

Table 1. Recognition rates using AANNs

Person	1	2	3	4	5	6	7
Rate	89.3	89.0	81.7	95.1	92.1	91.4	70.8

Table 2. Average confusion matrix using AANNs

96.6	0	0	0.7	0	2.7	0	0
0	96.1	0	0	0	0	3.9	0
3.3	0	86.0	0	0	10.7	0	0
0	1.7	0	89.4	0	0	8.9	0
0.5	0	0.2	0	98.6	0.2	0.4	0
26.3	0	1.2	0	0	72.5	0	0
0	14.7	0	4.7	0	0	80.6	0
0	1.9	0	0	0	2.8	5.3	90.0

Therefore, one may conclude that actions are well-recognized. The worst recognition rate (70.8%) is obtained for person 7 who presents a particular binary silhouette due to her clothing: she wears a long skirt and is the only person in the database with a skirt. Even if for this person, some actions with a very particular binary volume (e.g., “to sit down”) are well recognized, confusion still exists between other classes such as “to walk” or “to jump”. Table 2 presents the average confusion matrix on the 8 actions obtained by averaging the 7 confusion matrices corresponding to those 7 people.

The most poorly recognized action (72.5%) is action 6, ("to bend down",) sometimes confused with action 1 ("to crouch down") which is a nearly similar action.

5 Recognition with the Nearest Center

For this stage, the mean vector and the covariance matrix of each class is estimated with the training data. The recognition is done by searching the nearest center for the vector of features corresponding to the action that has to be recognized using Mahanalobis distance. The action is then assigned to the class of this center.

It could be interesting to consider a mixture of Gaussians to represent each class. However, the dimension of the database (about 45 sequences for each one of the 37 classes) is too low compared to the dimension of the feature space (14) to carry out this method. Tables 3 and 4 present the average recognition rates and confusion matrix obtained with the nearest center. Despite the differences between the rates for each person, the average recognition rates on the seven persons are approximately the same for both methods (88.1 for AANNs and 89.7 for the nearest center). In this case, the confusion stands between action 4 (“to sit up”) and action 7 (“to get up from bending”) which are similar, as well.

Table 3. Recognition rates using the nearest center

Person	1	2	3	4	5	6	7
Rate	97.0	88.8	82.3	95.0	92.7	91.1	69.8

Table 4. Average confusion matrix using the nearest center

93.9	0	0	0	0.7	5.4	0	0
0	92.1	0	0	0	0	7.9	0
4.6	0	85.9	0	0.5	8.4	0.6	0
0	3.3	0	77.1	0	0	19.6	0
0	0	0.4	0	98.0	0.9	0.4	0.2
6.9	1.3	0.5	0	0	91.0	0	0.3
0	6.6	0	2.4	0	0	90.7	0.3
0	6.8	0.8	0	0	0	3.2	89.1

6 Association of Classifiers

Results presented in the two previous sections show that classifiers do not have the same behavior. It often appears that if one classifier is wrong, the other one selects the true result. Therefore, it would be of interest to identify the cases where one classifier has to be preferred over the other, especially when the outcomes of the two classifiers are different. Thus, for each classifier, a "relevancy matrix" is constructed based on the training database. Let cl_n be the class returned by the nearest center classifier, cl_d the one returned by AANNs, and cl the true class. The cell (i,j) of the "relevancy matrix" provides the probability that the classifier returns the true result while the two classifiers respectively select classes i and j:

$$\begin{cases} M_n(i,j) = P(cl = cl_n \mid i,j) \\ M_d(i,j) = P(cl = cl_d \mid i,j) \end{cases}. \tag{4}$$

When both classifiers lead to the same result, the decision is evident. Otherwise, when the returned classes are different, the "relevancy matrix" will be used to decide among the two classes, which is the true class. Thus, if the nearest center classifier leads to class i and the AANN to class j, the expected true class is the one which maximizes the a posteriori probability given by:

$$\begin{cases} P(cl = i) = M_n(i,j) P(s_n / d_n) \\ P(cl = j) = M_d(i,j) P(s_d / d_d) \end{cases}. \tag{5}$$

Where d_n and d_d are the minimum distance generated by each individual classifier, and s is a logical variable equal to 1 in case of true result and 0 otherwise. It is assumed that $P(s/d)$ is a decreasing exponential function of the distance d:

$$P(s = 1 \mid d) = \exp(-\lambda d). \tag{6}$$

The parameter λ can be evaluated using the recognition results over the training set, by computing the observation likelihood:

$$L(\lambda) = \prod_{i/s_i=1} \exp(-\lambda d_i) \prod_{j/s_j=0} 1 - \exp(-\lambda d_j). \tag{7}$$

By maximizing the log-likelihood, λ satisfies the following relation:

$$-\sum_{i/s_i=1} d_i + \sum_{j/s_j=0} \frac{d_j \exp(-\lambda d_j)}{1-\exp(-\lambda d_j)} = 0\,. \tag{8}$$

The root λ can be found by iterated dichotomy since the left part of Equation (8) is a decreasing function. This method is applied to evaluate λ_n and λ_d, independently for each classifier.

Table 5 and 6 present the recognition rates and confusion matrix obtained with the fusion of classifiers.

Table 5. Recognition Rate Using Association of Classifiers

Person	1	2	3	4	5	6	7
Rate	95.1	93.0	86.6	95.7	94.1	94.1	68.4

Table 6. Average Confusion Matrix Using Association of Classifiers

95.3	0	0	0.7	0	4.0	0	0
0	92.8	0	0	0	0	7.2	0
4.6	0	86.5	0	0.5	8.4	0	0
0	1.2	0	87.8	0	0	11.0	0
0.5	0	0.2	0	98.6	0.2	0.4	0
8.2	0	0.5	0	0	91.3	0	0
0	10.3	0	4.4	0	0	84.9	0.3
0	1.3	0	0	0	2.8	3.4	92.5

As can be seen in Table 5, the recognition rates have improved for most persons compared to both classifiers examined independently (except for person 1 and 7). The average recognition rate over the 7 persons is a more relevant data: 89.7% for the nearest center, 88.1% for AANNs and 91.2% for the association. Furthermore, the disparity between the different classes has been reduced as can be seen on the diagonal of the confusion matrix. The lowest recognition rate (84.9%) is obtained for action 7 ("to get up from bending"), confused with action 2 ("to stand up"). This lower recognition rate is higher than it was in the previous cases: 77.1% for the nearest center classifier and 72.5% for AANNs.

7 Summary and Conclusions

In this work, a method to recognize certain actions of everyday life is proposed. Motion detection is initially obtained on each image. The 3D volume constructed for each sequence from the binary images resulting from detection, is characterized by its 3D geometrical moments. Action recognition is carried out by utilizing the fusion of two different classifiers on a database of 1662 sequences divided into 8 actions and carried out by 7 people.

The classifier association is achieved by featuring a “relevancy matrix” that identifies cases where a classifier has to be preferred over the other. By combining the performances of both classifiers a recognition rate of 91.2% is obtained on the database.

An extension of the number of actors in the database is envisioned to be more robust to the silhouette of the person and improve classification results. Furthermore, increasing the number of examples per class may lead to a finer modeling of each class.

References

1. Martin J. and Crowley J.L., An appearance based approach to gesture recognition, International Conference on Image Analysis and Processing, Florence, Italia, 1997.
2. Sun X., Chen C. and Manjunath B.S., Probabilistic motion parameter models for human activity recognition, International Conference on Pattern Recognition, pp. 443-446, 2002.
3. Yamato J., Ohya J. and Ishii K., Recognizing Human Action in Time-Sequential Images using Hidden Markov Models, Computer Vision and Pattern Recognition, Los Alamitos, IL, pp. 379-385, June 15-18, 1992.
4. Bobick A.F. and Davis J.W., The recognition of human movement using temporal templates, IEEE transactions on Pattern Analysis and Machine Intelligence, vol.23, n°3 march 2001.
5. Chomat O. and Crowley J.L., Probabilistic recognition of activity using local appearance, Computer Vision and Pattern Recognition, Colorado, USA, 1999.
6. Zelnik-Manor L. and Irani M., Event based analysis of video, Computer Vision and Pattern Recognition, pp. 123-130, 2001.
7. Shechtman E. and Irani M., Space time behavior based correlation, Conference on Vision and Patern Recognition, San Diego, CA, USA.
8. Blank M., Gorelick L., Shechtman E., Irani M. and Basri R., Actions as space-time shapes, International Conference on Computer Vision, Beijing, China, 2005.
9. Viola P.A. and Jones V., Rapid object detection using a boosted cascade of simple features, Computer Vision and Pattern Recognition, 2001.
10. Kuncheva L.I., Fuzzy vs non-fuzzy in combining classifiers designed by boosting, IEEE Transactions on Fuzzy Systems, 11 (6), 2003, 729-741.
11. Xu L., Krzyzak A., Suen C.Y., Methods of combining multiple classifiers and their applications to handwriting recognition. IEEE Trans Syst Man Cybern 23(3):418–435, 1992.
12. Reddy N.V.S, Nagabhushan P., A multi-stage neural network model for unconstrained handwriting recognition, IEEE Trans Syst Man Cybern 23(3):418-435, 1992.
13. Czyz J., Kittler J. and Vendendorpe, Combining face verification experts, International Conference on Pattern Recognition, vol 2, pp.28-31, 2002.
14. Belaroussi R., Prevost L. and Milgram M., Combining model-based classifiers for face localization, Journal of Advances in Information Fusion, to be published, 2006.
15. Tumer K. and Ghosh J., Linear and order statistics combiners for pattern classification, CoRR, 1999.
16. Mokhber A., Achard C., Qu X. and Milgram M., Action Recognition with global features, IEEE Human Computer Interaction, Workshop of the International Conference on Computer Vision, Beijing, China, 2005.

Adaptive Sparse Vector Tracking Via Online Bayesian Learning

Yun Lei, Xiaoqing Ding, and Shengjin Wang

Electronic Engineering Department, Tsinghua University,
Beijing 100084, P.R. China
{leiyun, dxq, wsj}@ocrserv.ee.tsinghua.edu.cn

Abstract. In order to construct a flexible representation for robust and efficient tracking, a novel real-time tracking method based on online learning is proposed in this paper. Under Bayesian framework, RVM is used to learn the log-likelihood ratio of the statistics of the interested object region to those of the nearby backgrounds. Then, the online selected sparse vectors by RVM are integrated to construct an adaptive representation of the tracked object. Meanwhile, the trained RVM classifier is embedded into particle filtering for tracking. To avoid distraction by the particles in background region, the extreme outlier model is incorporated to describe the posterior probability distribution of all particles. Subsequently, mean-shift clustering and EM algorithm are combined to estimate the posterior state of the tracked object. Experimental results over real-world sequences have shown that the proposed method can efficiently and effectively handle drastic illumination variation, partial occlusion and rapid changes in viewpoint, pose and scale.

1 Introduction

Visual tracking is to optimally estimate the state of the interested object within current frame according to the previously defined object representation. In practice, it is difficult to track appearance changed object with a fixed representation due to inevitable variation in viewpoints, pose and illumination conditions. In addition, cluttered backgrounds and partial occlusion also challenge visual tracker. Therefore, online learning with all available information for robust tracking is very necessary and it has been a popular research topic nowadays.

So far, different visual trackers with online learning mechanism can be mainly categorized to be generative model based [1, 2, 3, 4, 5, 6] and discriminative model based [7, 8, 9, 10]. WSL tracker [1] maintains object model with stable and transient statistics that are updated with online EM. Subspace based trackers update their corresponding models with incremental PCA [2], incremental SVD [3], and incremental Gramm-Schmidt process [4]. The template tracking with PCA based linear subspace model is investigated in [5]. With sequential GMM, online density based appearance model is updated for object tracking in [6]. The disadvantage of generative model based trackers are that they focus on how to model the interested object without consideration the cluttered backgrounds. Thus, they

N. Zheng, X. Jiang, and X. Lan (Eds.): IWICPAS 2006, LNCS 4153, pp. 35–45, 2006.

are apt to be distracted by similar background regions. For this reason, discriminative model based trackers are designed to resist drift from the interested object to similar background regions. In literature [7,9], different mechanisms are described to select discriminative features for tracking. In practice, a visual tracker depending on some sort of feature may fail to work when the foreground and nearby background regions are not discriminative enough in the specified feature space. As stated in [8], color feature affords limited power to discriminate an object from similar background regions (especially within gray image sequences), and an extension of the methods to different feature spaces for better performance is not obvious. Nguyen [8] proposed to model the foreground and background texture features with Gabor filters to handle severe aspect changes of foreground object. The foreground and background templates are adaptively updated with empirically predefined learning rate. However, improper learning rate will raise the specter of gradual drift. Ensemble tracking [10] trains an ensemble of weak classifiers to determine if a pixel belongs to an object or not, instead of explicitly representing the object. Then, mean shift algorithm [11] is implemented in the confidence map predicted with trained strong classifier to find the object location. Collins [12] has pointed out that spatially correlated background distractions could easily attract mean shift window and cause tracking failure.

Recently, the relevance vector machine (RVM) regression [13] has been used to build displacement expert for object tracking [14] in which the RVM expert predicts motion parameters of the interested object. The work of efficient tracking with RVM expert is an extension of support vector tracking [15] with sparse Bayesian learning theory. Nevertheless, the tracker is not tolerant to great variation of viewpoint, scale and articulation at the same time.

In essence, three key problems in visual tracking are how to construct a flexible representation of the interested object, to accurately estimate the target state with available observations, and to reliably update the target representation in time. To deal with the three problems, this paper intends to design a general framework of on-line Bayesian learning to extract useful information from all available observations for tracking, rather than to develop a visual tracker depending on some specified feature space.

This paper is organized as follows. Section 2 discusses the online Bayesian learning for visual tracking. Section 3 describes probabilistic state inference for particle filtering. Section 4 investigates how to update the object representation. Experimental results are demonstrated in Section 5, and some conclusions are drawn in Section 6.

2 Online Bayesian Learning Framework

At any time t, denote the state of a tracked object within image I_t by vector X_t, all state observations up to time t by $Z_t = \{z_0, ..., z_t\}$, and all image observations up to time t by $O_t = \{I_0, ..., I_t\}$. Standard Bayesian sequential estimation includes two recursive stages: prediction and update. Given all observations up to time $t-1$, the target state at time t is predicted by

$$p(X_t|O_{t-1}, Z_{t-1}) = p(X_t|Z_{t-1}) = \int p(X_t|X_{t-1})p(X_{t-1}|Z_{t-1})dX_{t-1}. \tag{1}$$

When observations I_t and z_t are available, the state can be update by

$$\begin{aligned} p(X_t|O_t, Z_t) &\propto p(I_t, z_t|X_t, O_{t-1}, Z_{t-1})p(X_t|O_{t-1}, Z_{t-1}) \\ &= p(I_t, z_t|X_t)p(X_t|Z_{t-1}) \\ &= p(I_t|X_t)p(z_t|X_t)p(X_t|Z_{t-1}), \end{aligned} \tag{2}$$

where $p(I_t|X_t)$ is the image observation likelihood which is very crucial for visual tracking, and $p(z_t|X_t)$ is the state observation likelihood which will be discussed in next section.

2.1 Image Observation Likelihood Formulation

Given state X_t of the interested object, image I_t can be divided into foreground region R_{FG} and background region R_{BG}, where $R_{FG} \cup R_{BG} = I_t$, and $R_{FG} \cap R_{BG} = \emptyset$. Denote $f(x, y)$ to be the feature value at pixel (x, y) within image I_t after mapping I_t into some feature space. Let $p_{on}(R_{FG}|X_t)$ be the likelihood of observing region R_{FG} given the representation of the tracked object, and $p_{off}(R_{BG}|X_t)$ be the likelihood of observing region R_{BG} from uninterested image regions. Then, the image observation likelihood can be decomposed as

$$\begin{aligned} p(I_t|X_t) &= p(R_{FG}, R_{BG}|X_t) \\ &= p_{on}(R_{FG}|X_t)p_{off}(R_{BG}|X_t) \\ &= \frac{p_{on}(R_{FG}|X_t)}{p_{off}(R_{FG}|X_t)} p_{off}(R_{FG}|X_t)p_{off}(R_{BG}|X_t) \\ &= \frac{p_{on}(R_{FG}|X_t)}{p_{off}(R_{FG}|X_t)} p_{off}(I_t|X_t). \end{aligned} \tag{3}$$

Since the likelihood $p_{off}(I_t|X_t)$ is independent of X_t, we have

$$p(I_t|X_t) \propto \frac{p_{on}(R_{FG}|X_t)}{p_{off}(R_{FG}|X_t)} = \exp\{l(R_{FG}|X_t)\}, \tag{4}$$

where $l(R_{FG}|X_t) = \log\{p_{on}(R_{FG}|X_t)/p_{off}(R_{FG}|X_t)\}$ is the log-likelihood ratio of the interested object distribution to background distribution. Expression (4) manifests that image observation likelihood $p(I_t|X_t)$ characterizes not the similarity between image region R_{FG} and the interested object representation, but the degree to which region R_{FG} discriminates the interested object from nearby background. However, a generative model based tracker just concentrates on the similarity, which explains why this sort of visual tracker is apt to be distracted by confused backgrounds.

Therefore, this paper will focus on online approximation of the log-likelihood ratio in (4) with statistical learning theory. Under this general framework, the discriminative information can be online learned for tracking. Consequently, the visual tracker designed in this paper will be fairly flexible, and can be easily extended to different feature spaces.

2.2 Sparse Bayesian Learning

During tracking process, the number of available samples for statistical learning is very limited and computational efficiency is also worthy serious consideration. In this paper, the log-likelihood ratio in (4) learned by RVM for its superior performance in sparse Bayesian learning [13]. Compared with SVM [16], the advantages of RVM include the benefits of probabilistic predictions, exceptional degree of sparsity, satisfactory generalization ability, and circumventing the constraint of Mercer's condition. Given a set of M-dim samples $\{\mathbf{x}_n\}_{n=1}^N$ along with corresponding labels $\{\mathbf{t}_n\}_{n=1}^N$, the standard probabilistic formulation of RVM is

$$\mathbf{t}_n = g(\mathbf{x}_n; \mathbf{w}) + \epsilon_n, \tag{5}$$

where additive noise ϵ_n is from zero-mean Gaussian process with variance σ^2. The scalar output of RVM is the linearly weighted sum of input samples:

$$g(\mathbf{x}_n; \mathbf{w}) = \sum_{i=1}^{N} \omega_i K(\mathbf{x}, \mathbf{x}_i) + \omega_0, \tag{6}$$

where $K : \mathbb{R}^M \times \mathbb{R}^M \to \mathbb{R}$ is the kernel function between two input vectors. The corresponding weights $\mathbf{w} = [\omega_0, ..., \omega_N]$ are determined by RVM training process. The popular choice of a zero-mean Gaussian prior distribution over $\mathbf{w}$ is preferred:

$$p(\mathbf{w}) = N(\mathbf{w}; \mathbf{0}, \mathbf{A}), \tag{7}$$

where the diagonal covariance matrix $\mathbf{A}$ contains individual hyper-parameters independently associated with every weight. With assumption of Bernoulli distribution for $p(\mathbf{t}|\mathbf{x})$, the likelihood $p(\mathbf{t}|\mathbf{w})$ can be formulated as follows for binary classification problem:

$$p(\mathbf{t}|\mathbf{w}) = \prod_{n=1}^{N} \sigma\{g(\mathbf{x}_n; \mathbf{w})\}^{\mathbf{t}_n} \left[1 - \sigma\{g(\mathbf{x}_n; \mathbf{w})\}\right]^{1-\mathbf{t}_n}, \tag{8}$$

where $\sigma(g) = 1/(1 + e^{-g})$ is the sigmoid function to convert real-valued output to probabilistic prediction. Utilizing Laplace approximation, the best weights are found according to $\mathbf{\Sigma} = (\mathbf{\Phi}^{\mathbf{T}}\mathbf{B}\mathbf{\Phi} + \mathbf{A})^{-1}$ and $\mathbf{w} = \mathbf{\Sigma}\mathbf{\Phi}^{\mathbf{T}}\mathbf{B}\mathbf{t}$, where $\mathbf{\Phi}$ is the design matrix with $\mathbf{\Phi}_{ij} = K(\mathbf{x}_i, \mathbf{x}_j)$, and $\mathbf{B} = diag(\beta_1, ..., \beta_N)$ is a diagonal matrix with $\beta_n = \sigma\{g(\mathbf{x}_n; \mathbf{w})\} \left[1 - \sigma\{g(\mathbf{x}_n; \mathbf{w})\}\right]$.

With the trained RVM classifier, the log-likelihood ratio of image region R_{FG} can be predicted by $l(R_{FG}|X_t) = g(R_{FG}; \mathbf{w})$. In order to suppress the possible estimation error of very large $\|l(R_{FG}|X_t)\|$, we adopt the sigmoid function to approximate image observation likelihood

$$p(I_t|X_t) = \frac{1}{1+\exp\{-l(R_{FG}|X_t)\}}. \tag{9}$$

Obviously, $p(I_t|X_t)$ preserves the linear property when $l(R_{FG}|X_t)$ is within range $[-2, 2]$.

3 Probabilistic State Inference

Particle filtering [17] is a sequential importance sampling method, which has proven to be a powerful tool for solving nonlinear/non-Gaussian tracking problems. Its key idea is to approximate required posterior distribution $p(X_t|O_t, Z_t)$ by a weighted set of samples $S_t = \{s_t^{(n)}, \pi_t^{(n)}|n = 1, ..., N_s\}$. The corresponding importance weight of each particle can be calculated by

$$\begin{aligned}\pi_t^{(n)} &= p(I_t, z_t|X_t = s_t^{(n)}) \\ &= p(I_t|X_t = s_t^{(n)})p(z_t|X_t = s_t^{(n)}),\end{aligned} \tag{10}$$

where $\sum_{n=1}^{N_s} \pi_t^{(n)} = 1$.

3.1 Dynamic Model

Define the state vector of sample s as $(x, y, R_x, R_y, \dot{x}, \dot{y}, \alpha)$, where (x, y) indicates the central location of the tracked object, (R_x, R_y) the scales in horizontal and vertical directions, $(\dot{x}, \dot{y})$ the central motion vector, and α the scale change velocity. In prediction stage, the state of sample s is propagated through the first order dynamic model

$$s_t = Hs_{t-1} + \mathbf{v}_{t-1}, \tag{11}$$

where matrix H characterizes the transition model, and $\mathbf{v}_{t-1}$ is a zero-mean multivariate Gaussian random variable. The random samples from Gaussian distribution are drawn with quasi-random sequence generator instead of pseudo-random sequence generator for fast convergence [18].

3.2 Statistical Observation Model

Given the generated set of particles $S_t = \{s_t^{(n)}, \pi_t^{(n)}|n = 1, ..., N_s\}$, assume the state observation likelihood is Gaussian distribution:

$$p(z_t|X_t = s_t^{(n)}) = N(s_t^{(n)}; \mu, V), \tag{12}$$

where μ is the mean and V is the covariance matrix. Usually, only a fraction of particles approach the true state of the tracked object, and others can be considered as outliers. In order to accurately estimate the true state of the target, all particles in S_t are clustered into groups with mean shift clustering [19]. The label of the group in which the particle with largest importance weight is assigned to be 1, and those of other groups are assigned to be 0. Thus, the zero-labeled particles are treated as outliers, and their corresponding image observation likelihoods are revalued by

$$p(I_t|X_t = s_t^{(n)}) = \min\{p(I_t|X_t = s_t^{(i)}) > 0; s_t^{(i)} \in S_t\}. \tag{13}$$

Then, the extreme outlier model [20] is utilized to convert seeking maximum likelihood of $\prod_{n=1}^{N_s} \pi_t^{(n)}$ to optimizing

$$\begin{aligned} h(\mu, V) &= \sum_n p(I_t|X_t = s_t^{(n)}) p(z_t|X_t = s_t^{(n)}) \\ &= \sum_n \eta_n N(s_t^{(n)}; \mu, V), \end{aligned} \tag{14}$$

where $\eta_n = p(I_t|X_t = s_t^{(n)})$. From the Jensen's inequality, we have

$$\log(h(\mu, V)) \geq \sum_n \log(\frac{\eta_n N(s_t^{(n)}; \mu, V)}{q_n})^{q_n}, \tag{15}$$

where $\sum_n q_n = 1$, and $q_n \geq 0$. Subsequently, EM algorithm is used to estimate μ and V with the following procedure.

Input: initial parameters μ_0 and V_0 estimated with all one-labeled particles by above mean shift clustering.

1. **E-step:** compute q_n-s with fixed μ_m and V_m,

$$q_n = \frac{\eta_n N(s_t^{(n)}; \mu, V)}{\sum_i \eta_i N(s_t^{(i)}; \mu, V)}. \tag{16}$$

2. **M-step:** update μ_m and V_m by

$$\mu_{m+1} = \sum_n q_n s_t^{(n)}, \tag{17}$$

$$V_{m+1} = \sum_n q_n (s_t^{(n)} - \mu_m)(s_t^{(n)} - \mu_m)^T. \tag{18}$$

4 Update Object Representation

Updating target representation is an important component of online learning for tracking. In order to design a visual tracker independent of color information, feature extraction modules with gray image as input are preferable. Lowe [21] proposed a scale invariant feature transform (SIFT), which has achieved outstanding performance as a reliable local region descriptor [22]. In this paper, the SIFT descriptor is utilized to represent the interested image region. For efficiency, eight orientation integral images [23] are precomputed with normalized image pixel values in range $[0, 1]$. The local histograms of oriented gradients within 4×4 subregions are stacked into a multidimensional feature vector. The kernel function employed to compute similarity between two input feature vectors with normalized lengths is the radial basis function:

$$K(x_i, x_j) = \exp\{-(\sqrt{2}\gamma)^{-2}\|\mathbf{x}_i - \mathbf{x}_j\|\}, \tag{19}$$

where the kernel width γ is very crucial for convergence of RVM training: too small kernel width leads to over-fitting, and too large one leads to under-fitting. Since the maximum Euclidean distance between two SIFT descriptors is $\sqrt{2}$, the value of γ is determined by $3.5\gamma = \sqrt{2}$ (99.95% confidence interval).

4.1 Create Initial Training Set

To learn the log-likelihood ratio of image observation in (4), an online training set including positive and negative samples is created as follows. Denote the initial location of the interested object by (x, y, R_x, R_y), the central locations of negative samples are uniformly generated on the circle with $\mathbf{d}_{neg} = \sqrt{R_x^2 + R_y^2}$ pixels away from the object center (x, y), and their corresponding scale perturbation is up to $\pm 40\%$. Likewise, the central locations of the positive samples are randomly generated with $\mathbf{d}_{pos}$ pixels away from (x, y), where $0 \leq \mathbf{d}_{pos} \leq 0.2\mathbf{d}_{neg}$. Their corresponding scale perturbation is up to $\pm 20\%$. To seek the trade-off between sampling density and RVM computational complexity $O(N^3)$, the sample size for positive set is $N_{pos} = 20$, and that for negative set is $N_{neg} = 40$. The selected sparse vectors by RVM training will be used to represent the interested object.

4.2 Update Ensemble of Sparse Vectors

Initially, let the object model be $U = \{u_1, u_2, ..., u_k\}$, where u_1,u_2,...,u_k are the selected sparse vectors from positive samples by RVM training. At any time $t > 0$, denote the feature descriptor of the tracked object region by u_t. If the image observation likelihood satisfies

$$0 < b \leq p(I_t|X_t) \leq a < 1, \tag{20}$$

then add current region descriptor u_t to the object model U by incremental augmentation $U = \{U, u_t\}$. If the number of elements in U is larger than N_{pos}, the oldest elements $|U| - N_{pos}$ will be removed to fix the model size to be $|U| = N_{pos}$. The parameter a in (20) is used to avoid redundancy resulting from too much similar region descriptors, and parameter b to resist incorrect addition of descriptors of the partially occluded regions to the object model. Empirical values determined by experiments are $a = 0.99$ and $b = 0.1$.

In addition, the RVM classifier will be retrained with positive samples from the object model U and negative samples randomly generated from the nearby backgrounds when current image observation likelihood $p(I_t|X_t = p(u_t))$ is below the threshold b. Therefore, the object model built with adaptive ensemble of sparse vectors not only affords discriminative information between tracked object and the nearby backgrounds, but also benefits from temporal fusion of stable tracking history.

5 Experiential Results

Experiments were conducted over video sequence captured in different scenarios to evaluate the performance of the proposed visual tracker, and some representative results are reported in this paper. The number of particles used for tracking in all experiments is 150.

5.1 Qualitative Comparisons

The *ThreePastShop2Cor.mpg* sequence (**Fig. 1**) has 1521 frames of 384×244 pixels (available at [24]). The interested pedestrian walks parallel with two nearby persons that cast challenge to the visual tracker since the three persons have similar appearances (in gray images), and the left most person changes his relative positions to the right most side during walking. The proposed tracker succeeds in locking on the interested pedestrian until it is occluded, and our tracking results are comparable with the discriminative model based tracker via online selection of Haar features [9].

Fig. 1. Tracking pedestrian among nearby walking persons. The frames 370, 472, 506, 523, 544, 576, 582, 621, 746, and 822 are shown.

To compare with the generative model based tracker adopting subspace learning, **Fig. 2** shows some difficult tracking frames in the *Dudek* sequence (available at [25]). The interested human face undergoes significant appearance changes, such as, occlusion by hand, taking the glass on and off, head rotation and scale variation. The proposed tracker affords comparable performance with the subspace learning based tracker in [4].

To demonstrate the flexibility of the proposed method, the tracking results in **Fig. 3** show the performance the proposed tracker in adapting to severe

Fig. 2. Tracking Human Face. The frames 1, 209,365, 695, 729, 935, 956, 975, 1096 and 1145 are shown.

illumination variation and continuous jitter of on-vehicle camera. In **Fig. 4**, the swift runner within the movie clip from *Forrest Gump* is tracked. The challenges include drastic variations in pose, viewpoint and scale. In addition, a portion of background pixels compassed within the rectangle boundary gives rise to appearance changes.

Fig. 3. Tracking car over on-vehicle sequence. The frames 1, 224, 388, 444, 455, 508, 711, 733, 1350 and 1520 are shown.

5.2 Computational Complexity

Let K_o be the quantized orientation bins of image gradients, the computational complexity for calculating integral images with resolution $N_h \times N_w$ is $O(N_h \times N_w \times K_o)$. Denote N_r to be the number of sparse vector selected by RVM, and N_s the number of the sampled particles. The complexity for particle filter tracking is about $O(N_r \times N_s)$ without considering EM optimization initialized by mean-shift clustering, and that of training RVM is $O\left((N_{pos} + N_{neg})^3\right)$.

On standard PC (P4 2.8GHz and 512M), the implementation of the proposed method coded in C++ language runs at 65 ms/frame for 384×288 video sequences with 150 particles. The time cost for calculating integral images of oriented

Fig. 4. Tracking swift runner. The frames 1, 36, 58, 78, 83 and 165 are shown.

gradients is about 53 ms/frame, while that needed for particle tracking with adaptive ensemble of sparse vectors is only 12 ms/frame.

6 Conclusions

The paper describes a novel real-time visual tracker via online Bayesian learning. As the experimental results reported, the proposed method can robustly track an object in the presence of drastic illumination, partial occlusion and rapid changes in pose, viewpoint and scale. The main contribution of this paper can be concluded as follows:

1. Online Bayesian learning of the image observation likelihood of the tracked object with RVM classification.
2. Temporal fusion of the selected sparse vectors into an adaptive representation of the tracked object for effective and efficient tracking.
3. Embedding trained RVM classifier into particle filtering.
4. Robust estimation of the target state with mean-shift initialized EM algorithm.

Beacuse of its generality, the proposed framework of online Bayesian learning could be extended to track different objects with various features. It remains future work to explore how to combine offline and online learning to improve visual tracker further.

References

1. Jepson, A., Fleet, D., EI-Maraghi, T.: Robust Online Appearance Models for Visual Tracking. PAMI **10** (2003) 1296-1311
2. Skocaj, D., Leonardis, A.:Weighted and robust incremental method for subspace learning. In: Proceedings of ICCV. (2003)
3. Ross, D., Lim, J., Yang, M-H.: Adaptive Probabilistic Visual Tracking with Incremental Subspace Update. In: Proceedings of ECCV. (2004)
4. Ho, J., Lee, K-C., Yang, M-H., Kriegman, D.: Visual Tracking Using Learned Linear Subspace. In: Proceedings of CVPR. (2004)
5. Matthews, I., Ishikawa, T., Baker, S.: The Template Update Problem. PAMI **6** (2004) 810-815
6. Han, B., Davis, L.: On-Line Density-Based Appearance Modeling for Object Tracking. In: Proceedings of ICCV. (2005)
7. Collins, R.T., Liu, Y.: On-line Selection of Discriminative Tracking Features. In: Proceedings of ICCV. (2003)
8. Nguyen, H.T., Smeulders, A.: Tracking Aspects of the Foreground against the Background. In: Proceedings of ECCV. (2004)
9. Wang, J., Gao, W., Chen, X.: Online Selecting Discriminative Tracking Features using Particle Filter. In: Proceedings of CVPR. (2005)
10. Avidan, S.: Ensemble Tracking. In: Proceedings of CVPR. (2005)
11. Comaniciu, D., Ramesh, V., Meer, P.: Kernel-Based Object Tracking. PAMI **5** (2003) 564-577
12. Collins, R.T., Liu, Y., Leordeanu, M.: Online Selection of Discriminative Tracking Features. PAMI **10** (2005) 1631-1643
13. Tipping, M.E.: Sparse Bayesian Learning and the Relevance Vector Machine. JMLR **1** (2001) 211-244
14. Williams, O., Blake, A., Cipolla, R.: Sparse Bayesian Learning for Efficient Visual Tracking. PAMI **8** (2005) 1-13
15. Avidan, S.: Support Vector Tracking. PAMI **8** (2004) 1064-1072
16. Vapnik, V.: The Nature of Statistical Learning Theory. Springer Verlag, New York (1995)
17. Arulampalam, M.S., Maskell, S., Gordon, N., Clapp, T.: A Tutorial on Particle Filters for Online Nonliner/Non-Gaussian Bayesian Tracking. Signal Processing **2** (2002) 174-188
18. Philomin, V., Duraiswami, R., Davis, L.: Quasi-Random Sampling for Condensation. In: Proceedings of ECCV. (2000)
19. Comaniciu, D., Meer, P.: Mean Shift: A Robust Approach Toward Feature Space Analysis. PAMI **5** (2002) 603-619
20. Zivkovic, Z., Krose, B.: An EM-like Algorithm for Color-Histogram-Based Object Tracking. In: Proceedings of CVPR. (2004)
21. Lowe, D.G.: Distinctive Image Features from Scale-Invariant Keypoints. IJCV **2** (2004) 91-110
22. Mikolajczyk, K., Schmid, C.: A Performance Evaluation of Local Descriptors. PAMI **10** (2005) 1615-1630
23. Viola, P., Jones, M.J.: Robust Real-Time Face Detection. IJCV **2** (2004) 137-154
24. http://homepages.inf.ed.ac.uk/rbf/CAVIAR/.
25. http://www.cs.toronto.edu/vis/projects/dudekfaceSequence.html.

Iterative Division and Correlograms for Detection and Tracking of Moving Objects

Rafik Bourezak and Guillaume-Alexandre Bilodeau

Departement of computer engineering
École Polytechnique de Montréal, P.O. Box 6079, Station Centre-ville
Montréal (Québec), Canada, H3C 3A7
rafik.bourezak@polymtl.ca, guillaume-alexandre.bilodeau@polymtl.ca

Abstract. This paper presents an algorithm for the detection and tracking of moving objects based on color and texture analysis for real time processing. Our goal is to study human interaction by tracking people and objects. The object detection algorithm is based on color histograms and iteratively divided interest regions for motion detection. The tracking algorithm is based on correlograms which combines spectral and spatial information to match detected objects in consecutive frames.

Keywords: Motion detection, background subtraction, iterative subdivision, objects tracking, correlograms.

1 Introduction

Nowadays, organizations that need a surveillance system can easily get low priced surveillance cameras but they still need many security agents to keep a permanent look at all time on all the monitors. This approach is not efficient, and in fact, most of the time video tapes or files are replayed to check on a particular event after it has happened. Thus, the automation of these systems is needed as it would allow automatically monitoring all the cameras simultaneously, and advising security agents only when a suspect event is on-going. This makes video surveillance an important and challenging topic in computer vision. A surveillance system is composed mainly of three different steps. The first step consists in detecting objects in motion. The second step is tracking, although some recent works combine these two first steps [1]. Finally, the third step is usually a high-level interpretation of the on-going events.

In this paper, we present an algorithm for each step. By opposition to previous works, for example [2] where algorithms are based on grayscale sequences and shape analysis, the developed algorithms are based on texture and color analysis to obtain more precise identification of objects.

If we briefly review existing approaches for motion detection, we note that for stationary cameras, most are based on a comparison with a reference image frame on a pixel by pixel basis [2,3]. Most important object detection algorithms are listed in [4]. An analysis of these methods show that they are sensitive to

N. Zheng, X. Jiang, and X. Lan (Eds.): IWICPAS 2006, LNCS 4153, pp. 46–55, 2006.

local variations and noise, and post-processing is often necessary to filter out erroneously labeled motion pixels. However, post-processing cannot fix detection errors involving large groups of pixels wrongly labeled on a local basis. To tackle this issue, we propose an algorithm that naturally filters out local variations by using color histograms on iteratively divided interest regions. Hence, contrarily to the usual strategy, here we first consider groups of pixels, and then gradually subdivide regions until a given precision is obtained. Motion detection is at the beginning a region-based process, and at the end it tends to a pixel-based method. However, by starting with regions, small perturbations are ignored and hence the quality of the detection and of the reference background is improved. Furthermore, color histograms are invariant to image scaling, rotation and translation, and hence allow focusing on regions with significant motion. Finally, by controlling the number of subdivisions, our object detection algorithm can be performed at different scale to adjust to the object shape precision needed for a given application. That is, a coarse or precise shape of moving objects can be obtained.

For the tracking step, works are often based on multiple hypotheses analysis [5], other on statistics [2,3]. We chose to use color and texture combined with some hypotheses analysis to determine new and previous objects in the scene. That is, we track by appearance.

Finally for the third step, we focus on tracking object relationships regardless of their identity. This will allow us analyzing specific behaviors of the detected objects such as the transportation of objects [2], or an illegal entry in a forbidden area [6]. Tracking generically, independently of the identity of objects will allow us to handle a larger set of objects without strong assumptions too early in the scene interpretation process. The contributions of this paper are a moving object detection algorithm that analyses the video frames based on regions of pixels and the use of correlograms in the HSV color space for object tracking. The first contribution allows a significantly less noisy detection of moving objects, and the second allows a robust appearance tracking of moving objects. The remainder of this paper is organized as follows. In section 2 preprocessing phase of video sequences is explained, along with the motion detection algorithm and possible post-processing. Section 3 presents the algorithms for the tracking and relationship analysis. Then, section 4 shows experimental results and their analysis. Finally, we conclude and present future works in section 5.

2 Methodology

Preprocessing is used to filter out noise and for color conversion. Then, the object detection algorithm is applied. To remove remaining shadows, it is possible to use some post-processing, though not necessary.

2.1 Preprocessing

Video capture is done in the RGB color space; however this color space is not suited for our application because small changes in the light intensity change significantly an object description. We prefer a color space less sensitive to light intensity. Thus, the HSV color space is used for all the processing because it provides direct control over brightness to normalize the light intensity V. It also focuses on the chromaticity present in Hue and Saturation. That is why H and S are given more importance in the quantization phase. Nonetheless, Hue is considered to be more reliable for color segmentation. So, the colors are quantized in 162 bins (18X3X3). Before converting from RGB to HSV space, a 3X3 median filter is applied to clean the image from acquisition noise.

2.2 Detection of Objects in Motion

The first step is to detect object in motion. This issue has been addressed by many algorithms [2,3,6]. In our application, we specifically need a time efficient algorithm that is not affected by brightness changes and noise. What we consider noise is object shadows, changes in the scene that are not of interest such as tree leaves motion, and also noise resulting from the acquisition which has not been cleaned by the median filter. To reduce the impact of noise naturally without many post-processing steps, we propose a method that is not limited to local pixel change. Instead, we consider groups of pixels to filter out noise by somewhat averaging changes over a window.

The idea is to split empirically the image into squared regions of the same size. At each step, color histograms of both reference frame H_{ref} and the current frame H_{cur} are calculated for each region. Then, the L_1 distance metric is used to measure the distance between both histograms.

The L_1 distance returns the level of difference, and it is defined as:

$$L_1 = \sum |H_{ref(i)} - H_{cur(i)}| \tag{1}$$

If L_1 is larger than a specified threshold, than the regions are different, and motion is detected in that region. The threshold is fixed as a percentage of the square size, according to the level of change we want to detect. That is, the smaller is the square size, the larger will be the value of the threshold. Typically, $Th_{i+1} = Th_i + 0.10$ with Th_0 =0.20. These values were set experimentally. Since histograms are normalized, changes in light intensity should not affect the threshold. More specifically, motion detection algorithm steps are:

1. The image is first split into squares of size X_1 by X_1, the value of X depends on the size of the objects we want to track. The larger the object is relatively to the frame, the larger is X (and vice versa). Let suppose X_1=N. (see white squares in Fig. 1a).
2. For each region, the histograms of both the current and reference frame are evaluated using the quantization described in section 2. Then, the L_1 distance is calculated between each pair of histograms. If according to L_1, the square regions are similar, no motion is detected in that region. Otherwise, we consider that motion is detected and label this region as an interest region to be further processed.

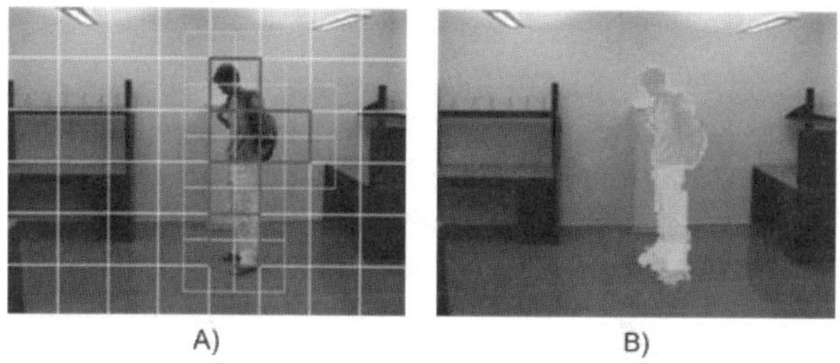

Fig. 1. A) Step one with N=64 (white square), and the first pass of step 2 and 3 (gray square). B) Final result with X_i=4 (y=4).

3. The interest regions identified at step 2 are split in four smaller squared region, that is $X_i = X_{i-1}/2$ (see the bold gray squares in Fig. 1a, to have a more accurate segmentation of the objects in motion. Also, to preserve small extremities of objects, we split in four outside boundaries regions and include the bordering quarters to the interest regions (see bordering grey squares in Fig. 1a. Then step 2 is repeated. The reference frame is updated with the content of the regions where no motion is detected. This way, the gradual changes in lighting is accounted for. This should allow our algorithm to perform reliably for outside scenes observed during extended time.
4. We repeat step 3 until $X_i == N/2y$, where y is a threshold fixed according to the desired level of precision. Fig. 1b shows the final result for region of 4 by 4 pixels.

At this point, the detection of objects in motion is completed. Compared to standard background subtraction algorithms, our method does not need a statistical background model. It provides efficiency with the control of the detected object shape precision, as coarse or precise shape of objects can be obtained based on the selected minimum region of interest size (see Fig. 2). Furthermore, the motion of small objects can be naturally filtered.

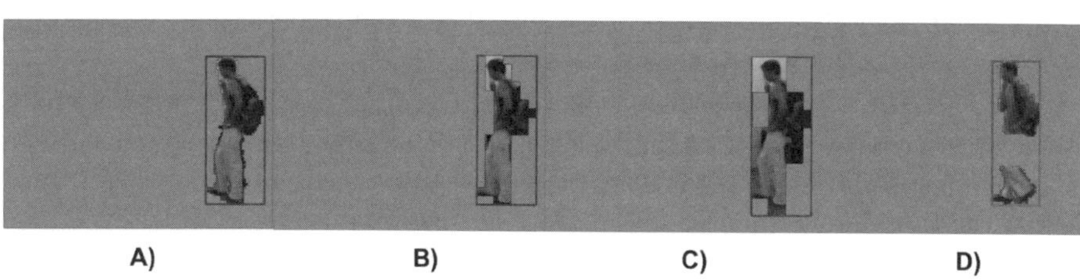

Fig. 2. Detecting and tracking moving objects. A) Object detection at fine scale, at frame 43, B) and C) object detection at coarser scales and D) fragmented object.

2.3 Postprocessing

Although, the detection algorithm filters out most of the noise, in some frames noise may persist because of strong shadows. This is caused by the fact that the floor has strong reflections, and these small reflection regions are in the area of squared interest regions containing motion. If such small regions are inside interest area where there is other motion for a number of a subdivision, they eventually end up at a scale where they have a significant impact of their own on the histogram of an interest region. That is why some noisy region may be included in the final segmentation. These noisy regions will be exclusively located near larger segmented region. They are removed using the algorithm proposed by Cucchiara *et al.* for shadow detection [9]. Note that, the HSV quantization of the frames and histogram difference threshold can be modified to avoid post processing. In our current work, we aim to do that.

3 Tracking of Object in Motion

The detected objects are tracked using correlograms which have been proven to be a better feature detector than histograms [7][8]. It is a two-dimensional matrix C that combines color and texture information by quantizing the spatial distribution of color. $C(i,j)$ indicates how many times color i co-occurs with color j according the spatial relationship given by the distance vector $V(dx,dy)$, where dx and dy represent the displacement in rows and columns respectively.

Let I be the image of width W and height H, the correlogram is defined as follows:

$$C(i,j) = |\{(x,y) =\in N^2, x < W, y < H | I(x,y) = i \wedge I(x+dx, y+dy) = j\}| \quad (2)$$

For every detected object its histogram and correlogram in the HSV space is calculated.

First, the histogram intersection is computed to verify globally if the objects are coarsely alike. Histogram intersection HI is defined as follows:

$$HI(x,y) = \min(H_p(i,j), H_o(i,j)) \quad (3)$$

Where H_p and H_o represents the color histogram of the object we are looking for and the classified one respectively.

Then correlogram intersection is calculated to compare in more precisely both objects if necessary. Correlogram intersection CI is used generally to check if an image contains another image. Here we used it to compare objects. It is defined as follows:

$$CI(x,y) = \min(C_p(i,j), C_o(i,j)) \quad (4)$$

where C_p and C_o represents the correlograms of the object we are looking for (Obj_p) and the classified one (Obj_o) respectively. Once the correlegram intersection is computed, the distance L_1 is calculated between C_p and CI. The closer is the distance to zero, the more likely the object is part of the other one.

The tracking algorithm works as follows:

1. The color histogram of the new object in the current frame and its correlogram are computed.
2. With each object in the previous scene, histograms intersection HI is computed. We assume that the object size does not change more than 15% from frame to frame. We believe that it is a reasonable assumption for human tracking.
3. The distance L_1 between H_p and HI is computed. If L_1 is larger than the threshold, then Obj_p is not the same as Obj_o. Otherwise, the correlogram intersection CI of Obj_p and Obj_o is computed. The distance L_1 between CI and C_p is computed. If it is smaller than a fixed threshold the objects are similar. Otherwise, they are different.
4. Steps 1, 2 and 3 are repeated for each object.

One problem that arises often in motion detection is that the object can be split into at least two parts being considered as two distinct objects. This can be caused by the fact that the background has the same color and texture as some parts of the object. This method overcomes the problem and tells if an object of the current frame has been parts of objects in the previous frame (and vice versa). This allows us to establish if fragments are part of the same object.

3.1 Tracking of Objects Relationships

Currently, for interpreting a scene, our algorithm cannot identify objects. However it can tell when an object A has been taken or left by another object B. This is also done using the correlograms intersection.

Case when an Object is Left. When an object A is left, using correlograms intersection we can determine that object A and object B were connected as object C in the previous frame. If object B gets far from A with a distance Z, than the algorithm determine that it was left by B. The distance Z is being used to determine whether A and B are fragments of C, or A is left by B. Currently, Z is simply represented by the distance between the centrods of the left Object A and the moving object B.

Case when an Object is Taken. When an object A is taken, using correlograms intersection we can determine that object A of the previous frame has been taken by object B to form object C. Objects are hence merged into one object. In future work, the system should be able to keep track of the objects separately even if they are temporarily merged.

4 Experiments

The algorithms described in the previous section were implemented on a 2.6 Ghz AMD Opteron(tm) and the presented sequence has been captured in an indoor scene under multiple light sources.

Fig. 2a shows the result of the motion detection algorithm presented in section 2. Inside the bounding box, the whole moving object is detected. Note that the region of the person includes background, partly because of the 4 by 4 pixels minimum square size. This effect is reduced using smaller square size. Larger square size gives coarser object regions. At some point in the sequence (Fig. 2d), the color and texture of the person legs and the background are similar. As many object detection algorithms this part is not detected. However, as explained in section 3, the tracking algorithm can determine that both parts belong to the same object present in previous frame because both fragment correlogram intersects with the correlogram of the whole object previously in the sequence. The tracking algorithm can also tell if a given object was split some times in the past using again correlogram intersection.

The bag is deposed in Fig. 3a; however it is still connected to the person, so the algorithm still consider them as one object. In Fig. 3b, although the bag and the person are separated; they are still considered as one object because they are close. This is cause by the choice of our distance threshold. A stronger criteria based on motion trajectory of objects is under development to obtain more robust results. Finally, in Fig. 3c the object gets far enough from the bag, so that our algorithm considers that the bag was set down by the person. Note that the body parts are still considered to be one object, because not only the distance between object is important, but also there appearance. Further work is on the way to segment objects from persons. For the moment, we have concentrated our efforts on assuring that the fragments of a single object are considered as such even if detection fails.

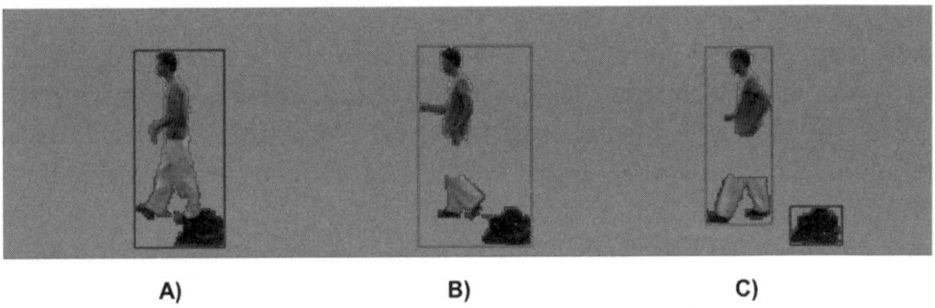

Fig. 3. Objects relationship processing A) at frame 88 B) at frame 91 C) at frame 93

Fig. 4 presents performances of the segmentation algorithm on Bootstrapping and Waving trees sequences presented in [10]. The proposed algorithm performs relatively well compared to the methods used on the same sequences. For the Bootstrapping sequence wrong segmentation that occurred is due to the strong reflection on the floor, and the strong lightning present in the scene; however the result is close to the ground truth, and all the present people has been detected. In the waving trees sequence, the waving of the tree leafs does not affect the segmentation algorithm. However some false positives occurred on the shirt of the person because it is green as the color of the background model for the same position in the image.

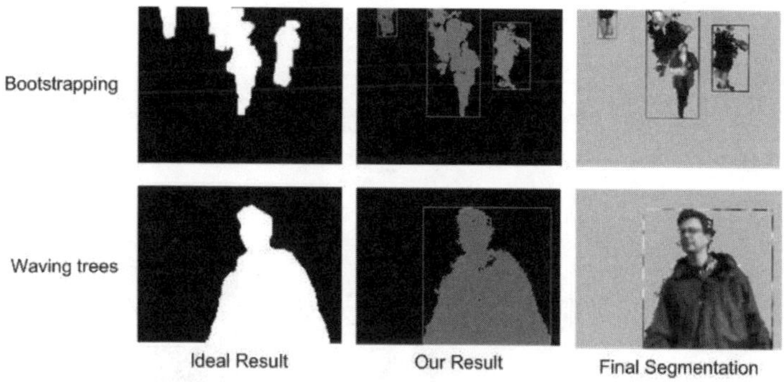

Fig. 4. Test of the segmentation algorithm on the test sequences presented in [10]

Fig. 5c and 5d is the frame 362 of the PETS 2001 dataset2 (camera2). In this outdoor sequence, objects to be detected are small relatively to the frame, so N is fixed to 32 and Th_0 remains equal to 0.20. The car is detected and tracked correctly since its color and texture are clear enough. When Th_0 is incremented to 0.30, in only 3 frames from the sequence the car is not detected because it is split in four parts, each part being in a different square region. This makes only small changes in these regions, thus the motion is not detected. Note that for the rest of the PETS sequence, where the there are persons walking on the road. They are too small to be detected at coarse scale and if the algorithm is applied directly at fine scale for all the images it looses its advantages since the noise has not been filtered at a coarse scale.

Table 1 shows quantitative results for the detection algorithm which has been applied to video sequences presented at Fig. 1 (100 frames of size 512X384) and Fig. 5 (frame 257 to frame 416). The algorithm was executed for both sequences. For each frame the false negative/positive motion detected squares of size 4X4 were counted and divided on the total number of squares in the image. Then, the average value for every sequence has been recorded in the table. Also, the frequency of lost objects (false negative objects) and wrongly detected objects (false positive objects) is shown. As we can see, if the objects to be detected are too small relatively to N and Th_0 is too large, motions regions are not detected very well and even some motion objects are totally lost for some frames because they do not make a significant change in the region's histogram. Meanwhile, when Th_0 is too small false positive regions increases creating in some frames false positive objects. Thus, when N is large relatively to motion objects, good results are achieved with a smaller Th_0 and vice versa. Furthermore, the execution time relative to the number of frames shows that the algorithm is time efficient.

Fig. 5. A), B) Detection and tracking of multiple people walking in an atrium and C), D) Detection and Tracking on frame 362 from pets dataset1 2001 camera2

Table 1. Quantitative evaluation of the detection algorithm

	N	Th_0	FP motion region (%)	FN motion region (%)	FP objects (%)	FN objects (%)	Total execution time (sec)
Sequence of Fig. 5b (160 frames)	64	0.10	0.20	0.017	0	0	13
		0.20	0.10	0.23	0	0.27	12
	32	0.20	0.18	0.017	0	0	15
		0.30	0.031	0.14	0	0.019	14
Sequence of Fig. 5d (100 frames)	64	0.20	0.14	0.04	0	0	20
		0.30	0.07	0.15	0	0.01	19
	32	0.20	0.13	0.017	0	0	16

FP: False postive, FN: False negative

5 Conclusion

In this paper we presented an algorithm for objects motion detection, tracking and interpretation of basic relationships. This algorithm is efficient, fast and does not require a background learning phase. Furthermore, the motion detection algorithm can be performed at different scale to adjust to the object shape precision needed for one application. Also, the motion of small objects can be naturally filtered as focus is only on interest regions. Results have demonstrated that this approach is promising as it performs adequately to detect and track object regions.

In future work, the detection algorithm will be adjusted to get a better segmentation of the object borders. Furthermore, an algorithm to process square regions where no motion is detected will be implemented to predict regions where the detected objects can hide based on color and textures. It will also permit to solve occlusion problems. Finally the algorithm will be tested in an outdoor scene and the object relationship algorithm will be improved using more robust criteria.

References

1. Lee, K.C., Ho,J.,Yang, M.H. ,Kriegman, D., Visual tracking and recognition using probabilistic appearance manifolds. Computer Vision and Image Understanding, 99 (2005) 303–331
2. Haritaoglu,I., Harwood,D., Davis,L.S., W4:Real-Time Surveillance of People and Their Activities. IEEE Transaction on Pattern Analysis and Machine Intelligence, Vol. 22, No.8, (2000) 809–830
3. Shoushtarian,B., Bez, E.: A practical adaptive approach for dynamic background subtraction using an invariant colour model and object tracking. Pattern Recognition Letters 26 (2005) 5–26
4. Cucchiara,R., Grana,C., Piccardi, M., Prati, A., Detecting Moving Objects, Ghosts, and Shadows in Video Streams. IEEE Transaction Pattern Analysis Machine Intelligence, Vol. 25, No. 10, (2003) 1337–1342
5. Zhou,Y.,Xu,W.Tao,H.,Gong, Y., Background Segmentation Using Spatial-Temporal Multi-Resolution MRF, in Proceedings of WACV/MOTION 2005, 8–13
6. Bodor,R., Jackson,B., Papanikolopoulos,P., Vision-Based Human Tracking and Activity Recognition, in Proceedings of the 11th Mediterranean Conference on Control and Automation, June 18-20, 2003.
7. Huang,J., Ravi Kumar,J.,Mitra,M.,Zhu,W.J., Spatial color indexing and applications, in Proceedings of 6th International Conference on Computer Vision, 4-7 Jan. 1998, 602–607
8. Ojala,T., Rautiainen,M., Matinmikko,E., Aittola,M., Semantic image retrieval with HSV correlograms, in Proceedings of 12th Scandinavian Conference on Image Analysis, Bergen, Norway, 2001, 621–627
9. Cucchiara,R., Grana,C., Piccardi.M., Prati,A., Sirotti, S., Improving Shadow Suppression in Moving Object Detection with HSV Color Information, in Proceedings Of IEEE International Conference on Intelligent Transportation Systems, August 2001, 334–339
10. Toyama,K., Krumm, J., Brumitt, B., Meyers, B., Wallflower: Principles and practice of background maintenance. In Proceedings of IEEE International Conference on Computer Vision, 1999, 255–261

Human Pose Estimation from Polluted Silhouettes Using Sub-manifold Voting Strategy

Chunfeng Shen, Xueyin Lin, and Yuanchun Shi

Key Lab of Pervasive Computing(MOE), Dept. of Computer Science & Technology,
Tsinghua University,
100084 Beijing, P.R. China
Spring98@mails.tsinghua.edu.cn
Lxy-dcs@mail.tsinghua.edu.cn, Shiyc@tsinghua.edu.cn

Abstract. In this paper, we introduce a framework of human pose estimation from polluted silhouettes due to occlusions or shadows. Since the body pose (and configuration) can be estimated by partial components of the silhouette, a robust statistical method is applied to extract useful information from these components. In this method a Gaussian Process model is used to create each sub-manifold corresponding to the component of input data in advance. A sub-manifold voting strategy is then applied to infer the pose structure based on these sub-manifolds. Experiments show that our approach has a great ability to estimate human poses from polluted silhouettes with small computational burden.

1 Introduction

Estimation of human pose from monocular videos is a challenging research topic, as environments may be very complicated. It makes this problem very tough because the extracted silhouette is always contaminated by shadow, occlusion between the body and background objects, etc.

A broad range of related works have considered this problem, which can be roughly classified as two major categories. The first one is generative model, which typically generates hypotheses of pose structure and chooses the most similar one to the observation. But inference involves complex search in high dimensional state spaces. Therefore, most researchers using generative model exert their efforts to make inference in high dimensional spaces tractable, e.g., covariance scaled sampling presented by Sminchisescu [1] and proposal maps driven MCMC by Lee [2]. However, the computational burden is still very heavy despite of introducing prior knowledges. Besides, initialization remains a great challenging problem, because bad initializations lead to explosive search steps.

The other one is discriminative method which recovers the pose structure from the input data directly. One kind of these approaches casts the pose estimation problem as a database retrieval task. That is, given a query feature, the database returns pose parameters with the most similar matching feature [3]. Shakhnarovich [4] uses hashing functions for fast approximate similarity search, and Athitsos [5] accelerates the query by introducing Lipschitz embeddings.

N. Zheng, X. Jiang, and X. Lan (Eds.): IWICPAS 2006, LNCS 4153, pp. 56–65, 2006.

More recently, discriminative methods based on manifold learning have attracted great attention of researchers for its extrapolating ability and less computation burden. Agarwal [6] uses Relevance Vector Machine, a sparse Bayesian nonlinear regression to map a feature space to a parameter space. Rosales [7] further splits the input space into several simpler ones, which have own mapping functions. Elgammal [8] also creates a mapping from the manifold to the input data using RBF interpolation framework in a close form. Lately, Scaled Gaussian Process Latent Variable Models (SGPLVM) [9] is widely used to learn the low dimensional embedding for optimizing mapping functions [10]. It learns a low-dimensional embedding of the high-dimensional pose data and provides a nonlinear probabilistic mapping from the latent space to the pose space [11].

One common problem of all above approaches is that they do not manipulate occlusion and shadow. Some researchers have considered this problem. For example, Grauman [12] proposed a multi-view shape and structure statistical model to recover other missing views based on one view without occlusion. But it must have at least one input view with high quality. Chang [13] decomposes complex cyclic motion into components and maintains coupling between components to deal with occlusion. However, the computational cost is still high.

In short, the discriminative methods mentioned above infer the pose structure by using every element of the input data. So the influence caused by occlusion and shadow can not be suppressed efficiently. We propose a manifold learning based method to estimate human poses. In our method, SGPLVM is used to learn the sub-manifold for each component of the input data (silhouette). Therefore, if one component feature appears in input data, all the body poses it supports can be indicated by its corresponding sub-manifold. During the inferring stage, a voting methodology is adopted to collect the supports from all the sub-manifolds, so that the latent variable corresponding to the intrinsic body configuration can be deduced by using a robust statistical method.

The main contributions and advantages of this paper include: 1) Propose a robust method of pose estimation given a polluted input silhouette with severe occlusion and shadow; 2) Low on-line computational burden of pose inference benefitted from the off-line sub-manifold learning; 3) Small training set required.

2 Problem Definition and Inference Framework

Our goal is to estimate pose structure y given input silhouette I. Here, I is composed of binary value where 1 means the foreground and 0 means the background obtained by background subtraction or color segmentation. Using "shape + structure" representation, pose structure y is defined as

$$y \equiv [y^1, \cdots, y^i, \cdots, y^d, \theta] \tag{1}$$

where y^i is the ith pixel value, d is the image size and θ is the vector of 3D joint angles. Suppose y is D-dimensional. If y is estimated, the joint angles θ and reconstructed silhouette $[y^1, \cdots, y^d]$ can be obtained simultaneously.

Although the dimension of y is very high, it can be embedded in a manifold with much lower latent dimension. Thus we can define a latent variable x in a low-dimensional space (as low as 2D in our problem), and use Gaussian Process [11] to create a mapping between x and y.

For a given input image I, we try to find a latent vector $\hat{x}$ whose corresponding high dimensional vector $\hat{y}$ is mostly similar to I. Then the solution is constrained near the trained manifold. Using Bayesian framework, finding optimal x can be formulated as a MAP (maximum a posterior) estimation problem,

$$\hat{x} = arg\max_x p(x|I) = arg\max_x p(I|x)p(x) \tag{2}$$

where $p(I|x)$ is the likelihood which can be estimated from the input image I, and $p(x)$ is the prior probability that can be calculated from the training data. The following sections will describe how to define these probabilities.

3 Learning Prior Probability Using Gaussian Process Model

Gaussian Process is used here for dimensional reduction and mapping creation between the latent variable and the high-dimensional input data. Moreover, it is also used to learn the prior probability $p(x)$. Here, SGPLVM [9] is applied.

3.1 SGPLVM

We briefly review the detail of SGLVM here. In contrast to other dimensionality reduction methods, SGPLVM models the likelihoods of the high-dimensional training data of pose structure $\{y_i\}_{i=1}^N$, $y_i \in \mathbb{R}^D$, as a Gaussian process for which the corresponding latent variables $\{x_i\}$ are initially unknown. Let $Y \equiv [y_1 - \mu, \cdots, y_N - \mu]^T$ be a training set where the means have been subtracted. Then the marginalized likelihood of Y is

$$p(Y|M) = \frac{|W|^N}{\sqrt{(2\pi)^{ND}|K|^D}} exp\left(-\frac{1}{2}tr\left(K^{-1}YW^2Y^T\right)\right), \tag{3}$$

where $M = \left\{\{x_i\}, \alpha, \beta, \gamma, \{w_i\}_{j=1}^D\right\}$ are the latent variables and model parameters; $W = diag(w_1, \cdots, w_D)$ is a diagonal matrix containing a scaling factor for each data dimension; and K is a $N \times N$ kernel matrix whose entry measures the similarity between two latent variables x_i, x_j using a RBF function with parameters α, β, and γ

$$K_{ij} = k\left(x_i, x_j\right) = \alpha exp\left(-\frac{\gamma}{2}\left\|x_i - x_j\right\|^2\right) + \beta^{-1}\delta_{x_i,x_j}, \tag{4}$$

where δ_{x_i,x_j} is the delta function. Then the negative log-likelihood of (3) is

$$L_{GP} = \frac{D}{2}ln|K| + \frac{1}{2}\sum_k w_k^2 Y_k^T K^{-1} Y_k + \frac{1}{2}\sum_i \|x_i\|^2 + ln\frac{\alpha\beta\gamma}{\prod_k w_k^N}. \tag{5}$$

By minimizing (5), the model parameters and latent variables corresponding to training samples can be learned.

3.2 Learning and Prediction Using GP Models

To reduce the algorithm complexity, we use the active set and the associated optimization algorithm. More details can be found in Lawrence's work [10].

Once the model parameters and the latent variables are learned, the joint probability of a new latent variable x and its associated pose y is given as [11]

$$p(x, y|M, Y) \propto \frac{1}{\sqrt{(2\pi)^{(N+1)D}\sigma(x)^{2D}}} exp\left(-\frac{\|W(y - f(x))\|^2}{2\sigma^2(x)}\right) exp\left(-\frac{x^T x}{2}\right). \tag{6}$$

Its negative log-likelihood is given by [9]

$$L(x, y) = \frac{\|W(y - f(x))\|^2}{2\sigma^2(x)} + \frac{D}{2} ln\sigma^2(x) + \frac{1}{2}\|x\|^2 \tag{7}$$

with

$$\begin{aligned} f(x) &= \mu + Y^T K_{I,I}^{-1} k(x) \\ \sigma^2(x) &= k(x, x) - k(x)^T K_{I,I}^{-1} k(x), \end{aligned} \tag{8}$$

where $K_{I,I}$ denotes the kernel matrix developed from the active set and $k(x) = [k(x_1, x), \cdots, k(x_N, x)]^T$, $x_i \in ActiveSet$.

It is obvious that, given a new latent variable x, the pose y, with the maximal probability can be predicted as

$$y = \mu + Y^T K_{I,I}^{-1} k(x). \tag{9}$$

From (6), the prediction probability at x is in direct proportion to

$$exp\left(-\frac{x^T x}{2}\right) \left(\sigma^2(x)\right)^{\frac{D}{2}}. \tag{10}$$

which is defined as the model prior $p(x)$.

Figure. 1 shows a learned two-dimensional embedding of a walk sequence, where the red points represent the latent variables corresponding to the training samples and image intensity value represents the model prior $p(x)$ with bright regions indicating high prediction probabilities.

4 Sub-manifold Learning for Each Component

This section presents a sub-manifold decomposition and voting strategy to estimate the likelihood $p(I|x)$ given the latent variable x.

4.1 Component Decomposition

For component decomposition in our method, pixel is taken as the component for convenience. By using component decomposition, $p(I|x)$ can be expressed as $p\left(I^1, \cdots, I^d|x\right)$, where I^i is the ith component of I. Here, I^i is binary which is

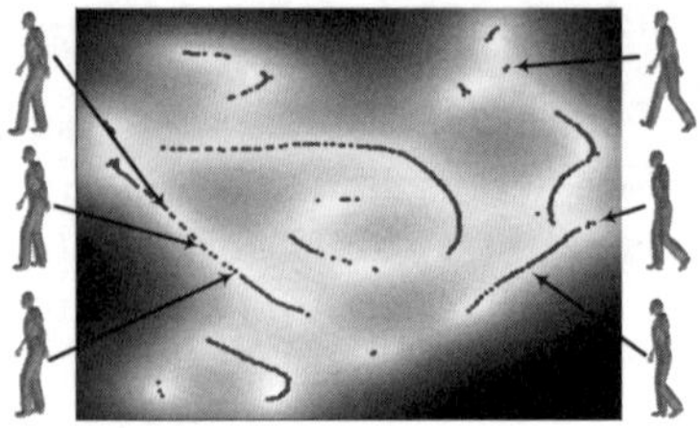

Fig. 1. The latent variable space learned by Gaussian Process in our experiment. The red points are latent variables associated with training samples. The model prior $p(x)$ is represented as intensity where white regions represent areas with high prior.

the value of I at the ith position of image coordinates. In section 3.2, Equ. (9) describes the relation between a latent variable x and its predicted pose y with the maximal probability. Writing it in decomposition manner we have

$$y^i = \mu^i + \left(Y^T K_{I,I}^{-1}\right)^i k(x) \tag{11}$$

where y^i represents the ith component having the same meaning with (1), μ^i is the ith entry of μ, and $\left(Y^T K_{I,I}^{-1}\right)^i$ is the ith row of matrix $Y^T K_{I,I}^{-1}$.

Obviously, all the poses whose ith component is foreground should be subjected to the following equation

$$\mu^i + \left(Y^T K_{I,I}^{-1}\right)^i k(x) = 1 \tag{12}$$

A binary map can be created to indicate whether the latent variables is subject to (12). We denote this map as the sub-manifold of the ith component. One example is shown in Fig. 2 with the bright blue regions indicating the sub-manifold with latent variables supporting the ith position of the input image to be the silhouette. This sub-manifold satisfying (12) is shown as the yellow curve.

4.2 Sub-manifold Learning

Since the silhouette is binary as 1 or 0, the constraint subjected to (12) is too strict, because the Gaussian Processes only provide continuous predictions. Therefore, an appropriate threshold is needed to translate the calculated values into binary values. The threshold value is determined based on the criteria of minimizing the misclassification risk by using the training data as

$$\hat{T}_i = arg\min_T \sum_n \left(y^i(n) > T\right) \oplus I^i(n) \tag{13}$$

Where $I^i(n)$ is the ith component value of the nth silhouette, and $y^i(n)$ is the prediction of $I^i(n)$ using the Gaussian Process. $\oplus$ is the exclusive or operator.

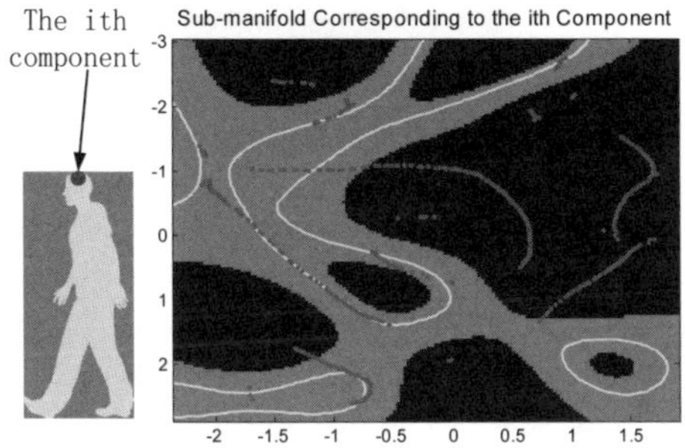

Fig. 2. The latent variable space and the sub-manifold corresponding to the ith component. Left: human silhouette and its ith component shown as the red point. Right: the latent variable space. The red points are latent variables of training data. The deep blue region is the embedding space and the bright blue one is the sub-manifold of the ith component, while the latent variables on the yellow curve are subject to Equ. (12).

Now the sub-manifold of each component expressed with the binary values can be modified as the following inequation

$$\mu^i + \left(Y^T K_{I,I}^{-1}\right)^i k(x) > \hat{T}^i \tag{14}$$

Then the binary sub-manifold calculated from (14) in the latent variable space are complex zones shown as a bright blue region in Fig. 2.

5 Inferring Pose by Sub-manifold Voting

The latent variable x can be obtained by maximizing the posterior probability as shown in (2). And the pose structure y can be estimated directly based on this latent variable. This section gives the specification of the observation probability $p(I|x)$, and the expression of the estimated pose structure y.

5.1 $p(I|x)$ Estimation

Different from most previous methods using regression to infer the pose structure directly, such as [8][6][12], we use a robust statistical method, sub-manifold voting strategy, to infer the most probable latent variable. All the latent variables on the sub-manifold corresponding to each component of input silhouette are voted to the latent variable space. Then the number of votes from all the sub-manifold at the latent variable x is accumulated which can be used to estimate the likelihood probability $p(I^1, \cdots, I^d|X)$.

As shown in Fig. 2, the bright blue regions indicate the sub-manifold with latent variables supporting the ith position of the input image to be the silhouette of the human body. It can also be expressed in the reverse way that if the value in some place of the sub-manifold image $S^i(x)$ is '1', its corresponding x value

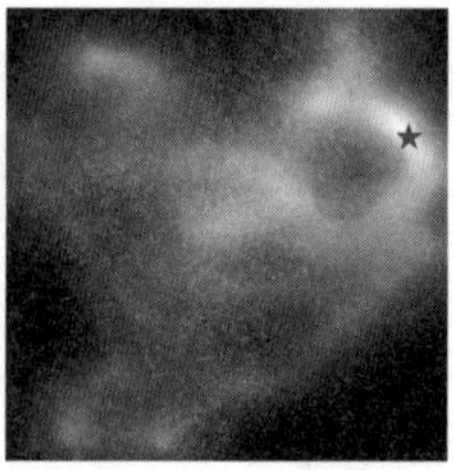

Fig. 3. Voting in embedding space. The distribution of posterior probability is illustrated as intensity and the red star represents the optimized latent variable using MAP.

is one of the candidates of the estimated latent variable. Since the computation of the sub-manifold of each component of pose vector y is independent of the input image, it can be calculated off-line during the training phase and stored in advance. Then the likelihood probability given a latent variable $p(I|x)$ can be estimated by sub-manifold voting as

$$p(I|x) \propto \sum_i S^i(x) \times I^i \tag{15}$$

where $S^i(x)$ is the sub-manifold value at x corresponding to the ith component, and I^i is the silhouette value at the ith component.

5.2 Posterior Probability Determination

By combining the definition of the prior and the likelihood probability from (10)(15), (2) can be converted as

$$\begin{aligned} \hat{x} &= arg\max_x exp\left(-\frac{x^T x}{2}\right)\left(\sigma^2(x)\right)^{-\frac{D}{2}} \sum_i S^i(x) I^i \\ \hat{y} &= \mu + Y^T K_{I,I}^{-1} k(\hat{x}) \end{aligned} \tag{16}$$

The distribution of posterior probability is shown in Fig. 3, where the latent variable with the maximal probability corresponds to the human pose we want to estimate.

6 Experiment

In this section, we show the performance of the proposed method by a series of experiments where the input silhouette images are polluted by occlusion or shadow. The pose parameters can be any description of pose structure, such as 3D joint angles, 3D joint positions, 2D joint positions and so on.

During the inference stage, the input data are human silhouettes which are obtained by simple background subtraction or color segmentation. In some of our experiments, the bounds of human body are labeled manually. But in other experiments, only very rough range of bound is provided in a single image which can be used to generate several candidate bounds.

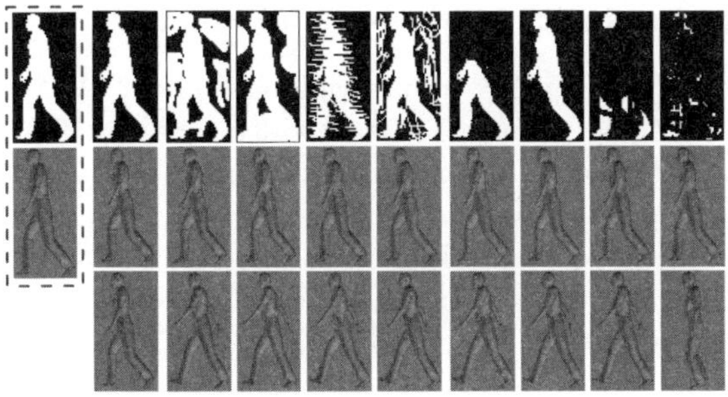

Fig. 4. Pose estimation of different kinds of polluted silhouettes by irregular noise. Left two in red dash box: the silhouette and the 3D structure of ground truth. Right: The first row shows the polluted silhouettes. The second row shows 3D pose structures estimated by our algorithm, and the third row is estimated by regression methods. The first column is used to test the algorithms using a unpolluted silhouette.

6.1 Pose Estimation for Irregular Noise

We demonstrate the proposed approach on whole body pose estimation of a walking sequence. The training data include 480 silhouettes with size 80×40 associated with 51-dimensional joint angles. The embedding space learned by Gaussian Process is shown as Fig. 1 where the red points represent the latent variables corresponding to the training data.

In order to test the robustness of our algorithm, two groups of images polluted to different extent are used. Firstly, we use graphics software to synthesize a human body pose as the ground truth shown in the red dashed box as shown in Fig. 4. The top image in the box is the silhouette and the bottom one is its associated 3D structure. By adding some noise to the silhouette of ground truth, we obtain several polluted images which can be taken as polluted by shadow or background subtraction error. The estimated results using our approach are given below the input silhouettes in the seconde row shown in Fig. 4. And the maximum error of silhouette reconstruction is below than 1%.

A method using regression similar to [8][6] is adopted here for comparison. The new pose x is obtained by minimizing the prediction error between the input data and prediction value as

$$\begin{aligned} x^* &= arg\min_x \|I - f(x)\|^2 \\ f(x) &= \mu + Y^T K_{I,I}^{-1} k(x) \end{aligned} \quad (17)$$

where $f(x)$ is the prediction given x, and I is the input silhouette. Therefore, a solution for x^* can be obtained by solving the over-constrained nonlinear equation. The estimated results using regressions are given below our results in the third row shown in Fig. 4. It is obviously that the pose estimated using regression method is very different from the ground truth. Since all the input dimensions are considered, the estimated results may be influenced greatly by the noise.

6.2 Real Sequences with Occlusion and Shadow

Here the result of a real sequence about walking is given. We recorded an indoor video with cluttered backgrounds. This test video contains 30 frames of a subject walking behind a chair and a board shown in Fig. 5.

For the existence of shadows and occlusion by the chair and the board, some parts of human body are missing. In stead of labeling human position manually, a rough search range is calculated automatically based on the result of background subtraction shown as the red dash box. Then some small sub-windows are generated in the search range, and the image patches in these sub-windows are taken as input. Since the maximal posterior can be obtained during the pose estimation from (16), the pose structure with the largest posterior of these sub-windows is taken as the best estimation result shown as the 3rd row in Fig. 5.

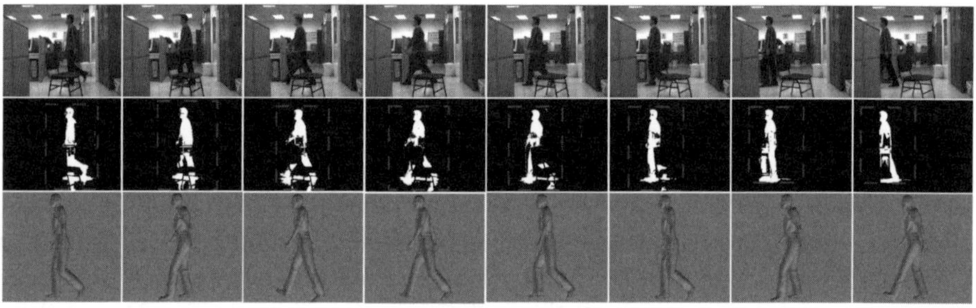

Fig. 5. Pose estimation of a walking sequence with occlusion and shadow. The 1st row: input images. The 2nd row: the silhouettes with the red dash box as the search range of human position. The 3rd row: 3D pose structures estimated by our algorithm.

Since the information of motion consistency is not used, the singularity can not be avoided for inference from 2D to 3D given only a single view. But the projected silhouettes of our results fit the input image very well which shows that our algorithm is very successful. One can overcome the singularity partially by using multi-views or continuous cues. From the experiment, the estimation results show that our algorithm can work very well in spite of the existence of occlusion and shadow at the same time.

7 Conclusion

A method of human pose estimation in complicated environments with occlusion and shadow is presented. In our method, the input data are decomposed as small components based on which the corresponding sub-manifolds are created. A robust statistical method, sub-manifold voting strategy, is used to fuse the voting results based on all the sub-manifolds and output the estimation.

We intend to explore several avenues to improve the performance of our algorithm in future work. The current algorithm needs a window to specify the body position. So we plan to integrate the estimation method into a tracking framework which can provide good candidate of body position. On the other hand, we also want to use this method to do posture recognition.

Acknowledgement. This research is supported partially by the National Grand Fundamental Research 973 Program of China (No. 2002CB312101) and the National Natural Science Foundation of China (No. 60433030).

References

1. Sminchisescu, C., Triggs, B.: Covariance scaled sampling for monocular 3d body tracking. In: Proc. IEEE Conf. Computer Vision and Pattern Recognition. Volume 1. (2001) 447–454
2. Lee, M.W., Cohen, I.: Proposal maps driven mcmc for estimating human body pose in static images. In: Proc. IEEE Conf. Computer Vision and Pattern Recognition. Volume 2. (2004) 334–341
3. zhou, H., Huang, T.: Okapi-chamfer matching for articulate object recognition. In: Proc. IEEE Int. Conf. Computer Vision. Volume 2. (2005) 1026–1033
4. Shakhnarovich, G., Viola, P.A., Darrell, T.: Fast pose estimation with parameter-sensitive hashing. In: Proc. IEEE Int. Conf. Computer Vision. Volume 2. (2003) 750–759
5. Athitsos, V., Sclaroff, S.: Estimating 3d hand pose from a cluttered image. In: Proc. IEEE Conf. Computer Vision and Pattern Recognition. Volume 2. (2003) 432–442
6. Agarwal, A., Triggs, B.: 3d human pose from silhouettes by relevance vector regression. In: Proc. IEEE Conf. Computer Vision and Pattern Recognition. Volume 2. (2004) 882–888
7. Rosales, R., Athitsos, V., Sigal, L., Sclaroff, S.: 3d hand pose reconstruction using specialized mappings. In: Proc. IEEE Int. Conf. Computer Vision. Volume 1. (2001) 378–387
8. Elgammal, A.M., Lee, C.S.: Inferring 3d body pose from silhouettes using activity manifold learning. In: Proc. IEEE Conf. Computer Vision and Pattern Recognition. Volume 2. (2004) 681–688
9. Grochow, K., Martin, S.L., Hertzmann, A., Popovic, Z.: Style-based inverse kinematics. ACM Trans. Graph. **23**(3) (2004) 522–531
10. Lawrence, N.D.: Gaussian process latent variable models for visualisation of high dimensional data. In: Proc. NIPs. (2003)
11. MacKay, D.: Introduction to gaussian processes. In: Proc. Neural Networks and Machine Learning. (1998) 133–165
12. Grauman, K., Shakhnarovich, G., Darrell, T.: Inferring 3d structure with a statistical image-based shape model. In: Proc. IEEE Int. Conf. Computer Vision. Volume 1. (2003) 641–648
13. Chang, C., Ansari, R., Khokhar, A.A.: Cyclic articulated human motion tracking by sequential ancestral simulation. In: Proc. IEEE Conf. Computer Vision and Pattern Recognition. Volume 2. (2004) 45–52

Kernel Modified Quadratic Discriminant Function for Facial Expression Recognition*

Duan-Duan Yang[1], Lian-Wen Jin[1], Jun-Xun Yin[1], Li-Xin Zhen[2], and Jian-Cheng Huang[2]

[1] Department of Electronic and Communication Engineering, South China University of Technology, 510640 Guangzhou, China
{ddyang, eelwjin, eejxyin}@scut.edu.cn
[2] Motorola China Research Center, 210000, Shanghai, P.R. China
{Li-Xin.Zhen, Jian-Cheng.Huang}@motorola.com

Abstract. The Modified Quadratic Discriminant Function was first proposed by Kimura et al to improve the performance of Quadratic Discriminant Function, which can be seen as a dot-product method by eigen-decompostion of the covariance matrix of each class. Therefore, it is possible to expand MQDF to high dimension space by kernel trick. This paper presents a new kernel-based method to pattern recognition, Kernel Modified Quadratic Discriminant Function(KMQDF), based on MQDF and kernel method. The proposed KMQDF is applied in facial expression recognition. JAFFE face database and the AR face database are used to test this algorithm. Experimental results show that the proposed KMQDF with appropriated parameters can outperform 1-NN, QDF, MQDF classifier.

1 Introduction

Statistical techniques have been widely used in various pattern recognition problems[1]. Statistical classifiers include linear discriminant function(LDF), quadratic discriminant function(QDF), Parzen window classifier, nearest-neighbor(1-NN) and k-NN rules, etc. Under the assumption of multivariate Gaussian density for each class, the quadratic discriminant function is obtained based on Bayes theory. The modified QDF(MQDF) proposed by Kimura et al. [2]aims to improve the computation efficiency and classification performance of QDF via eigenvalue smoothing, which have been used successfully in the handwriting recognition[2,3]. The difference from the QDF is that the eigenvalues of minor axes are set to a constant. The motivation be-hind this is to smooth the parameters for compensating for the estimation error on finite sample size.

* The paper is sponsored by Motorola Human Interface Lab Research Foundation(No.303D804372), New Century Excellent Talent Program of MOE(No.NCET-05-0736), NSFGD(No.04105938).

N. Zheng, X. Jiang, and X. Lan (Eds.): IWICPAS 2006, LNCS 4153, pp. 66–75, 2006.

On the other hand, kernel-based learning machines, e.g., support vector machines(SVMs)[4], kernel principal component analysis(KPCA)[5], and kernel Fisher discriminant analysis(KFD)[6,7,8], have been got much interest in the fields of pattern recognition and machine learning recently. The basic idea of kernel methods is finding a mapping such that, in new space, problem solving is easier(e.g. linear). But the mapping is left implicit. The kernel represents the similarity between two objects defined as the dot-product in this new vector space. Thus, the kernel methods can be easily generalized to a lot of dot-product (or distance) based pattern recognition algorithms. QDF and MQDF can also be seen as dot-product methods by eigen-decompostion of the covariance matrix. Therefore, it is nature that MQDF can be generalized to a new high-dimension space by kernel trick.

This paper proposes a new kernel-based method to pattern recognition, Kernel Modified Quadratic Discriminant Function(KMQDF), based on kernel methods and MQDF. For testing and evaluating its performance, the proposed KMQDF is applied for facial expression recognition(FER) on two face databases. Experimental results show that KMQDF with appropriated parameters can outperform 1-NN, QDF, MQDF classifier.

2 MQDF

In this section we would give a brief review the MQDF. Let us start with the Bayesian decision rule, which classifies the input pattern to the class of maximum a posteriori(MAP) probability out of class. Representing a pattern with a feature vector, the a posteriori probability is computed by Bayes rule:

$$P(w_i|x) = p(x|w_i)P(w_i)/p(x) \tag{1}$$

where $P(w_i)$ is the a priori probability of class, $p(x|w_i)$ is the class probability density function(pdf) and $p(x)$ is the mixture density function. Since $p(x)$ is independent of class label, the nominator of (1) can be used as the discriminant function for classification:

$$g(w_i|x) = p(x|w_i)P(w_i) \tag{2}$$

The Bayesian classifier is reduced to QDF under the Gaussian density assumption with varying restrictions. Assume the probability density function of each class is multivariate Gaussian

$$p(x|w_i) = \frac{1}{2\pi^{\frac{d}{2}}|\Sigma|_i^{\frac{1}{2}}} \exp[\frac{(x-\mu_i)^T \Sigma_i^{-1}(x-\mu_i)}{2}] \tag{3}$$

where μ_i and Σ_i denote the mean vector and the covariance matrix of class, respectively. Inserting (3) into (2), taking the negative logarithm and omitting the common terms under equal priori probabilities, the QDF is obtained as

$$g(w_i|x) = (x-\mu_i)^T \Sigma_i^{-1}(x-\mu_i) + \log|\Sigma_i| \tag{4}$$

The QDF is actually a distance metric in the sense that the class of minimum distance is assigned to the input pattern. By eigen-decompostion, the covariance matrix can be diagonalized as

$$\Sigma_i = B_i \Lambda_i B_i^T \tag{5}$$

where Λ_i is a diagonal matrix formed by the eigenvalues of Σ_i, B_i is formed by the corresponding eigenvectors.

According to (5), the QDF can be rewritten in the form of eigenvectors and eigen-values:

$$\begin{aligned} g(w_i|x) &= B_i^T(x-\mu_i)^T \Lambda_i^{-1} B_i^T(x-\mu_i) + \log|\Lambda_i| \\ &= \sum_{j=1}^{d} (\frac{1}{\lambda_{ij}})[\beta_{ij}^T(x-\mu_i)]^2 + \sum_{j=1}^{d} \log(\lambda_{ij}) \end{aligned} \tag{6}$$

Replacing the minor eigenvalues with a constant, the modified quadratic discriminant function [3] is obtained as follows:

$$\begin{aligned} g_2(w_i|x) &= \sum_{j=1}^{k} (\frac{1}{\lambda_{ij}})[\beta_{ij}^T(x-\mu_i)]^2 + \sum_{j=1}^{k} \log(\lambda_{ij}) \\ &\quad + \sum_{j=k+1}^{d} (\frac{1}{\delta_i})[\beta_{ij}^T(x-\mu_i)]^2 + (d-k)\log\delta_i \\ &= \sum_{j=1}^{k} (\frac{1}{\lambda_{ij}})[\beta_{ij}^T(x-\mu_i)]^2 + \sum_{j=1}^{k} \log(\lambda_{ij}) \\ &\quad + (\frac{1}{\delta_i}) r_i(x) + (d-k)\log(\delta_i) \end{aligned} \tag{7}$$

where k denotes the number of principal axed and $r_i(x)$ is the residual of subspace projection:

$$r_i(x) = \|x-\mu_i\|^2 - \sum_{j=1}^{k} [\beta_{ij}^T(x-\mu_i)]^2 \tag{8}$$

The (8) utilizes the invariance of Euclidean distance.

The advantage of MQDF is multifold. First, it overcomes the bias of minor eigen-values (which are underestimated on small sample size) such that the classification performance can be improved. Second, for computing the MQDF, only the principal eigenvectors and eigenvalues are to be stored so that the memory space is reduced. Third, the computation effort is largely saved because the projections to minor axes are not computed[3].

The parameter δ_i of MQDF can be set to a class-independent constant as the following equation[2,9]:

$$\delta_i = (tr(\Sigma_i) - \sum_{j=1}^{k} \lambda_{ij})/(d-k) = \sum_{j=k+1}^{d} \lambda_{ij}/(d-k) \tag{9}$$

where $tr(\Sigma_i)$ denotes the trace of covariance matrix.

3 Kernel MQDF

As a statistical algorithm, MQDF can detect stable patterns robustly and efficiently from a finite data sample. Embedding the data sample in a suitable feature by kernel trick, it is possible that MADF can perform better than in the original feature space. According to this idea, we subsequently present the new kernel-based method, KMQDF algorithm, in this section.

For a given nonlinear mapping Φ, the input data space IR^n can be mapped into the feature space H. As a result, a pattern in the original input space IR^n is mapped into a potentially much higher dimensional feature vector in the feature space H. Since the feature space H is possibly infinite dimensional and the orthogonality needs to be characterized in such a space, it is reasonable to view H as a Hilbert space. An initial motivation of KMQDF is to perform MQDF in the feature space H. However, it is difficult to do so directly because it is computationally very intensive to compute the dot products in a high-dimensional feature space. Fortunately, kernel techniques can be introduced to avoid this difficulty. The algorithm can be actually implemented in the input space by virtue of kernel tricks. The explicit mapping process is not required at all.

Given a set of M training samples $x(x_{i1}, x_{i2}, \ldots\ldots, x_{iM})$ in IR^n, labeled with the ith class, the covariance operator on the feature space H can be constructed by

$$\Sigma_i^{\Phi} = (\frac{1}{M}) \sum_{j=1}^{M} (\Phi(x_{ij}) - m_{i0}^{\Phi})(\Phi(x_{ij}) - m_{i0}^{\Phi})^T \tag{10}$$

where $m_0^{\Phi} = (\frac{1}{M}) \sum_{j=1}^{M} \Phi(x_{ij})$. In a finite-dimensional Hilbert space, this operator is generally called covariance matrix. Since every eigenvalue of a positive operator is nonnegative in a Hilbert space[10], it follows that all nonzero eigenvalues of are positive. It is the positive eigenvalues that are of interest to us. It is easy to show that every eigenvector of Σ_i^{Φ}, β can be linearly expanded by

$$\beta = \sum_{j=1}^{M} a_j \Phi(x_{ij}) \tag{11}$$

To obtain the expansion coefficients, let us denote $Q = [\Phi(x_{i1}) \ldots\ldots \Phi(x_{iM})]$, and form an $M * M$ Gram matrix $\tilde{R}_i = Q_i^T Q_i$,whose elements can be determined by virtue of kernel tricks:

$$\tilde{R}_{i(u,v)} = \Phi(x_{iu})^T \Phi(x_{iv}) = (\Phi(x_{iu}) \bullet \Phi(x_{iv})) = ker(x_{iu} \bullet x_{iv}) \tag{12}$$

We centralize $\tilde{R}_i$ by $R_i = \tilde{R}_i - 1_M \tilde{R}_i - \tilde{R}_i 1_M + 1_M \tilde{R}_i 1_M$, where $1_M = (\frac{1}{M})_{M \times M}$. On the other hand, We can denote Σ_i^{Φ} and R_i using Q_i as flowing:

$$\Sigma_i^{\Phi} = (\frac{1}{M})(Q_i - Q_i 1_M)(Q_i - Q_i 1_M)^T \tag{13}$$

$$R_i = (Q_i - Q_i 1_M)^T (Q_i - Q_i 1_M) \tag{14}$$

Consider an eignevector-eignevalue pair γ_i and λ_i of R_i, we have

$$\frac{1}{M}(Q_i - Q_i 1_M)(Q_i - Q_i 1_M)^T(Q_i - Q_i 1_M)\gamma_i = \frac{1}{M}\lambda_i(Q_i - Q_i 1_M)\gamma_i \quad (15)$$

Inserting (14) to (15),we can get

$$\Sigma_i^{\Phi}(Q_i - Q_i 1_M)\gamma_i = (\frac{\lambda_i}{M})(Q_i - Q_i 1_M)\gamma_i \quad (16)$$

Equation (16) implys that $(Q_i - Q_i 1_M)\gamma_i$, $\frac{\lambda_i}{M}$ is an eigenvetor-eigenvalue pair of Σ_i^{Φ} . Furthermore, the norm of $(Q_i - Q_i 1_M)\gamma_i$ is given by

$$\|(Q_i - Q_i 1_M)\gamma_i\|^2 = \gamma_i^T(Q_i - Q_i 1_M)^T(Q_i - Q_i 1_M)\gamma_i = \lambda_i \quad (17)$$

so that the corresponding normalized eigenvetor of Σ_i^{Φ} is $\beta_i = (Q_i - Q_i 1_M)\gamma_i/\sqrt{\lambda_i}$.

Calculate the orthonormal eigenvetors $r_{i1}, r_{i2} \dots r_{im}$ of R_i corresponding to the m largest positive eigenvalues, $\lambda_{i1} \leq \lambda_{i2} \dots \lambda_{im}$. The orthonormal eigenvetors $\beta_{i1}, \beta_{i2}, \dots, \beta_{im}$ of Σ_i^{Φ} corresponding to the m largest positive eignevalues, $\frac{\lambda_{i1}}{M}, \frac{\lambda_{i2}}{M}, \dots, \frac{\lambda_{im}}{M}$, which are $\beta_i = (Q_i - Q_i 1_M)\gamma_i/\sqrt{\lambda_i}, j = 1, 2, 3, \dots, m$.

Analogizing equation (7), in new feature space, we have KMQDF:

$$\begin{aligned} g_2^{\Phi}(w_i, x) &= \sum_{j=1}^{k}(\frac{1}{\lambda_{ij}^{\Phi}})[{\beta_{ij}^{\Phi}}^T(\Phi(x) - m_i^{\Phi})]^2 + \sum_{j=1}^{k}\log(\lambda_{ij}^{\Phi}) \quad (18) \\ &+ \sum_{j=k+1}^{d}(\frac{1}{\delta_{ij}^{\Phi}})[{\beta_{ij}^{\Phi}}^T(\Phi(x) - m_i^{\Phi})]^2 + (d-k)\log(\delta_i^{\Phi}) \\ &= \sum_{j=1}^{k}(\frac{M}{\lambda_{ij}})\left\{[(Q_i - Q_i 1_M)\gamma_i/\sqrt{\lambda_i}]^T[\Phi(x) - Q_i 1_{M\_v}]\right\}^2 \\ &+ \sum_{j=k+1}^{d}(\frac{1}{\delta_i^{\Phi}})\left\{[(Q_i - Q_i 1_M)\gamma_i/\sqrt{\lambda_i}]^T[\Phi(x) - Q_i 1_{M\_v}]\right\}^2 \\ &+ \sum_{j=1}^{k}\log(\frac{\lambda_{ij}}{M}) + (d-k)\log(\delta_i^{\Phi}) \\ &= \sum_{j=1}^{k}(\frac{M}{{\lambda_{ij}}^2})[{r_{ij}}^T(R_{it} - 1_M R_{it} - \tilde{R}_i 1_{M\_1} + 1_M \tilde{R}_i 1_{M\_1})]^2 \\ &+ \sum_{j=k+1}^{d}(\frac{1}{\delta_i^{\Phi}\lambda_{ij}})[{r_{ij}}^T(R_{it} - 1_M R_{it} - \tilde{R}_i 1_{M\_1} + 1_M \tilde{R}_i 1_{M\_1})]^2 \\ &+ \sum_{j=1}^{k}\log(\frac{\lambda_{ij}}{M}) + (d-k)\log(\delta_i^{\Phi}) \end{aligned}$$

where $R_{it} = [(\Phi(x_{i1}) \bullet \Phi(x)), (\Phi(x_{i2}) \bullet \Phi(x)), \ldots\ldots, (\Phi(x_{iM}) \bullet \Phi(x))]$,$1_{M\_v} = (\frac{1}{M})_{M\times 1}$ and $\delta_i = \sum_{j=k+1}^{d}(\frac{\lambda_{ij}}{M})/(d-k)$. We can utilizes the invariance of Euclidean distance to simply equation (18):

$$g_2^{\Phi}(w_i|x) = \sum_{j=1}^{k}(\frac{M}{\lambda_{ij}^{2}})[r_{ij}{}^{T}(R_{it} - 1_M R_{it} - \tilde{R}_i 1_{M\_1} + 1_M \tilde{R}_i 1_{M\_1})]^2 \quad (19)$$

$$+\sum_{j=1}^{k}\log(\frac{\lambda_{ij}}{M}) + \frac{1}{\delta_i^{\Phi}} r_i^{\Phi}(x) + (d-k)\log(\delta_i^{\Phi})$$

where

$$r_i^{\Phi}(x) = \left\|(\Phi(x) - m_i^{\Phi})\right\|^2 - \sum_{j=1}^{k}[\beta_{ij}^{\Phi}{}^{T}(\Phi(x) - m_i^{\Phi})]^2 \quad (20)$$

$$= (\Phi(x) \bullet \Phi(x)) - 2 * (1_{M\_1})^T \bullet R_{it} + (1_{M\_1})^T \tilde{R}_i (1_{M\_1})$$

$$-\sum_{j=1}^{k}(\frac{1}{\lambda_{ij}})[r_{ij}{}^{T}(R_{it} - 1_M R_{it} - \tilde{R}_i 1_{M\_1} + 1_M \tilde{R}_i 1_{M\_1})]^2$$

It is expected that the KMQDF algorithm can embed the data in a suitable feature space, in which we can use MQDF algorithm to discover pattern easily.

4 Facial Expression Recognition Using KMQDF

Facial expression recognition has been an active area of research in the literature for long time. The ultimate goal in this research area is the realization of intelligent and transparent communications between human beings and machines. Several facial expression methods have been proposed in the literature[11,12,13]. In recent years, facial expression recognition based on two-dimensional (2-D) digital images has received a lot of attention by researchers, because it doesn't involve 3-D measurements[13] and is suitable for real time application. A more detailed review on facial expression recognition can be found in[11].

4.1 Feature Extraction

In this paper, we use local Gabor filters to extract the features for facial expression recognition. Gabor features have been applied widely in the field of computer vision because of its powerful analysis ability in the conjoint time-frequency domain. Local Gabor filters[14] optimize the structure of global Gabor filters, which can achieve the same performance as global Gabor filters but involve less computation and storage.

Principle component analysis (PCA) and linear discriminant analysis (LDA) are two classical tools widely used in face analysis for data reduction. PCA seeks a projection that best represents the original data in a least-squares sense, and LDA seeks a projection that best separates the data in a least-squares sense. Many LDA-based algorithms suffer from the so-called *"small sample size problem"*(SSS)[15] which exists in high-dimensional pattern recognition tasks, where the number of available samples is smaller than the dimensionality of the samples. Facial expression recognition often meets this problem. The most famous solution to the SSS problem is to utilize PCA concepts in conjunction with LDA (PCA plus LDA)[16,17]. The effectiveness of the method has been demonstrated by [16,17,18,19].

In this paper, the process of the experiments consists of three steps. Firstly, local Gabor filters are used to extract the facial expression features as the description in[14]. Secondly, the local Gabor features will be reduced based on PCA plus LDA. Thirdly, the reduced features would be classified using 1-NN, MQDF and KMQDF respectively.

4.2 Experimental Data

Two face databases are used to test KMQDF. The first one is AR face database[19], a subset of AR database is used for our experiments. This subset includes 999 images of 126 individuals with 4 different facial expressions. The images corresponding to the 101 persons are chosen for training (799 samples), while the remaining images are used to test. We repeat the experiments 5 times by changing the training samples and testing samples to obtain an average recognition rate. The second one is JAFFE databases[18]. Total of use the 210 images of 10 individuals are used for our facial expression experiment. (Each expression of one person includes 3 samples). The images corresponding to 8 persons (168 samples) are used as the training samples. The residual images (42samples) are used to test. In the same way, we repeat the experiments 5 times by changing the training samples and testing samples. Fig.1 and Fig. 2 show some example images in AR and JAFFE database.

All images for the experiments are normalized (96*128 pixels) and aligned based on the position of the eyes as Fig.3 shows.

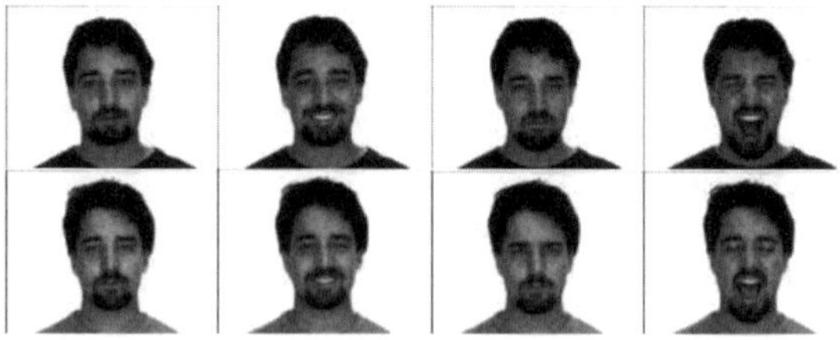

Fig. 1. Images of one person with 4 different facial expressions in the AR database

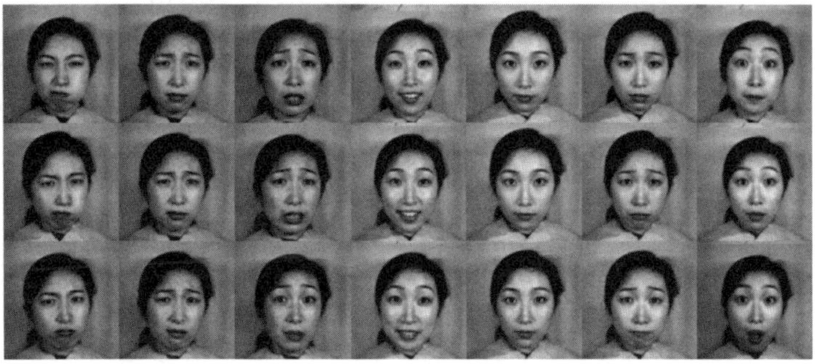

Fig. 2. Images of one person with 7 different facial expressions in the JAFFE database

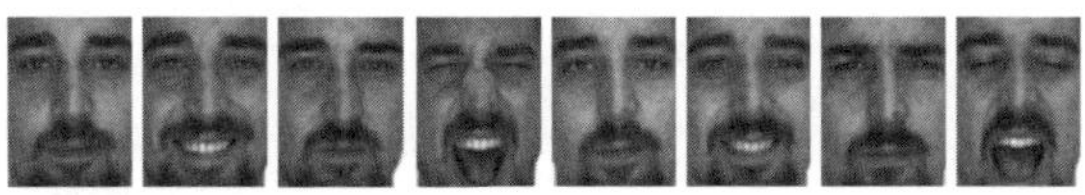

Fig. 3. Normalized images corresponding to the images in Fig.1

4.3 Experimental Results

A popular kernel, polynomial kernel, is involved in our tests:

$$ker(x, y) = (x \bullet y + 1)^d \tag{21}$$

To achieve the optimal recognition accuracy, the parameters of KMQDF(k in the equation (19) and d in the equation (21)) should be selected appropriately. Experiments show the optimal parameters are different for the different training set. Figure 4 gives an example that shows how the parameters of KMQDF affect the recognition accuracy. Table 1 and Table 2 give the results with the optical parameters on JAFFE and AR database respectively. In both Table1 and Table 2, $[T_1, T_2, \ldots, T_5]$ is used to index different testing sets.

From Table 1 and Table 2, it can be seen that the proposed KMQDF classifier with appropriated parameters can outperform the 1-NN, QDF, MQDF for the

Table 1. The recognition results on JAFFE DB

Test set	1-NN	QDF	MQDF	KMQDF
T1	71.43%	66.67%	69.05%	80.95%
T2	80.95%	69.04%	85.71%	85.71%
T3	66.67%	61.90%	71.43%	73.81%
T4	73.81%	50.00%	78.57%	78.57%
T5	76.19%	78.57%	78.57%	80.95%
Average	73.81%	65.24%	76.67%	**80.01%**

Table 2. The recognition results on AR DB

Test set	1-NN	QDF	MQDF	KMQDF
T1	86.5%	87.5%	87.0%	88.5%
T2	85.5%	84.5%	85.5%	86.5%
T3	85.5%	87.0%	86.5%	87.0%
T4	86.5%	87.5%	87.5%	88.0%
T5	86.0%	87.0%	87.5%	88.5%
Average	86.0%	86.7%	86.8%	**87.7%**

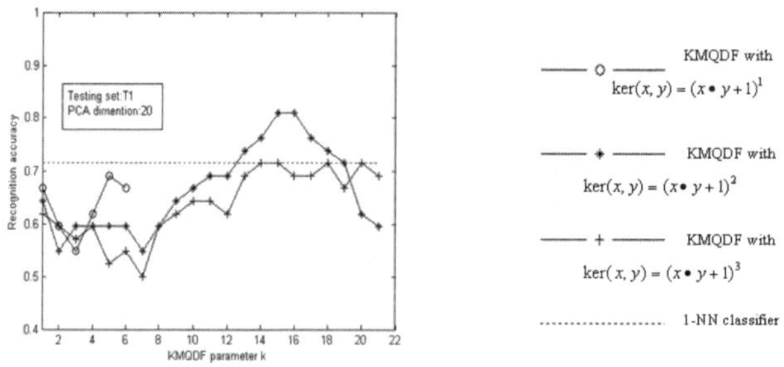

Fig. 4. Experiment results of T1 on the JAFFE database. X-axis is the modification parameter(k in the equation(19))of KMQDF.

facial expression recognition. Comparing with MQDF, an improvement of 3.3% recognition accuracy for JAFFE database and an improvement of 0.9% for AR database are obtained by the proposed kernel MQDF.

5 Conclusion

This paper presents a new kernel-based algorithm: Kernel MQDF, which can perform MQDF algorithm in a potentially much higher dimensional feature space. For testing its classifying capability, the proposed KMQDF is applied for facial expression recognition on the JAFFE face database and the AR face database. Experimental results show that the proposed KMQDF can outperform 1-NN, QDF, MQDF classifier.

Besides, as a new kernel-based algorithm, KMQDF may be expanded to solve other pattern recognition problems, such as characters recognition, face recognition etc, which merits our further study.

References

1. A.K.Jain, R.P.W.Duin, and J.mao, “Statistical pattern recognition: A review”, IEEE Trans-actions on Pattern Analysis and Machine Intelligence,vol.22,pp.4-37,Jan.2000.

2. F.Kimura, K.Takashina, S.Tsuruoka, and Y.Miyake, "Modified quadratic discriminant functions and the application to Chinese character recognition" IEEE Transactions on Pattern Analysis and Machine Intelligence, vol9,pp.149-153,Jan1987.
3. Liu CL, Sako H, Fujisawa H, "Discriminative Learning Quadratic Discriminant Function for Handwriting Recognition", IEEE Transaction on Neural networks Vol.15.No.2 March 2004.
4. V.Vapnik, the nature of stastical leaning Theory. New York: Springer, 1995.
5. B.Schölkopf, A. Smola, and K.-R.Müller, "Nonlinear ComponentAnalysis as a Kernel Eigenvalue Problem", Neural Computation,vol. 10, no. 5, pp. 1299-1319, 1998.
6. S.Mika, G.Rätsch, J. Weston, B. Schölkopf, and K.-R.Müller, "Fisher Discriminant Analysis with Kernels", Proc. IEEE Int'l Workshop Neural Networks for Signal Processing IX, pp. 41-48, Aug. 1999.
7. S.Mika, G.Rätsch, B.Schölkopf, A.Smola, J.Weston, and K.-R.Müller, "Invariant Feature Extraction and Classification in Kernel Spaces", Advances in Neural Information Processing Systems 12, Cambridge, Mass.: MIT Press, 1999
8. Jian Yang, Alejandro F. Frangi, Jing-yu Yang, David Zhang, "KPCA Plus LDA: A Complete Kernel Fisher Discriminant Framework for Feature Extraction and Recognition", IEEE Transactions on Pattern Analysis and Machine Intelligence, Vol. 27, No. 2, February 2005.
9. B.Moghaddam and A.Pentland, "Probabilistic visual learning for obeject representation", IEEE Transaction Pattern Analysis and Machining Intelligence, vol. 19,pp.696-710, July 1997.
10. W.Rudin, Functional Analysis. McGraw-Hill, 1973.
11. G. Donata, M.S.Bartlett, J.C.Hager, P.Ekman, and T.J.Sejnowski, "Classifying facial action", IEEE Transactions on Pattern Analysis and Machine Intelligence, vol. 21, pp.974-989, Oct.1999.
12. Y.Inada, Y.Xiao, and M.Oda, "facial expression recognition using Vector Matching of Special Frequency Components", IEICE Tech. Rep. TR-90-7,1990.
13. Y.Xiao, N.P.Chandrasiri, Y.Tadokora, and M.Oda, "Recognition of facial expressions using 2-d dct and neural network", Nerual network, vol. 9,no. 7,pp.1233-1240,1996.
14. Hong-Bo Deng,Lian-Wen Jin ,Li-Xin Zhen,Jian-Cheng Huang, "A New Facial Expression Recognition Method Based on Local Gabor Filter Bank and PCA plus LDA", Vol 11, no5, International Journal of Information Technology, 2005
15. K.Liu, Y.-Q.Cheng, J.-Y.Yang, and X.Liu, "An Efficient Algorithm for Foley-Sammon Optimal Set of Discriminant Vectors by Algebraic Method", Int'l J. Pattern Recognition and Artificial Intelligence, vol. 6, no. 5, pp. 817-829, 1992.
16. P.N.Belhumeur, J.P.Hespanha, and D.J.Kriegman, "Eigenfaces vs. Fisherfaces: Recognition using class specific linear projection", IEEE Trans. Pattern Anal. Machine Intell., vol. 19, pp. 711-720, July 1997.
17. D.L.Swets and J.Weng, "Using Discriminant Eigenfeatures for Image Retrieval", IEEE Trans. Pattern Analysis and Machine Intelligence, vol. 18, no.8, pp.831-836, Aug.1996.
18. Lyons M J, Budynek J, Akamatsu S. Automatic Classification of Single Facial Images. IEEE Transactions on Pattern Analysis and Machine Intelligence, 1999, 21(12): 1357-1362.
19. A.M.Martinez and R.Benavente, "The AR-face database",CVC Technical Report #24, June 1998.

3D Motion from Image Derivatives Using the Least Trimmed Square Regression*

Fadi Dornaika and Angel D. Sappa

Computer Vision Center
Edifici O, Campus UAB
08193 Bellaterra, Barcelona, Spain
{dornaika, sappa}@cvc.uab.es

Abstract. This paper presents a new technique to the instantaneous 3D motion estimation. The main contributions are as follows. First, we show that the 3D camera or scene velocity can be retrieved from image derivatives only. Second, we propose a new robust algorithm that simultaneously provides the Least Trimmed Square solution and the percentage of inliers- the non-contaminated data. Experiments on both synthetic and real image sequences demonstrated the effectiveness of the developed method. Those experiments show that the developed robust approach can outperform the classical robust scheme.

1 Introduction

Computing object and camera motions from 2D image sequences has been a central problem in computer vision for many years. More especially, computing the 3D velocity of either the camera or the scene is of particular interest to a wide variety of applications in computer vision and robotics such as calibration, visual servoing, etc. Many algorithms have been proposed for estimating the 3D relative camera motions (discrete case) [1,2] and the 3D velocity (differential case) [3]. While the discrete case requires feature matching and tracking across the images, the differential case requires the computation of the optical flow field (2D velocity field). All these problems are generally ill-conditioned.

This paper has two main contributions. First, we introduce a novel technique to the 3D velocity estimation using image derivatives only, therefore feature extraction and tracking are not required. Second, we propose a robust method that combines the Least Trimmed Square regression and the Golden Section Search algorithm where the number of inliers is not known *a priori*. In our work, we assume that the scene is far from the camera or it contains a dominant planar structure. Using image derivatives has been exploited in [4] to make camera intrinsic calibration. In our study, we deal with the 3D velocity of the camera or the scene. The paper is organized as follows. Section 2 states the problem. Section 3 describes the proposed approach. Experimental results on both synthetic and real image sequences are given in Section 4.

* This work was supported by the MEC project TIN2005-09026 and The Ramón y Cajal Program.

N. Zheng, X. Jiang, and X. Lan (Eds.): IWICPAS 2006, LNCS 4153, pp. 76–84, 2006.

2 Problem Formulation

Throughout this paper we represent the coordinates of a point in the image plane by small letters (x, y) and the object coordinates in the camera coordinate frame by capital letters (X, Y, Z). In our work we use the perspective camera model as our projection model. Thus, the projection is governed by the following equation were the coordinates are expressed in homogeneous form,

$$\lambda \begin{pmatrix} x \\ y \\ 1 \end{pmatrix} = \begin{pmatrix} f & s & x_c & 0 \\ 0 & r\,f & y_c & 0 \\ 0 & 0 & 1 & 0 \end{pmatrix} \begin{pmatrix} X \\ Y \\ Z \\ 1 \end{pmatrix} \tag{1}$$

Here, f denotes the focal length in pixels, r and s the aspect ratio and the skew and (x_c, y_c) the principal point. These are called the intrinsic parameters. In this study, we assume that the camera is calibrated, i.e., the intrinsic parameters are known. For the sake of presentation simplicity, we assume that the image coordinates have been corrected for the principal point and the aspect ratio. This means that the camera equation can be written as in (1) with $r = 1$, and $(x_c, y_c) = (0, 0)$. Also, we assume that the skew is zero (s = 0). With these parameters the projection simply becomes

$$x = f\,\frac{X}{Z} \text{ and } y = f\,\frac{Y}{Z} \tag{2}$$

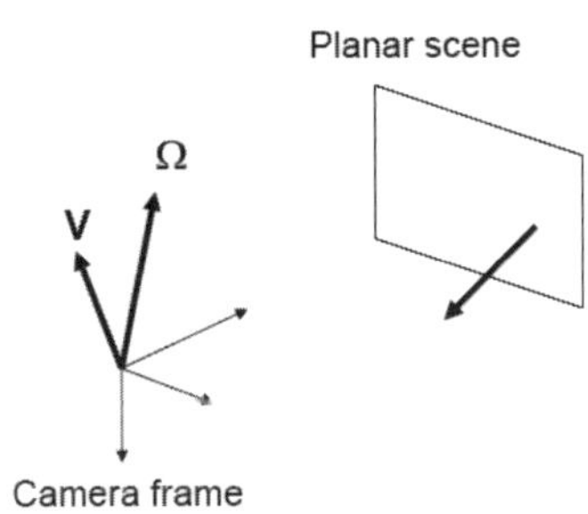

Fig. 1. The goal is to compute the 3D velocity from image derivatives

Let $I(x, y, t)$ be the intensity at pixel (x, y) in the image plane at time t. Let $u(x, y)$ and $v(x, y)$ denote components of the motion field in the x and y directions, respectively. This motion field is caused by the translational and rotational camera velocities $(\mathbf{V}, \boldsymbol{\Omega}) = (V_x, V_y, V_z, \Omega_x, \Omega_y, \Omega_z)$. Using the constraint that the gray-level intensity is locally invariant to the viewing angle and distance we obtain the well-known optical flow constraint equation:

$$I_x\,u + I_y\,v + I_t = 0 \tag{3}$$

where $u = \frac{\partial x}{\partial t}$ and $v = \frac{\partial y}{\partial t}$ denote the motion field. $I_x = \frac{\partial I}{\partial x}$ and $I_y = \frac{\partial I}{\partial y}$ denote the components of the spatial image gradient. They can be computed by convolution with derivatives of a 2D Gaussian kernel. The temporal derivative $I_t = \frac{\partial I}{\partial t}$ can be computed by convolution between the derivative of a 1D Gaussian and the image sequence.

We assume that the perspective camera observes a planar scene[1] described in the camera coordinate system by $Z = \alpha X + \beta Y + \gamma$. One can show that the equations of the motion field are given by these two equations:

$$u(x, y) = a_1 + a_2\, x + a_3\, y + a_7\, x^2 + a_8\, xy \tag{4}$$

$$v(x, y) = a_4 + a_5\, x + a_6\, y + a_7\, xy + a_8\, y^2 \tag{5}$$

where the coefficients are given by:

$$\begin{cases} a_1 = -f\,(\frac{V_x}{\gamma} + \Omega_y) \\ a_2 = (\frac{V_x}{\gamma}\,\alpha + \frac{V_z}{\gamma}) \\ a_3 = \frac{V_x}{\gamma}\,\beta + \Omega_z \\ a_4 = -f\,(\frac{V_y}{\gamma} - \Omega_x) \\ a_5 = (\frac{V_y}{\gamma}\,\alpha - \Omega_z) \\ a_6 = (\frac{V_y}{\gamma}\,\beta + \frac{V_z}{\gamma}) \\ a_7 = \frac{-1}{f}(\frac{V_z}{\gamma}\,\alpha + \Omega_y) \\ a_8 = \frac{-1}{f}(\frac{V_z}{\gamma}\,\beta - \Omega_x) \end{cases} \tag{6}$$

One can notice that the two solutions (V_x, V_y, V_z, γ) and $\lambda\,(V_x, V_y, V_z, \gamma)$ yield the same motion field. This is consistent with the scale ambiguity that occurs in the Structure From Motion problems. The case of a steady camera and a moving planar scene can be obtained by multiplying the right hand side of Eq.(6) by -1. Our goal is to estimate the instantaneous velocity $(\mathbf{V}, \boldsymbol{\Omega})$ as well as the plane orientation from the image derivatives (I_x, I_y, I_t).

In the sequel, we propose a two-step approach. In the first step, the eight coefficients are recovered by solving the system (3) using the Least Trimmed Square (LTS) regression and the Golden Section Search algorithm. In the second step, the 3D velocity as well as the plane orientation are recovered from Eq.(6) using a non-linear technique.

3 Approach

We assume that the image contains N pixels for which the spatio-temporal derivatives (I_x, I_y, I_t) have been computed. In practice, N is very large. In order to reduce this number, one can either drop pixels having small gradient components or adopt a low-resolution representation of the images. In the sequel, we

[1] Our work also addresses the case where the scene contains a dominant planar structure.

do not distinguish between the two cases, i.e., N is either the original size or the reduced one. By inserting Eqs.(4) and (5) into Eq.(3) we get

$$\begin{aligned} &I_x\, a_1 + I_x x\, a_2 + I_x y\, a_3 + I_y\, a_4 + I_y\, x\, a_5 + I_y\, y\, a_6 \\ &+(I_x x^2 + I_y\, x\, y)\, a_7 + (I_x\, x\, y + I_y\, y^2)\, a_8 = -I_t \end{aligned} \tag{7}$$

By concatenating the above equation for all pixels, we get the following over-constrained linear system:

$$\mathbf{G}\,\mathbf{a} = \mathbf{e} \tag{8}$$

where $\mathbf{a}$ denotes the column vector $(a_1, a_2, a_3, a_4, a_5, a_6, a_7, a_8)^T$.

It is well known that the Maximum Likelihood solution to the above linear system is given by:

$$\mathbf{a} = \mathbf{G}^{\dagger}\,\mathbf{e} \tag{9}$$

where $\mathbf{G}^{\dagger} = (\mathbf{G}^T\,\mathbf{G})^{-1}\,\mathbf{G}^T$ is the pseudo-inverse of the $N \times 8$ matrix $\mathbf{G}$. This solution is known as the Least Squares solution (LS). In practice, the system of linear equations may contain outliers. These outliers can be caused by local planar excursions and derivatives errors. Therefore, our idea is to estimate the 8 coefficients using robust statistics [5,6]. Statisticians have developed various kinds of robust estimators such as the Least Median of Squares (LMS) and the RANdom SAmpling Consensus (RANSAC).

3.1 Least Trimmed Square Regression

In this section, we briefly provide the principles of the linear Least Trimmed Square regression. The LTS regression has been proposed by Rousseeuw [6]. Its objective is to compute the unknown parameters (in our case, it is the vector $\mathbf{a}$) by minimizing

$$e = \sum_{i=1}^{h} (r^2)_{i:N} \tag{10}$$

where $(r^2)_{1:N} \leq \cdots (r^2)_{N:N}$ are the ordered squared residuals obtained for the linear system (e.g. (8)) associated with any value for the parameters. This is equivalent to finding the h-subset with the smallest least squares error. The LTS estimate is then the least square solution to this h-subset. The LTS objective function is smoother than that of the LMS. However, the implementation of LTS is less straightforward than the LMS. Notice that h corresponds to the percentage of non-contaminated data, that is, the percentage of inliers. In [7], an efficient implementation of the LTS has been proposed when h is known in advance. The proposed algorithm combines random sampling and an iterative C-step (Condensation step). The basic idea of the C-step is to start from an initial solution and update it iteratively by a Least Square estimator performed on another subset of constraints having the h smallest residuals.

Random sampling: Repeat the following three steps K times

1. Draw a random subsample of p different equations/pixels ($p \geq 8$).
2. For this subsample, indexed by k, compute the eight coefficients, i.e. the vector $\mathbf{a}_k$, from the corresponding p equations using a linear system similar to (8).
3. For this solution $\mathbf{a}_k$, determine the squared residuals with respect to the whole set of N equations. We have N residuals corresponding to the linear system (8). Sort these residuals and compute the trimmed sum $e_k = \sum_{i=1}^{N/2} (r^2)_{i:N}$. Note that this sum can be carried out using another number such as the *a priori* percentage of inliers.

Initial solution: Among the random solutions, keep the best solution, i.e., select the one that provides the smallest error.

Golden section optimization:

1. Select an initial bracketing interval $[\epsilon_a, \epsilon_b]$.
2. Split the bracketing interval into three segments $\epsilon_a, \epsilon_1, \epsilon_2, \epsilon_b$

$$\epsilon_1 = \epsilon_a + w\,(\epsilon_b - \epsilon_a), \text{ and } \epsilon_2 = \epsilon_b - w\,(\epsilon_b - \epsilon_a)$$

   where the fraction $w = (3 - \sqrt{5})/2 = 0.38197$ (see [8]).
3. For each percentage, perform several C-steps starting from the best solution found so far. This provides $\phi(\epsilon_a)$, $\phi(\epsilon_1)$, $\phi(\epsilon_2)$, and $\phi(\epsilon_b)$.
4. Compare $\phi(\epsilon_1)$ and $\phi(\epsilon_2)$, and update accordingly: i) the best solution, and ii) the bracketing interval such the new bracketing interval becomes either $[\epsilon_a, \epsilon_2]$ or $[\epsilon_1, \epsilon_b]$.
5. Generate a new percentage and form a new set of three segments.
6. Evaluate ϕ at the new generated percentage, ϵ. Go to step 4.

Fig. 2. Estimating the 8 coefficients using the LTS regression and the Golden Section Search algorithm

3.2 The Eight Coefficients

The algorithm provided by Rousseeuw assumes that the size of the subset, h, is known. In practice, however, h is not known. We propose an algorithm that simultaneously provides the LTS solution and the percentage of inliers.

Our problem consists in solving the 8-vector $\mathbf{a}$ using the over-constrained linear system (8). When the inlier percentage $\epsilon = \frac{h}{N}$ is unknown, we compute it by minimizing

$$\phi(\epsilon) = \frac{e(\epsilon)}{\epsilon^{\lambda}} \tag{11}$$

where λ is a predefined parameter (in all our tests described in the sequel, we used $\lambda = 6$). The above objective function $\phi(\epsilon)$ minimizes the trimmed error $e(\epsilon)$ while trying to use as many equations/pixels as possible. The minimization procedure is given a search interval $[\epsilon_a, \epsilon_b]$. Its assumes that in this interval the function has a single minimum and locates the minimum by iterative bracketing with the Golden Section Search algorithm [8]. By default, the minimum of ϕ is searched in the interval [0.5, 1.0] assuming that the inlier percentage is at least 50%. Specifying the interval more strictly improves the computational efficiency of the method. In our case, for an initial bracketing of 10%, about six iterations are sufficient to locate the minimum of $\phi(\epsilon)$ with an acceptable precision of 0.01, i.e. the interval becomes less the 1%. Figure 2 summarizes the proposed approach that estimates the vector **a** using the LTS principles and the Golden Section Search algorithm.

3.3 3D Velocity

Once the vector $\mathbf{a} = (a_1, a_2, a_3, a_4, a_5, a_6, a_7, a_8)^T$ is recovered, the 3D velocity and the plane parameters, i.e., $\frac{V_x}{\gamma}, \frac{V_y}{\gamma}, \frac{V_z}{\gamma}, \Omega_x, \Omega_y, \Omega_z, \alpha$ and β, can be recovered by solving the non-linear equations (6). This is carried out using the Levenberg-Marquardt technique [8]. In order to get an initial solution one can adopt assumptions for which Eq.(6) can be solved in a linear fashion. Alternatively, when tracking a video sequence the estimated velocity at the previous frame can be used as an initial solution for the current frame.

4 Experimental Results

Experiments have been carried out on synthetic and real images.

Fig. 3. A computer generated image of a 3D plane that is rotated about 60 degrees about an axis perpendicular to the optical axis

4.1 Synthetic Images

A synthetic planar scene was built whose texture is described by:

$$g(X_o, Y_o) \propto \cos(6\, X_o)\ (\sin(1.5\, X_o) + \sin(1.5\, Y_o))$$

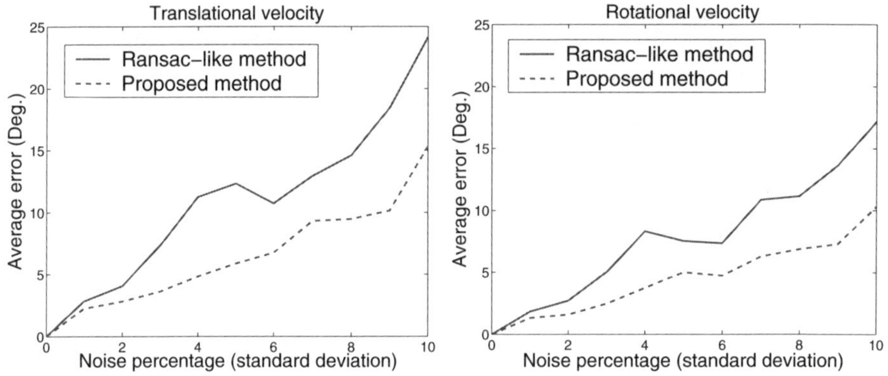

Fig. 4. Average errors obtained with a corrupted system (Gaussian noise and 10 % of outliers)

where X_o and Y_o where the 3D coordinates expressed in the plane coordinate system, see Figure 3. The resolution of the synthesized images was 160×160 pixels. The 3D plane was placed at 100cm from the camera whose focal length is set to 1000 pixels. A synthesized image sequence of the above planar scene was generated according to a nominal camera velocity $(\mathbf{V}_n, \boldsymbol{\Omega}_n)$. A reference image for which we like to compute the camera velocity was then fixed. The associated image derivatives can be computed or set to their theoretical values. Since we use synthetic data, the ground-truth values for the image derivatives as well as for the camera velocity are known. The nominal velocity $(\mathbf{V}_n(cm/s), \boldsymbol{\Omega}_n(rad/s))$ was set to $(10, 10, 1, 0.1, 0.15, 0.1)^T$. The corresponding linear system (8) was then corrupted by adding Gaussian noise and outliers to the spatio-temporal derivatives associated with each pixel. Our approach was then invoked to estimate the camera velocity. The discrepancies between the estimated parameters and their ground truth were then computed. In our case, the camera velocity was given by two vectors: (i) the scaled translational velocity, and (ii) the rotational velocity. Thus, the accuracy of the estimated parameters can be summarized by the angle between the direction of the estimated vector and its ground truth direction.

Figure 4 illustrates the obtained average errors associated with the camera velocity as a function of the Gaussian noise standard deviation. The solid curve corresponds to a RANSAC-like approach adopting a robust threshold (Eq.(8)), and the dashed curve to our proposed robust solution (Section 3). Each average error was computed with 50 random trials. As can be seen, unlike the RANSAC technique, our proposed method has provided more accurate solution. In the above experiment the percentage of outliers was set to 10%.

4.2 Real Images

The experiment was conducted on a 300-frame long video sequence of a moving scene (a newspaper) captured by a steady-camera, see Figure 5. The resolution

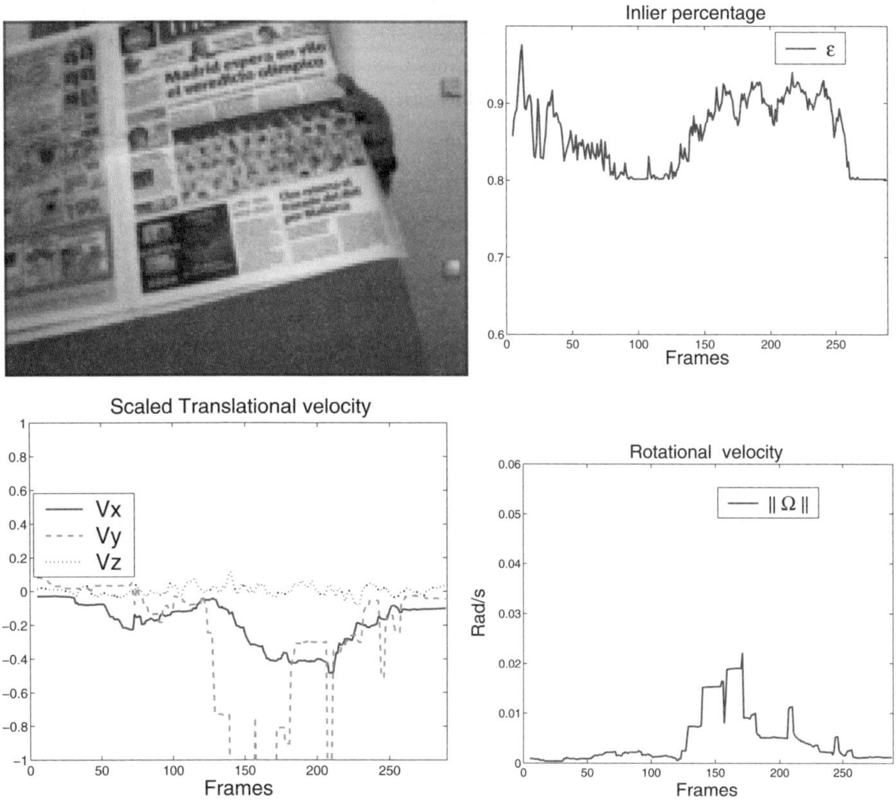

Fig. 5. Top: The used video and the estimated inlier percentage. **Bottom:** The estimated translational and rotational velocities.

is 160×120 pixels. We used 9 consecutive images to compute the temporal derivatives. The top-right shows the estimated inlier percentage. The bottom-left and bottom right show the estimated 3D translational velocity $(\frac{V_x}{\gamma}, \frac{V_y}{\gamma}, \frac{V_z}{\gamma})$ and the rotational velocity $||\boldsymbol{\Omega}||$, respectively.

Although, the ground-truth is not known, we have found that the estimated 3D motion was consistent with the video.

5 Conclusion

This paper presented an approach to the 3D velocity estimation from spatio-temporal image derivatives. The approach includes a novel robust estimator combining the LTS principles and the Golden Section Search algorithm.

References

1. Alon, J., Sclaroff, S.: Recursive estimation of motion and planar structure. In: IEEE Conference on Computer Vision and Pattern Recognition. (2002)
2. Weng, J., Huang, T.S., Ahuja, N.: Motion and Structure from Image Sequences. Springer-Verlag, Berlin (1993)
3. Brooks, M., Chojnacki, W., Baumela, L.: Determining the egomotion of an uncalibrated camera from instantaneous optical flow. Journal of the Optical Society of America A **14**(10) (1997) 2670–2677
4. Brodsky, T., Fermuller, C.: Self-calibration from image derivatives. International Journal of Computer Vision **48**(2) (2002) 91–114
5. Fischler, M., Bolles, R.: Random sample consensus: A paradigm for model fitting with applications to image analysis and automated cartography. Communication ACM **24**(6) (1981) 381–395
6. Rousseeuw, P.J., Leroy, A.: Robust Regression and Outlier Detection. John Wiley & Sons, New York (1987)
7. Rousseeuw, P.J., Driessen, K.V.: Computing LTS regression for large data sets. Estadistica **54** (2002) 163–190
8. Press, W.H., Teukolsky, S.A., Vetterling, W.T., Flannery, B.P.: Numerical Recipes in C. Cambridge University Press (1992)

Motion and Gray Based Automatic Road Segment Method MGARS in Urban Traffic Surveillance

Hong Liu, Jintao Li, Yueliang Qian, Shouxun Lin, and Qun Liu

Multilingual Interaction Technology and Evaluation Laboratory,
Institute of Computing Technology,
Chinese Academy of Sciences, Beijing 100080, China
hliu@ict.ac.cn

Abstract. This paper presents a novel method MGARS to automatic road area segmentation based on motion and gray feature for the purpose of urban traffic surveillance. The proposed method can locate road region by region growing algorithm with the fusion feature of motion information and grayscale of background image, which is independent to road marker information. An adaptive background subtraction approach using gray information is performed to motion segmentation. In region growing stage, start point that so called seed is selected automatically by motion centroid and local gray feature of background image. The threshold of region growing method is adaptively selected for different traffic scenes. The proposed method MGARS can effectively segment multi roads without manual initialization, and is robust to road surface pollution and tree shadow. The system can adapt to the new environment without human intervention. Experimental results on real urban traffic videos have substantiated the effectiveness of the proposed method.

1 Introduction

Automated visual traffic surveillance (AVTS) allows the visualization of vehicles on the road by using a single camera mounted in perspective view of the road scene that it is monitoring, thus enabling traffic-scene analysis [1]. In an AVTS system, moving vehicle detection is the basic task for other analysis. However, the performance of an AVTS system deteriorates when vehicles appear to occlude each other from the camera's point of view in a traffic video [2]. Failing to detect and resolve the presence of occlusion may lead to surveillance errors, including incorrect vehicle count, incorrect tracking of individual vehicles, and incorrect classification of vehicle type. As a result, methods for occlusion detection must be adopted in order to produce meaningful results [5]. These include stereo vision [6], an overhead camera with a viewing axis perpendicular to the road surface [7] or roadside mounted camera with a high position. Other researchers have done an extensive amount of work on occlusion detection and occlusion handling [5].

Occlusion problem is serious in urban traffic scenes for lower vehicle speed and little distance between vehicles than in highway scenes. In urban traffic monitoring, where camera is mounted roadside, occlusion is usually happened in far area. Instead of processing entire images, a computer vision system can analyze specific regions (the 'focus of attention') to identify and extract the features of interest [20]. So many papers

N. Zheng, X. Jiang, and X. Lan (Eds.): IWICPAS 2006, LNCS 4153, pp. 85 – 94, 2006.

propose to select better detect region with less vehicle occlusion. Tai [9] use detection line of each lane to detect whether the vehicle enters the detection region. Yu [10] use the Korean characters on each lane as the lane marks. Vehicle detection and shadow rejection are performed based on lane mark. But all the above detection region or detection lines are manually selected. In this case, the detection region is suited only to the current traffic video, which should be redefined for a new environment.

Region for vehicle detection can be seen as certain part of road area. In this paper, we focus on automatic road segment (ARS) approach, which is independent to any priori knowledge, such as road marker and camera viewing positions. Such a system would ease installation of the equipment due to its ability for self-initialization [11]. ARS is an important task for an adaptive traffic monitoring system. It enables the system to adapt to different environmental conditions.

In this paper, we propose a novel method MGARS for automatic road area segmentation in urban traffic video. The proposed method can locate road regions by the fusion feature of centroid of moving objects and gray of background image. The system block diagram is shown as Fig.1. An adaptive background subtraction approach using gray information is performed to motion segmentation. Then centroid of moving objects is obtained for next region growing process. Road regions are located using region growing method with automatically selecting seed points. The threshold of region growing method is adaptively selected for different traffic scenes. The proposed method can segment multi roads without manual initialization, and is robust to road surface pollution and tree shadow. Also it is independent to road marker information.

The rest of this paper is organized as follows. Section 2 provides a summary of previous work relevant to road segmentation in traffic video. The next three sections describe our proposed algorithm in details, and the results we obtained from experiments on a variety of traffic videos. Section 6 concludes by describing some of the important characteristics of our algorithm, and directions for future research.

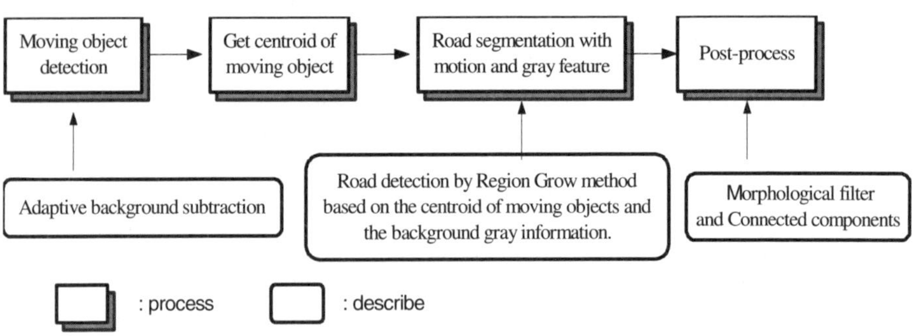

Fig. 1. Block diagram of automatic road segment method MRARS

2 Previous Work

In this section, we focus on road segment method in previous research. Real-time road segmentation is complicated by the great variability of vehicle and environmental conditions. Changing seasons or weather conditions, time of the day, dirt on the road, shadows. Because of these combined effects, robust segmentation is very demanding. The approaches in lane detection can be distinguished into two classes, namely lane-region detection and lane-border detection [4].

Lane-region approaches detect the lane with the changing intensity distribution along the region of a lane. For automatic vehicle guidance case, [18] assumes the road just in front of car, and take a few sample to capture the road color. Then flood-fill the road region using the sampled colors. The lane-region analysis can also be modeled as a classification problem, which labels image pixels into road and non-road classes based on particular features, which required extensive training process. Ref. [12] uses Gaussian distributions of (R,G,B) values to model the color classes. Ref. [13] use the hue, saturation, gray-value (HSV) space as more effective for classification. Besides color, the local texture of the image has been used as a feature for classification. Ref. [16] uses a normalized gradient measure based on a high-resolution and a low-resolution (smoothed) image, in order to handle shadow interior and boundaries. However changes in outdoor illuminations may change the road colors perceived by the camera and introduce errors in the classification. Ref. [11] uses motion information in lane detection. An activity map is used to distinguish between active areas of the scene where motion is occurring (the road) and inactive areas of no significant motion. But lane finding will false when the vehicles change their lane.

Lane-border detection method considers directly the spatial detection of lane characteristics. According the difference of lane characteristics, two general subclasses involve feature-driven approaches and model-driven approaches [4]. Feature-driven approaches are based on the detection of edges in the image and the organization of edges into meaningful structures (lanes or lane markings). The Road Markings Analysis (ROMA) system is based on aggregation of the gradient direction at edge pixels in real-time [14]. In general, edge feature suffer from noise effects, such as strong shadow edges sometime. The aim of model-driven approaches is to match the road edges with a deformable template, which is usually used in vehicle guidance. The Hough Transform is used to extract road boundaries from an image [17]. Ref. [15] use snakes to model road segments. Model-based approaches for lane finding have been extensively employed in stereo vision systems. Such pproaches assume a parametric model of the lane geometry, and a tracking algorithm estimates the parameters of this model from feature measurements in the left and right images. Model-driven approaches provide powerful means for the analysis of road edges and markings. However, the use of a model has certain drawbacks, such as the difficulty in choosing and maintaining an appropriate model for the road structure, the inefficiency in matching complex road structures and the high computational complexity [4].

3 Robust Motion Segmentation

3.1 Gray Based Background Subtraction

In recent years time-adaptive per pixel mixtures of Gaussians background models have been a popular choice for modeling complex and time varying backgrounds [6].

This method has the advantage that multi-modal backgrounds (such as moving trees) can be modeled. Different to Stauffer's method [19], we use only gray value of source image to construct background image.

In [19], each pixel is modeled as a pixel process; each process consists of a mixture of k adaptive Gaussian distributions. The distributions with least variance and maximum weight are isolated as the background. The probability that a pixel of a particular distribution will occur at time t is determined by:

$$P(X_t) = \sum_{i=1}^{k} \omega_{i,t} * \eta(X_t, \mu_{i,t}, \Sigma_{i,t}) \ . \tag{1}$$

where K is the number of Gaussian distributions, $\omega_{i,t}$ is the weight estimate of the ith Gaussian in the mixture at time t, $\mu_{i,t}$ and $\Sigma_{i,t}$ are the mean value and covariance matrix of the ith Gaussian at time t, and η is the Gaussian probability density function.

$$\eta(X_t, \mu_{i,t}, \Sigma_{i,t}) = \frac{1}{(2\pi)^{\frac{\pi}{2}} |\Sigma|^{\frac{1}{2}}} e^{-\frac{1}{2}(X_t - \mu_t)^T \Sigma^{-1} (X_t - \mu_t)}, \ \Sigma_{k,t} = \sigma_k^2 I \ . \tag{2}$$

In this paper we set k=3 Gaussians. An on-line k-means approximation algorithm is used for the mixture model. Every new pixel X_t is checked against the K existing Gaussian distribution. A match is found if the pixel value is within L = 2.5 standard deviation of a distribution. This is effectively per pixel per distribution threshold and can be used to model regions with periodically changing lighting conditions.

If the current pixel value matches none of the distributions the least probable distribution is updated with the current pixel values, a high variance and low prior weight. The prior weights of the K distributions are updated at time t according to:

$$\omega_{k,t} = (1-\alpha)\omega_{k,t-1} + \alpha(M_{k,t}) \ . \tag{3}$$

where α is the learning rate and $M_{k,t}$ is 1 for the model which matched the pixel and 0 for the remaining models. We set learning rate α =0.002. The changing rate in the model is defined by $1/\alpha$. That is means after 500 frames the background model well updated fully. After this approximation the weights are renormalized, the parameters μ and σ for the unmatched distributions remain the same. The parameters for the matching distribution are updated as follows:

$$\mu_t = (1-\rho)\mu_{t-1} + \rho X_t \ . \tag{4}$$

$$\sigma_t^2 = (1-\rho)\sigma_{t-1}^2 + \rho(X_t - \mu_t)^T (X_t - \mu_t) \ . \tag{5}$$

where

$$\rho = \alpha\eta(X_t | \mu_k, \sigma_k) \ . \tag{6}$$

For change detection a heuristic searches for the learnt distributions that have more supporting evidence. The Gaussians are ordered based on the ratio of ω/σ. This increases as the Gaussian's weight increases and its variance decreases. The first B distributions accounting for a proportion T of the observed data are defined as background. We set T=0.8 in this paper.

$$B = \arg\min_b \left(\sum_{k=1}^{b} \omega_k > T\right) \cdot \tag{7}$$

For the non-background pixel, we calculate the gray difference between this pixel in current image and in background model. Only the pixel with the difference over the threshold 10 is labeled as foreground pixel or motion pixel. Then the difference image is binary. In our experiments, the background model can be usually obtained within 100 to 200 sequence frames, which is good enough for the future segmentation process.

3.2 Obtain Centroid of Moving Object

After motion segmentation, the moving objects with their bounding boxes and centroids are extracted from each frame. The centroid (x,y) of a bounding box B corresponding to an object O is defined as follows:

$$x = \left(\sum_{i=0}^{N} x_i\right) \Big/ N,\ y = \left(\sum_{i=0}^{N} y_i\right) \Big/ N \ . \tag{9}$$

where N is the number of pixels belong to object O within bounding box B, x_i and y_i represent the x -coordinate and y -coordinate of the ith pixel in object O.

Fig.2 shows some results on an urban traffic video. Fib.2a is one source frame. The constructed background image is showed in Fig.2b, which use 100 sequence frames with moving objects. And the motion segment result on source image and binary image are presented as Fig.2c and Fig.2d. The motion centroids with 3×3 region after processing 200 sequence frames are show in Fig.2e.

Fig. 2a. Source image

Fig. 2b. Constructed background image

Fig. 2c. Motion segment

Fig. 2d. Binary image

Fig. 2e. Motion centroids

4 Motion and Gray Based Automatic Road Segmentation MGARS

In this section, we describe the proposed automatic road segment method using the feature of motion centroids and gray value of background image.

First a 3×3 Gaussian filter is performed on background image to reduce noise. Experimental results will show the effective of this smooth process.

The canny edge detection algorithm is known as the optimal edge detector. We use canny edge detection on background image to get edge information.

The region grow algorithm that is also called flood fill method is used in our system. Region growing process starts with some point, called "seed", fills the seed pixel neighborhoods inside which all pixel values are close to each other. This process is propagated until it reaches the image boundary or cannot find any new pixels to fill due to a large difference in pixel values.

This algorithm need some parameters: coordinates of the seed point inside the road area, threshold τ as maximal lower difference and maximal upper difference between the values of pixel belonging to the filled domain and one of the neighboring pixels to identify, type of connectivity. If connectivity is four, the region growing process tries out four neighbors of the current pixel otherwise the process tries out all the eight neighbors.

Ref. [18] uses flood fill method to extract the road region in front of moving vehicle in vehicle guidance. The seed is selected by priori knowledge, which make sure the seed must be in the road region. And the threshold is a constant value, which may not adapt to different scene.

In this paper, we propose a novel method MGARS to segment road regions automatically. The method consists of following stages:

1. Gray background image is divided into 10×10 pixel partitions without overlap.
2. For each partition, the number of moving centroid, mean and standard deviation of gray value and number of edge pixel are calculated. Partition containing motion centroids is called Centroid Partition here. The total number of Centroid Partition can also be calculated together.
3. From the bottom of background image, we search the proper Centroid Partition, which have number of motion centroids more than 2, standard deviation less then 10 and the number of edge pixel less than 20. Then the center of this Centroid Partition is selected as seed point for region growing process.
4. Process 8-connectivity region growing algorithm from the above seed point. If the gray value of neighbor pixel is similar to the gray value of seed point according to the threshold τ, this neighbor pixel is filled.
5. If 30 percent of pixels in a partition is filled, we define this Centroid Partition is filled. Calculate how many Centroid Partitions are filled. If there is enough Centroid Partitions (90 percent in our system) are filled by region growing process, the seed point search process can stop, else back to stage 3 to search the next proper seed point for region growing.
6. If the whole partitions in background image are searched, the region growing process can stop.

In stage 3, the strategy we choose proper Centroid Partition is considering the seed point should in the road region, which can be got by centroid of moving objects, and its neighbor region should relatively smooth. The method can select seed point avoid noise pixel, such as shadow, edge and road smut.

In stage 4, the min and max difference that is threshold τ is selected automatically. Here, we calculate the mean and standard deviation of all Centroid Partitions. If the standard deviation is less than 20, which means gray value of road region is so smooth, the threshold τ is set to 1, else the threshold τ is set to 2. The compare experiment is show in next section.

After region growing process, most of the road pixel is filled, then binary the result image. Post-processing stage using morphological filter is performed on binary image to remove small region and smooth the boundary of road region. Then road regions are labeled as connected components.

5 Experiments

The test video sequences were taken using a camera on roadside or cloverleaf junction in urban. The video was sampled at a resolution of 320×240 and a rate of 25 frames per second. We used only grays value of source video, and output a grayscale background model. Tests were performed on two representative sequences that might be commonly encountered in urban surveillance.

τ =1

Fig. 3a. Background image with seed position

Fig. 3b. Result of region grow

Fig. 3c. Edge of extracted road region

τ =2

Fig. 3d. Background image with seed position

Fig. 3e. Result of region grow

Fig. 3f. Edge of extracted road region

τ =3

Fig. 3g. Background image with seed position

Fig. 3h. Result of region grow

Fig. 3i. Edge of extracted road region

The first traffic scene with multi roads is medium shot. Fig.3 illustrate the road segment results using our proposed method. The first row in Fig.3 shows the results with threshold τ =1 in region growing process. Fig.3a displays the positions of proper Centroid Partition with seed point. Fig.3b is the result after region growing process from the selected seed point as in Fig.3a. After morphology filter, superimposition of the edges of road region onto the lighter original background image is shown in Fig.3c. It also demonstrates improvements possible using morphological filters in a post-processing stage. The results with threshold τ =2 and τ =3 are shown as the second and the third row of Fig.3. From the experiment results, we can conclude that if the threshold τ is lower, there will need more seed point to flood fill the whole road regions. But as Fig.3c shows lower threshold can not get well segment result if road region is non consistency in grayscale. The threshold τ =2 can get similar better result compared with threshold τ =3. The marker on the road region can be removed by post-process as shown in Fig.3f. In our system, for this video, threshold τ is automatically selected as 2 according to the standard deviation of all the Centroid Partitions. This experiment can also illustrate that our algorithm can detect multi road regions effectively.

τ =1

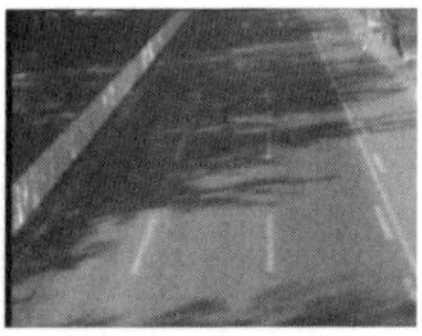

Fig. 4a. Background image with shadow

Fig. 4b. Result of region grow without smooth

Fig. 4c. Result of region grow with Gaussian smooth

τ =2

Fig. 4d. Result of region grow

Fig. 4e. Result of region grow with Gaussian smooth

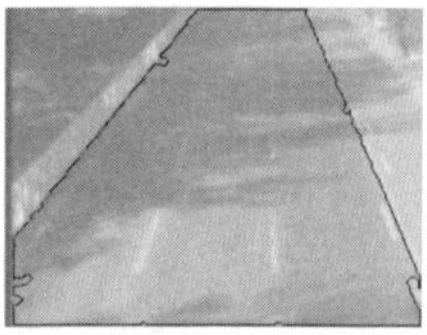

Fig. 4f. Edge of extracted road region

A typical traffic surveillance scene in urban was considered next where the challenge was due to the vigorous motion of the trees and the strong shadow on road surface. And the right part is pavement with moving person or bicycle. The result is shown in Fig.4. Fig.4a is the background image constructed, which has tree shadow on the road surface. Fig.4b is the result of flood filling by threshold τ =1 and without Gaussian filter on background image. While Fig.4c is the result by threshold τ =1 and after Gaussian filter, which can fill more road pixels than Fig.4b. Fig.4d is the result by threshold τ =2 without Gausssian filter while Fig.4e is by threshold τ =2 and after Gaussian filter. From the segment result, we can see that Gaussian filter on the source background image before region growing can get better segment results for it can smooth background image and remove many noise. Fig.4f is the final edge of road region after morphological filter. By the way, the left road is not extracted here for there is no moving vehicles appeared in 200 frames in which we get motion centroids. If we use more frames to get moving objects, moving vehicle will appear on the left road and it can also be extracted well.

In the experiment, our algorithm successfully segments out the entire road regions containing moving vehicles.

6 Discussion and Conclusions

In this paper, we present a novel method MGARS to automatically extract road region from traffic monitoring video. Fusion features with moving segmentation and gray of background image are used for region growing process to get road region. An adaptive background subtraction method is proposed and applied to several real life traffic video sequences to obtain more accurate motion information of the moving objects. Road regions are located using region growing method with automatically selecting seed by motion centroid and local gray feature of background image. The threshold of region growing method is adaptively selected for different traffic scenes. Satisfactory results were obtained in our experiment, and all the road areas with moving vehicles are successfully identified through our algorithm. The method shows robustness to variations in both road properties and illumination conditions. The algorithm is viewpoint independent. No manual initialization or prior knowledge of the road shape is needed, the method can also suit to curve road. The proposed method can detect multi roads together, and can adapt to the new environment without any human intervention.

Several problems occurred in the experiments. In the stage of motion segmentation, moving shadow is detected as moving object and the presence of occlusions between vehicles make centroid position of moving object is not the real centroid of moving vehicle. Also in some case, moving object contains moving person or bicycle, which will disturb the result of moving vehicle segmentation. Future improvements include using techniques that involve modeling of the motion of vehicles and pedestrians in order to produce a better classier. Moving shadow detect can also considered in the future research. Further, since the position of the centroid of a moving vehicle is recorded during the segment process, this information can be used in the future for extracting moving trajectory.

Acknowledgment

The research is sponsored by National Hi-Tech Program of China (No. 2004AA-114010, 2003AA111010).

References

1. Beymer, D., Malik, K.: Tracking Vehicles in Congested Traffic. Proc. IEEE Intelligent Vehicles Symp. (1996) 130–135
2. Yung, N. H. C., Lai, A.H.S.: Detection of Vehicle Occlusion Using a Generalized Deformable Model. Proc. IEEE Int. Symp. Circuits and Systems, 4 (1998) 154–157
3. Fathy, M., Siyal, M. Y.: A Window-based Image Processing Technique for Quantitative and Qualitative Analysis of Road Traffic Parameters. IEEE Trans. On Vehicle Technology, (1998) 1342–1349
4. Kastrinaki, V., Zervakis, M., Kalaitzakis, K.: A Survey of Video Processing Techniques for Traffic Applications. Image and Vision Computing 21(2003) 359-381
5. Clement, C.C.P., William, W.L.L., Nelson, H.C.Y.: A Novel Method for Resolving Vehicle Occlusion in a Monocular Traffic-Image Sequence. IEEE Trans. On Intelligent Transportation Systems, 5 (2004) 129-141
6. Rabie, T., Shalaby, A., Abdulhai, B., El-Rabbany, A.: Mobile Vision-based Vehicle Tracking and Traffic Control. Proc. IEEE 5th Int. Conf. Intelligent Transportation Systems, (2002) 13–18
7. Lai, A. H. S.: An Effective Methodology for Visual Traffic Surveillance. Ph.D. dissertation, Univ. Hong Kong, China, 2000
8. Ikeda, T., Ohnaka, S., Mizoguchi, M.:Traffic Measurement with a Roadside Vision System-Individual Tracking of Overlapped Vehicles. Proc. IEEE 13th Int. Conf. Pattern Recognition, 3 (1996) 859–864
9. Jen-Chao, T., Shung-Tsang, T.: Real-time Image Tracking for Automatic Traffic Monitoring and Enforcement Applications. Visual tracking. Image and Visison Computing, 22(2004) 640-649
10. Yu, M., Jiang G.Y., He S.L.: Land Mark Based Method for Vehicle Detection and Counting from Video. Chinese Journal of Scientific Instrument, 23(2002) 386-390
11. Stewart, B.D., Reading, I., Thomson, M.S., Binnie, T.D., Dickinson, K.W., Wan, C.L.: Adaptive Lane Finding in Road Traffic Image Analysis, Proc. of Seventh International Conference on Road Traffic Monitoring and Control, IEE, London (1994)
12. Thorpe, C., Hebert, M.H., Kanade, T., Shafer, S.A.: Vision and Navigation for the Carnegie–Mellon Navlab. IEEE Trans. on Pattern Analysis and Machine Intelligence 10 (3) (1988)
13. Betke, M., Haritaoglu, E., Davis, L.S.: Real-time Multiple Vehicle Detection and Tracking From a Moving Vehicle. Machine Vision and Applications 12 (2000) 69–83
14. Enkelmann, W., Struck, G., Geisler, J.: ROMA—a System for Model-based Analysis of Road Markings. Proc. of IEEE Intelligent Vehicles, Detroit (1995) 356–360
15. Yuille, A.L., Coughlan, J.M.: Fundamental limits of Bayesian Inference: Order Parameters and Phase Transitions for Road Tracking. IEEE Pattern Analysis and Machine Intelligence 22 (2) (2000) 160–173
16. Taylor, C.J., Malik, J. Weber, J.: A Real Time Approach to Stereopsis and Lane-Finding, IFAC Transportation Systems Chania, Greece (1997)
17. He, Y. H., Wang, H., Zhang B.: Color Based Road Detection in Urban Traffic Scenes, IEEE Trans. on Intelligent Transportation Systems. 5(2004) 309-318
18. Park, E., Tran, B., Arfvidsson, J.: Freeway Car Detection. CS 223B, Stanford, January 25, 2006
19. Stauffer, C., Grimson, W.: Adaptive Background Mixture Models for Real-Time Tracking. Proc. IEEE Conf. on Computer Vision and Pattern Recognition, (Fort Collins, CO), (1999)246–252
20. Bertozzi, M, Broggi, A., Fascioli, A.: Vision-based Intelligent vehicles: State of Art and Perspectives. Robotics and Autonomous System 32(2000) 1-16

A Statistically Selected Part-Based Probabilistic Model for Object Recognition

Zhipeng Zhao and Ahmed Elgammal

Computer Science Department, Rutgers University
110 Frelinghuysen Road, Piscataway, NJ 08854-8019, U.S.A
{zhipeng, elgammal}@cs.rutgers.edu

Abstract. In an object recognition task where an image is represented as a constellation of image patches, often many patches correspond to the cluttered background. If such patches are used for object class recognition, they will adversely affect the recognition rate. In this paper, we present a statistical method for selecting the image patches which characterize the target object class and are capable of discriminating between the positive images containing the target objects and the complementary negative images. This statistical method select those images patches from the positive images which, when used individually, have the power of discriminating between the positive and negative images in the evaluation data. Another contribution of this paper is the part-based probabilistic method for object recognition. This Bayesian approach uses a common reference frame instead of reference patch to avoid the possible occlusion problem. We also explore different feature representation using PCA an 2D PCA. The experiment demonstrates our approach has outperformed most of the other known methods on a popular benchmark data set while approaching the best known results.

Keywords: Computer vision, Pattern representation and modeling, Object detection, Class recognition, Feature selection.

1 Introduction

Object detection and class recognition is a classical fundamental problem in computer vision which has witnessed much research. This problem has two critical components: the representation of the images (image features) and recognizing the object class using this representation which requires learning models of objects that relate the object geometry to image representation. Both the representation problem, which attempts to extract features which capture the essence of the object, and the following classification problem are active areas of research and have been widely studied from various perspectives. The methods for recognition stage can be broadly divided into three categories: the 3D model-based methods, the appearance template search-based methods, and the part-based methods. 3D model-based methods ([20]) are successful when we can describe accurate geometric models for the object. Appearance based matching approaches are based on searching the image at different locations and different scales for best match for object 'template" where the object template can be learned from training data and act as a local classifier [18,15]. Such approaches are highly successful in modeling objects with wide within-class appearance variations such as in face

N. Zheng, X. Jiang, and X. Lan (Eds.): IWICPAS 2006, LNCS 4153, pp. 95–104, 2006.

detection [18,15] but they are limited when the within-class geometric variations are large, such as detecting a motorbike.

In contrast, object recognition based on dense local "invariant" image features have shown a lot of success recently [8,11,14,19,1,3,6,16,7] for objects with large within-class variability in shape and appearance. In such approaches objects are modeled as a collection of parts or local features and the recognition is based on inferring object class based on similarity in parts' appearance and their spatial arrangement. Typically, such approaches find interest points using some operator such as [9] and then extract local image descriptors around such interest points. Several local image descriptors have been suggested and evaluated, such as Lowe's scale invariant features (SIFT) feature [11], entropy-based scale invariant features [9,6] and other local features which exhibit affine invariance such as [2,17,13]. Other approaches that model objects using local features include graph-based approaches such as [5]. In this paper, we adopt a part-based method with a common reference frame. We also experiment with both PCA and 2D PCA [21] for image patch representation.

An important subtask in object recognition lies at the interface between feature extraction and their use for recognition. It involves deciding which extracted features are most suitable for improving recognition rate [19], because the initial set of features is large, and often features are redundant or correspond to clutter in the image. Finding such actual object features reduces the dimensionality of the problem and is essential to learn a representative object model to enhance the recognition performance. Weber *et al.* [19] suggested the use of clustering to find common object parts and to reject background clutter from the positive training data. In such approach large clusters are retained as they are likely to contain parts coming from the object. Similar approach has been used in [10]. However, there is no guarantee that large cluster will just contain only object parts. Since the success of recognition is based on using many local features, such local features (parts) typically correspond to low level feature rather than actual high level object parts. In this paper we introduce a statistical approach to select discriminative object parts out of a pool of parts extracted from the training images.

Contributions: The contribution of this paper is threefold. Firstly, we introduce a probabilistic Bayesian approach for recognition where object model does not need a reference part [6]. Instead object parts are related to a common reference frame. Secondly, we propose a novel approach for unsupervised selection of discriminative parts that finds features that best discriminate the positive and negative examples. Finally, we investigate PCA and 2D PCA for image patch representation in our experiment and did a comparison.

The organization of this paper is as follows. Section 2 describes our part-based probabilistic model, the recognition method and 2D PCA representation for image patch. Section 3 explains our statistical method for image patch selection. section 4 presents the results of applying the proposed methods on a benchmark dataset. Section 5 is the conclusion.

2 Part-Based Probabilistic Model

We model an object class as a constellation of image patches from the object, which is similar in spirit to [19], but we also model their relative locations to a common reference frame. In doing this, we avoid the problem of not detecting the landmark patch. We assume objects from the same class should always have the same set of image patches detected and these image patches are similar both in their appearance and their relative location to the reference frame. The recognition of an object in an image will be a high probability event of detecting similar image patches sharing a common reference frame. In our work, we use the centroid as the reference frame and use the image patches simultaneously to build a probabilistic model for the object class and the centroid.

2.1 Model Structure

The model structure is best explained by first considering recognition. Using m observed image patches v_k, $(k = 1, \dots, m)$, from an image V, the problem of estimating the probability $P(O, C|V)$ of object class O and its centroid C given V can be formulated as (assuming independence between the patches and using Bayes' rule):

$$P(O, C|V) = \frac{P(V|O, C)P(O, C)}{P(V)} = P(O, C) \prod_{k=1}^{m} \frac{P(v_k|O, C)}{P(v_k)} \tag{1}$$

We wish to approximate the probability $P(v_k|O, C)$ as a mixture of Gaussian model using the observed patches from the training data. We simplify this by clustering all the patches selected from the training data into n clusters, A_i, $i = 1, \dots, n$ according to their appearance and spatial information, which is the 2D offset to the centroid C. We can decompose $P(v_k|O, C)$ as

$$\begin{aligned} P(v_k|O, C) &= \sum_{i=1}^{n} P(v_k|A_i)P(A_i|O, C) \\ &= \frac{\sum_{i=1}^{n} P(v_k|A_i)P(O, C|A_i)P(A_i)}{P(O, C)} \end{aligned} \tag{2}$$

Substituting (2) in (1), we get

$$P(O, C|V) \propto \prod_{k=1}^{m} \frac{\sum_{i=1}^{n} P(v_k|A_i)P(O, C|A_i)P(A_i)}{P(v_k)} \tag{3}$$

While performing recognition, $P(v_k)$ can be ignored. Assuming that $P(C)$ and $P(O)$ are independent, we have

$$P(O, C|V) \propto \prod_{k-1}^{m} \sum_{i=1}^{n} P(v_k|A_i)P(O|A_i)P(C|A_i)P(A_i) \tag{4}$$

2.2 Learning

The task of learning is to estimate each term in (4) from the training data. We concatenate the image patches' appearance and spatial vectors as features in the image patches clustering process. Since the resulting clusters contain similar features, we can assume image patches from one cluster will follow normal distribution in both appearance and spatial subspaces. By calculating the sample mean and sample covariance matrix of the subspaces of these clusters, we can approximate the probability of v_k and C for each cluster $A_i, i = 1, \ldots, n$. We use μ_i^v and μ_i^c to denote the sample means for v_k and C, respectively, and Σ_i^v and Σ_i^c to denote the sample covariances for v_k and C, respectively. Then for cluster A_i we have $P(v_k|A_i) \sim \mathrm{N}(v_k|\mu_i^v, \Sigma_i^v)$ and $P(C|A_i) \sim \mathrm{N}(C|\mu_i^c, \Sigma_i^c)$.

The rest of the terms in (4), can be approximated using the statistics from each of the cluster $A_i, i = 1, \ldots, n$. If the Cluster A_i has n_i points of which n_{ij} belong to Class O_j, we can estimate the following: $P(A_i) = n_i / \sum_{i=1}^{n} n_i$ and $P(O_j|A_i) = n_{ij}/n_i$[1].

2.3 Recognition

Recognition proceeds by first detecting and selecting image patches, and then evaluating the probability of the event of detecting object features sharing a common reference frame, as described in section 2.1. By calculating the probability and comparing it to a threshold, the presence or the absence of the object in the image may be determined.

Equation 4 can be interpreted as a probabilistic voting where each patch gives a weighted vote for the object class and centroid given its similarity to each of the clusters. This formulation extends to handle scale variations by considering each pair of patches instead of each individual patch.

2.4 Image Feature Representation

The image patch feature concatenated from appearance and spatial information could be a high dimension vector. Usually PCA is applied to reduce the dimension while retaining much of the information. Recently Yang [21] has proposed 2D PCA for image representation. This method can easily evaluate the covariance matrix accurately to calculate the eigen vectors and also take less time. In this paper, we have experimented with both approaches and did a comparison.

3 Statistical Image Patch Selection

In an object recognition task where an image is represented as a constellation of image patches, often many patches correspond to the cluttered background. If such patches are used to build the model for object class recognition, they will adversely affect the recognition rate. In this section, we proposed a statistical method for selecting those images patches from the positive images which, when used individually, have the power of discriminating between the positive and negative images in the evaluation data.

We formulate the image patch selection problem in a statistical framework by selecting those images patches from the positive images which consistently appear in multiple

[1] It must be remarked that this model extends to modeling multiple object classes directly, however, since our problem consists of only one class, we have $P(O_j|A_i) = 1$.

instances of the positive images but only rarely appear in the negative images (barring some hypothetical and pathological cases). Intuitively, if an individual image patch from a positive image performs well in recognizing the images of the target object, a combination of a number of such image patches is likely to enhance the overall performance. This is because the individual classifiers, although weak, can synergistically guide the combined classifier in producing statistically better results.

Our approach is different from the Boosting method [16]. Boosting is originally a way of combining classifiers and its use as feature selection is an overkill. In contrast, our statistical method does not boost the previous stage but filters out the over-represented and undesirable clusters of patches corresponding to background. In spirit, our approach is similar to [4]. We formalize this intuitive statistical idea in the following straightforward yet effective method for selecting the characteristic image patches.

We select an image patch $v \in V^+$ from the positive images V^+ in the training data if it is able to discriminate between the positive and negative images in the evaluation data, $V_e = \{V_e^+, V_e^-\}$ with a certain accuracy. A complete description of this method requires describing the classification method using a single image patch and the accuracy threshold. For classifying an image $\mathcal{V} \in V_e$ in the evaluation set, using a single image patch $v \in V^+$, we first calculate the distance, $D(\mathcal{V}, v) = \min_{\nu \in \mathcal{V}} d(\nu, v)$, between $\mathcal{V}$ and v defined as the euclidean distance between v and the closest image patch from $\mathcal{V}$. For classifying the images in the evaluation data, we use a threshold, t on distance $D(\mathcal{V}, v)$; if $D(\mathcal{V}, v) < t$, the image $\mathcal{V}$ is predicted to contain the target object, otherwise not. Accordingly we can associate an error function, $\mathcal{E}r(\mathcal{V}, v, t)$ (defined below 5), which assumes a value 1 if and only if the classifier makes the mistake.

$$\mathcal{E}r(\mathcal{V}, v, t) = \begin{cases} 0, \text{ if } (D(\mathcal{V}, v) < t \wedge \mathcal{V} \in V_e^+) \vee \\ \qquad (D(\mathcal{V}, v) \geq t \wedge \mathcal{V} \in V_e^-) \\ 1, \text{ otherwise} \end{cases} \tag{5}$$

Clearly, the performance depends on the parameter t, so we find an optimal circular region of radius t_v around v which minimizes the error rate of the classifier on the evaluation data. Finally, only those image patches from the positive images are selected which have recognition rate above a threshold, θ. A description of this algorithm, in

Algorithm 3.1: SELECT PATCHES, $\widehat{H}(V^+, V_e, \theta)$

$\widehat{H} \leftarrow \emptyset$;
for each $v \in V^+$
do $\begin{cases} \textbf{for each } \mathcal{V} \in V_e \\ \quad \textbf{do } \left\{ D(\mathcal{V}, v) = \min_{\nu \in \mathcal{V}} d(\nu, v); \right. \\ t_v \leftarrow \arg\min_{t \in \mathbb{R}^+} \sum_{\mathcal{V} \in V_e} \mathcal{E}r(\mathcal{V}, v, t) \\ err \leftarrow \frac{1}{|V_e|} \sum_{\mathcal{V} \in V_e} \mathcal{E}r(\mathcal{V}, v, t_v) \\ \textbf{if } (err < \theta) \\ \quad \textbf{then } \left\{ \widehat{H} \leftarrow \widehat{H} \cup \{v\} \right. \end{cases}$

the form of a pseudocode, is given in Algorithm 3.1. This algorithm takes the positive image patches V^+, patches from the evaluation data V_e, and the threshold θ as input and outputs $\widehat{H} \subseteq V^+$, the subset of selected image patches.

4 Experiment

4.1 Data Set

The experiment was carried out using Caltech database [2]. This database contains four classes of objects: motorbikes, airplanes, faces, car rear end which have to be distinguished from image in the background data set, also available in the database. Each object class is represented by 450 different instances of the target object, which were randomly and evenly split into training and testing images. Of the 225 positive images set aside for selecting the characteristic image patches, 175 were used as the training images and the remaining 50 were spared to be used as evaluation data. In addition, the evaluation data also consisted of 50 negative images from the background.

4.2 Image Patch Detection and the Intensity Representation

We use region based detector [9] for detecting informative image patches. We perform normalization for intensity and rescaled the image patches to 11×11 pixels, thus representing them as a 121 dimension intensity vectors. Then we tried with both PCA and 2D PCA on these vectors to get a more compact 18 dimension intensity representation.

4.3 Experimental Setting

We extracted 100 image patches for each of the 175 training images, and 100 evaluation images. Following this, we applied the statistical image patch selection selection method for removing the image patches from the background. In this process, we built simple classifier from each image patch in the training images and selected the one which led to a classifier with classification error rate less than 24%, an empirically calculated value. Figure 1 shows results from the image patches selection, which removes a significant number of patches corresponding to background.

After the image patch selection process, we computed the centroid for each object in the image. We used 2-D offset between the image patch and the object centroid as the spatial feature for the image patch and concatenated it with the intensity feature vector as the feature representation for each image patch. We then used k-means algorithm for clustering them into 70 clusters (this number was empirically chosen) and calculated the mean and covariance for them.

4.4 Experimental Results

In the testing phase, we used Kadir & Brady's[9] feature detector for extracting the image patches. Then we calculated the probability of the centroid of a possible object in the image as an indicator of its presence.

[2] http://www.vision.caltech.edu/html-files/archive.html

Fig. 1. Image patch selection. The image patches are shown using a yellow circle on the images. The left column shows the image patches extracted by Kadir & Brady's feature detector. The right column shows image patches selected by the statistical method.

Figure 2 shows the computationally estimated frame for the object along with the image patches which contributed towards estimating this frame. Observe that the estimated frame was mainly voted by the image patches located on the object. It also shows some examples of misclassification. There are two major reasons for such misclassification. The first is the presence of multiple target objects in the image, as shown in the airplane example. In this scenario, there is no centroid which gets a strong probability estimation from the matched parts. The second is poor illumination conditions which seriously limits the number of initial image patches extracted from the object, as illustrated by the face example.

We compared our result to the state of the art results from [6] and [12]. Table 1 summarizes the recognition accuracy at the equal ROC points (point at which the true positive rate equals one minus the false positive rate) of our different approach: no part selection with PCA, part selection with PCA, part selection with 2D PCA and results from other recent methods. This shows that the result from 2D PCA representation

Fig. 2. This figure demonstrates the estimation of object frame in some typical testing image using statistical part selection. The estimated centroid is indicated by a rectangle. All the image patches contributed to this estimation are indicated by yellow circles. The bottom row of the images are some misclassification examples.

is similar that from PCA and our approach are comparable to other recent methods reporting equal ROC performance using this data set.

Table 1. Equal ROC performance of our different approaches and other recent methods

Dataset	No selection with PCA	statistial method with 2D PCA	statistical method with PCA	Fergus [6]	Opelt [12]
Airplane	54.2	95.8	94.4	90.2	88.9
Motorbike	67.8	93.7	94.9	92.5	92.2
Face	62.7	97.3	98.4	96.4	93.5
Car (rear)	65.6	98.0	96.7	90.3	n/a

5 Conclusion

We have presented a statistical method for selecting informative image patches for patch-based object detection and class recognition. The experiments show our approach surpasses the performance of many existing methods. Although this method has been demonstrated in the context of image patch selection, it is a general method suitable for selecting a subset of features in other applications. A natural extension of this method is by integrating the auxiliary information regarding spatial arrangement between image patches; one way for doing this currently under investigation. In future, we intend to further develop and disseminate this framework as a general method for selecting features by automatically determining various hyper-parameter, which are currently empirically calculated.

References

1. S. Agarwal and D. Roth. Learning a sparse representation for object detection. In *ECCV*, pages 113–130, 2002.
2. A. Baumberg. Reliable feature matching across widely separated views. pages 774–781.
3. E. Borenstein and S. Ullman. Class-specific, top-down segmentation. In *ECCV*, pages 109–124, 2002.
4. Gy. Dorkó and C. Schmid. Selection of scale-invariant parts for object class recognition. In *ICCV*, pages 634–640, 2003.
5. Pedro F. Felzenszwalb and Daniel P. Huttenlocher. Pictorial structures for object recognition. *IJCV*, 61(1):55–79, 2005.
6. R. Fergus, P. Perona, and A. Zisserman. Object class recognition by unsupervised scale-invariant learning. In *CVPR (2)*, pages 264–271, 2003.
7. R. Fergus, P. Perona, and A. Zisserman. A sparse object category model for efficient learning and exhausitive recognition. In *CVPR*, 2005.
8. M. Fischler and R. Elschlager. The representation and matching of pictorial structures, 1973. IEEE Transaction on Computer c-22(1): 67-92.
9. T. Kadir and M. Brady. Scale, saliency and image description. *IJCV*, 2001.
10. Thomas K. Leung and Jitendra Malik. Recognizing surfaces using three dimensional textons. In *ICCV (2)*, pages 1010–1017, 1999.

11. David G. Lowe. Object recognition from local scale-invariant features. In *Proc. of the International Conference on Computer Vision ICCV, Corfu*, pages 1150–1157, 1999.
12. Andreas Opelt, Michael Fussenegger, Axel Pinz, and Peter Auer. Weak hypotheses and boosting for generic object detection and recognition. In *ECCV (2)*, pages 71–84, 2004.
13. Frederik Schaffalitzky and Andrew Zisserman. Multi-view matching for unordered image sets, or "how do i organize my holiday snaps?". In *ECCV (1)*, pages 414–431, 2002.
14. Cordelia Schmid and Roger Mohr. Local grayvalue invariants for image retrieval. *IEEE PAMI*, 19(5):530–535, 1997.
15. H. Schneiderman and T. Kanade. A statistical method for 3d object detection applied to faces and cars. pages 45–51, 2000.
16. Antonio B. Torralba, Kevin P. Murphy, and William T. Freeman. Sharing visual features for multiclass and multiview object detection. In *CVPR*, 2004.
17. Tinne Tuytelaars and Luc J. Van Gool. Wide baseline stereo matching based on local, affinely invariant regions. In *BMVC*, 2000.
18. Paul Viola and Michael Jones. Robust real-time object detection. *International Journal of Computer Vision 2002.*
19. Markus Weber, Max Welling, and Pietro Perona. Unsupervised learning of models for recognition. In *ECCV (1)*, pages 18–32, 2000.
20. Haim J. Wolfson and Isidore Rigoutsos. Geometric hashing: An overview. *IEEE Computational Science & Engineering*, 4(4):10–21, /1997.
21. Jian Yang, David Zhang, Alejandro F. Frangi, and Jing-Yu Yang. Two-dimensional pca: A new approach to appearance-based face representation and recognition. *IEEE Trans. Pattern Anal. Mach. Intell.*, 26(1):131–137, 2004.

Approximate Vehicle Waiting Time Estimation Using Adaptive Video-Based Vehicle Tracking

Li Li[1] and Fei-Yue Wang[1,2]

[1] University of Arizona, Tucson AZ 85719, USA
[2] Chinese Academy of Sciences, Beijing 100080, China

Abstract. During the last two decades, significant research efforts had been made in developing vision-based automatic traffic monitoring systems in order to improve driving efficiency and reduce traffic accidents. This paper presents a practical vehicle waiting time estimation method using adaptive video-based vehicle tracking method. Specifically, it is designed to deal with lower image quality, inappropriate camera positions, vague lane/road markings and complex driving scenarios. The spatio-temporal analysis is integrated with shape hints to improve performance. Experiment results show the effectiveness of the proposed approach.

1 Introduction

Traffic monitoring and surveillance is one important research area of Intelligent Transportation Systems (ITS), which aims to collect real-time traffic flow data for road usage analysis and collisions warning. Automatic traffic monitoring is now world-widely accepted as an essential component of advanced traffic management systems [1]-[6].

To obtain accurate real-time data, various sensors/devices have been designed to estimate traffic parameters. Magnetic detectors and the sonar and microwave detectors are the most frequently used ones and proven to yield good performances [7]-[9]. But they are usually costly to install and maintain. In many recent approaches, vision based monitoring systems appears to be cheap and yet effective solutions, which are able to monitor wide areas and provide flexible estimations of traffic parameters [1]-[6], [10]-[24].

Object (vehicle, pedestrian, bicyclist) tracking is the basic function of a traffic monitoring system. Numerous algorithms had been proposed for accurate and real-time vision based vehicle tracking tasks. Image based object detection using edge/shape hints attracts great interests now [10]-[13]. Usually, the potential traffic participators are first separated from the background scene. Then, to enable precise classification of the moving objects, some characteristics such as length, width, and height are further recovered and examined. Finally, the found objects will be tracked to extract the associated traffic parameters. For instance, adaptive thresholding is a simple but not so effective method, which supposes that vehicles are compact objects having different intensity form their background. Thus, to threshold intensities in regions assumes to be able to separate

N. Zheng, X. Jiang, and X. Lan (Eds.): IWICPAS 2006, LNCS 4153, pp. 105–114, 2006.

the vehicle from the background. But false detection of shadows or missed detection of vehicles with similar intensities as theirs environment cannot be avoid [15]-[16]. Motion based vehicle detection/tracking is another popular method in traffic monitoring systems. For instance, vehicle detection using optical flow was discussed in [17]-[18]. Since it is time consuming, many research addresses on fast optical flow calculation design. Background-frame differencing and inter-frame differencing are also important methods [19]-[24]. They were proven to be fast and reliable vehicle detection/tracking methods in many literals. However, all the above approaches cannot thoroughly solve all traffic monitoring problems due to variation of lighting condition, vehicle shapes and sizes.

To try to keep up with the steps of U.S., European and Japan, several developing countries begin to apply cutting edge traffic monitoring and management techniques to alleviate their fast growing traffic congestions and accidents. However, the researchers in these countries are now facing the following new challenges:

- because the financial budget for installing city traffic monitoring systems is limited, the obtained image qualities are often therefore limited;
- due to the same reason, these cameras are frequently installed at inappropriate positions, which leads to notable view field and vehicle occlusions problems;
- the lane markings are often vague and diminished, since they are often painted tens of years ago;
- mixed traffic flow, which simultaneously contains pedestrians, bicyclists, motors and vehicles, makes the vehicle waiting time hard to estimate;
- the traffic laws might be violated occasionally or even frequently, which obviously introduce difficulties for traffic parameter extraction.

Under such conditions, most known methods cannot yield acceptable results standalone without modifications. Therefore, a new traffic monitoring system is proposed in this paper as shown in Fig.1. It detects potential vehicles using spatio-temporal analysis at first. Then, it further examines these interested areas based on vehicle/road shape information and driving rules to filter the disturbances caused by pedestrians and vehicle occlusions. Finally, Section 6 concludes the whole paper.

To give a detailed explanation, the rest of this paper is arranged as follows: Section 2-3 analyze driving environment learning; Section 4 examines vehicle detection and identification algorithms; and Section 5 discusses how to track vehicle and estimate average waiting time.

2 Lane Markings Detection

Lane detection is unnecessary in vehicle tracking, if the camera is set at an appropriate position. However, if this condition cannot be met, it is an essential step in order to determine the vehicle's relative position to the lanes/roads.

One difficulty here is to detect the vague and diminished lane markings, especially when parts of the lanes are occluded by vehicles and pedestrians. To solve this problem, the following adaptive algorithm is proposed and employed.

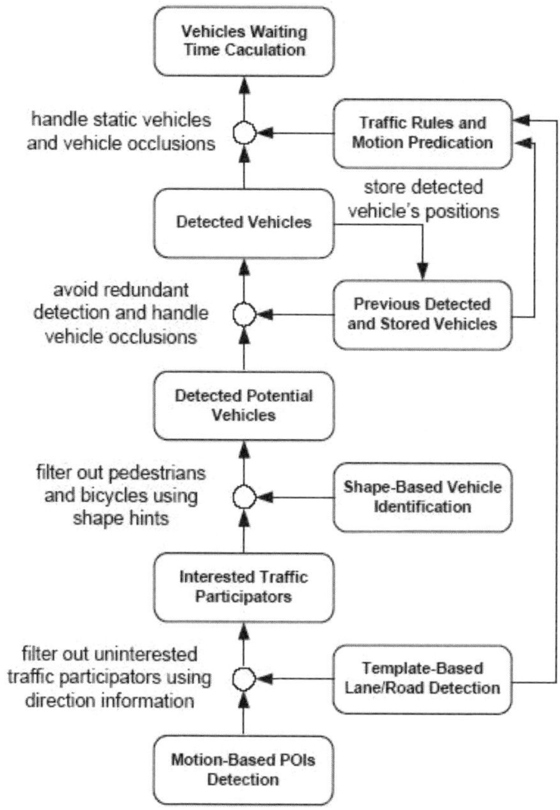

Fig. 1. The proposed traffic monitoring system workflow

Adaptive Lane Markings Detection Algorithm:

1) Set an initial edge detection threshold σ_e;
2) Use Canny edge detection algorithm to detect those apparent edges regarding to σ_e and filter out the unexpected margin lines generated by camera problems;
3) Set an initial line detection threshold σ_l;
4) Use Hough Transformation and *a priori* road shape templates to find the potential lane markings in the obtained edge image;
5) Gradually increase σ_l until only one line is selected as the dominant lane line. If the dominant lane line cannot be determined by choosing different σ_l, adjust σ_e and go back to step 1);
6) Store the found lane marking line and its direction θ_l;
7) Use Canny edge detection algorithm to detect as much edges as possible with a lower threshold σ_e.
8) Set an relatively lower line detection threshold σ_l;
9) Use Hough Transformation to find other lane by only searching potential lines with angles similar to θ_e;

10) Adjust σ_l and go back to step 8), if too many or too few lanes are found based on *a priori* knowledge of lane sum. If problem still cannot be solved, Adjust σ_e and go back to step 7).
11) Eliminate false lines by calculating their distances to the dominant lane marking line.

(a) (b)

Fig. 2. (a) lane markings detection results; (b) division of monitoring area

Lane detection does not need to be carried out frequently. Namely, once or twice a day would be enough. In most situations, to model the lane markings as lines will yield acceptable results. If really needed, those template-based lane detection algorithms, i.e. the one described in [25]-[26], will be applied. However, this will introduce significant calculation cost.

Fig.2(a) shows lane detection example, where the 5th line (top to bottom, same as follows) indicates the dominant lane marking line, and the 6th and 7th lines are the other detected lane marking lines. And the first four lines indicate disturbance lines which has similar angles of the lane markings. They are eliminated by check their distances to the dominant lane marking line. If the distance is relatively large comparing to other found lane lines, the corresponding line will be considered as out of Area of Interest (AOI) and eliminated. The two vertical margin (left and right) lines caused by camera problems are intensionally discarded. The Hough transformation referring point is the top left corner.

3 Environment Learning and Vehicle Detection

Similar to [27], in order to improve tracking performance, an image got from the video is divided into three areas as shown in Fig.2(b): distant view, near view and disappear areas. In Area 1 (distant view), all the moving objects will be labeled and memorized. While in the Area 2 (near view), only the objects approximately moving alone the lane direction will be further examined. Any vehicle moves from

Area 1 into Area 2 will be tracked, even it stops. The lane direction information will help a lot to remove the disturbances caused by vehicles and bicyclist moving in the opposite directions. If vehicles move from Area 2 into Area 3 (disappear areas), it will soon be discarded after a short time, or several frame equivalently.

The area sizes are determined by the focus and range of view of the camera. Due to the image quality limits of the applied camera, the motion detection threshold for the objects moving in Area 1 is set smaller than that used for Area 2. Notice that vehicles usually have larger size than pedestrians and bicyclists, the proposed motion-based vehicle detection algorithm is designed as:

Adaptive Vehicle Detection Algorithm:

1) Set an initial motion detection threshold σ_{m1} for Area 1;
2) Use frame differencing algorithm to detect moving object. If less than 5 objects are detected on average, choose a smaller σ_{m1} and go to step 1); otherwise, if more than 10 objects are detected, chose a larger σ_{m1} and go to step 1). The sum of the vehicles here is estimated by lane sum and previous traffic records;
3) Choose an motion detection threshold σ_{m2} so that $\sigma_{m1} \approx \sigma_{m2}$. Here 1.5 is an scale factor chosen by considering the applied camera quality;
4) Filter out the objects using lane direction information generated by optical flow estimation.

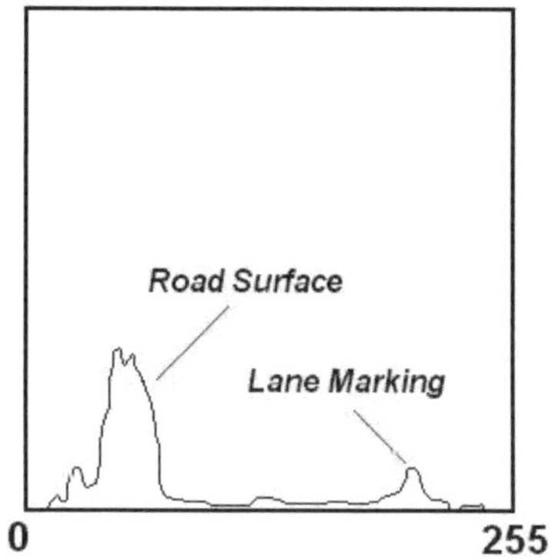

Fig. 3. Diagram of two peaks in the histogram of the road areas

To detect all potential road participators in the complex driving scenarios, frame differencing is employed to deal with multiple moving objects first. Then, background differencing is used to get the more precise contours of the moving objects. The road areas is determined by color hints like what proposed in [12]-[14] and the lane information obtained above. Particularly, the road surface color is retrieved from the images that satisfy the following two heuristic rules:

- no (moving) objects are detected on the road areas;
- the shape of the gray histogram of road areas roughly fits the passed record. This could partly reduce the effect of varied lighting conditions. Normally, there will only exist two apparent peaks in the histogram as shown in Fig.3, which indicate dark road surface and light lane markings respectively.

4 Vehicle Identification

To distinguish vehicles, motors and bicyclists in the real time is a difficult problem, since the size information cannot be easily retrieved in the images obtained here. Thus, shape information is employed here similar to what discussed in [28]-[29].

Knowledge-based methods employ *a priori* knowledge to find potential vehicles in an image. Comparing to the following frequently considered cues: vehicle geometry structures, shadow beneath the vehicle, texture, symmetry, color, rear-lights, horizontal overlap assumption yields better results here. Due to low image quality, vehicle texture and color information cannot be properly used here. Moreover, since the traffic monitoring systems is required to work in cloudy day time, shadow and rear-lights cues do not work well, either.

It is frequently assumed that road vehicles, especially cars and lesser extent lorries, consists of a large number of horizontal structures, particularly windows and bumpers. For example, the horizontal overlap assumption was used in [28] to each image column may result in several Areas of Interest. The horizontal edge response in each image column is summed and smoothed with a triangular filter. And each locally maximal peak which is extracted from the smoothed column responses will indicate a potential vehicle. A similar method is used to here to roughly identify bicyclists, motors and vehicles. More specifically, is could be described as follows:

Adaptive Vehicle Identification Algorithm:

1) Determine the Areas of Interests (AOI) using motion detection. If the width of an AOI is larger than a pre-selected threshold σ_w, than split this AOI into two AOIs from the middle. Repeat this action until all the widths of AOIs are shorter than σ_w;
2) Set a relatively large edge detection threshold than what is used for lane detection, i.e, set $\hat{\sigma_e} \approx \sigma_e$;
3) Use Canny edge detection algorithm to detect the edges for each AOI found with $\hat{\sigma_e}$, then obtain the edge response column sums for each AOI;
4) Distinguish the detected objects based on the heuristic rules listed as below:
   i. if the width of an AOI is larger than a pre-selected threshold $\bar{\sigma_w}$, it may not be a motor;
   ii. if the height of an AOI is larger than a pre-selected threshold $\bar{\sigma_h}$, it indicates a vehicle;
   iii. if there exit two or more than two dominant peaks in the edge response column sums, or equivalently there exits apparent valley(s), it must indicate bicyclists;

iv. if there exits only one dominant peak in the edge response column sums plot, it usually indicates a motor;
v. if there is a flat top in the edge response column sums plot, it often indicates a vehicle.

Since the image quality is limited and AOI are much smaller than the whole image, the obtained response column sums plot usually need to be averagely smoothed to easily find the peaks/valleys/top.

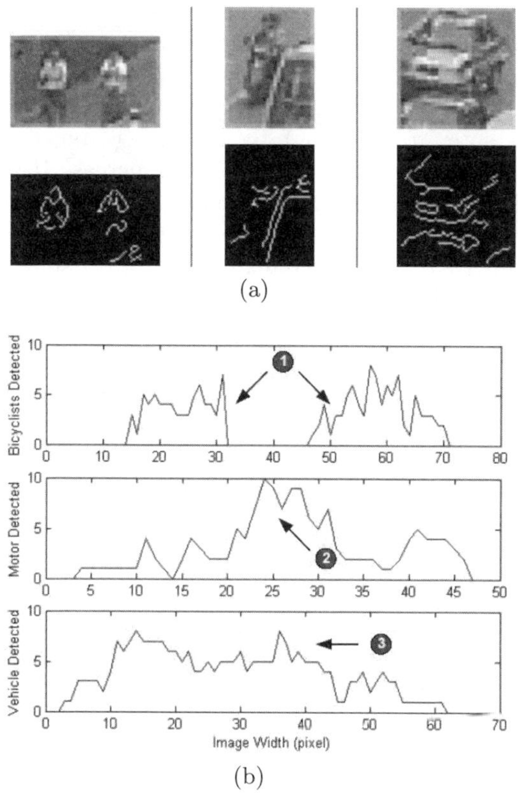

Fig. 4. (a) detected traffic participators: (left) bicyclists, (middle) motor, (c) commercial vehicles; (b) the associated edge response column sums plot

Fig.4(a) shows several typical examples of detected objects. Usually, bicyclists are detected only because two or more than two bicyclists moving to the same direction side by side. Thus, there usually exit valleys between peaks as shown in Fig.4(b).1. The windows, plates and bumpers add significant edge information to vehicles comparing to bicyclists and motors (a single hill), which results in a relatively flat top in the edge response column sums plot, see Fig.4(b).3. Besides, vehicles usually generate larger AOI than bicyclists and motors. These hints cannot perfectly distinguish a vehicle from bicyclists or a motor, however, experiments shows it works well in many cases and fast enough to guarantee real-time processing.

5 Vehicle Waiting Time Calculation

In order to apply optimal traffic light control and relieve traffic congestion, the average vehicle waiting time needs to be approximately estimated. Due to varied passenger capacity and occupancy, different vehicles/motors waiting times will be scaled by proper factor first and then added up together.

The most difficult problem is to calculate the waiting time for the stopped vehicles. Here, a simple yet effective method is applied. It assumes that all the identified vehicles enter from Area 1 to Area 2 will be registered with their approximate positions and labeled with an auto-increase ID, respectively. The waiting time of such a vehicle will be accumulated until it leaves Area 2 to Area 3, or after a pre-determined die-away time span, i.e. ten minutes. Any start to move vehicles in Area 2 will be compared to the registered vehicles (mainly position information and traffic rules) to check whether it is a new vehicle or not. However, the traffic rules used here consider all the possible driving scenarios including the illegal driving behaviors.

However, the proposed approach makes wrong tracking when the following cases occur in the practical experiments:

- a vehicle drives backward for a notable distance will be recognized as a new vehicle or simply discarded;
- some vehicles cannot be detected if the vehicle queue is too long and extents out of view;
- track-trailers might be recognized as two vehicles;
- the system cannot work well under foggy or heavy rain conditions. New types of traffic monitoring systems are still in bad need for those cities where such bad weathers are easily encountered.

Further discussions and experiments will be carried out to improve the tracking performance of the proposed system and make it more practicable for the fast growing transportation markets in the near future.

6 Conclusion

To fast track vehicles in complex driving scenarios, a video-based traffic monitoring system is discussed in this paper. Both motion vehicle motion and shape information is considered to accurately recognize commercial vehicles and motors from varied road objects including pedestrians and bicyclists. Experiment results show the effectiveness of this method.

Acknowledgement

This work was supported in part by the Federal Department of Transportation through the ATLAS Center at the University of Arizona, and Grants (60125310, 60334020, 2002CB312200, 2004AA1Z2360, 2004GG1104001) from China. We would like to thank Mr. Tao Yang for help collecting experimental data for testing and evaluation in this paper.

References

1. R. M. Inigo, "Traffic monitoring and control using machine vision: a survey," IEEE Transactions on Industrial Electronics, vol. 32, no. 3, pp. 177-185, 1985.
2. I. Masaki, "Machine-vision systems for intelligent transportation systems," IEEE Intelligent Systems, vol. 13, no. 6, pp. 24-31, 1998.
3. V. Kastrinaki, M. Zervakis, and K. Kalaitzakis, "A survey of video processing techniques for traffic applications," Image and Vision Computing, vol. 21, no. 4, pp. 359-381, 2003.
4. W. Hu, T. Tan, and L. Wang, et. al, "A survey on visual surveillance of object motion and behaviors," IEEE Transactions on Systems, Man and Cybernetics, Part C, vol. 34, no. 3, pp. 334-352, 2004.
5. P. Mirchandani and F.-Y. Wang, "RHODES to Intelligent Transportation Systems," IEEE Intelligent Systems, vol. 20, no. 1, pp. 10-15, 2005.
6. L. Li, J. Song, and F.-Y. Wang, et. al, "New developments and research trends for intelligent vehicles," IEEE Intelligent Systems, vol. 20, no. 4, pp. 10-14, 2005.
7. J. Scarzello, D. Lenko, and R. Brown, et. al, "SPVD: A magnetic vehicle detection system using a low power magnetometer," IEEE Transactions on Magnetics, vol. 14, no. 5, pp. 574-576, 1978.
8. T. Uchiyama, K. Mohri, and H. Itho, et. al, "Car traffic monitoring system using MI sensor built-in disk set on the road," IEEE Transactions on Magnetics, vol. 36, no. 5, pp. 3670-3672, 2000.
9. S. Kitazume and H. Kondo, "Advances in millimeter-wave subsystems in Japan," IEEE Transactions on Microwave Theory and Techniques, vol. 39, no. 5, pp. 775-781, 1991.
10. M. Fathy and M. Y. Siyal, "A window-based image processing technique for quantitative and qualitative analysis of road traffic parameters," IEEE Transactions on Vehicular Technology, vol. 47, no. 4, pp. 1342-1349, 1998.
11. X. Li, Z.-Q. Liu and K.-M. Leung, "Detection of vehicles from traffic scenes using fuzzy integrals," Pattern Recognition, vol. 35, no. 4, pp. 967-980, 2002.
12. S. Gupte, O. Masoud, and R. F. K. Martin, et. al, "Detection and classification of vehicles," IEEE Transactions on Intelligent Transportation Systems, vol. 3, no. 1, pp. 37-47, 2002.
13. D. M. Ha, J.-M. Lee, and Y.-D. Kim, "Neural-edge-based vehicle detection and traffic parameter extraction," Image and Vision Computing, vol. 22, no. 5, pp. 899-907, 2004.
14. B. Coifman, D. Beymer, and P. McLauchlan, et. al, "A real-time computer vision system for vehicle tracking and traffic surveillance," Transportation Research Part C, vol. 6, pp. 271-288, 1998.
15. Y. Park, "Shape-resolving local thresholding for object detection," Pattern Recognition Letters, vol. 22, no. 8, pp. 883-890, 2001.

16. W. Enkelmann, "Interpretation of traffic scenes by evaluation of optical flow fields from image sequences," IFAC Control Computers, Communications in Transportation, 1989.
17. B. Maurin, O. Masoud, and N. P. Papanikolopoulos, "Tracking all traffic: computer vision algorithms for monitoring vehicles, individuals, and crowds," IEEE Robotics and Automation Magazine, vol. 12, no. 1, pp. 29-36, 2005.12-17, 2003.
18. N. Hoose, "IMPACT: an image analysis tool for motorway analysis and surveillance," Traffic Engineering Control Journal, pp. 140-147, 1992.
19. N. Paragios and G. Tziritas, "Adaptive detection and localization of moving objects in image sequences," Signal Processing: Image Communication, vol. 14, pp. 277-296, 1999.
20. N. Paragios and R. Deriche, "Geodesic active contours and level sets for the detection and tracking of moving objects," IEEE Transactions on Pattern Analysis and Machine Intelligence, vol. 22, no. 3, pp. 266-280, 2000.
21. E. Sifakis and G. Tziritas, "Fast marching to moving object location," Proceedings of International Conference on Scale Space Theories in Computer Vision, 1999.
22. E. Sifakis, I. Grinias, and G. Tziritas, "Video segmentation using fast marching and region growing algorithms," EURASIP Journal on Applied Signal Processing, pp. 379-388, 2002.
23. R. Cucchiara, M. Piccardi, and P. Mello, "Image analysis and rule-based reasoning for a traffic monitoring system," IEEE Transactions on Intelligent Transportation Systems, vol. 1, no. 2, pp. 119-130, 2000.
24. R. Cucchiara, C. Grana, and M. Piccardi, et. al, "Detecting moving objects, ghosts, and shadows in video streams," IEEE Transactions on Pattern Analysis and Machine Intelligence, vol. 25, no. 10, pp. 1337-1342, 2003.
25. S. Lakshmanan and D. Grimmer, "A deformable template approach to detecting straight edges in radar images," IEEE Transactions on Pattern Analysis and Machine Intelligence, vol. 18, no. 4, pp. 438-443, 1996.
26. B. Ma, S. Lakshmanan, and A. O. Hero, "Simultaneous detection of lane and pavement boundaries using model-based multi-sensor fusion," IEEE Transactions on Intelligent Transportation Systems, vol. 1, no. 3, pp. 135-147, 2000.
27. D. R. Magee, "Tracking multiple vehicles using foreground, background and motion models," Image and Vision Computing, vol. 22, no. 2, pp. 143-155, 2004.
28. N. D. Matthews, P. E. An, and C. J. Harris, "Vehicle detection and recognition in grey-scale imagery," The Second International Workshop on Intelligent Autonomous Vehicles, pp. 1-6, 1995.
29. Z. Sun, R. Miller, and G. Bebis, "A real-time precrash vehicle detection system," Proceedings of the Sixth IEEE Workshop on Applications of Computer Vision, pp. 171-176, 2002.

Mouth Region Localization Method Based on Gaussian Mixture Model

Kenichi Kumatani and Rainer Stiefelhagen

Universitaet Karlsruhe (TH), Interactive Systems Labs, Am Fasanengarten 5,
76131 Karlsruhe, Germany
k_kumatani@ieee.org, stiefel@ira.uka.de

Abstract. This paper presents a new mouth region localization method which uses the Gaussian mixture model (GMM) of feature vectors extracted from mouth region images. The discrete cosine transformation (DCT) and principle component analysis (PCA) based feature vectors are evaluated in mouth localization experiments. The new method is suitable for audio-visual speech recognition. This paper also introduces a new database which is available for audio visual processing. The experimental results show that the proposed system has high accuracy for mouth region localization (more than 95 %) even if the tracking results of preceding frames are unavailable.

1 Introduction

Facial feature localization methods have recently undergone much attention. In particular, a mouth feature plays an important role for many applications such as automatic face recognition, facial expression analysis and audio visual automatic speech recognition.

However, automatic mouth localization is especially difficult because of the various changes of its shape and person dependent appearance. In addition, the better localization accuracy and faster response speed should be achieved at the same time. Many systems use skin color, the vertical and horizontal integration of pixel values in a face image[1]-[4]. However those systems are generally not robust for the significant change of illumination conditions.

Some researchers have tried to find the precise lip contour [5]-[7]. However, most of applications don't need it. For example, in audio visual speech recognition, the image of a mouth region is preferred [12].

Lienhart et al. applied the detector tree boosted classifiers to lip tracking [8]. And they showed that their tracking system achieved high accuracy and small execution time per frame. However, we found that their method often fails to localize a mouth area at a frame level. In addition, an eye image is often misrecognized as a mouth. Actually they refined the trajectory of mouth by post-processing approach. Although some errors at a fame level can be recovered by such a post-processing, better accuracy at each frame is of course preferred.

The method based on Gaussian mixture models (GMM) [9][10] is one of the promising approaches since its performance is very high. And it can easily adjust the accuracy and computation cost by configuring the parameters such as a number of

N. Zheng, X. Jiang, and X. Lan (Eds.): IWICPAS 2006, LNCS 4153, pp. 115 – 124, 2006.

mixtures. In the GMM based methods, the feature vector representation is a main issue for the improvement of the performance.

In this paper, we present a new mouth region localization method based on GMM, which doesn't need prohibitively heavy calculation. This paper is organized as the followings: Section 2 describes the training algorithm of GMM and section 3 describes the new mouth region localization method. Then section 4 presents the database used in experiments. In section 5, experimental results are depicted and discussed.

2 Training Algorithm

First this section defines a mouth template image to be localized. Then feature vectors used in this paper are explained. This paper evaluates two kinds of feature representation: (1) discrete cosine transformation (DCT) based feature vector [9] and (2) principle component analysis (PCA) based feature vector. After that, we describe how to construct GMM of the feature vectors.

2.1 Mouth Template

In order to construct the template images of a mouth, consistent rules for labeling are required. In our system, the width of a mouth region is defined from a left lip corner to the right one. And the height is defined from nostrils to a chin. Accordingly the mouth templates include non-lip area. Figure 1 shows the samples of the template images. By containing non-lip area such as the nostrils, template images can have robust information to locate a mouth region because nostrils don't change largely. If we use a lip image only, a mouth region more often fails to be localized because of the significant change of lip shape. It is noteworthy that the movements of nostrils might have useful information for audio-visual speech recognition. All mouth images are scaled to the same size in training stage which is the average size over the training images. Thus, the original ratio of the width to the height is not kept the same.

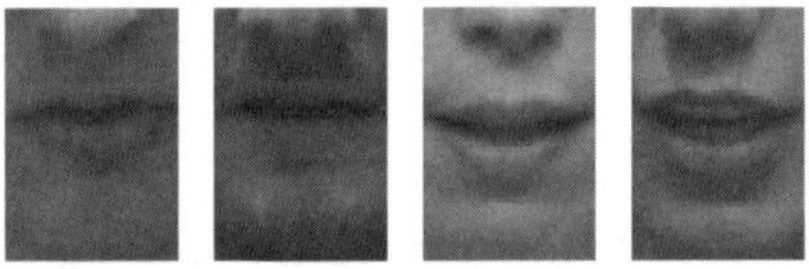

Fig. 1. This figure shows the samples of the mouth template images for training. Note that these samples are scaled to the same size.

2.2 DCT Based Feature Vector

Let $\boldsymbol{I}$ denote the image normalized by histogram equalization and its size is $\boldsymbol{M}$x$\boldsymbol{N}$. Then, the 2-D DCT transformation is computed as:

$$D_{u,v} = \sum_{m=0}^{M-1}\sum_{n=0}^{N-1}\left[C_i \times C_j \times \cos(u\pi \frac{2m+1}{2M}) \times \cos(v\pi \frac{2n+1}{2N}) \times I_{m,n} \right] . \quad (1)$$

After that, the matrix $D_{u,v}$ is converted into a vector using a zigzag scan.

2.3 PCA Based Feature Vector

Let $\boldsymbol{x}$ denote the vector converted from the normalized image. This approach calculates the followings.

(1) The mean of the vectors $\overline{\mathbf{x}}$,
(2) The covariance matrix $\boldsymbol{C}$ of the vectors,
(3) The eigenvectors, $\boldsymbol{\varphi}_i$ and the corresponding eigenvalues λ_i of $\boldsymbol{C}$ (sorted so that $\lambda_i \geq \lambda_{i+1}$),

After these values are calculated, a feature vector is represented as:

$$\mathbf{y} = \boldsymbol{\Phi}^T (\mathbf{x} - \overline{\mathbf{x}}) \ . \tag{2}$$

where the matrix $\boldsymbol{\Phi}$ consists of the $\boldsymbol{t}$ eigenvectors corresponding to the largest eigenvalues.

Although both methods can de-correlate the elements of an image and compress vector size efficiently, the feature vectors obtained by PCA are more dependent of the training data. Therefore, PCA based feature vector can deteriorate if there is a gap between training and test data.

2.4 Training GMM

After feature vectors are calculated, those vectors are classified into k classes by K-mean algorithm. A mixture weight, mean and covariance of a mixture are obtained by dividing the number of samples belonging to the class by the total number of samples and calculating a mean and covariance from the samples in the class, respectively.

2.5 Multi-resolution GMM

To improve the efficiency of the search, we use the multi-resolution framework. In this framework, after the mouth region in a coarse image is located, the estimated location is refined in a series of finer resolution image.

For each training and test image, our system constructs the image pyramid where the higher level has the lower resolution. The base image at level 0 has the original resolution. Subsequent levels are formed by half resolution image sub-sampled from the ones at the one lower level. At each level, GMM is build from the corresponding resolution images. The sizes of feature vectors are kept the same over all levels.

2.6 Mouth Region Localization Based on GMM

Figure 2 shows the basic flow chart of our mouth localization system at each level of the pyramid. Given an input image, the image with the same size as a window is cropped. The window is translated over all pixels of an input image and scaled. Our system scales the window in two ways: (1) with the same original ratio of the width to the height and (2) without keeping that ratio. The process (2) is important because the mouth template images during the training are resized to the same size without keeping the original ratio due to the change of mouth shape. However, scaling without keeping the ratio leads to extremely heavy computation. Thus, our system changes that ratio within the range from the training data. Then, feature vector is calculated from the cropped image, as mentioned in section 2. Note that the cropped image is normalized by histogram equalization. After that, the likelihood of the feature vector is computed with the GMM. The position and size which gives the maximum likelihood are estimated as the mouth region.

First the above process is performed for the lowest resolution image in the pyramid. In order to avoid converging to the local minima, ***n*** candidates are kept at each level. At the next level, the search area is limited based on the ***n*** candidates. Those steps are repeated until the candidate is found at the finest resolution.

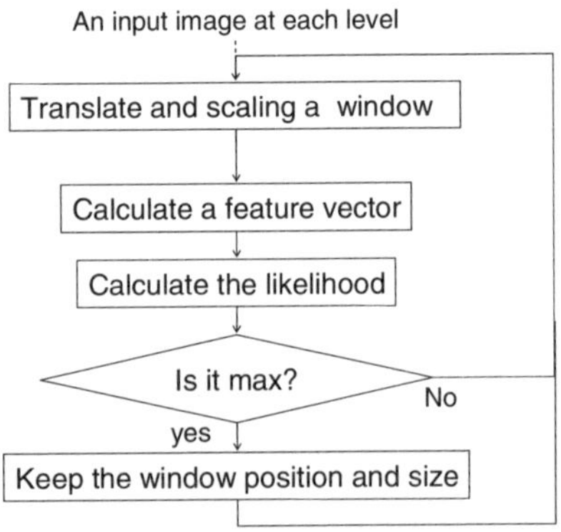

Fig. 2. This figure shows the basic flow chart of the mouth localization system. This process is repeated from the lowest resolution image to the highest resolution image.

3 Database for Experiments

This section describes the specification of the new database we recorded. Though this paper addresses only the video processing, the database contains speech data and is available for audio visual processing.

Figure 3 describes the layout of equipments at the recording. Three pan-tilt-zoom (PTZ) cameras are set at different angles for a subject. A cross talking microphone is put on speaker's ear. Three kinds of video data and two kinds of audio data are recorded. The cameras and microphones are connected to different computers. Audio and video data streams are synchronized with network time protocol (NTP). Figure 4 shows the sample images which are taken at 0, 45 and 90 angles, respectively. The speakers utter English alpha-numeric strings and English sentences extracted from TIMIT database. 39 male and 9 female are recorded.

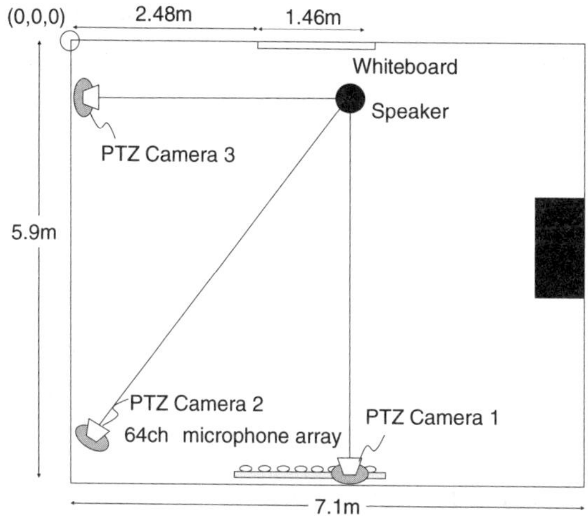

Fig. 3. The layout of equipments at the recording is described

Fig. 4. This figure shows the sample images

4 Experiment

4.1 Experimental Conditions

Table 1 shows the details of experimental conditions. The subjects in test data are not included in training data. In this experiment, images have always only one face. Note that we decide the size of mouth templates at level 0 from the average size over all training images. In this experiment, only frontal faces are used.

4.2 Experimental Results and Discussions

Figure 5 and 6 represent the accuracy of mouth region localization by DCT and PCA based feature vector, respectively. The line 'D*N*' presents results when the dimension of a feature vector is *N*. Thus, the line 'D16' indicates results when a 16 dimensional vector is used. The horizontal axis (x-axis) of each figure represents the average distance Di between the manually labeled points and automatically estimated positions as

$$Di = \frac{1}{4}\sum_{l-1}^{4}\left|\mathbf{p}_{corr}^{(l)} - \mathbf{p}_{est}^{(l)}\right| \qquad (3)$$

where $\mathbf{p}^{(1)} \cdots \mathbf{p}^{(4)}$ are positions of an upper left, upper right, bottom left and bottom right of a mouth region, respectively. $\mathbf{p}_{corr}^{(l)}$ and $\mathbf{p}_{est}^{(l)}$ mean the labeled and estimated positions, respectively. The smaller Di means that system can localize a mouth area more precisely.

Table 1. Experimental conditions

A kind of parameter	Value
Training data	2113 images 30 subjects
Test data	319 images 18 subjects
The number of mixtures	50
The number of candidates kept at each level	8
The size of mouth templates at level 0 (width, height)	65, 105
The maximum pyramid level	3
Dimensions of feature vectors	16, 24, 32, 48, 54
The number of mixtures	50, 80

The vertical axis (y-axis) represents the cumulative probability of x-axis value which is also associated with the accuracy of mouth localization system. For example, figure 5 shows that the mouth regions are correctly estimated with probability 0.97 (accuracy 97 %) by DCT based vector of 54 dimensions when $Di \geq 15$. On the other hand, Figure 6 shows that the accuracy of 95 % is achieved by PCA based method under the same condition as the above. Comparing Figure 5 with Figure 6, one can see that the mouth can be located more accurately and stably when the PCA based feature is used. However, we found that PCA based method rarely estimate the mouth region far from the correct position. In other words, the completely different area is seldom detected as a mouth region. We consider that those errors occur because the mouth shape is not included in the training data. Note that DCT computation is faster than PCA.

In Figure 7 and Figure8, experimental results are shown when the system uses GMMs with 50 Gaussians (50 mixtures) and 80 Gaussians (80 mixtures). In both figures, the line ‘M*I*(D*N*)’ stands for GMM with *I* mixtures and a *N* dimensional feature vector. Accordingly, the line ‘M50(D48)’ indicates the cumulative probabilities when GMM with 50 mixtures and a 48 dimensional feature vector are used. Figure 7 shows experimental results when the DCT based feature vector is used. And results are shown in Figure 8 when the PCA based feature vector is used. Generally by increasing the number of mixtures, we can achieve the better performance for the classification of training data. However, in the case that too many mixtures are used for a few training data, the performance gets worse because of data sparseness. From Figure 8, one can clearly confirm the degradation of the performance when 80 mixtures are

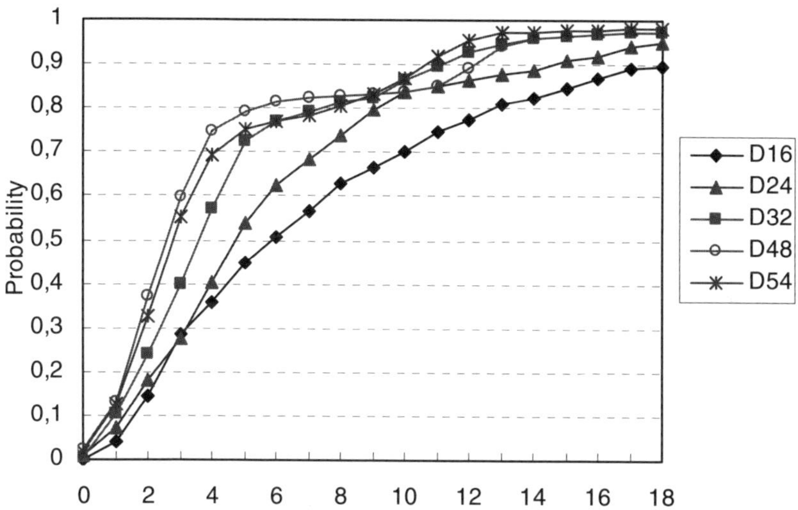

Fig. 5. This figure presents accuracy of mouth localization by DCT based feature vector. In this figure, 'D16' stands for a 16 dimensional feature vector. Accordingly, the line 'D16' (*with diamond symbols*) indicates the accuracy when a 16 dimensional feature vector is used.

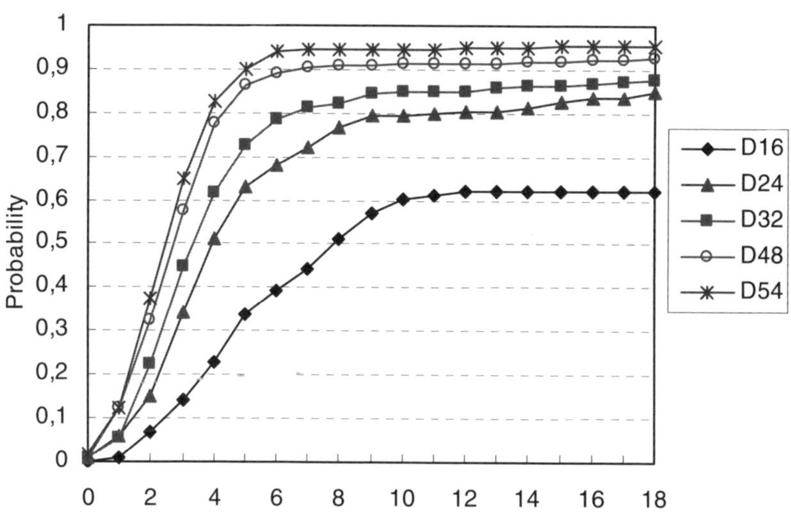

Fig. 6. This figure presents accuracy of mouth localization by PCA based feature vector. In this figure, 'D16' stands for a 16 dimensional feature vector. Accordingly, the line 'D16' (*with diamond symbols*) indicates the accuracy when a 16 dimensional feature vector is used.

used since it's too much. However, a situation is more complicated when the DCT based feature vector is used. The combination of the number of mixtures and the number of dimension influences the performance. For example, even if the number of mixtures is a little big, the improvement might be obtained by decreasing the number

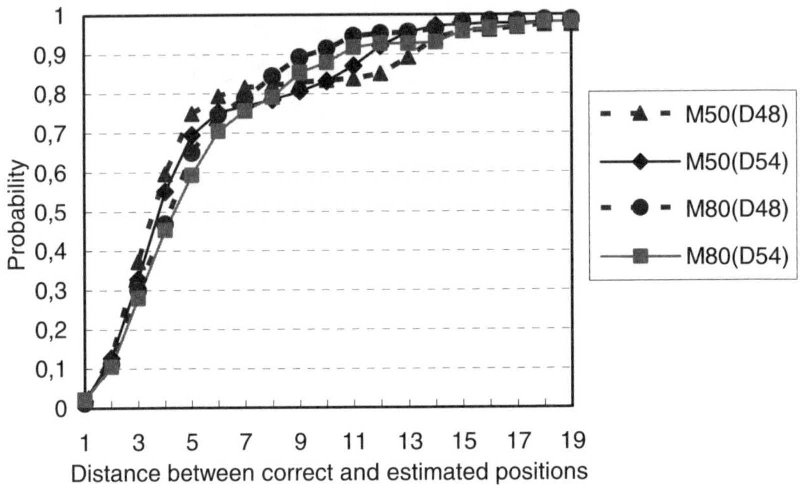

Fig. 7. This figure shows accuracy of mouth localization for the number of mixtures by DCT based feature vector. In this figure, 'M50(D48)' stands for GMM with 50 mixtures and a 48 dimensional feature vector. Accordingly, the line 'M50(D48)' (*the dotted line with triangle symbols*) indicates the accuracy when GMM with 50 mixtures and a 48 dimensional feature vector are used.

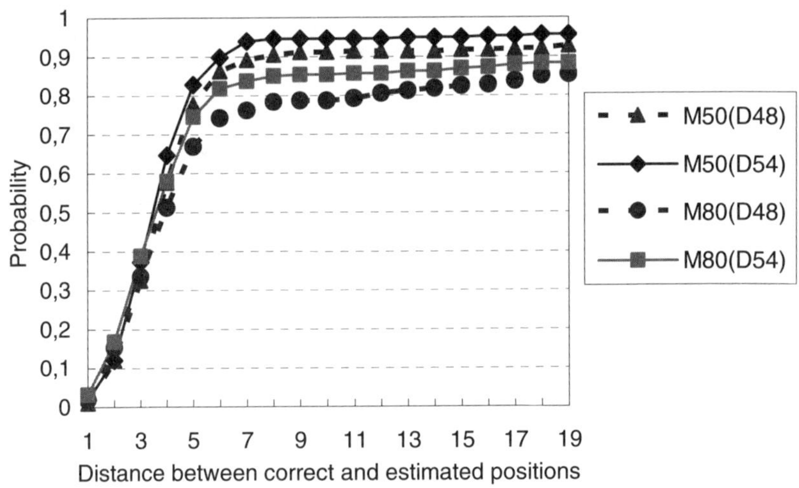

Fig. 8. This figure shows accuracy of mouth localization for the number of mixtures by the PCA based feature vector. In this figure, 'M50(D54)' stands for GMM with 50 mixtures and a 54 dimensional feature vector. Accordingly, the line 'M50(D54)' (*the solid line with diamond symbols*) indicates the accuracy when GMM with 50 mixtures and a 54 dimensional feature vector are used.

of dimensions. In fact, when 80 mixtures and 48 dimensions are set (M80(D48)), the best performance is achieved, as shown in Figure 7. Setting too many mixtures also leads to heavy computation.

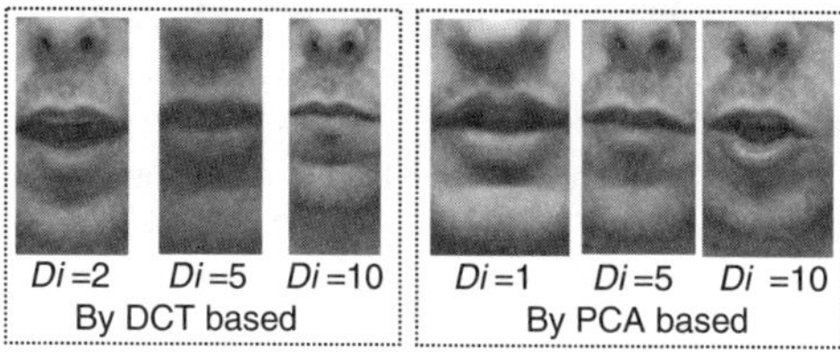

Fig. 9. Examples of result images are depicted. Di is defined in Equation 3 and the same as x-value in Figure 5-8.

Figure 9 shows examples of the mouth images estimated by the DCT and PCA based methods. The DCT based method tends to lose the edge of a chin, as shown in the image above $Di = 10$ of Figure 9, where Di is defined in Equation 3. Note again that Di is also the same as x-value in Figure 5-8. The inaccurate localization of a chin is the main reason why the DCT is less accurate than PCA.

5 Conclusion

We have successfully developed the accurate mouth localization system, which achieved the localization rate 95 % for our database if the average pixel distances Di is more than 6 (see Figure 6). It also proved that PCA based feature can improve the accuracy of the mouth localization. In the future, we are going to embed this method into audio visual speech recognition system.

Acknowledgments

This work was sponsored by the European Union under the integrated project CHIL, Computers in the Human Interaction Loop (http://chil.server.de).

References

1. Vladimir Vezhnevets, Stanislav Soldatov, Anna Degtiareva: Automatic Extraction of Frontal Facial Features. Proc. Asian Conf. on Computer Vision, Vol. 2., Jeju (2004) 1020-1025
2. Xingquan Zhu, Jianping Fan, Ahmed K. Elmagarmid: Towards Facial Feature Extraction and Verification for Omni-face Detection in Video/images, Proc. the IEEE Int. Conf. on Image Processing, Vol. 2., New York (2002) 113-116
3. Ying-li Tian, Takeo Kanade, Jeffrey F. Cohn: Lip Tracking by Combining Shape, Color and Motion. Proc. Asian Conference on Computer Vision , Taipei (2000) 1040-1045
4. Selin Baskan, Mehmet Mete Bulut, Volkan Atalay: Projection based Method for Segmentation of Human Face and its Evaluation. Pattern Recognition Letters, Vol. 23., (2002) 1623-1629

5. Haiyuan Wu, Taro Yokoyama, Dadet Pramadihanto, Masahiko Yachida: Face and Facial Feature Extraction from Color Image. Proc. Int. Conf. on Automatic Face and Gesture Recognition, Killington (1996) 345-350
6. Mark Barnard, Eun-Jung Holden, Robyn Owens: Lip Tracking using Pattern Matching Snakes. In Proc. Asian Conf. on Computer Vision, Melbourne (2002) 23-25
7. Juergen Luettin: Visual Speech and Speaker Recognition. PhD thesis, Department of Computer Science, University of Sheffield (1997)
8. Rainer Lienhart, LuHong Liang, Alexander Kuranov: A Detector Tree of Boosted Classifiers for Real-time Object Detection and Tracking. Proc. IEEE Int. Conf. on Multimedia and Expo, Baltimore (2003) 277-280
9. Jintao Jiang, Gerasimos Potamianos, Harriet J. Nock, Giridharan Iyengar, Chalapathy Neti: Improved Face and Feature Finding for Audio-visual Speech Recognition in Visually Challenging Environments. Proc. IEEE Int. Conf. on Acoustics, Speech and Signal Processing, Vol. 5., Montreal (2004) 873-876
10. Kah-Kay Sung, Tomaso Poggio: Example-based Learning for View-based Face Detection. IEEE Trans. on Pattern Analysis and Machine Intelligence, Vol. 20., (1998) 39-51
11. Gerasimos Potamianos, Chalapathy Neti, Juergen Luettin, Iain Matthews: Audio-Visual Automatic Speech Recognition: An Overview. Issues in Visual and Audio-Visual Speech Processing, G. Bailly, E. Vatikiotis-Bateson, and P. Perrier (Eds.), MIT Press, 2004.

Traffic Video Segmentation Using Adaptive-K Gaussian Mixture Model

Rui Tan, Hong Huo, Jin Qian, and Tao Fang

Institute of Image Processing and Pattern Recognition, Shanghai Jiao Tong University, Shanghai 200240, China
{tanrui, huohong, qianjinml, tfang}@sjtu.edu.cn

Abstract. Video segmentation is an important phase in video based traffic surveillance applications. The basic task of traffic video segmentation is to classify pixels in the current frame to road background or moving vehicles, and casting shadows should be taken into account if exists. In this paper, a modified online EM procedure is proposed to construct Adaptive-K Gaussian Mixture Model (AKGMM) in which the dimension of the parameter space at each pixel can adaptively reflects the complexity of pattern at the pixel. A heuristic background components selection rule is developed to make pixel classification decision based on the proposed model. Our approach is demonstrated to be more adaptive, accurate and robust than some existing similar pixel modeling approaches through experimental results.

1 Introduction

In video based surveillance applications, a basic and important approach called background subtraction is widely employed to segment moving objects in the camera's field-of-view through the difference between a reference frame, often called background image, and the current frame [1]. The accuracy of the background image quite impacts on output quality of the whole system, but the task to retrieve an accurate background is usually overlooked in many video based surveillance systems. It is complicated to develop a background modeling procedure that keeps robust in changeful environment and for longtime span.

The simplest background reconstruction scheme adopts the average of all historical frames as the background image, which contains both real background component and foreground component. Consequently, the arithmetic average method causes confusion. As an improved version, Running Gaussian Average [1] is employed instead of arithmetic average, for each pixel (x, y), current background value $B_j(x, y)$ is given by

$$B_j(x, y) = \alpha I(x, y) + (1 - \alpha)B_{j-1}(x, y), \tag{1}$$

where $I(x, y)$ is current intensity, $B_{j-1}(x, y)$ is last background value and α is a learning rate often chosen as trade-off between the stability of background and the adaptability for quick environmental changes. Confusion problem also can

N. Zheng, X. Jiang, and X. Lan (Eds.): IWICPAS 2006, LNCS 4153, pp. 125–134, 2006.

not be avoided in this approach. Autoscope system [2] adopts such approach but a background suppression procedure is needed to eliminate the confusion. Temporal Median Filter [1], a nonparametric, welcomed and applicable approach, uses temporal median value of recent intensities in a length-limited moving window as the background at each pixel. Temporal Median Filter can generate an accurate background image under the assumption that the probability of real background in sight is over 0.5 in initialization phase, and the computational load of Temporal Media Filter is predictable. But it will totally fail when foreground takes up more time than background. N. Friedman et al. [3] first use Gaussian Mixture Model (GMM) to model the pixel process. Their model contains only three Gaussian components corresponding to road background, moving vehicles and dynamic casting shadows. Meaning of their approach lies in pixel modeling and a wise EM framework to train GMM, but it is not clear if the real scene doesn't fit such a three components pattern. C. Stauffer et al. [5], [6] work out a successful improvement based on N. Friedman et al.'s model. They model each pixel process as a GMM with K Gaussian components, where the constant K is from 3 to 5, and then employ a heuristic rule to estimate background image. In their approach, the number of components, K, is a pre-defined constant for each pixel. Reversible Jump Markov chain Monte Carlo (RJMCMC) methods can be used to construct GMM with an unknown number of components [10], but there is no realtime version of RJMCMC for video processing. In this paper, we try to present an engineering oriented and realtime approach to construct GMM with an unknown number of components through a modified EM procedure. As a result, complicated regions in the video is described by more components adaptively, and simple regions with fewer components vice versa.

The rest of this paper is organized as follows: Section 2 briefly introduces GMM modeling using EM algorithm. AKGMM learned by a modified EM procedure and a heuristic background components selection rule are proposed in Section 3. In section 4, comparative experimental results are analyzed and section 5 concludes this paper.

2 Related Work

Parametric probabilistic approaches in image processing usually treat each pixel independently and try to construct a statistical model for each pixel [3], [4], [6]. GMM is such a prevalent model usually trained using an iterative procedure called Expectation Maximum algorithm (EM algorithm). EM algorithm is introduced briefly in this section.

Considering the values of a particular pixel over time as a pixel process, its history becomes

$$\chi = \{x_j = I_j(x, y)\}_{j=1}^{n}, \tag{2}$$

where $I_j(x, y)$ is grayscale or color vector at time j for pixel (x, y). A mixture model of Gaussian distributions can be set up on χ at this pixel to gain on the underlying PDF [7],

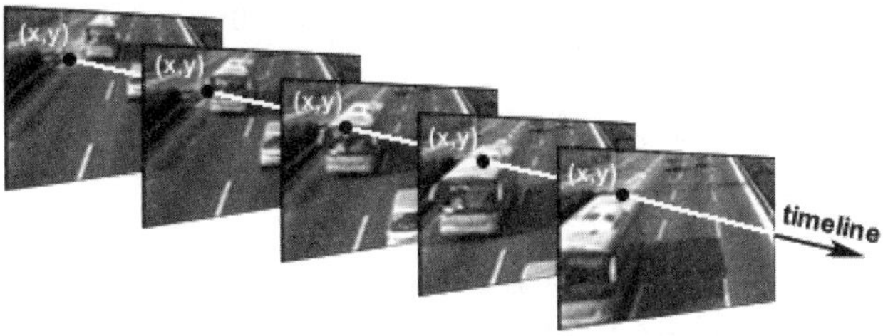

Fig. 1. A pixel process is constituted by values of a particular pixel over time. For each pixel in the frame, a statistical model is built upon the corresponding pixel process.

$$f(x|\Theta) = \sum_{i=1}^{K} \omega_i \eta(x|\Theta_i), \tag{3}$$

where ω_i is the normalized weight of ith Gaussian component C_i, so $\sum_{i=1}^{K} \omega_i = 1$; $\eta(x|\Theta_i)$ is PDF for C_i which can be replaced by

$$\eta(x|\Theta_i) = \frac{1}{\sqrt{2\pi\sigma_i}} \exp[-\frac{1}{2}(\frac{x-\mu_i}{\sigma_i})^2]. \tag{4}$$

Theoretically, the Maximum-Likelihood root of parameters $\Theta = \{\omega_i, \Theta_i\}_{i=1}^{K}$ can be found but in hidden form [7]. In practice, mixture models can be learned using EM [3], [8]. Because of the requirement of realtime system, an online EM version [3], [9] was proposed which converges to local expectation maximum point with high probability. In this variant of EM, three sufficient statistics, N_i, S_i, Z_i are considered, where N_i represents the count of samples belonging to C_i; S_i is the sum of these samples, $S_i = \sum_{x_j \in C_i} x_j$; Z_i represents the sum of the outer product of these samples, $Z_i = \sum_{x_j \in C_i} x_j^2/n$. Consequently, the model parameters can be calculated from these sufficient statistics as follow,

$$\omega_i = \frac{N_i}{\sum_{k=1}^{K} N_k}, \quad \mu_i = \frac{S_i}{N_i}, \quad \sigma_i^2 = \frac{1}{N_i} Z_i - \mu_i^2. \tag{5}$$

When a new sample x_j comes in, these sufficient statistics are updated as follow,

$$\begin{aligned} N_i^j &= N_i^{j-1} + P(X \in C_i | X = x_j, \Theta^{j-1}), \\ S_i^j &= S_i^{j-1} + x_j P(X \in C_i | X = x_j, \Theta^{j-1}), \\ Z_i^j &= Z_i^{j-1} + x_j^2 P(X \in C_i | X = x_j, \Theta^{j-1}), \end{aligned} \tag{6}$$

where

$$P(X \in C_i | X = x_j, \Theta) = \frac{P(X \in C_i, X = x_j | \Theta)}{P(X = x_j | \Theta)} = \frac{\omega_i \eta(x_j|\Theta_i)}{f(x_j|\Theta)}, \tag{7}$$

and we choose $\{N_i^0, S_i^0, Z_i^0\}_{i=1}^{K}$ as initial values of these sufficient statistics. From the updated $\{N_i^j, S_i^j, Z_i^j\}_{i=1}^{K}$, we can compute Θ^j. If the underlying PDF is stationary, Θ^j will converge to local expectation maximum point with high probability in long run [3], [9].

3 Adaptive-K Gaussian Mixture Model

R. Bowden et al. have successfully segmented low resolution targets using C. Stauffer et al.'s fixed K model [11], and they argue that it is not suitable for large scale targets segmentation [11]. The detailed information of large moving objects' appearance, i.e., color, texture and etc, makes the pattern of pixels in the track of objects much complicated. In other words, the objects' track regions hold a complex pattern mixed with background components and kinds of object appearance components, but other regions hold just a stable background pattern. And in practice, the difference among different regions, which is impacted by many factors, i.e., acquisition noise, light reflection, camera's oscillation caused by wind, is also complicated. It is not suitable to describe every pixel in field-of-view using a mixture model with fixed K Gaussian components as C. Stauffer et al. did [5], [6]. We try to describe those pixels with complex pattern using more Gaussian components adaptively, in other words, bigger K at those pixels, and those simple pixels using fewer components vise versa. In such strategy, a more accurate description of the monitoring region is expected. In video based traffic surveillance applications, vehicles which are relatively large size targets are tracked.

3.1 Pixel Modeling

When the first video frame comes in, a new Gaussian component is created at each pixel with the current grayscale as its mean value, an initially high variance, and low prior weight. In the following, at each pixel, a new instance is used for updating the model using (6) if a match is found. A match is defined as a pixel value within 2.5 standard variance of a component. If no match is found, a new Gaussian component is created and no existing component is disposed.

Then, two problems arise: those three sufficient statistics, $\{N_i, S_i, Z_i\}$, increase unlimitedly while more frames are captured; K may also increase unlimitedly at a particular pixel, so the computational load will increase drastically. Firstly, if $\sum_{i=1}^{K} N_i^{j-1} < L$, $\{N_i, S_i, Z_i\}$ are updated using (6); otherwise we define a forgetting rate as follow,

$$\beta = \frac{\sum_{i=1}^{K} N_i^{j-1}}{\sum_{i=1}^{K} N_i^{j-1} + 1}, \tag{8}$$

then those sufficient statistics are updated using

$$\begin{aligned} N_i^j &= \beta[N_i^{j-1} + P(X \in C_i | X = x_j, \Theta^{j-1})], \\ S_i^j &= \beta[S_i^{j-1} + x_j P(X \in C_i | X = x_j, \Theta^{j-1})], \\ Z_i^j &= \beta[Z_i^{j-1} + x_j^2 P(X \in C_i | X = x_j, \Theta^{j-1})]. \end{aligned} \tag{9}$$

As a result, $\sum_{i=1}^{K} N_i$ will be a constant near by L which is an equivalent time constant.

Secondly, every L frames, each Gaussian component is checked at any pixel whether coefficient of some component C_k, that is ω_k, is below a pre-defined threshold ω_{T}. If inequality $\omega_k < \omega_{\mathrm{T}}$ holds, component C_k is discarded because the inequality means there are too few evidences to support that component which is inspired by low-probability events. $1/L$ is a reasonable value for ω_{T}, because a component supported by less than one evidence in L frames shouldn't be maintained. After a number of frames are processed, K will adaptively reflects the complexity of pattern at each pixel, in other words, we can set up a more accurate description of the monitoring region. In this case, computational cost is mainly allocated for complicated regions, such as tracks of the moving objects. Figure 2(b) shows a K-image formed by the components' number at each pixel, where grayscale encodes K accumulated by 200 frames using AKGMM. As our expectation, pixels in the three lanes have more Gaussian components than pixels in other areas, i.e., barriers by the road.

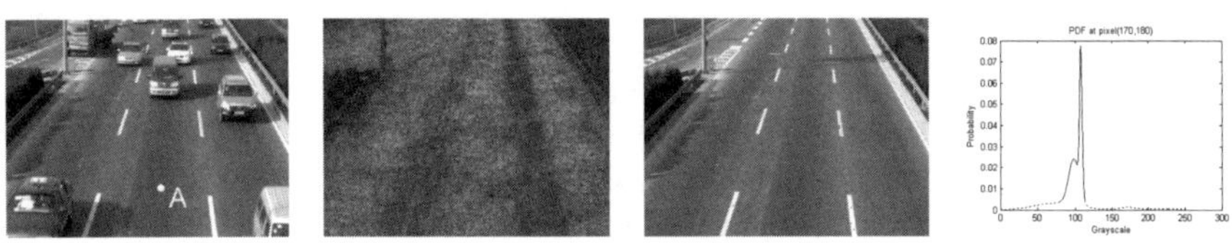

(a) (b) (c) (d)

Fig. 2. (a) Monitoring scene on a highway; (b) shows a image formed by the components' number where grayscale encodes K; (c) is the background image formed by mean value of the first Gaussian component at each pixel; (d) plots PDF at point A labeled in (a)

3.2 Background Estimation

For GMM, measurement ω/σ is proposed to be positively related to the probability of being background component [5], [6]. Heuristically, C. Stauffer et al. select the first B components in the sequence of all components ordered by ω/σ as background, where

$$B = \arg\min_b \left(\sum_{i=1}^{b} \omega_i > T\right). \tag{10}$$

In such strategy, T is a threshold related to occupancy in traffic applications. Such background estimation may fail in some cases, i.e., large flow volume, traffic jam, if the background is just judged from occupancy.

A searching procedure is developed to estimate background in our framework. Assume the first component in the sequence of components ordered by ω/σ must be a part of background, and background components set $\mathbf{B}$ includes only the first component initially while the other components are labeled non-background. In the iterative searching phase, a non-background component $C_{\rm nb}$ is labeled background and included into **B** if

$$\mu_{\rm nb} \in [\mu_{\rm b} - 3\sigma_{\rm b}, \mu_{\rm b} + 3\sigma_{\rm b}], \quad \exists C_{\rm b} \in \mathbf{B}, \tag{11}$$

where $\mu_{\rm nb}$ is mean value of $C_{\rm nb}$; $C_{\rm b}$ is some background component with mean value $\mu_{\rm b}$ and standard variance $\sigma_{\rm b}$. The iteration ends until no such component $C_{\rm nb}$ can be found. If a background image is needed, we choose the mean value of the first component of **B**, in which elements are also ordered by ω/σ, at any pixel to form the background image. Figure 2(c) shows such a background image accumulated by the first 100 frames. Figure 2(d) plots PDF at point A labeled in Fig.2(a), in which five components are included. Solid line represents two background components selected by our searching procedure, and dotted line represents the other three non-background components. Our experimental results will show that our simple iterative procedure generates accurate background model in many traffic cases.

3.3 Foreground Segmentation

In terms of the background components set **B** updated in the previous searching procedure, a new grayscale at pixel (x, y) is identified as moving vehicle if the current grayscale matches no component in **B** when dynamic casting shadow is out of consideration.

If vehicles cast moving shadows, non-background pixels should be segmented into vehicles and their casting shadows, otherwise the foreground segmentation will be enlarged wrongly. Many shadow detection algorithms are proposed, but most of them are too complex. In our framework, we adopt a simple shadow detection algorithm called Normalized Cross-Correlation algorithm (NCC algorithm) proposed by Julio et al. [12] to refine the segmentation if dynamic casting shadow exists. NCC explores the relationship between casting shadow and background, that is, the intensity of shadowed pixel is linear to the corresponding background, so the background image provided by AKGMM is used to detect shadows.

An example of the segmentation refinement applied to the original frame with shadow is depicted in Fig.3(b). In this figure, white areas correspond to moving vehicles and gray areas correspond to shadow detection. Figure 3(c) shows the final foreground segmentation result after applying morphological operators to eliminate gaps and isolated pixels.

4 Experimental Results

Following comparative experiments demonstrate the performance of our proposed algorithm on two groups of traffic image sequences. Dataset A is recorded

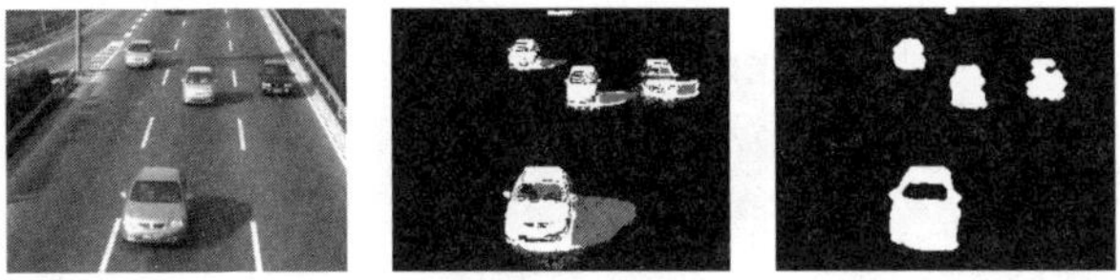

(a) (b) (c)

Fig. 3. Segmentation result using AKGMM and NCC. (a) is the original frame; (b) shows the segmentation (shadowed pixels are represented by light gray); (c) is morphological post-processing result after shadow removal.

on a highway; dataset B is by an intersection on a ground road, and the camera oscillates drastically in the wind. The video size is 320x240 and shadow detection is incorporated in following experiments. In order to distinguish our framework from C. Stauffer et al.'s, we name their model Fixed-K Gaussian Mixture Model (FKGMM) in the following.

4.1 Reflection

In this experiment, FKGMM maintains 3 components at each pixel, while the average of components' number in AKGMM is about 6. In the Fig.4(d), we can see there are more false alarm pixels in the output of FKGMM, and our shadow areas have better texture than theirs. Whenever a large vehicle passes by the camera, reflection from the large vehicle impacts on the quantification of the camera in the whole field-of-view. Column 2 and 3 show the difference between the two models in such case. In FKGMM, a meaningful component may be substituted by a new one which is inspired by the sudden reflection to keep K as a constant. Consequently, the sudden reflection is classified as dynamic casting shadow. In contrast, AKGMM gives a more accurate background description, and no component will be destroyed by the sudden reflection, so AKGMM works better in such cases.

4.2 Camera's Oscillation

In outdoor applications, camera's oscillation caused by wind should be taken into consideration. In this robustness experiment in case of camera's oscillation, 5 components are maintained and the threshold T in (10) is set to 0.5 for FKGMM. The background selected by FKGMM will be unimodal at most pixels. As a result, edges of the ground marks and static objects by the road are identified as non-background because of the oscillation. By increasing T, FKGMM will behave better because the background becomes multimodal, but the confusion problem will occur as analyzed in next subsection. The K-image of AKGMM depicted in Fig.5(d) illuminates that these edges are described more accurately. After an opening then a closing morphological operation, our framework takes on better robustness than C. Stauffer et al.'s.

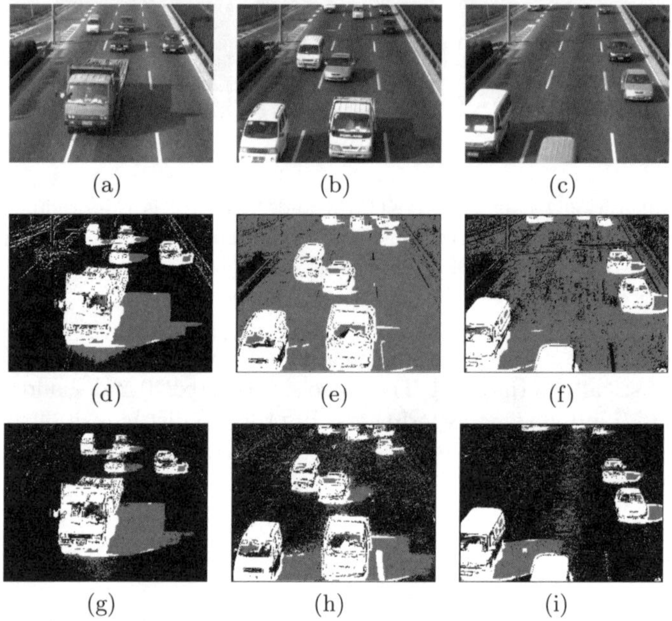

Fig. 4. Corresponding segmentations on dataset A. Top row: the original images at frames 1443, 2838, 2958. Middle row: the corresponding segmentation using C. Stauffer et al.'s model (shadowed pixels are represented by light gray). Bottom row: the segmentation using AKGMM.

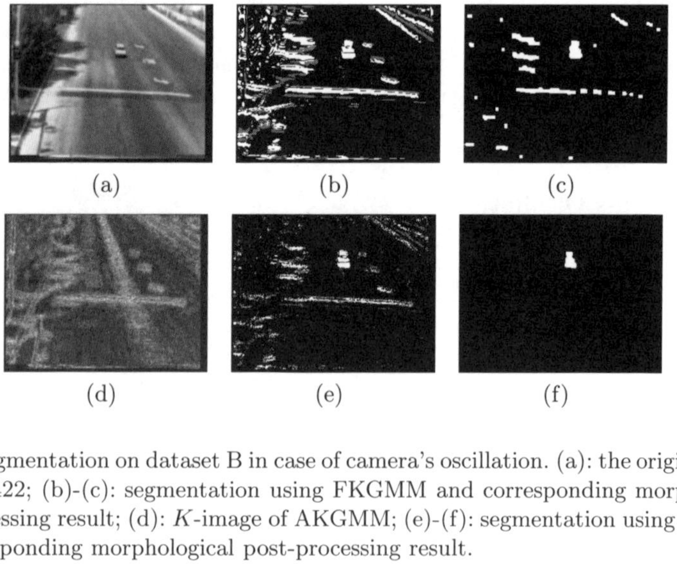

Fig. 5. Segmentation on dataset B in case of camera's oscillation. (a): the original image at frame 422; (b)-(c): segmentation using FKGMM and corresponding morphological post-processing result; (d): K-image of AKGMM; (e)-(f): segmentation using AKGMM and corresponding morphological post-processing result.

4.3 Stationary Vehicles

In front of intersections, vehicles occasionally stop to wait for pass signal. To detect stationary vehicles is a typical problem in video based traffic surveillance. In dataset B, the vehicles stop for about 15 seconds, 375 frames equivalently, every 45 seconds' pass. Figure 6(a) and Fig.6(d) represent such a move-to-stop process for about 4 seconds. The threshold T is adjusted to 0.9 to keep FKGMM robust in oscillation. The Gaussian components which correspond to the stationary vehicles grow so quickly that these components are included into background according to (10). Consequently, the stationary vehicles incorporate into background as showed in Fig.6(e). In our framework, the incorporation occurs provided that the stationary vehicles cover those pixels more frames than the time constant L. By choosing an appropriate L, our system keeps robust both in camera's oscillation and stationary vehicles case.

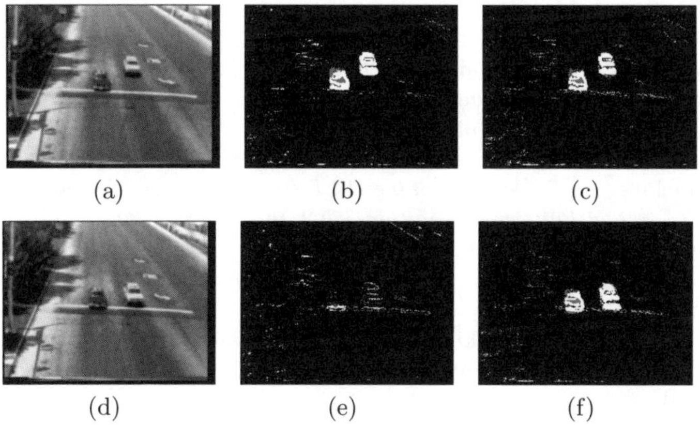

Fig. 6. Segmentation on dataset B in case of stationary vehicles. (a): original image at frame 1680; (b)-(c): segmentation of (a) using FKGMM and AKGMM; (d) original image at frame 1768; (e)-(f): segmentation of (d) using FKGMM and AKGMM.

5 Conclusions and Future Work

A visual traffic surveillance application oriented, probabilistic approach based large scale moving objects segmentation strategy is presented in this paper. In our strategy, a modified online EM procedure is used to construct Adaptive-K Gaussian Mixture Model at each pixel, and a heuristic background components selection rule is developed to generate accurate background and make pixel classification decision. Our approach shows good performance in terms of adaptability, accuracy and robustness, but the computational load is unpredictable because of the very adaptability. We can constrain the computational load by applying our approach just in small Region of Interest (ROI). Reasonable heuristic background estimation rules and adaptability for kinds of environmental changes need more study. Some intro-frame tasks, such as vehicle tracking, can be studied based on the object segmentation.

Acknowledgements. This research is supported in part by Demonstrative Research of WSN Application in Transportation Systems administered by Shanghai Science and Technology Committee under grant 05dz15004.

References

1. M. Piccardi, "Background Subtraction Techniques: A Review," in *2004 IEEE International Conference on Systems, Man and Cybernetics*, pp.3099-3104.
2. P. G. Michalopoulos, "Vehicle Detection Video Through Image Processing: The Autosope System," *IEEE Trans. on Vehicular Technology*, vol.40, No.1, February 1991.
3. N. Friedman and S. Russell, "Image Segmentation in Video Sequences: A Probabilistic Approach," in *Proceedings of the 13th Conference on Uncertainty in Artificial Intelligence(UAI)*, San Francisco, 1997.
4. C. R. Wren, A. Azarbayejani, T. Darrell, and A. P. Pentland, "Pfinder: Real-time Tracking of the Human Body," *IEEE Trans. on Pattern Analysis and Machine Intelligence*, vol.19, No.7, July 1997.
5. C. Stauffer and W.E.L. Grimson, "Adaptive Background Mixture Models for Read-Time Tracking," in *Proceedings of the IEEE Computer Society Conference on Computer Vision and Pattern Recognition*, vol.2, pp.246-252, 1999.
6. C. Stauffer and W.E.L Grimson, "Learning Patterns of Activity Using Real-Time Tracking," *IEEE Trans. on Pattern Analysis and Machine Intelligence*, vol.22, No.8, August 2000.
7. Z. R. Yang and M. Zwolinski, "Mutual Information Theory for Adaptive Mixture Models," *IEEE Trans. on Pattern Analysis and Machine Intelligence*, vol.23, No.4, April 2001.
8. A. Dempster, N. Laird, and D. Rubin, "Maximum Likelihood From Incomplete Data via the EM Algorithm," *Journal of the Royal Statistical Society*, 39(Series B):1-38, 1977.
9. R. M. Neal and G. E. Hinton, "A View of the EM Algorithm That Justifies Incremental, Sparse, and Other Variants," *Learning in Graphical Models*, pp.355-368, 1998.
10. S. Richardson and P.J. Green, "On Bayesian Analysis of Mixtures with an Unknown Number of Components," *Journal of the Royal Statistical Society*, 60(Series B):731-792, 1997.
11. P. KaewTraKulPong and R. Bowden, "An Adaptive Visual System for Tracking Low Resolution Colour Targets," in *Proceedings of British Machine Vision Conference 2001*, vol.1, pp.243-252, Manchester UK, September 2001.
12. Julio Cezar Silveira Jacques Jr, C. R. Jung, and S. R. Musse, "Background Subtraction and Shadow Detection in Grayscale Video Sequences," in *Proceedings of SIBGRAPI 2005-Natal-RN-Brazil*, 2005.

EM-in-M: Analyze and Synthesize Emotion in Motion

Yuichi Kobayashi[1] and Jun Ohya[2]

[1] Toppan Printing Co.,ltd., Information Technology Research Laboratory, 1-3-3 Suido, Bunkyo-ku, Tokyo, Japan
Yuichi.Kobayashi@toppan.co.jp
[2] Waseda University, Graduate school of GITS, 1-3-10 Nishi-Waseda, Shinjuku-ku, Tokyo, Japan
ohya@waseda.jp

Abstract. We have been researching the relationship between human motion and emotion. In this paper, our purpose is to extract motion features specific to each emotion. We propose a new approach for motion data analysis, which applies the higher order Singular Value Decomposition(HOSVD) direct to the motion data and the wavelet analysis to the synthesized data with SVD. The HOSVD models the mapping between persons and emotions. The model can synthesize a complete data acting with each emotion for a given new person. The wavelet analysis extracts each motion feature from the synthesized data for each emotion. Some experimental results using motion capture data for "gait" action and 6 emotions – "angry, joy, sad and so on" show that our method can synthesize novel gait motions for a person by using the extracted motion elements and can extract some features specific to each emotion.

1 Introduction

With the spreading popularity of sensing technology or the growing needs of security, the analysis of human motion is now the hot area of research. Recently, several researches which describe and archive the precise motion of typical dance have been reported[1],[2]. Though, our interests concentrate on human motions of general people in daily life.

We have studied the mechanism of human impressions mainly with images[3] and our current interest is to study human psychological responses to time-variate stimuli, from the view point of *Kansei* information processing.

In the literature of motion analysis and synthesis research, there have been model based and non-model based methods. Most model based ones are based on hidden markov model[4],[5] and non-model based ones are based on PCA or tensor technique. In this paper, our purpose is to extract motion features specific to each emotion and the method, which can synthesize motion specific to each emotion, is adequate for our purpose. For a simple implementation, we use the tensor method proposed by Vasilescu[6] to extract human motion signatures individualizing their movements from sample motions. We applied this algorithm to motion data which measured several action patterns with several emotions for each subject. According to this method, corpus of motion data spanning multiple persons and actions is organized as higher order array or tensor which defines multi linear operators over a set of vector spaces.

N. Zheng, X. Jiang, and X. Lan (Eds.): IWICPAS 2006, LNCS 4153, pp. 135 – 143, 2006.

2 The Analyze and Synthesize Methods

2.1 The Higher Order SVD

Given a corpus of body motion data of different persons and different emotions, we decompose them into two separate subspaces – the person subspace and the emotion subspace.

We use a third-order tensor $\mathcal{A} \in R^{N \times K \times T}$ to represent the human motion configuration, N is the number of persons, K is the number of emotions and T is the number of joint feature time samples. We can decompose tensor $\mathcal{A}$ using the higher order singular value decomposition which is known as the N-mode SVD. N-mode SVD is a generalization of SVD that orthogonalizes N spaces as mode-n product of N orthogonal spaces:

$$\mathcal{A} \times_1 \mathbf{U}_1 \times_2 \mathbf{U}_2 \times_3 \cdots \times_n \mathbf{U}_n \cdots \times_N \mathbf{U}_N \tag{1}$$

Here, $\mathcal{A}$ is called as core tensor which governs the interaction between the mode matrices $\mathbf{U}_n$, for $n = 1, \cdots, N$. Mode matrix $\mathbf{U}_n$ contains the orthonormal vectors spanning the column space of the matrix $\mathbf{A}_{(n)}$ that results from the mode-n flattening of $\mathcal{A}$.

N-mode SVD algorithm for decomposing $\mathcal{A}$ is :

1. for $n = 1, \cdots, N$, calculate matrix $\mathbf{U}_n$ in (1) by calculating the SVD of the flattened matrix $\mathbf{A}_{(n)}$ and setting $\mathbf{U}_n$ to be the left matrix of the SVD.
2. solve for the core tensor as follows

$$\mathcal{S} = \mathcal{A} \times_1 \mathbf{U}_1^T \times_2 \mathbf{U}_2^T \cdots \times_n \mathbf{U}_n^T \cdots \times_N \mathbf{U}_N^T \tag{2}$$

It can be calculated in a matrix representation, e.g.,

$$\mathbf{S}_{(n)} = \mathbf{U}_n^T \mathbf{A}_{(n)} (\mathbf{U}_{n-1} \otimes \mathbf{U}_{n-2} \cdots \otimes \mathbf{U}_N \cdots \otimes \mathbf{U}_{n+2} \otimes \mathbf{U}_{n+1})^T , \tag{3}$$

where $\otimes$ is the matrix Kronecker product.

Suppose given motion sequences of several persons, we define a data set tensor $\mathcal{D}$ with size $P \times E \times J$, where P is the number of persons, E is the number of emotions and J is the number of joint feature time samples.

$$\mathcal{D} = \mathcal{S} \times_1 \mathbf{P} \times_2 \mathbf{E} \times_3 \mathbf{J} \tag{4}$$

The person matrix $\mathbf{P} = [\mathrm{p}_1 \cdots \mathrm{p}_\mathrm{n} \cdots \mathrm{p}_\mathrm{P}]^T$ whose person specific row vectors p_n^T span the space of person parameters, encodes per-person invariances across emotions. The emotion matrix $\mathbf{E} = [\mathrm{e}_1 \cdots \mathrm{e}_\mathrm{m} \cdots \mathrm{e}_\mathrm{E}]^T$ whose emotion specific row vectors e_m^T span the space of emotion parameters, encodes the invariances for each emotion across different person. The joint angle matrix **J** whose row vectors span the space of joint angles are the eigen motions that are normally computed by PCA.

$$\mathcal{B} = \mathcal{S} \times_2 \mathbf{E} \times_3 \mathbf{J} \tag{5}$$

defines a set of basis matrices for all the motion features associated with all emotions.

$$\mathcal{C} = \mathcal{S} \times_1 \mathbf{P} \times_3 \mathbf{J} \tag{6}$$

defines a set of basis matrices for all the motion features associated with all persons. After extracting $\mathcal{S}$, **E**, and **J** , we have a generative model that can observe motion data of a new person performing one of these emotions e and synthesize the remaining emotions for this new person in the equation

$$\mathcal{D}_{p,e} = \mathcal{B}_e \times_1 \mathbf{p}^T , \tag{7}$$

where $\mathcal{B}_e = \mathcal{S} \times_2 \mathbf{e}_e{}^T \times_3 \mathbf{J}$ and $\mathcal{D}_{p,e}$ is a $1 \times 1 \times T$ tensor and flattening this tensor in the person mode yields the matrix $D_{p,e(person)}$, which can be denoted as $\mathbf{d}_e^T$. A complete set of new person is synthesized as follows:

$$\mathcal{D}_p = \mathcal{B} \times_1 \mathbf{p}^T \tag{8}$$

If several emotions $\mathbf{d}_{ek}^T$ are observed, the person parameters are computed as follows:

$$\mathbf{p}^T = \mathbf{d}_{ek}^T \times \mathbf{B}_{ek\,(person)}^{-1} \tag{9}$$

Similarly, given a known person with an unknown emotion, we can synthesize all the persons in the database with the same emotions:

$$\mathcal{D}_e = \mathcal{C} \times_2 \mathbf{e}^T \tag{10}$$

If several persons are observed performing the same emotion $\mathbf{d}_{pk}$, the emotion parameters are computed as follows:

$$\mathbf{e}^T = \mathbf{d}_{pk}^T \times \mathbf{C}_{pk\,(emotion)}^{-1} \tag{11}$$

2.2 Wavelet Analysis

As long as observing wave forms as a time sequence, wavelet analysis is considered to be effective. We applied wavelet transform to the synthesized data described in previous section. In wavelet analysis, the wavelet function needs to be selected adequately to data. We tried daubechies' wavelet family[7] and selected db6 (in case of N=6 out of dbN), experimentally.

2.3 Feature Extraction Process

The flow of our emotion feature extraction is follows:

1. to measure motion capture data with gait action expressing each emotion.
2. to collect all the subject's motion data for the same emotion.
3. to apply the HOSVD to the motion data, which are spanned the space of all subjects , all emotions and all joints.
4. to synthesize other emotions' motion from a new gait motion data with neutral emotion by formulae (9) or (11).

5. to apply the wavelet analysis including multi-resolution decomposition and re-composition to the synthesized motion and extract each emotion specific motion feature.

3 Motion Data Acquisition

All the human motion was recorded using a Motion Star system. Subject wore a hub system(as shown in Fig.1), which sends each sensor's 3D information to the server wirelessly. Server detects 18 markers and computes each 3D position relative to a fixed lab coordinate frame. Each marker is placed on forehead, throat, both shoulders, elbows and wrists, sternum, low back, both waists, knees, ankles and toes of a human subject. A subject walks on the wood support about 3 times 3 square meter in diagonal or stands on the center of the support. We indicate a subject to walk or stand with each emotion – we select 1 neutral emotion and 6 emotions -angry, disgust, fear, joy, sad and surprise – based on Ekman's facial research[8].

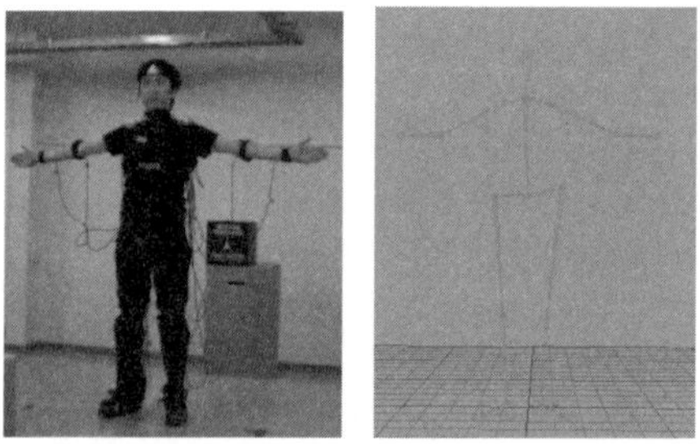

Fig. 1. Left image shows a subject who takes a T-stance pose wearing magnetic sensors. Right image shows a skelton image which connects each sensor with line.

3.1 Subjects

In order to collect a training data, 4 subjects (2 male and 2 female) are selected from young actors and actresses who belong to a theater company.

3.2 Action Patterns

As an action pattern – gait is adopted because its routine action in our daily life is considered to be adequate to analyze. Gait action is considered to have a distinctive routine motion common between people, which is independent on an emotion specific motion. Subjects are instructed to perform gait action in 3 seconds expressing each emotion and repeat many times.

4 Results and Discussions

We focus on the lean of body and the angle between arms or legs, and analyze each joint angles and joint velocity. Three joint angles are analyzed - the angle between body and upper arm, upper arm and front arm, upper leg and lower leg. All matrix computation is performed using Matlab 7.0.

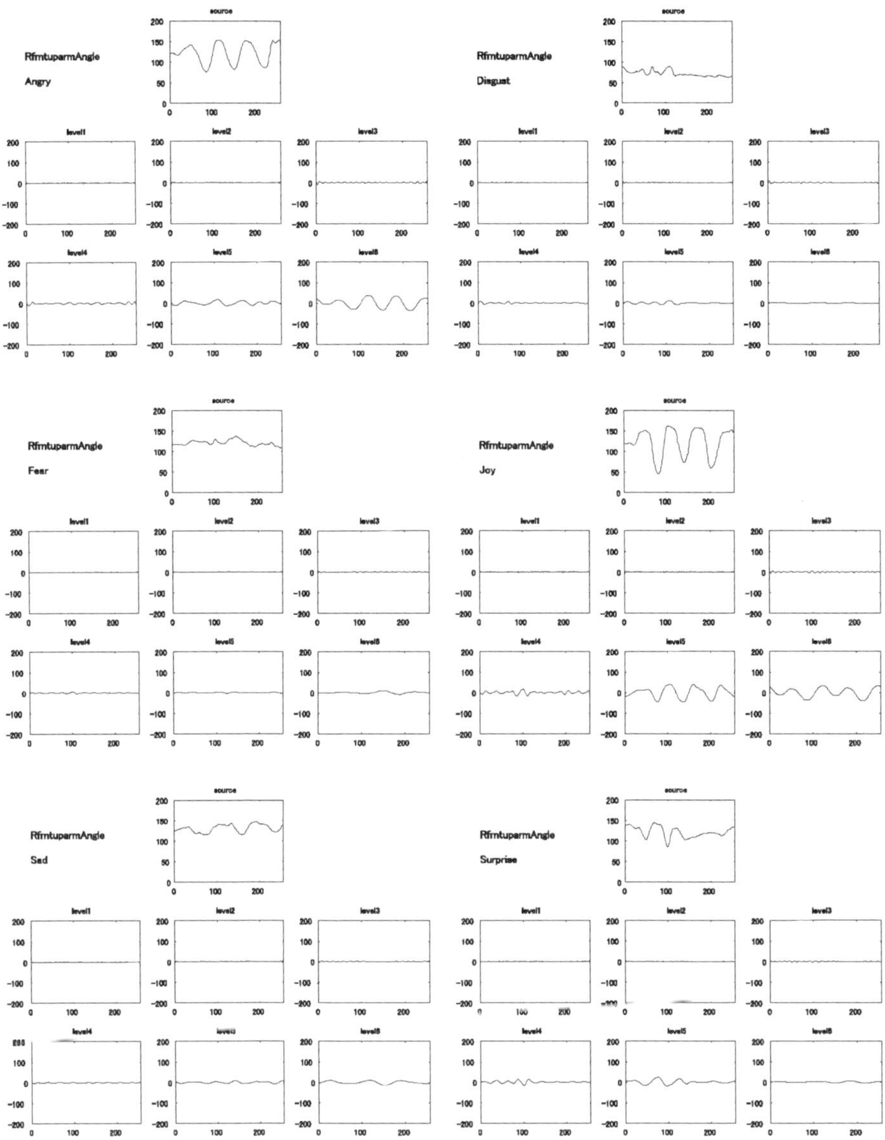

Fig. 2. Wavelet decomposed waveform for each resolution level: the case of angle between right upper and front arm for each emotion center top graph shows raw data – angle time sequence, below 6 graphs show recomposed waveform by wavelet transform and inverse wavelet transform with each resolution level

Fig. 2, Fig.3 and Fig.4 show the example of wavelet analyses for the angle time sequence between upper and front arm, between upper arm and upper body, and between lower and upper leg, respectively. These angles reflect the crook of elbow and mainly the motion of front arm, the arm motion forward or backward of the upper

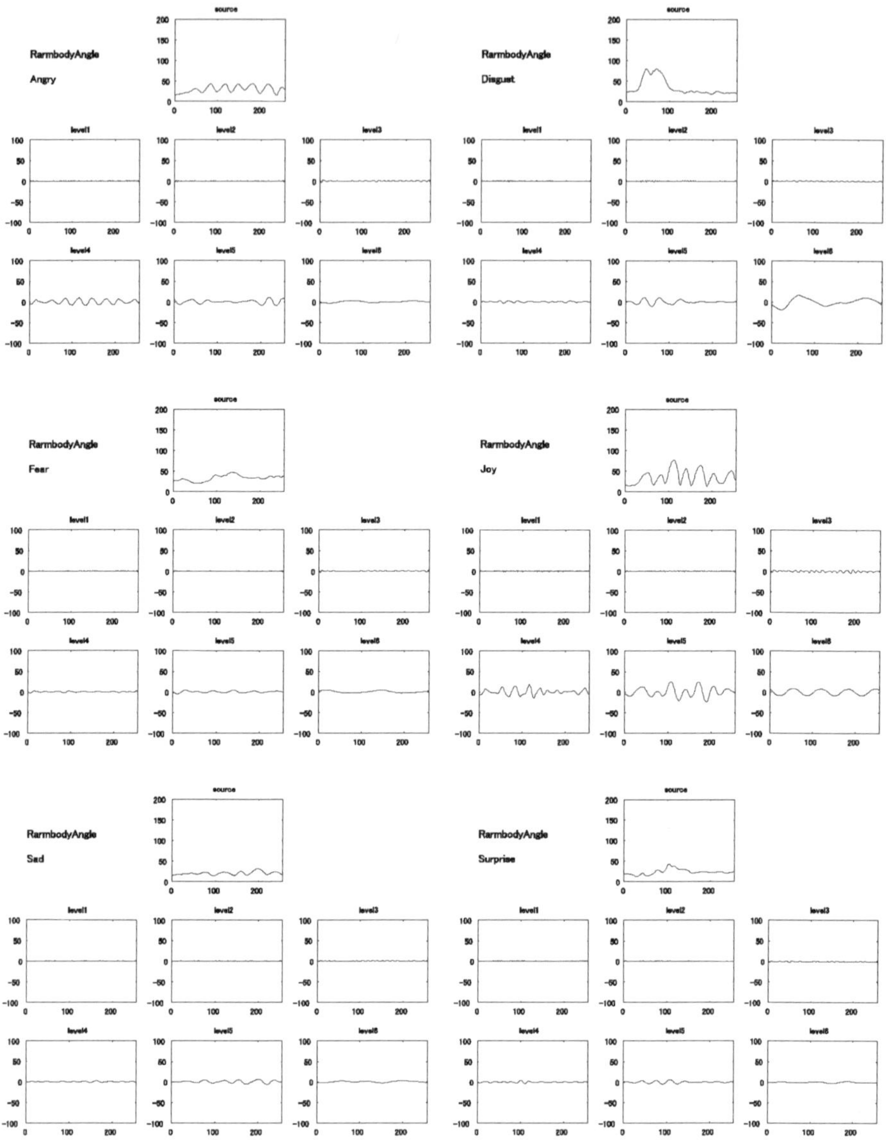

Fig. 3. Wavelet decomposed waveform for each resolution level: the case of angle between right upper body and upper arm for each emotion center top graph shows raw data – angle time sequence, below 6 graphs show recomposed waveform by wavelet transform and inverse wavelet transform with each resolution level

body and the bending of knee, respectively. In these graphs, "source" means a raw synthesized signal for each emotion and "level" means a temporal scale (level 1,2,…,5 correspond to time cycle with $2^1,2^2,\ldots,2^5$ frames, respectively. Here, 1 frame corresponds to 1/60 second). Lower level reflects fine motion and higher reflects

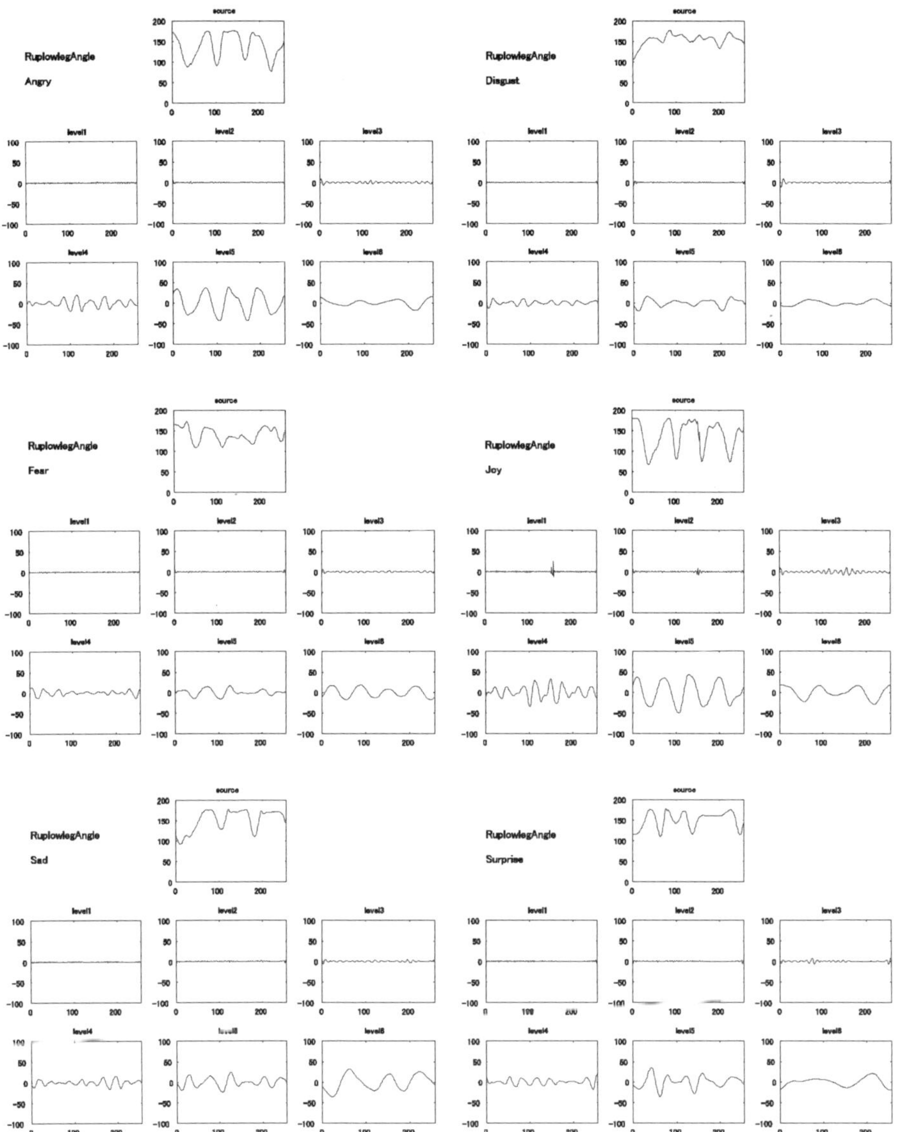

Fig. 4. Wavelet decomposed waveform for each resolution level: the case of angle between right lower and upper leg for each emotion center top graph shows raw data – angle time sequence, below 6 graphs show recomposed waveform by wavelet transform and inverse wavelet transform with each resolution level

larger motion. From these figures, angry and joy show clear periodic peaks in higher level 5 and 6, but fear, disgust and sad show no clear peaks at any temporal scale. These means that angry and joy show periodic motion, while disgust, fear and sad show irregular motion on arm. Fig.4 reflects the leg motion, each emotion shows

Table 1. Extracted motion features for each emotion

emotion	tempo	wave feature
The angle between upper & front arm		
neutral	normal	periodicity, synchronicity over scales
angry	faster	large & steep peaks repeated in longer period
disgust	random	short periodicity, clear peak irregular but continual
fear	faster	short periodicity, tiny peaks
joy	normal	continual steep peak in short period, synchronous between scales
sad	irregular	a little change, no clear peak
surprise	slower	temporal large peak which decays
The angle between upper arm & upper body		
neutral	normal	clear periodicity at large scales
angry	slower	synchronous to gait, stronger the right side
disgust	normal	frequent small peaks at fine scale
fear	unclear	tiny peaks at fine scale
joy	normal	large clear peaks, synchronous over scales
sad	slow	no peaks
surprise	normal	temporal large peak which decays
The angle between lower & upper leg		
neutral	normal	stronger periodicity with larger scale
angry	a bit slower	a bit stronger periodicity at each scale
disgust	a bit faster	strong periodicity at middle scale,
fear	unclear	tiny peaks at each scale
joy	faster	strong periodicity synchronous between scales
sad	a bit slower	small peaks at the edge of periodic wave
surprise	slow	large peaks which decays

clear peaks at several scales. Angry and joy show strong continual peaks especially at level 5, while disgust and surprise show a irregular peaks. This means that angry and joy hold leg's periodic motion, but disgust and surprise break it. Fear and sad show a periodic alternation of a steep peak and a mild peak at mid scale. This reflects a sluggish gait. Total motion features for each emotion extracted by wavelet analysis are summarized in Table 1.

5 Conclusion and Future Extensions

We propose a motion analysis and synthesis method based on the higher order SVD and wavelet analysis, in order to extract motion features specific to emotions. Our method applies the higher order SVD to the motion time sequence acted with each emotion and compute a mapping model between persons and emotions. The generative model synthesizes a novel person's motion data acting each emotion or a known person's motion data with the other emotions. Experimentally, our method can synthesize a new person's each motion sequence with other emotions. The analyses applying a wavelet transform to the synthesized data can extract each motion feature for each emotion.

Experimentally, in gait action, we confirmed our method could extract motion feature for each emotion. For example, gait with angry or joy gave an enhancing motion of gait action, joy gave the continual enhancing effect of gait motion both arm and leg. Angry gives the enhancing effect on bending arm or leg and the periodicity of swinging arms is lost. While, disgust, fear, and sad show a depressed motion of gait action, arms are kept lifting and legs show a sluggish gait motion. In the case of surprise, an instant large motion which decays is shown in each joint, and so forth.

In future work, we plan to investigate psychological responses to the animated data generated using our synthesized motion data and construct a motion corpus specific to each emotion.

References

1. T.Kim, S.I.Park and S.Y.Shin : Rhythmic-motion synthesis based on motion-beat analysis, ACM Trans. on Graphics, Vol.22, No.3,(2003) 392-401
2. T.Shiratori, A.Nakazawa and K.Ikeuchi: Detecting Dance Motion Structure through Music Analysis, IEEE ICAFGR,(2004) 857-862
3. Y.Kobayashi, J.Ohya, Z.Zhang: Cognitive bridge between haptic impressions and texture images for subjective image retrieval. Proc. of IEEE ICME, (2004) 2239-2242
4. M.Brand and A. Hertzmann: Style machines, Proc. of ACM SIGGRAPH, (2000) 183-192
5. A.Sundaresan, A.Roy Chowdhury and R.Chellappa: A hidden markov model based framework for recognition of humans from gait sequences, Proc. of IEEE ICIP, Vol.2 (2003) 93-96
6. Vasilescu M.A.O., Human Signatures: Analysis, Synthesis, Recognition. Proc. of ICPR, Vol.3.(2002) 456-460
7. I.Daubechies, "Ten Lectures On Wavelets", Society for Industrial and Applied Mathematics, (1995)
8. P.Ekman, Facial Expressions of Emotion : an old Controversy and New Findings, Philosophical Transactions of the Royal Society, London, B335: (1992) 63 - 69

Discriminant Transform Based on Scatter Difference Criterion in Hidden Space

Cai-kou Chen [1,2] and Jing-yu Yang [2]

[1] Department of Computer Science and Engineering, Yangzhou University, 225001 Yangzhou, China
yzcck@126.com

[2] Department of Computer Science and Engineering, Nanjing University of Science and Technology, 210094 Nanjing, China
yangjy@public1.ptt.js.cn

Abstract. In this paper, a novel feature extraction method based on scatter difference criterion in hidden space is developed. Its main idea is that the original input space is first mapped into a hidden space through a kernel function, where the feature extraction is conducted using the difference of between-class scatter and within-class scatter as the discriminant criterion. Different from the existing kernel-based feature extraction methods, the kernel function used in the proposed one is not required to satisfy Mercer's theorem so that they can be chosen from a wide range. It is more important that due to adoption of the scatter difference as the discriminant criterion for feature extraction, the proposed method essentially avoids the small size samples problem usually occurred in the kernel Fisher discriminant analysis. Finally, extensive experiments are performed on a subset of FERET face database. The experimental results indicate that the proposed method outperforms the traditional scatter difference discriminant analysis in recognition performance.

1 Introduction

Over the last years, nonlinear variants of linear algorithms have become possible by the so-called "kernel trick", originally introduced in SVMs [1]. Basically, the linear algorithms are written in the form of dot products which are substituted by kernel functions which directly compute the dot products in a high-dimensional nonlinear space. Kernel Fisher discriminant analysis (KFD) [2, 3], the famous one of them, has widely been applied to many pattern recognition problems and its good performance is available. However, KFD has two intrinsic limitations. First, it always encounters the difficulty of singularity of the within-class scatter matrix in feature space, which is the same one as its linear version, LDA. A number of regularization techniques [4-7] that might alleviate this problem have been suggested. Unfortunately, most of the approaches discard the discriminant information contained in the null space of the within-class covariance matrix, yet this information is very effective for the small sample size. Recently, a novel classifier, referred to as maximum scatter difference classifier (MSDC), is presented [8]. Its main idea is that one finds the optimal projection direction depended on the difference of between-class scatter and within-class

N. Zheng, X. Jiang, and X. Lan (Eds.): IWICPAS 2006, LNCS 4153, pp. 144 – 151, 2006.

scatter (SD) rather than their ratio (i.e., the Fisher criterion), which avoids the problem of the small sample size in nature. MSDC, however, extracts only an optimal projection vector for the resulting classification, which is insufficient for multi-class classification task. Second, the kernel functions used in KFD must satisfy the Mercer's condition or they have to be symmetric and positive semidefinite. However, kernel functions available are limited and have mainly the following ones: polynomial kernel, Gaussian kernel, sigmoidal kernel, spline kernel, and others. The limited number of kernel functions restrains the modeling capability for KFD when confronted with highly complicated applications.

To overcome the above-mentioned weaknesses of KFD, a novel feature extraction method, named as discriminant transform based on scatter difference criterion in hidden space (HSDD) is proposed in this paper. Different from KFD, the proposed HSDD method adopts SD as projection criterion. As a result, it is not required to calculate the inverse of within-class scatter matrix and the trouble of singularity is avoided essentially. Motivated by the hidden function mapping used in radial basis function networks (RBFs), we will extend the range of usable kernels that are not required to meet the Mercer's condition. A new kernel function for nonlinear mapping, called similarity measurement, is employed in the method. Finally, the proposed method has been used in face recognition. The experimental results on the FERET face database indicate the proposed method is effective and encouraging.

The rest of this paper is organized as follows: Section 2 describes the principle and algorithm of HSDD. In Section 3, experimental results on the FERET face image databases demonstrate the effectiveness and efficiency of HSDD. Finally, conclusions are presented in Section 4.

2 Principle and Method

2.1 Hidden Space

Let $\mathbf{X}=\{\mathbf{x}_1, \mathbf{x}_2, \ldots, \mathbf{x}_N\}$denote the set of N independently and identical distributed (i.i.d.) patterns. Define a vector made up of a set of real-valued functions $\{\varphi_i(\mathbf{x})|i=1, 2, \ldots, n_1\}$, as shown by

$$\varphi(\mathbf{x}) = [\varphi_1(\mathbf{x}), \varphi_2(\mathbf{x}), \ldots, \varphi_{n_1}(\mathbf{x})]^{\mathrm{T}}, \tag{1}$$

where $\mathbf{x} \in \mathbf{X} \subset \mathbb{R}^n$. The vector $\varphi(\mathbf{x})$ maps the points in the n-dimensional input space into a new space of dimension n_1, namely,

$$\mathbf{x} \xrightarrow{\varphi} \mathbf{y} = [\varphi_1(\mathbf{x}), \varphi_2(\mathbf{x}), \ldots, \varphi_{n_1}(\mathbf{x})]^{\mathrm{T}}. \tag{2}$$

Since the set of functions $\{\varphi_i(\mathbf{x})\}$ plays a role similar to that of a hidden unit in radial basis function networks (RBFNs), we refer to $\varphi_i(\mathbf{x})$, $i=1, \ldots, n_1$, as hidden functions. Accordingly, the space, $\mathbb{Y} = \{\mathbf{y} \mid \mathbf{y} = [\varphi_1(\mathbf{x}), \varphi_2(\mathbf{x}), \ldots, \varphi_{n_1}(\mathbf{x})]^{\mathrm{T}}, \mathbf{x} \in \mathbf{X}\}$, is called the hidden space or feature space.

Now consider a special kind of hidden function: the real symmetric kernel function $k(\mathbf{x}_i, \mathbf{x}_j) = k(\mathbf{x}_j, \mathbf{x}_i)$. Let the kernel mapping be

$$\mathbf{x} \xrightarrow{k} \mathbf{y} = [k(\mathbf{x}_1, \mathbf{x}), k(\mathbf{x}_2, \mathbf{x}), ..., k(\mathbf{x}_N, \mathbf{x})]^{\mathrm{T}} . \tag{3}$$

The corresponding hidden space based on $\mathbf{X}$ can be expressed as $\mathbb{Y} = \{\mathbf{y} \mid \mathbf{y} = [k(\mathbf{x}_1, \mathbf{x}), k(\mathbf{x}_2, \mathbf{x}), \ ..., \ k(\mathbf{x}_N, \mathbf{x}), \mathbf{x} \in \mathbf{X}]^{\mathrm{T}}$ whose dimension is N.

It is only the symmetric for kernel functions that is required, which will extend the set of usable kernel functions in HSDD while the rigorous Mercer's condition is required in SVMs. Some usual hidden functions are given as follows: sigmoidal kernel: $k(\mathbf{x}_i, \mathbf{x}_j) = S(v(\mathbf{x}_i \cdot \mathbf{x}_j) + c)$, Gaussian radial basis kernel : $k(\mathbf{x}_i, \mathbf{x}_j) = \exp(-\frac{\|\mathbf{x}_i - \mathbf{x}_j\|^2}{2\sigma^2})$, polynomial kernel: $k(\mathbf{x}_i, \mathbf{x}_j) = (\alpha(\mathbf{x}_i \cdot \mathbf{x}_j) + b)^d$, $\alpha > 0, \ b \geq 0$, and d is a positive integer.

In what follows, we will define a new kernel mapping directly based on two-dimensional image matrix rather than one-dimensional vector.

Definition 1. Let $\mathbf{A}_i$ and $\mathbf{A}_j$ are two $m \times n$ image matrices. A real number s is defined by

$$s(\mathbf{A}_i, \mathbf{A}_j) = \frac{tr(\mathbf{A}_i \mathbf{A}_j^{\mathrm{T}} + \mathbf{A}_j \mathbf{A}_i^{\mathrm{T}})}{tr(\mathbf{A}_i \mathbf{A}_i^{\mathrm{T}} + \mathbf{A}_j \mathbf{A}_j^{\mathrm{T}})}, \tag{4}$$

where $tr(\mathbf{B})$ denote the trace of a matrix $\mathbf{B}$. The number $s(\mathbf{A}_i, \mathbf{A}_j)$ is referred to as the *similarity measurement* of both $\mathbf{A}_i$ and $\mathbf{A}_j$.

According to the definition 1, it is easy to show that the similarity measurement s has the following properties:

(1) $s(\mathbf{A}_i, \mathbf{A}_j) = s(\mathbf{A}_j, \mathbf{A}_i)$;

(2) $s(\mathbf{A}_i, \mathbf{A}_j) = s(\mathbf{A}_i^{\mathrm{T}}, \mathbf{A}_j^{\mathrm{T}})$;

(3) $-1 \leq s(\mathbf{A}_i, \mathbf{A}_j) \leq 1$, if $s(\mathbf{A}_i, \mathbf{A}_j) = 1$, then $\mathbf{A}_i = \mathbf{A}_j$.

From the above properties, it is clear to see that $s(\mathbf{A}_i, \mathbf{A}_j)$ represents the relation of similarity between two image matrices, $\mathbf{A}_i$ and $\mathbf{A}_j$. If the value of $s(\mathbf{A}_i, \mathbf{A}_j)$ approaches one, the difference of both $\mathbf{A}_i$ and $\mathbf{A}_j$ reaches zero, which shows that $\mathbf{A}_i$ is nearly the same as $\mathbf{A}_j$.

Definition 2. A mapping $\varphi: \mathbb{R}^{m \times n} \to \mathbb{R}^N$ is defined as follows,

$$\varphi = s(.,\mathbf{A}) = [s(\mathbf{A}_1, \mathbf{A}), s(\mathbf{A}_2, \mathbf{A}), ..., s(\mathbf{A}_N, \mathbf{A})]^T . \tag{5}$$

The mapping φ is called the *similarity kernel mapping*. Thus, the hidden space associated with φ is given by $\mathbb{Z} = \{\mathbf{z} \mid \mathbf{z} = [s(\mathbf{A}_1, \mathbf{A}), s(\mathbf{A}_2, \mathbf{A}), ..., s(\mathbf{A}_N, \mathbf{A}), \mathbf{A} \in \mathbf{X}]^{\mathrm{T}}$.

2.2 Feature Extraction Based on Scatter Difference Criterion in Hidden Space

Suppose $\mathbf{X} = \{\mathbf{A}_i\}$, $i = 1,2,...,N$ is a set of $m \times n$ training images, which contains c pattern classes, $\omega_1, \omega_2, ..., \omega_c$. According to the definition 2, each training image, $\mathbf{A}_i$,

$i=1, \ldots, N$, is mapped to the hidden space $\mathbb{Z}$ through the similarity kernel mapping φ. Let $\mathbf{z}_i$ be the mapped image in $\mathbb{Z}$ of the original training image $\mathbf{A}_i$, that is,

$$\mathbf{z}_i = [s(\mathbf{A}_1, \mathbf{A}_i), s(\mathbf{A}_2, \mathbf{A}_i), \ldots, s(\mathbf{A}_N, \mathbf{A}_i)]^{\mathrm{T}} . \tag{6}$$

The mean vector, covariation matrix, and prior probability of the ith class in the hidden space $\mathbb{Z}$ are, respectively, denoted by $\boldsymbol{\mu}_i$, $\mathbf{K}_i$, and $P(\omega_i)$. Then, the between-class scatter matrix and within-class scatter matrix in $\mathbb{Z}$ are defined as follows.

$$\mathbf{K}_b = \sum_{i=1}^{c} P(\omega_i)(\boldsymbol{\mu}_i - \boldsymbol{\mu})(\boldsymbol{\mu}_i - \boldsymbol{\mu})^{\mathrm{T}} , \tag{7}$$

$$\mathbf{K}_w = \sum_{i=1}^{c} P(\omega_i)\mathbf{E}\left\{(\mathbf{z}-\boldsymbol{\mu}_i)(\mathbf{z}-\boldsymbol{\mu}_i)^{\mathrm{T}} \mid \omega_i\right\} = \sum_{i=1}^{c} P(\omega_i)\mathbf{K}_i , \tag{8}$$

where $\mathbf{E(M)}$ is the expectation of a matrix $\mathbf{M}$, $\mathbf{K}_i = \mathbf{E}\left\{(\mathbf{z}-\boldsymbol{\mu}_i)(\mathbf{z}-\boldsymbol{\mu}_i)^{\mathrm{T}} / \omega_i\right\}$, and $\boldsymbol{\mu} = \mathbf{E}\{\mathbf{z}\} = \sum_{i=1}^{c} P(\omega_i)\boldsymbol{\mu}_i$ denotes the total mean vector of training samples.

From the scatter matrices defined above, the scatter difference criterion is defined as follows,

$$J_s(\mathbf{w}) = \mathbf{w}^{\mathrm{T}}(\mathbf{K}_b - \mathbf{K}_w)\mathbf{w} , \tag{9}$$

where $\mathbf{w}$ is any N-dimensional vector in the hidden space $\mathbb{Z}$. The vector $\mathbf{w}^*$ maximizing the criterion function $J_s(\mathbf{w})$ is chosen as an optimal projection direction for HSDD. Thus, the projected feature vectors in the direction reach its maximum class separability.

Theorem 1. The optimal projection vector is the unitary vector that maximizes $J_s(\mathbf{w})$, i.e., the unitary eigenvector of the matrix $\mathbf{K}_b$-$\mathbf{K}_w$ corresponding to the largest eigenvalue.

Proof. The problem to solve the optimal discriminant vector $\mathbf{w}^*$ maximizing $J_s(\mathbf{w})$ in Eq. (9) is equivalent to the following one,

$$\underset{\|\mathbf{w}\|=1}{Max}\, J_s(\mathbf{w}) = \underset{\|\mathbf{w}\|=1}{Max}\, \mathbf{w}^{\mathrm{T}}(\mathbf{K}_b - \mathbf{K}_w)\mathbf{w} = \underset{\|\mathbf{w}\|=1}{Max} \frac{\mathbf{w}^{\mathrm{T}}(\mathbf{K}_b - \mathbf{K}_w)\mathbf{w}}{\mathbf{w}^{\mathrm{T}}\mathbf{w}} . \tag{10}$$

Since

$$\frac{\mathbf{w}^T(\mathbf{K}_b - \mathbf{K}_w)\mathbf{w}}{\mathbf{w}^T\mathbf{w}} = \frac{\mathbf{w}^T(\mathbf{K}_b - \mathbf{K}_w)\mathbf{w}}{\mathbf{w}^T \boldsymbol{I}\mathbf{w}} , \tag{11}$$

where $\mathbf{I}$ is an identity matrix. Note that the formula (11) is a rayleigh quotient in the space $\mathbb{Z}$. According to the extreme value property of the rayleigh quotient [9], the optimal discriminant vector $\mathbf{w}^*$ maximizing $J_s(\mathbf{w})$ corresponds to the unitary eigenvector of the matrix $\mathbf{K}_b$-$\mathbf{K}_w$ with the largest eigenvalue. □

In general, it is not enough to have only one optimal projection vector. We usually need to select a set of projection vectors maximizing the criterion function $\boldsymbol{J}_s(\mathbf{w})$.

Corollary 1. A set of best discriminant vectors maximizing $\boldsymbol{J}_s(\mathbf{w})$ in Eq. (9) are taken as the orthonormal eigenvectors of the following eigenequation (12) corresponding to the first d largest eigenvalue, that is,

$$(\mathbf{K}_b - \mathbf{K}_w)\mathbf{w}_j = \lambda_j \mathbf{w}_j\,, \quad j = 1,...,d\,. \tag{12}$$

Finally, the obtained optimal discriminant vectors, say $\mathbf{w}_1$, $\mathbf{w}_2$, ..., $\mathbf{w}_d$, are used for feature extraction in the space $\mathbb{Z}$.

It is clear that unlike the KFD methods based on the Fisher criterion, which fails to calculate its optimal discriminant vectors when the within-class scatter matrix $\mathbf{K}_w$ is of singularity, which usually occurs in its real-world applications, it is always easy to compute the optimal projection directions of HSDD no matter the matrix $\mathbf{K}_w$ is singular or not. In addition, the eigendecomposition for HSDD simply bases on the matrix $\mathbf{K}_b$-$\mathbf{K}_w$ rather than the matrix $\mathbf{K}_w^{-1}\mathbf{K}_\mathbf{b}$, which is used in the conventional KFD methods. Thus, the computation time consumed by HSDD is much smaller than one by KFD.

2.3 Feature Extraction

Let $\mathbf{w}_1,\cdots,\mathbf{w}_d$ denote a set of optimal discriminant vectors extracted by Eq. (12). Given a training image $\mathbf{A}$, we can obtain the discriminant feature vector $\mathbf{y}$ by the following transformation:

$$\mathbf{y} = \mathbf{W}^T\mathbf{z} \tag{13}$$

where,

$$\mathbf{W}=[\mathbf{w}_1, \mathbf{w}_2, \cdots, \mathbf{w}_d]$$

$$\mathbf{z} = [s(\mathbf{A}_1,\mathbf{A}), s(\mathbf{A}_2,\mathbf{A}),..., s(\mathbf{A}_N,\mathbf{A})]^T\,.$$

3 Experiments

The proposed method was applied to face recognition and tested on a subset of the FERET face image database [10, 11]. This subset includes 1400 images of 200 individuals (each individual has 7 images). It is composed of the images named with two-character strings: "*ba*", "*bd*", "*be*", "*bf*", "*bg*", "*bj*", and "*bk*". These strings indicate the kind of imagery, see [11]. This subset involves variation in facial expression, illumination, and poses ($\pm 15^0$ and $\pm 25^0$). In our experiment, the facial portion of each original image was cropped based on the location of eyes and, the cropped image was resized to 80×80 pixels and pre-processed by histogram equalization. The seven images of one person in the FERET face database are shown in Figure 1.

Fig. 1. Seven cropped images of one person in the FERET face database

In our experiment, three images of each subject are randomly selected for training, while the remainder is used for testing. Thus, the total number of training samples is 200×3=600 and the total number of testing samples is 200×4=800. Apart from the similarity measurement kernel, two popular kernels are involved in our tests. One is the polynomial kernel $k(\mathbf{x},\mathbf{y})=(\mathbf{x}\cdot\mathbf{y}+1)^T$ and the other is the Gaussian RBF kernel $k(\mathbf{x},\mathbf{y})=\exp(-\|\mathbf{x}-\mathbf{y}\|^2/\sigma)$. KFD and HSDD are, respectively, used for testing and comparison. A minimum-distance classifier is employed for classification. For the sake of conciseness, KFD and HSDD with the polynomial kernel, the Gaussian RBF kernel and the similarity measurement kernel are, respectively, denoted by KFD_P, KFD_G, KFD_S, HSDD_P, HSDD_G and HSDD_S. The above experiments are repeated 10 times. In each time, the training sample set is chosen at random so that the training sample sets are different for each test. The average recognition rate across 10 times of each method over the variation of dimensions is plotted in Fig. 2. In addition, the average CPU time consumed for training and testing, and the best recognition rates are given in Table 1.

From Fig. 1 and Table 1, we can see that HSDD_S is superior to KFD's, HSDD_G, and HSDD_P in recognition accuracy. The result verifies the effectiveness of similarity measurement as kernel function. In addition, the speed of three methods

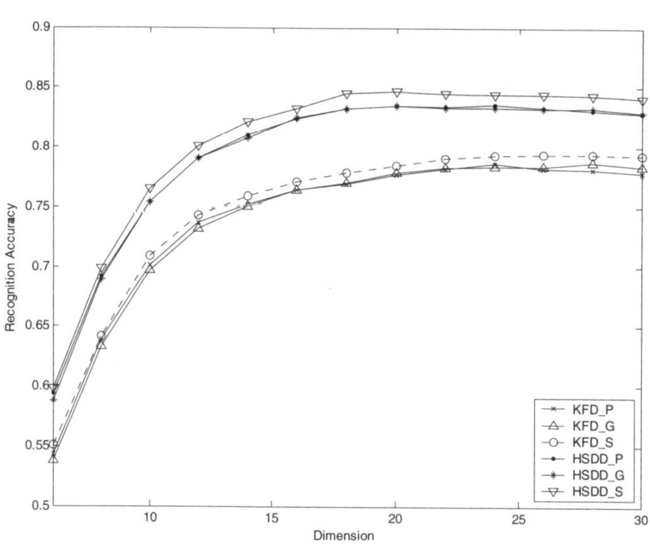

Fig. 2. The average recognition rate (%) across 10 tests of each method with the variation of dimensions

Table 1. The average CPU time (s) consumed for training and testing and the top recognition rates (%) of the four methods (CPU: Pentium 2.4GHZ, RAM: 640Mb)

Method	KFD_P	KFD_G	KFD_S	HSDD_P	HSDD_G	HSDD_S
Recognition rate	78.61	78.83	79.13	82.45	82.47	83.25
CPU time	97.86	125.15	99.25	48.21	59.96	41.09

of HSDD_S, HSDD_G, and HSDD_P is faster than KFD's. This result is reasonable since the proposed algorithms are based on the scatter difference criterion rather than the Fisher criterion adopted in KFD, which saves much time due to avoid the computation of the inverse of the within-class scatter matrix.

4 Conclusion

A new feature extraction method, coined discriminant transform based on scatter difference criterion in hidden space, is developed in this paper. Compared to the existing KFD methods, HSDD has two prominent advantages: first, it is free to the singularity of the within-class scatter matrix so that the computation time required is reduced considerably; second, since the kernel is no longer required to meet the Mercer's condition, the range of kernel functions available is widened. As a result, one may find more desirable kernel according to the present problem itself. Our experiments demonstrate that the proposed method is effective and efficient.

Acknowledgements

We wish to thank the National Science Foundation of China, under Grant No. 60472060, the University's Natural Science Research Program of Jiangsu Province under Grant No 05KJB520152, and the Jiangsu Planned Projects for Postdoctoral Research Funds for supporting this work.

References

1. V. Vapnik. The Nature of Statistical Learning Theory. Springer, N.Y., 1995.
2. S. Mika, G. Rätsch, J. Weston, B. Schölkopf, and K.-R. Müller. "Fisher discriminant analysis with kernels", IEEE International Workshop on Neural Networks for Signal Processing IX, Madison (USA), August, 1999, pp. 41-48.
3. S. Mika, A.J. Smola, and B. Schölkopf. An improved training algorithm for kernel fisher discriminants. In T. Jaakkola and T. Richardson, editors, Proceedings AISTATS 2001, San Francisco, CA, 2001, pp. 98-104,
4. S. Mika, G. Rätsch, J Weston, B. Schölkopf, A. Smola, and K.-R. Müller, Constructing descriptive and discriminative non-linear features: Rayleigh coefficients in kernel feature spaces. IEEE Trans. Pattern Anal. Machine Intell. 25(5) (2003) 623-628.
5. G. Baudat and F. Anouar. Generalized discriminant analysis using a kernel approach, *Neural Computation*. 12 (10) (2000) 2385-2404.

6. M. H. Yang, Kernel Eigenfaces vs. kernel Fisherfaces: face recognition using kernel methods, Proceedings of the Fifth IEEE International Conference on Automatic Face and Gesture Recognition (RGR'02), Washington D. C., May, 2002, 215-220.
7. Hua Yu, Jie Yang. A direct LDA algorithm for high-dimensional data—with application to face recognition, Pattern Recognition. 34(10) (2001) 2067-2070.
8. Fengxi Song, Shuhai Liu, Jingyu Yang, et al., Maximum scatter difference classifier and its application to text categorization, Computer Engineering. 31(5) (2005) 890-896
9. Cheng Yun-peng. Matrix theory (in chinese). Xi'an: Northwest Industry University Press, 1999.
10. P. J. Phillips, H. Moon, S. A. Rizvi, and P. J. Rauss, "The FERET Evaluation Methodology for Face-Recognition Algorithms", IEEE Trans. Pattern Anal. Machine Intell., 2000, 22 (10), pp.1090-1104.
11. P. J. Phillips, The Facial Recognition Technology (FERET) Database, http://www.itl.nist.gov/iad/humanid/feret/feret_master.html.

Looking for Prototypes by Genetic Programming

L. P. Cordella[1], C. De Stefano[2], F. Fontanella[1], and A. Marcelli[3]

[1] Dipartimento di Informatica e Sistemistica
Università di Napoli Federico II,
Via Claudio, 21 80125 Napoli – Italy
{cordel, frfontan}@unina.it

[2] Dipartimento di Automazione, Elettromagnetismo, Ingegneria dell'Informazione e Matematica Industriale
Università di Cassino
Via G. Di Biasio, 43 02043 Cassino (FR) – Italy
destefano@unicas.it

[3] Dipartimento di Ingegneria dell'Informazione e Ingegneria Elettrica
Università di Salerno
84084 Fisciano (SA) – Italy
amarcelli@unisa.it

Abstract. In this paper we propose a new genetic programming based approach for prototype generation in Pattern Recognition problems. Prototypes consist of mathematical expressions and are encoded as derivation trees. The devised system is able to cope with classification problems in which the number of prototypes is not a priori known. The approach has been tested on several problems and the results compared with those obtained by other genetic programming based approaches previously proposed.

1 Introduction

Several modern computational techniques have been introduced in the last years in order to cope with classification problems [1,2,3]. Among others, evolutionary computation (EC) techniques have been also employed. In this field, genetic algorithms [4,5] and genetic programming [6,7] have mostly been used. The former approach encodes a set of classification rules as a sequence of bit strings. In the latter approach instead, such rules, or even classification functions, can be learned. The technique of Genetic Programming (GP) was introduced by Koza [7] and has already been successfully used in many different applications [8,9], demonstrating its ability to discovering underlying data relationships and to representing them by expressions. Only recently, classification problems have been faced by using GP. In [10], GP has been used to evolve equations (encoded as derivation trees) involving simple arithmetic operators and feature variables. The method was tested on different type of data, including images. In [11], GP has also been employed for image classification, adding exponential functions, conditional functions and constants to the simple arithmetic operators. In both the above quoted approaches, the data set is divided in a number c of *clusters* equal to the number of predefined classes. Thus, these approaches do not take into account the existence of subclasses within one or more of the classes in the analyzed data set.

N. Zheng, X. Jiang, and X. Lan (Eds.): IWICPAS 2006, LNCS 4153, pp. 152–159, 2006.

We present a GP based method for determining a set of prototypes describing the data in a classification problem. In the devised approach, each prototype is representative of a cluster of samples in the training set, and consists of a mathematical expression involving arithmetic operators and variables representing features. The devised method is able to generate a variable number of expressions, allowing us to cope with those classification problems in which single classes may contain not a priori identifiable subclasses. Hence, a fixed number of expressions (prototypes) may not be able to effectively classify all the data samples, since a single expression might be inadequate to express the characteristics of all the subclasses present in a class. The proposed approach, instead, is able to automatically find the number of expressions needed to represent all the possible subclasses present in the data set.

According to our method, the set of prototypes describing the classes makes up a *single* individual of the evolving population. Each prototype is encoded as a derivation tree, thus an individual is a list of trees, called *multitree*. Given an individual and a sample, classification consists in attributing the sample to one of the classes (i.e. in associating the sample to one of the prototypes). The recognition rate obtained on the training set when using an individual is assigned as fitness value to that individual. At any step of the evolution process, individuals are selected according to their fitness value. At the end of the process, the best individual obtained, constitutes the set of prototypes to be used for the considered application.

A preliminary version of this method was presented in [12], where prototypes consisted of simple logical expressions.

The method presented here has been tested on three publicly available databases and the classification results have been compared with those obtained by the preliminary version of the method and with another GP based method presented in the literature [10].

2 Description of the Approach

In the approach proposed here, a prototype representing a class or subclass consists of a mathematical expression, namely an inequality, that may contain a variable number of variables connected by the four arithmetic operators (+,-,*,/). Each variable x_i, $(i = 1, \ldots, n)$ represents a particular feature. Note that an inequality characterizes a region of the feature space delimited by an hypersurface. Given an expression E and a sample represented by a feature vector $\mathbf{x}$, we say that E *matches* the sample $\mathbf{x}$ if the values in $\mathbf{x}$ satisfy the inequality E. Training the classifier is accomplished by the EC paradigm described in Section 3 and provides a set of labeled expressions to be used as prototypes. Different expressions may have the same label in case they represent subclasses of a class.

Given a data set and a set of labeled expressions, the classification task is performed in the following way: each sample of the data set is matched against the set of expressions and *assigned* to one of them (i.e. to a class or subclass) or rejected. Different cases may occur:

1. The sample is matched by just one expression: it is assigned to that expression.
2. The sample is matched by more than one expression with different number of variables: it is assigned to the expression with the smallest number of variables.
3. The sample is matched by more than one expression with the same number of variables and different labels: the sample is rejected.
4. The sample is matched by no expression: the sample is rejected.

Hereinafter, this process will be referred to as *assignment* process, and the set of samples assigned to the same expression will be referred to as *cluster*.

3 Learning Classification Rules

As already said, the prototypes to be used for classification are given in terms of inequalities, thus they may be thought of as computer programs and can be generated by adopting the GP paradigm. Our GP based system starts by randomly generating a population of p individuals. An individual is made by a set of prototypes each encoded as a derivation tree, so that it is a *multitree* (i.e. a list of trees). The number of trees making up an individual will be called *length* of the individual: in the initial population, it ranges from 2 to L_{max}. Afterwards, the fitness of the initial individuals is evaluated. In order to generate a new population, first the best e individuals are selected and copied in the new population so as to implement an elitist strategy. Then $(p - e)/2$ couples of individuals are selected using the tournament method and manipulated by using two genetic operators: crossover and mutation. The crossover operator is applied to each of the selected couples, according to a chosen probability factor p_c. Then, the mutation is applied to the obtained individuals according to a probability factor p_m. Finally, these individuals are added to the new population. The process just described is repeated for N_G generations. In order to implement the above system the following steps must be executed:

- definition of the structure to be evolved;
- choice of the fitness function;
- definition of the genetic operators.

In the following each of these steps is detailed.

3.1 Structure Definition

In order to generate syntactically correct expressions (i.e., prototypes), a nondeterministic grammar is defined. A grammar $\mathcal{G}$ is a quadruple $\mathcal{G} = (\mathcal{T}, \mathcal{N}, S, \mathcal{P})$, where $\mathcal{T}$ and $\mathcal{N}$ are disjoint finite alphabets. $\mathcal{T}$ is the *terminal alphabet*, whereas $\mathcal{N}$ is the *non-terminal alphabet*. S, is *the starting symbol* and $\mathcal{P}$ is the set of *production rules* used to define the strings belonging to the language. The grammar employed is given in Table 1.

Each individual consists of a variable number of derivation trees. The root of every tree is the symbol S that, according to the related production rule, can be replaced only by the string "C". The symbol C can be replaced by any mathematical expression obtained by recursively combining variables, representing features, and operators.

Table 1. The context free grammar used for generating the expressions employed as prototypes. In the right column, the probability of being chosen for each of the right side clause is shown.

Number	Rule	Probability
1	$S \longrightarrow C$	1.0
2	$C \longrightarrow [E > V] \mid [E < V]$	equiprobable
3	$E \longrightarrow PFD \mid P$	0.4, 0.6
4	$D \longrightarrow PFD \mid P \mid V$	0.5, 0.25, 0.25
5	$F \longrightarrow * \mid + \mid / \mid -$	equiprobable
5	$P \longrightarrow x_0 \mid x_1 \mid \ldots \mid x_N$	equiprobable
6	$V \longrightarrow +0.XX \mid -0.XX$	equiprobable
7	$X \longrightarrow 0\|1\|2\|3\|4\|5\|6\|7\|8\|9$	equiprobable

Summarizing, each individual is a list of derivation trees whose leaves are the terminal symbols of the grammar defined for constructing the set of inequalities. The set of inequalities making up an individual is obtained by visiting each derivation tree in depth first order and copying into a string the symbols contained in the leaves. In such string, each inequality derives from the corresponding tree in the list. To reduce the probability of generating too long expressions (i.e. too deep trees) the action carried out by a production rule is chosen on the basis of fixed probability values (shown in the last column of Table 1). Moreover, an upper limit has been imposed on the total number of nodes contained in an individual, i.e. the sum of nodes of each tree. Examples of individuals are shown in Fig. 1.

The matching process is implemented by an automaton which accepts as input an expression and a sample and returns as output the value true or false depending on the fact that the sample matches or not the expression.

3.2 Training Phase and Fitness Function

The aim of the training phase is that of generating the prototypes. The system is trained with a set containing N_{tr} samples. During training, the fitness of each individual in the population has to be evaluated. This process implies the following steps:

1. The assignment of the training set samples to the expressions belonging to the individual is performed. After this step, n_i ($n_i \geq 0$) samples will have been assigned to the i-th expression. The expressions for which $n_i > 0$ will be referred to as *valid*, whereas the ones for which $n_i = 0$ will be ignored in the following steps.
2. Each valid expression is labeled with the label most widely represented in the corresponding cluster.
3. The recognition rate (on the training set) of the individual is evaluated and assigned as fitness value to that individual.

In order to favor those individuals able to obtain good performances with a lesser number of expressions, the fitness of each individual is increased by k/N_e, where N_e is the number of expressions in the individual and k is a constant.

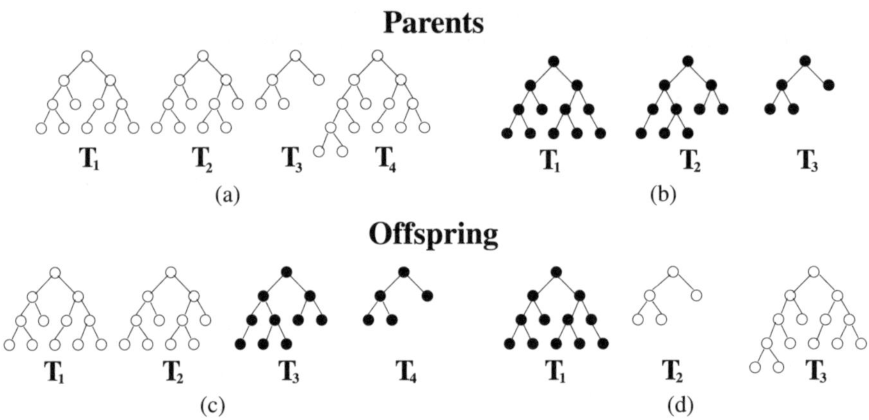

Fig. 1. An example of application of the crossover operator. The top figures (a and b)show a couple of individuals involved as parents of the crossover operator. The bottom figures (c and d) show the offspring obtained after the application of the operator. In this case case, t_1 and t_2 ha been chosen respectively equal to 2 and 1.

3.3 Genetic Operators

The choice of encoding the individuals as lists of derivation trees (see Section 3.1) allows us to implementing the genetic operators in a simple way.

The crossover operator is applied to two individuals I_1 and I_2 and yields two new individuals by swapping parts of the lists of the initial individuals (see Figure 1). Assuming that the lengths of I_1 and I_2 are respectively L_1 and L_2, the crossover is applied in the following way: the first individual is split in two parts by randomly choosing an integer t_1 in the interval $[1, L_1]$, so generating two multitrees $I_1^{'}$ and $I_1^{''}$, respectively of length t_1 and $L_1 - t_1$. Analogously, by randomly choosing an integer t_2 in the interval $[1, L_2]$, two multitrees $I_2^{'}$ and $I_2^{''}$ are obtained from I_2. Two new individuals are obtained: the first, by merging $I_1^{'}$ and $I_2^{''}$ and the second by merging $I_2^{'}$ and $I_1^{''}$.

It is worth noting that the implemented crossover operator allows us to obtain individuals of variable length. Hence, during the evolution process, individuals made of a variable number of prototypes can be evolved.

The mutation operator is independently applied to every tree of an individual I with probability p_m. More specifically, given a tree T_i, the mutation operator is applied by randomly choosing a single nonterminal node in T_i and then activating the corresponding production rule in order to substitute the subtree rooted under the chosen node.

4 Experimental Results

Three data sets have been used for training and testing the previously described approach. The sets are made of real data and are available at UCI site (http://www.ics.uci.edu/~mlearn/MLSummary.html) with the names IRIS, BUPA and Vehicle.

IRIS is made of 150 samples of iris flowers of three different classes, equally distributed in the dataset. Four features, namely sepal length, sepal width, petal length and petal width, are used for describing the samples. BUPA is made of 345 samples representing liver disorder using six features. Two classes are defined. The samples of the data set Vehicle are feature vectors representing 3D vehicle images. The data set has 846 samples distributed in four classes: 18 features characterize each sample.

In order to use the grammar shown in Table 1 the feature values of the data sets taken into account have been normalized in the range $[-1.0, 1.0]$. Given a not normalized sample $\mathbf{x} = (x_1, \ldots, x_N)$, every feature x_i is normalized using the formula: $x_i = (x_i - \overline{x}_i)/2\sigma_i$ where $\overline{x}_i$ and σ_i, respectively represent the mean and the standard deviation of the i-th feature computed over the whole data set.

Each dataset has been divided in two parts, a training set and a test set. These sets have been randomly extracted from the data sets and are disjoint and statistically independent. The first one has been used during the training phase to evaluate, at each generation, the fitness of the individuals in the population. The second one has been used at the end of the evolution process to evaluate the performance of our method. In particular, the recognition rate over the test set has been computed using for classification the best individual generated during the training phase.

The values of the evolutionary parameters, used in all the performed experiments, have been heuristically determined and are: Population size = 500; Tournament size = 6; Elithism size = 5; Crossover probability = 0.5; Mutation probability = 0.3; Number of Generations = 300; Maximum number of nodes in an individual = 1000; maximum length of an individual = 20. The value of the constant k (see Subsection 3.2) has been set to 0.1.

In order to investigate the generalization power of our system, i.e. a measure of its performance on new data, the recognition rates both on training and test sets have been taken into account for the different considered data sets. In Figure 2 such recognition rates, evaluated every 50 generations in a typical run, are displayed for BUPA and Vehicle data sets. It can be seen that the recognition rate increases with the number of generations both for the training set and for the test set. The best recognition rates occur in both cases nearby generation 250 and then remain stationary.

The proposed approach has been compared with another GP based approach previously proposed in [10]. Furthermore, the results obtained by the preliminary version of the method [12] are also shown for comparison. The substantial difference between the new and the old version of the method consists in the form of the encoded expressions: in [12] each expression contains a variable number of logical predicates connected by Boolean operators. Each predicate represents an assertion establishing a condition on the value of a particular feature of the samples. This implies that the hypersurfaces

Table 2. The recognition rates R_{new}, R_{old} and R_{Muni} obtained respectively by the method presented here, its preliminary version and the method presented in [10]

Data sets	$\mathbf{R}_{\text{new}}$	R_{old}	R_{Muni}
IRIS	**99.6**	99.4	98.67
BUPA	**78.6**	74.3	69.87
Vehicle	**70.2**	66.5	61.75

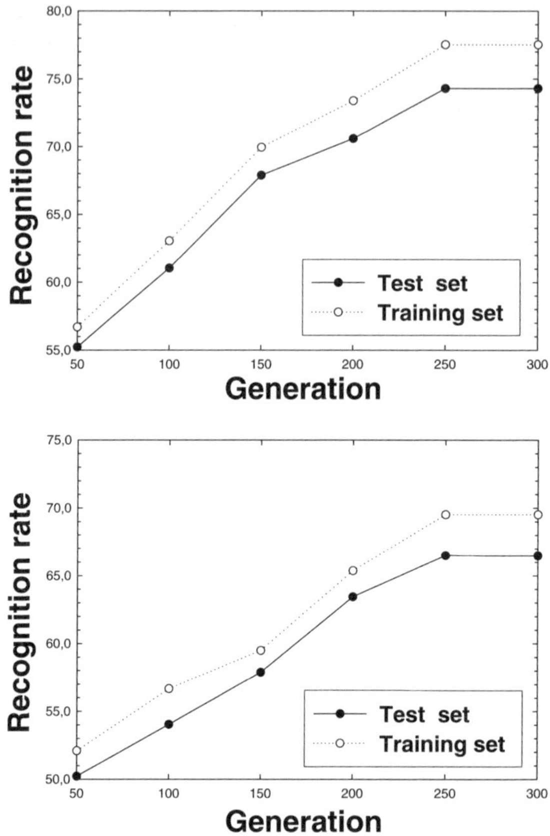

Fig. 2. Typical runs for BUPA (top) and Vehicle (bottom) datasets

separating the regions of the feature space belonging to different classes can only be hyperplanes parallel to the axes. In the new version of the method such hypersurfaces are of polynomial type, thus enabling a more effective separation between classes.

In Table 2 the recognition rates achieved on the test set by the three methods are shown. The results have been obtained by using the 10-fold cross validation procedure. Since the GP approach is a stochastic algorithm, the recognition rates have been averaged over 10 runs. Hence, 100 runs have been performed for each data set. Note that, in [10], the number of prototypes is a priori fixed, while in our method it is automatically found. The results show that the proposed method outperforms those used for comparison on all the data sets taken into account, confirming the validity of the approach.

5 Conclusions

A new GP based approach to prototype generation and classification has been proposed. A prototype consists of a set of mathematical inequalities establishing conditions on feature values and thus describing classes of data samples. The method is able to automatically find the number of clusters in the data, without forcing the system to find a predefined number of clusters. This means that a class is neither necessarily represented by one single prototype nor by a fixed number of prototypes. A remarkable feature of our method is that the hypersurfaces separating the regions of the feature space belonging to different classes are of polynomial type, thus enabling an effective separation between classes. The results show that the proposed method outperforms those used for comparison.

References

1. Duda, R.O., Hart, P.E., Stork, D.G.: Pattern Classification. John Wiley & sons, Inc. (2001)
2. Zhang, G.P.: Neural networks for classification: a survey. IEEE Transactions on Systems, Man, and Cybernetics, Part C **30** (2000) 451–462
3. Quinlan, J.R.: C4.5: programs for machine learning. Morgan Kaufmann Publishers Inc. (1993)
4. Holland, J.H.: Adaptation in Natural and Artificial Systems: An Introductory Analysis with Applications to Biology, Control and Artificial Intelligence. MIT Press (1992)
5. Goldberg, D.E.: Genetic Algorithms in Search, Optimization and Machine Learning. Addison-Wesley Longman Publishing Co., Inc. (1989)
6. Koza, J.R.: Genetic Programming: On the Programming of Computers by Means of Natural Selection. MIT Press, Cambridge, MA, USA (1992)
7. Koza, J.R.: Genetic programming II: automatic discovery of reusable programs. MIT Press, Cambridge, MA, USA (1994)
8. Sette, S., Boullart, L.: Genetic programming: principles and applications. Engineering Applications of Artificial Intelligence **14** (2001) 727–736
9. Bastian, A.: Identifying fuzzy models utilizing genetic programming. Fuzzy Sets and Systems **113** (2000) 333–350
10. Muni, D.P., Pal, N.R., Das, J.: A novel approach to design classifiers using genetic programming. IEEE Trans. Evolutionary Computation **8** (2004) 183–196
11. Agnelli, D., Bollini, A., Lombardi, L.: Image classification: an evolutionary approach. Pattern Recognition Letters **23** (2002) 303–309
12. Cordella, L.P., De Stefano, C., Fontanella, F., Marcelli, A.: Genetic programming for generating prototypes in classification problems. In: Proceedings of the 2005 IEEE Congress on Evolutionary Computation. Volume 2., IEEE Press (2005) 1149–1155

Identifying Single Good Clusters in Data Sets

Frank Klawonn

Department of Computer Science
University of Applied Sciences Braunschweig/Wolfenbuettel
Salzdahlumer Str. 46/48
D-38302 Wolfenbuettel, Germany
f.klawonn@fh-wolfenbuettel.de
http://public.rz.fh-wolfenbuettel.de/~klawonn/

Abstract. Local patterns in the form of single clusters are of interest in various areas of data mining. However, since the intention of cluster analysis is a global partition of a data set into clusters, it is not suitable to identify single clusters in a large data set where the majority of the data can not be assigned to meaningful clusters. This paper presents a new objective function-based approach to identify a single good cluster in a data set making use of techniques known from prototype-based, noise and fuzzy clustering. The proposed method can either be applied in order to identify single clusters or to carry out a standard cluster analysis by finding clusters step by step and determining the number of clusters automatically in this way.

Keywords: Cluster analysis, local pattern discovery.

1 Introduction

Cluster analysis aims at partitioning a data set into clusters. It is usually assumed that, except for some noise data, most of the data can be assigned to clusters. However, when we are interested in detecting local patterns, standard clustering techniques are not suited for this task.

In various applications, cluster analysis is applied, although the focus is on detecting single interesting patterns, instead of partitioning the data set. For instance, cluster analysis is very often applied in the context of gene expression data in order to find groups (clusters) of genes with a similar expression pattern. The approach described in this paper was also motivated by an analysis of gene expression data where we applied standard clustering in the first step [4], but the main intention of the biologists was to find local patterns instead of a global partition into clusters. However, there are many other areas like the analysis of customer profiles where local patterns are of high interest.

A number of different approaches for the detection of local patterns have already been proposed and studied in the literature. For categorical data, numerous variants of the a priori algorithm for finding frequent item sets and association rules are very popular [8]. Scan statistics [7,3] can be used to search for local peaks in continuous data sets. However, due to the high computational

N. Zheng, X. Jiang, and X. Lan (Eds.): IWICPAS 2006, LNCS 4153, pp. 160–167, 2006.

costs, they are not suited for high-dimensional data and are very often applied in the context of geographical clusters, for instance places with an unusually high rate of a certain disease. In [9] a statistical approach is described that tries to circumvent the high computational costs of scan statistics by restricting the search space for the price of sub-optimal solutions. In this paper, we do not follow the more statistical idea of finding regions with high densities in the data space, but clusters that are more or less well separated from the rest of the data.

Fig. 1. An example data set

Figure 1 shows an almost ideal example of a data set we consider here. It contains an almost well-separated cluster close to the top-left of the figure made of 200 data points, whereas the other 600 data points are scattered all over the data space and do not form meaningful clusters. Of course, figure 1 serves only illustration purposes, real data sets will have more than two dimensions.

The approach presented in this paper follows the concept of prototype-based cluster analysis, however, trying to find only one single cluster at a time. From the perspective of the single cluster, that we are trying to find in one step, data not belonging to this cluster is considered as noise. Therefore, we incorporate the idea of noise clustering into our approach. Section 2 provides a brief overview on the necessary background of prototype and objective function-based clustering including noise clustering. In section 3 the new approach is introduced in detail. Short comments on application scenarios are provided in section 4, before we conclude the paper with a perspective on future work.

2 Prototype- and Objective Function-Based Clustering

In prototype-based clustering clusters are described by certain parameters that determine the prototype of the cluster. In the most simple case of c-means clustering, the prototype has the same form as a data object, assuming that clusters correspond more or less to (hyper-)spheres. Nevertheless, more flexible cluster shapes can also be covered by using more sophisticated prototypes. Cluster shapes might range from ellipsoidal shapes of varying size to non-solid clusters in the form of lines, hyperplanes or shells of circles and ellipses, the latter being more interesting in the area of image analysis. In this paper, we only mention c-means prototypes for our approach. However, our approach can be easily applied to any other cluster shape that is used in prototype-based clustering. For an overview on different cluster shapes and an introduction to objective function-based clustering we refer for instance to [5].

Once the form of the prototype is chosen, the idea of most prototype-based clustering techniques is to minimize the following objective function

$$f = \sum_{i=1}^{c} \sum_{j=1}^{n} u_{ij}^m d_{ij} \qquad (1)$$

under the constraints

$$\sum_{i=1}^{c} u_{ij} = 1 \qquad \text{for all } j = 1, \ldots, n. \qquad (2)$$

It is assumed that the number of clusters c is fixed. We will not discuss the issue of determining the number of clusters here and refer for an overview to [1,5]. The set of data to be clustered is $\{x_1, \ldots, x_n\} \subset \mathbb{R}^p$. d_{ij} is some distance measure specifying the distance between datum x_j and cluster i, for instance the (quadratic) Euclidean distance of x_j to the ith cluster centre in the case of c-means clustering. u_{ij} is the membership degree of datum x_j to the ith cluster. In the case of classical deterministic clustering, we require $u_{ij} \in \{0, 1\}$. However, here we will need the more general concept of fuzzy clustering and allow $u_{ij} \in [0, 1]$. The parameter $m > 1$, called fuzzifier, controls how much fuzzy clusters may overlap. The constraints (2) lead to the name probabilistic clustering, since in this case the membership degree u_{ij} can also be interpreted as the probability that x_j belongs to cluster i.

The parameters to be optimized are the membership degrees u_{ij} and the cluster parameters that are not given explicitly here. They are hidden in the distances d_{ij}. Since this is a non-linear optimization problem, the most common approach to minimize the objective function (1) is to alternatingly optimize either the membership degrees or the cluster parameters while considering the other parameter set as fixed.

Davé [2] introduced the technique of noise clustering. Noise clustering uses the same objective function as (1). However, one of the clusters – the noise cluster – does not have any prototype parameters to be optimized. All data objects have a fixed (large) distance δ to this noise cluster. In this way, data objects that are far away from all other clusters are assigned to the noise cluster.

3 Identifying Single Clusters

As mentioned in the introduction, we are not interested in partitioning the data set, but in finding single clusters step by step. In order to find one single cluster, we adopt the idea of prototype-based clustering reviewed in the previous section.

We can simplify the notation, since we do not have to deal with c clusters, but only with two clusters: The proper cluster, we want to identify, and the noise cluster. We denote the membership degree of data object x_j to the cluster to be identified by u_j and its distance to this cluster by d_j. According to the constraint (2), the membership degree to the noise cluster is $1 - u_j$. The distance to the noise cluster is denoted by δ. We also choose $m = 2$ as the fuzzifier. This means that the objective function (1) including the constraints (2) simplifies to

$$f_1 = \sum_{j=1}^{n} u_j^2 d_j + (1 - u_j)^2 \delta^2. \tag{3}$$

The distance δ to the noise cluster influences the possible size of the single cluster, we want to identify. The larger the noise distance, the larger the single cluster can be. However, we are not able to specify δ a priori. In [6] an approach was proposed that also considers a single cluster together with a noise cluster. There, the noise distance δ is varied. Starting from a very large value δ is decreased in small steps until it reaches zero. While δ decreases, data objects are moved from the proper cluster to the noise cluster. The proper cluster is identified by analysing the fluctuation of the data from the proper cluster to the noise cluster. Although effective, this approach requires high computational costs for the repeated clustering while δ is decreasing. Also the analysis of the fluctuation of the data is not trivial.

In this paper, we try to adapt δ automatically during the clustering process. Therefore, we extend the objective function (3) by three further terms. We want our proper cluster to be well-separated from the remaining data, i.e. from the noise cluster. When the proper cluster is well separated from the noise cluster, membership degrees should tend to the values zero and one. There should be few data with intermediate values. Assuming $u_j \in [0, 1]$, the following term is maximal, if $u_j \in \{0, 1\}$ holds for all data objects j. It is minimal, if all u_j are equal to 0.5.

$$f_2 = \sum_{j=1}^{n} u_j^2 + (1 - u_j)^2 \tag{4}$$

It is also desirable, that our proper cluster is not empty and all data are assigned to the noise cluster. The term

$$f_3 = \sum_{j=1}^{n} u_j^2 \tag{5}$$

is maximised, when data objects are assigned to the proper cluster with high membership degrees.

Finally, we need an additional condition for the noise distance δ. Otherwise, if we could choose δ freely, minimizing (3) would automatically lead to $\delta = 0$. The fourth term

$$f_4 = \delta \tag{6}$$

should be maximised in order to favour larger values δ. A large δ also means that the proper cluster can be larger.

The objective function, we want to minimize for identifying the single cluster, is a linear combination of these four terms. Since only (3) should be minimized, whereas the other three should be maximised, we choose a negative coefficient for (4), (5) and (6). The overall objective function to be minimized is

$$f = \frac{a_1}{n} f_1 - \frac{a_2}{n} f_2 - \frac{a_3}{n} f_3 - a_4 f_4. \tag{7}$$

We have introduced the factor $\frac{1}{n}$ for the first three terms, in order to make the choice of the coefficients independent of the number of data. $\frac{1}{n} f_1$ is the weighted average distance, weighted by the membership degrees, of the data to the two clusters. $\frac{1}{n} f_2$ can be interpreted as an indicator of how well separated the proper cluster is from the remaining data. It can assume values between 0.5 and 1. $\frac{1}{n} f_3$ corresponds to the proportion of data in the proper cluster. The final term f_4 is already independent of the number of data.

The parameters in f to be optimized are

- the membership degrees $u_j \in [0, 1]$ ($j \in \{1, \ldots, n\}$),
- the noise distance $\delta > 0$ and
- the cluster prototype parameters that are hidden in the distances d_j.

In order to apply the alternating optimization scheme, we have to find the optimal values for each set of parameters, while the other parameters are considered as fixed.

Taking the partial derivative of f with respect to u_j leads to

$$\frac{\partial f}{\partial u_j} = 2\frac{a_1}{n} u_j d_j^2 - 2\frac{a_1}{n}\delta^2 + 2\frac{a_1}{n} u_j \delta^2 - 2\frac{a_2}{n} u_j - 2\frac{a_2}{n} u_j + 2\frac{a_2}{n} - 2\frac{a_3}{n} u_j. \tag{8}$$

For a minimum, it is necessary that the partial derivative is zero. Setting (8) to zero, we obtain

$$u_j = \frac{a_1 \delta^2 - a_2}{a_1 d_j^2 + a_1 \delta^2 - 2a_2 - a_3}. \tag{9}$$

The partial derivative of f with respect to δ is

$$\frac{\partial f}{\partial \delta} = 2\frac{a_1}{n}\delta\sum_{j=1}^{n}(1-u_j)^2 - a_4,$$

leading to

$$\delta = \frac{a_4}{2a_1\frac{1}{n}\sum_{j=1}^{n}(1-u_j)^2}. \tag{10}$$

The cluster prototype parameters occur only in the distances d_j and therefore only in the term f_1 of the objective function. Therefore, the derivation for the cluster prototype parameters is the same as for standard fuzzy clustering. In the most simple case of a fuzzy c-means prototype, the prototype is a vector $v \in \mathbb{R}^p$ like the data objects. The corresponding equation for v is then

$$v = \frac{\sum_{j=1}^{n} u_j^2 x_j}{\sum_{j=1}^{n} u_j^2}. \tag{11}$$

The four coefficients $a_1, \ldots, a_4$ determine, how much influence the corresponding terms in the objective function have. Since only the proportions between these coefficients and not their absolute values play a role in the optimization, we can choose $a_1 = 1$ without loss of generality. Therefore, equations (9) and (10) can be simplified to

$$u_j = \frac{\delta^2 - a_2}{d_j^2 + \delta^2 - 2a_2 - a_3} \tag{12}$$

and

$$\delta = \frac{a_4}{2\frac{1}{n}\sum_{j=1}^{n}(1-u_j)^2}, \tag{13}$$

respectively.

The principal algorithm to find a single cluster is then as follows:

1. Choose $a_2, a_3, a_4 \geq 0$.
2. Choose $\varepsilon > 0$ for the stop criterion.
3. Initialise v and δ (randomly or as described in section 4).
4. Update the u_j's according to equation (12).
5. Update δ according to equation (13).
6. Update v according to equation (11) (or to the corresponding equation, if other than fuzzy c-mean prototypes are considered).
7. Repeat steps 4,5,6 until v is not changed significantly anymore, i.e. until $\| v^{\text{new}} - v^{\text{old}} \| < \varepsilon$.

In step 4 we have to make sure that $0 \leq u_j \leq 1$ holds. In order to satisfy this condition, we define a lower bound for the noise distance δ. When we want the denominator in (12) to be positive, even for small distances d_j or at least for distances about $d_j = a_3$, we have to require that $\delta^2 \geq 2a_2$, i.e. $\delta \geq \sqrt{2a_2}$ holds. Therefore, we define $\delta = \sqrt{2a_2}$ in case (13) yields a value smaller than $\sqrt{2a_2}$. For very small values of d_j this might still lead to a negative denominator in (12).

It is obvious that we should choose $u_j = 1$ in these cases, i.e. assign the data object x_j fully to the very close proper cluster.

Recommendations for the choice of the parameters a_2, a_3, a_4 will be provided in the next section.

4 Application Scenarios

The main objective of identifying a single cluster is still to find the correct cluster prototype and to assign the corresponding data correctly to the cluster. Therefore, the most important term in the objective function (7) is f_1. Since we assume $a_1 = 1$, the other parameters should be chosen smaller than one. Our experiments with various data sets have shown that in most cases $a_4 \approx a_3 \approx 10a_2$ is a suitable relation between the coefficients. The crucial point is then the choice of the parameter a_2. Since this coefficient determines also the minimal noise distance, it should depend on the expected distances d_j in the data set. When we assume that the data set is normalised to the unit hyper-cube, the distance values d_j still depend on the dimension p of the data and $a_4 \approx (p \cdot 0.1)^2$ worked quite well.

In the example data set from figure 1 our algorithm is able to identify the cluster in the top left correctly, depending on the initialisation. As long as the initial cluster centre v is not too far away from the dense data cluster – the initial prototype does not have to be within the data cluster – the cluster will be identified correctly. However, when the initial prototype v is too far away from the cluster to be identified, the cluster might not be found. We cannot expect this, since our algorithm does not carry out any explicit scanning of the data set. Therefore, we recommend to carry out standard c-means clustering and use the resulting cluster centres as initialisations for our algorithm. The initial value for δ can then be based on the average distance of the data to the corresponding cluster. We have applied this technique to gene expression data and were able to identify clusters relevant from the biological point of view. Due to the limited space, we cannot discuss the details of this application here.

5 Conclusions

We have proposed an efficient approach to identify single clusters. Future work will focus on the influence of the choice of the coefficients a_2, a_3, a_4 to be chosen in our algorithm as well as on results using more complex cluster prototypes.

References

1. Bezdek, J.C., Keller, J., Krishnapuram, R., Pal, N.R.: Fuzzy Models and Algorithms for Pattern Recognition and Image Processing. Kluwer Academic Publishers, Boston, (1999)
2. Davé, R.N.: Characterization and Detection of Noise in Clustering. Pattern Recognition Letters **12** (1991) 657–664

3. Duczmal, L., Assunção, R.: A Simulated Annealing Strategy for the Detection of Arbitrarily Shaped Spatial Clusters. Computational Statistics & Data Analysis **45** (2004) 269–286
4. Georgieva, O., Klawonn, F., Härtig, E.: Fuzzy Clustering of Macroarray Data. In: Reusch, B. (ed.): Computational Intelligence, Theory and Applications. Springer-Verlag, Berlin (2005) 83–94
5. Höppner, F., Klawonn, F., Kruse, R., Runkler, T.: Fuzzy Cluster Analysis. Wiley, Chichester (1999)
6. Klawonn, F., Georgieva, O.: Identifying Single Clusters in Large Data Sets. In: Wang, J. (ed.): Encyclopedia of Data Warehousing and Mining. Idea Group, Hershey (2006) 582–585
7. Kulldorff, M.: A Spatial Scan Statistic. Communications in Statistics **26** (1997) 1481–1496
8. Zhang, C., Zhang, S.: Association Rule Mining. Springer-Verlag, Berlin (2002)
9. Zhang, Z., Hand, D.J.: Detecting Groups of Anomalously Similar Objects in Large Data Sets. In: Famili, A.F., Kook, J.N., Peña, J.M., Siebes, A. (eds.): Advances in Intelligent Data Analysis VI. Springer-Verlag, Berlin (2005) 509–519

A New Simplified Gravitational Clustering Method for Multi-prototype Learning Based on Minimum Classification Error Training

Teng Long and Lian-Wen Jin

Department of Electronic and Communication Engineering,
South China University of Technology,
510640 Guangzhou, China
{tenglong, eelwjin}@scut.edu.cn

Abstract. In this paper[1], we propose a new simplified gravitational clustering method for multi-prototype learning based on minimum classification error (MCE) training. It simulates the process of the attraction and merging of objects due to their gravity force. The procedure is simplified by not considering velocity and multi-force attraction. The proposed hierarchical method does not depend on random initialization and the results can be used as better initial centers for K-means to achieve higher performance under the SSE (sum-squared-error) criterion. The experimental results on the recognition of handwritten Chinese characters show that the proposed approach can generate better prototypes than K-means and the results obtained by MCE training can be further improved when the proposed method is employed.

1 Introduction

Many real world problems of pattern classification are non-linear separable. Multi-prototype learning and classification can solve many such problems by forming complex boundary for each class of patterns. It is especially suitable for recognition of handwritten characters because characters of one category are usually written in different styles by different people [2]. The recognition accuracy can be improved significantly when multiple prototypes are well designed and a multi-prototype minimum distance classifier is employed [1][2]. Prototype selection by hand is not guaranteed to build an optimal prototype set and it is not practical for recognition of Chinese characters of which the number of categories is more than 3,000. So it is necessary to make effort on automatic prototype learning to build optimal prototype sets for classifiers. As a well known statistical clustering technique, K-means [3] is usually used to build the multiple prototypes [2][9]. The prototypes obtained by K-means can be further fine tuned to achieve much higher recognition accuracy by some prototype learning methods such as learning vector quantization (LVQ) [4] and minimum classification

[1] The paper is sponsored by New Century Excellent Talent Program of MOE (No.NCET-05-0736), NSFGD (No.04105938).

N. Zheng, X. Jiang, and X. Lan (Eds.): IWICPAS 2006, LNCS 4153, pp. 168–175, 2006.

error (MCE) training [5][6]. The empirical rules of LVQ have not enough of a mathematical basis to guarantee design optimality and the convergence mechanism has not been mathematically elaborated [7]. The MCE training which has quite similar rules as an improved version of LVQ aims at minimizing a smooth approximation function of the error rate. It can be used to adjust the initial prototype set iteratively under the minimum classification error criterion to generate high quality prototypes [6]. However, does the selection of the initial prototype set affect the local minimum finally converged by MCE training?

In this paper, we introduce a new simplified gravitational clustering method for multi-prototype learning based on MCE training. It simulates the process of the attraction and merging of objects due to their gravity force. The procedure is simplified by not considering velocity and multi-force attraction. The proposed hierarchical clustering method does not depend on thresholds which are usually required by agglomerative hierarchical clustering and density-based clustering [11]. And it does not have random initialization problems which may lead to incorrect results in K-means algorithm. The method gives not only a reasonable clustering result but also better initial centers for K-means to achieve higher performance under SSE (sum-squared-error) criterion. It can be used to generate initial prototypes for the multi-prototype learning based on MCE. Experiments were carried out on the recognition of handwritten Chinese characters and proved the efficiency of our method. The recognition performance of the 4-prototypes template generated by the proposed hybrid method is even higher than the 8-prototypes template generated by traditional K-means method. The results also indicate that when the initial prototype set is improved by our method the fine tuned prototype set obtained by MCE training achieves better performance as well.

2 A New Simplified Gravitational Clustering

The gravitational clustering algorithm was first proposed in [10], and has been discussed in a recent paper [8]. It iteratively simulates the movement of each object due to the gravity force during a time interval and check for possible merge. As it simulates the whole physical process, the velocity of each object needs to be recalculated after each time interval based on a co-efficient of the air resistance and the vector sum of the gravity forces, which the object experiences from all other objects remaining in the physical system [8].

We simplify the process by making an assumption that if each time only one pair of objects which are likely to meet and merge first are freed to move and merged, at the same time other objects are fixed and not affected by the movement and mergence, the final clustering result can still well describe the characteristics of the spatial distribution of the objects.

The simplified gravitational clustering (SGC) is performed as follows:

Step 1. Let $\{X_1, X_2, \ldots, X_N\}$ be a set S of N objects on D dimensions. Set all objects' initial mass as:

$$m_i = 1, i = 1, 2, \ldots, N. \quad (1)$$

Step 2. Find the pair of objects which are most likely to meet and merge first by the following equation:

$$\{X_i, X_j\} \text{ } if \text{ } \{i,j\} = \arg\min_{i,j}(\|X_i - X_j\| \times \frac{m_i + m_j}{2}) \tag{2}$$

Step 3. Merge the pair of objects to generate a new object. The mass of the new object is given by:

$$m_t = m_i + m_j \tag{3}$$

And the position of the new object is the centroid of the pair of objects:

$$X_t = \frac{m_i X_i + m_j X_j}{m_i + m_j} \tag{4}$$

Step 4. Add the new object X_t to the set S and delete the objects X_i and X_j from it.

Step 5. Terminate if the number of objects in the set S reaches k which is the desired number of clusters, otherwise, go to step 2.

The final remaining objects can represent the clusters by their positions. It can be easily proved that their positions are the centroids of all the objects merged to them no matter what the merging sequence is. Thus if the cluster number k is 1, the result is the centroid of all objects which is the same as the K-means algorithm.

The eq. (2) is important which determines the merging sequence. It is defined by the assumption that heavier objects move together more slowly. This makes the cluster centers distributed more equally and avoid to get centers at the outliers because of some lonely points, which is also a drawback of the K-means algorithm. It is not the same as the traditional gravitational clustering which is based on gravity theory [8], in which heavier objects have stronger gravity forces and move together earlier than light objects at the same distance. Experiments convinced us the measurement employed in eq. (2) is a good and robust choice for clustering and multi-prototype learning as well.

Because the new object generated by the mergence is located at the centroid of all the objects merged to it, the results should be the same as the K-means algorithm if the final partition of the objects given by the SGC is the same as the partition which the K-means gives. However, the SGC method does not guarantee the SSE criterion. So it can be combined with the K-means algorithm. When the centers obtained from the SGC are used as the initial centers for the K-means, the clustering results get better under the SSE criterion. The Fig. 1 shows an example, in which the cluster centers obtained by three methods, K-means, SGC and the combined are given. From the results, it can be seen that the traditional K-means algorithm with random initialization can lead to incorrect clustering results. It is also shown that the results given by the SGC are slightly different from the K-means after combined. This leads to fewer iterations of K-means in the hybrid method.

Fig. 1. An example of the clustering results ("+" represents the centers obtained by the K-means, "×" for the SGC method and "o" for the combined)

In Fig. 2, a real world example is shown. The data points are the projection of the training samples' LDA-based features of the handwritten Chinese character "王" on the first two dimension plain. The training samples are used in the experiments in section 4. As the number of clusters is fixed, the clustering method for the prototype generation should be able to generate descriptive prototypes for the spatial distribution of the sample points while the number of clusters is not an optimal one. The example shows that with some random initialization, the K-means generate much less descriptive prototypes than the proposed method.

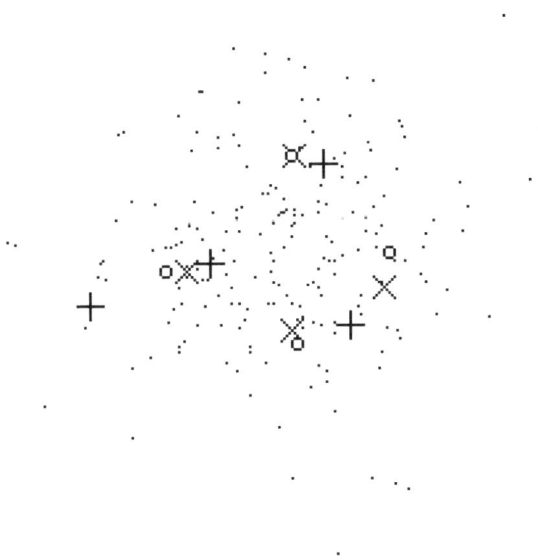

Fig. 2. A real world example of clustering results ("+" represents the centers obtained by the K-means, "×" for the SGC method and "o" for the combined)

3 Multi-prototype Learning Based on Minimum Classification Error Training

We employed the same LDA-based Gabor feature extraction as which is discussed in [6] for the recognition of handwritten Chinese characters. All the prototypes are represented by 256-dimensional LDA-based feature vectors. The clustering methods are used to generate the multi-prototype template from the training samples. In this paper, the three clustering methods, K-means, SGC and the combined method are used to generate the prototypes respectively and the performances are compared. All of them are unsupervised clustering methods.

As the prototype learning is a supervised process, the supervised clustering methods such as LVQ and MCE can achieve better performance than the unsupervised clustering methods for prototype generation. We employed the MCE training technique as the multi-prototype learning method to fine tune the prototype sets obtained from the unsupervised clustering. It is the same as [6] but the learning strategy is modified. In our MCE training, all the training samples are used to update the prototypes no matter the samples are correctly recognized or not. In our experiment, this strategy performed better than the one used in [6].

4 Experiments

Several experiments were performed on the recognition of handwritten Chinese characters. All the experiments were based on the recognition of 3755 categories of level 1 Chinese characters in GB2312-80 which is a national Chinese character set standard. We randomly selected 250 samples for each category from the China 863 National Handwriting Database HCL2000. 200 samples among them were used as training set and other 50 samples formed the testing set, i.e. 751,000 samples for train-ing and 187,750 samples for testing in total.

In the first experiment, we tested the recognition performance on the templates of different number of prototypes generated by different clustering methods. The processing time was about 40, 175 and 200 seconds for the K-means, SGC and the combined method respectively when building the 4-prototypes template using the C++ programming language compiled program. The computation environment was on a PC with an Intel P4 3.0G CPU and 512M memory. The curves of the results are shown in Fig. 3. The results show it clearly that the multi-prototype classifier is much better than the single-prototype one. The recognition accuracy can be improved more than 2 percent by using an 8-prototypes template generated by the proposed method. They also indicate that by using the combined clustering method, the performance of 4-prototypes template is even better than which of 8-prototypes template generated by the traditional K-means method.

In the second experiment, we tried to find out how the performance is affected by the different tries of random initial points for K-means algorithm. The recognition results are listed in Table 1. By choosing the best result of 8-prototypes template obtained by K-means, the recognition rate of 90.21% is still lower than the rate of 4-prototypes template generated by the combined method, which is 90.22%. This indicates that not only the storage of the templates but also the recognition time can be saved 50% to achieve the same performance by using the proposed hybrid method.

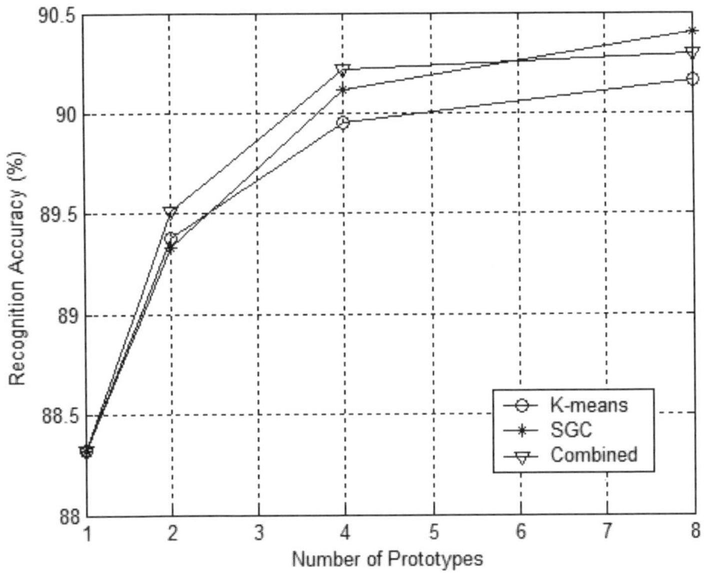

Fig. 3. Recognition performance of the different number of prototypes templates generated by the different clustering methods

Table 1. Recognition accuracy (%) of using K-Means with 10 different random initializations

Number of prototypes	Recognition accuracy by 10 different random initializations	Mean
4	89.94, 90.00, 89.97, 90.00, 89.91, 90.04, 89.96, 89.96, 89.96, 89.95	89.97
8	90.18, 90.18, 90.15, 90.19, 90.20, 90.10, 90.21, 90.20, 90.14, 90.17	90.17

In the third experiment, the MCE training was performed to fine tune the 4-prototypes template. Fig. 4 shows the learning curves for MCE training on open-test. It indicates that the recognition rate can be improved another 2 percent by using the MCE training. It also shows that the local minimum converged by MCE training can be improved by choosing a better initial prototype set. From the figure, it seems that the prototype sets obtained by the SGC and the combined method converged to the same local minimum even the performances of them are different at the beginning.

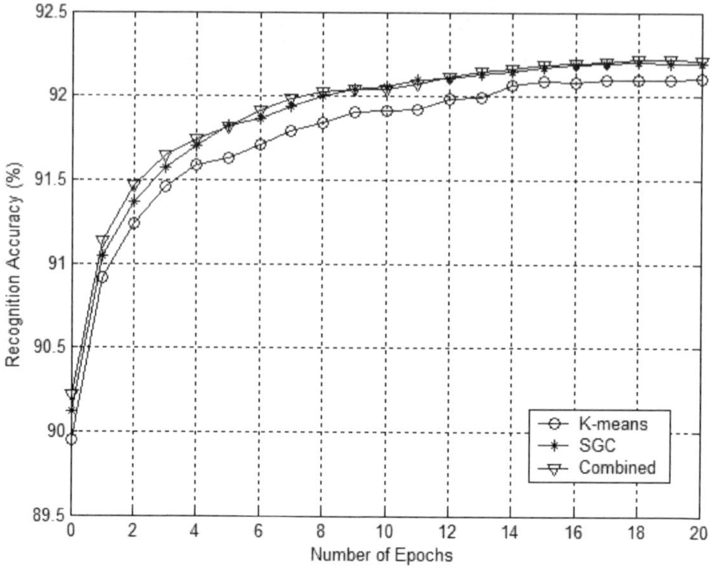

Fig. 4. Learning curves for MCE training on open-test: recognition accuracies (%) as a function of epoch number by the different initial templates obtained by the different clustering methods

5 Conclusion

In this paper, we have introduced a new simplified gravitational clustering method for multi-prototype learning based on MCE training. It's a hierarchical agglomerative clustering method which does not depend on thresholds or random initialization. The main idea is to find equally distributed centers to better describe the spatial distribution of the sample data by using a modified distance. The results of the proposed method can be used as the initial centers for K-means to achieve higher performance under the SSE criterion. Experiments on the recognition of handwritten Chinese characters proved the efficiency of the proposed method. As the number of the prototypes can be reduced to achieve the same performance, the proposed technique saves not only the storage of the templates but also the computation time of the recognition. The experiments also showed us an interesting result that the prototypes obtained by MCE training can be further improved by choosing a better initial prototype set.

References

1. Liu, C.-L., Jaeger, S., and Nakagawa, M.: Online Recognition of Chinese Characters: The State-of-the-Art. IEEE Trans. on Pattern Analysis and Machine Intelligence, Vol. 26, No. 2, (2004) 198–213

2. Rahman, A.F.R., Fairhurst, M.C.: Multi-prototype Classification: Improved Modeling of the Variability of Handwritten Data using Statistical Clustering Algorithms. Electronics Letters, Vol. 33, No. 14, (1997) 1208–1210
3. Kanungo, T., et al: An Efficient k-Means Clustering Algorithm: Analysis and Implementation. IEEE Trans. on Pattern Analysis and Machine Intelligence, Vol. 24, No. 7, (2002) 881–892
4. Kohonen, T.: The Self-Organizing Map. IEEE Proceedings, Vol. 78, No. 9, (1990) 1464–1480
5. Juang, B.-H. and Katagiri, S.: Discriminative Learning for Minimum Error Classification. IEEE Trans. on Signal Processing, Vol. 40, (1992) 3043–3054
6. Huo, Q., Ge, Y., Feng, Z.-D.: High Performance Chinese OCR Based on Gabor Features, Discriminative Feature Extraction and Model Training. Proc. ICASSP 2001, Vol. 3, (2001) 1517–1520
7. Katagiri, S., Juang, B.-H., Lee, C.-H.: Pattern Recognition Using a Family of Design Algorithms Based Upon the Generalized Probabilistic Descent Method. IEEE Proceedings, Vol. 86, No. 11, (1998) 2345–2373
8. Chena, C.-Y., Hwanga, S.-C., Oyanga, Y.-J.: A statistics-based approach to control the quality of subclusters in incremental gravitational clustering. Pattern Recognition, Vol. 38, (2005) 2256–2269
9. Wang, Q., et al: Match between Normalization Schemes and Feature Sets for Handwritten Chinese Character Recognition. Proc. ICDAR 2001, (2001) 551–555
10. Wright, W.E.: Gravitational Clustering. Pattern Recognition, Vol. 9 (1997) 1149–1160
11. Berkhin, P.: Survey of Clustering Data Mining Techniques. Technical Report, Accrue. Software Inc., San Jose, CA, USA, 2002

Speaker Identification and Verification Using Support Vector Machines and Sparse Kernel Logistic Regression

Marcel Katz, Sven E. Krüger, Martin Schafföner, Edin Andelic, and Andreas Wendemuth

IESK, Cognitive Systems
University of Magdeburg, Germany
marcel.katz@e-technik.uni-magdeburg.de

Abstract. In this paper we investigate two discriminative classification approaches for frame-based speaker identification and verification, namely Support Vector Machine (SVM) and Sparse Kernel Logistic Regression (SKLR). SVMs have already shown good results in regression and classification in several fields of pattern recognition as well as in continuous speech recognition. While the non-probabilistic output of the SVM has to be translated into conditional probabilities, the SKLR produces the probabilities directly.

In speaker identification and verification experiments both discriminative classification methods outperform the standard Gaussian Mixture Model (GMM) system on the POLYCOST database.

1 Introduction

The use of speaker recognition and its applications is already widespread, e.g. access to a private area or in telephone banking systems, where it is important to verify that the person prompting the credit card number is the owner of the card.

The field of speaker recognition can be divided into two tasks, namely *speaker identification* and *speaker verification*. The speaker identification task consists of a set of known speakers or *clients* (closed-set) and the problem is to decide which person from the set is talking.

In speaker verification the recognition system has to verify if a person is the one he claims to be (open-set). So the main difficulty in this setup is that the system has to deal with known and unknown speakers, so-called *clients* and *impostors* respectively.

In speech and speaker recognition Gaussian mixtures are usually a good choice in modeling the distribution of the speech samples both in continuous speech recognition with multi-state left-to-right *Hidden Markov Models* (HMMs) and for text-independent approaches with single-state HMMs [1]. It has to be noted that good performance of GMMs depends on a sufficient amount of data for the parameter estimation. In speaker recognition the amount of speech data of

N. Zheng, X. Jiang, and X. Lan (Eds.): IWICPAS 2006, LNCS 4153, pp. 176–184, 2006.

each client is limited. Normally, only a few seconds of speech are available and so the parameter estimation might not be very robust. Especially if the data is limited, SVMs show a great ability of generalization and a better classification performance than GMMs. Also, in continuous speech recognition SVMs were integrated into HMMs to model the acoustic feature vectors [2].

There have been several approaches of integrating SVMs into speaker verification environments. One method is not to discriminate between frames but between entire utterances. These utterances have different lengths and so a mapping from a variable length pattern to a fixed size vector is needed. Several methods like the *Fisher-kernel* [3] map the resulting score-sequences of the GMMs into a high dimensional *score-space* where a SVM is then used to classify the data in a second step, e.g. [4].

2 GMM Based Speaker Recognition

In the past several years there has been a lot of progress in the field of speaker recognition [5][1]. State of the art systems are based on modeling a speaker-independent *universal background model* (UBM) which is trained on the speech of a large number of different speakers. For each client of the system a speaker-dependent GMM is then derived from the background model by adapting the parameters of the UBM using a *maximum a posteriori* (MAP) approach [6].

The GMM is the weighted sum of M component Gaussian densities given by:

$$p(\mathbf{x}|\lambda) = \sum_{i=1}^{M} c_i \, \mathcal{N}(\mathbf{x}|\boldsymbol{\mu}_i, \boldsymbol{\Sigma}_i) \tag{1}$$

where c_i is the weight of the i'th component and $\mathcal{N}(\mathbf{x}|\boldsymbol{\mu}_i, \boldsymbol{\Sigma}_i)$ is a multivariate Gaussian with mean vector $\boldsymbol{\mu}_i$ and the covariance matrix $\boldsymbol{\Sigma}_i$.

The mixture model is trained using standard methods like the *Expectation Maximization* (EM) algorithm. Finally the probability that a test-sentence $\mathbf{X} = \{\mathbf{x}_1, ..., \mathbf{x}_N\}$ is generated by the specific speaker model λ is calculated by the log-likelihood over the whole sequence:

$$\log P(\mathbf{X}|\lambda) = \sum_{i=1}^{N} \log P(\mathbf{x}_i|\lambda). \tag{2}$$

Given a set of speakers the task of speaker identification is to deduce the most likely client C from a given speech sequence:

$$\hat{C}_k = \operatorname*{argmax}_k P(\mathbf{X}|\lambda_k). \tag{3}$$

In the case of speaker verification the decision of accepting a client is usually based on the ratio between the summed log likelihoods of the specific speaker models and the background model. Defining the probability $P(\mathbf{X}|\lambda_k)$ as the probability of client C_k producing the sentence $\mathbf{X}$ and $P(\mathbf{X}|\boldsymbol{\Omega})$ as the probability of the background model, the client is accepted if the ratio is above a speaker-independent threshold δ:

$$\log \frac{P(\mathbf{X}|\lambda_k)}{P(\mathbf{X}|\mathbf{\Omega})} > \delta. \tag{4}$$

This results in two possible error rates, the first one is the *false-reject* (FR) error rate ($P_{Reject|Target}$): the speaker is the claimed client but the likelihood-ratio of equation (4) is lower than the threshold. The second error rate is the *false-accept* (FA) error rate: the speaker is not the claimed one but the likelihood-ratio is higher than δ and the speaker is accepted ($P_{Accept|NonTarget}$).

For the performance measure of a speaker verification system the *decision cost function* (DCF) is given. The DCF is defined as a weighted sum of the FR and the FA probabilities:

$$\begin{aligned} C_{det} = \; & C_{FR} \times P_{Reject|Target} \times P_{Target} \\ & + C_{FA} \times P_{Accept|NonTarget} \times (P_{NonTarget}) \end{aligned} \tag{5}$$

with the predefined weights C_{FR}, C_{FA} and prior probabilities P_{Target}, $P_{NonTarget} = 1 - P_{Target}$.

3 Support Vector Machines

Support Vector Machines (SVM) were first introduced by Vapnik and developed from the theory of *Structural Risk Minimization* (SRM) [7]. We now give a short overview of SVMs and refer to [8] for more details and further references. SVMs are linear classifiers that can be generalized to non-linear classification by the so-called *kernel trick*. Instead of applying the linear methods directly to the input space $\mathbb{R}^d$, they are applied to a higher dimensional *feature space* $\mathcal{F}$ which is nonlinearly related to the input space via the mapping $\Phi : \mathbb{R}^d \to \mathcal{F}$. Instead of computing the dot-product in $\mathcal{F}$ explicitly, a *kernel function* $k(\mathbf{x}_i, \mathbf{x}_j)$ satisfying Mercer's conditions is used to compute the dot-product. A possible kernel function is the Gaussian *radial basis function* (RBF) kernel:

$$k(\mathbf{x}_i, \mathbf{x}_j) = \exp\left(\frac{-\|\mathbf{x}_i - \mathbf{x}_j\|^2}{2\sigma^2}\right). \tag{6}$$

Suppose we have a training set of input samples $\mathbf{x} \in \mathbb{R}^d$ and corresponding targets $y \in \{1, -1\}$.The SVM tries to find an optimal separating hyperplane in $\mathcal{F}$ by solving the quadratic programming problem:

$$W(\alpha) = \sum_{i=1}^{N} \alpha_i - \frac{1}{2} \sum_{i=1}^{N} \sum_{j=1}^{N} \alpha_i \alpha_j y_i y_j k(\mathbf{x}_i, \mathbf{x}_j) \tag{7}$$

under the constraints $\sum_{i=1}^{N} \alpha_i y_i = 0$ and $0 < \alpha_i < C \; \forall i$. The parameter C allows us to specify how strictly we want the classifier to fit to the training data.

The output of the SVM is a distance measure between a pattern and the decision boundary:

$$f(\mathbf{x}) = \sum_{i=1}^{N} \boldsymbol{\alpha}_i k(\mathbf{x}_i, \mathbf{x}) + b \tag{8}$$

where the pattern $\mathbf{x}$ is assigned to the positive class if $f(\mathbf{x}) > 0$. For the posterior class probability we have to model the distributions $P(f|y = +1)$ and $P(f|y = -1)$ of $f(x)$ computing the probability of the class given the output by using Bayes' rule [9] :

$$P(y = +1|\mathbf{x}) = g(f(\mathbf{x}), A, B) = \frac{1}{1 + \exp(Af(x) + B)} \tag{9}$$

where the parameters A and B can be calculated by a maximum likelihood estimation [9].

4 Sparse Kernel Logistic Regression

Considering again a binary classification problem with targets $y \in \{0, 1\}$, the success probability of the sample $\mathbf{x}$ belonging to class 1 is given by $P(y = 1|\mathbf{x})$ and $P(y = 0|\mathbf{x}) = 1 - P(y = 1|\mathbf{x})$ that it belongs to class 0.

In Kernel Logistic Regression we want to model the posterior probability of the class membership via equation (8). Interpreting the output of $f(\mathbf{x})$ as an estimate of a probability $p(\mathbf{x}, \boldsymbol{\alpha})$ we have to rearrange equation (8) by the *logit* transfer function

$$logit\{P(\mathbf{x}, \boldsymbol{\alpha})\} = \log \frac{P(\mathbf{x}, \boldsymbol{\alpha})}{1 - P(\mathbf{x}, \boldsymbol{\alpha})} = f(\mathbf{x}) \tag{10}$$

which results in the probability:

$$P(\mathbf{x}, \boldsymbol{\alpha}) = \frac{1}{1 + \exp(-f(\mathbf{x}))}. \tag{11}$$

If we assume that the training data is drawn from a Bernoulli distribution conditioned on the samples $\mathbf{x}$, the negative log-likelihood (NLL) $l\{\boldsymbol{\alpha}\}$ of the conditioned probability $P(y|\mathbf{x}, \boldsymbol{\alpha})$ can be written as

$$\begin{aligned} l\{\boldsymbol{\alpha}\} = &- \sum_{i=1}^{N} y_i f(\mathbf{x}_i) - \log\left(1 + \exp(f(\mathbf{x}_i))\right) \\ &+ \frac{\lambda}{2} \|f\|^2 \end{aligned} \tag{12}$$

with the ridge-penalty $\frac{\lambda}{2}\|f\|^2 = \boldsymbol{\alpha}^T \mathbf{K} \boldsymbol{\alpha}$ to avoid over-fitting to the training data [10]. $\mathbf{K}$ is defined as the kernel matrix with entries $\mathbf{K}_{ij} = k(\mathbf{x}_i, \mathbf{x})$. To minimize the regularized NLL we set the derivatives $\frac{\partial l\{\boldsymbol{\alpha}\}}{\partial \alpha}$ to zero and use the

Newton-Raphson algorithm to iteratively solve equation (12). This algorithm is also referred to as *iteratively re-weighted least square* (IRLS), e.g. [11]:

$$\boldsymbol{\alpha}^{new} = \left(\mathbf{K} + \lambda \mathbf{W}^{-1}\right)^{-1} \mathbf{z} \tag{13}$$

with the *adjusted response*

$$\mathbf{z} = \left(\mathbf{K}\boldsymbol{\alpha}^{old} + \mathbf{W}^{-1}(\mathbf{y} - \mathbf{p})\right) \tag{14}$$

where $\mathbf{p}$ is the vector of fitted probabilities with the i'th element $P(\boldsymbol{\alpha}^{old}, \mathbf{x}_i)$ and $\mathbf{W}$ is the $N \times N$ weight matrix with entries $P(\boldsymbol{\alpha}^{old}, \mathbf{x}_i)(1 - P(\boldsymbol{\alpha}^{old}, \mathbf{x}_i))$ on the diagonal.

A sparse solution can be achieved if we involve only basis functions corresponding to a subset S of the training set $\mathcal{R}$:

$$f(\mathbf{x}) = \sum_{i=1}^{q} \boldsymbol{\alpha}_i k(\mathbf{x}_i, \mathbf{x}) \quad q \ll N \tag{15}$$

with q training samples. If we apply equation (15) instead of (8) in the IRLS algorithm we get the following sparse formulation:

$$\boldsymbol{\alpha}^{new} = \left(\mathbf{K}_{Nq}^{T} \mathbf{W} \mathbf{K}_{Nq} + \lambda \mathbf{K}_{qq}\right)^{-1} \mathbf{K}_{Nq}^{T} \mathbf{W} \tilde{\mathbf{z}} \tag{16}$$

with $\tilde{\mathbf{z}} = \left(\mathbf{K}_{Nq}\boldsymbol{\alpha}^{old} + \mathbf{W}^{-1}(\mathbf{y} - \mathbf{p})\right)$, the $N \times q$ matrix $\mathbf{K}_{Nq} = k(\mathbf{x}_i, \mathbf{x}_j); \mathbf{x}_i \in \mathcal{R}, \mathbf{x}_j \in S$ and the $q \times q$ regularization matrix $\mathbf{K}_{qq} = k(\mathbf{x}_i, \mathbf{x}_j); \mathbf{x}_i, \mathbf{x}_j \in S$.

This sparse variant was introduced by [11]. The SKLR aims to minimize the NLL iteratively by adding training samples to a subset S of selected training vectors until the algorithm converges to some value. Starting with an empty subset we have to minimize the NLL for each $\mathbf{x}_l \in \mathcal{R}$ of the training set:

$$\begin{aligned} l\{\mathbf{x}_l\} = & -\mathbf{y}^T(\mathbf{K}_{Nq}^{l}\boldsymbol{\alpha}^{l}) + \mathbf{1}^T \log(1 + \exp(\mathbf{K}_{Nq}^{l}\boldsymbol{\alpha}^{l})) \\ & + \frac{\lambda}{2} \boldsymbol{\alpha}^{l^T} \mathbf{K}_{qq}^{l} \boldsymbol{\alpha}^{l} \end{aligned} \tag{17}$$

with the $N \times (q+1)$ matrix $\mathbf{K}_{Nq}^{l} = k(\mathbf{x}_i, \mathbf{x}_j); \mathbf{x}_i \in \mathcal{R}, \mathbf{x}_j \in S \cup \{\mathbf{x}_l\}$ and the $(q+1) \times (q+1)$ regularization matrix $\mathbf{K}_{qq}^{l} = k(\mathbf{x}_i, \mathbf{x}_j); \mathbf{x}_i, \mathbf{x}_j \in S \cup \{\mathbf{x}_l\}$. Then we add the vector for which we get the highest decrease in NLL to the subset:

$$\mathbf{x}_l^{*} = \underset{\mathbf{x}_l \in \mathcal{R}}{\operatorname{argmin}}\, l\{\mathbf{x}_l\}. \tag{18}$$

While in the original Newton-Raphson algorithm we iteratively estimate the parameter $\boldsymbol{\alpha}$ applying the IRLS algorithm we can use a one step approximation here [11]. In each step we approximate the new $\boldsymbol{\alpha}$ with the fitted result from the current subset S which we estimated in the previous minimization process.

5 Multi-class Problems

Naturally, kernel logistic regression could be extended to multi-class problems. But for comparison with binary classifiers like the SVM we decided to use a common one-versus-one approach where $C(C-1)/2$ classifiers learn pairwise decision rules [12], which is easier than solving C large problems. The pairwise probabilities $\mu_{ij} \equiv P(q_i|q_i \text{or} q_j, \mathbf{x})$ of a class q_i given a sample vector $\mathbf{x}$ belonging to either q_i or q_j are transformed to the posterior probability $P(q_i|\mathbf{x})$ by [13]:

$$P(q_i|\mathbf{x}) = 1/\left(\sum_{j=1,j\neq i}^{C} \frac{1}{\mu_{ij}} - (C-2)\right). \tag{19}$$

6 Experiments

For all experiments we used the POLYCOST dataset [14]. This dataset contains 110 speakers (63 females and 47 males) from different European countries. The dataset is divided into 4 baseline experiments (BE1-BE4), from which we used the text-independent set BE4 for speaker identification and the text-dependent set BE1 for the speaker verification experiments.

In the feature extraction the speech data is divided into frames of 25ms at a frame rate of 10ms and a voiced/unvoiced decision is obtained using a pitch detection algorithm. Only the voiced speech is then parameterized using 12 Mel-Cepstrum coefficients as well as the frame-energy. The first and the second order derivatives are added, resulting in feature vectors of 39 dimensions. The parameters of the baseline GMM models were estimated using the HTK toolkit [15].

For the identification experiments we used 2 sentences of each speaker for the training and 2 sentences as development test set. The evaluation set contains up to 5 sentences per speaker, all in all 664 true identity tests. From every speaker there is a total amount of only 10 to 20 seconds of free speech for the training and about 5 seconds per speaker for the evaluation. The parameters of the different classifiers were validated on the development set.

Table 1. Speaker Identification experiments on the POLYCOST database using different classification methods

Classifier	IER (%)
GMM	10.84
SVM	8.89
SKLR	8.58

The utterances are classified to that speaker with the highest speaker-model score defined in equation (3). Because of the fact that all speakers are known to the system, the error rate is simply computed as *Identification Error Rate*

(IER). As can be seen in table 1, both the SVM and the SKLR classifiers clearly outperform the GMM baseline system. The SKLR classifier decreases the IER of the baseline system by about 20.8% relatively.

In the verification experiments the sentence "Joe took father's green shoe bench out" is given as a fixed password sentence shared by all clients. The classifiers are trained on 4 sentences of each speaker. We used the same parameters as in the identification experiments. For the GMM environment a

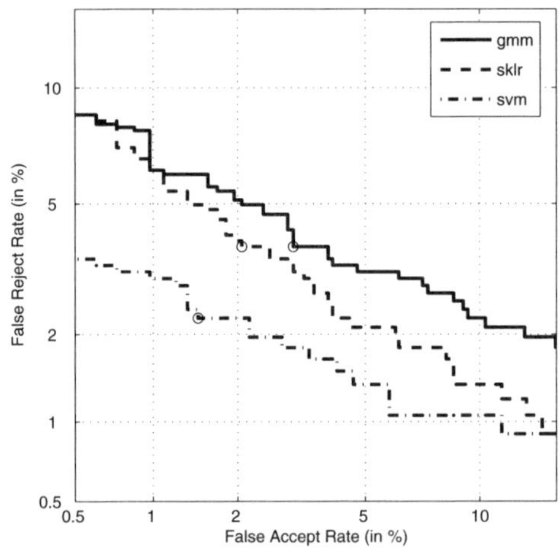

Fig. 1. DET curves for the three systems on the POLYCOST-BE1 verification task

gender-independent background model is trained by 22 non-client speakers from the POLYCOST database. The evaluation test consists of 664 true client tests and 824 impostor trials. The results of the three classifiers are given in figure 1 as *detection error tradeoff* (DET) plot. The DET shows the tradeoff between *false-rejects* (FR) and *false-accepts* (FA) as a decision threshold [16].

Additionally we report the *Equal Error Rate* (EER) and the DCF as performance measure in table 2. The parameters of the cost function used in the experiments are $C_{FR} = 10$, $C_{FA} = 1$ and $P_{Target} = 0.01$. As one can see in the table, the DCF of the evaluation test is reduced from 0.034 of the GMM baseline system to 0.019 of the SVM system.

Table 2. Comparison of the EER and the DCF for three systems on the POLYCOST-BE1 speaker verification task

Classifier	EER (%)	DCF
GMM	4.09	0.034
SVM	2.16	0.019
SKLR	3.31	0.029

While the SVM clearly outperforms the GMM baseline, the SKLR performs only slightly better than the GMM system. This might be due to the fact that there was no special parameter estimation on the verification task and so the SVM exhibits a better generalization performance than the SKLR.

7 Conclusion

In this paper we presented two discriminative methods for frame-based speaker identification and verification. Both methods outperform the GMM baseline in the speaker recognition experiments. Because the decision process depends directly on the discrimination of the different speaker models there is no need for a score normalization by a background model. The advantage of the SKLR is that it directly models the posterior probability of the class membership.

The main drawback of the discriminative classification methods is the time and memory consuming parameter estimation, so that it is not possible to use larger datasets directly. One idea is not to use a multi-class method like the one-versus-all or one-versus-one approach of section 5 but to use a fixed set of background speakers. The speech sentences are then classified in a one-versus-background approach which is computational more effective if the background set is not to large.

In our future research we will extend the verification system to larger datasets and different speech conditions, like telephone and cellular speech.

References

1. D. Reynolds, "An overview of automatic speaker recognition technology," in *Proc. IEEE International Conference on Acoustics, Speech, and Signal Processing*, vol. 4, 2002, pp. 4072–4075.
2. S. E. Krüger, M. Schafföner, M. Katz, E. Andelic, and A. Wendemuth, "Speech recognition with support vector machines in a hybrid system," in *Proc. EuroSpeech*, 2005, pp. 993–996.
3. T. Jaakkola and D. Haussler, "Exploiting generative models in discriminative classifiers," in *Advances in Neural Information Processing Systems*, M. Kearns, S. Solla, and D. Cohn, Eds., vol. 11. Cambridge, MA, USA: MIT Press, 1999, pp. 487–493.
4. V. Wan and S. Renals, "Speaker verification using sequence discriminant support vector machines," *IEEE Transactions on Speech and Audio Processing*, vol. 13, no. 2, pp. 203–210, 2005.
5. M. Przybocki and A. Martin, "NIST speaker recognition evaluation chronicles," in *Proceedings of ODYSSEY - The Speaker and Language Recognition Workshop*, 2004.
6. D. Reynolds, T. Quatieri, and R. Dunn, "Speaker verification using adapted gaussian mixture models," *Digital Signal Processing*, vol. 10, pp. 19–41, 2000.
7. V. N. Vapnik, *The Nature of Statistical Learning Theory*, 2nd ed., ser. Information Science and Statistics. Berlin: Springer, 2000.
8. C. Burges, "A tutorial on support vector machines for pattern recognition," *Data Mining and Knowledge Discovery*, vol. 2, no. 2, pp. 121–167, jun 1998.

9. J. Platt, "Probabilistic outputs for support vector machines and comparisons to regularized likelihood methods," in *Advances in Large-Margin Classifiers*, P. Bartlett, B. Schölkopf, D. Schuurmans, and A. Smola, Eds. Cambridge, MA, USA: MIT Press, oct 2000, pp. 61–74. [Online]. Available: http://research.microsoft.com/~jplatt/abstracts/SVprob.html
10. A. Hoerl and R. Kennard, "Ridge regression: Biased estimation for nonorthogonal problems," *Technometrics*, vol. 12, pp. 55–67, 1970.
11. J. Zhu and T. Hastie, "Kernel logistic regression and the import vector machine," *Journal of Computational and Graphical Statistics*, vol. 14, pp. 185–205, 2005.
12. T. Hastie and R. Tibshirani, "Classification by pairwise coupling," in *Advances in Neural Information Processing Systems 10*, M. I. Jordan, M. J. Kearns, and S. A. Solla, Eds. Cambridge, MA, USA: MIT Press, jun 1998.
13. D. Price, S. Knerr, L. Personnaz, and G. Dreyfus, "Pairwise neural network classifiers with probabilistic outputs," in *Advances in Neural Information Processing Systems 7*, G. Tesauro, D. Touretzky, and T. Leen, Eds. Cambridge, MA, USA: MIT Press, 7 1995, pp. 1109–1116.
14. H. Melin and J. Lindberg, "Guidelines for experiments on the polycost database," in *Proceedings of a COST 250 workshop on Application of Speaker Recognition Techniques in Telephony*, Vigo, Spain, 1996, pp. 59–69.
15. S. Young, G. Evermann, D. Kershaw, G. Moore, J. Odell, D. Ollason, D. Povey, V. Valtchev, and P. Woodland, *The HTK Book*, Cambridge University Engineering Department, 2002.
16. A. Martin, G. Doddington, T. Kamm, M. Ordowski, and M. Przybocki, "The det curve in assessment of detection task performance," *Proc. EuroSpeech*, vol. 4, pp. 1895–1898, 1997.

Monitoring Abnormal Patterns with Complex Semantics over ICU Data Streams*

Xinbiao Zhou, Hongyan Li**, Haibin Liu,
Meimei Li, Lvan Tang, Yu Fan, and Zijing Hu

National Laboratory on Machine Perception,
School of Electronics Engineering and Computer Science,
Peking University, 100871, P.R. China
{zhouxb, lihy, liuhaibin, limm, tangla, efan, huzijing}@cis.pku.edu.cn

Abstract. Monitoring abnormal patterns in data streams is an important research area for many applications. In this paper we present a new approach MAPS(Monitoring Abnormal Patterns over data Streams) to model and identify the abnormal patterns over the massive data streams. Compared with other data streams, ICU streaming data have their own features: pseudo-periodicity and polymorphism. MAPS first extracts patterns from the online arriving data streams and then normalizes them according to their pseudo-periodic semantics. Abnormal patterns will be detected if they are satisfied the predicates defined in the clinician-specifying normal patterns. At last, a real application demonstrates that MAPS is efficient and effective in several important aspects.

1 Introduction

Nowadays, many applications generate data streams and an increasing need is arising to distinguish different status on the fly such as normal and abnormal, for instance, network intrusion detection, and telecommunication fraud detection. Static data sets could be considered to be a fixed process such as normal distribution, however a data stream has a temporal dimension, and it's necessary to spot the potential abnormities over time for further inspection. Thus monitoring abnormal patterns is an important area in data stream settings and has received considerable attention in various communities[1][2][3][4][19][20].

1.1 Goals and Challenges

Medical data monitoring is an important application area of data stream; the ICU(Intensive Care Unit) is equipped with many advanced machines from all kinds of vital sign monitoring equipment to life support equipments. Those equipments dynamically measure the patient's physiological functions continuously,

* This work is supported by Natural Science Foundation of China(NSFC) under grant number 60473072.

** Hongyan Li is the corresponding author.

N. Zheng, X. Jiang, and X. Lan (Eds.): IWICPAS 2006, LNCS 4153, pp. 185–194, 2006.

and generate a large amount of data streams, what the clinicians may have difficulties in getting information from the data stream, not only may the amount of information available be greater than can be assimilated, but the clinical environment provides distractions with other tasks, still worse, current monitors flood clinicians with false alarms, providing further unnecessary distraction. Therefore detecting anomalies in the data streams is urgently needed, the changes represent the patients status, and the aim of this paper is to support the abnormal pattern semantics and improving the treating quality. There are three major

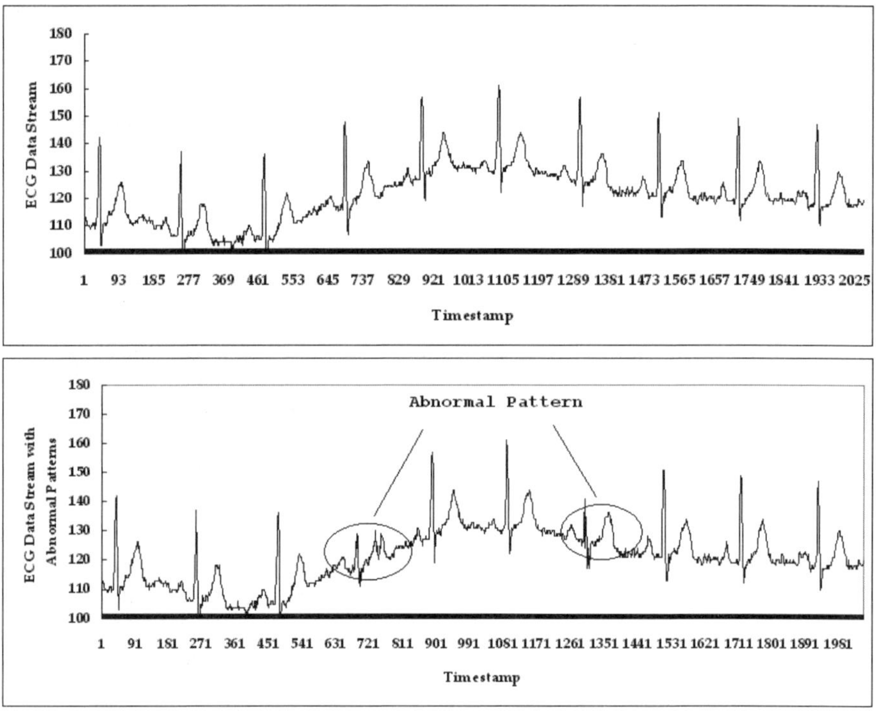

Fig. 1. ECG Data streams

challenges to fulfill the tasks we declare above:

- The ICU data streams which output in a high-frequency often involves stochastic process. This feature greatly complicates the problem of modeling and prediction. Previous methods often become fruitless when they encounter such a situation;
- Data streams in the ICU environment always contains pseudo-periodic data in which outliers exists, which also increase the difficulty in monitoring abnormal patterns;

- Another striking feature of ICU data streams is polymorphism:For a specific application, the data stream has certain semantics[4], but the changes of the same kind of streams may have different semantics. In ICU data streams, the changes of streams have diverse semantics for different patients or diseases.

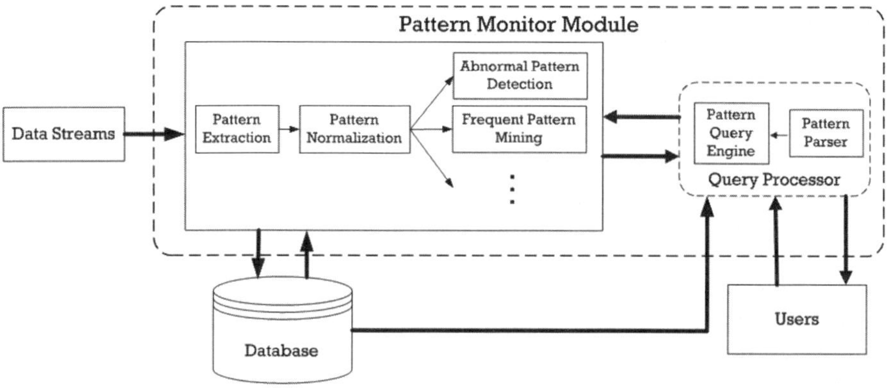

Fig. 2. Overview of the Pattern Monitor Module in DESC

1.2 Our Contributions

We have implemented a patient-based prototype information system from the perspective of clinicians – Data Stream Engine based Clinical information system[6] [7](DSEC). DSEC consists of 6 modules: preprocessing, data queue, query network, load shedder, pattern monitor and query output. Figure.2 depicts the overview of the pattern monitor module in our system. Our implementation introduces a new model of pseudo-periodic streams and presents a new algorithm— to spot the abnormities occurring in data streams. Real application cases show that MAPS do a good work while dealing with pseudo-periodic and polymorphic data streams.

1.3 Paper Outlines

The outline of this paper is as follows: In section 2 we discuss the related work on abnormal pattern monitoring in data stream environment. Section 3 presents the pseudo-periodic model we apply to process the data streams. Section 4 gives the implementation of our algorithm in detail and analysis the complexity of the algorithm. The application of our method in several aspects are presented in Section 5. At last, Section 6 summarizes the whole paper and discusses the future work.

2 Related Work

Detection of changes in data stream has been discussed in [16], the proposed method provides meaningful description and quantification of these changes, and on the assume, the method provide statistical guarantees on the reliability of detected changes and also provide quantification and descriptions of the changes, but the method is based on the assumption that the points in the streams are independently generated, and the description of changes only is meaningful in statistics, and our method detect the change with semantics for specific application.

MAIDS[14] is a general-purpose tool for data stream analysis and is designed to process high rate and multi-dimensional stream data. MAIDS adopts a flexible tilted time window framework throughout all of the functional modules. The pattern monitoring module, *StreamPatternFinder*, has been constructed to discover frequent patterns and sequential patterns. The underlying algorithm essentially adopts the extended frequent pattern growth approach which discovers frequent patterns for the interested sets of items specified by users. However, the main idea of counting approximate frequent pairs in MAIDS can't easily handle the continuous semantics in high-frequent data streams, because monitoring abnormal patterns by summing up its frequency is a relative long-term process and not feasible in ICU environment.

Lilian Harada[13] proposed an improved method base on the IBM string matching algorithm. It efficiently detect some complex temporal patterns over data streams. The method scans the data stream with a sliding window and checks the data inside the window to see if they satisfy the pattern predicates. But it only fit for discrete data, which changes relatively slow.

Researches on specific data stream focus on financial applications, Huanmei Wu[17] proposes a 3-tier online segmentation and pruning algorithm according to the stock market's zigzag shape, and defines an alternative similarity subsequence measure, it also introduces the event-driven online similarity matching to reduce system burden, but it only considers single stream. StatStream[5] treats pair-wise correlated statistics in an online fashion, focusing on similarity for whole streams, not on subsequence similarity, and the weight of different stream subsequence is not considered.

Our work differs from previous research in several aspects. The problem addressed here is application driven, and we focus on the abnormity detection to support some aspects in the complex intrinsic semantics of the stream[4]. And the existing techniques similarity matching do not address appropriately the special concerns in abnormity detection in support of semantics.

3 Pseudo-periodicity Semantics in ICU Data Streams

The ICU data streams often exhibit great regularity without exactly repeating. For example, heartbeats always have the characteristic lub-dub pattern which occurs again and again, yet each recurrence differs slightly from each other. Some beats are faster, some slower, some are stronger and some weaker. Sometimes a beat may be missed due to several reasons. Nonetheless, the overriding regularity of the heartbeat is its most striking feature. Our method models such near repetition using the idea of pseudo-functions.

Definition 1. *A data stream is an ordered sequence of records with a timestamp:* $\{(s[0], t_0),(s[1], t_1), \ldots\}$*, where each of* $s[i]$ *can have* z *attributes* $a[0], \ldots, a[z-1]$*. An attribute can be quantitative or categorical.*

In ICU data streams, for example, there are many attributes representing different physiological meanings, such as end expiratory pressure, exhaled minute volume, and spontaneous minute volume. Every attribute is an indispensable part of stream and they are correlated with each other.

Definition 2. *A predicate* p *specifies the conditions for any of the* z *attributes of a record stream* $r[i]$*.*

e.g. $p[j] = f_{j0}(r[i].a[0])$ AND ... AND $f_{j(z-1)}(r[i].a[z-1])$, where $f_{jt}(r[i].a[t])$ can be a conjunction of inequalities of involving attribute a[t] of record $r[i]$ with a constant, or with attribute a[t] of the next record $r[i+1]$.

Definition 3. *A stream pattern is an ordered list of* m *predicates* $p[0], \ldots, p[m]$ *which are satisfied by* m *consecutive records of the data stream.*

A function $f(t)$ is said to be periodic of a period T if $f(t) = f(t+T)$ for all t. In general, T is the smallest value for which it holds. However, many phenomena in the real life is just repetitious and not strictly periodic, such as the heartbeat of humans. The property of exhibiting great regularity without being periodic is considered to be pseudo-periodic in our models, because it is quite different from the periodicity although there are several similarities between them.

Definition 4. *A stream* s *is pseudo-periodic if the attributes of* s *satisfied the following function :*

$$PP(t) = \sum_i \alpha_i F(\omega_i t + \varphi_i) \tag{1}$$

where $PP(t)$ *represents a pseudo-periodic functions and* $F(t)$ *is a template functions of* $PP(t)$*.*

Note that, the ω_i is a stretching parameters which lengthens or shortens the period and the φ_i is a translating parameter which represents nonuniform timing of the progress, such as the acceleration or deceleration of heartbeats in our models.

While we are transforming the pseudo-periodic data streams into periodic ones, we should achieve unbiased estimation of the ω_i and φ_i using the ρ-norm. This is defined to be the norm induced by the inner product :

$$\langle f, pp \rangle_\rho \equiv \lim_{k \to \infty} \frac{1}{2k} \int_{-k}^{k} f(t)pp(t)dt \tag{2}$$

In the equation(3), $f(t)$ and $pp(t)$ are periodic functions of periods T_f and T_{pp}. T_f and T_{pp} need not be the same numerically. So we can get that

$$||f||_\rho = \sqrt{\langle f, f \rangle_\rho} \tag{3}$$

4 Monitoring Abnormal Patterns over ICU Data Streams

4.1 Modeling the Pseudo-periodical Data Streams

Most of existing pseudo-periodic model are aiming to process continuous signals, discrete data sets have rarely been paid much attention to. The shortcoming of the upper functions is that they can be only applied to continuous infinite signals. When we implements the methods in discrete time and data driven, we should expand the functions to meet the realistic conditions. To apply these functions to finite data sets, we should suppose the template function $f(t)$ is defined by n points in a period T. And then we can calculate the ρ-inner product as the ℓ_2-inner product normalized by the size of the support of the template, which can be depicted as the following formula :

$$\langle \mathbf{f}_\omega, \mathbf{pp} \rangle_\rho \equiv \frac{\langle \mathbf{f}_\alpha, \mathbf{pp} \rangle}{N_\omega} \equiv \frac{1}{N_\omega} \sum_{t=1}^{N_\omega} f(\omega t) pp(t) \tag{4}$$

The purpose of modeling phenomena exhibiting cyclical patterns with pseudo-periodic functions is that we can decompose the patterns into a periodic data set with a set of parameters. These parameters define the deviations of the original pattern from the true periodicity.

At each local period, $f(\omega t)$ can be obtained from $F(t)$. Our algorithm extracts $pp(t)$ from $PP(t)$ with an proper translation and then estimates the three parameters α_i, ω_i, φ_i. In the practical implementation, it is more convenient to use the parameter ψ_i other than φ_i. The two variable are related by :

$$\varphi_i \equiv \sum_{j=0}^{j<i} \frac{2\pi}{\omega_j} + \psi_i \tag{5}$$

With appropriate $f(\omega t)$ and $pp(t)$, the cost function at the ith pseudo-periodic can be computed in the following way :

$$\begin{aligned} D(\omega, \varphi, \alpha) &= ||\alpha f(\omega t + \varphi) - pp(t)||_p^2 \\ &= ||\alpha f(\omega t + \varphi)||^2 - 2\langle \alpha f(\omega t + \varphi), pp(t) \rangle_\rho + ||pp(t)||^2 \end{aligned} \tag{6}$$

Theorem 3.1 in [10] shows that in the formula 5 the first and third terms on the right side are translation and stretch invariant, and guarantees that both $||f||_\rho$ and $||pp||_\rho$ are independent of ω and φ.

According to the previous statement, in order to find the best representation of $PP(t)$, we should find the minimum value of $D(\omega, \varphi, \alpha)$. Now the problem of minimizing $D(\omega, \varphi, \alpha)$ is equivalent to maximizing

$$\bar{D}(\omega, \varphi, \alpha) = \langle \alpha f(\omega t + \varphi), pp(t) \rangle_\rho \tag{7}$$

To achieve this goal, we choose the steepest descent method. So the parameters can be updated with the following formula:

$$\omega_{k+1} = \omega_k - \lambda_\omega \frac{d\bar{D}}{d\omega} \approx \omega_k - \lambda_\omega \frac{\bar{D}(\omega_k) - \bar{D}(\omega_k + \Delta\omega)}{\Delta\omega}$$

$$\varphi_{k+1} = \varphi_k - \lambda_\varphi \frac{d\bar{D}}{d\varphi} \approx \varphi_k - \lambda_\varphi \frac{\bar{D}(\varphi_k) - \bar{D}(\varphi_k + \Delta\varphi)}{\Delta\varphi} \tag{8}$$
$$\alpha_{k+1} = \alpha_k - \lambda_\alpha \frac{d\bar{D}}{d\alpha} \approx \alpha_k - \lambda_\alpha \frac{\bar{D}(\alpha_k) - \bar{D}(\alpha_k + \Delta\alpha)}{\Delta\alpha}$$

The algorithm will stop and consider the current parameters to be satisfactory when all the three derivatives change sign and meet the conditions: $|\frac{d\bar{D}}{d\alpha}| < \epsilon_\alpha$, $|\frac{d\bar{D}}{d\omega}| < \epsilon_\omega$, $|\frac{d\bar{D}}{d\varphi}| < \epsilon_\varphi$.

4.2 MAPS: Monitoring Abnormal Patterns over Data Streams

In this part, we will show that how MAPS monitors the anomalies in high-rate arriving data streams. MAPS is composed of three parts, the main part *Monitor_Pattern*, two sub-part *Normalize_Pattern* and *Check_Abnormity*.

Algorithm 1. Monitor_Pattern

Input: Data stream S and normal periodic pattern p.
Output: Abnormal patterns list AP_list.

```
for i = 1...k do
   Window_i ← first m_i records from the data stream
end for
while not at the end of stream S do
   for i = 1...k do
      Divide the window into disjoint sub-windows
         according to their repetition
      for each sub-window do
         NP_item ← Normalize_Pattern()
         Append NP_item to NP_list
      end for
      for each element in NP_list do
         AP_list ← Check_Abnormity()
      end for
   Delete the window and report the abnormity, GOTO step 1
   end for
end while
```

The main part of MAPS provides a framework of extracting patterns from online data streams. The algorithm in Monitor_Pattern reduces the problem from the streaming data scenario to the problem of comparing two sample sets. We also assume that only a bounded amount of memory is available, and in the DESC the size of the data stream is much larger than the amount of available memory.

Normalize_Pattern accomplishes the task of choose a template function and then calculate the appropriate values of parameters ω, φ and α.

Algorithm 2. Normalize_Pattern

Input: Sample normal pattern P and pseudo-periodic pattern pP.
Output: Normalized pattern list NP_list.

```
Calculate the cost function D̄(ω, φ, α)
Calculate the partial function of dD̄/dα, dD̄/dω, dD̄/dφ respectively.
ω ← 0, φ ← 0, α ← 0
while |dD̄/dα| > ε_α or |dD̄/dω| > ε_ω or |dD̄/dφ| > ε_φ do
    ω ← ω − λ_ω (D̄(ω) − D̄(ω+Δω)) / Δω
    φ ← φ − λ_φ (D̄(φ) − D̄(φ+Δφ)) / Δφ
    α ← α − λ_α (D̄(α) − D̄(α+Δα)) / Δα
end while
return the normalized pattern αf(ωt + φ)
```

The correlations between two stream patterns can be measured with the $PearsonR$ model. $PearsonR$ defines the correlation between two patterns o_1 and o_2 as :

$$R_\epsilon = \frac{\sum (o_1 - \bar{o_1})(o_2 - \bar{o_2})}{\sqrt{(o_1 - \bar{o_1})^2 \times (o_2 - \bar{o_2})^2}} \tag{9}$$

where $\bar{o_1}$ and $\bar{o_2}$ are the mean of all attributes values in o_1 and o_2, respectively.

Algorithm 3. Check_Abnormity

Input: Normalize pattern list NP_list and sample abnormal pattern list SAP_list.
Output: Abnormal pattern list AP_list.

```
for each item in the SAP_list
    for each item in the NP_list
        if R(item_SAP, item_NP) ≤ R_ε
            Append item_NP to AP_list
        end if
    end for
end for
```

5 Application Case

As we mentioned in the introduction, we have developed a clinical information system, DSEC, to assist doctors and nurses in medical decision support. This prototype system have several novel features in addition to abnormal pattern monitoring: 1) A complete data stream processing and querying architecture for medical application; 2) a load-shedding mechanism[8] used to avoid system crash when high data rate occurs; 3)friendly graphic user interface facilitating the analysis the high volume stream data. Fig.3. illustrates the system architecture of DSEC.

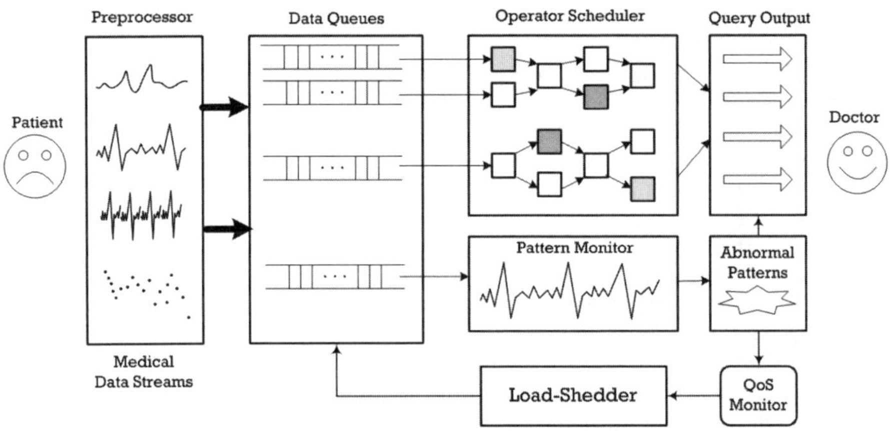

Fig. 3. System Architecture of DSEC

6 Conclusion and Future Work

Our work focuses on the monitoring abnormal patterns over ICU data streams. The algorithm we proposed has the following desirable characteristics:

- it represents complex repetitive phenomena as a periodic process with a set of parameters and defines the deviation of the process from true periodicity.
- The algorithm MAPS goes deep into the intrinsic semantics in the ICU data streams and efficiently identifies the anomalies just in a single pass of streams.
- Normal patterns and thresholds can be automatically adjusted according to the specification of clinicians. The design has greatly improved the flexibility and scalability of the module. This also solved the polymorphism mentioned above.

Future research can proceed in several directions. One possibility is to dynamically change the weight of each streams according to the feedback of the monitoring result. Because in multi-dimensional data streams, each stream has its own repetitious features and semantic meanings. Still another problem is combining the distribute feature with current semantics analysis, so we can get more precise and efficient methods to monitor the patients' states.

References

[1] B. Babcock, S. Babu, M. Datar, R. Motwani, and J. Widom. Models and Issues in Data Stream Systems. In SIGMOD POS, 2002.

[2] D. Abadi, D. Carney, U. Cetinternet, M. Cherniack, C. Convey, S. Lee, M. Stonebraker, N. Tatbul, S. Zdonik. Aurora: A New Model and Architecture for Data Stream Management. In VLDB Journal, August 2003.

[3] S. Chandrasekharan et al. TelegraphCQ: Continuous dataflow processing for an uncertain world. CIDR, 2003.

[4] David Maier, Jin Li, Peter Tucker, Kristin Tufte, and Vassilis Papadimos. Semantics of Data Streams and Operators. ICDT 2005, LNCS 3363, pp. 37-52, 2005.

[5] Y. Zhu and D. Shasha. StatStream: Statistical Monitoring of Thousands of Data Streams in Real Time. VLDB, pages 358-369, 2002.

[6] Yu Fan, Hongyan Li, Zijing Hu, Jianlong Gao, Haibin Liu, ShiweiTang, Xinbiao Zhou. DSEC: A data stream engine based clinical information system, APWEB 2006, Harbin.

[7] Yu Fan, Hongyan Li: ICUIS: A Rule-Based Intelligent ICU Information System. In Proceedings of IDEAS04-EH, September 29-31, 2004, China.

[8] Zijing Hu, Hongyan Li, Baojun Qiu, Lv-an Tang, Yu Fan, Haibin Liu, Jianlong Gao, Xinbiao Zhou. Using Control Theory to Guide Load Shedding in Medical Data Stream Management System. Advances in Computer Science - ASIAN 2005.

[9] Ting Yin, Hongyan Li, Zijing Hu, Yu Fan, Jianlong Gao, Shiwei Tang. A Hybrid Method for Detecting Data Stream Changes with Complex Semantics in Intensive Care Unit.Advances in Computer Science - ASIAN 2005.

[10] W.A.Sethares. Repetition and pseudo-periodicity, Tatra Mountains Mathematical Publications, Pulication 23, 2001.

[11] Steven M. Kay. Fundamentals of staticstical signal processing volume I estimation theory volume II detection theory. 2002.8

[12] Ryszard S. Michalski, Ivan Bratko, Miroslav Kubat. Machine learning and data mining methods and applications 2003.

[13] Lilian Harada. Detection of complex temporal patterns over data stream. Information System 29(2004)439-459.

[14] Y. Dora Cai, David Clutter, Greg Pape, Jiawei Han, Michael Welge, Loretta Auvil.MAIDS: Mining Alarming Incidents from Data Streams, ACM SIGMOD 2004.

[15] L.Gao, Xiao Yang,and Sean Wang. Continually evaluating similarity-based pattern queries on a streaming time series, in Proceedings of the 2002 ACM SIGMOD International Conference on Management of Data, June 2002, pp.370-381.

[16] Daniel Kifer, ShaiBen-David, Johannces Gehrke. Detecting change in Data Streams. In Proceedings for the 30th VLDB Conference, Toronto, Canada, 2004.

[17] Huanmei Wu, Betty Salzberg, Donghui Zhang. Online Event-driven Subsequence Matching over Financial Data Streams. SIGMOD 2004 Paris, France.

[18] Charbonnier S. ,Becq G. , Biot L.. Online segmentation algorithm for continuously monitored data in Intensive Care Units. IEEE Transactions on Biomedical Engineering, Vol.51, pp.484-492, Mars 2004.

[19] S. Muthukrishnan. http://athos.rutgers.edu/ muthu/stream-1-1.ps/DataStreams: Algorithms and Applications.

[20] http://www-db.stanford.edu/stream/

Spatial-temporal Analysis Method of Plane Circuits Based on Two-Layer Cellular Neural Networks

Masayoshi Oda[1], Yoshifumi Nishio[1], and Akio Ushida[2]

[1] Dept. of Electrical and Electronic Engineering, Tokushima University, Japan
[2] Dept. Mechanical and Electrical Electronic Engineering, Tokushima Bunri University, Japan

1 Introduction

Recently, the operational speeds of the integrated circuits are increasing rapidly. There have been many researches about transmission lines because they are very important for designing high performance integrated circuits. As well as transmission lines, the analysis of the power distribution of printed circuit boards becomes more and more important [1-3]. The analysis of the power distribution is important for designing decoupling capcitors. In the power distribution analysis, the finite element method is often applied. However, in the finite element method, in order to obtain the accurate results, we have to discretize the object into the many small elements and to solve large scale equations. It is very time consuming to solve those large scale equations by conventional degital computing.

We have proposed an efficient method to solve large scale equation of the plane circuits using Cellular Neural Networks (CNNs) [4-7]. Since the large processing ability of CNNs, there have been many papers about the applications for adopting CNNs for analyzing spatio-temporal phenomena such as pattern formations and traveling waves [6-8]. In our method, we transform the plane into corresponding equivalent circuit, and analyze the equivalent circuit using CNNs [9-10]. In this paper, we verify the accuracy of the proposed method and investigate its capability for various kinds of the simulation models. We show how transform the plane into the equivalent circuit in section 2. The concept of CNNs is explained in section 3. In section 4, we show how analyze the voltage propagation using CNNs and illustrative examples of our simulations.

2 Plane Circuits

As the operating speed of the integrated circuits increases, many complicated phenomena such as the signal/power integrity are occured. In the high speed integrated circuits, analyzing the power distribution of the power/groung plane is important for designing the decoupling capacitors. Analysis of power distributions are classified into three classes by modeling methods, full-wave electromagnetic model, modified nodal model and lumped circuits model. Full-wave

N. Zheng, X. Jiang, and X. Lan (Eds.): IWICPAS 2006, LNCS 4153, pp. 195–204, 2006.

electromagnetic model is based on the physical electromagnetic field equations. Although this model is most accurate model, solving those equations needs much time and computation.

The partial-element equivalent circuit (PEEC) methods is often adopted for analyzing the power distribution of the multi-layer printed circuit bords[3,11]. In this method, the power/ground plane is discretized spatially and approximated by linear R, L, C, and G elements. Fig. 1 shows the transformation of the plane into the equivalent circuit.

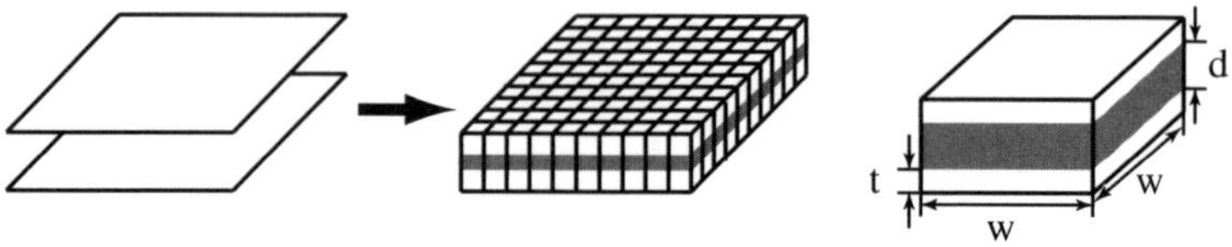

(a) Plane discretization

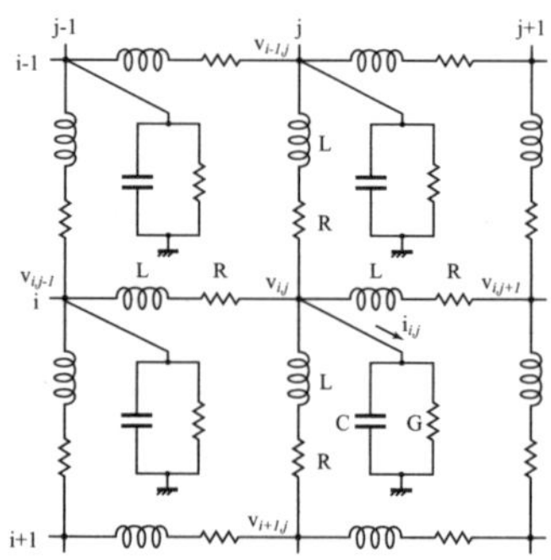

(b) Plane circuit

Fig. 1. Transformation of the plane

The magnitudes of these parameters are decided by the discretization size and the physical characteristics of the plane;

$$R = \frac{2}{\sigma_c t} + 2\sqrt{\frac{\pi f \mu_0}{\sigma_c}}, \quad L = \mu_0 d, \quad G = 2\pi f C \tan\delta, \quad C = \epsilon_0 \epsilon_r \frac{w^2}{d}, \tag{1}$$

where
ϵ_0: dielectric constant in vacuum, ϵ_r: relative dielectric constant,
μ_0: magnetic permeability in vacuum, σ_c: resistivity of the conductor,
δ: loss tangent of the conductor, f: operating freaquency.
The state equations of equivalent circuit are described as follows;

$$\begin{cases} \dfrac{dv_{i,j}}{dt} = -\dfrac{G}{C} v_{i,j} + \dfrac{1}{C} i_{i,j}, \\ \dfrac{di_{i,j}}{dt} = -\dfrac{R}{L} i_{i,j} + \dfrac{1}{L}(v_{i-1,j} + v_{i+1,j} + v_{i,j-1} + v_{i,j+1} - 4v_{i,j}). \end{cases} \tag{2}$$

Normalizing by

$$\tau = \frac{1}{\sqrt{LC}} t, \tag{3}$$

we have

$$\begin{cases} \dfrac{dv_{i,j}}{d\tau} = -G\sqrt{\dfrac{L}{C}} v_{i,j} + \sqrt{\dfrac{L}{C}} i_{i,j}, \\ \dfrac{di_{i,j}}{d\tau} = -\dfrac{R}{L} i_{i,j} + \dfrac{1}{L}(v_{i-1,j} + v_{i+1,j} + v_{i,j-1} + v_{i,j+1} - 4v_{i,j}). \end{cases} \tag{4}$$

If we discretize the plane into $n \times n$ elements, we have to solve $2n^2$ differential equations. In order to obtain accurate results, we have to discretize the plane into many small elements and to solve large scale equations. It takes much time to solve these large scale equations by conventional digital computers.

3 Solving Plane Circuits Via Cellular Neural Networks

Cellular Neural Networks (CNNs) have been established by combining the concepts of neural networks and cellular automata [4,5]. Since its speed advantage of the processing, CNNs have been noted as applications for the image processing and solvind partial differential equations in last two decades.
CNNs have the array structure consisting of fundamental elements, called *cell.* Each cell connects its neighbor cells and makes contribution each other. The cell can be implimented by simple analog circuit. Because of constructive simplicity, CNNs are suited for LSI implimentation.

In our research, we adapt the two-layer cellular neural networks. The concept of multi-layer CNNs has been proposed and its high proccessing abilities have been reported. Fig. 2 shows the cell structure of two-layer CNNs.

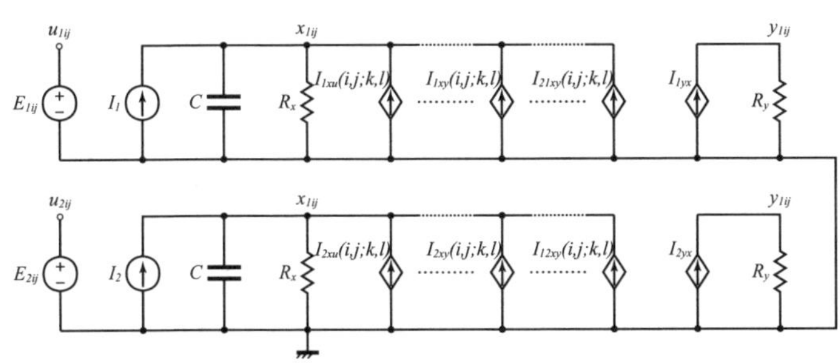

Fig. 2. Cell structure of two-layer CNN

Assuming $R_x = R_y = 1[\Omega]$ and $C = 1[\mathrm{F}]$ for simplicity, the state equation of the cell is described as follow;

$$\begin{cases} \dfrac{dx_{1ij}}{dt} = -x_{1ij} + \displaystyle\sum_{C(k,l)\in N_r(i,j)} A_1(i,j;k,l)y_{1kl} \\ \quad + \displaystyle\sum_{C(k,l)\in N_r(i,j)} B_1(i,j;k,l)u_{1kl} + \displaystyle\sum_{C(k,l)\in N_r(i,j)} C_1(i,j;k,l)y_{2kl} + I_1, \\ \dfrac{dx_{2ij}}{dt} = -x_{i,j} + \displaystyle\sum_{C(k,l)\in N_r(i,j)} A_2(i,j;k,l)y_{2kl} \\ \quad + \displaystyle\sum_{C(k,l)\in N_r(i,j)} B_2(i,j;k,l)u_{2kl} + \displaystyle\sum_{C(k,l)\in N_r(i,j)} C_2(i,j;k,l)y_{1kl} + I_2, \end{cases} \tag{5}$$

where u_{ij}, x_{ij} and y_{ij} indicate the input voltage, the state voltage and the output voltage of $C(i,j)$, respectively. In general CNNs, the output voltages are defined by the following piecewise linear function,

$$\begin{cases} y_{1ij} = \dfrac{1}{2}\left(|x_{1ij}+1| - |x_{1ij}-1|\right), \\ \\ y_{2ij} = \dfrac{1}{2}\left(|x_{2ij}+1| - |x_{2ij}-1|\right). \end{cases} \tag{6}$$

In state equations, the coefficients $\boldsymbol{A}$ and $\boldsymbol{B}$ indicate the weights of connectivity between the connected neighbor cells. The output of the first layer contribute to the state of the second layer and the output of the second layer contribute to the state of the first layer. The connectivity between the first layer and the second layer is described by coefficient $\boldsymbol{C}$. These coefficients are given by matrix form and they are called *cloning templates*. The behavior of CNNs is decided by these cloning templates.

In our method, we solve the large scale equations which obtained by discretizing the plane using the two-layer CNN. Both state equations of the plane and the CNNs have local interconnection. Comparing (4) and (5), we can apply each discretized element to each CNN cell. Then we have following cloning templates.

$$\begin{aligned} \boldsymbol{A}_1 &= \begin{pmatrix} 0 & 0 & 0 \\ 0 & 1 - G\sqrt{\frac{L}{C}} & 0 \\ 0 & 0 & 0 \end{pmatrix}, \boldsymbol{B}_1 = \boldsymbol{0}, \boldsymbol{C}_1 = \begin{pmatrix} 0 & 0 & 0 \\ 0 & \sqrt{\frac{L}{C}} & 0 \\ 0 & 0 & 0 \end{pmatrix}, I_1 = 0. \\ \boldsymbol{A}_2 &= \begin{pmatrix} 0 & 0 & 0 \\ 0 & 1 - R\sqrt{\frac{C}{L}} & 0 \\ 0 & 0 & 0 \end{pmatrix}, \boldsymbol{B}_2 = \boldsymbol{0}, \boldsymbol{C}_2 = \begin{pmatrix} 0 & \sqrt{\frac{C}{L}} & 0 \\ \sqrt{\frac{C}{L}} & -4\sqrt{\frac{C}{L}} & \sqrt{\frac{C}{L}} \\ 0 & \sqrt{\frac{C}{L}} & 0 \end{pmatrix}, I_2 = 0. \end{aligned} \tag{7}$$

Since the discretized model is linear, we redefine the output equations as follows,

$$\begin{cases} y_{1ij} = x_{1ij}, \\ \\ y_{2ij} = x_{2ij}. \end{cases} \tag{8}$$

In following section, we carry out the simulations based on the fourth-order Runge-Kutta method, and are applied the fixed boundary condition [12]. The size of CNN array is 100 × 100. We assume the physical characteristic of the plane, $t = 0.03$[mm], $d = 0.2$[mm], $\sigma_c = 5.8 \times 10^7$[S/m] and $\epsilon_r = 4.7$.

4 Direction Difference of the Lattice-Like Structure

Preceding the simulation, we confirm the accuracy of the equivalent circuits. If the plane is uniform, at the points whose distance from an arbitrary point in Euclidean space are the same, the observed phenomena must be the same.

First, we set the discretization size $w = 2.0$[mm]. Assuming the dielectric loss can be neglected, we have following cloning templates;

$$\begin{aligned} \boldsymbol{A}_1 &= \begin{pmatrix} 0\,0\,0 \\ 0\,1\,0 \\ 0\,0\,0 \end{pmatrix}, \boldsymbol{B}_1 = \boldsymbol{0}, \boldsymbol{C}_1 = \begin{pmatrix} 0 & 0 & 0 \\ 0 & 17.4 & 0 \\ 0 & 0 & 0 \end{pmatrix}, I_1 = 0, \\ \boldsymbol{A}_2 &= \begin{pmatrix} 0\,0\,0 \\ 0\,1\,0 \\ 0\,0\,0 \end{pmatrix}, \boldsymbol{B}_2 = \boldsymbol{0}, \boldsymbol{C}_2 = \begin{pmatrix} 0 & 0.058 & 0 \\ 0.058 & -0.23 & 0.058 \\ 0 & 0.058 & 0 \end{pmatrix}, I_2 = 0. \end{aligned} \quad (9)$$

We set the impulse voltage at $(50, 50)$ and simulate the transient response. We measure the voltage at three points $(46, 53)$, $(47, 54)$ and $(50, 55)$ which distance from the impulse is the same. Measured results are shown in Fig. 3 (b). As a

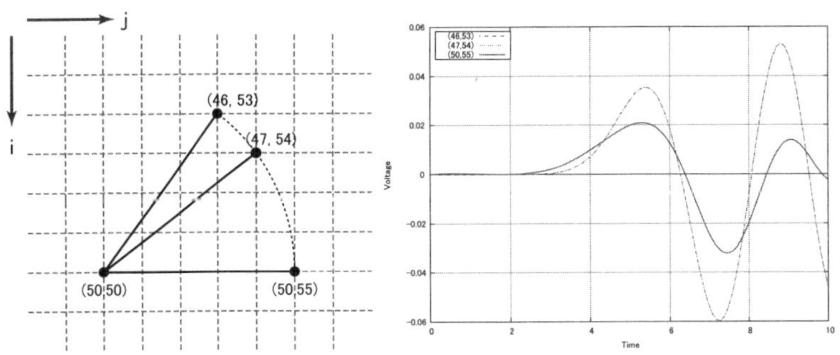

(a) Location of the points (b) Measured results

Fig. 3. Direction difference ($w = 2.0$[mm])

result, the measured voltages at $(46, 53)$ and $(47, 54)$ are completely the same value. However, the measured voltages at $(50, 55)$ do not agree with the voltage at $(46, 53)$ or $(47, 54)$. The difference proceeds from the lattice-like structure of the equivalent circuit. Moreover, the voltages oscillate widely.

We reset the discretization size smaller, $w = 0.4$[mm], and the impulse voltage around $(50, 50)$ as the area, not as the point. Then, the cloning templates are given as follows;

$$\boldsymbol{A}_1 = \begin{pmatrix} 0\,0\,0 \\ 0\,1\,0 \\ 0\,0\,0 \end{pmatrix}, \boldsymbol{B}_1 = \boldsymbol{0}, \boldsymbol{C}_1 = \begin{pmatrix} 0 & 0 & 0 \\ 0 & 86.9 & 0 \\ 0 & 0 & 0 \end{pmatrix}, I_1 = 0,$$
$$\boldsymbol{A}_2 = \begin{pmatrix} 0\,0\,0 \\ 0\,1\,0 \\ 0\,0\,0 \end{pmatrix}, \boldsymbol{B}_2 = \boldsymbol{0}, \boldsymbol{C}_2 = \begin{pmatrix} 0 & 0.012 & 0 \\ 0.012 & -0.048 & 0.012 \\ 0 & 0.012 & 0 \end{pmatrix}, I_2 = 0. \quad (10)$$

As well as the above simulation, we simulate the transient response and measure the voltage at the same three points. Note that since we reset the discretization size, the cordinates of the points are replaced as shown in Fig. 4 (a). The

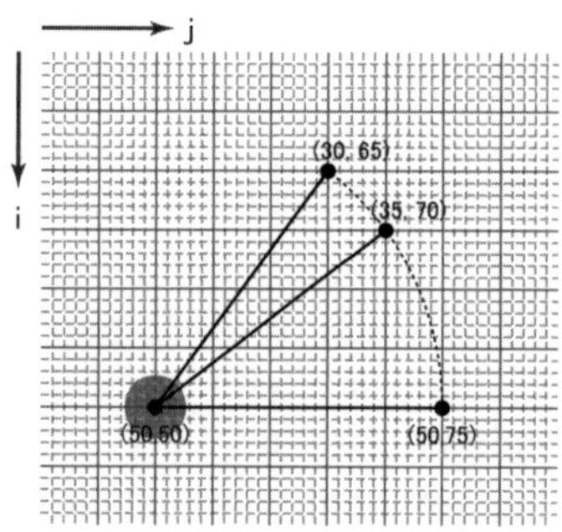

(a) Location of the points

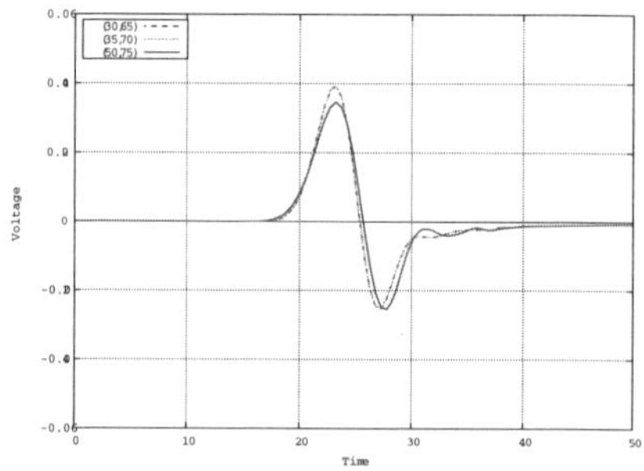

(b) Measured results

Fig. 4. Direction difference ($w = 0.4$[mm]).

measured results are shown in Fig. 4 (b). We can see that difference between $(50, 75)$ and $(30, 65)$ or $(35, 70)$ is smaller than previous case and the oscilations converge immediately. In following simulations, we adapt the same way.

5 Illustrative Examples

In this section, we show some interesting examples of our simulations.

5.1 Uniform Plane

We simulate the voltage propagation on the uniform plane. We assume two-impulse voltage shown in Fig. 5 and simulate how the voltage propagates on the plane. Fig. 6 shows the snap shots of the transient state. We can see the voltage propagates spatially and the voltage waves interfere each other.

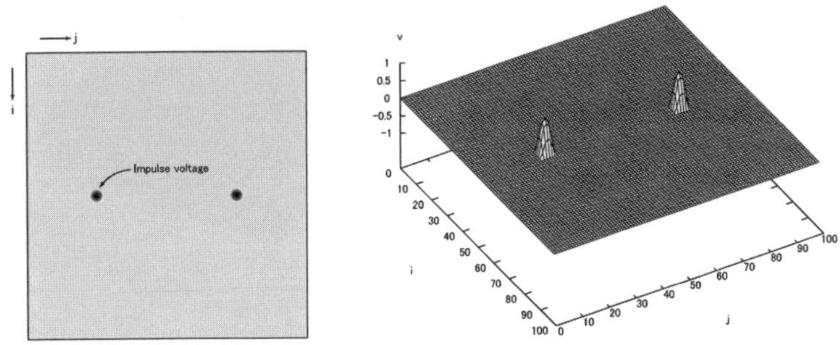

(a) Layout of the impulse voltage (b) Snap shot of the impulse voltages

Fig. 5. Initial State of the two-impulse voltage

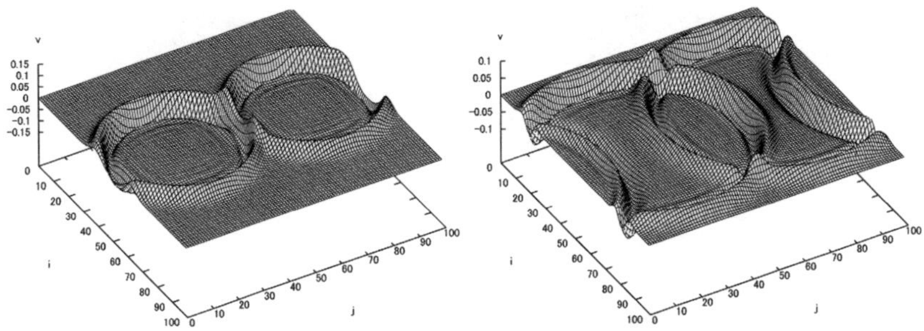

(a) $\tau = 25.0$ (b) $\tau = 40.0$

Fig. 6. Transient response for two-impulse

5.2 Irragular Shaped Plane

Next, we simulate the voltage propagation on the irragular shaped plane. Our method can be adjusted to analyze the arbitrary shaped plane easily. As an example, we simulated the plane shown in Fig. 7. As well as the above simulation, we assume the impulse voltage and simulate how the voltage propagate on the plane. Fig. 8 shows the snap shot of the voltage propagation. We can see the voltage propagates along the conductor strips.

5.3 External Input

The above method can simulate only the transient response for the initial state. Now, we modify the equivalent circuit to be able to simulate the phenomena which the plane has external inputs. The improved model is shown in Fig.9.

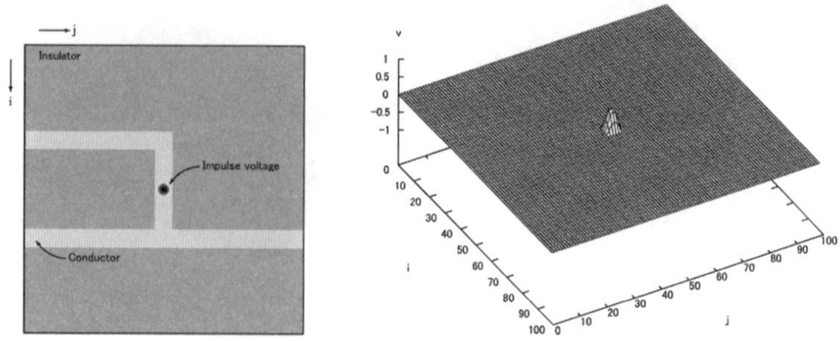

(a) Simulated plane (b) Snap shot of the impulse voltage

Fig. 7. Initial state for the irragular plane

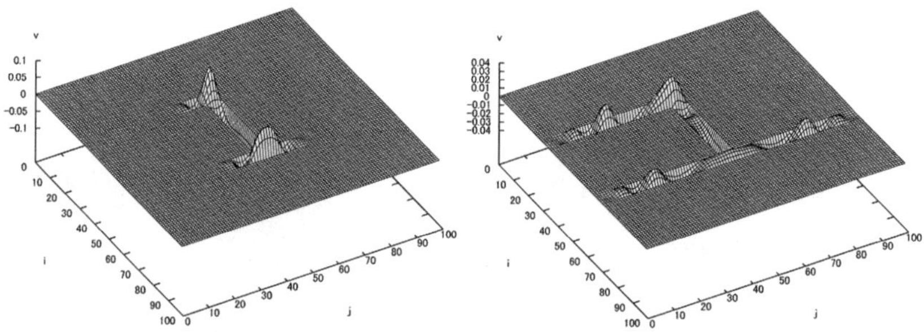

(a) $\tau = 30.0$ (b) $\tau = 70.0$

Fig. 8. Transient response of the irragular plane

Then the state equations of the equivalent circuit are given as follows;

$$\left\{\begin{aligned}\frac{dv_{i,j}}{d\tau} &= -G\sqrt{\frac{L}{C}}v_{i,j} + \sqrt{\frac{L}{C}}i_{i,j} + \sqrt{\frac{L}{C}}J_{i,j},\\ \frac{di_{i,j}}{d\tau} &= -\frac{R}{L}i_{i,j} + \frac{1}{L}(v_{i-1,j} + v_{i+1,j} + v_{i,j-1} + v_{i,j+1} - 4v_{i,j}).\end{aligned}\right. \tag{11}$$

Hence, we have the following cloning templates;

$$\begin{aligned}\boldsymbol{A}_1 &= \begin{pmatrix} 0 & 0 & 0 \\ 0 & 1 - G\sqrt{\frac{L}{C}} & 0 \\ 0 & 0 & 0 \end{pmatrix}, \boldsymbol{B}_1 = \begin{pmatrix} 0 & 0 & 0 \\ 0 & \sqrt{\frac{L}{C}} & 0 \\ 0 & 0 & 0 \end{pmatrix}, \boldsymbol{C}_1 = \begin{pmatrix} 0 & 0 & 0 \\ 0 & \sqrt{\frac{L}{C}} & 0 \\ 0 & 0 & 0 \end{pmatrix}, I_1 = 0,\\ \boldsymbol{A}_2 &= \begin{pmatrix} 0 & 0 & 0 \\ 0 & 1 - R\sqrt{\frac{C}{L}} & 0 \\ 0 & 0 & 0 \end{pmatrix}, \boldsymbol{B}_2 = \boldsymbol{0}, \boldsymbol{C}_2 = \begin{pmatrix} 0 & \sqrt{\frac{C}{L}} & 0 \\ \sqrt{\frac{C}{L}} & -4\sqrt{\frac{C}{L}} & \sqrt{\frac{C}{L}} \\ 0 & \sqrt{\frac{C}{L}} & 0 \end{pmatrix}, I_2 = 0.\end{aligned} \tag{12}$$

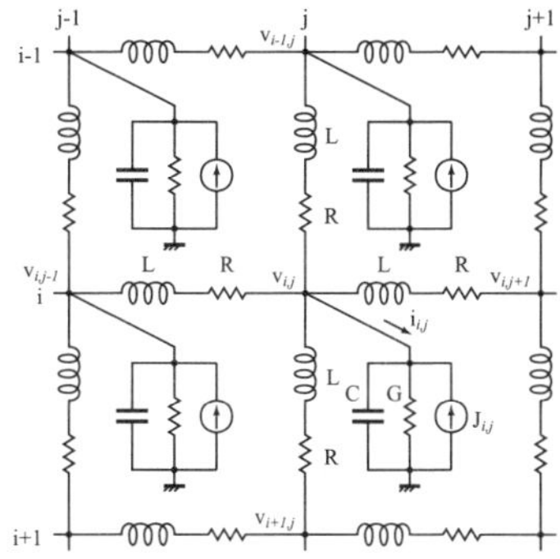

Fig. 9. Modified plane circuit

As an example, we simulate the transient response of the pulse input on the uniform plane. We set the pulse input $J_{i,j}$ around $(50, 50)$. Fig. 10 shows the snap shot of the transient response for pulse input.

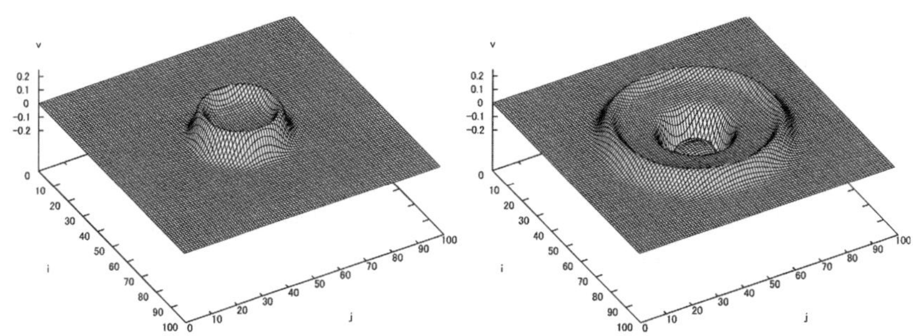

(a) $\tau = 15.0$ (b) $\tau = 30.0$

Fig. 10. transient response for the pulse

6 Conclusion

In this paper, we showed that the power distribution of the power/ground plane of printed circuit boards can be analyzed by two-layer CNNs. We adopt the PEEC method to approximate the characteristic of the plane and solve the circuit equations of the plane circuit using CNNs. Although our research is only the simulations, CNN will provide for a solution with higher seepd than any other known methods. Moreover, in our method, it is easy to simulate various planes with changing parameters because we use the cloning templates as the characteristics of the plane.

References

1. D. Herrell and B. Becker, "Modeling of Power Distribution Systems for High Performance Microprocessors," *IEEE Trans. Adv. Packag.*, vol. 22, pp. 240-248, 1999.
2. J. Kim and M. Swaminathan, "Modeling of Irregular Shaped Distribution Planes using Transmission Matrix Method," *IEEE Trans. Adv. Packag.*, vol. 24, pp. 334-346, 2001.
3. Y. Kim, H. Yoon, S. Lee, G. Moon, J. Kim, and J. Wee, "An Efficient Path-Based Equivalent Circuit Model for Design, Synthesis, and Optimization of Power Distribution Networks in Multilayer Printed Circuit Boards," *IEEE Trans. Adv. Packag.*, vol. 27, no. 1, pp. 97-106, 2004.
4. L. O. Chua, and L. Yang, "Cellular Neural Networks: Theory," *IEEE Trans. Circuits Syst.*, vol. 35, no. 10, pp. 1257-1272, 1988.
5. L. O. Chua, and L. Yang, "Cellular Neural Networks: Application," *IEEE Trans. Circuits Syst.*, vol. 35, no. 10, pp. 1273-1290, 1988.
6. T. Roska, L. O. Chua, D. Wolf, T. Kozek, R. Tetzlaff, and F. Puffer, "Simulating Nonlinear Waves and Partial Differential Equations via CNN —Part I: Basic Technique," *IEEE Trans. Circuits Syst.*, vol. 42, no. 10, pp. 807-815, 1995.
7. T. Kozek, L. O. Chua, T. Roska, D. Wolf, R. Tetzlaff, F. Puffer, and K. Lotz, "Simulating Nonlinear Waves and Partial Differential Equations via CNN —Part II: Typical Examples," *IEEE Trans. Circuits Syst.*, vol. 42, no. 10, pp. 816-819, 1995.
8. Z. Yang, Y. Nishio, and A. Ushida, "Generation of Various Types of Spatio-Temporal Phenomena in Two-Layer Cellular Neural Networks," *IEICE Trans. on Fundamentals*, vol. E87-A, no. 4, pp. 864-871, 2004.
9. M. Oda, Z. Yang, Y. Nishio, and A. Ushida, "Analysis of Two-Dimensional Conductive Plates Based on CNNs," Proceedings of RISP International Workshop on Nonlinear Circuits and Signal Processing (NCSP'05), pp. 447-450, Mar. 2005.
10. Y. Tanji, H. Asai, M. Oda, Y. Nishio, and A. Ushida, "Fast Timing Analysis of Plane Circuits via Two-Layer CNN-Based Modeling," Proceedings of IEEE International Symposium on Circuits and Systems (ISCAS'06), pp. 3738-3741, May 2006.
11. A. Ushida, Y. Tanji, and Y, Nishio, "Analysis of Two-Dimensional Circuits Based on Multi-conductive Theorem," *IEICE Tech. Report*, no. NLP-97-16, pp. 25-29, 1997.
12. P. Thiran, "Influence of Boundary Conditions on the Behavior of Cellular Neural Networks," *IEEE Trans. Circuits Syst.*, vol. 40, no. 3, pp. 207-212, 1993.

Feature-Based Synchronization of Video and Background Music

Jong-Chul Yoon, In-Kwon Lee, and Hyun-Chul Lee

Dept. of Computer Science, Yonsei University, Korea
media19@cs.yonsei.ac.kr, iklee@yonsei.ac.kr, kennyd@cs.yonsei.ac.kr

Abstract. We synchronize background music with a video by changing the timing of music, an approach that minimizes the damage to music data. Starting from a MIDI file and video data, feature points are extracted from both sources, paired, and then synchronized using dynamic programming to time-scale the music. We also introduce the music graph, a directed graph that encapsulates connections between many short music sequences. By traversing a music graph, we can generate large amounts of new background music, in which we expect to find a sequence which matches the video features better than the original music.

1 Introduction

Background music (BGM) enhances the emotional impact of video data. Here, BGM means any kind of music played by one or more musical instruments, and should be distinguished from sound effects, which are usually short sounds made by natural or artificial phenomena. We introduce a method that synchronizes BGM with motion in video data. Well-synchronized BGM helps to immerse the audience in the video, and can also emphasize the features of the scenes.

In most cases of film production, the picture comes first and music and sound effects are usually added once the picture is completed [1]. In order to obtain music that synchronizes with a particular video, we have to hire a composer. Since this approach is expensive, it is more common, especially in a small production or home video, to fit existing recorded music to the video after it has been produced. But, it is not simple to find a piece of music that matches the video scene. One may have to go through several scores, and listen to many selections in order to find a suitable portion for a given scene. Furthermore, it is still hard to match the selected music with every significant feature of the video.

Our goal is the automatic generation of synchronized video by choosing and modifying the music sequence, with the aim of avoiding drastic changes which make damage to music. Our system analyzes MIDI and video data to find the optimal matches between features of the music and the video using DP (Dynamic Programming). This is followed by modification of the time domain, so as to match the musical features while preventing noticeable damage.

We also exploit the music graph [2], as a music rearrangement method. Similar to a motion graph [3,4,5], a music graph encapsulates connections between

N. Zheng, X. Jiang, and X. Lan (Eds.): IWICPAS 2006, LNCS 4153, pp. 205–214, 2006.

several music sequences. Music can be generated by traversing the graph and then smoothing the resulting melody transitions. The music graph can be utilized in our synchronization system to generate new tunes that will match the video better than the original music.

The contributions of our research can be summarized as follows:

- We introduce a feature-based matching method which can extract the optimal matching sequence between the background music and video.
- We introduce a stable time warping method to modify the original music that can prevent noticeable damage to the music.
- Using the music graph, we can generate novel background music which has better coherence with video than the original music.

2 Related Work

There has been a lot of work on synchronizing music (or sounds) with video. In essence, there are two classes of approach, depending on whether one is modifying a video clip for given music, or vice versa.

Foote et. al [6] computed the novelty score at each part of the music, and analyzed the movements of the camera in a video. Then, a music video can be generated by matching an appropriate video clip to each part of the original music. Another segment-based matching method was introduced by Hua et. al [7]. Since home video, which is pictured from typical people, has low quality and unnecessary clips, Hua et. al calculated the attention score of each video segment as the method for extracting important shots. Using the beat analysis of video data, they attempted to create a coherent music tempo and beat. Then, the tempo and beat of given background music can be adjusted by the computed tempo and beat. Mulhem et. al [8] introduced aesthetic rules, which are commonly used by real video editors, as a method of video composing.

In addition to the previous research that considered the composing of video segments, Jehan [9] suggested a method to control the video time domain and synchronized the feature points of both video and music. Using the temporary data manually given, he adjusted the dance clip by time-warping for the synchronization to the background music. Our method is similar to this method, but we considered the reverse direction: the time-warping of music.

Yoo et. al [10] suggested a method to generate long background music sequences from a given music clip using a music texture synthesis technique. Lee et. al [2] introduced a music graph concept that is an utility for synchronization of music and the motion in the character animation. Since the video is more commonly used than animation scenes, we adapted the music graph to the method for a video-based BGM generater.

3 Feature Extraction

We will represent a video clip in the time interval $[t_b, t_e]$ as a multidimensional curve, $A(t) = (a_1(t), a_2(t), ..., a_n(t)), t_b < t < t_e$, which is called a feature curve.

Each of the component functions $a_i(t)$ represent a quantitative or qualitative property of the video clip, such as:

- Shot Boundary.
- Camera Movement (Panning, Zoom-in/out).
- The movement of any object in the video clip.
- An arbitrary function specified by the user.

Similar to the video clip, the BGM can also be represented by a multidimensional BGM curve, which we will write $M(s) = (m_1(s), m_2(s), ..., m_m(s)), s_b < s < s_e$. Each component function $m_i(s)$ represents any quantitative or qualitative property of the music, such as:

- Note pitch, duration, or velocity (volume).
- Inter-onset interval (duration between consecutive notes).
- Register (interval between highest and lowest pitches).
- Fitness for a fixed division (see Equation 3).
- Chord progression.
- Feeling of the music.
- An arbitrary function specified by the user.

Collecting such samples from the BGM is not easy when its source is analogue or digital sound data. A MIDI file makes extraction of the necessary data much easier. In the following subsections, we will look at some examples of how feature points are obtained from the video and BGM curves.

3.1 Video Feature Extraction

There are several methods for feature extraction of video in computer vision and image processing. Ma et. al [11] suggested the feature extraction method using the motion of object, variance of human face appearing in the video, and camera movement. Foote [6] used the variance of brightness to compute the feature points. In our work, for analyzing the camera movement, we use ITM (Integral Template Matching) method, which was introduced by Lan [12]. Using ITM, we can extract the shot boundary, and analyze the dominant motion of camera and its velocity at the same time. The ITM system uses MAD (Mean Absolute Difference) method to derive the camera movement. The time instances having sharp local maximum MAD can be considered as shot boundaries. We can also determine DM (Dominant Motion) of the camera by considering the camera motion having minimum MAD. The equation of MAD is defined by:

$$MAD(\Delta x) = \frac{1}{N} \sum_{x \in T} |L_i(x) - L_{i+1}(x + \Delta x)| \tag{1}$$

where Δx is a translation of image basis, and L_i is ith frame of the video. We use three types of Δx, especially vertical, horizontal and zoom in(out). After computing dominant motion, we assume that the changing points of DM as feature points.

The features of a video clip are influenced by shot boundary and variation of camera movement dominantly. Additionally, we extract the other features from each shot. Inside an single shot, we applied the Camshift [13] method for tracking the object played in the shot clip. Using Camshift, we can analyze the movement of the user selected object (see Figure 1). By tracking the trajectory of the selected region, we can construct the positional curve $p(t)$ of the selected object.

The component feature curves $a_i(t)$ are converted into feature functions $f_i(t)$ that represent the scores of the candidate feature points. For example, an $f_i(t)$ can be derived from $a_i(t)$ as follows:

$$f_i(t) = \begin{cases} q & \text{if } a_i'(t) = 0 \text{ and } a_i''(t) > 0 \\ 0 & \text{otherwise} \end{cases}, \tag{2}$$

where q is a predefined score corresponding to the importance of the features. For example, we use 1.0 as a shot boundary score, and 0.8 as a camera movement score. The score of the object movement can be computed to be proportional to the secondary derivative of the positional curve. Finally, the video feature function $F(t)$ can be computed by merging the component feature functions $f_i(t)$. The user can select either one feature function or merge several functions together to give an overall representation of the video.

Fig. 1. Object Tracking using Camshift

3.2 Music Feature Extraction

In our work, low-level data such as note pitch and note velocity (volume) can be extracted from MIDI files, and these data can be used to analyze higher-level data such as chord progressions [14]. These data are represented in separate BGM curves that can either be *continuous* or *bouncing*. The note velocity (volume) $m_1(s)$ in Figure 2(a) is a continuous function which represents the change in note volume through time. By contrast, the fitness function $m_2(s)$, which determines whether a note is played near a quarter note (a note played on the beat), is of the bouncing type. For example, the fitness function $m_2(s)$ can be defined as follows:

$$m_2(s) = \begin{cases} |s - s_k| & \text{if a note exist in } [s_k - \epsilon, s_k + \epsilon] \\ 0 & \text{otherwise} \end{cases}, \tag{3}$$

$$s_k = k\Delta s,\ \Delta s = \frac{s_e - s_b}{4N_m} \quad (k = 0, 1, 2, \cdots), \tag{4}$$

where ϵ is a small tolerance, and N_m is the number of bars of the BGM; thus Δs is the length of a quarter note. (Note that the time signature of the BGM in Figure 2 is $\frac{4}{4}$). Feature points can be extracted from the BGM curves in various ways depending on the kind of data we are dealing with. For example, we may consider the local maximum points of the note velocity (volume) curve to be the features of this curve, because these are notes that are played louder than the neighboring notes.

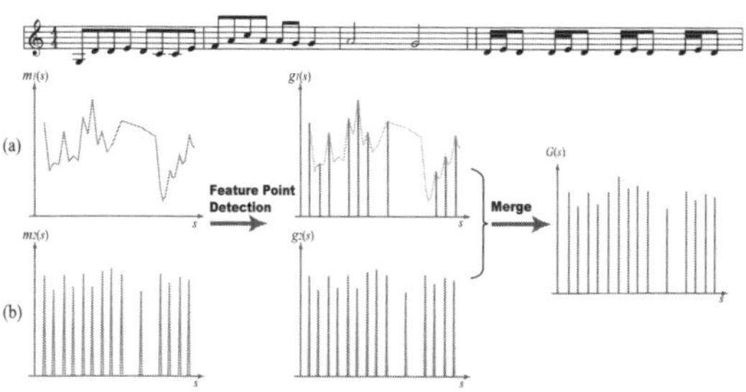

Fig. 2. An example of BGM curves and feature point detection: (a) note velocity (volume); (b) fitness to quarter note

The BGM curves $m_i(s)$ are converted into the feature functions $g_i(s)$, as shown in Figure 2. In some cases, the fitness function can be used directly as the feature function since it represents discrete data. For example, $m_2(s)$ is inverted in order to represent how well the note fits a quarter note:

$$g_2(s) = \begin{cases} \dfrac{1}{m_2(s)} & \text{if } m_2(s) \neq 0 \\ 0 & \text{otherwise} \end{cases}, \tag{5}$$

Finally, the BGM feature function $G(s)$ can be computed by merging the normalized component feature functions. The user can select either one feature function or merge several feature functions together to form the final representation of the music.

4 Synchronization Using DP Matching

DP matching is a well-known method for retrieving similarities in time series data such as speech or motion. Using DP matching, we can find the partial sequence from the given BGM that best matches the video clip, while also pairing the feature points from the video and music. And to synchronize the music and video, we modify the music using feature pairs that will not cause severe damage to the music.

4.1 DP Matching

The DP matching method does not require the video and music to be of the same time length. However, we will assume that the music sequence is longer than the video so that we are sure there is enough music for the video. Following Section 3, we assume that $F(t)$, $t_b \leq t \leq t_e$, and $G(s)$, $s_b \leq s \leq s_e$, are the feature functions for the video and music, respectively. For DP matching, we use t_i, $i = 1, ..., T$, and s_j, $j = 1, ..., S$, which consist, respectively, of T and S sampled feature points of $F(t)$ and $G(s)$, and which satisfy $F(t_i) > 0$ and $G(s_j) > 0$, for all i and all j. Note that we place default sample feature points at the boundary of each feature function, such that $t_1 = t_b$, $t_T = t_e$, $s_1 = s_b$, and $s_S = s_e$. The distance $d(F(t_i),\ G(s_j))$ between a video feature point and a BGM feature point can be given by the following formula:

$$d(F(t_i),\ G(s_j)) = c_0(F(t_i) - G(s_j))^2 + c_1(t_i - s_j)^2, \tag{6}$$

where c_0 and c_1 are weight constants that control the relative influence of the score difference and the time distance. The DP matching method calculates $d(F(t_i),\ G(s_j))$ using a matching matrix $q(F(t_i),\ G(s_j))$, of dimension $T \times S$. The matching matrix is calculated as follows:

$$q(F(t_1),\ G(s_j)) = d(F(t_1),\ G(s_j)) \quad (j = 1, ..., S) \tag{7}$$

$$q(F(t_i),\ G(s_1)) = d(F(t_i),\ G(s_1)) + q(F(t_{i-1}),\ G(s_1)) \quad (i = 2, ..., T) \tag{8}$$

$$q(F(t_i),\ G(s_j)) = d(F(t_i),\ G(s_j)) + min \begin{pmatrix} q(F(t_{i-1}),\ G(s_j)) \\ q(F(t_{i-1}),\ G(s_{j-1})) \\ q(F(t_i),\ G(s_{j-1})) \end{pmatrix} \quad (i = 2, ..., T, \quad j = 2, ..., S) \tag{9}$$

$$D(F,\ G) = min\{q(F(t_T),\ G(s_j)) \mid 1 \leq j \leq S\}. \tag{10}$$

Here $q(F(t_T), G(s_j))$ is the total distance between the video feature point sequence F and the partial BGM feature point sequence of G, when $F(t_T)$ matches $G(s_j)$. Moreover, $D(F, G)$ is the total distance between F and the partial sequence of G starting from s_1. In order to find the optimal match, we increase the starting time of G from s_1 to s_{S-T} and calculate the matching matrix again until we get the minimum value of $D(F, G)$. This dynamic programming algorithm naturally establishes the optimal matching pairs of motion and music feature points with time complexity $O(N^3)$, where $N = \max(T, S)$.

4.2 Music Modification

Now we synchronize the feature points by time-scaling the music to match the feature pairs obtained from DP matching. First we plot the feature pairs and interpolate the points using a cubic B-spline curve [15]. The reason we use curve interpolation is to minimize the perceptual tempo change around the feature pairs. Once an interpolation curve $C(u) = (s(u), t(u))$ has been computed, each music event, occurring at a time $s_* = s(u_*)$, is moved to $t_* = t(u_*)$ (see Figure 3(a)).

Before we apply the scaling to the music, we discard the points that will give large local deformations and lead to abrupt time scaling of the music. The points to be discarded are further than a user-specified threshold from the least-squares line, which approximates all the feature pairs. The red points in Figure 3(a) are removed, producing the new curve illustrated in Figure 3(b). This new curve will change the tempo of the music locally, with natural ritardando and accelerando effects.

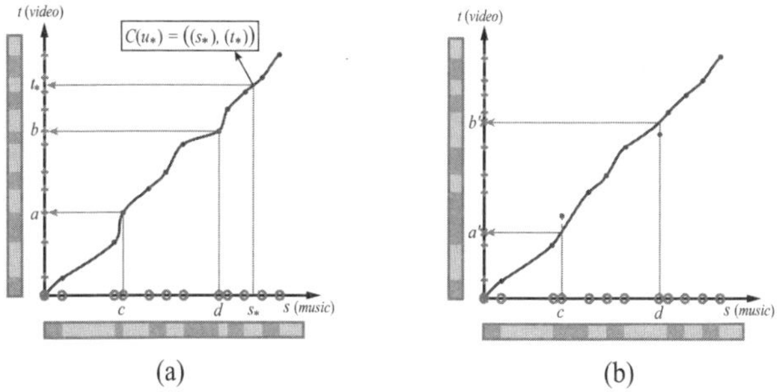

Fig. 3. Music time-scaling using B-spline curve interpolation. The red circles on the s-axis indicate the feature points of the BGM, and the red crosses on the t-axis indicate the feature points of the video: (a) all feature pairs used to interpolate the curve; (b) after removal of feature pairs that will damage the music.

5 Music Graph

The music graph [2] encapsulates connections between several music sequences. New sequences of music can be generated by traversing the graph and applying melody blending at the transition points. The goal of the music graph is to retain the natural flow of the original music, while generating many new tunes.

A traversal of the music graph begins at a vertex selected by the user. Because every edge in the music graph is weighted by the chord distance, the next edge in the traversal can be selected by a random process, influenced by the score, as in a Markov chain [16], which is used as a standard tool for algorithmic composition in computer music [17,18].

The system randomly traverses the music graph repeatedly (100 times in our work), retrieving new music sequences. We expect that some of these will synchronize more effectively with the motion than the original music clips. We measure the disparity between each new music sequence and the given video using the DP matching distance function, and select the sequence corresponding to the minimum distance.

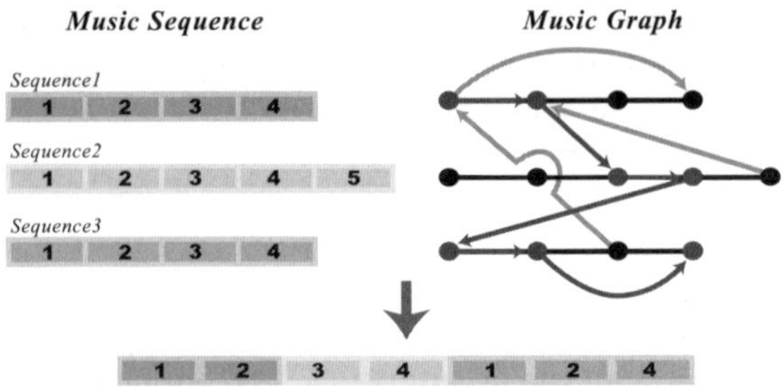

Fig. 4. Basic concept of Music graph

6 Results

In our experiments, we used two video clips, showing Flybar and scenes of Venice; and the music data have various genres including classic, waltz, and dance.

We synchronized the Flybar (Figure 5(a)) clip with *Light Character Polka* BGM which is composed by Johann Strauss. The length of the video clip is 43 seconds and the BGM is 198 seconds. We used the fitness of quaternote as a main feature score of the music, and used the shot boundary, camera movement and object movement as a video feature score.

The other one is the scenes of Venice (Figure 5(b)). We used *An der schönen blauen Donau*, which was composed by Johann Strauss, as a BGM. The length of the video clip is 33 seconds and the BGM is 201 seconds. We also used the fitness of quaternote as a feature score of the music, and use the shot boundary as a video feature score.

In the case of the Flybar video, we used the movement of objects as a dominant feature of the synchronization, while for the Venice scene, we used the shot boundary as a dominant term, for generating the similar effects to any music video. Although there are some non-uniform shot changes, we could create a nicely synchronized video by the music modification.

The next example used the music graph. Using the single BGM, *Gm sonata Op. 49* which was composed by Beethoven, we constructed the music graph. The original music is composed with two main parts, a piano solo and orchestral

Fig. 5. Sample video clip: (a) Flybar (b) Scenes of Venice

music. As a result of similarity analysis, we extracted 329 transitions in the resulting music graph. By traversing the music graph, we synchronized the features of the Flybar video and the synthesized music. Consequently, more dynamic BGM is composed which is more coherent with movement of object than any original music. Table 1 shows the comparison of the synchronization using the original BGM and synthesized BGM generated by music graph.

Table 1. Music graph can generate more synchronized BGM (having less DP matching distance) compared with original BGM

BGM	Length	Distance of DP matching
'Gm sonata Op. 49'	168 sec	8.92
Music graph	44 sec	7.09

7 Conclusion

We have suggested a method to synchronize background music and video using DP matching and the music graph. Our method matches the feature points extracted from the music and video by time scaling the music. By modifying of music a little, we can minimize the changes to the original data necessary to synchronize the feature points.

The music graph is a new way to synthesize new music from a directed graph of music clips. It has various applications. In this paper we show how it can be used to generate well-synchronized background music for the given video. There are several factors that could make the music graph more useful. Replacing random search with systematic traverse methods, as used in motion graph research [4,5], is one possibility. Additionally, we could extend the functions for transition distance and melody blending to consider melodic or rhythmic theories.

Using the difference of DP matching, we can measure the suitability of BGM. Using our database system, we can extract the most suitable BGM by comparison of the matching score. However, to synchronize the mood of BGM and video, maybe the user must select the BGM candidates.

At a higher level, it may be possible to parameterize both music and video in terms of their emotional content [19]. Synchronizing emotions could be a fascinating project.

Acknowledgement. This work was supported by the Ministry of Information & Communications, Korea, under the Information Technology Research Center(ITRC) Support Program.

References

1. Burt, G.: The Art of Film Music. Northeastern University Press (1996)
2. Lee, H.C., Lee, I.K.: Automatic synchronization of background music and motion in computer animation. In: Proceedings of the EUROGRAPHICS 2005. (2005) 353–362

3. Kovar, L., Gleicher, M., Pighin, F.: Motion graphs. In: Proceedings of ACM SIGGRAPH. (2002) 473–482
4. Arikan, O., Forsyth, D.: Interactive motion generation from examples. In: Proceedings of ACM SIGGRAPH. (2002) 483–490
5. Lee, J., Chai, J., Reitsma, P., Hodgins, J., Pollard, N.: Interactive control of avatars animated with human motion data. In: Proceedings of ACM SIGGRAPH. (2002) 491–500
6. Foote, J., Cooper, M., Girgensohn, A.: Creating music videos using automatic media analysis. In: Proceedings of ACM Multimedia 2002. (2002) 553–560
7. Hua, X.S., Lu, L., Zhang, H.J.: Ave - automated home video editing. In: Proceedings of ACM Multimedia 2003. (2003) 490–497
8. Mulhem, P., Kankanhalli, M.S., Hassan, H., Yi, J.: Pivot vector space approach for audio-video mixing. In: Proceedings of IEEE Multimedia 2003. (2003) 28–40
9. Jehan, T., Lew, M., Vaucelle, C.: Cati dance: self-edited, self-synchronized music video. In: Proceedings of SIGGRAPH Conference Abstracts and Applications. (2003) 27–31
10. Yoo, M.J., Lee, I.K., Choi, J.J.: Background music generation using music texture synthesis. In: Proceedings of the International Conference on Entertainment Computing. (2004) 565–570
11. Ma, Y.F., Lu, L., Zhang, H.J., Li, M.J.: A user attention model for video summarization. In: Proceedings of ACM Multimedia 2002. (2002) 553–542
12. Lan, D.J., Ma, Y.F., Zhang, H.J.: A novel motion-based. representation for video mining. In: Proceedings of IEEE. International Conference on Multimedia and Expo. (2003) 469–472
13. Bradski, G.R.: Computer vision face tracking as a component of a perceptual user interface. In: Proceedings of Workshop on Applications of Computer Vision. (1998) 214–219
14. Rowe, R.: Machine Musicianship. MIT Press (2004)
15. Hoscheck, J., Lasser, D.: Fundametals of Computer Aided Geometric Design. AK Peters (1993)
16. Trivedi, K.: Probability & Statistics with Reliability, Queuing, and Computer Science Applications. Prentice-Hall (1982)
17. Cambouropoulos, E.: Markov chains as an aid to computer assisted composition. Musical Praxis **1** (1994) 41–52
18. Trivino-Rodriguez, J.L., Morales-Bueno, R.: Using multiattribute prediction surffix graphs to predict and generate music. Computer Music Journal **25** (2001) 62–79
19. Bresin, R., Friberg, A.: Emotional coloring of computer-controlled music performances. Computer Music Journal **24** (2000) 44–63

An Integration Concept for Vision-Based Object Handling: Shape-Capture, Detection and Tracking*

Matthias J. Schlemmer, Georg Biegelbauer, and Markus Vincze

Automation and Control Institute,
Vienna University of Technology,
1040 Vienna, Austria
{ms, gb, vm}@acin.tuwien.ac.at
http://www.acin.tuwien.ac.at

Abstract. Combining visual shape-capturing and vision-based object manipulation without intermediate manual interaction steps is important for autonomic robotic systems. In this work we introduce the concept of such a vision system closing the chain of shape-capturing, detecting and tracking. Therefore, we combine a laser range sensor for the first two steps and a monocular camera for the tracking step. Convex shaped objects in everyday cluttered and occluded scenes can automatically be re-detected and tracked, which is suitable for automated visual servoing or robotic grasping tasks. The separation of shape and appearance information allows different environmental and illumination conditions for shape-capturing and tracking. The paper describes the framework and its components of visual shape-capturing, fast 3D object detection and robust tracking. Experiments show the feasibility of the concept.

1 Introduction

A lot of detection and tracking methods have been introduced to computer vision, visual servoing gets more and more important in robotic applications and some approaches for visual learning techniques have been presented. However, these techniques are usually dissociated from each other and the connections between them are manually at best.

In this work we present a concept of a vision system that guides the manipulation of convex shaped objects. Robotic applications such as visual servoing or grasping tasks are the goal. Our main contribution is the closing of the gap between shape-capturing, detecting and tracking the object, integrating the individual vision steps in a fully automatic way. The approach is to show the object once to the robot vision system. It is scanned by a laser range sensor that derives a volumetric object description for further detection and tracking. Performing the detection in a totally different environment (e.g. in a home environment on

* This work is supported by the European project MOVEMENT (IST-2003-511670) and by the Austrian Science Foundation grants S9101-N04 and S9103-N04.

N. Zheng, X. Jiang, and X. Lan (Eds.): IWICPAS 2006, LNCS 4153, pp. 215–224, 2006.

potential object places) is possible and results in the object pose, which is the starting pose for the subsequent tracker. This monocular tracker uses the 3D-pose as well as the 3D-object model delivered during the shape-capturing step for continuously updating the pose of the object. Appearance information for the tracker (cues in any form, i.e., interest points in the system proposed) is derived not until now, i.e., from the actual scene – discoupling the illumination and environmental conditions of the shape-capturing and the manipulation steps.

The paper is structured as follows: After an overview of related approaches in the next section, the main concept, the reasons for using Superquadrics and the discrete vision steps are described in detail in Section 2. First experiments are given in Section 3 and further work is outlined in Section 4.

1.1 State of the Art

Kragic and Christensen [7] clearly outline the desire for a fusion of shape and appearance information in robotic servoing and grasping. They emphasize the lack of robustness of model based techniques when trying to track line features of highly textured objects. Their solution is the usage of training images and their projection into the eigenspace. In contrast to this, we are integrating two different sensors, namely a laser scanner for providing the object model (= shape-capturing step) as well as the starting pose of the object in the scene (= detection step) and a CCD-camera (= tracking step). In contrast to the former (shape), the latter exploits appearance information. The problem of line features lies in our understanding not only in textured objects but also in situations where occlusions occur and especially when handling non-rectangular objects. We aim to solve both with our framework.

Currently information for the different tasks is often provided manually. In [5], [6], model databases are required containing local information about the model. Our contribution is a framework that allows model data, initial pose information as well as interest points for the tracking part to be automatically provided by the sensors.

Moreover our framework operates an automatic vision system including the object capturing process for size and shape parameters without any user interaction. Pioneer work in learning for 3D object recognition was done by Mukherjee et al. [14] and an approach for vision-based active learning for robot grasping tasks was introduced by Salganicoff [16]. Our learning – we call it shape-capturing – differs from the latter contributions in that way that we understand the learning process as a coded object description temporarily stored for further processing rather than classifying objects to similar groups by comparing them in a database.

A recent work by Taylor et al. [18] uses a similar full system assembly as we do. They, too, combine a laser scanner with vision but stereo instead of monocular. Their approach is finding geometrically primitive objects (bowls, cylinders, boxes) in a scene without previous learning. To achieve this, a scene segmentation is performed using surface curvature. The main difference to our work is that we divide this step into two parts: shape-capturing (see Sec. 2.1)

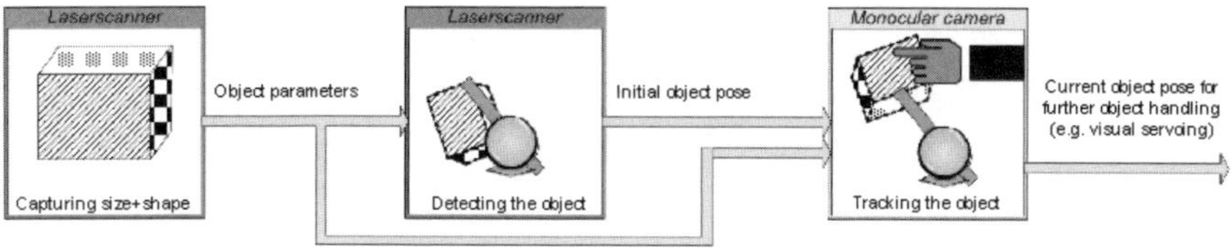

Fig. 1. Concept of our perceptual system: The fully automatic sequence starts with the object capturing where the size and shape parameters are gained that are used for subsequent object detection and tracking in an occluded and cluttered scene

and detection of the learned object in the scene (Sec. 2.2). That way, we avoid the computational expensive segmentation and enable the handling of convex objects with less geometric constraints than [18].

Concerning the tracking part, we like to pick a recent paper by Yoon et al. [19] who presented a combination of a laser scanner and a camera for a tracking task. The selection of line features for the tracking is done manually from the range image – allowing to track complex objects (such as a toy lorry).

2 Concept

Fig. 1 shows the overall concept. First, the target object is shown unoccluded to the laser scanner which automatically derives shape and size parameters storing them in terms of a Superquadric model description (see Sec. 2.1). Detection (Sec. 2.2) is performed in the real-world scene without further user interaction as the parameters are already known from shape-capturing. The detection leads to the pose (position and orientation) of the object, starting the tracking part (Sec. 2.3) that additionally uses the object dimension acquired in the capturing step. The output, i.e., the updated pose, can be used for any further robotic task: grasping, visual servoing and so on. Fig. 2 shows the experimental assembly of the system with the vision equipment and the linear axis.

Stereo vision is usually prone to show weak accuracy and problems arise when dealing with not or weakly textured objects. Our approach aims at delivering the pose of an object with respect to the robot arm in order to be able to perform visual servoing, grasping tasks etc., which all needs high accuracy. The combination of a laser scanner and a colour camera requires a single parametric description of the object to be handled that can be passed along the different steps. Multiple parametric models have been introduced for 3D object recovery. Superquadrics are perhaps the most popular because of several reasons. The compact shape can be described with a small set of parameters ending up in a large variety of different basic shapes. The recovery of Superquadrics has been well investigated and even global deformations can be easily adopted [17]. Additionally, they can be used as volumetric part-based models desirable for robotic manipulations. These advantages cannot be found in other geometric entities, which predestine the Superquadric model for our application. For further information regarding Superquadrics, please refer to [1].

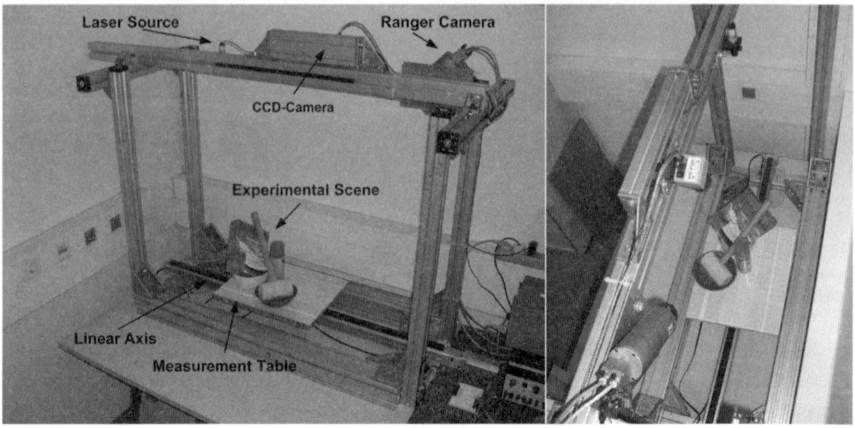

Fig. 2. Experimental sensor assembly with laser source and the ranger camera, the CCD camera for the tracking and a measurement table where the scene for the experiment in Fig. 4 is arranged

The usage of Superquadrics for a system such as ours has several advantages. First of all, Superquadrics are purely shape-based, which frees us from using approximately the same illumination conditions when acquiring the shape, detecting and tracking the object. Second, it enables the possibility to describe a large variety of different objects especially with the extension of global deformations. Most everyday objects such as commodity boxes, cups or tin cans can be described or well approximated. Third, Superquadrics use only a small set of parameters therefore providing a very compact description of the object's surface. This implies a fourth advantage: The computation of the 3D-model coordinates that is necessary for the tracking part, can numerically be solved in a straight-forward manner.

2.1 Capturing the Shape of the Object

Before a robot can handle a convex shaped object, the vision system needs information about it. We propose a shape-capturing step by showing the object to the system and extracting its geometric properties. We use a laser range finder to acquire a range image in which the 3D shape of the object has to be directly recovered. As many sides of the object as possible (i.e., no degenerate view) and no other objects should be visible to the laser scanner. Due to the symmetry of most every-day objects one view is sufficient.

2.2 Detecting the Object

The task of this module is to scan the scene of interest to obtain a single-view range image and detect the object in process real time. The method needed for this purpose must robustly handle object occlusions in a cluttered scene. In order to achieve fast detection results a probabilistic approach is used to verify pose hypotheses of the learned model. For keeping the computational effort low, the search process is structured in a two-level hierarchy.

First the low-level search (probabilistic pose estimation) is RANSAC-based [3] with samples on sub-scaled raw data to speed up the Superquadric recovery using the Levenberg-Marquardt [13] minimization. The best fit of the low level search is again refined finding the optimal pose which is saved.

Second the high level selection (pose verification) is necessary due to faulty detections in the low level search results. To resolve these ambiguities a ranked voting [15] of the pose hypotheses is applied considering three constraints: the quality of fit, the number of points on the Superquadric surface and the number of the Superquadric's interior points.

The hierarchical two-level search achieves a fast and robust detection result especially in cluttered scenes. Because of fitting the learned object model to local surface patches and verify them globally within the refinement step, disconnected surface patches can be associated to one entire part. This enables a robust detection of partly occluded objects. For more details on this algorithm please refer to [2]. The detected pose of the object is the initialization for the subsequent tracking with a monocular camera and the recovered shape and size parameters from the shape-capturing process provide the required model to the tracker.

2.3 Tracking the Object

Provided with starting pose information from the detection step, our tracker projects the Superquadric, acquired during the shape-capturing step, into the current camera image. The usage of Superquadrics involves the possibility of a fast computation of the convex hull which provides the boundaries of the projected object, within which interest points are now searched using any detector, e.g. hessian-laplace or harris-affine (a very good comparison can be found in [11]). For each detected point, a descriptor [12] is saved that contains its properties. Here again, any descriptor may be used, e.g. SIFT [9]. The main focus lies on good repeatability as the majority of detected points should be found again in the next frame with a very similar descriptor. However, timing behaviour is of course also a very important issue. Note that the appearance information of the object for the tracking is obtained directly from the actual scene situation, enabling the handling of different illumination and occlusion conditions of the model acquisition and the tracking step. The interest points are finally reprojected into the image for computation of the object coordinates. Here another strength of the used model stands out: A Superquadric describes the closed surface of an object, hence, the computation of the intersection point of the ray of sight through the interest point and the model immediately delivers the 3D-model coordinates of this point. This enables the association of every detected interest point in 2D with its 3D-coordinates on the object.

The tracking loop works as follows: Interest points are searched in the 2D-neighborhood of the points found in the previous image. Correspondences between the points in the two frames are established via comparing their signatures. Finally, the pose is determined using the algorithm by Lu et al. [10]. The image points from the current image are taken as observed 2D-points and the corresponding points from the previous tracking step provide the 3D object coordinate information. For handling wrong matches, the RANSAC [3] method is applied using the number of point votes and selecting the best result respectively the mean of the largest pose cluster in case of multiple equal votes. The interest points of the current frame are again projected onto the object model and the interest point positions are stored in object coordinates for the next tracking step. All interest points are used for the matching with the next frame, independently of whether they have been used when matching with the previous image or not. Thus, the overall number of points for the tracking may vary and newly appearing points are seamlessly integrated into the tracking process. This way, appearing sides of the object that were occluded before are available for supporting the tracking process. In this way problems with rotational motions are reduced.

2.4 Calibrating the System

First, the sensors have to be calibrated individually for the sake of accuracy. Second, the coordinate systems of the scanner and the camera must be registered onto each other for executing an automatic sequence of the different steps.

The calibration of the laser scanner is done using the geometrical approach. With a 3D calibration object with markers on at least two different planes, the pose of the laser plane and the extrinsic parameters of the camera can be calculated as described in [4].

The tracking camera is calibrated with the calibration tool *Camcalb*, introduced in [20]. This tool provides the intrinsic camera parameters in order to undistort the camera images for enhancement of tracking robustness and additionally gives the extrinsic parameters (position and orientation of the calibration plate) for fulfilling the last calibration step:

Laser coordinate system and camera coordinate system are finally registered via transformation between the respective world coordinate systems. This leads to the possibility of transforming the target object's position and orientation obtained by the laser scanner during the detection step into the coordinate system of the tracking camera.

3 Experimental Results

Fig. 3 shows an uncluttered scene for tracking a cylinder (one of the basic Superquadric shapes). The object (3a) is scanned (3b) and a Superquadric is fitted (3c). Scanning the scene (3d) leads to the location of the learned Superquadric (3e). This provides the starting pose (3f) for the tracker (3g–3i).

Table 1 shows the parameters of the Superquadric – both ground-truth and the captured values.

Fig. 4 shows another whole vision sequence as presented in this paper for a more complex example. Again, we chose an every-day commodity item as object

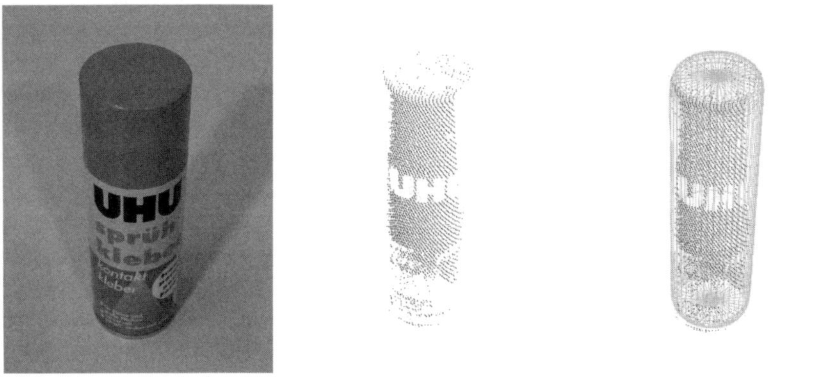

(a) Object of interest (b) Range image of object (c) Fitted Superquadric

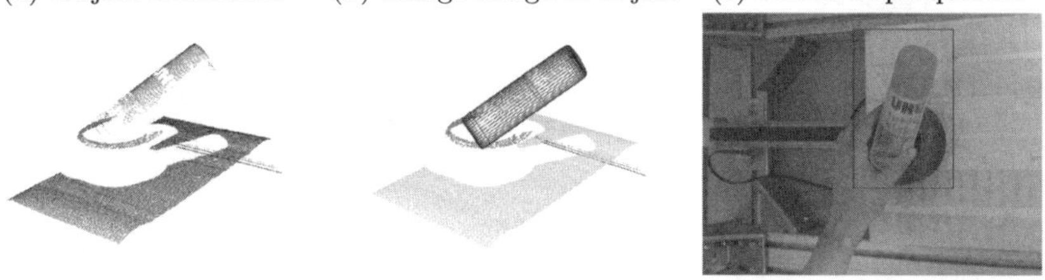

(d) Range image of scene (e) Detection of the object (f) Tracker starting frame

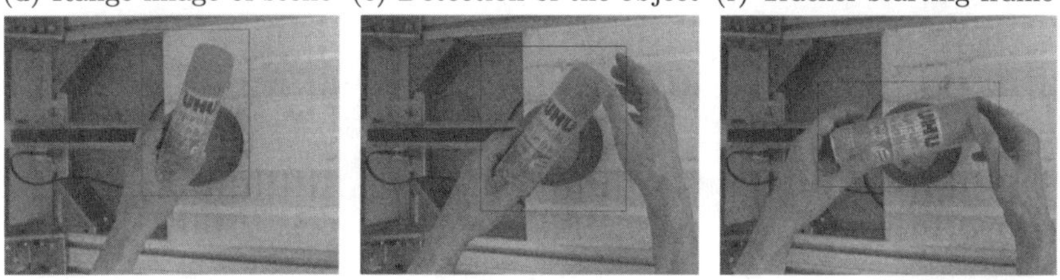

(g) Tracking frame #7 (h) Tracking frame #11 (i) Tracking frame #16

Fig. 3. Experiment 1: Handling of a cylinder. Capturing model (first row), Detecting (second row) and Tracking (last row). The reprojected pose is depicted as mesh-grid.

to be retrieved and tracked, this time a rectangular rice box. Table 2 sums up the parameters retrieved by the shape-capturing step. Although the accuracy of the shape-capturing is deficient on the shortest side of the object, tracking is not affected. This leads back to the derivation of the tracking cues, i.e. the interest points, from the actual scene whereas an edge-detector would be misdirected.

Note that during detection (second row of Fig. 4), the rice box now lies in an arbitrary position and is partially occluded by the white bowl, the tin can as well as the mallet shaft. The reprojected white lines in the last two rows refer to the pose of the tracker. The white points are the locations of the interest points. The matching example on the right of the third row is a zoomed clip of frame #18. The black dots indicate the positions where interest points have been found in the previous step, the white dots the locations of the points in the current frame. Note that there are some white points that have no match with

(a) Object of interest

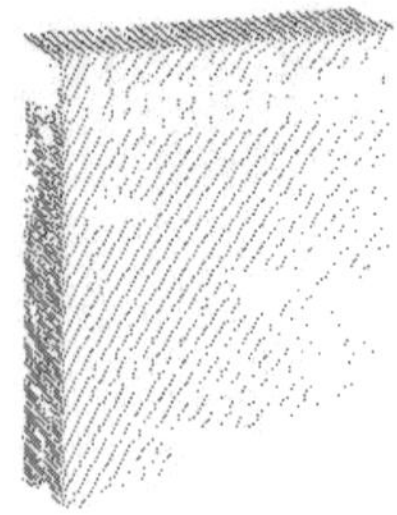

(b) Object range image

(c) Fitted Superquadric

(d) Occluded object

(e) Scene range image

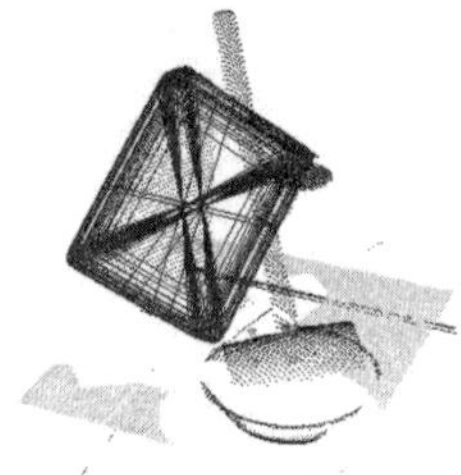

(f) Detected object

(g) Starting pose

(h) Matching example

(i) Frame #1

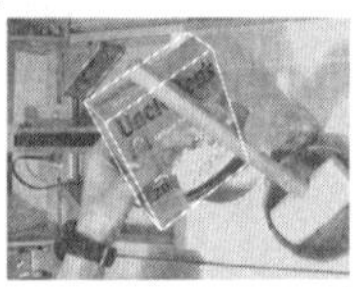

(j) Frame #18

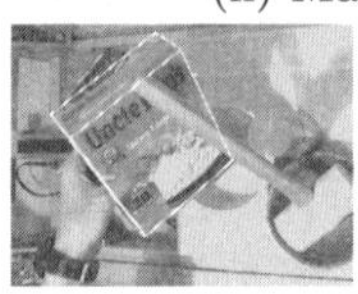

(k) Frame #23

(l) Frame #28

Fig. 4. Experiment 2: Fig. (a) to (c): Capturing the object parameters; Fig. (d) to (f): Detection of the object in the scene; Fig. (g): Starting pose of the object; Here, the pose is depicted as white lines; Fig. (h): Matching example: Black dots from frame #17 are matched with white dots from frame #18; Fig. (i) to (l): Some tracking frames

black ones (no white chain). Nevertheless, these points are stored for the next iteration as they may possibly be matched with points of frame #19.

Furthermore the occlusion caused by the mallet shaft is dynamic during tracking due to the motion of the rice box. Additionally, the hand coming from the left also occludes a part of the box. Finally, even the number of visible faces of the box changes. Nevertheless, the pose is recovered with sufficient accuracy.

Table 1. Summarized learned Superquadric size and shape parameters of the tin can

parameter	*size [mm]*			*shape*			
	a_1	a_2	a_3	ϵ_1	ϵ_2	k_x	k_y
model	24.5	24.5	85.2	0.1	1.0	0.0	0.0
true object	26.5	26.5	86.5	0.0	1.0	0.0	0.0

Table 2. Summarized learned Superquadric size and shape parameters of the rice box

parameter	*size [mm]*			*shape*			
	a_1	a_2	a_3	ϵ_1	ϵ_2	k_x	k_y
model	96.8	74.9	27.1	0.2	0.1	0.0	0.0
true object	95.0	75.0	22.5	0.0	0.0	0.0	0.0

4 Conclusion and Further Work

With this work we presented a vision concept that closes the gap between capturing the shape of a convex object and handling it in a cluttered and occluded scene – in an automatic way. The fusion of shape and appearance proved to be well suited for this purpose. A laser range scanner for retrieving object parameters as well as for detecting the object in the scene, is combined with a monocular CCD camera that is liable for the tracking part. This concept has been shown to provide a stable solution for shape-capturing, detecting and tracking different Superquadric shapes as cylinders and boxes.

As further work, tests – including timing analysis and quantitative evaluation – of the system will be done on our existing pan-tilt laser range sensor. Accessibility and grasping analysis will follow as soon as we mount the unit on a mobile platform. As extension for this concept, the shape-capturing and detection of more complex objects will be tackled. These objects may be expressed by a composition of several Superquadrics. This requires a learning process that parses subparts of an object automatically [8]. The current bottleneck of the tracker as far as timing is concerned is the 3D pose estimation. To achieve camera frame rate, code optimization has to be done and matching robustness must be increased in order to reduce the number of required RANSAC-iterations. Furthermore, the additional usage of cues as for example edges may also support the robustness of the monocular pose estimation.

References

1. A. H. Barr, *Superquadrics and Angle Preserving Transformations*, IEEE Computer Graphics and Applications, 1981, Vol. 1(1), pp. 11-23
2. G. Biegelbauer and M. Vincze, *Fast and Robust 3D Object Detetction Using a Simplified Superquadric Model Description*, Proceedings of the 7th Conference on Optical 3-D Measurement Techniques, 2005, Vol. 2, pp. 220-230

3. M.A. Fischler and R.C. Bolles, *Random Sample Consensus: A Paradigm for Model Fitting with Applications to Image Analysis and Automated Cartography*, Communications of the ACM, 1981, Vol. 24, pp. 381-395
4. J. Haverinen and J. Röning, *A 3-D Scanner Capturing Range and Color for the Robotics Applications*, 24th Workshop of the Austrian Association of Pattern Recognition OEAGM/AAPR, 2000, pp. 41-48
5. H.-Y. Jang et al., *A Visibility-Based Accessibility Analysis of the Grasp Points for Real-Time Manipulation*, IEEE/RSJ International Conference on Intelligent Robots and Systems, 2005, pp. 3111-3116
6. S. Kim et al., *Robust model-based 3D object recognition by combining feature matching with tracking*, Proceedings of the IEEE International Conference on Robotics and Automation, 2003, Vol.2, pp. 2123-2128
7. D. Kragic and H.I. Christensen, *Model based techniques for robotic servoing and grasping*, Proceedings of the IEEE/RSJ International Conference on Intelligent Robots and System, 2002, Vol.1, pp. 299-304
8. A. Leonardis and A. Jaklic, *Superquadrics for segmenting and modeling range data*, IEEE Transactions on Pattern Analysis and Machine Intelligence, 1997, Vol. 19(11), pp. 1289-1295
9. D. Lowe, *Distinctive image features from scale-invariant keypoints*, International Journal of Computer Vision, 2004, Vol. 60(2), pp. 91-110
10. C.P. Lu et al., *Fast and Globally Convergent Pose Estimation from Video Images*, IEEE Transactions on Pattern Analysis and Machine Intelligence 22 (June 2000), No. 6, pp. 610-622
11. K. Mikolajczyk et al., *A Comparison of Affine Region Detectors*, International Journal of Computer Vision, 2005, Vol. 65(1/2), pp. 43-72
12. K. Mikolajczyk and Cordelia Schmid, *A performance evaluation of local descriptors*, IEEE Transactions on Pattern Analysis and Machine Intelligence, 2005, Vol. 27(10), pp. 1615-1630
13. J.J. Moré, *The Levenberg-Marquardt Algorithm: Implementation and Theory*, Numerical Analysis - Lecture Notes in Mathematics, Springer Verlag, 1977, Vol. 630, pp. 105-116
14. S. Mukherjee and S.K. Nayar, *Automatic generation of GRBF networks for visual learning*, Proceedings of the IEEE International Conference on Computer Vision, 1995, pp. 794-800
15. B. Parhami, *Voting Algorithms*, Machine Learning (IEEE Transactions on Reliability), 1994, Vol. 43(4)pp. 617-629
16. M. Salganicoff, *Active Learning for Vision-Based Robot Grasping*, Machine Learning (Kluwer), 1996, Vol. 23(2)pp. 251-278
17. F. Solina and R. Bajcsy, *Recovery of Parametric Models from Range Images: The Case for Superquadrics with Global Deformations*, IEEE Transactions on Pattern Analysis and Machine Intelligence, 1990, Vol. 12(2), pp. 131-147
18. G. Taylor and L. Kleeman, *Integration of robust visual perception and control for a domestic humanoid robot*, Proceedings IEEE/RSJ Int. Conf. on Intelligent Robots and Systems, 2004, Vol.1, pp. 1010-1015
19. Y. Yoon et al., *A New Approach to the Use of Edge Extremities for Model-based Object Tracking*, Proceedings of the IEEE International Conference on Robotics and Automation, 2005, pp. 1883-1889
20. M. Zillich and E. Al-Ani, *Camcalb: A user friendly camera calibration software*, Workshop of the Austrian Association of Pattern Recognition OEAGM/AAPR, 2004, pp.111-116

Visual Information Encryption in Frequency Domain: Risk and Enhancement

Weihai Li[1] and Yuan Yuan[2]

[1] Department of Electronic Engineering and Information Science,
University of Sciences and Technology of China, Hefei, Anhui 230027, P.R. China
whli@ustc.edu.cn

[2] School of Computing and Applied Science, Aston University,
Birmingham B4 7ET, United Kingdom
yuany1@aston.ac.uk

Abstract. Focusing on the encryption of digital image and video, this paper reports an intrinsic weakness of all existing discrete-cosine-transform (DCT) based algorithms. This serious weakness of DCT is analyzed theoretically and then demonstrated practically. As an instance, a novel attack algorithm is proposed to acquire the sketch information from the encrypted data without any pre-knowledge of the encryption algorithm. Thereafter, to solve this problem, a full inter-block shuffle (FIBF) approach is developed and it can be employed to improve the encryption security in all DCT-based algorithms, such as JPEG, MPEG and H.26x.

1 Introduction

Recently, with the rapid incensement of visual information, digital image and video encryption approaches have been widely studied upon many important data resources, such as military satellite images, patent design blueprints, and visual net meetings [1,2,3]. These applications always require ultra-high security level to keep the image and/or video data confidential between users, in other word, it is essential that nobody could get to know the content without a key for decryption. Moreover, it worth emphasizing that a video segment normally contains a number of single frames. Therefore, from this point of view, image encryption can be regarded as a basis of video encryption (Note that: video motion vector should also be encrypted). So, this paper mainly focuses on digital image encryption.

Previous image encryption algorithms can be classified into three major categories:

- *Spatial domain-based* [4]: this category always treats an image as a set of single pixels and does not consider too much about (1) the correlation among pixels within an image and (2) the characteristics of individual images. There-fore, modern encrypting algorithms can be utilized upon images, which are processed as general data without considering size, redundancy, and other is-sues. In these algorithms, the general encryption usually destroy the correlation among pixels and thus make the encrypted images incompressible;

N. Zheng, X. Jiang, and X. Lan (Eds.): IWICPAS 2006, LNCS 4153, pp. 225–234, 2006.

- *Frequency domain-based* [7,8,9,10,11,12]: aiming at reducing the size of the encrypted image for network applications etc., a number of image encryption algorithms have been developed in transform domain to keep the result images compressible. The most popular frequency domains are: Wavelet transform [12] and discrete-cosine-transform (DCT) [8,9,10,11]. As an efficient and effective domain, 8×8 DCT-based algorithms[1] have been widely employed, e.g., signs flipping [7], DC and non-zero ACs scramble [8], intra-block shuffle [9], DC splitting and intra-block shuffle [9], and inter-block shuffle [10,11]. These algorithms are different in secrecy and affection of compression ratio, while the proper combination of different methods may give better performance and security; and
- *Entropy coding based* [5,6]: this is a complex class of image encryption approaches. Herein, we only give a brief description because it is not our major concern and not used as frequently as the frequency domain-based ones. In these encryption algorithms, different entropy coding tables are chosen by keys [5,6], and which causes compression ratio reduced slightly. Such as the algorithms of enciphering headers, these entropy coding based algorithms have also some disadvantages: (1) an encrypted image is invisible without the right key. Such if a user has an invisible image, s/he can not judge whether the image file is destroyed or the key is wrong; and (2) the more serious thing is that it makes quantum state amplification possible since only the right key can make encrypted image visible, and that causes quantum exhausting attack realizable.

These existing DCT-based image encryption algorithms worked in many applications and gave satisfactory results as well. Unfortunately, a serious problem is ignored: The ability of image information protection is hard to be examined. In fact, the securities of these image encryption algorithms are mostly evaluated by eyes. This is certainly an insecure and unreasonable way. As a result, many algorithms in DCT-based encryption systems seem to be good, but most of them may leak out the sketch information of the encrypted images even though the attacker has no pre-knowledge about the encryption algorithm and the key.

This paper reports an intrinsic weakness of conventional DCT-based image encryption approaches and then gives an enhanced method to avoid this problem in applications. This paper is organized as follows: Section 2 briefly introduces previous work on DCT-based image encryption. In Section 3, based on theoretical analysis, a novel scheme is reported to attack conventional encryption approaches. This newly proposed scheme is named as *non-zero-counting attack* (NZCA). Section 4 then gives a *full inter-block shuffle* (FIBS) solution, which improves the existing DCT-based image encryption approaches to avoid the NZCA-liked attacks. Finally, Section 5 concludes and states future work.

2 DCT-Based Encryption Approaches (DBEA)

DCT-based algorithms are normally established based on image sub-blocks, which are sized 8 pixels by 8 pixels. When DCT coefficients in one sub-block are encrypted, the

[1] In this paper, 8×8 size is used for analyzing the DCT-based algorithms.

inverse DCT (IDCT) cannot reconstruct the original sub-block. The key criterions are compression ratio, computing complexity and key quantity etc. There are two kinds of encryption techniques: scramble and shuffle. [5,6,7,8,9,10,11]

Previously, a number of image encryption algorithms have been proposed and successfully employed based on DCT, such as:

- *Signs flipping* [7]: This method treats signs as bit stream (negative as 1 and positive as 0), and encrypt them with a key. From another point of view, signs flipping can be regarded as a special case of the most significant bits (MSB) scramble, which will be introduced below;
- *DC and non-zero ACs scramble* [8]: Scramble of DC coefficients, averages of pixels in each sub-block, can change energy amplitudes and demolish image impression. Scramble of AC coefficients can destroy image texture and make image baffling. It has been noticed that only DC coefficients scramble or only AC coefficients scramble cannot obtain high security, so that both DC and AC coefficients should be scrambled. To keep high compression ratio, zeros are usually not scrambled. Sometimes, only several most significant bits (MSBs) are scrambled in order to save key bits;
- *Intra-block shuffle* [9] and *DC splitting and intra-block shuffle* [9]: The early method of shuffle is to shuffle all intra-block coefficients simply. However, DC coefficient is often larger than AC coefficients, and easy to be located and restored. To avoid this bug, DC coefficient can be split into two parts: four lowest bits set to DC coefficient and highest bits set to AC63 position, the highest frequency component, and then all coefficients are shuffled. Coefficients shuffle changes energy distribution in frequency domain, and makes encrypted image incomprehensible. At the same time, coefficients shuffle ruins the effect of zigzag scan and reduces compression ratio observably. An improvement is to divide the 64 coefficients into several bands and limit shuffle within each band. Different bands relate to different security levels. Shuffle more bands will obtain higher security; and
- *Inter-block shuffle* [10,11]: Another shuffle method is inter-block shuffle. To simplify algorithm complexity, two kinds shuffle are ordinarily adopted. The simpler one takes sub-block as basic unit, and shuffle all sub-blocks. The security of this algorithm is low since it is just like a *jigsaw puzzle* for image sub-blocks. The other algorithm takes all coefficients of the same frequency position as a group, and shuffle within each group. Usually, shuffle of low frequency coefficients can make image incomprehensible.

These above algorithms have different characteristics and therefore are suitable for different applications. Moreover, by properly combining (some of) them, better performance and security may be achieved.

Figure 1 shows several image encryption results. The original Lena image is given in the top-left, which is sized 512×512. The top-right and bottom-left sub-figures show experimental results of the original image encrypted by a scramble and a intra-block shuffle algorithms respectively. Finally, a combination algorithm of scramble and shuffle is performed and the result is shown in the bottom-right sub-figure. In the experiments: (1) the employed scramble algorithm is: DC and non-zero AC coefficients scramble. Data to be scrambled should have at least 10 bits, otherwise 0 was inserted ahead for positive data or 1 was inserted for negative data; and (2) the shuffle algorithm employed here is: DC splitting and intra-block shuffle. Shuffle table is generated and changed base the key.

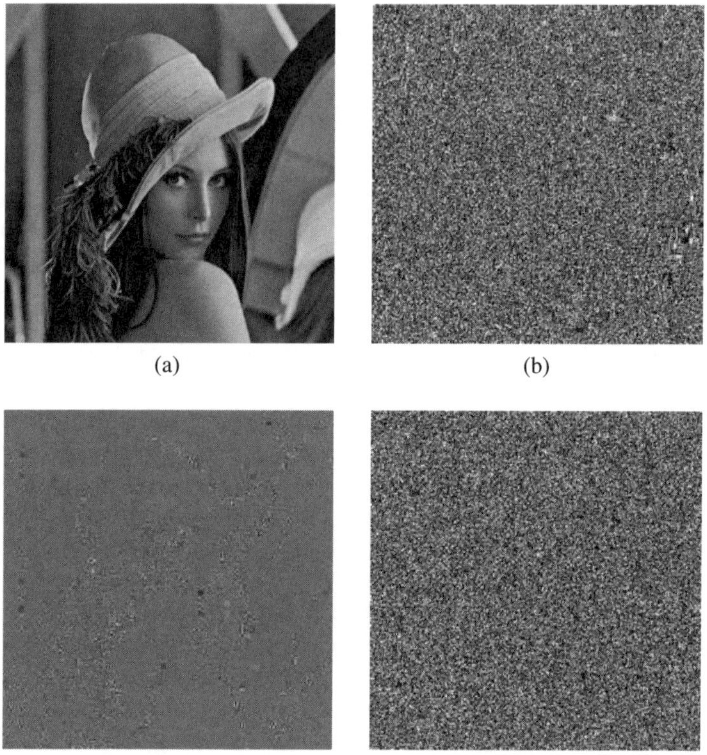

(a) (b)

(c) (d)

Fig. 1. Existing DCT-based image encryption algorithms. (a) The original Lena image. (b) The result image encrypted with DC and non-zero ACs scramble. (c) The result image encrypted with DC splitting and intra-block shuffle. (d) The result image encrypted with both scramble and shuffle - the combination result of the algorithms used in (b) and (c).

Note that: some obscure edges are still perceptible in the shuffle result, Figure 1(c). This phenomenon exists because: there are often large AC coefficients when a sub-block contains edge information. Thereafter these large AC coefficients usually cause strong dark-to-light visual effect, even if they are shuffled to other locations. These eye-catcher sub-blocks results in the obscure edges.

3 Non-Zero-Counting Attack (NZCA): Risk of DBEA

The encrypted images in Figure 1 appear to be security, unfortunately they can still leak some information, i.e., the security of encrypted images cannot be guaranteed by these conventional encryption algorithms. For instance, in this Section, a novel attack scheme, named non-zero-counting attack (NZCA), is designed to catch the sketch information from encrypted images without pre-knowledge about the encryption algorithm.

As a sample attack scheme, the NZCA is thus proposed based on the below fact: In an 8×8 DCT-based encryption algorithm, the zero coefficients in each image sub-block are usually not scrambled (alternatively, increases by one in the algorithm of DC splitting and intra-block shuffle) to keep high compression ratio (a successive series of zeros benefits the run-length coding after zigzag scan). In other word, some frequency band information is not encrypted. On the other hand, the image sub-blocks, which contain much edge information, usually have more non-zero coefficients than the smooth sub-blocks. Moreover, sub-blocks with different textures often have different amounts of non-zero coefficients, and there will be a large number of non-zero coefficients if a sub-block is chaotic. This means that: the amount of non-zero coefficients implies some characteristics, especially texture and edge information, of the corresponding sub-block.

As illustrated in Figure 2, the amounts of non-zero coefficients for Figure 1(a). It shows the percent of sub-blocks, which contain n non-zero coefficients, to the total sub-blocks.

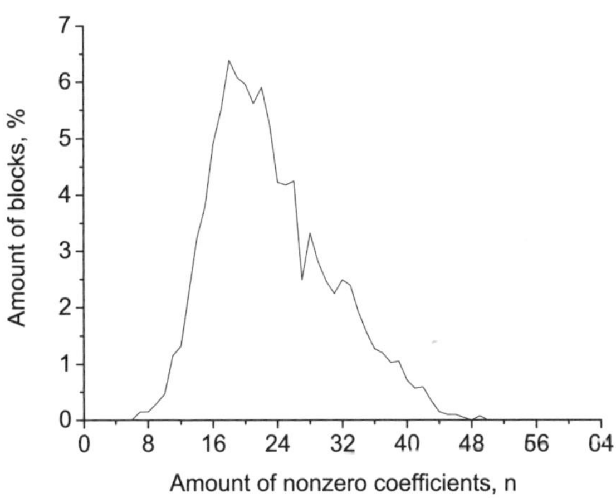

Fig. 2. The statistical results of non-zero coefficients for Figure 1(a)

This sample attack algorithm is introduced in Table 1. Several key issues of this algorithm are then stated and analyzed individually.

Parameter selection: Experimental results show that the NZCA algorithm works in most cases. Figure 3 shows some broken results of Figure 1(d) with different pairs of parameters r1 and r2. It can be drawn from Figure 3 that broken sketches benefit from proper selections of r1 and r2. An interesting phenomenon is noticed that Figure 3(b) is somehow like inverse of Figure 3(c), and vice versa. Then it is known that 25 is a proper threshold of inner sub-blocks and edge sub-blocks. Images are different from

Table 1. Non-Zero-Counting Attack (NZCA)

Step	Content
Input	Encrypted images I_E.
Output	Decrypted (sketch) images I_{DE}.
1	To generate the statistical chart of non-zero coefficients for I_{DE}.
2	To determine thresholds $r1$ and $r2$ to define emphasized region.
3	For each 8×8 sub-block B_E in I_E,
4	To get the amount of non-zero coefficients (including DC coefficient) n.
5	To computer the pseudo-luminance value Y of each sub-block by: $Y = \begin{cases} 255 - 50 \times n/r1 & (n < r1) \\ 50 + 100 \times (r1 + r2 - 2n)/(r2 - r1) & (r1 \leq n \leq r2) \\ 255 - 50 \times (64 - n)/(64 - r2) & (n > r2) \end{cases}$
6	In I_{DE}, assign the value of all 64 pixels within B_E with the Y value.
7	End.
8	If the I_{DE} is not good enough, repeat 1-7.

one to another; therefore, it is hard to decide the best parameters. As in the machine learning fields, *parameter tuning* is a very popular mechanism and has been widely used. In this case, abundant experiences are desirable. Moreover, an adaptive scheme will also be an important future work as stated later.

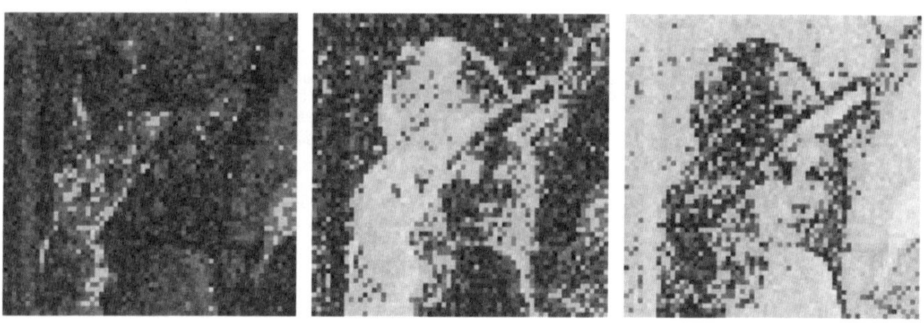

(a) (b) (c)

Fig. 3. Broken results of encrypted image Figure 1(d). (a) $r1 = 11, r2 = 39$; (b) $r1 = 11, r2 = 25$; (c) $r1 = 26, r2 = 39$.

Target encryption algorithms: The attack scheme is performed on Figure 1(d), in which both scramble and shuffle are employed. In fact, it can be noticed from Table 1 that the NZCA algorithm is independent of the encryption algorithm. It is worth emphasizing that: some background edges are ignored in Figure 2(d). This is because that they are defocused and not as sharp as foreground edges.

Image resolution: As introduced before, in most of the DCT-based processes, the minimum units are sub-blocks sized 8 pixels by 8 pixels. Therefore, in the attack results (sketches), all details within one sub-block cannot be captured. In other word, what can be got is mosaic-liked images, but that is enough for human to recognize the major content of the target image. As we know, human's vision system is sensitive on low-frequency parts, and this NZCA attack scheme can exactly show such information to attackers.

It is nature that if the image has higher resolution, more sub-blocks will be contained and fewer details will be included in a sub-block, in that case, the attack results (sketches) will be much clearer — the higher the image resolutions, the better the attack performances.

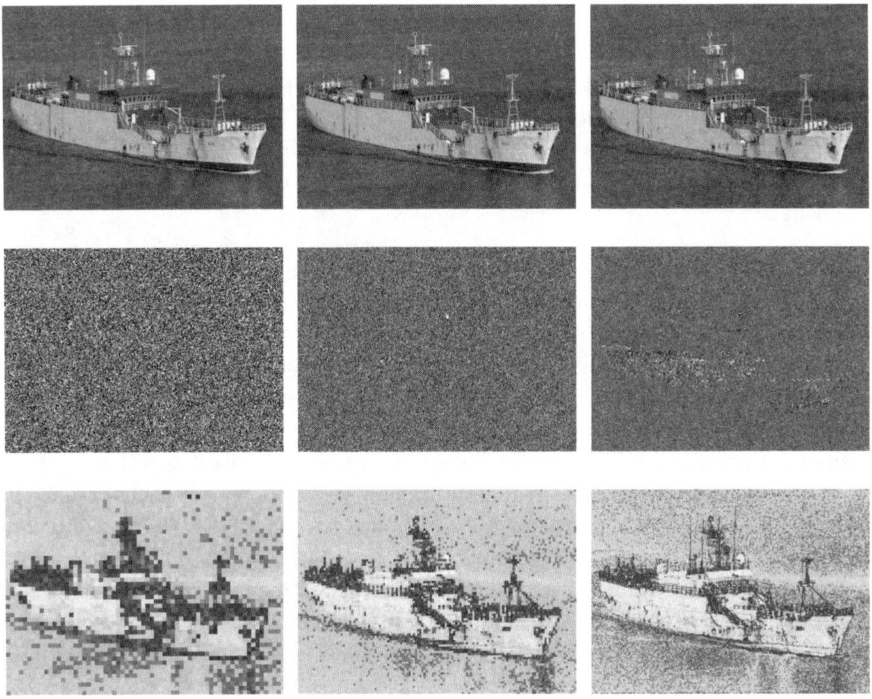

Fig. 4. Non-zero-counting attack (NZCA) effects at different resolutions. The first row shows original images of different sizes, say, 525×375, 1050×750, and 2100×1500, respectively, from left to right. The second row shows the encrypted images. The bottom row provides the broken sketches.

In addition, in modern digital image processing systems, people usually keep and transform high quality/resolution images, especially for some sensitive application fields, e.g., military satellite images etc. So, this attack algorithm can work more effectively. Experiments were carried out to show the performance of NZCA upon the same image of different resolutions, which is shown in Figure 4. When the original image size is around 2100×1500, the attack result can show not only the major content but also some details. Herein, obviously we can see that: the conventional DCT-based image/video encryption algorithms are not safe any longer.

4 Full Inter-Block Shuffle (FIBS): Enhancement of DBEA

In Section 3, we introduced a kind of serious attack algorithms for DCT-based image encryption. To guarantee the security of image communication, it is essential to develop an effective approach to stand against the NZCA attack. By taking this issue into account: the NZCA algorithm is based on the precondition of unchanged amounts of non-zero coefficients in each sub-block (not caring the influence of DC coefficient splitting), there are two options to enhance the conventional DCT-based encryption algorithms:

- *Zeros to non-zeros*: To change some zeros to non-zeros according to the keys may make the algorithm(s) stronger against the NZCA attack. However, it meanwhile increases the amount of non-zeros greatly, and will decrease compression ratio hugely. Therefore, it is not a good method; and
- *Coefficients inter-block shuffle*: This solution does not change the total amount of non-zeros, but their locations only. As a result, the compression ratio is slightly changed.

Theoretically, by shuffling the inter-block coefficients, the NZCA attack should be avoid to some extent. Unfortunately, thing is not such easy and there are some key issues to study, i.e., *which and how many coefficients to shuffle?*

To simplify the inter-block procedure, the shuffle is usually carried on upon coefficients of the same frequency position. It is therefore normally enough to make image incomprehensible by shuffling merely the lowest frequency coefficients. How-ever, it is not to withstand the NZCA attack. The reason can be described as follows: Human naked eyes are not sensitive to small high frequency components, especially when the image looks chaotic. So, it is enough for human eyes security to shuffle only some low frequency coefficients. However the NZCA algorithm is more sensitive to high frequency components than low frequency ones, since low frequency ones are often non-zero. Even if low frequency coefficients are shuffled, the NZCA can still catch texture information from high frequency coefficients. This analysis is confirmed by experiment results shown in Figure 5.

In general, a partial inter-block shuffle can benefit the image encryption algorithm, but it is not enough to withstand the NZCA attack. Therefore, in this paper, a full inter-block shuffle (FIBS) is proposed and examined as in the last column in Figure 5. Herein, note that: comparing with computation cost, security is a bigger concern for image encryption applications.

In Figure 5, it can be seen that when the 10 lowest coefficients are shuffled, the encrypted image looks incomprehensible, but the broken sketch is almost as clear as Figure 1(d). Even when the 30 lowest coefficients shuffled, the broken sketch is still recognizable. Thus, it can be concluded that shuffle of almost all coefficients is necessary to withstand the NZCA attack. When the shuffle procedure is random enough, the amount of non-zero coefficients of each sub-block will be close to their average value as shown in Figure 5. Then all possible information is covered up and the security of encrypted image is ensured.

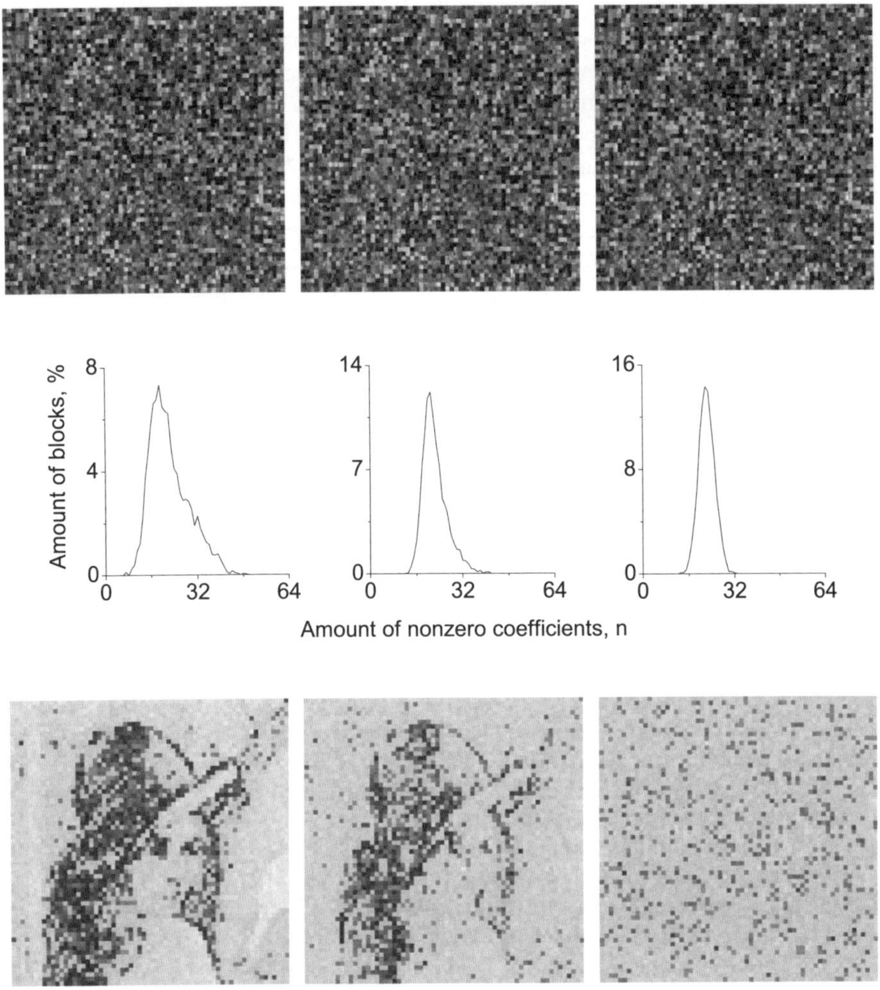

Fig. 5. Full inter-block shuffle (FIBS). The last column shows the advantage of FIBS against the NZCA attack, the corresponding bands are 0-63. The first two columns stand for partial inter-block shuffles on bands 0-9 and 0-29 respectively. The top row gives encrypted images by inter-block shuffle; the middle row gives the statistical charts of these encrypted images, while the last row provides attack results with $r1 = 26$ and $r2 = 39$.

5 Conclusion and Future Work

In this paper, conventional discrete-cosine-transform (DCT) based image encryption algorithms are reported to be unsafe and have big potential to be attacked. This kind of attack algorithms are based on the invariant amounts of non-zero coefficients of the 8×8 DCT image sub-blocks. There are very few non-zero coefficients if a sub-block is smooth or gradual, on the other hand, more non-zero coefficients can be gain if a sub-block contains much edges information. In general, the amount of non-zero coefficients implies some characteristics of the original image. As a sample, a non-zero-counting attack (NZCA) scheme is introduced to generate a rough sketch of the original image by setting pseudo-luminance values for each sub-block. To avoid the NZCA-liked attack, a solution, named full inter-block shuffle (FIBS), is then developed to enhance these encryption algorithms in JPEG, MPEG, H.26x, etc. The FIBS is demonstrated to effectively destroy the invariance of non-zero coefficient amount. Therefore, the existing DCT-based image encryption algorithms are enhanced to be much securer. An adaptive parameter selection procedure of the NZCA attack, the complexity reduction of the FIBS, and other information hiding strategies [13] will be our future work.

References

1. Macq, B. M., Quisquater, J.-J.: Cryptology for Digital TV Broadcasting. Proceedings of the IEEE (1995) **83**(6) 944–957
2. Iskender, A., Li, G.: An Empirical Study of Secure MPEG Video Transmissions. Proceedings of the Symposium on Network and Distributed System Security (1996) 137–144
3. Qiao, L., Nahrstedt, K.: A New Algorithm for MPEG Video Encryption. Proceeding of the First Int'l Conf. on Imaging Science, Systems and Technology (1997) 21–29
4. Zhang, X., Liu, F., Jiao, L.: An Image Encryption Arithmetic Base on Chaotic Sequences. Journal of Image and Graphics (2003) **8A**(4) 374–378
5. Li, C., Han, Z.: The New Evolution of Image Encryption Techniques. Information and Control (2003) **32**(4) 339–343,351
6. Lian S., Wang Z.: MPEG Video Encryption Algorithm Based on Entropy Encoding and Encryption. Mini-Micro Systems (2004) **125**(12) 2207–2210
7. Shi, C., Bharat, B.: A Fast MPEG Video Encryption Algorithm. Proceedings of the 6th ACM Int'l Conf. on Multimedia (1998) 81–88
8. Lu, Y., Yang, W, Chen, L.: Encryption Algorithm for the Image in the Frequency Domain. Computer Engineering and Application (2003) **39**(14) 130–131,172
9. Tang, L.: Methods for Encrypting and Decrypting MPEG Video Data Efficiently. Proceedings of the Fourth ACM Int'l Conf. on Multimedia (1996) 219–229
10. Liu, X., Eskicioglu, A. M.: Selective Encryption of Multimedia Content in Distribution Networks: Challenges and New Directions. IASTED Int'l Conf. on Communications, Inter-net and Information Technology (2003) 527–533
11. Lian, S., Sun, J, Wang, Z.: Quality Analysis of Several Typical MPEG Video Encryption Algorithms. J. of Image and Graphics (2004) **9**(4) 483–490
12. Zeng, W., Lei, S.: Efficient Frequency Domain Selective Scrambling of Digital Video. IEEE Trans. Multimedia (2003) **5**(1) 118–129
13. Li, X., Yuan, Y., Tao, D.: Artistic Mosaic Series Generation. Int. J. of Image and Graphics (2006) **6**(1) 139–154

Automatic 3D Face Model Reconstruction Using One Image

Chen Lu and Yang Jie

Institute of Image Processing and Pattern Recognition,
Shanghai Jiao tong University, 800 Dongchuan Road, Shanghai, China
{dalureal, jieyang}@sjtu.edu.cn

Abstract. In this paper, we reconstruct the corresponding 3D face model using only one 2D image. 3D feature points are obtained by optimally approximating 2D feature points set with defined similarity. Then, a shape model is reconstructed by the warp function algorithm. Finally, a realistic face model is created through texture mapping with registration method such as affine transform. Results show that the models we reconstruct are comparatively realistic, and they can be used for face recognition or computer animation. The computation speed is also satisfying.

Keywords: face reconstruction, similarity, optimal approximation, texture mapping.

1 Introduction

Face recognition with PIE (pose, illumination, and expression) is a challenging problem. It is hard to solve this problem only through dealing with 2D images. However, incorporation of computer graphics provides a possible solution. If a corresponding 3D model is reconstructed and added with some PIE or animation, it is comparatively easy for recognition.

3D face model reconstruction has greatly developed recently. Methods using three images to reconstruct are prevalent [1], [2], [3] and easy to implement. But they can not be applied to all situations because it is difficult to obtain such ideal images at any time. So we concentrate on the instance with a monocular vision. Recently, Volker Blanz et al. [4] used a 3D morphable model to fit the image by optimization procedure. They acquired their models by a series of processes: linear combination, some rotation, illumination parameters and cost function. Their optimal matching was a complex process, and it took about 4.5 minutes on a workstation with a 2GHz P4 processor. Besides, Dalong Jiang et al. [5] used an integrated face reconstruction method for face recognition. They located key facial points by an alignment algorithm, then reconstructed a geometric model, and extracted texture to the model at last. This method simply calculated the weights used for linear combination. So it is better to devise more sophisticated methods to enhance realisiticity

N. Zheng, X. Jiang, and X. Lan (Eds.): IWICPAS 2006, LNCS 4153, pp. 235–243, 2006.

In this paper, we generate a corresponding 3D model only using one frontal image fast. Choosing a frontal image is because it can provide maximal information for reconstruction. However, such reconstruction is an ill-posed problem, so how to achieve optimal approximation is the key. It contains two essentials: how to obtain the optimal shape model and how to best map texture onto the shape model. Any fault will badly affect the realisticity of the model. So we take the 3D face model database into consideration and obtain finer weights using a statistic method for linear combination, which is an easily accepted idea.

There are two steps for model reconstruction: shape reconstruction and texture mapping. First, we locate some feature points since the warp function needs them. 3D feature points can be obtained with a weight vector by optimally approximating 2D feature points with defined similarity. And 2D feature points can be located by some prevalent method. So far the well-studied methods include ASM (Active Shape Model) [6], AAM (Active Appearance Model) [7].Then, the shape model can be reconstructed by an elastic warp function algorithm TPS (Thin-Plate Spline) [8]. Finally, we get a real face model by texture mapping with registration method such as affine transform. Results show that the models we reconstruct are comparatively realistic, and they can be used for face recognition or computer animation. The computation speed is also satisfying.

The rest of this paper is organized as follows. Two basic assumptions are made on top of this section. Shape reconstruction based on similarity optimal approximation is introduced in section 3. Section 4 provides the texture mapping algorithm. Experimental results are given in section 5 and conclusion is drawn in section 6.

2 Basic Assumptions

We use the optimal approximation method to handle this problem. How to reconstruct an optimal model is the key issue in this paper. Before our generation, we make the following assumptions:

(1) The models are neutral expression, and their coordinates have been rectified without need to perform any rotation transformation.

(2) 3D optimal feature points can be obtained by the weights during the process of optimally approximating 2D target feature points.

3 Shape Reconstruction

In this section, we elucidate the method which is used to generate the 3D shape model automatically. We select a frontal facial image under the condition of normal illumination and neutral expression for reconstruction. Then, two procedures are applied to yield the desired model, namely, (1) shape reconstruction and (2) texture mapping. The framework of 3D model reconstruction shows in Fig. 1. And the following subsections will describe these two procedures in detail.

3.1 Feature Points Extraction

The extracted feature points fall into two categories: model feature points and target image feature points. The 3D model feature points are manually selected on the sample models off-line to ensure precision. We select 60 feature points on every 3D sample model and project them to obtain the corresponding 2D projection feature points, which will be used for the optimal approximation (discussed later). 100 male and 100 female facial models are used for the sake of statistic computation later.

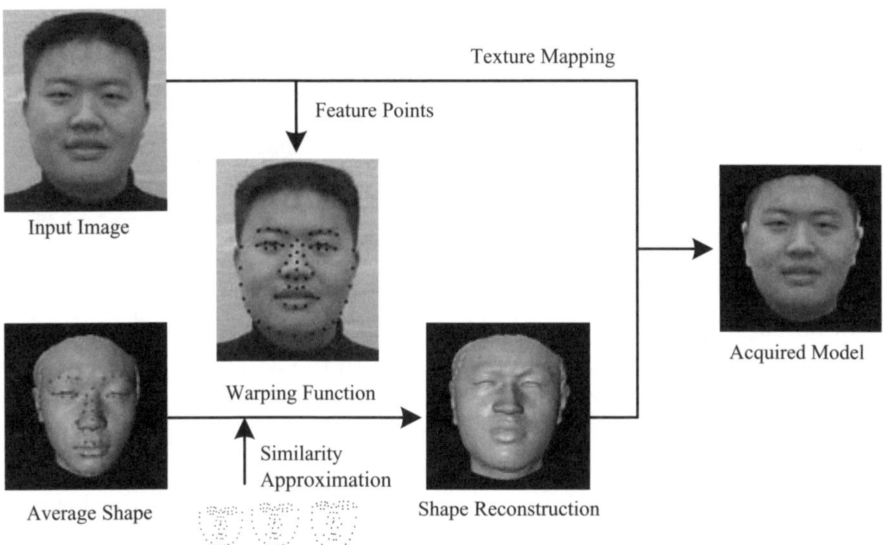

Fig. 1. The framework of 3D face model reconstruction

As for the target feature points, we can extract them by some automatic algorithms, which ensures our procedure fully automatic. Here we choose ASM algorithms [6] to acquire 60 corresponding facial target feature points in the same order.

3.2 Optimal Approximation

According to the assumptions above, we can use a weight vector to approximate the 3D optimal feature points. We write the selected 3D model feature points in the column vector form as $S_i = (X_1, Y_1, Z_{1,} ... X_n, Y_n, Z_n)^T$. Where m is the number of sample models, and n is the number of selected feature points. Here $m = 200$, $n = 60$. X, Y, Z are the spatial coordinates of the 3D model feature points. In order to acquire the corresponding 3D optimal feature points based on the 3D model feature points, we use the weight vector ω to calculate them. So the corresponding 3D optimal feature points can be written as:

$$S_{opt} = \sum_{i=1}^{m} \omega_i S_i \ . \tag{1}$$

Where S_{opt} are the generated 3D optimal feature points. Generally, we make such constraints as $\omega_i \geq 0$ and $\sum_{i=1}^{m} \omega_i = 1$.

Also according to the assumptions, we can get the optimal weight vector based on the 2D projection feature points. Similarly, let $S' = (X_1', Y_1', ...X_n', Y_n')^T$ be the vector of 2D optimal feature points and we can write the generated 2D optimal feature points as:

$$S'_{opt} = \sum_{i=1}^{m} \omega_i S'_i \ . \tag{2}$$

Let the 2D target feature points on the target image are $S_0 = (X_1, Y_1, ... X_n, Y_n)^T$. We intent to minimize the following square error function

$$\varepsilon^2 = ||S_0 - \sum_{i=1}^{m} \omega_i S'_i||^2 = \min \ . \tag{3}$$

According to Tukey's bi-weight method [9], a series of normally distributed weights can be obtained, which conforms well to the natural laws. However, it is no easy to work out those ones. So, here, we define a new measure named similarity to help work out the optimal weights.

Definition of Similarity. It's a key issue to define the match degree between the 2D projected feature points and those on the target image. And so does to get the optimal solution of linear combination. We define four criteria to evaluate the resemblance of two facial feature points. They are: (1) the accumulated angle error, (2) the variance of angles, (3) the variance of length and (4) the variance of length proportion.

As show in Fig. 2, we first calculate the mean point of 60 feature points

$$(\bar{X}, \bar{Y}) = (\sum_{i=1}^{n} X_i, \sum_{i=1}^{n} Y_i) \ . \tag{4}$$

as basic point. Then, before computing the similarity, we define:

$$\rho_i^k = ||(X_i^k, Y_i^k) - (\bar{X}^k, \bar{Y}^k)|| \ . \tag{5}$$

$$\theta_i^k = \arcsin \frac{L_i^k}{\rho_i^k}, L_i^k = \frac{|b * (X_i^k - \bar{X}^k) - (Y_i^k - \bar{Y}^k)|}{\sqrt{1+b^2}} \ . \tag{6}$$

$$\lambda_i^k = \frac{||(X_i^k, Y_i^k) - (\bar{X}^k, \bar{Y}^k)||}{||(X_i^0, Y_i^0) - (\bar{X}^0, \bar{Y}^0)||} \ . \tag{7}$$

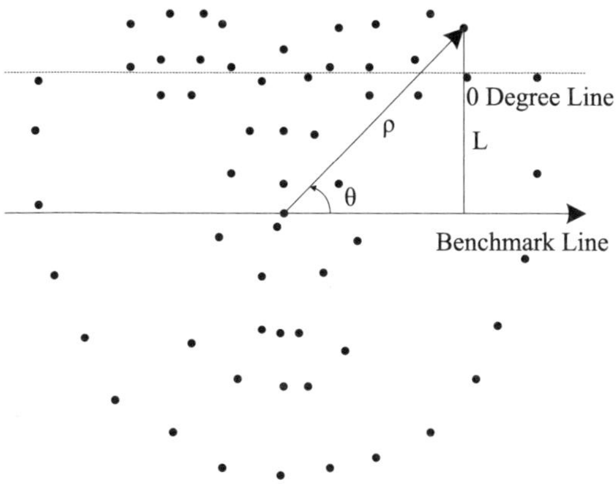

Fig. 2. Several essentials for calculating similarity. ρ: the distance from current point to basic point, θ: the angle from benchmark line to current line, L: the distance from current point to the benchmark line

Here, $i = 1, 2, ...n$, and $k = 0, 1, 2, ...m$.When $k = 0$, the formulas and the parameters represent those of the target feature points. When $k = 1, 2, ...m$, they represent those from the 2D projected feature points. L represents the distance from the feature point to the benchmark line.

For every S', we make:

(1) the accumulated angle error: $\theta^k_{Dif} = \sum \Delta\theta = \sum\limits_{i=1}^{n} (\theta^k_i - \theta^0_i)$

(2) the variance of angles: $\theta^k_{Var} = \frac{1}{n}\sum(\Delta\theta)^2 = \frac{1}{n}\sum\limits_{i=1}^{n} (\theta^k_i - \theta^0_i)^2$

(3)the variance of length: $\rho^k_{Var} = \frac{1}{n}\sum(\Delta\rho)^2 = \frac{1}{n}\sum\limits_{i=1}^{n} (\rho^k_i - \bar{\rho}^k)^2$

(4) the variance of length proportion: $\lambda^k_{\text{Var}} = \frac{1}{n}\sum(\Delta\lambda)^2 = \frac{1}{n}\sum\limits_{i=1}^{n} (\lambda^k_i - \bar{\lambda}^k)^2$

in (3) and (4), $\bar{\rho}^k = \frac{1}{n}\sum\limits_{i=1}^{n} \rho^k_i$, $\bar{\lambda}^k = \frac{1}{n}\sum\limits_{i=1}^{n} \lambda^k_i$, respectively. So, we define four components of similarity to evaluate the match degree between the projection feature points and target ones. Finally, we add the four components with certain weights, and the total similarity ξ^k is calculated as follows:

$$\xi^k = a_0\theta^k_{Dif} + a_1\theta^k_{Var} + a_2\rho^k_{Var} + a_3\lambda^k_{\text{Var}} . \tag{8}$$

where a_0, a_1, a_2, a_3 are the weights for adjusting the best similarity.

Optimal Weights. In the above section, we have given the formula of approximation expression based on weights. Now we can evaluate this expression using the devised similarity measure. Here, the similarity measure is actually error measure, as opposed to the common sense of similarity. The purpose is to assign greater weights for those of small similarity and at the same time to make the outliers have zero or small weights in order to minimize the error.

So, we use the method named normal weight. The weights are defined as:

$$\omega^k = \frac{1}{\sqrt{2\pi\sigma}} e^{\frac{(\xi^k)^2}{2\pi\sigma^2}} . \tag{9}$$

Where $\sigma^2 = \frac{1}{m}\sum_{k=1}^{m}(\xi^k - \bar{\xi})^2$, and $\bar{\xi} = \frac{1}{m}\sum_{k=1}^{m}\xi^k$.

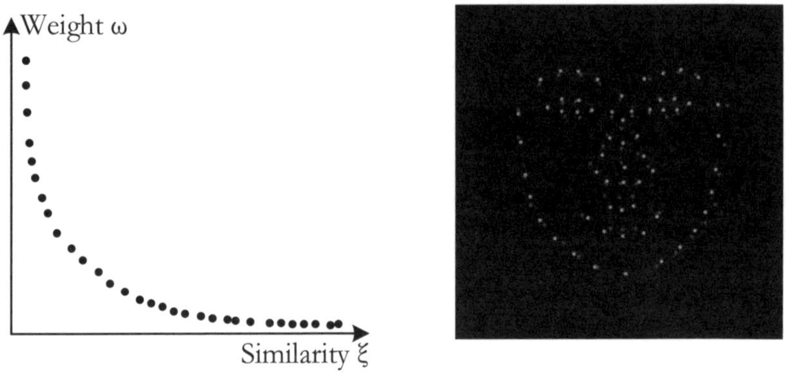

Fig. 3. The optimal weights and optimal similarity approximation

We let $\omega_i = \omega^i$ for the sake of unification. To satisfy the constraints above, we normalize $\omega_i = \frac{\omega_i}{\sum_{i=1}^{m}\omega_i}$. The optimal weights and optimal similarity approximation show in Fig. 3.

3.3 Warping Using TPS

Just as described above, we have acquired correspondent 3D optimal feature points S_{opt}, we may reconstruct the shape model by elastic warp function. Here, we use an improved TPS (Thin-plate Spline) algorithm.

$$f(x, y, z) = a_1 + a_x x + a_y y + a_z z + \sum_{i=1}^{n} w_i U(P_i - (x, y, z)) . \tag{10}$$

The new coordinates can be calculated using such formula. This does work to other radial basic function, such as linear, Gaussian, multi-quadric, etc. The reconstructed shape model shows in Fig. 4.

4 Texture Mapping

Since we got shape model, we may acquire satisfying model by texture mapping. For better registration, we extract correspondent texture information by such method as affine transform.

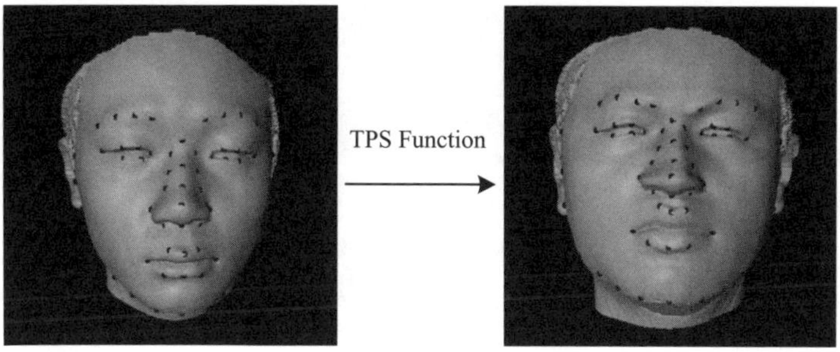

Fig. 4. The reconstructed shape model after elastic warp

Affine transform is calculated as follows:

$$I' = c * I + o \,. \tag{11}$$

Here, c and o represent scale and offset respectively. As defined before, we simply calculate the two items as:

$$c = \frac{\frac{1}{n}\sum_{i=1}^{n} ||(X_i', Y_i') - (\bar{X}', \bar{Y}')||}{\frac{1}{n}\sum_{i=1}^{n} ||(X_i, Y_i) - (\bar{X}, \bar{Y})||}, o = (\bar{X}', \bar{Y}') - (\bar{X}, \bar{Y}) \,. \tag{12}$$

And for the profile texture information, we refer to Jiang's algorithm [5].

5 Experimental Results

For each input images, we locate the 60 target feature points with the ASM method automatically, and reconstruct their corresponding 3D models. Experimental results show as follows:

(1) Computation speed

We do experiment for more than 200 images. It will take about 3.8S on a workstation with a 2GHz P4 processor, which is enormously less than the one according to the Voker Blanz's method, and less than the one from Jiangs' too.

(2) Realisticity

To such an ill-product problem, how to evaluate the realisticity of the model is difficult. Actually, the aim we reconstruct such a 3D face model is for face recognition. In order to demonstrate the advantage of our algorithm, we save a 2D projection image when the model is frontal. Then, we use it to reconstruct correspondent model, and compare it with the original one. Experimental results show that our algorithm has perfect regenerative property. The results show in Fig. 5.

Also, we may acquire the model with PIE by changing some parameters, which is useful for recognition or animation. Fig. 6 shows the model with PIE.

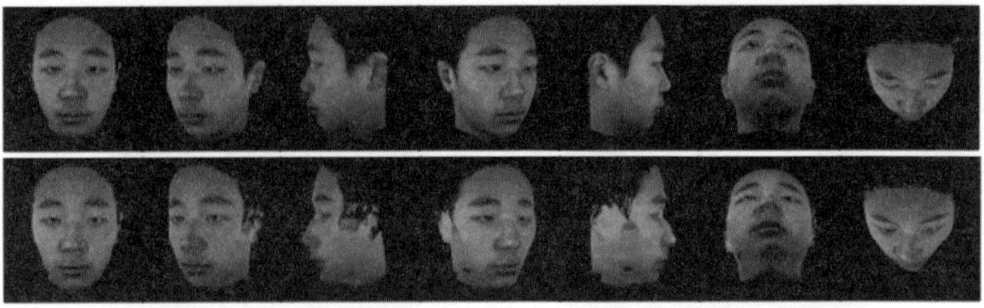

Fig. 5. The model reconstructed compares with the original one. The upper model is the one already exist in the database, and we change its poses at degree 0, -30, -90, 30, 90, up 45, down 45. The reconstructed model through our method is described underneath, so do its poses

(a) (b) (c)

Fig. 6. Face model with PIE. (a) face pose after 30 degree left rotation (b) face illumination with left spot lighting (c) face expression of surprise

(3) Some disadvantages

Our algorithm does work well when reconstructing shape model, but attention should be paid the texture mapping. Texture is very sensitive to the input image and the registration. So we should improve our algorithm more about this in the future work.

Such algorithm does less work to the face image with glasses. Since we have no models with glasses, we could not generate such model with various depths. Besides, how to estimate whether a face is with glasses is still a challenging problem.

6 Conclusion

In this paper, we reconstruct a corresponding 3D face model using only one 2D image. 3D feature points can be obtained by optimally approximating 2D feature points set using defined similarity. Then, shape model can be reconstructed by warp function algorithm. Finally, we get real face model by texture mapping with registration method such as affine transform. Results show that the models we reconstruct are comparatively realistic, and they can be used for face recognition or computer animation. The computation speed is also satisfying.

Except for profile information, the models we reconstruct have extraordinary added information, which will do help to recognition.

Acknowledgments. Portions of the research in this paper use the BJUT-3D Face Database.

References

1. Wang Kun, Zheng Nanning: Realistic Face Modeling with Robust Correspondences, Vol. 00, IV (2004) 997-1002
2. Mandun Zhang, Linna Ma, Xiangyong Zeng, Yangsheng Wang: Imaged-Based 3D Face Modeling, CGIV (2004) 165-168
3. A-Nasser Ansari, Mohamed Abdel-Mottaleb: Face Modeling Using Two Orthogonal Views and a Generic Face Model, IEEE, ICME, (2003) 289-292
4. V. Blanz and T. Vetter: Face Recognition Based on Fitting a 3D Morphable Model, IEEE transactions on PAMI, Vol. 25, No. 9, Sept (2003) 1063-1074
5. Dalong Jiang, Yuxiao Hu, Shuicheng Yan, Lei Zhang, Hongjiang: Efficient 3D reconstruction for face recognition, Pattern Recognition 38 (2005) 787-798
6. T. F. Cootes, C. J. Taylor, D. H. Cooper, and J. Graham: Active Shape Models-Their Training and Application, Computer Vision and Image Understanding, Vol. 61, No. 1, Jan (1995) 38-59
7. Timothy F. Cootes, Gareth J. Edwards, and Christopher J. Taylo: Active Appearance Models, IEEE transactions on PAMI, Vol. 23, No. 6, June (2001) 681-685
8. Fred L. Bookstein: Principle Warps: Thin-Plate Splines and the Decomposition of Deformation, IEEE transactions on PAMI, Vol. 11, No. 6,June (1989) 567-585
9. Hoaglin, C. F. Mosteller, and J. W. Tukey: Understanding Robust and Exploratory Data Analysis, New York: John Wiley (1983) 348-349

Cognitive Approach to Visual Data Interpretation in Medical Information and Recognition Systems

Lidia Ogiela[1], Ryszard Tadeusiewicz[2], and Marek R. Ogiela[2]

[1] AGH University of Science and Technology, Faculty of Management,
Al. Mickiewicza 30, PL-30-059 Kraków, Poland
logiela@agh.edu.pl

[2] AGH University of Science and Technology, Institute of Automatics
{rtad, mogiela}@agh.edu.pl

Abstract. This paper will demonstrates that Computational Intelligence methods based on picture grammar can be efficiently applied to the development of intelligent diagnosis support systems. The computational intelligence methods in the form o linguistic formalism can facilitate an in-depth semantic analysis of the medical patterns and visualizations. The main objective is to present the possibilities of medical structure meaning description and computer interpretation based on selected examples of hand and spinal cord images. Presented further procedures for semantic description and reasoning will be based on the model of cognitive analysis which can imitate the process of reasoning in human mind. The application of such methods allow to detect and classify the most important lesion in the analysed structures.

1 Introduction

The development of soft-computing techniques, based on the analysis taking advantage of graph image grammars, has had a significant impact on the development of medical information systems: they enable interpretation of the meaning of some diagnostic image classes. Together with the use of such techniques, information sys-tems were directed at possibilities that enable an in-depth semantic analysis aimed at formulating diagnostic recommendations and supporting the tasks associated with automatic medical diagnostics. In the field of image analysis where advanced tech-niques are used, of huge importance became the structural methods of applying graph and tree formalisms. Information systems constructed on such methods are directed at attempts to automatically understand the semantics of analysed images, and therefore at their content meaning interpretation. The cognitive resonance process are very similar in operation to the model of human visual perception [1,7]. During semantic analysis there are looking for coincidence between expectations concerning the registered cases and their actual features. The outcome of these results is that these methods gain in importance and can be used on a wider scale to support the meaning of diagnostic interpretation of selected image classes.

N. Zheng, X. Jiang, and X. Lan (Eds.): IWICPAS 2006, LNCS 4153, pp. 244–250, 2006.

The analysis of images conducted in this paper will go in the direction to evaluate the possibilities of expansive graph grammar application for the recognition and intelligent meaning analysis of wrist radiogrammes, and spinal cord CT examinations. In the paper we defined effective, syntactic analyser algorithms for classes describing both cases of morphological elements falling within physiological norms, and, for selected cases of diseases showing their symptoms as visible irregularities on analysed visualizations.

2 Processing of Medical Visualizations

All kinds of images analysed here were, before their analysis, subject to preprocessing aimed at showing structure contours and their identification enabling a later search of the spanned graph with a selected width analysis technique.

In order to obtain a structure description in the form of a graph it is necessary to conduct pre-processing operations first. These result in the separating of the individual parts of medical structures. Among such operations the most important are the image segmentation and the operation of spanning the graph on the selected parts. To extract individual structures and separate their contours on the examined images we tried to used the histogram programming algorithm and the method of structure separation as described in the paper [6]. After image segmentation further stages of analysis composed of image coding used terminal symbols of the introduced language, and shape approximation.

As a result of the execution of such stages it is possible to obtain a new image representation in the form of hierarchic semantic tree structures and subsequent production steps of this representation from the initial grammar symbol [4,7].

In intelligent cognitive system the recognition of whether a given representation of the actual image belongs to a class of images generated by languages defined by one of possible number of grammars. Such grammars can be considered to belong to sequential, tree and graph grammars while recognition with their application is made in the course of a syntactic analysis performed by the system [7].

The main element of a correctly functioning diagnosis support system is, analysis preparation of a cognitive method of disease units and pathological lesions as occurring in the hand, and spinal cord. The cognitive analysis contained in the DSS system is aimed to propose an automatic correct interpretation method of these extremely complicated medical images. Such images are difficult to interpret due to the fact that various patients have various morphologies of the imaged organs. This is true both of the correct state and if there are any disease lesions. The skeletal, and nervous systems, similarly as most elements of the human body, is not always correctly built and fully developed from the birth. The anatomy and pathomorphology differentiate between a number of developmental defects of these systems. It often occurs that these systems for the first couple of years functions correctly and only after some time there are some troubles with theirs functioning.

3 Grammar Classification of Hand Images

The hand images analysis described in this paper has focused primarily on the analysis of the number and spatial relations between individual wrist bones. An intelligent interpretation of the analysed cases can enable the identification of lesions such as occurrence of *os centrale* or other additional wrist bones. It may also point to a lack of or lesions in the shape of scaphoid or capitate bones as well as their synostoses with other wrist parts. As the development of research and syntactic image recognition techniques progress, analyses will become increasingly more complex. This means that more and more subtle irregularities in their number, build and mutual location in the wrist will be detected.

Real example of hand image showing pathological lesion in the form of wrist bone necrosis has been shown on figure 1.

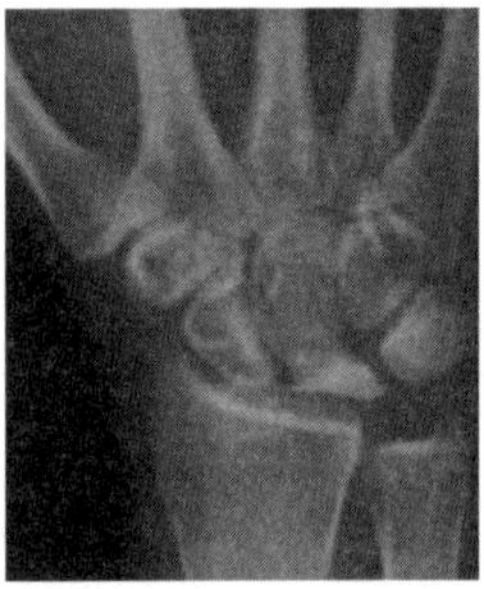

Fig. 1. Image showing lesions in the form of a vascular necrosis of lunate

For the analysed hand images it is necessary to define an appropriate linguistic formalism that is an appropriate graph grammar defining a language. The language is defined in such a way that one could describe using it, without any ambiguities, every image representing a spatial system composed of elements similar to the wrist bone system. In this way we create a tool, which describes all possible the shapes and locations of wrist bones, both the correct ones and the pathological ones. The linguistic formalism that we propose in this paper to execute the task of mirroring real medical image forms into graph formulas fit for computer processing, will be an expansive graph grammar [7].

The analysis of hand images was performed using the grammar defined below.

$$G_{sc} = (N, \Sigma, \Gamma, P, S), where, \qquad (1)$$

Non-terminal set of peak labels N= {ST, ULNA SCAPHOID, LUNATE, TRIQUETRUM, PISIFORM, TRAPEZIUM, TRAPEZOID, CAPITATE, HAMATE, m1, m2, m3, m4, m5}.

Terminal set of peak labels Σ = {r, u s, l, t, p, tm, tz, c, h, m1, m2, m3, m4, m5}

Γ - edge label set, Start symbol S=ST, P - is a finite production set presented on figure 2.

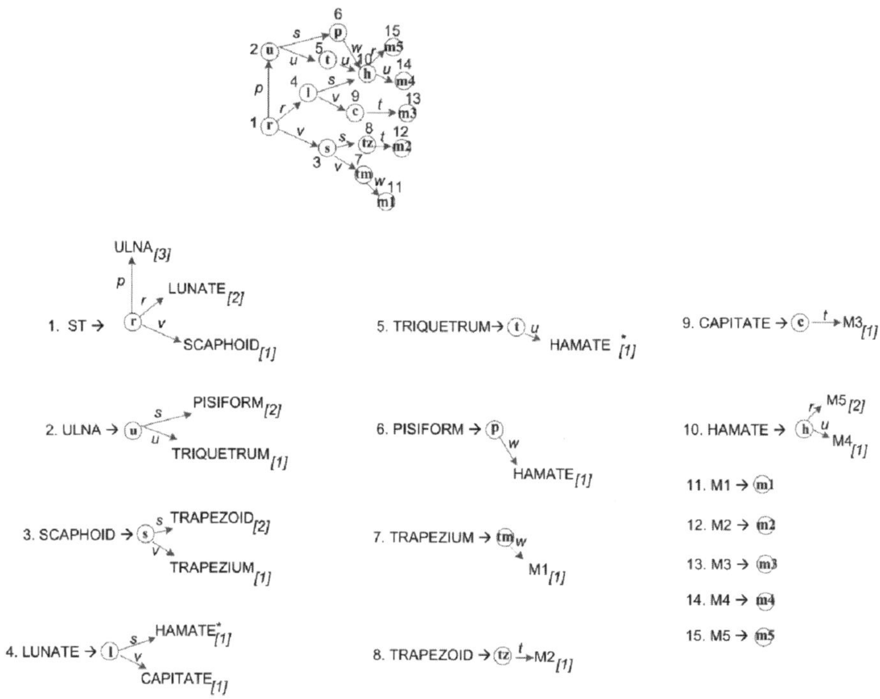

Fig. 2. Production set introducing a representation of the correct build and the number of bones in the wrist

4 Spinal Cord Images Interpretation

For the cognitive analysis of spinal cord images the following attributed grammar has been proposed:

$$G_{sc} = (\Sigma_N, \Sigma_T, P, ST) \tag{2}$$

where: Σ_N - stands for a set of non-terminal symbols (intermediary in the process of image description generation), Σ_T - stands for a set of terminal symbols (final symbols describing shape features), P - stands for a production set, ST - stand for the grammar start symbol.

Σ_N = {CHANGE, STENOSIS, DILATATION, TUMOR, N, D, S}, Σ_T = {n, d, s} Apart from these, the following meaning was given to terminal elements present in the description:

n∈[-11°, 11°], d∈(11°, 180°), s∈(-180°, -11°), ST = CHANGE

P production set has been defined as in Table 1.

The proposed grammar makes it possible to detect various kinds of spinal cord or meningeal stenoses characteristic for neoplastic lesions and inflammatory processes of the spinal cord. Figure 3, 4, 5 present images of the spinal cord with a visible deformation, and the diagrams of the spinal cords. The bold lines represents the area of occurrence of the anomalies within the structure of the spinal cords. The set of chords, cross-cutting the spinal cord in subsequent points perpendicularly to its axis demonstrate how the width diagram was made.

Table 1. Production set defining pathological signs

Pathological sign	Grammar description	Semantic actions
Dilation/cyst	1. $CHANGE \rightarrow DILATATION$ 2. $DILATATION \rightarrow D\ N\ S \mid D\ N \mid D\ S$	$Sign$ = dilatation
Neoplasm	3. $CHANGE \rightarrow TUMOR$ 4. $TUMOR \rightarrow D\ S\ D\ S \mid S\ D\ S\ N \mid$ $\mid \mathrm{S\ D\ S\ D} \mid \mathrm{D\ S\ D\ N}$	$Sign$ = tumor
Compression	5. $CHANGE \rightarrow STENOSIS$ 6. $STENOSIS \rightarrow S\ N\ D \mid S\ D \mid S\ N$	$Sign$ = stenosis
Elements of the detected lesions	7. $N \rightarrow n \mid n\ N$ 8. $D \rightarrow d \mid d\ D$ 9. $S \rightarrow s \mid s\ S$	*Sign= location; length; diameter, quantity, severity*

Spinal cord width diagrams (figure 3, 4, 5) present, in the most concise form, the results of spinal cord morphology analysis. It is the most precious source of information when one is looking for pathological lesions and it contains all-important data about the examined fragment of central nervous system. At the same time it ignores all spinal cord image details unimportant from the diagnostic point of view. Image 3, 4, 5 presents an example of results obtained by the author in the course of examinations for a given disease case.

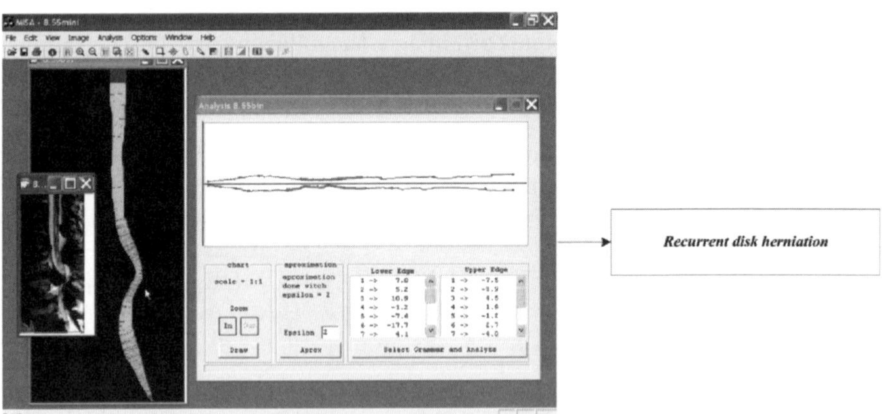

Fig. 3. Spinal cord and width diagram. Diagnostic description of spinal cord lesions with disk hernation detected as a result of cognitive analysis.

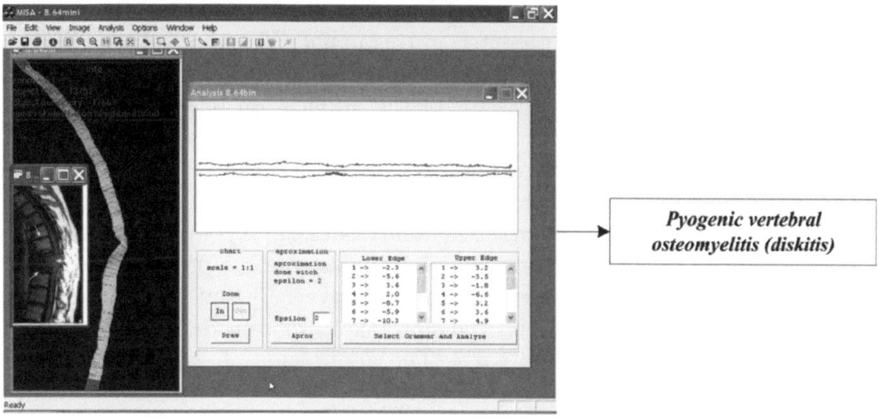

Fig. 4. Spinal cord and width diagram. Diagnostic description of spinal cord lesions with arachnoid cyst detected as a result of syntax analysis.

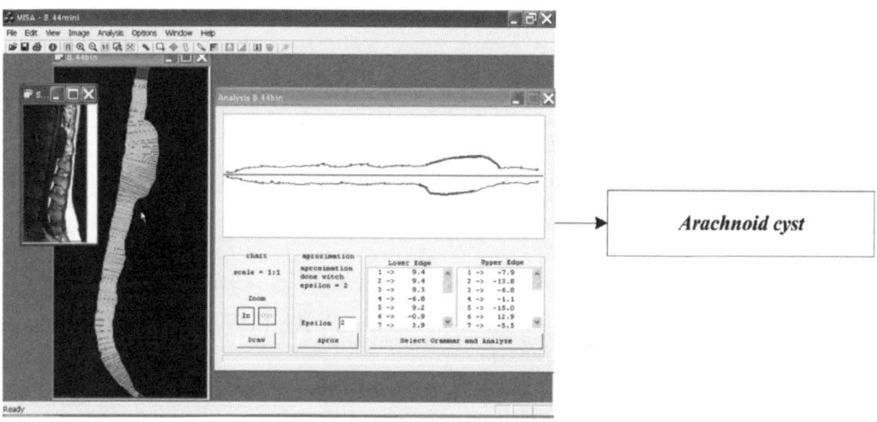

Fig. 5. Spinal cord and width diagram. Diagnostic description of spinal cord lesions with diskitis detected as a result of cognitive analysis.

The results presented here have been achieved by the application of attribute grammar and they are an example of the cognitive approach to the medical data considered here. The type of lesion detected here has been assigned based on its location and on morphometric parameters determined by the grammar semantic procedures.

5 Conclusions

In order to perform meaning analysis on presented images with the use of a linguistic mechanism as described in this paper, the MISA (Medical Image Syntax

Analyser) computer system has been developed. This enables the analysis and classification of kinds images presented in this paper. The application efficiency of cognitive analysis procedures, using this system, reach the level of 90,5%. These results are obtained as a result of the application of semantic analysis algorithms conducted in reasoning modules of the proposed system and based on semantic actions assigned to structural rules.

The use of proposed grammars is an important step towards the application of structural graph methods in practical analysis tasks of complex multi-object images. This is an important expansion of previous research on the use of structural application methods for medical image analysis [7] that related primarily to single structures or organs and did not take into consideration the analysis of objects composed of many parts. The application of structural methods can therefore significantly expand the possibilities offered by traditional medical information systems and medical diagnostic support systems. Moreover, such procedures could create semantic PACS system components that, in their operation, will support the semantic categorisation and indexation of various diagnostic images, including such images that show the complex medical structures of organs.

Acknowledgement

This work was supported by the AGH University of Science and Technology under Grant No. 10.10.120.39.

References

1. Albus, J. S., Meystel, A. M.: Engineering of Mind - An Introduction to the Science of Intelligent Systems. Wiley (2001)
2. Bankman I.(ed.): Handbook of Medical Imaging: Processing and Analysis. Academic Press (2002)
3. Burgener, F. A., Kormano, M.: Bone and Joint Disorders. Thieme Stuttgart (2001)
4. Duda, R. O., Hart, P. E., Stork, D. G.: Pattern classifications, 2nd Edition. Willey (2001)
5. Khan M. G.: Heart Disease Diagnosis and Therapy. Williams & Wilkins Baltimore (1996)
6. Ogiela, M. R., Tadeusiewicz, R.: Nonlinear Processing and Semantic Content Analysis in Medical Imaging - A Cognitive Approach. IEEE Transactions on Instrumentation and Measurement **54(6)** (2005) 2149–2155
7. Tadeusiewicz, R., Ogiela, M. R.: Medical Image Understanding Technology. Springer Berling-Heildelberg (2004)

Modelling the Human Visual Process by Evolving Images from Noise

Sameer Singh, Andrew Payne, and Roman Kingsland

Research School of Infomatics
Loughborough UK
{s.singh, a.m.payne, r.l.kingsland}@lboro.ac.uk

Abstract. The modelling of human visual process is considerably important for developing future autonomous agents such as mobile robots with vision capability. The future efforts will be directed at using this knowledge to develop powerful new algorithms that mimic the human vision capability. In this paper we focus on the process of how the human eye forms an image. We use genetic algorithms to synthetically model this process and interpret the results on different types of objects. In particular, we investigate which of the image properties stabilise early and which ones later, i.e. as the image forms iteratively, does the shape appear before the texture?

1 Introduction

Considerable effort has been spent on computational modelling of human vision. The human eye has variable resolution capability (e.g. foveal vision is of high resolution whereas peripheral vision is of low resolution). The foveal and peripheral capabilities of the human eye have been the inspiration for a range of computer vision algorithms for describing attentive mechanisms and image compression. However, the process of how the image forms has not been fully investigated. The rod and cone cells within the human eye are stimulated to give us day and night vision. This is a complex process in which an image is stabilisied and formed starting from noise. Two example scenarios can illustrate this process: (a) Imagine opening your closed eyelids very slowly; (b) Move from a very dark room to another room with dim lighting. In both cases, the retinal image is formed of the scene starting from noise (the dark scene with your eyes closed or in a dark room). The seamless quality in the images that you see is possible because human vision updates images, including the details of motion and color, on a time scale so rapid that a "break in the action" is almost never perceived. The range of color, the perception of seamless motion, the contrast and the quality, along with the minute details, that most people can perceive make "real-life" images clearer and more detailed than any seen on a television or movie screen. The efficiency and completeness of your eyes and brain is unparalleled in comparison with any piece of apparatus or instrumentation ever invented. We know this amazing function of the eyes and brain as the sense of vision. The image formation process can be modelled as discrete. We can formulate the following question. As the image is formed, which properties of the

N. Zheng, X. Jiang, and X. Lan (Eds.): IWICPAS 2006, LNCS 4153, pp. 251–259, 2006.

image (colour, texture, shape, etc.) stabilise earlier and which take longer? The rate at which texture, shape and other image primitives are organised, on the basis of which we interpret what is in the scene, is important to study for understanding the human response times. If a human observer has to react to an image (e.g. label it, take action, etc.) then how long will they take?

In this paper we use genetic algorithms to evolve images from random (noise). The use of genetic algorithms for image evolution has been significantly limited even though they have been widely used for a range of image processing operations as discussed in section 2. In particular we focus on images with different content, e.g. low texture content (snow, sky, water), high texture regularity (cloth, grass, path), bright colours (starfish, fire) and variable texture and colour (garden, hair). The process of pixel manipulation (chromosome encoding, mutation and crossover) and assigning a fitness function is not trivial. We discuss these issues in section 3. In section 4 we present our results. We first detail the image properties we aim to monitor with increasing GA iterations. Thereafter we present our results and interpret them.

2 GAs in Image Processing

Genetic algorithms (GAs) are robust search mechanisms based on the theoretical workings of biological systems. They are based on the concepts of reproduction, cross-over and mutation to evolve coded populations to find the maximum of some described fitness function. GAs have been used in a variety of different aspects of image processing. In [2], morphological filters for the purpose of film dirt removal from archival film material were designed using genetic algorithms. Morphological filters can remove noise in images while preserving the structure. Their design can be complex and GAs are well suited to optimisation problems that are difficult to model. Rather than using user input for the fitness function, a training set is artificially created by selecting a small noise-free region of the image and creating noise within it. The best filter in terms of a fitness function is the filter created under constraint that returns the artificially noisy section to its original state.

Colour quantisation, also referred to as colour image segmentation, is a likely area of image processing for genetic algorithms. The evaluation of methods, however, is a difficult task with no clear standard method [3]. Homogeneous regions extracted with the K-Means clustering method was used as the fitness function in [4] and the segmentation problem is treated as an unsupervised clustering problem. The GA was used for finding the most natural clusters. This method, while producing reasonable results, was crude in the sense that most of the parameterisation of the algorithm was experimentally optimised. None of the parameter optimisations were discussed.

In [5], evolutionary simulation methods have been used to enhance contrast in greyscale images by evolving the contrast curve. Through each generation, user input is required to determine the fitness of the modified contrast curve. The proposal would be impractical as at least several hundred images would have to be reviewed by a user. In light of this, it was suggested to use multiple regression techniques to simulate user input. In their tests, they found that this method of image enhancement performed at least as well as the conventional alternative, histogram equalisation. In some cases, the results were greatly improved with the evolutionary technique. Their method, however, does not take into consideration any local image variations that might be hurt in viewability terms by a uniform contrast enhancement. The use of subjective fitness functions has been used in other systems and was suggested as a viable method in [1] when the fitness function would otherwise be too difficult to design and the users' aesthetics are required.

In [6], the authors proposed a method of histogram equalisation by encoding four parameters of the statistical scaling histogram equalisation as a genome. The fitness is performed automatically as opposed to the user-subjective fitnesses in previous works. It is noted that a good contrast and enhanced image has a higher number of pixels laying on edges in the image. To this, the fitness is evaluated by performing the statistical scaling using the genome's four parameters, edge detecting, and counting edge pixels. Generally, this method outperformed traditional histogram equalisation methods.

GAs have been used to select an optimal set of standard image processing tools to best enhance an image in [7,8]. Genomes are coded as strings representing a set of image processing functions. In [7], the genomes strings were sectioned based on the refinement of parameters for each individual operation. The encompassed the simple operations of hue thresholding, brightness thresholding, smoothing, edge enhancement, contraction, expansion, and reversion. In [8], a slightly different approach was taken where the genomes are encoded as a series of instructions and parameters randomly selected and ordered. In both, the fitness is determined based on the difference between the enhanced image and some predefined goal image either given as a objective or as a comparison of training data. A genetic programming method similar to these genetic algorithm methods is presented in [9] in which the random combination of processing sequences are evaluated.

3 Pixel Manipulation Using a GA

In this paper we develop a methodology for evolving a target image from noise (random valued pixels). The target image serves as the final desired output image. This is a challenging process since pixel based chrosmosomes are very large in size and convergence can be very slow. In the following sections we will describe a method for genome encoding, crossover, mutation, and evaluation designed for the direct manipulation of pixels using a GA.

3.1 Genome Operations

Unlike the methods previously discussed, the approach we describe here deals with direct pixel manipulation. To this end, the genome encoding is a direct mapping of and nxm image to an nxm array of valid RGB values. Freedom for pixel evolution is key so no constraints have been placed on the genome outside of the fitness functions. The genomes are initialised with random integer values between 0 and 255 independantly for all values in R, G and B. Crossover is performed as a uniform crossover producing children as the random combinations of seperate R, G and B components of the parent genomes. Mutation is performed by randomly changing values in R, G and B at a very small probability. The new value is chosen by the old value -a shift value randomly selected between 0 and some variation limit. The variational limit is set initially to a large value, say 255, and then is re-evaluated at after every generation so that as the GA converges, the variation of pixels is less severe.

The objective, or fitness function, of the GA is the combination of several fitness functions. First, we must consider the fitness of the pixels in relation to the given image. By definition, the pixel difference between two images is defined by the Euclidean distance as:

$$d(I,J) = \sum_{i=0}^{n}\sum_{j=0}^{m} |\boldsymbol{I(i,j)} - \boldsymbol{J(i,j)}|$$

where I and J are the images and $\boldsymbol{I(i,j)}$ is defined as the vector of colour components {r,g,b} at pixel (x,y). We modify this value using the inverse exponential cumulative distribution function (CDF) to more steeply penalise large difference values as

$$d(I,J) = \sum_{i=0}^{n}\sum_{j=0}^{m} \frac{-log(1 - \boldsymbol{I(i,j)} - \boldsymbol{J(i,j)})}{\lambda}$$

assuming, in this case, that the difference between colours is normalised between 0 and 1. The inverse CDF produces a steeper response curve to large values as shown in Figure 1. The steeper response effects the convergence by requiring on average fewer generations to achieve a better closer pixel match seen in Figure 2.

3.2 Feature Fitness Functions

In order to show this encoding can be used for image enhancement, we propose using a series of feature fitness functions combined together with the image structure fitness function discussed above. The combination would have to show preference to the image structure so that the image would remain visually representative of the original. We approach the combination of these features as a multicriterion optimisation problem. While considered a naive approach [10], the weighted sum combination of fitness satisifies the need for computational simplicity. In our problem, any extra population requirement for the fitness function can be seen as a hinderance as pixel-coding genomes is already a large memory overhead. The combining for the fitness functions is then defined as

$$F = f_s \sum_{i=0}^{n} \omega_i f_i c_i$$

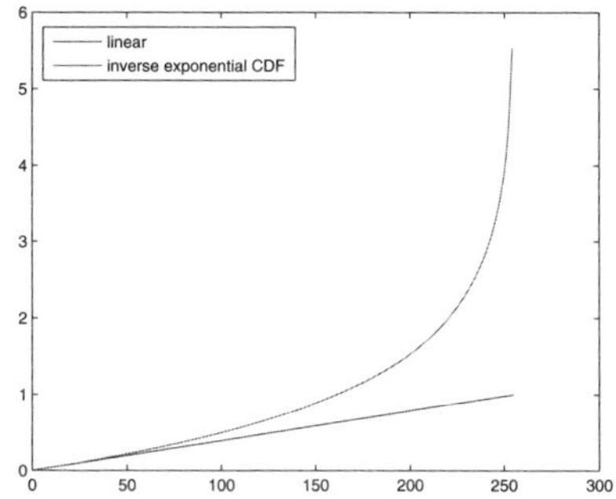

Fig. 1. Inverse exponential CDF against a linear Euclidean distance

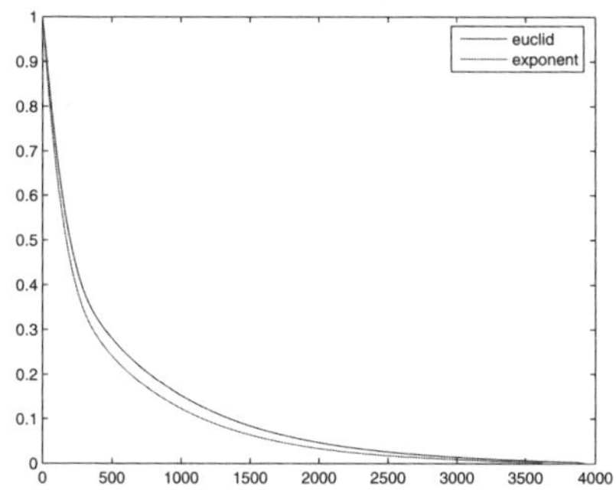

Fig. 2. Over ten runs on the same image, the exponential had in the same generation a better result than the simple Euclidean and converged 310 generations more quickly

where f_s is the structural fitness, ω_i is a weighting for the feature, f_i, and c_i is a normalisation factor for the fitness so that all the fitness functions fall between the same range. For our purposes, we use a common weighting factor for the fitness functions such that $\omega = \frac{1}{2(n+1)}$. This asserts that the supporting feature fitness functions are suppressed equally and effectively against the structural fitness function.

4 Results

We first test the GA's ability to mutate a pixel-coded genome to converge on a given image using the structural fitness described by the inverse exponential CDF. We take a total of ten images including cloth, fire, garden, grass, hair, path, sky, snow, starfish and water. Each image is of size 50x50 pixels. We initialise the genetic algorithm with random pixels representing the chromosome with the aim of reproducing these images in separate trials. The GA runs for a maximum of 450 iterations. After every 10 iterations, the fitness is evaluated as the difference between the following features of the reconstructed and target image: colour pixel difference, contrast, correlation, energy and homogeneity (Haralick [11]). Table 1 shows these feature values on the original images.

Table 1. Original image texture features

Image	pixel diff.	contrast	correlation	energy	homogeneity
cloth	0.4264	0.4343	0.2040	0.7867	0.4264
fire	0.1714	0.9438	0.1579	0.9186	0.1714
garden	0.9278	0.5869	0.0845	0.7014	0.9278
grass	0.3988	0.2819	0.3385	0.8213	0.3988
hair	0.4906	0.6337	0.1564	0.7950	0.4906
path	0.2384	0.6381	0.3034	0.8835	0.2384
sky	0.0302	0.8917	0.6972	0.9849	0.0302
snow	0.0588	0.8728	0.5112	0.9727	0.0588
starfish	0.6208	0.8547	0.1121	0.7872	0.6208
water	0.0620	0.8758	0.4424	0.9690	0.0620

Table 2 shows the final fitness value on the ten images using the GA. The best possible fitness is 0 which implies that the target image has been perfectly reconstructed.

Table 2. The final fitness values after GA convergence across ten different images evolved from random noise

Image	pixel diff.	contrast	correlation	energy	homogeneity
cloth	0.0001	0.0151	0.0082	0.0045	0.0048
fire	0.0041	0.0020	0.0021	0.0011	0.0021
garden	0.0128	0.0024	0.0000	0.0002	0.0007
grass	0.0031	0.0020	0.0062	0.0023	0.0005
hair	0.0021	0.0025	0.0051	0.0007	0.0009
path	0.0001	0.0020	0.0062	0.0022	0.0047
sky	0.0014	0.0037	0.0148	0.0058	0.0018
snow	0.0089	0.0183	0.0542	0.0203	0.0092
starfish	0.0027	0.0057	0.0004	0.0002	0.0012
water	0.0020	0.0090	0.0185	0.0059	0.0045

The following conclusions can be drawn from Table 2: (a) The most accurate pixel based reconstruction of images is possible for cloth and path; The least accurate case is garden; (b) In terms of contrast, the best reconstructed images are fire, grass and path; The least accurate cases are snow and cloth; (c) On correlation, energy and homogeneity measures, garden is the best reconstructed image and snow the worst case. The summed pixel difference percentages are calculated on the assumption that on average, the pixel difference of noise from a given image is 128 per channel. From these results, we can see that the GA can effectively generate the goal image from noise using the fitness function. We then need to test the GAs ability to mutate the pixel-coded genome to convergence given the extra components of shifting the mean channel histograms of the image by a fixed amount in each channel. In the red and blue channels, the shift is -25 and in the green, the shift is +25. Results are shown in Table 3.

Table 3. Pixel difference and Harlick texture feature results across the same ten images evolved from random noise compared, taking into account histogram shift features, against their respective expected goal images

Image	pixel diff.	contrast	correlation	energy	homogeneity
cloth	0.1218	0.1486	0.0652	0.0063	0.0254
fire	0.0481	0.1343	0.0555	0.0288	0.0649
garden	0.1023	0.0873	0.0078	0.0036	0.0091
grass	0.0370	0.0297	0.0002	0.0453	0.0176
hair	0.1781	0.3951	0.1647	0.0420	0.0944
path	0.1419	0.2689	0.2106	0.2417	0.1239
sky	0.0717	0.2498	0.3318	0.3808	0.1183
snow	0.1371	0.0384	0.0882	0.0226	0.0192
starfish	0.0551	0.1812	0.0189	0.0200	0.0255
water	0.1363	0.0653	0.1322	0.0501	0.0327

There are a couple of issues that we must concern ourselves in these results. The first is that for most of the image convergence implies a weakening correlation in texture. This is attributed to the lack of any texture features represented in the fitness function. The weakness in the fitness function is clearly shows here that convergence can be achieved through pixel values alone as opposed to any global or regional view of the image. The second concern is that for the path image, the structure and texture were all but lost leading to a divergence from expected pixel results and the textural features of the image.

Finally in Figure 3, we show the changes in these features through increasing GA iterations. We include three other fitness features, namely Edge Magnitude, Signal to Noise Ratio and Regional Pixel Standard Deviation. We find that most features stabilise (no longer change) after: Cloth: (200 iterations) Fire: (350 iterations); Garden: (200 iterations); Grass: (250 iterations); Hair: (250 iterations); Path: (300 iterations); Sky: (400 iterations); Snow (900 iterations); Starfish: (250 iterations); and Water (350 iterations). This shows that most image objects are easy to reconstruct in a short amount of time, whereas objects with fine texture such as water, fire, sky and snow take much longer. If we monitor the change in features over iterations, we observe that image contrast increases most rapidly, whereas the signal to noise ratio takes the longest to stabilise. Most notably the edge information becomes visible quite early on which suggests that the structure of objects in an image appear much earlier than the fine details such as colour and texture (as evidenced by the slow rate of increase of other

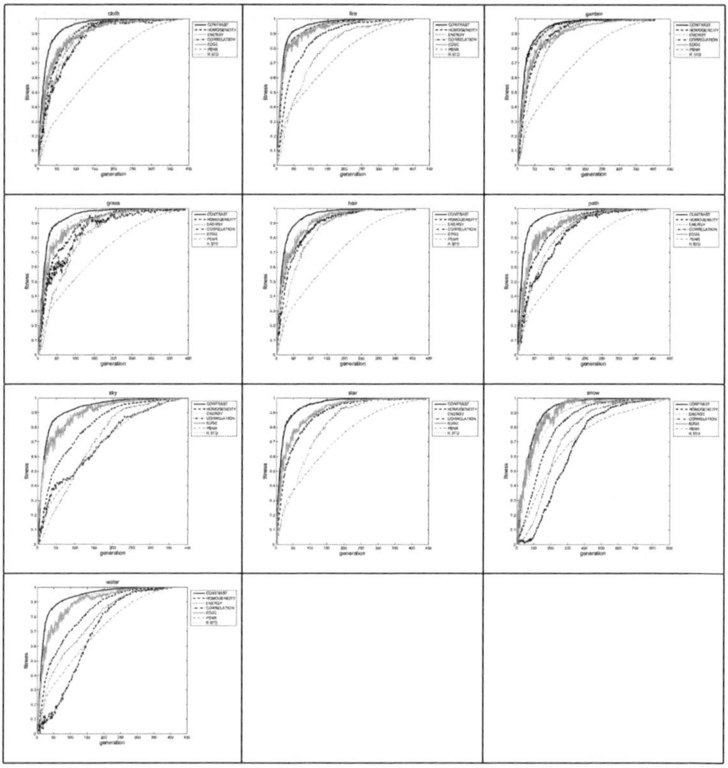

Fig. 3. The change in feature fitness on 9 sample images that are evolved from random for a maximum of 450 generations

features). It is also important to note that the feature fitness (except for signal to noise ratio) increases exponetially. Hence, the basic details of the image do not take much time to form however the fine details take much longer.

In future work, these plots can be correlated with the human response time. Consider a controlled experiment with a human observer with closed eyes. As they open their eyes in a controlled manner, they can describe what they see in the image, e.g. how clear is the contrast, can they see the edges, can they label the scene, etc. If these plots correlate well with respect to the response time then we have a good methodology based on GA that mimics the human visual system. Furthermore, such responses and plots can be correlated on a larger set of images, grouped by type (image categories can be created based on its texture, shape and colour content).

5 Conclusions

In this paper, we have described a method of pixel-based genome encoding for image reconstruction with GAs. This is different from the usual GA image techniques as it treats the image as a large data optimisation problem as opposed to a parametric optimisation. First, we demonstrated that it is possible to achieve close convergence on image generation from randomly initialised noisy genomes. This served to show that our fitness function was sufficient to reproduce the given image. Following this, we showed that modifying the fitness functions to combine the fitness functions manipulating image features lead to reasonable reproductions of the given image with considerations of the feature modifications. These reproductions confirm that the direct pixel manipulation method of GA-based image reconstruction is a viable technique. Furthermore, we analysed which image features stabilise earlier than later with increasing GA generations. Further work is now needed on correlating these findings with the actual human eye behaviour under controlled experimental conditions.

References

1. C. Bounsaythip, J. Alander, "Genetic Algorithms in Image Processing - A Review", Proc. of the 3rd Nordic Workshop on Genetic Algorithms and their Applications, Metsatalo, Univ. of Helsinki, Helsinki, Finland, pp. 173-192. 1997.
2. S. Marshall, N. R. Harvey, D. Greenhalgh, "Design of Morphological Filters Using Genetic Algorithms", Mathematical Morphology and Its Applications to Image Procesing, 1994.
3. Y.J. Zhang, "A Survey on Evaluating Methods for Image Segmentation", Pattern Recognition 29(8), pp. 1335-1246, 1996.
4. V. Ramos, F. Muge, "Image Colour Segmentation by Genetic Algorithms", RecPad 2000 Portugese confererncе on Pattern Recognition, pp. 125-129, 2000.
5. C. Munteanu, A. Rosa, "Evolutionary Image Enhancement with User Behaviour Modelling", Proceedings of the 2001 ACM Symposium on Applied Computing, pp. 316 - 320, 2001.
6. C. Munteanu, A. Rosa, "Towards Automatic Image Enhancement Using Genetic Algorithms", Proceedings of the IEEE conference on Evolutionary Computation, Vol. 4, pp. 1535-1542. 2000.
7. K. Otobe, K. Tanaka, M. Hirafuji, "Knowledge Acquisition on Image Processing Based On Genetic Algorithms", Proceedings of the IASTED International Conference on Signal and Image Processing, pp 28-31, 1998.
8. S. P. Brumby, N. R. Harvey, S. Perkins, R. B. Porter, J. J. Szymanski, J. Theiler, J. J. Bloch, "A Genetic Algorithm for Combining New and Existing Image Processing Tools for Multispectral Imagery", Proceedings of SPIE, 2000.
9. R. Poli, "Genetic Programming for Image Analysis", Proceedings of Genetic Programming, pp. 363-368, 1996.
10. C. A. Coello, "An Updated Survey of GA-Based Multiobjective Optimisation Techniques", ACM Computing Surveys, Vol. 32, No. 2, June 2000.
11. R. M. Haralick, K. Shanmugam and I. Dinstein, "Textural features for image classification", IEEE Transactions on System, Man, Cybernetics, vol. SMC-3, pp. 610-621, 1973.

A Novel Recovery Algorithm of Incomplete Observation Matrix for Converting 2-D Video to 3-D Content

Sungshik Koh

Insan Innovation Telecom Co., Ltd.,
524-19, Unnam-dong, Gwangsan-gu, Gwnagju, 506-812, Korea
phdkss@chosun.ac.kr

Abstract. This paper studies on new recovery of incomplete observation matrix for converting existing 2-D video sequences to 3-D content. In situations when converting previously recorded monoscopic video to 3-D, several entries of the observation matrix have not been observed and other entries have been perturbed by the influence of noise. In this case, there is no simple solution of SVD factorization for shape from motion. In this paper, a new recovery algorithm is proposed for recovering missing feature point, by minimizing the influence of noise, using iteratively geometrical correlations between a 2-D observation matrix and 3-D shape. The results in practical situations demonstrated with synthetic and real video sequences verify the efficiency and flexibility of the proposed method.

1 Introduction

In order to provide sufficient 3-D content, it is important to convert existing 2-D video clip into 3-D content [1], [2]. In real life video clips, these projections are not visible along the entire image sequence due to occlusion and a limited field of view. Thus, the observation matrix is incomplete. In this case, there are actually some weak points in matrix factorization. Many researchers have developed 3-D reconstruction methods using SVD factorization methods in difference ways. The matrix collects 2-D trajectories of projections of feature points (FPs) [3]-[8] or other primitives [9]-[12]. Sub-optimal solutions were proposed in [3] and [13]. Tomasi and Kanade [3] proposed that the missing FPs of the observation matrix are 'filled in', in a sequential and heuristic way, using SVD of observed partial matrices. Jacobs [13] improved their method by fitting an unknown matrix of a certain rank to an incomplete noisy matrix resulting from measurements in images, which is called Linear Fitting (LF). However, his method presents no approach to determine whether the incomplete matrix is stable or unstable. Guerreiro and Aguiar [14] proposed Expectation-Maximization (EM) and Two-Step (TS) iterative algorithm. The algorithms converged to the global optimum in a very small number of iterations. However, the performance of both EM and TS are influenced by noisy observation.

In the paper, a new missing FP estimation method that is executed under noisy observation matrix is proposed and it is compared with LF, EM and TS. The experimental results demonstrate that the proposed algorithm is more robust than LF, EM and TS, with respect to the sensibility to noise.

N. Zheng, X. Jiang, and X. Lan (Eds.): IWICPAS 2006, LNCS 4153, pp. 260 – 269, 2006.

2 Novel Missing FP Estimation

3-D reconstruction error is dependant on the total viewing angle and the total number of frames [15]-[18]. In practice, several entries of the matrix may not be observed or be observed with noise due to occlusion, image low resolution, and so on. By this reason, the 3-D reconstruction error is relative to the number of available image frames. It means that, when the observation matrix has noisy entries, the more the number of image frames gives the better result. Therefore, in order to obtain accurate 3D-contents it is obviously essential that the missing FPs of the observation matrix must be estimated accurately. In this section, some specific geometry between the noise of the 2-D observation matrix and the error of 3-D shape is described.

2.1 3-D Error Space and Its Parameters

In order to evaluate the precision of the 3-D shape reconstructed from a noisy observation matrix, the 3-D error space is introduced as follows:

i) For recovering a missing FP ($\boldsymbol{p}_m$), its initial position ($\boldsymbol{p}_t + \Delta\boldsymbol{e}$) is first fit roughly and three FPs ($\boldsymbol{p}_{bA}$, $\boldsymbol{p}_{bB}$, and $\boldsymbol{p}_{bC}$) are randomly selected, which are called bias FPs being neighbors of the missing FP ($\boldsymbol{p}_m$), on the same 2-D image plane. Next, new FPs ($\boldsymbol{q}_i$) are added, which are called Reference Points (RPs), on a circular pattern ($r = \Delta\boldsymbol{c}_i$) centering on the missing FP ($\boldsymbol{p}_m$). The aspects are shown in Fig. 1(a), where Π_2 is a reference plane composed of $\boldsymbol{q}_i$ on the 2-D image plane and $\overrightarrow{\boldsymbol{p}_m\boldsymbol{q}_i}$ is a reference vector (RV) composed of $\boldsymbol{p}_m$ and $\boldsymbol{q}_i$ on the 2-D image plane.

$$\boldsymbol{p}_m = \boldsymbol{p}_t + \Delta\boldsymbol{e}, \tag{1}$$

$$\boldsymbol{q}_i = \boldsymbol{p}_m + \Delta\boldsymbol{c}_i, \quad i = 1,2,\cdots,Z, \tag{2}$$

where $\boldsymbol{p}_t$, $\Delta\boldsymbol{e}$, $\boldsymbol{q}_i$, and $\Delta\boldsymbol{c}_i$ are a true FP, a noise vector, RPs, and circle radius on the 2D image plane, respectively.

ii) Using affine SVD factorization, the roughly fitted FP ($\boldsymbol{p}_m$), three bias FPs ($\boldsymbol{p}_{bA}$, $\boldsymbol{p}_{bB}$, and $\boldsymbol{p}_{bC}$), and circular RPs ($\boldsymbol{q}_i$) are reconstructed to $\boldsymbol{P}_m^*$, ($\boldsymbol{P}_{bA}^*$, $\boldsymbol{P}_{bB}^*$, and $\boldsymbol{P}_{bC}^*$), and $\boldsymbol{Q}_i^*$ on the 3-D reconstruction space, respectively (see Fig. 1(b)).

$$\boldsymbol{Q}_i^* = \boldsymbol{P}_m^* + \Delta\boldsymbol{C}_i^*, \tag{3}$$

where $\boldsymbol{P}_m^*$ and $\Delta\boldsymbol{C}_i^*$ are the reconstructed RPs and its circular parameter on 3-D reconstruction space. The symbol '*' means a perturbation.

iii) A 3-D error space is defined as the coordinates of 3-D point vectors without perturbation, which are transformed from three Euclidean distances between three bias FPs ($\boldsymbol{P}_{bA}^*$, $\boldsymbol{P}_{bB}^*$, and $\boldsymbol{P}_{bC}^*$) and a FP ($\boldsymbol{P}^*$) on 3-D reconstruction space. For example, the $\boldsymbol{P}_m$ on 3-D error space can be transformed from the missing FP ($\boldsymbol{P}_m^*$) on 3-D reconstruction space by three Euclidean distances between three bias FPs and the missing FP on the same 2-D image plane as

$$\boldsymbol{P}_m = (L_A, L_B, L_C), \tag{4}$$

where $L_A = \left\| \overrightarrow{P_m^* P_{bA}^*} \right\|$, $L_B = \left\| \overrightarrow{P_m^* P_{bB}^*} \right\|$, and $L_C = \left\| \overrightarrow{P_m^* P_{bC}^*} \right\|$. Also the circular RPs (Q_i^*) can be also expressed as Q_i on the 3-D error space as

$$Q_i = (L_{Ai}, L_{Bi}, L_{Ci}), \tag{5}$$

where $L_{Ai} = \left\| \overrightarrow{P_m^* P_{bA}^*} \right\|$, $L_{Bi} = \left\| \overrightarrow{P_m^* P_{bB}^*} \right\|$, and $L_{Ci} = \left\| \overrightarrow{P_m^* P_{bC}^*} \right\|$, $i = \{1, 2, \cdots, Z\}$.

This aspect is shown in Fig. 1(c), where Π_3 is a reference plane composed of Q_i on the 3-D error space and $\overrightarrow{P_m Q_i}$ is a Reference Vector (RV) composed of P_m and Q_i on the same 3-D error space.

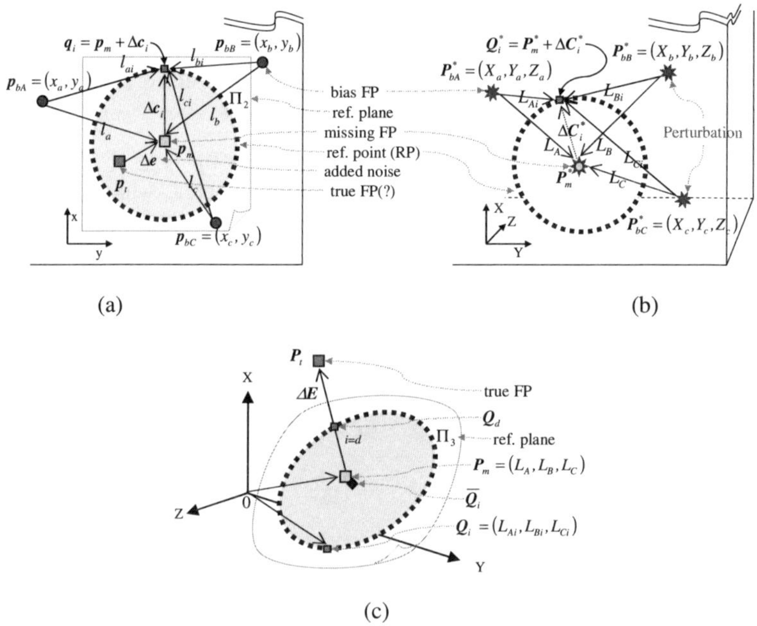

Fig. 1. Comparison of some parameters on 2-D image plane, 3-D reconstruction space, and 3-D error space. (a) noisy FP, three bias FPs and circular RPs on 2-D image plane. (b) parameters reconstructed from (a) on 3-D reconstruction space. (c) parameters transformed from (b) on 3D error space.

2.2 Geometrical Correlations Between Two Reference Plane Π_2 and Π_3

Assume that the noise vectors of a 2-D FP and the error vectors of its 3-D reconstructed FP are perpendicular to the camera optic axis and have approximately the same orientation and the nearly proportional size to each other. According to our considerations, the relationships between two reference planes Π_2 and Π_3 are analyzed on the 2-D image plane and the 3-D error space. In investigating the geometrical correlations, the following motivating facts are found:

Plane: Since 2-D RVs are on a plane Π_2, the 3-D RVs are also approximately located on a plane Π_3.

$$\Pi_2 = \{\overrightarrow{p_m q_i},\ i = 1,2,...,Z\},\ \Pi_3 \cong \{\overrightarrow{P_m Q_i},\ i = 1,2,...,Z\}. \quad (6)$$

Pattern: If the RPs on Π_2 are distributed on a circular pattern, then the RPs on Π_3 are distributed on an ellipse and are very close to be circular.

$$\{q_i\}\text{: circular pattern on } \Pi_2,\ \{Q_i\}\text{: ellipse pattern on } \Pi_3. \quad (7)$$

Symmetry: If two of any RVs on Π_2 exist on symmetrical positions with p_m, then their positions on Π_3 are nearly symmetric.

$$\overrightarrow{p_m q_{i_a}} \cong -\overrightarrow{p_m q_{i_b}} \Leftrightarrow \overrightarrow{P_m Q_{i_a}} \cong -\overrightarrow{P_m Q_{i_b}}. \quad (8)$$

Size: If two of any RVs on Π_2 are in the same direction with different sizes, then the RVs on Π_3 keep their magnitude relationships and ratios relative to the size.

$$\left\|\overrightarrow{p_m q_{i_a}}\right\| < \left\|\overrightarrow{p_m q_{i_b}}\right\| \Leftrightarrow \left\|\overrightarrow{P_m Q_{i_a}}\right\| < \left\|\overrightarrow{P_m Q_{i_b}}\right\|, \quad (9)$$

Angle: If three RVs on Π_2 are arranged in some angles, then the RVs on Π_3 are also arranged similarly, while keeping the relationship of magnitude and ratio around the angle.

$$\angle q_i p_m q_{i+1} < \angle q_i p_m q_{i+2} \Leftrightarrow \angle Q_i P_m Q_{i+1} < \angle Q_i P_m Q_{i+2}. \quad (10)$$

According to the above investigations, it can be observed that there are these geometrical correlations such as plane, pattern, symmetry, size, and angle between on Π_2 and Π_3. These aspects are always true for not only synthetic images but also real images. Therefore, the estimation algorithm for estimating the missing FPs can be derived using above facts in the next section.

2.3 Geometrical Estimation of Missing FP

When a FP deviates from its observation matrix position, its 3-D point reconstructed by affine SVD factorization is also misaligned. In this section, we estimate the noise vector of the missing FP using the geometrical correlations described previously. Since $P_m(L_A, L_B, L_C)$ and $Q_i(L_{Ai}, L_{Bi}, L_{Ci})$ are transformed from (3) on the 3-D error space, an error vector of a missing FP can be expressed as

$$\Delta E = \overrightarrow{P_m P_t}, \quad (11)$$

where P_t is the true FP on 3D error space. Because P_t is unknown parameter, an approximate P_t' is substituted. It can be obtained from a sub-matrix without missing FP. Also the relationship is satisfied with $P_t' \cdot \overline{Q}_i \cong P_t \cdot \overline{Q}_i'$, where $\overline{Q}_i$ is the mean of Q_i s. Hence, the approximate error vector can be represented as

$$\Delta E' = \overrightarrow{P_m P_t'} = P_t' \langle\times\rangle \left(\overline{Q}_i \langle/\rangle \overline{Q}_i' - (1,1,1)\right), \quad (12)$$

where $P\langle\times\rangle Q \equiv (x_1 x_2, y_1 y_2, z_1 z_2)$ and $P\langle/\rangle Q \equiv \left(\frac{x_1}{x_2}, \frac{y_1}{y_2}, \frac{z_1}{z_2}\right)$ for $\begin{cases} P = (x_1, y_1, z_1) \\ Q = (x_2, y_2, z_2) \end{cases}$.

If $\|\Delta E'\| \neq 0$, this means some noise exists in $\boldsymbol{P}_m$ on 3D error space and also in $\boldsymbol{p}_m$ of (1). In order to obtain the noise vector ($\Delta \boldsymbol{e}'$) of the missing FP on Π_2, we first calculate the error vector from the parameters represented on Π_3 of the 3D error space.

$$\Theta_d = \underset{d \in i}{\boldsymbol{argmin}} \|\Psi_i\|^2, \quad for\ \Psi_i = \boldsymbol{cos}^{-1}\left(\frac{\left\|\overrightarrow{\boldsymbol{P}_m \boldsymbol{P}_t'}\right\| \cdot \left\|\overrightarrow{\boldsymbol{P}_m \boldsymbol{Q}_i}\right\|}{\overrightarrow{\boldsymbol{P}_m \boldsymbol{P}_t'} \cdot \overrightarrow{\boldsymbol{P}_m \boldsymbol{Q}_i}} \right), \tag{13}$$

$$A_d = \frac{\left\|\overrightarrow{\boldsymbol{P}_m \boldsymbol{P}_t'}\right\|}{\left\|\overrightarrow{\boldsymbol{P}_m \boldsymbol{Q}_d}\right\|}, \; d \in \{1, 2, \cdots, Z\}, \tag{14}$$

where Θ_d is the minimum angle between $\overrightarrow{\boldsymbol{P}_m \boldsymbol{P}_t'}$ and $\overrightarrow{\boldsymbol{P}_m \boldsymbol{Q}_d}$, and A_d is the ratio of the size of $\overrightarrow{\boldsymbol{P}_m \boldsymbol{P}_t'}$ based on $\overrightarrow{\boldsymbol{P}_m \boldsymbol{Q}_d}$. Next, according to the geometrical correlations, the noise vector of the missing FP on Π_2 is derived from (13) and (14) as

$$\theta_d = \boldsymbol{\cos}^{-1}\left(\frac{\left\|\overrightarrow{\boldsymbol{p}_m \boldsymbol{q}_d}\right\| \cdot \left\|\overrightarrow{\boldsymbol{p}_m \boldsymbol{q}_1}\right\|}{\overrightarrow{\boldsymbol{p}_m \boldsymbol{q}_d} \cdot \overrightarrow{\boldsymbol{p}_m \boldsymbol{q}_1}} \right), \tag{15}$$

$$\alpha_d = A_d \left\|\overrightarrow{\boldsymbol{p}_m \boldsymbol{q}_d}\right\|. \tag{16}$$

Therefore, the missing FP ($\boldsymbol{p}_m$) can be updated as

$$\tilde{\boldsymbol{p}}_t = \boldsymbol{p}_m - \Delta \boldsymbol{e}', \tag{17}$$

where $\Delta \boldsymbol{e}' \equiv f(\alpha_d, \theta_d)$, which is a vector with magnitude α_d and angle θ_d. If $\|\Delta E'\|$ is larger than the predefined threshold, then $\tilde{\boldsymbol{p}}_t$ is set up to $\boldsymbol{p}_m$ and the above procedure is repeated until the position converses sufficiently close to the true position.

3 Analysis of Two Recovery Approaches for Multi-frame

To test our algorithm for multi-frame, two recovery approaches here are examined. Generally, the noise level of missing FPs may be higher than the potential noise level within noisy observation data. As much as possible, the missing FPs have to be estimated until the potential noise level. To solve this problem, we introduce two recovery approaches. The necessary three frames without missing FPs are called sub-observation matrix or simply sub-matrix. The rest frames are allowed with or without them. The two approaches are described in detail with Fig. 2. Red circles and Black squares are missing FPs by tracking failure and by occlusions, respectively. Here, Approach–I always uses four frames which are a sub-matrix consisting of the first three frames and one frame with missing FPs. On the other hand, Approach-II uses variable sub-matrix. That is, although the size of initial sub-matrices of Approach–I and Approach-II are the same, the size of the sub-matrix for Approach–I is fixed but that of the sub-matrix for Approach–II is increased gradually after solving each frame.

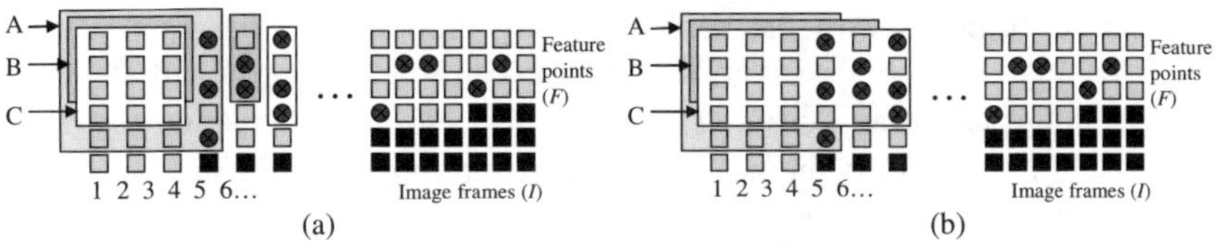

Fig. 2. Recovering sequences. (a) Approach–I (A,B,C,$\cdots$). (b) Approach–II (A,B,C,$\cdots$).

4 Experimental Results

In this section, we describe experiments that illustrate the behavior of the proposed algorithm using synthetic and real video sequences. The evaluation of our method is confirmed through experimental results by comparing with other approaches, LF, EM and TS.

4.1 Synthetic Video Sequence

For synthetic cube, we preset camera configuration as shown in Fig. 3(a), a cube is set on a 3-D world with a set of cameras. The size of the cube is 1x1x1 [unit], and the cube contains eight 3-D corner points. All points are tracked from 20 image frames taken to cover 180 degrees. The cube is placed with its centroid at 2.5[unit] from the first camera. The cameras are pointed towards the centroid of the cube. Fig. 3(b) presents a pattern of the missing FPs. The positions of its entries in the observation matrix are corrupted with holes. Yellow squares represent successfully tracked entries. Red circles denote missing FPs that are not received initially, this result in some holes in the observation matrix. For confirming the convergence of the proposed geometrical approach, we set the following reference points. The RPs ($\boldsymbol{q}_{\mathrm{i}}$, $i = 1,2,\cdots,10$) around a missing FP ($\boldsymbol{p}_{\mathrm{m}}$) are located at the constant interval angles on a circle and its radius is set up to $\Delta c_i = 0.2$ [unit]. The number of RPs has no limitation because the proposed algorithm is able to use the geometrical correlations if the number of reference points is greater then three (see Fig. 1).

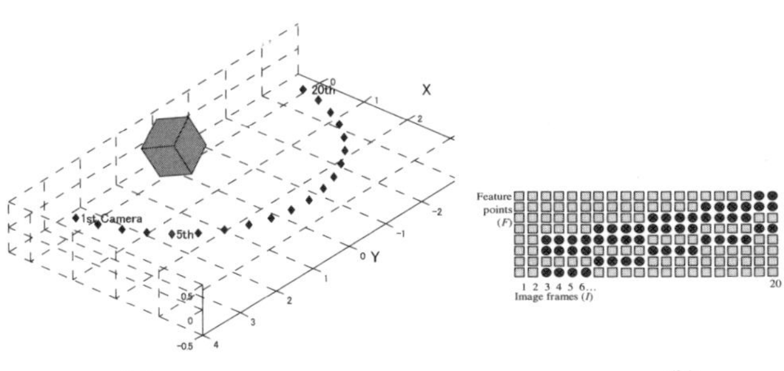

Fig. 3. Synthetic cube sequence. (a) camera configurations around a 3D cube. (b) pattern of missing FPs (Red) in the observation matrix.

In order to compare with the performance of Approach-I and Approach-II for multi-frame, Fig. 4 shows the criterion and the reconstructed shapes with iteration 10 times. The white Gaussian noise (*Δε*) is embedded into an observation matrix (**W**) and the added noise (*Δe*) is the position error of the roughly estimated missing FPs. Some symbols are defined as follows: S_0 is the 3-D shape reconstructed from **W** which will is used as a criterion, S_s from the sub-matrix of **W′**, S_a from **W′**, and S_1 and S_2 are the 3-D shapes after recovering by Approach-I and Approach-II, respectively.

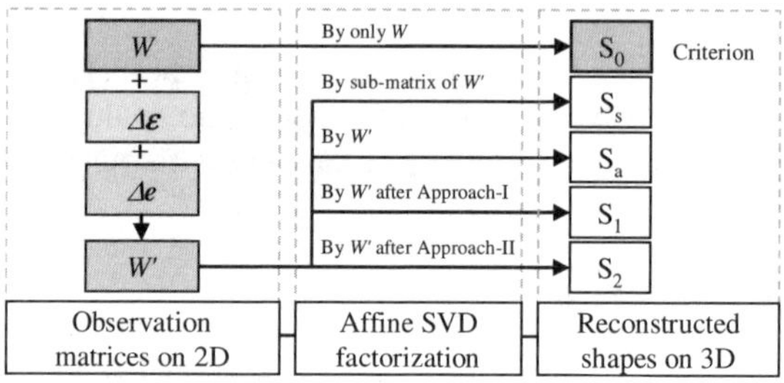

Fig. 4. Criterion and reconstructed 3-D shapes

Table 1 represents their 3D-*RMS* errors. When *Δε*=0 and *Δe*=0.1, $|S_0\text{-}S_a|$ is 0.004828, due to the effect of only added noise. For only white Gaussian noise, in the case of *Δε*=0.001 and *Δe*=0, $|S_0\text{-}S_a|$ is 0.000095. When the absent of added noise, $|S_0\text{-}S_s|$ is larger then $|S_0\text{-}S_a|$. Similarly, $|S_0\text{-}S_1|$ is larger then $|S_0\text{-}S_2|$. It means that the larger the number of image frames, the smaller the 3D-*RMS* error under the influence of noise. Anyway, $|S_0\text{-}S_2|$ in all cases are nearly the same to $|S_0\text{-}S_a|$ in the case of no added noise. More precisely, the reconstructed results after recovering using Approach-II is almost nearly equal to the result using all frames with absence of added noise. According to the results, we can draw the Approach-II is the best.

Table 1. 3D-*RMS* errors for synthetic cube sequence

Δε [unit]	0	0.001	0.001	0.001
Δe [unit]	0.1	0	0.02	0.1
$\lvert S_0\text{-}S_s\rvert$	0	0.000437	0.00437	0.000437
$\lvert S_0\text{-}S_a\rvert$	0.004828	0.000095	0.01000	0.004857
$\lvert S_0\text{-}S_1\rvert$	0	0.000285	0.00282	0.000280
$\lvert S_0\text{-}S_2\rvert$	0	0.000111	0.00110	0.000110

Fig. 5(a)-(b) plot the 2D-*RMS* errors and 3D-*RMS* errors under various noise distributions. The results of the proposed algorithm by Approach-II are superior to that of the LF, EM, and TS algorithms for 10 times iteration, as the proposed method is designed to minimize the influence of noise. Improved results can be achieved after greater iterations.

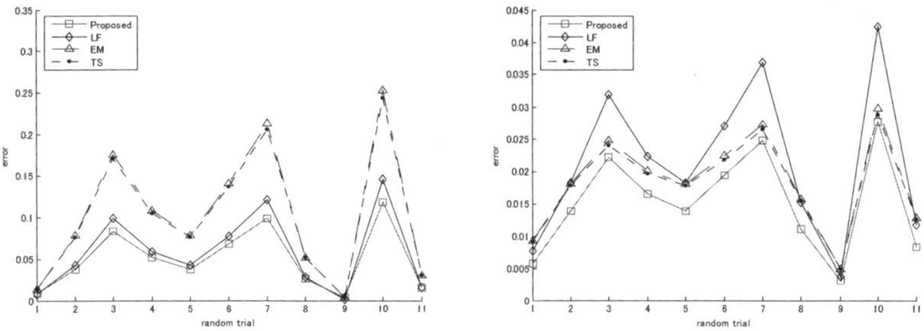

(a) (b)

Fig. 5. *RMS* errors under influence of noise level from zero to 0.1 [unit]. (a) 2-D reprojection errors (2D-*RMS*). (b) 3-D reconstruction errors (3D-*RMS*).

4.2 Real Video Sequence

In order to test the proposed algorithm on real data, the entries of an observation matrix are tracked over the 30-frame 'toyhotel' sequence. The 3rd frame (480x512) is presented in Fig. 6(a), where the tracked FPs are denoted by symbol '+'. The FPs

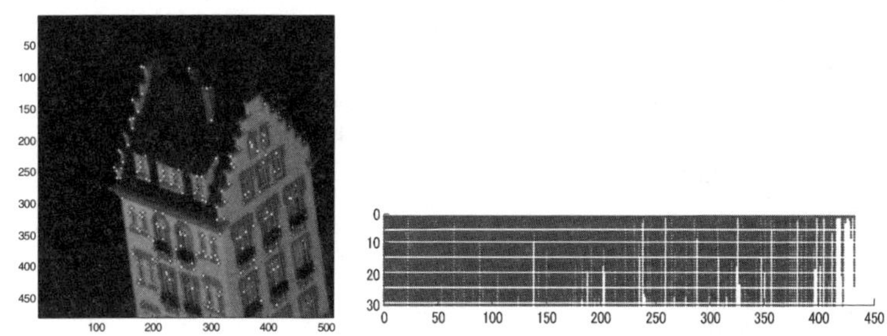

(a) (b)

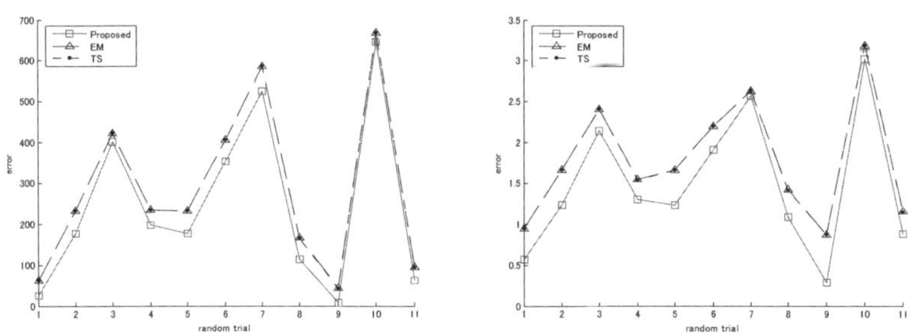

(c) (d)

Fig. 6. Real video sequence and *RMS* errors. (a) 3rd frame of hotel sequence with the tracked FPs. (b) observation matrix (30x442). (c) 2-D reprojection errors (2D-*RMS*). (d) 3-D reconstruction errors (3D-*RMS*).

were extracted by the Harris interest operator [19]. The observation matrix of the video frames is presented in Fig. 6(b), where red points are the observed entries. The proposed algorithm is verified against noise distribution from zero to 2 [pixel]. In the real data, Jacobs' method cannot be solved because of excessive sensitivity for high level of noise. Therefore, the proposed method is only compared with EM and TS, except for LF method. Fig. 6(c)-(d) illustrates the results of the estimated missing FPs. The proposed method by Approach-II leads to results of greater accuracy in various levels of noise. In addition, the trend of the 2D-*RMS* errors and 3D-*RMS* errors for real sequence closely follow that of the synthetic sequence. Therefore, it can be confirmed that the proposed method provides more satisfied results not only for the synthetic sequences, but also for real sequences.

5 Conclusions

To solve the problem of missing FPs for converting 2-D video sequence to 3-D content, a new recovery algorithm is presented by minimizing the influence of noise. The main idea is to estimate missing FPs by the geometrical correlations between 2-D image plane and 3-D error space. The achievements of the proposed system are presented using experimental results for synthetic and real sequences. In the results, it can be confirmed that our recovery algorithm can provide more accurate estimation results than the LF, EM, and TS algorithms' in various levels of noise by handling directly the orientation and distance of the missing FPs.

In the near future, our system will support the real-time creation of 3-D video material from 2-D video with self-occluding objects. Furthermore, the proposed method will assist 3-D content creation by advancing 3-D TV significantly and increasing its attractiveness.

References

1. C. Fehn, P. Kauff, M. Op de Beeck, F. Ernst, W. I.Jsselsteijn, M. Polleys, L. Van Gool, E. Ofek and I. Sexton : An Evolutionary and Optimized Approach on 3D-TV. In Proc. IBC02 (2002) 357-365
2. M. op de Beeck, P. Wilinski, C. Fehn, P. Kauff, W. I.Jsselsteijn, M. Polleys, L. Van Gool, E. Ofek and I. Sexton : Towards an Optimized 3D Broadcast Chain. In Proc. SPIE IT-Com02 (2002) 357-365
3. Tomasi and T. Kanade : Shape and motion from image streams under orthography: A factorization method. Int. J. of Computer Vision, vol.9-2 (1992) 137-154
4. Sturm, P., Triggs, B.: A factorization based algorithm for multi-image projective structure and motion. In Proc. ECCV, vol. 2, Cambridge, UK (1996) 709-720
5. Poelman, C.J., Kanade, T. : A paraperspective factorization method for shape and motion recovery. IEEE Trans. on PAMI, vol.19-3 (1997) 206-218
6. Morita, T., Kanade, T. : A sequential factorization method for recovering shape and motion from image streams. IEEE Trans. on PAMI, vol.19-8 (1997) 858-867
7. Aguiar, P.M.Q., Moura, J.M.F. : Rank 1 Weighted Factorization for 3D Structure Recovery: Algorithms and Performance Analysis. IEEE Trans. on PAMI, vol.25-9 (2003) 1134-1149

8. Irani, M., Anandan, P. : Factorization with uncertainty. In Proc.ECCV, Dublin, Ireland (2000) 539-553
9. Shapiro, L., : Affine Analysis of Image Sequences. Cambridge University Press (1995)
10. Quan, L., Kanade, T. : A factorization method for affine structure from line correspondences. In Proc. IEEE CVPR, San Francisco CA, USA (1996) 803-808
11. Morris, D., Kanade, T. : A unified factorization algorithm for points, line segments and planes with uncertainty models. In Proc. IEEE ICCV (1998) 696-702
12. Aguiar, P.M.Q., Moura, J.M.F. : Three-dimensional modeling from two dimensional video. IEEE Trans. on Image Processing, vo.10-10 (2001)1544-1551
13. D. Jacobs : Linear fitting with missing data for structure-from-motion. In Proc. CVIU, vol.82 (2001) 57-81
14. Rui F. C. Guerreiro, Pedro M. Q. Aguiar : Estimation of Rank Deficient Matrices from Partial Observations: Two-Step Iterative Algorithms. In Proc. EMMCVPR (2003) 450-466
15. Zhaohui Sun, V. Ramesh, and A. Murat Tekalp : Error characterization of the factorization method. Computer Vision and Image Understanding, vol.82 (2001) 110-137
16. K. Daniilidis and M. Spetsakis : Understanding noise sensitivity in structure from motion, Visual Navigation (1996) 61–88
17. D. D. Morris, K. Kanatani, and T. Kanade : Uncertainty modeling for optimal structure from motion. In Vision Algorithms: Theory and Practice, Lecture Notes in Computer Science, Springer-Verlag, Berlin/New York, vol.1883 (2000) 200–217
18. R. Szeliski and S. B. Kang : Shape ambiguities in structure-from-motion. IEEE Trans. on PAMI. vol.19 (1997) 506–512
19. C. J. Harris and M. Stephens : A Combined Corner and Edge Detector. In Proc. Alvey Vision Conf. (1998) 147-151

Study on the Geolocation Algorithm of Space-Borne SAR Image

Xin Liu, Hongbing Ma, and Weidong Sun

Remote Sensing Laboratory, Department of Electronic Engineering,
Tsinghua University,
100084 Beijing, China
{xin-liu04, hbma, wdsun}@mails.tsinghua.edu.cn

Abstract. SAR (Synthetic Aperture Radar) images have been widely used nowadays, as the SAR system is capable of scanning the earth surface objects into high resolution images. Before the SAR images are used, the geolocation step is needed to locate arbitrary pixels in an image accurately. Geolocation is very important in geometric rectification, geocoding, as well as object location and detection in the SAR image. In this paper, we propose a novel geolocation algorithm, which is a hybrid of an iterative algorithm and the conventional analytic algorithm based on Range-Doppler (RD) location model. First a new analytic algorithm adopted in our approach is presented. Next, in order to correct the geometry and terrain height, an iterative routine is integrated into the procedure. The experiment results indicate that our algorithm is efficient and can achieve higher accuracies compared with three state-of-the-art location algorithms.

1 Introduction

With the rapid development of the SAR technology, SAR products have been widely used in diverse fields recently, such as forestry, agriculture, geology, oceanography etc.. Despite the popularity of SAR products, the geometric distortion problem caused by variable terrain hampers the further application of the SAR images, and also inhibits the collocation of SAR images with geographically referenced information acquired from other sources. In order to better utilize the SAR images, we need to accurately locate every pixel in the SAR image in order to eliminate the inherent geometric distortions. The process of the pixel location is called geolocation. It is very important in the geometric rectification, and can be used to locate objects in the SAR images.

An important issue in geolocation or pixel location is the construction of the geolocation model. Up to now, many models have been proposed, including Konecny model, Leberl model, Polynomial model and RD (Range-Doppler) model [1,2,5,6]. These models can be divided into two categories: models based on radar collinear equation, such as Konecny model and Leberl model, and RD model. Compared with the former one, the RD model is deduced from the principle of SAR imagery and can work without the attitude angle of the sensor or

N. Zheng, X. Jiang, and X. Lan (Eds.): IWICPAS 2006, LNCS 4153, pp. 270–280, 2006.

any reference points. Thus the RD model has become the main pixel location method recently, especially when applied on the space-borne SAR images.

The process of solving the geolocation model is identical to the process of pixel location. Pixel location plays an important role in real applications for several reasons as given below. Firstly, it is a key procedure to rectify the geometric distortion of the SAR images. The pixel location result has a major impact on the accuracy of ortho-rectification and geocoding of SAR images. Secondly, the geometric rectification methods based on GCP (Ground Control Point) or DEM (Digital Elevation Model) can surely achieve very high accuracy. However, one major drawback of these methods is that they can not be applied to SAR images that are acquired from areas without topography map or DEM. In contrast, the absolute pixel location method is able to work as long as the platform ephemeris data are provided. The term "absolute" means that the location process is done only with the metadata in the SAR product and without any extra information, such as GCP and DEM, which is defined in the specification recommended by CEOS (Committee on Earth Observations Satellites) [3].

This paper is organized in five parts as follows. Section 2 briefly introduces the principle of the RD model. In Section 3, after several algorithms solving the model are discussed, our algorithm is presented. Section 4 presents some experiment results and shows that our algorithm is efficient and can achieve a high accuracy. Section 5 concludes.

2 RD Geolocation Model

In this section, we give a brief introduction to the RD geolocation model. In 1981, Brown proposed an absolute pixel location method which can locate an arbitrary pixel in the SAR image without any reference points or control points [4]. Curlander developed the Range-Doppler geolocation theory on the SEASAT SAR based on Brown's work [5,6]. Most RD geolocation models used now are based on the Curlander's RD theory.

SAR, as a kind of active remote sensor, can provide a precise distance between the sensor and the target and the Doppler frequency of the echo wave. In the imagery process, the absolute location of the image pixel can be determined by these two factors. We can obtain the distance between the sensor and target according to the echo delay time. All the points on the ground with the same distance to the sensor form a circle. According to the Doppler shift, we could infer that all the points on the ground with the same Doppler frequency form a hyperbola (Fig. 1). The two curves intersect at four points. The left/right ambiguity is resolved by our knowledge of the side of the platform from which the radar beam is directed, while the branch of the hyperbola is indicated by the sign of the Doppler shift.

Fig. 1 gives the SAR geolocation model defined in the GEI (Geocentric Equatorial Inertial) coordinate system. In the GEI system, the earth center is the origin, the x axis points toward the vernal equinox and the z axis points to the north pole, the y axis completes a right-handed system. As the principle of the RD geolocation theory introduced above, for a fixed target on the ground, its position vector $\boldsymbol{R}_t = (x_t, y_t, z_t)^T$ satisfies three equations: (1) Range equation, (2) Doppler equation, and (3) Earth model equation.

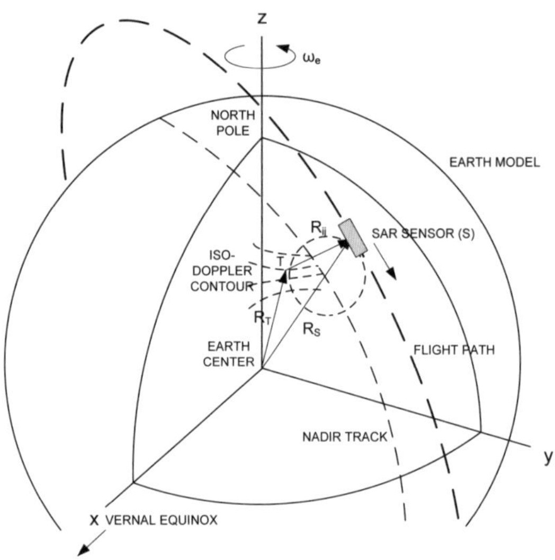

Fig. 1. GEI coordinate system illustrating a graphical solution for the pixel location equations [8]

The range equation is given by

$$R = | \boldsymbol{R}_s - \boldsymbol{R}_t | \tag{1}$$

where R is the distance between the sensor and the target, $\boldsymbol{R}_s$ and $\boldsymbol{R}_t$ are the sensor and the target position vectors, respectively.

The Doppler equation is given by

$$f_d = -\frac{2}{\lambda}\frac{(\boldsymbol{R}_s - \boldsymbol{R}_t)(\boldsymbol{V}_s - \boldsymbol{V}_t)}{|\boldsymbol{R}_s - \boldsymbol{R}_t|} \tag{2}$$

where λ is the radar wavelength, f_d is the Doppler frequency, and $\boldsymbol{V}_s$, $\boldsymbol{V}_t$ are the sensor and the target velocity vectors, respectively.

The third equation is the earth model equation. An oblate ellipsoid can be used to model the earth's shape as follows

$$\frac{x_t^2 + y_t^2}{(R_e + h)^2} + \frac{z_t^2}{R_p^2} = 1 \tag{3}$$

where R_e is the radius of earth at the equator, h is the local target elevation relative to the assumed model, and R_p, the polar radius, is given by

$$R_p = (1 - f)(R_e + h) \tag{4}$$

where f is the flattening factor.

The target location as given by its position vector $\boldsymbol{R}_t = (x_t, y_t, z_t)^T$, is determined from the simultaneous solution of Eqn. (1), Eqn. (2) and Eqn. (3) for the three unknown target position parameters, as illustrated in Fig. 1.

3 Algorithms

After the construction of the RD geolocation model, we begin to discuss the algorithms solving the model in this section. The process of solving the model is actually identical to the process of the absolute pixel location of the SAR image, that is, given the row index and the column index (i, j) of a pixel in the image, the longitude and latitude of the pixel can be calculated according to the RD model. The three basic equations introduced above was proposed by Curlander in 1982. Curlander also analyzed the location accuracy and the sources of the location errors. However, Curlander didn't present the details about how to solve the model.

In recent years, several algorithms have been proposed for the above problem and can be classified into two categories: numerical algorithms and analytic algorithms. We'll first introduce these algorithms and then present our approach.

3.1 Numerical Algorithm

Alaska Satellite Facility implemented a numerical algorithm in its public open software processing SAR images [8]. We refer this method as ASF algorithm.

The main idea of the ASF algorithm is to adjust the attitude of the sensor using the given Doppler centroid frequency and the slant range, then calculate the target position vector with the attitude. The details can be found in [8]. The advantage of the ASF algorithm is its high location accuracy. Its main drawback is that many iterative steps used in the routine reduce its efficiency heavily.

3.2 Analytic Algorithm

Li (1983) proved that the analytic solution can be archived if the earth is regarded as a sphere with the local radius, but he didn't give the specific solution [9]. Xiaokang Yuan (1997) is the first to implement an analytic algorithm for the absolute geolocation based on the RD model. He conducted intensive analysis on this algorithm and its location errors in theory [10]. However, he didn't try any experiments or use any SAR product to verify his algorithm. We refer this algorithm as AGM (Analytic Geolocation Method). Jingping Zhou developed a new algorithm based on the AGM algorithm [7]. He called this algorithm Relative Geolocation Method. We denote this algorithm with RGM for short.

The analytic algorithms need no iterative steps, and their main procedures are as follows: Firstly, we can calculate the position of the nadir. If the spherical angel of the target relative to the nadir could be calculated, we can get the target position. The main advantage of the analytic algorithms are their efficiency compared with the ASF algorithm. However, their low location accuracy makes them of little practice.

3.3 Our Algorithm – An Ierative Analytic Algorithm

In order to improve the location accuracy while keeping a moderate efficiency, we incorporate the iterative step into the analytic algorithm. As a result, we implement a new algorithm that outperforms the above ones.

Since the reference coordinate system used in most SAR products is ECR (Earth Centered Rotating) system, our model and algorithm is also implemented in this reference frame. As shown in Fig. 2, in the ECR system, the Z axis points toward the north pole, the X axis points toward the prime meridian, and the Y axis completes a right-handed system. The only difference between the GEI system and the ECR system is the earth rotating angle, thus the basic three equations, Eqn. (1), Eqn. (2) and Eqn. (3) have the same forms in the ECR coordinate system as they are in the GEI system. It should be noted that $\boldsymbol{V}_t = 0$ in the ECR coordinate system.

Now we first present the new analytic algorithm adopted in our approach. As shown in Fig. 2, a local coordinate system is constructed, in which the platform is the origin and so called PCS (Platform Coordinate System). In the PCS, the z axis points from the earth center to the sensor, the y axis is perpendicular to the plane determined by the z axis and the velocity of the sensor, and the x axis completes a right-handed system. It is noted that the x axis direction is close to the sensor's velocity, but they are not identical in most cases.

The point S' intersected by the line lying between the sensor S and the earth center O, and the earth surface is called nadir. Given the sensor position vector $\boldsymbol{R}_s$, we can get the longitude and the latitude of the nadir S' and thus the length of OS', R_L, called the local radius. With a small area around the nadir, the earth surface can be regarded as a sphere, so we can assume that $R_t = OT = OS' = R_L$, where R_t is the magnitude of the target position vector.

In the triangle $\triangle OST$, we have

$$\cos\alpha = \frac{R_s^2 + R^2 - R_t^2}{2R_s R} \tag{5}$$

where R_s is the magnitude of the sensor position vector and $\alpha = \angle OST$.

As shown in Fig. 3, T' is the projection of the target T onto the xy plane, and $\beta = \angle xST'$, the angle with which the x axis needs to revolve clockwise to the vector $\overrightarrow{ST'}$ direction. The range vector from the sensor to the target $\boldsymbol{R}$ is determined by its magnitude R and α, β angle. Since R is given in advance and we have got α, the problem left is to compute β.

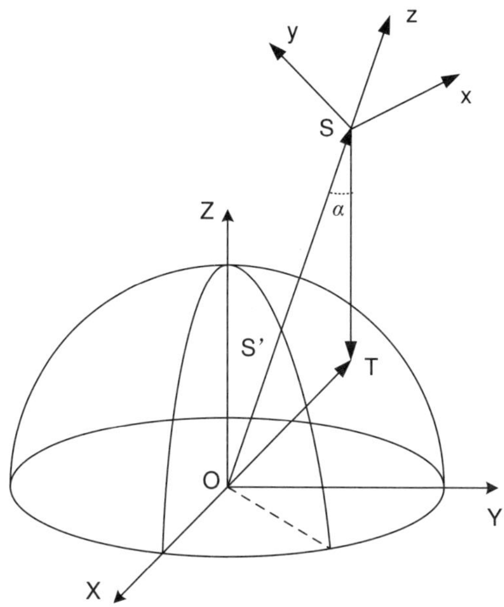

Fig. 2. ERC coordinate system illustrating our algorithm

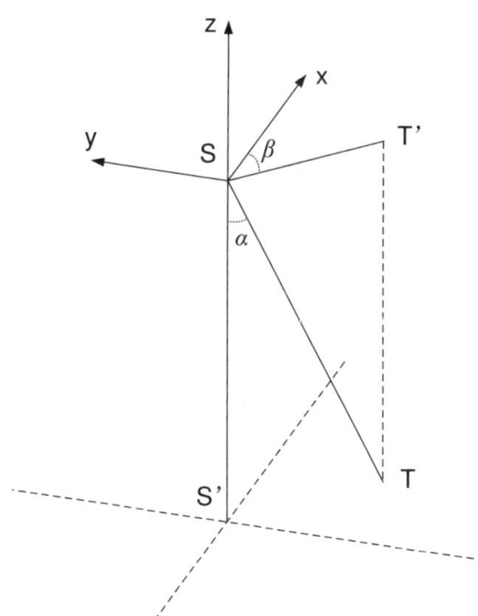

Fig. 3. Illustration of the local coordinate system

The coordinate transformation matrix from the local coordinate system to the ECR system $\boldsymbol{M}$ is given by

$$\boldsymbol{M} = \{\, \boldsymbol{x}_e, \boldsymbol{y}_e, \boldsymbol{z}_e\} \tag{6}$$

where $\boldsymbol{x}_e$, $\boldsymbol{y}_e$, $\boldsymbol{z}_e$ are the unit vectors of the three axes of the local coordinate system. According to the definition of the local coordinate system, we have

$$\begin{cases} \boldsymbol{z}_e = \dfrac{\boldsymbol{R}_s}{|\boldsymbol{R}_s|} \\ \boldsymbol{y}_e = \dfrac{\boldsymbol{R}_s \times \boldsymbol{V}_s}{|\boldsymbol{R}_s||\boldsymbol{V}_s|} \\ \boldsymbol{x}_e = \boldsymbol{y}_e \times \boldsymbol{z}_e \end{cases} \tag{7}$$

Eqn. (7) shows that the transformation matrix $\boldsymbol{M}$ is the function of the sensor position vector and velocity vector. The sensor velocity vector in the local coordinate system $\boldsymbol{V}'_s = (v_x, v_y, v_z)^T$ is given by

$$\boldsymbol{V}'_s = \boldsymbol{M}^{-1}\boldsymbol{V}_s \tag{8}$$

The range vector $\boldsymbol{R}$ in the local coordinate system $\boldsymbol{R}'$ is given by

$$\boldsymbol{R}' = R\boldsymbol{P} \tag{9}$$

where $\boldsymbol{P} = (x_p, y_p, z_p)^T$ is the unit vector in vector $\boldsymbol{R}$ direction, and is given by

$$\begin{cases} x_p = \sin\alpha\cos\beta \\ y_p = -\sin\alpha\sin\beta \\ z_p = -\cos\alpha \end{cases} \tag{10}$$

In the local coordinate system, the Doppler equation becomes

$$f_d = -\frac{2}{\lambda R}\boldsymbol{R}'\boldsymbol{V}'_s = -\frac{2}{\lambda}\boldsymbol{P}\boldsymbol{V}'_s \tag{11}$$

Substituting from $\boldsymbol{V}'_s = (v_x, v_y, v_z)^T$ and Eqn. (10), we get

$$f_d = -\frac{2}{\lambda}[v_x\sin\alpha\cos\beta + v_y(-\sin\alpha\sin\beta) + v_z(-\cos\alpha)] \tag{12}$$

Simplifying the equation above, we have

$$A\cos\beta + B\sin\beta + C = 0 \tag{13}$$

where

$$\begin{cases} A = -\dfrac{2}{\lambda}v_x\sin\alpha \\ B = \dfrac{2}{\lambda}v_y\sin\alpha \\ C = \dfrac{2}{\lambda}v_z\cos\alpha - f_d \end{cases} \tag{14}$$

By solving the equation above, we have

$$\cos\beta = \frac{-AC \pm B\sqrt{A^2 + B^2 - C^2}}{A^2 + B^2} \tag{15}$$

where the $\pm$ ambiguity is resolved by the knowledge of the sensor pointing direction, we get + when the direction is right and - when it is left. Now we have both α and β. After inserting them into Eqn. (10), we get the vector $\boldsymbol{P}$. Then the slant range vector $\boldsymbol{R}$ is given by

$$\boldsymbol{R} = \boldsymbol{M}\boldsymbol{R}' = \boldsymbol{M}R\boldsymbol{P} = R\boldsymbol{M}\boldsymbol{P} \tag{16}$$

Inserting this equation into $\boldsymbol{R} = \boldsymbol{R}_t - \boldsymbol{R}s$, we get the target position vector $\boldsymbol{R}_t$,

$$\boldsymbol{R}_t = \boldsymbol{R}_s + \boldsymbol{R} = \boldsymbol{R}_s + R\boldsymbol{M}\boldsymbol{P} \tag{17}$$

At last, we can calculate the longitude and the latitude of the target according to its position vector $\boldsymbol{R}_t$.

Now we have presented a new analytic location algorithm. Next, we'll introduce the iterative steps into it to implement our algorithm. The detailed procedures are given as follows:

(1) Get R_L, R_t according to the above method.
(2) Calculate α using Eqn. (5).
(3) According to the location algorithm presented above, we can get the position vector $\boldsymbol{R}_t = (x_t, y_t, z_t)^T$ of the target and its longitude, latitude and elevation (L_t, δ_t, h).
(4) Calculate $R'_L = R_t - h$. If $|R'_L - R_L| < 0.01$, then stop the iteration and export the result (L_t, δ_t). Otherwise, let $R_L = R'_L$ and return to step (2).

4 Experiment

4.1 Data Set

The data used for experiments are four scenes of EAR SAR imagery product, three of which are acquired in Zengcheng district of Guangdong Province and the forth one was acquired in Xiamen city in Fujian Province. The basic attributes of the SAR images are listed in Table 1.

Table 1. Basic attributes of the SAR imagery products for the experiment

Index	District	Product Type	Scene Identification	Radar direction	Image size
1	Zengcheng	ERS-1.SAR.PRI	18-Aug-97	Right look	8173×8000
2	Zengcheng	ERS-1.SAR.PRI	9-Jun-97	Right look	8173×8000
3	Zengcheng	ERS-1.SAR.PRI	22-Sep-97	Right look	8173×8000
4	Xiamen	ERS-2.SAR.PRI	27-Feb-98	Right look	8200×8000

4.2 Evaluation Method

Using the Corners. The SAR processor will save the longitude and the latitude of the four corners of the SAR image into the product metadata when generating level 1B product from level 0 product. Therefore we can use geolocation algorithms to locate these four corners, compare the location results with the longitude and the latitude of the four corners given in the metadata and calculate the errors between them to evaluate the location accuracy of the algorithm.

Assume the longitude and the latitude of the four corners given in the metadata are (L_n, δ_n), $n = 1, 2, 3, 4$. By locating the pixels of the four corners, we get the location results, (L'_n, δ'_n), $n = 1, 2, 3, 4$. The average errors in the longitude and the latitude, E_L and E_δ respectively, are given by

$$E_L = \frac{1}{4}\sum_{n=1}^{4} |L'_n - L_n| \tag{18}$$

$$E_\delta = \frac{1}{4}\sum_{n=1}^{4} |\delta'_n - \delta_n|. \tag{19}$$

which are regarded as the evaluation guideline.

Using GCP. We could manually collect some GCPs comparing the SAR image with the topography map in the same district. The following procedures are similar to those of the former evaluation method. We locate the pixels corresponding to these GCPs, and compare the location results with the position results acquired from the topography map.

Efficiency Evaluation. Since it is time consuming to locate all the pixels in the image, we just locate part of the image to test the efficiency performance of the algorithms. We could locate the first, the middle and the last row of the SAR image using the same algorithm and note down the time consumed.

4.3 Results

The evaluation results using the corners are provided in Table 2.

Table 2 shows that for the longitude, the location accuracies of the ASF, the RGM and our algorithm are nearly the same. Our algorithm has the least average error while the AGM algorithm has the largest one. For the latitude, the location accuracies of the ASF, the AGM and our algorithm are almost the same, and the AGM has the least average error while the RGM has the largest one. The accuracy for the latitude of our algorithm is only a little worse than that of the AGM algorithm. We can see that the results from all the four scenes have the same conclusion. Taking the accuracies in both longitude and latitude into account, we can find our algorithm outperforms the other three.

Table 2. Evaluation results using the corners (unit: 10^{-5}degree)

Algorithms	1		2		3		4	
	E_L	E_δ	E_L	E_δ	E_L	E_δ	E_L	E_δ
ASF	36.627	144.67	59.32	161.4	56.187	151.98	25.994	110.25
AGM	374.14	114.95	397.57	131.67	393.18	122.26	364.77	80.023
RGM	46.689	1333.6	69.476	1352.9	66.274	1345.3	37.469	1328.3
Our Algorithm	29.214	134.51	30.562	151.2	35.209	141.75	36.654	99.658

Table 3. Efficiency performance of the algorithms (unit: second)

Algorithm	Time
ASF	20.6
AGM	2.1
RGM	2.1
Our Algorithm	10.9

With regard to the efficiency, we select one of the four images to test the performance of the algorithms and the results are shown in Table 3.

Table 3 demonstrates that although our algorithm is still slower than the two analytic algorithms, its efficiency has improved dramatically compared with the ASF algorithm.

In summary, our algorithm can achieve a higher accuracy while keeping a moderate efficiency. Considering the performances in both accuracy and efficiency, we can find that our algorithm obviously outperforms the other three.

5 Conclusions and Future Work

In this paper, a novel geolocation algorithm of SAR images is proposed based on an iterative analytic method. The experiment results show that our algorithm is superior to the other three approaches widely used in real applications.

The location accuracies of current geolocation algorithms are all subject to the platform ephemeris errors. The product types of the experiment data used in the paper are all ERS SAR products, the platform ephemeris of which has a high accuracy. In order to validate the robustness of our algorithm, we'll use other types of SAR products for experiment.

References

1. Konecny, G., Schuhr, W.: Reliability of Radar Image Data. 16th ISPRS Congress, Comm, **3**. Tokyo (1988)
2. Leberl, F.: Radargrammetry for Iamge Interpretation. ITC Technical Report. (1978)
3. Radarsat International: Technical Documents For Radarsat Network Stations. (1997)

4. Brown, W.E.:Application of SEASAT SAR Digitally Corrected Imagery for Sea Ice Dynamics, Amer. Geophys Union Spring 1981 Meeting (1981)
5. Curlander, J.C.: Location of Space-borne SAR Imagery. IEEE Transaction on Geoscience Remote Sensing, Vol. 20, **3** (1982) 359–364
6. Curlander, J.C., McDonough, R. N.: Synthetic Aperture Radar: Systems and Signal Processing. New York (1991)
7. Jinping Zhou: Development of Two Practical R-D Location Model and Precision Comparison Between Them. Journal of Remote Sensing, Vol. 5, **3** (2001) 191–197
8. Coert Olmsted: Alaska SAR Facility Scientific SAR User's Guide. `http://www.asf.alaska.edu/reference/general/SciSARuserGuide.pdf` (1993)
9. Li, F.K., Johnson, W.T.K.: Ambiguities in Spaceborne Synthetic Aperture Radar System. IEEE Transaction on Aerospace and Electronic Systems, Vol. 19, **3** (1983) 389–396
10. Xiaokang Yuan: The Location Method for Targets in Satellite-borne SAR. Aerospace Shanghai, **6** (1997) 51–57
11. Erxue Chen, Zengyuan Li: Study on the Geocoding Algorithm of Space borne SAR Image. High Technology Letters, **2** (2000) 56–62
12. Erxue Chen: Study on Ortho-rectification Methodology of Space-borne Synthetic Aperture Radar Imagery [D]. Chinese Academy of Forestry, Beijing (2004)

Perceptual Image Retrieval Using Eye Movements

Oyewole Oyekoya and Fred Stentiford

University College London, Adastral Park,
Ipswich United Kingdom IP5 3RE
{o.oyekoya, f.stentiford}@adastral.ucl.ac.uk

Abstract. This paper explores the feasibility of using an eye tracker as an image retrieval interface. A database of image similarity values between 1000 Corel images is used in the study. Results from participants performing image search tasks show that eye tracking data can be used to reach target images in fewer steps than by random selection. The effects of the intrinsic difficulty of finding images and the time allowed for successive selections were also investigated.

1 Introduction

Images play an increasingly important part in the lives of many people. There is a critical need for automated management, as the flow of digital visual data increases and is transmitted over the network. Retrieval mechanisms must be capable of handling the amount of data efficiently and quickly. Existing systems are capable of retrieving archiving material according to date, time, location, format, file size, etc. However, the ability to retrieve images with semantically similar content from a database is more difficult.

One of the major issues in information searching is the problem associated with initiating a query. Indeed lack of high-quality interfaces for query formulation has been a longstanding barrier to effective image retrieval systems [19]. Users find it hard to generate a good query because of initial vague information [18] (i.e. "I don't know what I am looking for but I'll know when I find it"). Eye tracking presents an adaptive approach that can capture the user's current needs and tailor the retrieval accordingly. Understanding the movement of the eye over images is an essential component in the research.

Research in the applications of eye tracking is increasing, as presented in Duchowski's review [3] of diagnostic and interactive applications based on offline and real-time analysis respectively. Interactive applications have concentrated upon replacing and extending existing computer interface mechanisms rather than creating a new form of interaction. The tracking of eye movements has been employed as a pointer and a replacement for a mouse [5], to vary the screen scrolling speed [12] and to assist disabled users [1]. Dasher [20] uses a method for text entry that relies purely on gaze direction. In its diagnostic capabilities, eye-tracking provides a comprehensive approach to studying interaction processes such as the placement of menus within web sites and to influence design guidelines more widely [10]. The imprecise nature of saccades and fixation points has prevented these approaches from yielding benefits over conventional human interfaces. Fixations and saccades are used to

N. Zheng, X. Jiang, and X. Lan (Eds.): IWICPAS 2006, LNCS 4153, pp. 281 – 289, 2006.

analyze eye movements, but it is evident that the statistical approaches to interpretation (such as clustering, summation and differentiation) are insufficient for identifying interests due to the differences in humans' perception of image content. More robust methods of interpreting the data are needed. There has been some recent work on document retrieval in which eye tracking data has been used to refine the accuracy of relevance predictions [16]. Applying eye tracking to image retrieval requires that new strategies be devised that can use visual and algorithmic data to obtain natural and rapid retrieval of images.

Traditional approaches of image retrieval suffer from three main disadvantages. Firstly there is a real danger that the use of any form of pre-defined feature measurements will be unable to handle unseen material. Image retrieval systems normally rank the relevance between a query image and target images according to a similarity measure based on a set of features. Pre-determined features can take the form of edges, colour, location, texture, and others. Secondly the choice of low-level features is unable to anticipate a user's high-level perception of image content. This information cannot be obtained by training on typical users because every user possesses a subtly different subjective perception of the world and it is not possible to capture this in a single fixed set of features and associated representations. Thirdly descriptive text does not reflect the capabilities of the human visual memory and does not satisfy users' expectations. Furthermore the user may change his/her mind and may also be influenced by external factors.

An approach to visual search should be consistent with the known attributes of the human visual system and account should be taken of the perceptual importance of visual material. Recent research in human perception of image content [7] suggests the importance of semantic cues for efficient retrieval. Relevance feedback mechanisms [2] is often proposed as a technique for overcoming many of the problems faced by fully automatic systems by allowing the user to interact with the computer to improve retrieval performance. This reduces the burden on unskilled users to set quantitative pictorial search parameters or to select images (using a mouse) that come closest to meeting their goals. This has prompted research into the viability of eye tracking as a natural input for an image retrieval system. Visual data can be used as input as well as a source of relevance feedback for the interface. Human gaze behaviour may serve as a new source of information that can guide image search and retrieval.

Human eye behaviour is defined by the circumstances in which they arise. The eye is attracted to regions of the scene that convey what is thought at the time to be the most important information for scene interpretation. Initially these regions are pre-attentive in that no recognition takes place, but moments later in the gaze the fixation points depend more upon either our own personal interests and experience or a set task. Humans perceive visual scenes differently. We are presented with visual information when we open our eyes and carry out non-stop interpretation without difficulty. Research in the extraction of information from visual scenes has been explored by Yarbus [21], Mackworth and Morandi [9] and Hendersen and Hollingworth [6]. Mackworth and Morandi [9] found that fixation density was related to the measure of informativeness for different regions of a picture and that few fixations were made to regions rated as uninformative. The picture was segmented and a separate group of observers were asked to grade the rate of informativeness. Scoring the informativeness of a region provides a good insight into how humans perceive a scene or image. Henderson and Hollingworth [6] described semantic informativeness as the meaning of an image region and visual informativeness as the structural information. Fixation positions were more influenced by the former compared to the latter. The determination of informativeness and corresponding eye movements are influenced by task demands [21].

Previous work [13] used a visual attention model to score the level of informativeness in images and found that a substantial part of the gaze of the participants during the first two seconds of exposure is directed at informative areas as estimated by the model. Subjects were presented with images with clear regions-of-interest and results showed that these attracted eye gaze on presentation of the images studied. This led credence to the belief that the gaze information obtained from users when presented with a set of images could be useful in driving an image retrieval interface. More recent work [14] compared the performance of the eye and the mouse as a source of visual input. Results showed faster target identification for the eye interface than the mouse for identifying a target image on a display.

In this paper, experiments are described that explore the viability of using the eye to drive an image retrieval interface. Preliminary work was reported in [15]. In a visual search task, users are asked to find a target image in a database and the number of steps to the target image are counted. It is reasonable to believe that users will look at the objects in which they are interested during a search [13] and this provides the machine with the necessary information to retrieve a succession of plausible candidate images for the user.

2 Data and Apparatus

1000 images were selected from the Corel image library. Images of 127 kilobytes and 256 x 170 pixel sizes were loaded into the database. The categories included boats, landscapes, vehicles, aircrafts, birds, animals, buildings, athletes, people and flowers. The initial screen (including the position of the target image) is shown in Figure 1. Images were displayed as 229 x 155 pixel sizes in the 4 x 4 grid display.

An Eyegaze System [8] was used in the experiments to generate raw gazepoint location data at the camera field rate of 50 Hz (units of 20ms). A clamp with chin rest provided support for chin and forehead in order to minimize the effects of head movements, although the eye tracker does accommodate head movement of up to 1.5 inches (3.8cm). Calibration is needed to measure the properties of each subject's eye before the start of the experiments. The images were displayed on a 15" LCD Flat Panel Monitor at a resolution of 1024x768 pixels. The loading of 16 images in the 4 x 4 grid display took an average of 100ms on a Pentium IV 2.4GHz PC with 512MB of RAM. Gaze data collection and measurement of variables were suspended while the system loaded the next display. The processing of information from the eye tracker is done on a 128MB Intel Pentium III system with a video frame grabber board.

Fig. 1. Standard start screens for all participants

A measure [17] was used to pre-compute similarity scores between all pairs of images in the database. Images are presented in a 4 by 4 grid with target image presented in the top left corner of the display. The user is asked to search for the target image and on the basis of the captured gaze behaviour, the machine selects the most favoured image. The next set of 15 images are then retrieved from the database on the basis of similarity scores and displayed for the next selection. The session stops when the target image is found or a prescribed number of displays is reached.

A random selection strategy (the machine randomly selects the most favoured image) was employed to provide a performance base-line which any more intelligent approach would need to exceed.

3 Experiment Design

3.1 Selection of Target Images

It was found that as the number of randomly retrieved images in each display was increased, the likelihood of finding the target image also increased. A histogram plot of the frequency distribution of steps to target for every image in the database revealed the easy-to-find and hard-to-find images. 4 easy-to-find and 4 hard-to-find target images were picked for the experiment. These are shown in Figure 2.

Fig. 2. Target Images (Four easy-to-find images on the right and four hard-to-find images on the left)

3.2 Experimental Procedure

Thirteen unpaid participants took part in the experiment. Participants included a mix of students and university staff. All participants had normal or corrected-to-normal vision and provided no evidence of colour blindness.

One practice run was allowed to enable better understanding of the task at hand and to equalise skill levels during the experiment. Participants understood that there would be a continuous change of display until they found the target but did not know what determines the display change. The display change is determined by eye selection of an image, using the sum of all fixations of 80ms and above on an image position, up to a fixation threshold. Two fixation thresholds of 400ms and 800ms were employed as a factor in the experiment. The display included either no randomly retrieved image (all 15 images are selected on the basis of similarity scores) or one randomly retrieved image (one image is randomly selected from the database). Participants performed 8 runs, using all image types (easy-to-find and hard-to-find). Four treatment combinations of the two fixation thresholds (400ms and 800ms) and two randomly-retrieved levels (0 and 1) were applied to each image type. Any sequence effect was minimised by randomly allocating each participant to different sequences of target images. The first four runs were assigned to each image type. There was a 1 minute rest between runs. The maximum number of steps to target was limited to 26 runs.

4 Results and Discussion

Three dependent variables, the number of steps to target, the time to target (F_1), and the number of fixations (F_2) of 80ms and above were monitored and recorded during the experiment. 8 dependent variables were recorded for each participant. The average figures are presented in Table 1.

Table 1. Analysis of Human Eye Behaviour on the Interface (rounded-off mean figures)

Image Type	Fixation Threshold	Randomly-retrieved	Target not found (frequency)	Steps to target	Time to target (seconds)	Fixation Numbers
Easy-to-find	400ms	0	38.5%	14	34.944	99
		1	53.8%	18	36.766	109
	800ms	0	38.5%	14	55.810	153
		1	15.4%	11	51.251	140
Hard-to-find	400ms	0	69.2%	23	52.686	166
		1	84.6%	23	50.029	167
	800ms	0	92.3%	24	104.999	327
		1	69.2%	19	83.535	258

104 figures were entered for each dependent variable into repeated measures ANOVA with three factors (image type, fixation threshold and randomly-retrieved).

The results of the ANOVA performed on the steps to target revealed a significant main effect of image type, $F(1,12)=23.90$, $p<0.0004$ with fewer steps to target for easy-to-find images (14 steps) than the hard-to-find images (22 steps). Easy-to-find target images were found in fewer steps by participants than the hard-to-find images as predicted by the evidence obtained using the random selection strategy.

The main effect of the fixation threshold was not significant with $F(1,12)=1.50$, $p<0.25$. The main effect of randomly-retrieved was also not significant, $F(1,12)=0.17$, $p<0.69$. Generally, the influence of including one randomly retrieved image in each display produced little or no difference in the steps to target, time to target and fixation numbers. Even when compared with the random selection tool, the steps to target did not significantly differ. All two-factor and three-factor interactions were not significant.

The analysis of the time to target produced similar results to the analysis of the number of fixations. There was a significant main effect of image type, $F_1(1,12)=24.11$, $p<0.0004$, $F_2(1,12)=21.93$, $p<0.0005$, with shorter time to target and fewer fixations for easy-to-find images (40.468s and 125 fixations) than the hard-to-find images (71.331s and 229 fixations). The main effect of the fixation threshold was also similarly significant with $F_1(1,12)=18.27$, $p<0.001$ and $F_2(1,12)=16.09$, $p<0.002$. There were more fixations and more time was spent on hard-to-find images than the easy-to-find images. This is consistent with the conclusion of Fitts et al [4] that complex information leads to longer fixation durations and higher fixation numbers.

In line with the steps to target, the main effect of randomly-retrieved was also not significant, $F_1(1,12)=1.49$, $p<0.25$ and $F_2(1,12)=0.76$, $p<0.40$.

Image type interacted with the fixation threshold, $F_1(1,12)=8.04$, $p<0.015$ and $F_2(1,12)=5.84$, $p<0.032$, and an analysis of simple main effects indicated a significant difference in time to target and fixation numbers for the fixation thresholds when hard-to-find images were presented, $F_1(1,12)=20.00$, $p<0.001$ and $F_2(1,12)=16.25$, $p<0.002$, but interestingly, no significant difference when easy-to-find images were presented, $F_1(1,12)=3.62$, $p<0.08$ and $F_2(1,12)=3.57$, $p<0.08$. There was no significant difference in the time to target and fixation numbers between the threshold levels for the easy-to-find images as opposed to the hard-to-find images. In other words, setting a higher threshold did not significantly differ when either 400ms or 800ms was used for the easy-to-find images, but it did for the hard-to-find images. However, the steps to target did differ for both image types under either of the threshold conditions. A future experiment will be needed to investigate whether the thresholds can be reduced further, at least for the easy-to-find images.

The same treatment combinations experienced by all participants were applied to the random selection tool to obtain 104 dependent variables (steps to target). By combining the variables, 208 figures were entered into a mixed design multivariate ANOVA with two observations per cell and three factors (selection mode, image type and randomly-retrieved). The average figures are presented in Table 2.

Table 2. Comparison of Eye and Random Selection (rounded-off mean figures)

Selection Mode	Image Type	Randomly-retrieved	Target not found (frequency)	Steps to target
Eye gaze	Easy-to-find	0	38.5%	14
		1	34.6%	15
	Hard-to-find	0	80.8%	23
		1	76.9%	21
Random selection	Easy-to-find	0	57.7%	20
		1	38.5%	16
	Hard-to-find	0	96.2%	25
		1	92.3%	26

In summary the results of the ANOVA revealed a main effect of the selection mode, $F(2,23)=3.81$, $p<0.037$, with fewer steps to target when the eye gaze is used (18 steps) than when random selection is used (22 steps). There was also a main effect of image type, $F(2,23)=28.95$, $p<0.00001$ with fewer steps to target for easy-to-find images (16 steps) than the hard-to-find images (24 steps).

Further analysis of simple main effect revealed that there was a significant difference between the modes for the hard-to-find images, $F(2,23)=3.76$, $p<0.039$ as opposed to the easy-to-find images, $F(2,23)=2.02$, $p<0.16$.

The participants using the eye tracking interface found the target in fewer steps than the automated random selection strategy and the analysis of simple effect attributed the significant difference to the hard-to-find images. This meant that the probability of finding the hard-to-find images was significantly increased due to human cognitive abilities as opposed to the indiscriminate selection by random selection. Some did not reach the hard target after 26 successive displays. Future experiment will concentrate on improving the chances of getting to the target using information extracted from the scan path.

5 Conclusions

Experiments have shown that an eye tracking interface together with pre-computed similarity measures yield a significantly better performance than random selection using the same similarity information. A significant effect on performance was also observed with hard-to-find images. This was not seen with easy-to-find images where with the current database size a random search might be expected to perform well.

An eye controlled image retrieval interface will not only provide a more natural mode of retrieval but also have the ability to anticipate the user's objectives coupled with user relevance feedback, thereby retrieving images extremely rapidly and with a minimum of thought and manual involvement. In future interfaces, eye tracking will not only be used as a rapid and continual information gathering tool for input to improve query formulation but also to build up a visual behavioural pattern using the time series information from the data. The ensuing interface will require a model for matching possible interests between images in the database. Visually similar regions will need to be linked between all regions within the images present in the database. Adaptive algorithms could then be used to improve the model for individual users.

Acknowledgement

The authors acknowledge the support of BT Research and Venturing, SIRA and the Engineering and Physical Sciences Research Council in this work. The work has been conducted within the framework of the EC funded Network of Excellence (MUSCLE)[11].

References

1. Corno F., Farinetti L. and Signorile I., A cost effective solution for eye-gaze assistive technology, IEEE Int. Conf. on Multimedia and Expo, August 26-29, 2002, Lausanne.
2. Cox I.J., Miller M. L., Minka T. P., Papathomas T. V., and Yianilos P. N., The Bayesian image retrieval system, PicHunter: theory, implementation, and Psychophysical experiments. IEEE Trans. on Image Processing, (2000) Vol. 9, No 1.
3. Duchowski, A. T., A Breadth-First Survey of Eye Tracking Applications. Behaviour Research Methods, Instruments, & Computers (BRMIC), (2002) 34(4), pp.455-470.
4. Fitts, P.M., Jones, R.E., and Milton, J.L., Eye Movement of Aircraft Pilots during Instrument-Landing Approaches. Aeronautical Engineering Review 9, (1950) 24-29.

5. Hansen J.P., Anderson A.W., and P. Roed, Eye gaze control of multimedia systems. Symbiosis of Human and Artifact (Y. Anzai, K. Ogawa, and H. Mori (eds), Vol 20A, Elsevier Science, (1995) pp 37-42.
6. Henderson John M. and Hollingworth Andrew, High-Level Scene Perception. Annual Reviews Psychology (1999) 50:243-71.
7. Itti, L., Automatic foveation for video compression using a neurobiological model of visual attention. IEEE Trans. on Image Processing, 13(10) (2004) 1304-1318.
8. LC Technologies Inc. - http://www.eyegaze.com/
9. Mackworth, N., and Morandi, A., The gaze selects informative details within pictures. Perception and Psychophysics 2 (1967) 547–552.
10. McCarthy, J, Sasse, M.A. & Riegelsberger, J., Could I have the menu please? An eye tracking study of design conventions. Proceedings of HCI2003, 8-12 Sep 2003, Bath, UK.
11. Multimedia Understanding through Semantics, Computation and Learning, Network of Excellence. EC 6th Framework Programme. FP6-507752. http://www.muscle-noe.org/
12. Numajiri T., Nakamura A., and Kuno Y., Speed browser controlled by eye movements. IEEE Int Conf. on Multimedia and Expo, August 26-29, Lausanne, (2002).
13. Oyekoya O. K., Stentiford F. W. M., Exploring Human Eye Behaviour Using a Model of Visual Attention, International Conference on Pattern Recognition, Cambridge UK, August (2004).
14. Oyekoya O. K., Stentiford F. W. M., A Performance Comparison of Eye Tracking and Mouse Interfaces in a Target Image Identification Task, 2nd European Workshop on the Integration of Knowledge, Semantics & Digital Media Technology, London, 30th Nov - 1st Dec, (2005).
15. Oyekoya O. and Stentiford F., An eye tracking interface for image search. Eye Tracking Research & Applications symposium (ETRA'06), San Diego, (2006).
16. Puolamäki K., Salojärvi J., Savia E., Simola J., Kaski S., Combining Eye Movements and Collaborative Filtering for Proactive Information Retrieval. In Proceedings of the 28th ACM Conference on Research and Development in Information Retrieval (SIGIR) 2005.
17. Stentiford F. W. M., Attention Based Similarity, to appear in Pattern Recognition (2006).
18. Urban J., Jose J.M., van Rijsbergen C.J., An adaptive approach towards content-based image retrieval. Proc. of the Third International Workshop on Content-Based Multimedia Indexing (CBMI'03), (2003) pp. 119-126.
19. Venters, C.C., J.P. Eakins and R.J. Hartley, The user interface and content based image retrieval systems. Proc. of the 19th BCS-IRSG Research Colloquium, Aberdeen, April (1997).
20. Ward D.J. and MacKay D.J.C., Fast hands-free writing by gaze direction. Nature 418 pp 838, Aug. 22 (2002).
21. Yarbus, A., Eye Movements and Vision. Plenum Press, New York (1967).

A Pseudo-hilbert Scan Algorithm for Arbitrarily-Sized Rectangle Region

Jian Zhang[1], Sei-ichiro Kamata[1], and Yoshifumi Ueshige[2]

[1] Waseda University, Graduate School of Information, Production and System
808-0135 Kitakyushu, Japan
zj_jay@toki.waseda.jp, kam@waseda.jp
[2] Institute of Systems & Information Technologies
808-0135 Kitakyushu, Japan
usehige@isit.or.jp

Abstract. The 2-dimensional Hilbert scan (HS) is a one-to-one mapping between 2-dimensional (2-D) space and one-dimensional (1-D) space along the 2-D Hilbert curve. Because Hilbert curve can preserve the spatial relationships of the patterns effectively, 2-D HS has been studied in digital image processing actively, such as compressing image data, pattern recognition, clustering an image, etc. However, the existing HS algorithms have some strict restrictions when they are implemented. For example, the most algorithms use recursive function to generate the Hilbert curve, which makes the algorithms complex and takes time to compute the one-to-one correspondence. And some even request the sides of the scanned rectangle region must be a power of two, that limits the application scope of HS greatly. Thus, in order to improve HS to be proper to real-time processing and general application, we proposed a Pseudo-Hilbert scan (PHS) based on the look-up table method for arbitrarily-sized arrays in this paper. Experimental results for both HS and PHS indicate that the proposed generalized Hilbert scan algorithm also reserves the good property of HS that the curve preserves point neighborhoods as much as possible, and gives competitive performance in comparison with Raster scan.

1 Introduction

A space-filling curve is a continuous mapping of a one-dimensional interval into a two-dimensional area (a plane-filling function) or a three-dimensional volume. Among the space-filling curves, the Hilbert curve is known to preserve point neighborhoods as much as possible. This trait makes it useful in multidimensional signal processing. Especially, with the rapid development of digital image processing, the Hilbert curve, as a scan technique, is applied widely in digital image processing, such as image compression [1,8], clustering an image [2,9] and so on [10,11]. Currently there also have been several algorithms [3-6] for 2-dimensional Hilbert scan, such as the Kamata algorithm [3,4], the Agui algorithm [5] and the Quinqueton algorithm [6]. However, these algorithms more or

N. Zheng, X. Jiang, and X. Lan (Eds.): IWICPAS 2006, LNCS 4153, pp. 290–299, 2006.

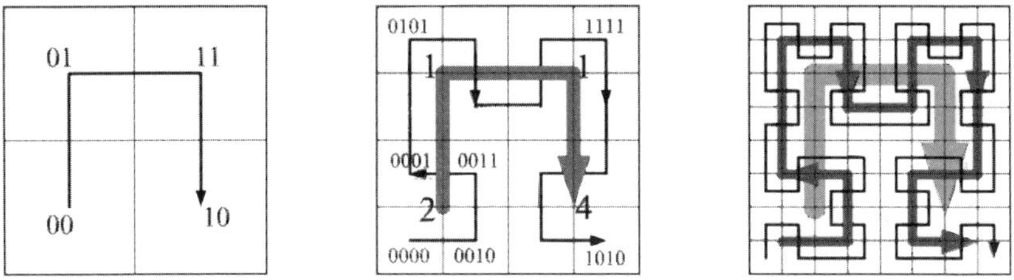

(a) 2×2 (b) 4×4 (c) 8×8

Fig. 1. Original 2-D Hilbert scan

less have some restrictions. For example, the Agui algorithm and the Quinqueton algorithm use the recursive functions to generate the curve, which makes the algorithm complex and takes time to compute the one-to-one mapping correspondence, so it is very difficult to apply them in the real-time systems. And the Kamata algorithm has the strict restriction on the size of rectangle region which required that one side of the scanned rectangle should be even and the both sides should have the same division times. Therefore, to relax these limitations for general application, Hilbert scan needs to be improved up to be proper to an arbitrary-sized rectangle region. In the paper, based on the look-up table method, we proposed a novel Hilbert scan algorithm to generate mapping pattern for arbitrarily-sized arrays. And this generalized Hilbert scan is called as 2-D Pseudo-Hilbert scan (PHS). The proposed algorithm is suitable for real-time processing and easy to be implemented in hardware. Furthermore, like as HS, PHS can also preserve the spacial neighborhood relationships in a rectangle region, which has been confirmed by the experimental results.

2 A Pseudo-hilbert Scan Algorithm

The Peano curve published in 1890 is a locus of points in N-dimensional space. It was an analytical solution of a space-filling curve. Fig. 1 shows three curves with different resolutions, (a)2×2, (b)4×4, (c)8×8. In the figure, the binary numbers express the address alignment.

2.1 The Address Assignment

In this subsection, we define the expression of a point in a rectangle with size l_x and l_y. In order to discuss expediently, we assume $l_x \geq l_y$. The coordinate of a point is denoted as (X, Y), and the rectangle is represented as

$$R(l_x, l_y) = \{X, Y | 0 \leq X < l_x, 0 \leq Y < l_y\}. \quad (1)$$

Then the division times of each side can be calculated by the following equations,

$$M_x = \log_2(\frac{l_x}{2}), M_y = \log_2(\frac{l_y}{2}), \quad (2)$$

where the operator $\lfloor z \rfloor$ means the integer part of a real number z. As $l_x \geq l_y$, it is easy to get $M_x \geq M_y$. Thus, the address of a point in $R(l_x, l_y)$ can be expressed as a $2(M_x+2)$-bit binary number,

$$\underbrace{\overbrace{x_{M_x+2}y_{M_x+2}}^{2bits}\overbrace{x_{M_x+1}y_{M_x+1}}^{2bits}\cdots\cdots\overbrace{x_1y_1}^{2bits}}_{2(M_x+2)bits}. \tag{3}$$

And the coordinates of a point (X, Y) can be expressed as two (M_x+2)-bit binary numbers,

$$X = x_{M_x+2}x_{M_x+1}\cdots\cdots x_2x_1 \tag{4}$$

$$Y = y_{M_x+2}y_{M_x+1}\cdots\cdots y_2y_1 \tag{5}$$

where x_m and y_m $(1 \leq m \leq M_x+2)$ are 0 or 1. Note that, $(M_x - M_y)$-bit binary number $y_{3+\bigtriangledown M-1}y_{3+\bigtriangledown M-2}\cdots y_3$ equals to 0 in the binary sequences $y_{M_x+2}y_{M_x+1}\cdots\cdots y_2y_1$. So the memory can be saved effectively by eliminating these bits. However, for simplicity, we use (M_x+2)-bit binary number to represent address in the paper.

2.2 The Division Rules of a Rectangle

Since the size of a rectangle is arbitrary, its values are not always the power of 2. Thus we proposed a new division method to split the sides of a rectangle. Each side of the scanned region must be subject to following "Division Rule":

1. $l(0) = l$, $k = 0$;
2. If $2 \cdot 2^{M-k} \leq l(k) < 3 \cdot 2^{M-k}$, we split $l(k)$ into 2^{M-k} and $l(k) - 2^{M-k}$;
   If $l(k) = 3 \cdot 2^{M-k}$, we split $l(k)$ into 2^{M-k} and $2 \cdot 2^{M-k}$;
   If $3 \cdot 2^{M-k} < l(k) < 4 \cdot 2^{M-k}$, we split $l(k)$ into $2 \cdot 2^{M-k}$ and $l(k) - 2 \cdot 2^{M-k}$;
3. $k = k + 1$, make the results of k-th splitting equal to $l(k)$. Until $k = M$, the division is completed. Otherwise, skip to step 2 and divide $l(k)$ sequentially.

So based on the above division rules, the vertical side of a rectangle $R(l_x, l_y)$ can be divided for M_y times, the horizontal side can be divided for M_x times. However, in order to make the scan comply to Hilbert scan in global sense (that is, the scanning of blocks submits to the Hilbert scan), we should divide the vertical side and horizontal side for the same times. So the splitting times of a rectangle are M_y times $(M_y \leq M_x)$, and then the rectangle can be divided into $2^{M_y} \times 2^{M_y}$ blocks. Thus we can make use of Hilbert curve to scan $2^{M_y} \times 2^{M_y}$ blocks. The scan from the k-th depth nodes to the $(k+1)$-th depth nodes is ordered by look-up tables, where $k = 1, 2, \cdots, M_y$. In the following, we introduce the look-up tables for HS in 2-D space.

2.3 The Hilbert Scan of Block

Hilbert curves (parent region) $R(2^M, 2^M)$ includes four sub-rectangle regions (child region) which are congruent with $R(2^{M-1}, 2^{M-1})$. As shown in Fig.2, we

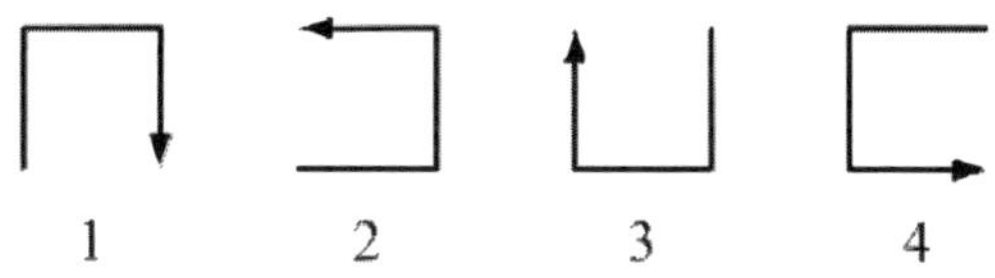

Fig. 2. The basic patterns of 2-D Hilbert curves (the number 1-4 means curve type)

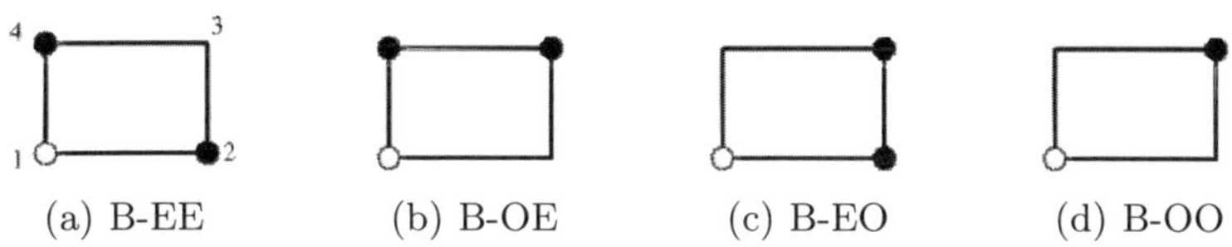

Fig. 3. The scanning manners of four templates of block, when the entry is point 1

use four 2-D Hilbert curves to connect these four congruent sub-rectangle regions. Each curve is identified by the number (from 1 to 4), which is curve type. For creating the addresses, we prepare two look-up tables. One is a terminal table $\boldsymbol{T}^2_{trm}$ and the other is an induction table $\boldsymbol{T}^2_{ind}$, which are shown as follows respectively:

$$\boldsymbol{T}^2_{trm} = (T^2_{trm}[\gamma][i]) = \begin{pmatrix} 00\ 01\ 11\ 10 \\ 00\ 10\ 11\ 01 \\ 11\ 10\ 00\ 01 \\ 11\ 01\ 11\ 10 \end{pmatrix}, \boldsymbol{T}^2_{ind} = (T^2_{ind}[\gamma][i]) = \begin{pmatrix} 2\ 1\ 1\ 4 \\ 1\ 2\ 2\ 3 \\ 3\ 4\ 4\ 1 \\ 3\ 4\ 4\ 1 \end{pmatrix},$$

where γ is the curve type, and $T^2_{trm}[\gamma][i]$ and $T^2_{ind}[\gamma][i]$ represents the elements of the two tables, respectively. For example, Fig.1 (a) shows the addresses and curve types in four child regions, in the case where the curve type $\gamma = 1$. Thus we can arrange the four addresses according to the first row of terminal table, that is,

$$00 \longrightarrow 01 \longrightarrow 11 \longrightarrow 10. \tag{6}$$

And Fig.1 (b) shows the curve types in the order of scanning child regions, which is obtained according to the first row of induction table as follows,

$$2 \longrightarrow 1 \longrightarrow 1 \longrightarrow 4. \tag{7}$$

2.4 Scanning Manner

Considering all the four types of rectangle region (l_x-l_y)—E-E, E-O, O-E and O-O (E and O represent even length and odd length), the $2^{M_y} \times 2^{M_y}$ blocks can be classified into the four templates which are shown in Fig.3. In the figure $\circ$ denotes the entry and $\bullet$ denotes the exit, they express the scanning manner of the points in a block. It is noted that Fig.3 described only one case when the entry point located number 1. During the scan procedure, according to the end point of previous block, we can decide the entry of the current scanned block. And based on the value of $(M_y + 1) - th$ depth nodes we select the point of exit.

To make a summary, the whole Pseudo-Hilbert scan algorithm is shown in the following. It shows our Pseudo-Hilbert scan algorithm for generating all addresses ($(2M_x+2)$-bit binary number) in a rectangle region $R(l_x, l_y)$. As initial condition, the value of $\gamma(0)$ equals one.

Pseudo-Hilbert scan

```
program Address assignment in a rectangle (Output)

      /* Address assignment of the blocks */
for i_0 = 1,2,...,4
  α_0 = T_trm[γ(0)][i(0)]
  γ(1) = T_ind[γ(0)][i(0)]
  l(1) = division(l(0), α_0)
      ⋮         ⋮
 for i_m = 1,2,...,4
    α_m = T_trm[γ(m)][i(m)]
    γ(m+1) = T_ind[γ(m)][i(m)]
    l(m) = division(l(m-1), α_m)
        ⋮         ⋮
   for i_{M_y-1} = 1,2,...,4
      α_{M_y-1} = T_trm[γ(M_y-1)][i(M_y-1)]
      l(M_y) = division(l(M_y-1), α_{M_y})
   /* Computation of address in each block */
      b = block_type(l(M_y))
      if b = B_OE or B_OO
        if it is the first block
          go to scanning_1
        else
          go to scanning_8
      else if b = B_EO
        if it is the first block
          go to scanning_2
        else
          go to scanning_7
      else
        s = scanning_type((M_y), γ(M_y-1))
        go to scanning_s

    scanning_1:
        for i = 0,1,...,l_x-1
          for j = 0,1,...,l_y-1
          α = ij
          output < α_0 ··· α_{M_y-1}α_{M_y} >
```

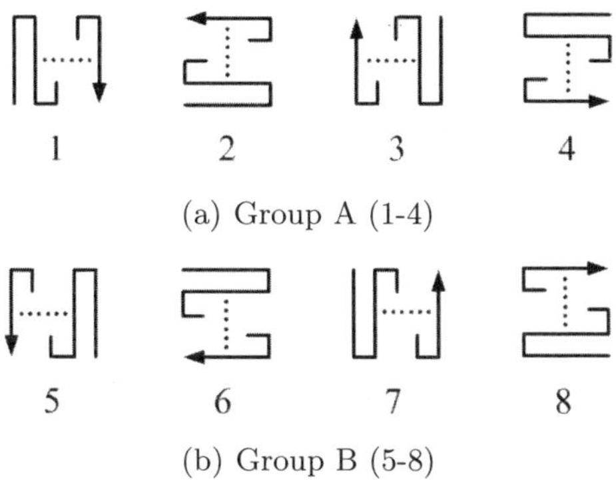

Fig. 4. Two group of scanning curves (the number 1-8 means the manner of scan)

$\vdots \qquad \vdots$

scanning_8:
  $for\ i = 0, 1, \cdots, l_y - 1$
    $for\ j = l_x - 1, \cdots, 1, 0$
    $\alpha = ji$
    $output < \alpha_0 \cdots \alpha_{M_y-1}\alpha_{M_y} >$

(The algorithm generating 2-D Pseudo-Hilbert curve.)

From the algorithm, it can be seen that at the m-th splitting, we obtain two-bit binary number α_m from the terminal table $\boldsymbol{T}_{trm}$. And from the induction table $\boldsymbol{T}_{ind}$, we obtain the curve type $\gamma(m+1)$ for the next splitting. In the algorithm, $\boldsymbol{l}(m)$ is a vector which represents the two sides $(l_x(m), l_y(m))$ of a rectangle. We use the function "division( )" to split each side into two parts according to "Division-Rule" and then to choose the two sides $(l_x(m+1), l_y(m+1))$ corresponding to the address α_m, which are X- and Y- side respectively. Here, $m(0 \leq m \leq M_y)$ is the number of splits. The procedures above are performed until $m = M_y$, so that we obtain the upper $2M_y$ bits $(\alpha_0\alpha_1 \cdots \alpha_{M_y-1})$ in each address. In the following steps, we compute the lower $2(M_x - M_y + 2)$ bits α_{M_y}. Firstly, we use the function "block_type( )" to obtain the block type according to the two sides $\boldsymbol{l}(M_y)$. Then, using the function "scanning_type( )", we select the scanning curve of a block from scanning_1 to scanning_8 shown in Fig.4, and we obtain the remnant binary number α_{M_y}.

In order to explain the algorithm, we give an example of a rectangle region $R(5,5)$. After 1 time division, $R(5,5)$ can be divided into 4 blocks including all types of blocks mentioned above—$\{B(l_x, l_y)|(l_x, l_y) = (3,3), (3,2), (2,2), (2,3)\}$, where $B(l_x, l_y)$ represents a block with the size $l_x \times l_y$. Each block is identified by the number (from 1 to 4), which is the order of the block scan. Fig.5 shows the

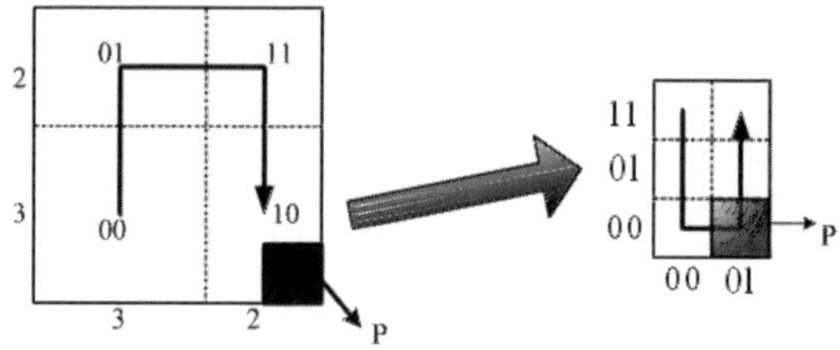

Fig. 5. An example of the address assignment to the lattice point "p" using Pseudo-Hilbert scan

address for lattice point "P" which is located at $(X, Y) = (4, 0)$. Since $M_y = 1$, the address of "P" needs $6(= 2M_y + 4)$-bit binary number to represent. We compute the address by the following steps:

1. $i(k)$, $\gamma(k)$, $\alpha(k)$ and b are a scanning order, a curve type, an address, and a block type respectively, where k means k-th splitting. $\gamma(0) = 1$ is given.
2. This step is the computation of the upper 2 bits in the address to "P". According to the division rule, we obtained four subrectangles expressed in section 3.2 (Fig.5). Fig.5 shows that "P" is in the shaded region. So we get $i(0) = 4$, and we know $\gamma(0) = 1$. Then, we obtain $\alpha_1 = T_{trm}[\gamma(0)][i(0)] = T_{trm}[1][4] = 4$.
3. This step is the computation of the lower 4 bits of the address. The block with $\alpha_1 = 10$ is congruent with $B(2, 3)$. Thus according to PHS algorithm, scanning_7 is selected as the scanning manner. So it is known that the entry point is $(3, 2)$ and the order of the point "P" is the forth among the six lattice points in the forth block. So we obtained $\alpha_2 = 0100$.
4. Hence, the address of "P" is $\alpha_1\alpha_2 = 100100$.

PHS algorithm is performed through referring to the look-up tables and scanning manner function in a block. Table 1 shows a comparison of storage memory and computation complexity with our method and recursive method.

Table 1. Comparison of computation complexity and storage memory

Method	Computation complexity	Storage memory
Our method	$O(4^{M_y} l_x l_y)$	64
Recursive method	$O(2^{4M_y + M_y 2^{M_y+1}})$	$10M_y$

3 Experiments and Results

Three examples of pseudo-Hilbert scan are shown in Fig.6 with different resolution, (a)64×64, (b)100×100, (c)97×123. When the size of both sides are power

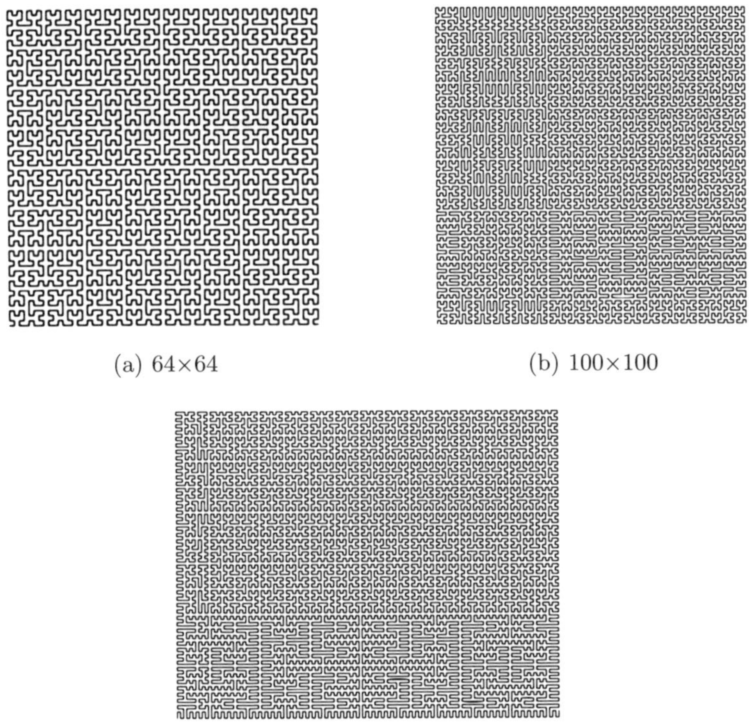

(a) 64×64 (b) 100×100

(c) 123×97

Fig. 6. Examples of Pseudo-Hilbert scan for different size of rectangle

of 2, the Pseudo-Hilbert curve is the same as Hilbert curve as shown in Fig.6 (a). Comparing Fig.6 (a) with (b) and (c), it can be seen easily that PHS submits to HS on the level of blocks, and in details the most segments of Pesudo-Hilbert curve have the same structure as HS. So it can be concluded that the PHS has the similar property of HS that scan curve preserves point neighborhoods as much as possible. In order to demonstrate the neighborhoods property of PHS, we made a statistical simulation by computer, which is resemble as the method provided by T. Agui[5]. This statistical simulation has the following tow steps,

1. Take two points $a(x_1, y_1)$, $b(x_2, y_2)$ randomly, where $1 \leq x_1, x_2 \leq M$ and $1 \leq y_1, y_2 \leq N$ (M and N represent the horizontal length and vertical length of a rectangle, respectively).
2. Then, calculate the square Euclidean distance d ($d \in [0, (M-1)^2+(N-1)^2]$) and the scanning length l ($l \in [0, M \cdot N]$) between these two points.

$$d = (x_2 - x_1)^2 + (y_2 - y_1)^2; \tag{8}$$

$$N(d) = N(d) + 1; \tag{9}$$

$$L(d) = L(d) + l; \tag{10}$$

where N and L are two vectors.

After many enough recursive trials (Step 1 and 2), we can compute the mean scanning length by the following equation.

$$L(d) = L(d)/N(d) \tag{11}$$

In Fig.7, we show the relationship between $L(d)$ and d. Fig.7 (a) is the case of HS with size 64×64. Fig.7 (b) and (c) show the PHS and Raster scan respectively, with the same size 97×123. From Fig.7 (a) and (b), it can be seen that the trends of the both curves are nearly the same, which proved that PHS can also preserve point neighborhoods as much as possible. For comparison between Pseudo-Hilbert scan and Raster scan as shown in Fig.7 (b) and (c), it is clearly that between the $L(d)$ and d, the proportional relationship of PHS is much better than that of the Raster scan. Especially with the increasing of L, this superiority becomes greatly obvious.

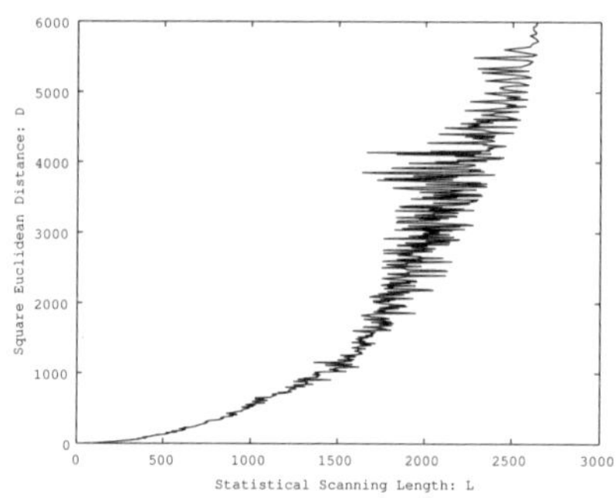

(a) Hilbert scan, 64×64

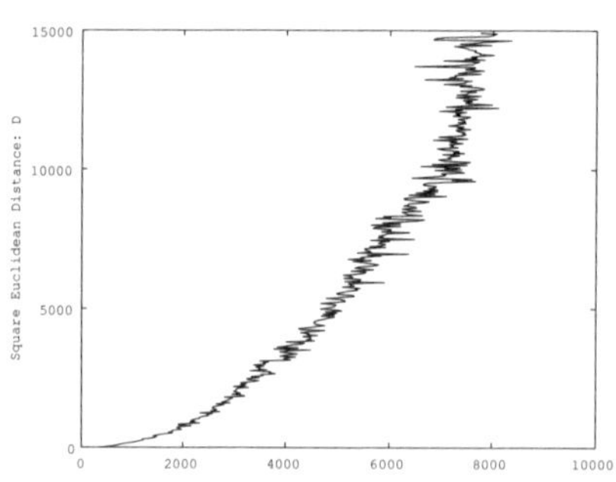

(b) Pseudo-Hilbert scan, 97×123

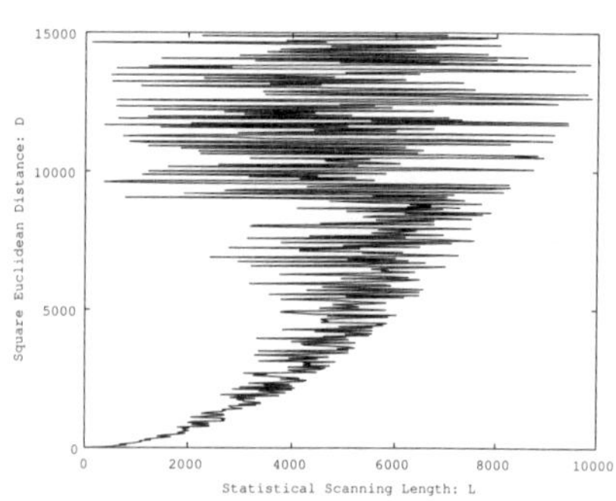

(c) Raster scan, 97×123

Fig. 7. Relation between mean square Euclidean distance and the scanning length between two points

4 Conclusions

In this paper, we proposed a Pseudo-Hilbert scan algorithm. The proposed algorithm, based the look-up table method, has lower computational complexity and faster scan. Thus the algorithm is suitable for application of real-time systems. Furthermore, PHS is proper for any arbitrarily-sized rectangle region. Thus the constraints in HS are significantly relaxed, which enlarges the application of the 2-D Hilbert curve. At the end of paper, the results of simulation is shown. Through the simulation results, it can be demonstrated that the neighborhood property of PHS can also work as well as HS. A future problem to be solved is a generalization of our algorithm for 3-D and N-D Pseudo-Hilbert scan.

References

1. S. Biswas, "Hilbert Scan and Image Compression," Proc. of IEEE Int. Conf. on Pattern Recognition. Pp.201-210(2000).
2. Bongki Moon, H. V. Jagadish and Christow Faloutsos, "Analysis of the Clustering Properties of the Hilbert Space-Filling Curve," IEEE Trans. Knowledge and Data Engineering, Vol. 13, No. 1, pp.124-141(2001).
3. S. Kamata et al and Y. Bandoh, "An Address Generator of a Pseudo-Hilbert Scan in a Rectangle Region," Proc. of IEEE Int. Conf. on Image processing, pp.707-710(1997).
4. S. Kamata, R. O. Eason and Y. Bandou, "A New Algorithm for N-Dimensional Hilbert Scanning," IEEE Trans. Image Processing, Vol. 8, No. 7, pp.964-973(1999).
5. T. Agui, T. Nagae and M. Nakajima, "Generalized Peano scans for arbitrary-sized arrays," IEICE Trans. Info. and Syst., E74, 5, pp.1337-1342(1991).
6. J. Quinqueton and M. Berthod, "A locally adaptive Peano scanning algorithm," IEEE Trans. Pattern Anal. Mach. Intell., PAMI-3, 4, pp. 409-412(1981).
7. D. Hilbert, "Uber die stetige Abbildung einer Linie auf ein Flachenstuck," Mathematische Annalen, 38, pp. 459-460(1891).
8. G. Melnikov and A. K. Katsaggelos, "A Jointly Optimal Fractal/DCT Compression Scheme," IEEE Trans. Multimedia, vol. 4, No. 4, pp.413-422(2002).
9. H. V. Jagadish, "Linear Clustering of Objects with Mutiple Atributes," Int. Conf. on Management of Data, pp.332-342(1990).
10. C. Jose, G. Michael, D. Ronald and G. Avelino, "Data-Partitioning using the Hilbert Space Filling Curves: Effect on the Speed of Convergence of Fuzzy ARTMAP for Large Database Problems," Neural Networks, vol. 18, No. 7, pp.967-984(2004).
11. L. Tian, S. Kamata, K. Tsuneyoshi and H. J. Tang, "A Fast and Accurate Algorithm for Matching Images using Hilbert Scanning Distance with Threshold Elimination Function," IEICE Trans. E89-D, No. 1, pp.290-297(2006).

Panoramas from Partially Blurred Video

Jani Boutellier and Olli Silvén

Machine Vision Group
Department of Electrical and Information Engineering
P.O.Box 4500, FI-90014 University of Oulu, Finland
{bow, olli.silven}@ee.oulu.fi

Abstract. Numerous high-quality image stitching algorithms have been published in the recent years. Mosaics created by these methods are of high quality if the input images are not distorted. However, if the source images are blurred, parts of the resulting mosaic will be blurred also. In this paper we propose a method to create high-quality panoramas from video sequences that contain also low-quality frames. Moreover, our method is computationally efficient, which makes it attractive for hand-held devices. The algorithm uses motion detection to display correctly moving objects in the sequence. The colors of the mosaic are also balanced to handle changes in camera exposure times.

1 Introduction

Image stitching is used to combine several images into one wide-angled mosaic image. Traditionally mosaic images have been constructed from a few separate photographs, but nowadays that video recording has become commonplace, it is possible to consider also video sequences as a source for mosaic images. When a mosaic image is constructed from single photographs, the procedure is straightforward because the amount of images is rather limited. With video sequences, the situation is different. Even a short video clip contains vast amounts of data, that is mostly redundant due to large overlaps between frames.

Because of the overlap, it is clear that not all frames from the sequence are needed to construct a mosaic that covers the whole scene. The frame selection process has been researched only little [1],[2] and until now, it has been assumed that the video frames are of good quality. Practically this is not the case, since pictures are often taken freehand, which leads to blurred images in many occasions. In this paper we will propose a new method to select the best frames from a video sequence and then create a high-quality panorama from those images.

2 Related Work

The whole process of creating a mosaic image consists of several smaller tasks, of which image registration is the most important one. Stitching algorithms use both feature-based [2] and direct approaches [3], [4] in the registration process.

N. Zheng, X. Jiang, and X. Lan (Eds.): IWICPAS 2006, LNCS 4153, pp. 300–307, 2006.

The definitions and properties of these two fundamentally different methods are explained well in the survey of Zitová and Flusser [5].

An image stitching algorithm also needs to use some kind of motion detection to avoid the distortion of moving objects [3]. This problem and its solutions are covered extensively in the survey of Radke [6]. In stitching applications, Davis [3] solved the problem by drawing the seams around moving objects by Dijkstra's algorithm. In the method created by Zhu [4] the moving objects were extracted by differencing three successive frames and defined further by calculating an active contour for each object.

Once the registration and motion detection is done, the images can be stitched. The stitching process consists of local blending operations and of radiometric adjustments. The paper of Zomet [7] contains a good comparison of image blending methods and also proposes a new approach of optimizing the stitching result by a gradient-based cost function. Szeliski proposed a simple, local blending method to eliminate seam artifacts [8]. Xiao [9] reduced the exposure differences of an image pair by setting the mean and standard deviation of the registered image to be the same as that of the reference image.

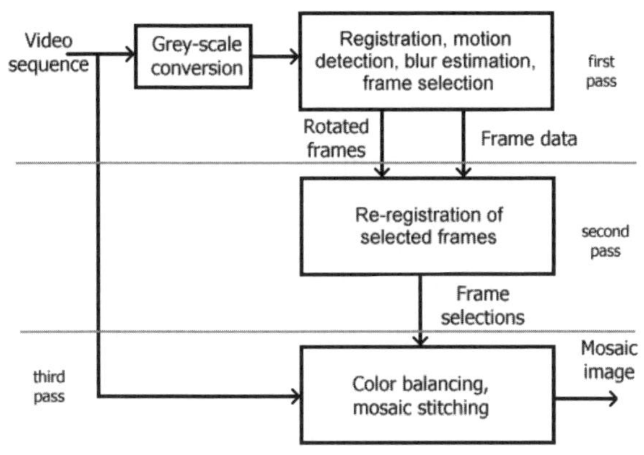

Fig. 1. Block diagram of our algorithm

3 The Algorithm

The issue of selecting the best frames for an image mosaic has not been addressed until now. The work closest to ours has been made by Li [1]. In the method of Li the amount of distortion caused by rotation and perspective is evaluated and a suitable subset of images is chosen to form a mosaic. Also Hsu [2] has selected frames for the construction of a panorama. He has only considered the criteria of suitable overlap.

Our method relies on the recent image registration method of Vandewalle [10], that can register blurred, rotated and translated frames. After registration, motion detection is performed to each frame. The frames used for stitching are selected by estimating their quality by a couple of different parameters. Our algorithm tries to use as few frames as possible, since the seams are the places where the image quality is most probably degraded.

The image sequence is processed in three phases, as depicted in Figure 1. In the first phase the frames are registered consecutively, so that each frame n is registered against frame *n-1*. The consecutive registration approach ensures that the overlap between frames is as large as possible. This makes registration and motion detection more robust. Simultaneously with the registration, the amount of motion blur is calculated. The best frames are selected for the mosaic based on their quality. The choices depend on the amount of moving objects and motion blur in the frames. Also, the frames are selected so that their mutual offset is as large as possible.

After the frames have been chosen, the centermost frame is selected as the root frame. A shortest spanning tree is constructed between frames based on their mutual translations. Then each selected frame is re-registered against its parent [11]. This ensures that the accumulated registration errors from the first phase disappear and that the registration is performed optimally.

In the final phase of the algorithm, the selected frames are stitched together. In the stitching process we use the method of Xiao [9] to minimize color differences caused by variable exposure times. Finally, the small geometric and photometric misalignments are compensated by a bilinear weighting function [8].

3.1 Projection and Camera Motion Model

We used the idea of *manifold projection*, originally introduced by Peleg [12]. In manifold projection a thin strip is taken from the center of each frame to be used in the construction of the mosaic image. Peleg states that the frames can be registered accurately by a rigid camera motion model if it is assumed that significant motion parallax or change of scale does not occur. Manifold projection offers excellent image quality, since frames do not have to be projected to a different surface for the construction of the mosaic. Manifold projection is also quick to process.

3.2 Motion Blur Estimation

Motion blur is determined simultaneously with the first-phase registration. The image registration method of Vandewalle requires the calculation of the amplitude spectrum for each image to be registered. The spectrum is now also used for blur estimation by calculating the amount of high-frequency components in it. Vandewalle states that the frequencies above a certain limit ρ_{max} need to be discarded in the registration process, since those frequencies contain alias if the image is blurred. The darkened area in Figure 2 depicts the frequency area from ρ_{max} to the maximum frequency, which we use to estimate the amount of blur. If the sum of the frequencies in the area is small, it means that sharp image

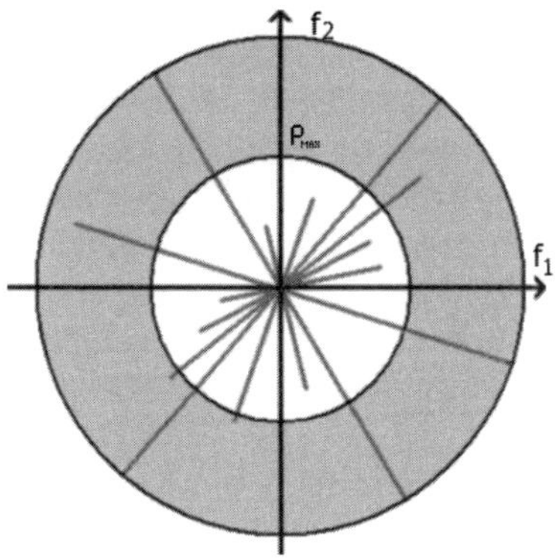

Fig. 2. An amplitude spectrum of a fictional image. The darkened area depicts the high-frequency area that is used to estimate the image blur.

details are absent due to blurring. A large sum tells us that the frame is free of blur.

Of course, these values can only be used for comparing frames that depict roughly the same scene, since the scene contents also affect the result.

3.3 Frame Selection

The frame selection process is a matter of weighting the importance of different frame features. According to experiments, the presence of moving objects is the most important criteria, since the most severe artifacts are created in the stitching process by moving objects that get clipped. The factor of second highest importance was chosen to be the amount of blur. Finally, frames that are farther away from the previous selected frame, are preferred.

In practice each frame gets a quality value that is calculated from the aforementioned factors and this can be implemented successfully in many different ways. The quality values are computed for a certain scope of frames at a time. The scope encompasses the frames that have a suitable translation with respect of the previous selected frame, as depicted in Figure 3.

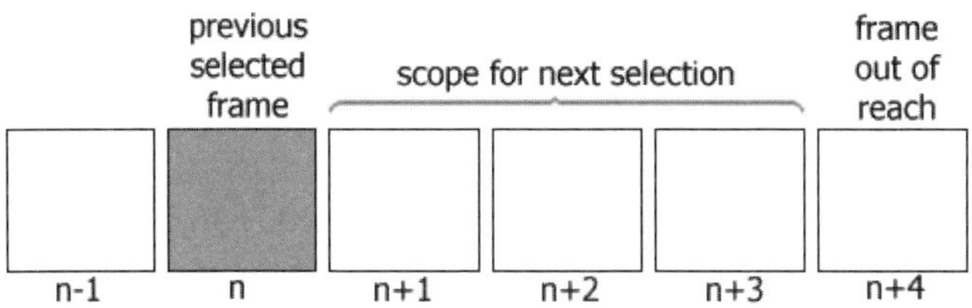

Fig. 3. The scope of frame selection

3.4 Stitching Phase

Once the best frames have been selected, the mosaic may be created. First of all, the colors are balanced between adjacent frames in the way that Xiao used in his paper [9]. The merging of two images is most critical in the area where the images meet. This seam area can be processed in many ways, but we have chosen bilinear weighting [8], since it produces good results compared to the amount of calculations it requires. It is important to remember that more sophisticated seam handling is beneficial only when the registration step produces erroneous results.

In our method blending is done with a gaussian weighting mask similarly to [13] if no moving objects are present. If there are moving objects, the seam is drawn outside the boundaries of moving objects.

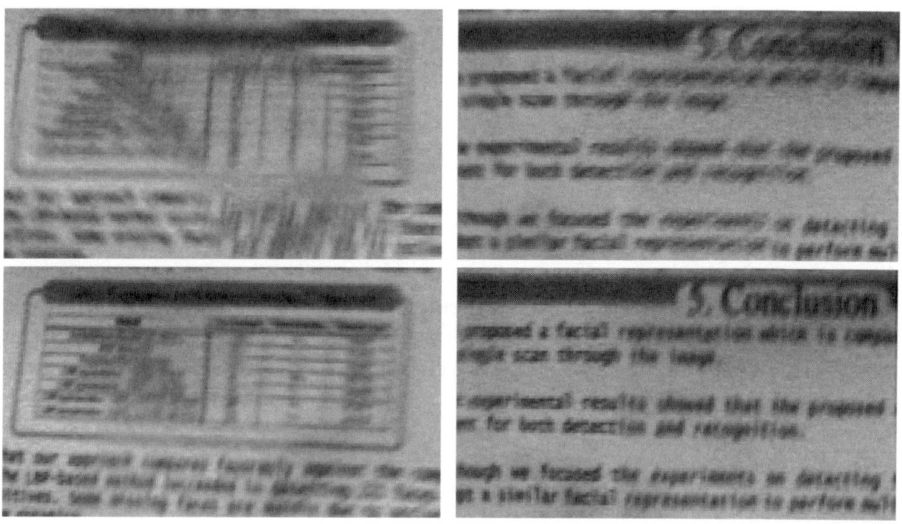

Fig. 4. The images in the top row are a small detail from a mosaic that was created without frame selection. The images in the bottom row show the corresponding areas from a mosaic that was constructed with frame selection. All of the images are magnified and even the best frames in this sequence were somewhat blurred.

4 Experimental Results

The algorithm was tested with many different video sequences containing moving objects and motion blur. The sequences we used were recorded freehand by a couple of different cameras. The consequence of freehand recording was that the frames were rotated slightly to unpredictable directions and that some

Table 1. The effect of blur detection to image quality (PSNR)

Sequence	With blur detection	No blur detection
Example A	27.0	25.0
Example B	29.1	26.8

Fig. 5. Mosaic images created by our algorithm. The cut in the trees in the top image is real, not a stitching error.

unintentional camera tilt was also present. In other words, the sequences were taken in very practical conditions. Mosaic results can be seen in Figure 5 and Figure 6.

The impact of frame selection to the mosaic quality was tested by creating the same mosaic with blur detection and without it. Corresponding areas from both mosaics were compared against a blur-free input frame with the standard PSNR [14] measure. The results can be seen in Table 1 and magnified and cropped details from both examples are shown in Figure 4.

According to these tests the algorithm produced high-quality results with very good computational efficiency. On a 3.0 GHz desktop computer running Matlab 7.1 the execution speed was over 4 frames per second (with frame size 352x288).

We used rather broad strips (34% of the frame width) from frames to construct the panorama images with manifold projection.

Fig. 6. A 360 degree panorama constructed by our method. For viewing purposes the panorama is cut in two pieces.

5 Conclusion

We have presented a stitching algorithm with the novel idea of evaluating the frames and selecting the best ones for the mosaic. The presented algorithm is capable of handling moving objects in the video sequence and can correct problems caused by varying lighting conditions. The method is also computationally efficient, which makes it attractive for hand-held devices.

References

1. Li, J.S., Randhawa, S.: Improved video mosaic construction by selecting a suitable subset of video images. In: CRPIT '04: Proceedings of the 27th conference on Australasian computer science, Darlinghurst, Australia, Australian Computer Society, Inc. (2004) 143–149
2. Hsu, C.T., Cheng, T.H., Beuker, R.A., Horng, J.K.: Feature-based video mosaic. In: Proceedings of the International Conference on Image Processing. Volume 2., Vancouver, Canada (2000) 887–890
3. Davis, J.: Mosaics of scenes with moving objects. In: CVPR '98: Proceedings of the IEEE Computer Society Conference on Computer Vision and Pattern Recognition, Washington, DC, USA, IEEE Computer Society (1998) 354–360
4. Zhu, Z., Xu, G., Riseman, E., Hanson, A.: Fast generation of dynamic and multi-resolution 360 degrees panorama from video sequences. In: Proceedings of the IEEE International Conference on Multimedia Computing and Systems. Volume 1., Florence, Italy (1999) 400–406
5. Zitová, B., Flusser, J.: Image registration methods: a survey. Image and Vision Computing **21**(11) (2003) 977–1000

6. Radke, R.J., Andra, S., Al-Kofahi, O., Roysam, B.: Image change detection algorithms: a systematic survey. IEEE Transactions on Image Processing **14**(3) (2005) 294–307
7. Zomet, A., Levin, A., Peleg, S., Weiss, Y.: Seamless image stitching by minimizing false edges. IEEE Transactions on Image Processing **15**(4) (2006) 969–977
8. Szeliski, R.: Video mosaics for virtual environments. IEEE Computer Graphics & Applications (1996) 22–30
9. Xiao, F., Wu, H.Z., Xiao, L., Tang, Y., Ma, W.J.: Auto method for ambient light independent panorama mosaics. In: Proceedings of International Conference on Machine Learning and Cybernetics. Volume 6., Shanghai, China, IEEE (2004) 3851–3854
10. Vandewalle, P., Süsstrunk, S., Vetterli, M.: A Frequency Domain Approach to Registration of Aliased Images with Application to Super-Resolution. EURASIP Journal on Applied Signal Processing (special issue on Super-resolution) (2005)
11. Marzotto, R., Fusiello, A., Murino, V.: High resolution video mosaicing with global alignment. In: Proceedings of the IEEE Computer Society Conference on Computer Vision and Pattern Recognition. Volume 01., Los Alamitos, CA, USA, IEEE Computer Society (2004) 692–698
12. Peleg, S., Herman, J.: Panoramic mosaics by manifold projection. In: CVPR '97: Proceedings of the 1997 Conference on Computer Vision and Pattern Recognition (CVPR '97), Washington, DC, USA, IEEE Computer Society (1997) 338–343
13. Heikkilä, M., Pietikäinen, M.: An image mosaicing module for wide-area surveillance. In: VSSN '05: Proceedings of the third ACM international workshop on Video surveillance & sensor networks, New York, NY, USA, ACM Press (2005) 11–18
14. Bovik, A., Gibson, J., Bovik, A., eds.: Handbook of Image and Video Processing. Academic Press, Inc., Orlando, FL, USA (2000)

Salience-Preserving Image Composition with Luminance Consistency

Zhenlong Du, Xueying Qin, Wei Hua, and Hujun Bao

State Key Lab of CAD&CG, Zhejiang University, P.R. China
{duzhl, xyqin, huawei, bao}@cad.zju.edu.cn

Abstract. Image composition is a frequently-used editing technique. Existed approaches rarely consider the issue of luminance consistency. In this paper, an image composition method with salience preservation is proposed, which focuses on how to achieve the luminance consistency. Our method includes salience determination, whitepoint correction and luminance adjustment. Salience depends not only on luminance, but also on chrominance, an approach fully exploiting the difference of luminance and chrominance is suggested. A whitepoint correction schema by aligning the principle color axes is presented. Meanwhile, the luminance consistency composition is formulated as a nonlinear optimization with respect to the salience constraint, hence the composition could achieve the consistent luminance and preserve the appropriate salience.

1 Introduction

Image composition and separation are two kinds of primary image manipulations. The composition is generally served for putting the different parts of image/images together to produce a novel image. Quite a few people regard that if all parts are present, the easy operation like *copy* and *paste* is enough to compose them. However, whether these parts bear the same or similar illumination is hard to guarantee, and the inconsistent lighting causes the composition to be unrealistic. To our knowledge, there are few literatures discussing this issue. In this paper, we concentrate on how to compose images with the consistent luminance.

(a) Patch (b) Background (c) Composition

Fig. 1. Image Composition

N. Zheng, X. Jiang, and X. Lan (Eds.): IWICPAS 2006, LNCS 4153, pp. 308–316, 2006.

Some definitions, including *patch*, *background* and *composition*, are introduced in advance for the presentation necessity. *Patch* is the extracted image used for composition, for instance, the region bounded by the red contour in Fig. 1(a). *Background* is the composition target of *patch*, as the illustration of Fig. 1(b). *Composition* is the merging result of *patch* and *background*. Essentially speaking, *patch* is the source of composition, it tells "what" should be composed, *background* describes the location, that is, "where" is the composition place, and *composition* is the "result" of blending *patch* and *background*.

Seamless image composition should gratify three consistencies: perspective, geometry and illumination. When the patch and background bear the compatible depth and harmonic size, the consistent luminance is critical to final composition. Most commercial softwares adopt the schema of uniformly adjusting the patch luminance, which is based on the shifting whitepoint. But even the patch and background have the same whitepoint, they still can hold the compatible dynamic range. That is, after the uniform luminance adjusting, the patch might appear too dim or bright. Hence, to maintain the same whitepoint as well as the harmonious dynamic range is necessary to image composition.

Keeping the features of a patch is also crucial to image composition. In [5,6] the gradient is used as the image features, and it is retained during manipulations. Sun et al [2] proposed the Poisson-based matting method, in which gradient vector served as the guidance field, and the transparency scalar is extracted under the Dirichlet boundary condition. However, in image composition, directly specifying the surrounding luminance via Dirichlet boundary condition may produce unfavorable results when the luminance of the patch is very discrepant with the one of the background. In the paper the luminance of background is exploited for adjusting the one of patch. Additionally, Fattal et al [6] suggested an approach which the image feature is maintained during the dynamic range compression, our method is an inverse to [6], we adjust the patch's dynamic range to match the one of background.

Humans' eyes can distinguish object not by the absolute luminance and chrominance, but by the relative ones. Humans' visual perception depends on the salience, which describes the exciting location and degree to eye. Gooch et al [1] presented a method which could transform the color image to gray one with salience preservation, and the differences of luminance and chrominance between pixels are utilized to evaluate the salience. We employ the approach of [1] for measuring the salience contained within the patch. The difference between the literature [1] and our method is that the goal of literature [1] is to keep as much feature as possible, while ours is to adjust the dynamic range according to the salience.

The rest of the paper is organized as follows: in next section we review the related works. In section 3, we present three subproblems of our approach: salience determination, adjusting the patch luminance by color axes alignment, luminance modification with salience preservation. In section 4, we present some results, and draw our conclusions in the last section.

2 Related Work

In this section the issues, including the gradient domain manipulation, dynamic range modulation and salience evaluation, are briefly reviewed.

The poisson PDE is the widely-used approach to perform the image composition. However, it is difficult to pleasingly handle two kinds of composition: the patch with large size, the existence of outstanding difference in chrominance and luminance between the patch and background.

Gradient is an important image feature, which is exploited for many image manipulations. Levin [3] proposed an image stitching approach, in which the similarity based on the gradient between the input and stitched images is constructed, and used for stitching. As we know, the same gradients don't mean the same illuminations. When the distinct luminance difference exists in images, only depending upon the gradient is hard to achieve the pleasing effect.

Maintaining the appropriate dynamic range between the patch and the background is necessary for image composition. The taken images of the same object under different illumination appear different dynamic range. Therefore, by modulation of dynamic range, the same patch could be placed into the different illumination background. Existing methods [7,9] are focus on how to compress the dynamic range of image so as to display it on displaying devices with limited dynamic range, and simultaneously preserve the significant cues, while we modify the dynamic range of patch for bearing the apparent visual cues.

Salience depends on the chrominance and luminance besides the dynamic range. The conventional conversion from color image to gray image is uniformly mapping the dynamic range, and easily causes the loss of salience. Gooch et al [1] proposed a method for efficiently measuring the salience, which fully take advantages of the difference of chrominance and luminance. Meanwhile, since a signed color distance based on salience is constructed, the visual cues is significantly preserved in Gooch's demonstrations.

3 Image Composition with Luminance Consistency

3.1 Salience Determination

The salience expresses the conspicuity which most excites the eyes' attention [11,12]. The salience map is a scalar field which describes all pixels' salience. The salience of the patch and the background are different, and the inharmonic luminance between them further magnifies the salience difference, consequently the composition gives rise to the unrealistic perception. In this paper, the patch's salience is used for achieving the consistent composition.

CIE La^*b^* color space is adopted by lots of image manipulations for its strong separating capability between color luminance and chrominance, in which the chrominance plane is composed by the orthogonal a^* and b^* axes. In La^*b^* color space, luminance has little correlation with chrominance. No matter which kind of color space is employed, the color difference need to be evaluated firstly. Besides the conventional color distance estimation, Rubner et al [8] proposed the

EMD (Earth Mover's Distance) to measure the dissimilarity of two images, which allows for partial matches and could reflect the perceptual distance (ground distance) to some extent. The salience in [1] is significantly preserved in transforming the color image to gray one. Salience more corresponds with the perception than EMD, hence it is exploited in the paper.

Salience is related to illuminance and chrominance. For any two pixels $\mathbf{r}$ and $\mathbf{s}$, let $\Delta L_{\mathbf{rs}}$ be their luminance difference $(L_{\mathbf{r}} - L_{\mathbf{s}})$, $\Delta A_{\mathbf{rs}}$ and $\Delta B_{\mathbf{rs}}$ separately be the difference of a^* and b^* channels, and $\Delta C_{\mathbf{rs}}$ be the chrominance difference $(\Delta A_{\mathbf{rs}}, \Delta B_{\mathbf{rs}})$. Gooch [1] introduced the parameter θ for signifying the chrominance variation towards lightening or darkening, and the chrominance plane is divided into two parts along the perpendicular direction to θ, different θ denotes different chrominance alteration. Most importantly, Gooch suggested a criteria to weight the salience embedded within the image, which is adopted in our approach.

$$\delta(\alpha,\theta)_{\mathbf{rs}} = \begin{cases} \Delta L_{\mathbf{rs}} & \text{if } |\Delta L_{\mathbf{rs}}| > \text{crunch}(\|\overrightarrow{\Delta C}_{\mathbf{rs}}\|) \\ \text{crunch}(\|\overrightarrow{\Delta C}_{\mathbf{rs}}\|) & \text{if } \overrightarrow{\Delta C}_{\mathbf{rs}} \cdot \overrightarrow{v_\theta} \geq 0 \\ \text{crunch}(-\|\overrightarrow{\Delta C}_{\mathbf{rs}}\|) & \text{otherwise} \end{cases} \tag{1}$$

Where $\overrightarrow{\nu_\theta} = (\cos\theta, \sin\theta)$, and *crunch* is the hyperbolic crunch function, in which small values are preserved but large ones approach the given threshold α. Eq. (1) presents the salience evaluation by the luminance and chrominance differences. And it is consistent with the visual experience of human, in which the salience depends not only on the luminance, but also on the chrominance.

$$A_{\mathbf{r}} = \sum_{\mathbf{s}} \delta_{\mathbf{rs}} \tag{2}$$

The salience sum defined by Eq. (2) reflects the global salience, which essentially is the *affinity* referred in [10].

(a) Original Image (b) Salience (c) Colorbar

Fig. 2. Salience

Fig. 2(a) shows the patch used in this paper. The evaluated salience map by Eq. (1) and Eq. (2) and the used colorbar are displayed in Fig. 2(b) and 2(c), respectively. It is obvious that the salience map depends on the luminance and chrominance together. Meanwhile, it corresponds to visual cues.

3.2 Color Axes Alignment

The patch and the background are often taken under the different illumination, hence they have the different white point. White point somewhat reflects the color distribution, which is determined by the principle color axes. The approach of aligning the principle color axes between the patch and the background is exploited for adjusting the chrominance of patch. And the modified patch is used for further adjusting in the following section.

Let C_p and C_b be the color matrix of patch and background, C_c be the color matrix of the patch after composition. The principle color axes of C_p, C_c and C_b are evaluated by SVD method. That is, $C_p = U_p S_p V_p^T$, $C_c = U_c S_c V_c^T$ and $C_b = U_b S_b V_b^T$, where S_p, S_c and S_b denote the principle color axes of C_p, C_c and C_b, respectively. In fact, S_c is equivalent to S_b, hence the principle color axes of

(a) (b) (c) (d)

(e)

Fig. 3. Color Axes Alignment

$C_c = U_c S_c V_c^T$ is replaced by S_b for adjusting the white point of the patch, this is, $C_c = U_c S_b V_c^T$.

In Fig. 3(e), four pink rectangles, labelled by letters a, b, c and d, serve as different background images to correct the white point of patch (Fig. 2(a)), and the corresponding results are showed in Fig. 3(a), 3(b), 3(c) and 3(d), respectively. For the same patch, when the different background is employed for correcting the patch's white point, the patch shows the different chrominance.

3.3 Luminance Adjustment

Luminance adjustment is to cause the patch to bear the salience. After the alignment of principle color axes, the chrominance of the patch and the background has been very similar. However, the patch is still lack of salience. In this section, a salience preservation method is presented, which is accomplished by modifying the luminance of patch. The modification involves two aspects: local and global. Local adjustment is referred to the operation within the current and neighboring pixels, while the global one is concerned with the manipulation among the current and non-neighboring pixels.

Luminance adjustment within the gradient domain easily produce the blurry effect, hence the salience is not well preserved. In [4,13,14], the optimization method is employed, which could achieve better effects and maintain the fine details, therefore in this paper the luminance adjusting is also based on the optimization approach.

(a) (b) (c)

(d) Poisson (e) Photoshop (f) Our Method

Fig. 4. Composition Compare

Let Ω be the pixel set of patch, $(\mathbf{r}, \mathbf{s})$ be a pair of pixels, which $\mathbf{r}$ and $\mathbf{s}$ may be adjacent, or non-adjacent. The luminance adjustment with salience constraint is formulated as that.

$$\min_{L} f(L) = \sum_{(\mathbf{r},\mathbf{s})\in\Omega} ((L_{\mathbf{r}} - L_{\mathbf{s}}) - \omega\delta_{\mathbf{rs}})^2 \tag{3}$$

where $L_{\mathbf{r}}$ and $L_{\mathbf{s}}$ denote the luminance of pixel **r** and **s**, respectively. $\delta_{\mathbf{rs}}$ is the evaluated salience in section 3.1. $\omega(0 \leq \omega \leq 1)$ is the adjustable scalar of salience holding degree. Higher ω is able to preserve stronger salience, while lower ω is capable of keeping weaker salience. If ω is zero, the composition degenerates to the naive "copy" and "paste" operations.

Luminance adjustment is performed within the whole patch.

4 Results

In Fig. (4), three groups of results are demonstrated, which are composed by the Fig. 2(a) with the Fig. 4(a), 4(b) and 4(c), respectively. Each group compares the composition of Poisson [5], Photoshop and our method, which are orderly illustrated in the first, second and third column of Fig. 4(d), 4(e) and 4(f). From the comparison, we can notice that the part of Poisson composition appears too dim or too bright, but the patch is entirely merged into the background. The composition of Photoshop could not keep the salience, while our composition result preserve the salience well, while still keep the consistent luminance.

It should be noted that our schema emphasizes the luminance consistency between the patch and the background, while could maintain the salience of the patch. Photoshop accomplishes the composition by globally adjusting the patch luminance, and the final composition depends on the user manipulation skill. Our schema considers the influence of the background, and the luminance adjustment is subject to the background luminance as well as salience. Additionally, in the shown examples Poisson can not generate the pleasing composition, but the patch is fully merged into the background, while the results from Photoshop and ours do not fully mix the patch with the background, this issue is solved in our future investigation.

5 Conclusion

Luminance consistency is an important issue in image composition. Global adjustment could not achieve the consistent luminance and preserve the salience. In this paper a novel image composition method is proposed, which could preserve the patch salience. Different white point between patch and background influences the composition, hence the white point of patch is corrected by the method of principle color axes alignment. Meanwhile, the patch luminance is nonlinearly adjusted with the constraint of salience. Experiments show that our method could achieve the consistent illumination composition, especially when the illumination between patch and background is significantly different.

It should be noted that Poisson method could well perform the image composition when the background luminance around the patch boundary approximates to be a constant. Meanwhile, Photoshop is able to achieve the pleasing composition when the patch and the background have the similar whitepoint.

How to harmonically transmit the luminance along the patch boundary is solved in our recent work. In future, we would investigate the video composition with salience preservation.

Acknowledgement

The work is supported by National Basic Research Program (China) Grant 2002CB312102, and Natural Science Foundation(China) Grant 60373035, 60021201, 60203014.

References

1. A.A. Gooch, S.C. Olsen, J. Tumblin, B. Gooch: Color2Gray: Salience-Preserving color removal, In Proc. of SIGGRAPH'2005, 2005.
2. J. Sun, J. Jia, C.-K. Tang, H.-Y. Shum: Poisson matting, In Proc. of SIGGRAPH'2005, 2005.
3. A. Levin, A. Zomet, S. Peleg, Y. Weiss: Seamless image stitching in the gradient domain, In Proc. of ECCV'2004, 2004.
4. A. Levin D. Lischinski, Y. Weiss: Colorization using optimization, In Proc. of SIGGRAPH'2004, 2004.
5. P. Pérez, M. Gangnet, A. Blake: Poisson Image Editing, In Proc. of SIGGRAPH'2003, 2003.
6. R. Fattal, D. Lischinski, M. Werman: Gradient domain high dynamic range compression, In Proc. of SIGGRAPH'2002, 2002.
7. J. Tumblin, G. Turk: LCIS: A boundary hierarchy for detail-preserving contrast reduction, In Proc. of SIGGRAPH'2001, 2001.
8. Y. Rubner, C. Tomasi, L.J. Guibas: The earth mover's distance as a metric for image retrieval, IJCV, vol. 40, no. 2, pp. 99-121, Nov. 2000.
9. P.E. Debevec, J. Malik: Recovering high dynamic range radiance maps from photographs, In Proc. of SIGGRAPH'1997, 1997.
10. Y. Weiss: Segmentation using eigenvectors: a unifying view, In Proc. of ICCV'1999, 1999.
11. L. Itti, C. Koch: Computational modeling of visual attention, Nature Reviews Neuroscience, vol. 2, no. 3, pp. 194-223, Mar. 2001.
12. L. Itti, C. Koch, E. Niebur: A model of saliency-based visual attention for rapid scene analysis, IEEE PAMI, vol. 20, no. 11, pp. 1254-1259, Nov. 1998.
13. K. Rasche: Re-coloring images for Gamuts of lower dimensions, In Proc. of Eurographics'2005, 2005.
14. T. Welsh, M. Ashikhmin, K. Mueller: Transferring color to greyscale images, In Proc. of SIGGRAPH'2002, 2002.

Filament Enhancement by Non-linear Volumetric Filtering Using Clustering-Based Connectivity

Georgios K. Ouzounis and Michael H.F. Wilkinson

Institute of Mathematics and Computing Science, University of Groningen
P.O. Box 800, 9700 AV Groningen, The Netherlands

Abstract. Shape filters are a family of connected morphological operators that have been used for filament enhancement in biomedical imaging. They interact with connected image regions rather than individual pixels, which can either be removed or retained unmodified. This prevents edge distortion and noise amplification, a property particularly appreciated in filtering and segmentation. In this paper we investigate their performance using a generalized notion of connectivity that is referred to as "clustering-based connectivity". We show that we can capture thin fragmented structures which are filtered out with existing techniques.

1 Introduction

Biomedical data sets often contain curvi-linear, dendritic or other filamentous structures of interest which are susceptible to acquisition noise. Enhancing these structures can be of particular importance to certain medical applications and many methods have been proposed [3]. Some common drawbacks among them is noise amplification and edge distortion while they can also be computationally expensive.

In mathematical morphology, a family of operators called *connected filters* has been developed which interact with regions characterized by some notion of connectivity. According to these filters, *connected regions* can either be removed or retained unmodified based on a pre-specified attribute (shape in this case) but new edges cannot emerge. This edge and therefore shape-preserving property makes connected filters competitive to existing morphological methods for filament enhancement such as the multi-scale approach in [11].

The objects targeted are thin, plate-like (Fig. 1) and elongated structures which are often fragmented at higher gray-levels according to the standard connectivity. We aim at countering this with a further improvement of the method presented in [11]. This is by using a more general notion of connectivity termed *clustering-based connectivity* [8, 9] which models object clusters as individual connected regions. We demonstrate our findings and compare them to the existing method using three different 3-D data sets. In each case we study the parameters which maximize the filter's performance in association with the underlying clustering-based connectivity.

Following this section there is a short reference to the concept of connectivity and connectivity openings complemented by the notion of clustering-based connectivity. In Section 3 the shape filters and their extensions to gray-scale are presented while in Section 4 we discuss their applications to 3-D medical data sets. The work is summarized with some conclusions in Section 5.

N. Zheng, X. Jiang, and X. Lan (Eds.): IWICPAS 2006, LNCS 4153, pp. 317–327, 2006.

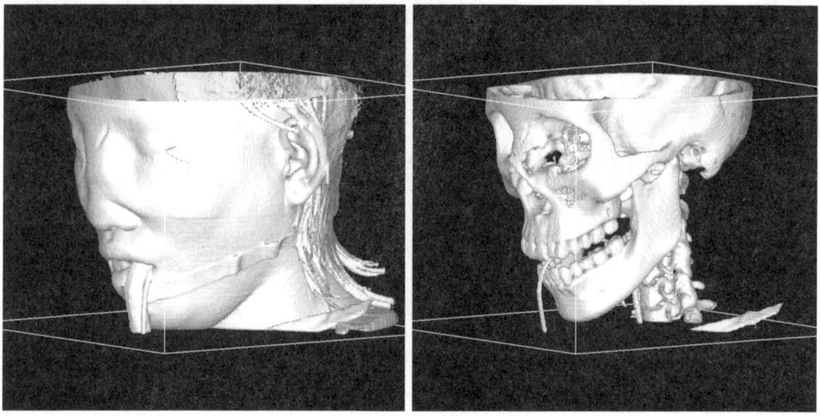

Fig. 1. 3-D Shape filtering using 26 connectivity: The image on the left illustrates an isosurface projection of a human head at isolevel 208. Increasing the isolevel to visualize the skull removes important details. The image on the right illustrates a shape filter enhancing the thin, plate-like structures comprising the skull and all the noise at an isolevel 96.

2 Theory

2.1 Connectivity Classes and Openings

The set-theoretic notion of connectivity in discrete spaces such as $\mathbb{Z}^2$ describes how groupings are realized in digital images. Connectivity in mathematical morphology is given by *connectivity classes*, a construct defined as:

Definition 1. *Let E be an arbitrary (non-empty) set. A family $\mathcal{C} \subseteq \mathcal{P}(E)$ is called a* connectivity class *if it satisfies:*

1. $\emptyset \in \mathcal{C}$ *and for all* $x \in E$, $\{x\} \in \mathcal{C}$,
2. *for any* $\{A_i\} \subseteq \mathcal{C}$ *for which* $\bigcap A_i \neq \emptyset \Rightarrow \bigcup A_i \in \mathcal{C}$

Members of $\mathcal{C}$ are called *connected sets* [8, 9] and Definition 1 means that both the empty set and singleton sets are connected, and any union of connected sets which have a non-empty intersection is also connected.

Addressing objects in binary images is often more practical using *connected components* or *grains* which are connected parts of an object of maximal extend, i.e. they are connected and not smaller than any other connected part of the same object. Writing this explicitly, we say that C is a connected component of a binary image X if there is no set $C' \supset C$ such that $C' \subseteq X$ and $C' \in \mathcal{C}$.

Connected components are groupings of connected sets containing a certain point $x \in E$ in their intersection. The operator Γ_x to access them is called a *connectivity opening* marked by x and is given by:

$$\Gamma_x(X) = \bigcup \{A_i \in \mathcal{C} \mid x \in A_i \text{ and } A_i \subseteq X\} . \quad (1)$$

Furthermore, $\forall x \notin X$, $\Gamma_x(X) = \emptyset$. Connectivity openings are characterized by three properties; they are *anti-extensive*, *increasing* and *idempotent* operators. For a given set X each property implies the following:

1. Anti-extensiveness: $\Gamma_x(X) \subseteq X$,
2. Increasingness: if $X \subseteq Y \Rightarrow \Gamma_x(X) \subseteq \Gamma_x(Y)$,
3. Idempotence : $\Gamma_x(\Gamma_x(X)) = \Gamma_x(X)$.

The operator Γ_x is explicitly related to a connectivity class $\mathcal{C}$ if satisfying the set of conditions given by Serra [8] (also in [6]) in the following theorem:

Theorem 1. *The datum of a connectivity class $\mathcal{C}$ on $\mathcal{P}(E)$ is equivalent to the family $\{\Gamma_x \mid x \in E\}$ of openings on x such that:*

1. *every Γ_x is an algebraic opening,*
2. *for all $x \in E$, we have $\Gamma_x(X) = \{x\}$,*
3. *for all $X \subseteq E$, $x, y \in E, \Gamma_x(X)$ and $\Gamma_y(X)$ are equal or disjoint,*
4. *for all $X \subseteq E$, and all $x \in E$, we have $x \notin X \Rightarrow \Gamma_x(X) = \emptyset$.*

Connectivity openings characterize uniquely the connectivity class they are associated with and there is a one-to-one correspondence between the two.

2.2 Clustering-Based Connectivity

Connected components of X according to $\mathcal{C}$ are separated by elements of the background. If however the distance separating them is smaller than the size of a given structuring element (SE), it is possible to define a *cluster* [1,6,9] in a *child* connectivity class $\mathcal{C}^\psi$, where ψ denotes a structural operator referred to as *clustering*. Following is a list summarizing the properties required to define a clustering:

1. ψ is increasing and extensive.
2. $\psi(\mathcal{C}) \subseteq \mathcal{C}$.
3. For a family $\{X_i\}$ in $\mathcal{P}(E)$ such that $\psi(X_i) \in \mathcal{C}, \forall\ i$, and $\bigcap_i X_i \neq \emptyset \Rightarrow \psi(\bigcup X_i) \in \mathcal{C}$.
4. ψ does not create connected components; i.e., if $\forall x \in C$, $C = \Gamma_x(\psi(X)) \Rightarrow X \cap C \neq \emptyset$.
5. ψ treats the clusters of X independently; i.e., if $\forall x \in C$, $C = \Gamma_x(\psi(X)) \Rightarrow \psi(X \cap C) = C$.

More details on each item are given in [1]. Typically, ψ is either a dilation or a closing and generates a mask image, called the *connectivity mask* by expanding X.

Definition 2. *Let $\mathcal{C}$ be a connectivity class in $\mathcal{P}(E)$ and ψ be an increasing and extensive operator on $\mathcal{P}(E)$. Then*

$$\mathcal{C}^\psi = \{X \in \mathcal{P}(E) \mid \psi(X) \in \mathcal{C}\} \tag{2}$$

is a clustering-based *connectivity class for which $\mathcal{C} \subseteq \mathcal{C}^\psi$.*

If, for ψ the above five properties hold, and furthermore, $\psi(\emptyset) = \emptyset$ and

$$\psi(X \cap \Gamma_x(\psi(X))) = \Gamma_x(\psi(X)), \tag{3}$$

we have a *strong clustering* [1].

Definition 3. *Let $\{\Gamma_x \mid x \in E\}$ be the connectivity openings associated with $\mathcal{C}$. If ψ is a strong clustering on $\mathcal{P}(E)$, the family of connectivity openings $\{\Gamma_x^\psi \mid x \in E\}$ associated to $\mathcal{C}^\psi$ are given by*

$$\Gamma_x^\psi(X) = \begin{cases} \Gamma_x(\psi(X)) \cap X, & \textit{if } x \in X \quad \text{(4a)} \\ \emptyset, & \textit{otherwise} \quad \text{(4b)} \end{cases}$$

In the following, every time we use the term clustering we mean a strong clustering.

3 Shape Filters

Filtering a binary image based on the attributes of its connected components requires a criterion T commonly given by:

$$T(C) = (Attr(C) \geq \lambda) \tag{5}$$

where $Attr$ is some attribute value of a connected component C and λ a pre-selected threshold. Components that satisfy (5) are retained while the rest are removed. Binary attribute filters in the anti-extensive case can be categorized to attribute openings or thinnings depending on whether the attribute criterion is increasing or not. The case that $Attr(C)$ is non-increasing implies that for any two nested components C_1 and C_2,

$$C_1 \subseteq C_2 \nRightarrow Attr(C_1) \leq Attr(C_2), \tag{6}$$

i.e. their attributes need not be ordered in the same way. Comparing the attribute value of a connected component against λ is by means of a trivial thinning Φ_T on the output of the connectivity opening of (1). The trivial thinning is an anti-extensive, idempotent and non-increasing operator defined as $\Phi_T : \mathcal{C} \to \mathcal{C}$ which for a connected component $C \in \mathcal{C}$ yields C if $T(C)$ is true, and $\emptyset$ otherwise. Furthermore, $\Phi_T(\emptyset) = \emptyset$. For a binary image X, the attribute thinning is given by:

$$\Phi^T(X) = \bigcup_{x \in E} \Phi_T(\Gamma_x(X)). \tag{7}$$

Attribute thinnings sensitive to structures of a given shape are called *shape filters*. The filamentous structures that we investigate, are thin elongated structures that are characterized by a high trace of the moment of inertia tensor $I(C)$ compared to their volume $V(C)$. For 3-D data sets, $I(C)$ has a minimum for a sphere and increases rapidly as the object becomes more elongated [11]. It is defined as:

$$I(C) = \frac{V(C)}{4} + \sum_{\mathbf{x} \in \mathbf{C}} (\mathbf{x} - \overline{\mathbf{x}})^2 \tag{8}$$

and scales with size to the fifth power whereas the volume scales with the third power of the size. Therefore the ratio

$$Attr(C) = \frac{I(C)}{V^{5/3}(C)} \tag{9}$$

is a purely shape dependent attribute which together with (7) defines a filter sensitive to elongated shapes.

Connected filters in general rely on some notion of connectivity. In the case of (7) the term $\Gamma_x(X)$ relates the filter to the connectivity class $\mathcal{C}$ and the connected components it returns are unique. Extending connected filters to sets characterized by second-generation connectivity is by replacing the connectivity opening with the associated operator. For clustering-based connectivity this is Γ_x^{ψ}.

The cases in which the attribute criterion of a filter is increasing, like the volume of a 3-D connected component $V(C)$, extend to gray-scale trivially [4, 5] based on the principle of threshold superposition [2]. For the non-increasing, translation and shift invariant shape descriptor of (9), gray-scale attribute filters based on either type of connectivity can be computed efficiently using the *subtractive filtering rule* [10]. This is a non-pruning, tree-based filtering strategy in which if a tree node (corresponding to a connected component of the thresholded image at level h) is reduced in gray-scale, its descendants are lower by the same amount. It is realized on a tree structure for second-generation connectivity representation termed the *Dual-Input Max-Tree* algorithm that is based on [7] and extended details can be found in [4, 5]. The experiments that follow are based on this arrangement.

4 Experiments

In this section we experiment with the 3-D shape filter discussed in Section 3, using clustering-based connectivity. In this first approach to non-linear volumetric filtering using this specific type of second-generation connectivity, the objective is to enhance and extract filamentous details from a number of noisy biomedical data sets. The present study investigates the factors that affect the performance of the proposed filter. We identify five critical parameters namely: (i) the neighborhood of each volume element in 3-D, (ii) the size of the structuring element to be used, (iii) the type of clustering operator ψ, i.e. a dilation or a closing, (iv) the way the attributes are calculated (on X or $\psi(X)$) and (v) the attribute threshold used with the filter.

The first data set is an isosurface projection of an 8 bit, $256 \times 256 \times 256$ rotational b-plane CT-angiogram (CTA) of the arteries of the right half of a human head (Fig. 2). A contrast agent was used and an aneurysm is present. The volume contains a dense cloud of low intensity noise centered within the structures of interest. To generate the connectivity mask we consider the first three parameters listed earlier. For volume sets it is common to use a 26 neighborhood since a 6 neighborhood often results in "loosely" connected components. Masks generated by a dilation expand the original set creating a number of structures of previously disconnected elements. In noisy backgrounds, this can result in grouping the noise elements to high attribute structures and create connections with the structures of interest. Using structural closings instead, the unwanted

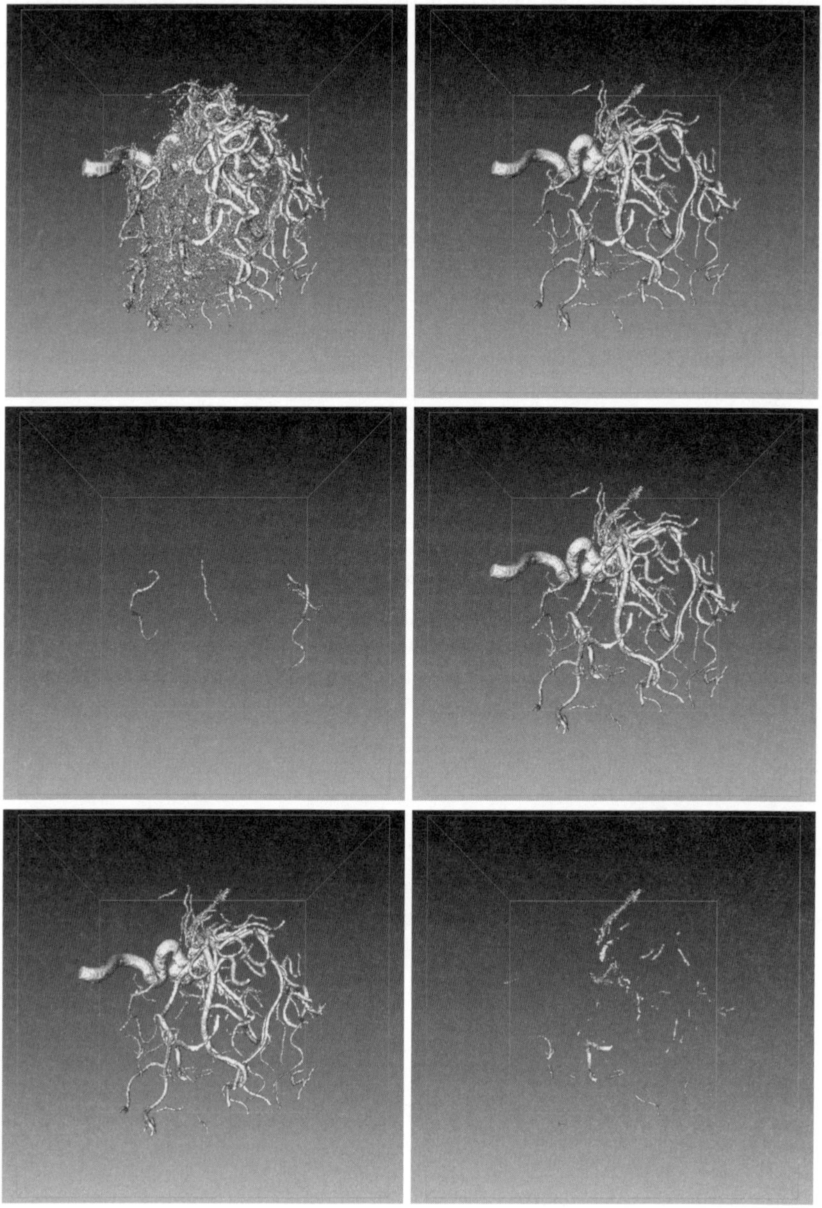

Fig. 2. Isosurface projections of a CTA scan containing an aneurysm and the output of the elongation filter based on standard connectivity (both at isolevel 0). The middle row shows the filtered outputs using a mask based on a dilation and a closing respectively. The bottom row shows the difference volumes between the filter outputs using clustering-based connectivity based on a closing vs. a dilation and based on a closing vs. the standard connectivity. Most vessel-like structures are preserved using a closing-based connectivity.

connections between small objects tend to break apart while structures merged by wide bridging regions are maintained. This is illustrated at the middle row of Fig. 2 where the image on the left shows the response of an elongation filter with λ=3 using a mask based on a dilation with a cubic SE of size $3 \times 3 \times 3$. The image on the right is the response of the same filter using a mask by a structural closing instead. It is evident that a dilation even with a relatively small SE merges most of the noise together with the blood vessels creating a structure with large overall volume and small elongation. Filtering removes all but certain regions disconnected from the clustered volume. The results can be compared with the filter response using standard, 26-connectivity - top right image. The bottom row shows the difference volumes between the filter responses. In the left image we compare the responses using a closing and a dilation. It can be seen that most of the structure of interested is lost. The right image shows the difference in the response using a closing-based clustering connectivity and the standard connectivity. We see a number of elongated structures missed by the filter using standard connectivity. With the closing-based connectivity, these vessel fragments are merged with the overall structure and hence they are retained.

The second data set shown at the top left image of Fig. 3, is a $256 \times 342 \times 243$, 8-bit confocal microscopy volume of a pyramidal neuron. The noise density here is not as high as the previous data set, but the filamentous structures (the dendrites in this case) are fragmented at low levels. Filtering using standard connectivity removes noise together with a considerable fraction of the dendrites. If the volume is clustered however, nearby fragments are connected into a single entity with overall elongation greater than the threshold λ and hence are retained. The top right image shows the result of an elongation filter with λ=2 using the standard connectivity at a 26 neighborhood.

Creating a mask with a structural closing is often not sufficient to counter the issue of noise clustering. Noise can be clustered in arbitrary arrangements and along arbitrary orientations. Two examples are illustrated at the first two images of Fig. 4 where both clustered arrangements have a similar elongation measure (attributes computed on the clustered sets are referred to as *C-attributes*). If the elongation measure is computed based on the expanded sets as illustrated at the corresponding connectivity masks at the last two images, the attributes of the two clustered arrangements are separated by a larger margin that distinguishes easier compact from elongated clusters. Attributes computed on the expanded sets of the mask are referred to as *M-attributes*.

The two images of the middle row of Fig. 3 illustrate the filter response with a connectivity mask generated by a structural closing with a cubic SE of size $5 \times 5 \times 5$ and corresponding C- and M-attributes respectively. The difference volumes computed between the responses with C-attributes, and M-attributes vs. 26-connected filtering, respectively, are shown at the bottom row. It can be seen that together with a considerable fraction of the dendrites claimed by the filter based on clustering connectivity, computing M-attributes outperforms the output based C-attributes which fails to deal with clustered noise effectively. The top first four images are isosurface projections at level 1 and the last two at level 0.

The last data set is a $256 \times 256 \times 124$, 8-bit, phase contrast magnetic resonance angiogram (MRA) of a human head. In this experiment we target the blood vessels and experiment with the size of the SE to be used along ψ in generating the connectivity

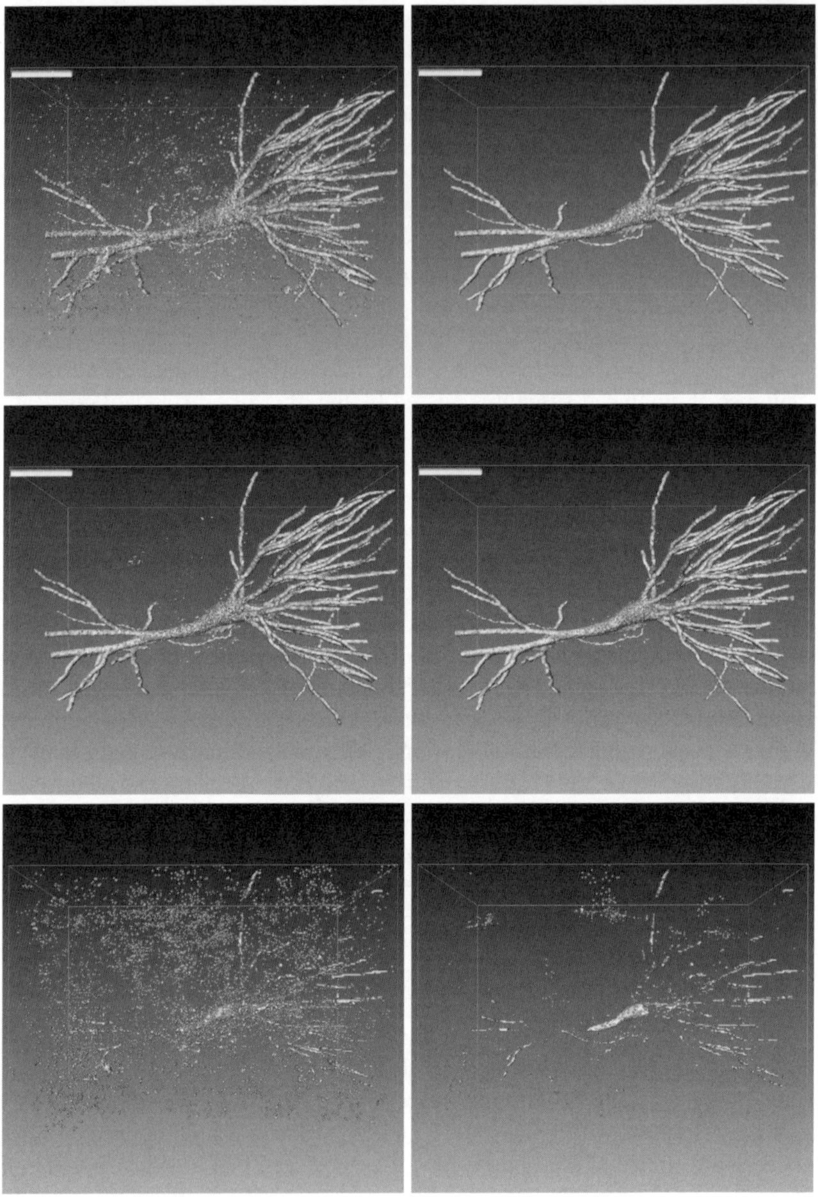

Fig. 3. Isosurface projections of the neuron and the output of the elongation filter based on the standard connectivity, both at isolevel 1. The middle row illustrates the filter performance by computing the structure attributes based on the clustered volume and based on the expanded volume which constitutes the mask. The bottom row shows the difference volumes between the C-attributes vs. 26-connected filtering, and between the M-attributes vs. 26-connected filtering.

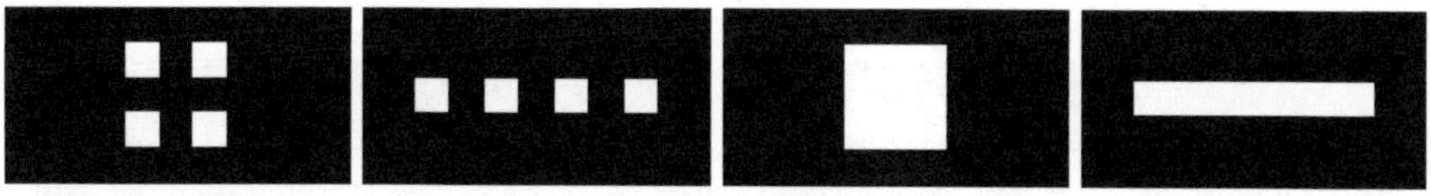

Fig. 4. The elongation measures of the clustered sets X and Y (first and second image from the left) are similar if the we compute the C-attributes. The M-attributes instead are computed on $\psi(X)$ and $\psi(Y)$ (third and fourth image from the left respectively) and obviously the elongation of $\psi(X)$ is smaller compared to that of $\psi(Y)$.

mask. The top left image of Fig. 5 shows the input volume at isolevel 50 (details start to appear only after this threshold). The top right image and the two at the middle row (starting from the left) show the responses of an elongation filter with $\lambda = 2$ using standard connectivity, and clustering connectivity based on masks by a $3 \times 3 \times 3$ and $5 \times 5 \times 5$ cubic SE respectively (at isolevel 5). The filter uses M-attributes and from the difference volumes between the responses of the filter using clustering connectivity with 3^3-based mask vs. standard connectivity and with 5^3-based mask vs. standard connectivity, it can be seen that both deal relatively well with clustered noise (isolevel 1) and they both capture vessel fragments but at a varying detail. To examine their in-between differences we also compute the difference volume between the output with 3^3-based mask vs. 5^3-based mask and the reverse (Fig. 6). The left image illustrates that with an increasing size of SE, the overall signal intensity in the vessels is reduced, though there is no distortion. On the other hand as the size of the SE increases the number of fragments captured increases as well, as shown in the righthand image. This also contributes to some additional clustered noise. In general the size of the SE can only be determined by the amount of detail required and a quantitative evaluation is only possible given the ground truth.

5 Discussion

In this paper we compared the performance of connected filters for filament enhancement, based on classical connectivity and clustering-based connectivity. From the difference volumes produced in the previous section it can be seen that the 3-D shape filter, sensitive to elongated structures, captures filamentous details in greater accuracy when dependent upon an underlying clustering-based connectivity. This is because fragments of the filamentous structures are clustered with their original body, contributing to an overall elongation attribute greater than their own if treated separately.

The parameters influencing the performance of the filter have also been studied and we demonstrated how each one affects the filter response and in what way. A comparison with different elongation thresholds has not been carried out since it is obvious that as the value of λ increases the more elements will be filtered out. This can be useful for capturing highly elongated structures. In the case of blood vessels the handling of each vessel separately involves a different type of second-generation connectivity called *contraction-based connectivity* which is not studied here.

A drawback of filters relying on a clustering-based connectivity is that of noise clustering. We minimize this effect by considering the structure attributes based on the

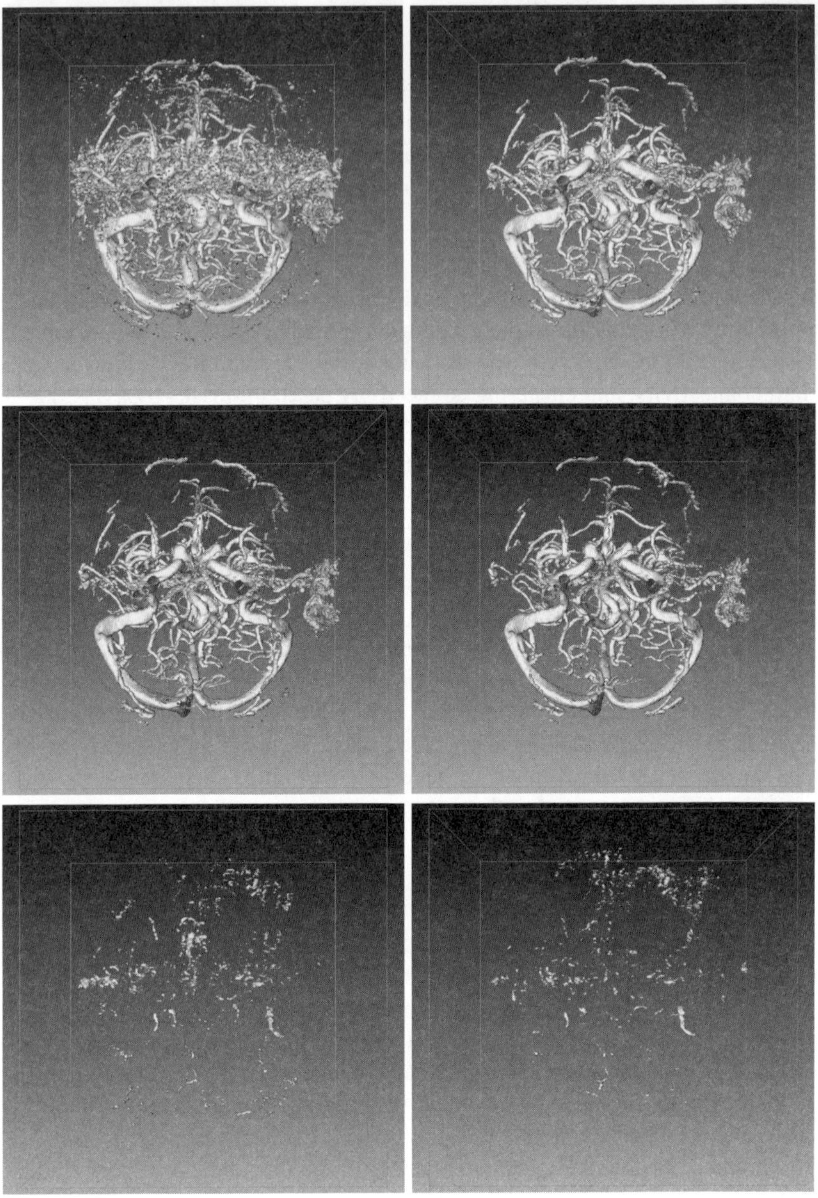

Fig. 5. Isosurface projection of the MRA at isolevel 50 and the output of the elongation filter based on the standard connectivity at isolevel 5. The middle row illustrates the filter outputs using a clustering-based connectivity with masks generated by a structural closing with a cubic SE of size $3 \times 3 \times 3$ and $5 \times 5 \times 5$ respectively. The bottom row shows the difference volumes between the two filter outputs compared against the volume generated by the filter based on standard connectivity.

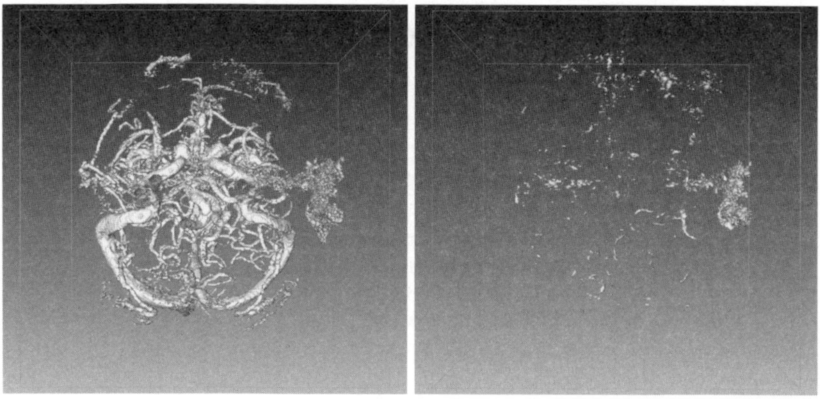

Fig. 6. The difference volumes between a filter based on the 3^3-based mask vs. the 5^3-based mask, and the reverse, at isolevel 1

connectivity mask instead of the clustered volume. We are currently working on further improvements by creating connectivity masks with adaptive structuring elements sensitive only to the direction of elongation.

References

1. U.M. Braga-Neto and J. Goutsias. Connectivity on complete lattices: New results. *Comp. Vis. Image Understand.*, 85:22–53, 2002.
2. P. Maragos and R. D. Ziff. Threshold superposition in morphological image analysis systems. *IEEE Trans. Pattern Anal. Mach. Intell.*, 12(5):498–504, 1990.
3. M. Orkisz, M. Hernández-Hoyos, P. Douek, and I. Magnin. Advances of blood vessel morphology analysis in 3D magnetic resonance images. *Mach. Vis. Graph.*, 9:463–471, 2000.
4. G. K. Ouzounis and M. H. F. Wilkinson. Mask-based second-generation connectivity and attribute filters. *IEEE Trans. Pattern Anal. Mach. Intell.*, 2005. submitted.
5. G. K. Ouzounis and M. H. F. Wilkinson. Second-order connected attribute filters using max-trees. In C. Ronse, L. Najman, and E. Decencire, editors, *Mathematical Morphology: 40 Years On; Proc. 7th Int. Symp. Math. Morphology*, pages 65–74. Springer-Verlag, 2005.
6. C. Ronse. Set-theoretical algebraic approaches to connectivity in continuous or digital spaces. *Journal of Mathematical Imaging and Vision*, 8:41–58, 1998.
7. P. Salembier, A. Oliveras, and L. Garrido. Anti-extensive connected operators for image and sequence processing. *IEEE Trans. Image Proc.*, 7:555–570, 1998.
8. J. Serra, editor. *Image Analysis and Mathematical Morphology. II: Theoretical Advances.* Academic Press, London, 1988.
9. J. Serra. Connectivity on complete lattices. *Journal of Mathematical Imaging and Vision*, 9:231–251, 1998.
10. E. R. Urbach and M. H. F. Wilkinson. Shape-only granulometries and grey-scale shape filters. In H. Talbot and R. Beare, editors, *Mathematical Morphology; Proc. 6th Int. Symp. Math. Morphology*, pages 305–314, Collingwood, Australia, 2002. CSIRO Publishing.
11. M. H. F. Wilkinson and M. A. Westenberg. Shape preserving filament enhancement filtering. In W. J. Niessen and M. A. Viergever, editors, *Proc. MICCAI'2001*, volume 2208 of *Lecture Notes in Computer Science*, pages 770–777, 2001.

Applying Preattentive Visual Guidance in Document Image Analysis

Di Wen[1,2] and Xiaoqing Ding[1,2]

[1] Department of Electronic Engineering, Tsinghua University
[2] State Key Laboratory of Intelligent Technology and Systems
Beijing 100084, P.R. China
{wendi, dxq}@ocrserv.ee.tsinghua.edu.cn

Abstract. In this paper, we present a novel methodology on document image analysis (DIA) which harnesses the mechanism of preattentive visual guidance in human vision. Summarizing the psychophysical discoveries on preattentive vision, we propose two types of computational simulations of this biological process: the visual similarity clustering and visual saliency detection, based on which we implement a novel biological plausible way to guide the interpretation of document images. Experimental results prove the efficiency of these two computational processes, whose outputs can be further utilized by other task-oriented DIA applications.

Keywords: Document image analysis, preattentive visual guidance, texture synthesis, dynamic clustering, visual saliency.

1 Introduction

Detecting and segmenting semantic contents from document images is a challenging task. In recent years, there have been proposed dozens of matured algorithms in the document image analysis (DIA) domain, oriented at different application scenarios. Some of them are quite successful in automatically converting specific classes of paper-based documents, in batches, into their electronic counterparts [1, 2, 3, 4]. However, little attention has been paid to the adaptability of the DIA methods while they are encountered with constantly switching environments, such as from simple layouts to complex layouts, from upright to geometric distorted images, from clean background to clutter background etc. As a result, current DIA systems are quite specialized for specific class of samples and quite demanding for image quality, which greatly reduce the usability of OCR techniques. In this paper, we propose a new attempt towards a generic DIA approach adapting to various cases. Our original idea is motivated by the mechanism of preattentive visual guidance in human vision.

In the literature, most DIA methods process binary images by investigating simple geometric features. For example, the famous RLSA method [1] discriminates text and non-text contents by the distance between foreground pixels and extracts text contents after a run-length smearing preprocessing. But unfortunately, RLSA method is sensitive to noise, page orientation and font size, making it unsuitable for constructing adaptive systems. Another branch of methods, referred to as the connected component

N. Zheng, X. Jiang, and X. Lan (Eds.): IWICPAS 2006, LNCS 4153, pp. 328 – 338, 2006.

aggregation methods [5, 6], utilize alignment and spacing consistency of text components and perform a bottom-up hierarchical reconstruction of document layouts. Such bottom-up methods can be well suited for segmenting arbitrary layouts, only if the text line aggregation results are reliable. In many cases this is hard to achieve by using only geometric features and local merging scheme without any global directive. Furthermore, analysis on binary connected components is also unreliable in noisy, skewed and irregular document images. Limited by such disadvantages, the bottom-up methods are inadequate to discriminate text and non-text contents robustly. To make full use of image appearance in document analysis, some researchers proposed the texture-based methods [7, 8, 9, 10], which model each homogeneous region in document images as a texture pattern. By extracting texture statistics as features, dynamic or static classifier techniques are applied to classify the image pixels as text or non-text. Frequently used texture features include Gabor responses [7], morphological masked pixel values [8, 10], wavelet coefficients [9] etc. Although the texture-based methods model the visual appearance of different contents in document images, the texture features they used are derived from mathematical perspectives and hence are not biological plausible. Therefore, it is hard to tell how well these texture features can characterize unknown visual patterns, which is an important factor to realize adaptability.

Based on the above observation, we consider a brand-new adaptive DIA solution from the biological plausible perspective. Summarizing the latest discoveries in psychophysical research on preattentive vision, we propose a novel computational model in this paper to simulate the preattentive visual guidance mechanism in human vision in document image analysis. The model contains two kinds of computations: visual similarity clustering (VSC) and visual saliency detection (VSD). The former one simulates the categorical characteristics of preattentive vision in summarizing homogeneous regions. And the latter one simulates the visual center-surround characteristics to spot salient regions. This two-part information is further combined to guide visual search of specific document contents. Initial experimental results show that the computation of VSC and VSD results are quite adaptive and highly complementary, which is helpful for robust segmentation of various document images.

The rest of the paper will be arranged as follows. In section 2, we introduce our computational model for preattentive visual guidance. The implementation of VSC and VSD processes is illustrated in details in section 3 and section 4 respectively. Experimental results are demonstrated in section 5, followed by the conclusion and discussion in section 6.

2 Computational Model for Preattentive Visual Guidance

Human vision is highly robust in capturing useful objects out of distracter elements in the visual field. Such adaptive power is attributed to the visual guidance mechanism deployed in the primary visual cortex. That is, the high-level cognitive functionality is not to be executed at every position in the scene. On the contrary, the visual guidance mechanism serves as a system bottle-neck to direct the interpretation of the whole scene [11]. Until now, most researchers agree that the major work of preattentive visual guidance is contributed by low-level neurons, which investigate simple visual properties throughout the scene in very short instant simultaneously [12]. Psychophysical experiments have shown that some visual searching task can be finished accurately within 200~250 milliseconds, which is too short for serial attention to be involved. The visual properties affirmed in such experiments are called *pre-attentive* [12].

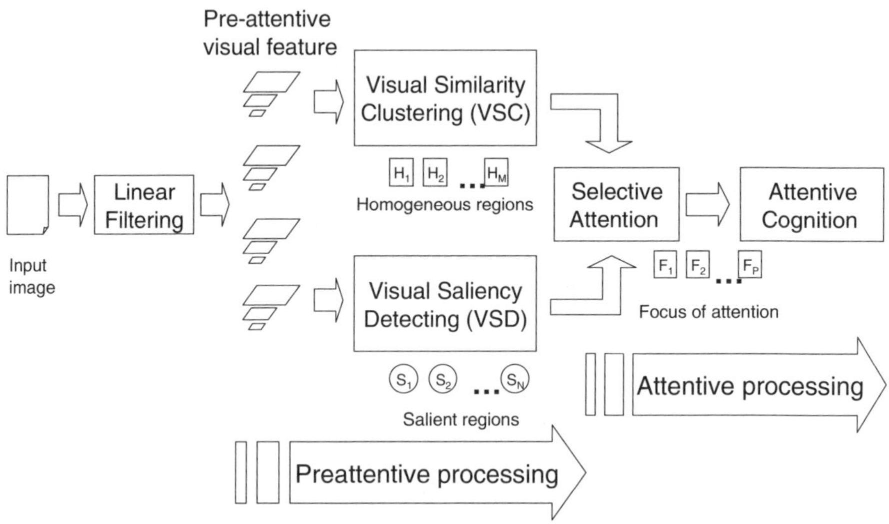

Fig. 1. Our computational model for preattentive visual guidance in DIA

In this paper, we notice two types of visual hints that can be discerned in the preattentive vision: visual similarity and visual saliency. Mathematical representation of the former has been conjectured by Julesz and further proven by psychophysical and computational experiments [13, 14, 15]. Also, computational models for the latter has also been focused in recent years by Treisman, Ullman, Koch and Itti etc. [11, 16, 17, 18]. Motivated by these two streams of research efforts, we propose in this paper a computational model characterizing the preattentive visual guidance mechanism in document image analysis. As shown in figure 1, the input image is first decomposed by series of preattentive feature channels. Then these separated feature maps will go through two independent processes: visual similarity clustering (VSC) and visual saliency detection (VSD). The VSC process categorizes homogeneous regions by measuring quantitative visual similarity. On the other hand, the VSD process points out salient regions different from their neighbors. Both of these two processes compute only preattentive visual properties. In a document image, the VSC results are useful in aggregating homogeneous text contents; while the VSD results provides us with hints to find out conspicuous titles, separating lines, edges and graphics etc. In the following stage called selective attention, which is oriented to specific object extraction task, a series of focuses of attention (FOA) will be determined by consulting the VSC and VSD results. The final attentive cognition of various document contents will be executed in these selective FOAs serially.

3 Visual Similarity Clustering

To discuss the subjective visual similarity perception, we must first find out a numerical way to measure it quantitatively. Before the studies on human vision system, this problem had no generic solution. The early characteristic features for texture were merely proposed according to mathematical convenience or task dependant heuristics [19]. Later, physiological research on visual cortex revealed the spatial/frequency representation of image in human vision system. Such discovery inspired researches to use spatial/frequency localized filters as generic texture feature extractors. In 1995, Heeger and Bergen accomplished the first texture synthesis experiment by matching the histograms of image pyramids between the synthesized and target images [14]. Their experiments reveal that image pairs with closely matched histograms also share similar visual appearance. Later, Zhu etc. offered a stricter mathematical framework to ensure the convergence of histogram matching and further argued that marginal histogram statistics pooled from Gabor filters can serve as generic features to characterize various homogeneous textures [15, 20]. Based on Zhu's work, Liu developed the quantitative measurement of visual similarity between two image patterns, based on the χ^2-distance of Gabor histogram features [19]. His work was applied in texture classification.

In our work, we are interested to use visual similarity measurement in document image segmentation, which is a variant case of texture classification. So the first problem is how to characterize visual patterns in the document images by representative texture features. And second, the similarity-based segmentation should be self-adaptive to various document images. Since the definite texture classes can not be statically defined among different document images (even the pattern for text contents varies greatly in different pages), the best way to accomplish adaptability is through dynamic clustering. Therefore, our major implementation problem in VSC is: first, to select a series of representative filters and histogram bins to extract the Gabor histogram features from document images; and second, to derive a mathematical plausible way to cluster the features so as to obtain adaptive segmentation results.

To solve the first problem, we must investigate in what scale that the document contents will illustrate homogeneous visual textures. Generally speaking, font sizes of the perceptible text contents in document images vary from 2 pts to 32 pts (we regard that characters with sizes bigger than 32 pts can not be treated as homogeneous texture). In the very low resolution, text contents demonstrate line pattern and character blob pattern. With increasing resolution, the character stroke pattern will gradually emerge. These three patterns can be well captured by Gabor and Laplacian of Gaussian filters. Therefore, we first prepare a bank of filters containing Gabor filters (denoted as ***G***) and Laplacian of Gaussian filters (denoted as ***LoG***) covering consecutive scales and orientations in frequency domain. The mathematical expressions of these two kinds of filters are as follows:

$$Gabor(x, y \mid T, \theta) = \exp\{-\frac{1}{2T^2}[4(x\cos\theta + y\sin\theta)^2 + (-x\sin\theta + y\cos\theta)^2]\} \cdot \exp\{-j\frac{2\pi}{T}(x\cos\theta + y\sin\theta)\} \quad (1)$$

$$LoG(x, y \mid T) = C(x^2 + y^2 - T^2)\exp(-\frac{x^2 + y^2}{T^2}) \quad (2)$$

To capture the three typical texture patterns of text contents from 2 pts to 32 pts, we choose parameters $T = \sqrt{2}, 2, 4, 6, 8, 10$ and $\theta = 0^\circ, 45^\circ, 90^\circ, 135^\circ$, which results in a filter bank $\mathcal{B}$ consisting 24 ***G*** filters (only use cosine components) and 6 ***LoG*** filters. To further select representative filters from these 30 filters, a visual similarity testing experiment is performed. That is, we choose a sufficient set $\mathcal{S}$ from $\mathcal{B}$, with whose histograms we can fully characterize the visual appearance of the referenced image $\boldsymbol{I}_{\text{obs}}$, which we pick up as typical visual pattern from document images. The filter selection process is presented in [21], in which we followed the Minimax entropy principle and used Markov Chain Monte Carlo sampling [15] to match the histograms between the synthesized and original images. By matching the histograms from more and more filter channels, the synthesized image become more and more similar to the referenced image. The experiment finally selects the following 13 filters to form the representative filter set $\mathcal{S}$:

1. $\boldsymbol{G}(\boldsymbol{T}, \boldsymbol{\theta})$, $\boldsymbol{T} = 2, 4$, and $\boldsymbol{\theta} = 0^\circ, 45^\circ, 90^\circ, 135^\circ$;
2. $\boldsymbol{G}(\boldsymbol{T}, \boldsymbol{\theta})$, $\boldsymbol{T} = 6$, and $\boldsymbol{\theta} = 0^\circ, 90^\circ$;
3. ***LoG***($\boldsymbol{T}$), $\boldsymbol{T} = 2, 4, 6$.

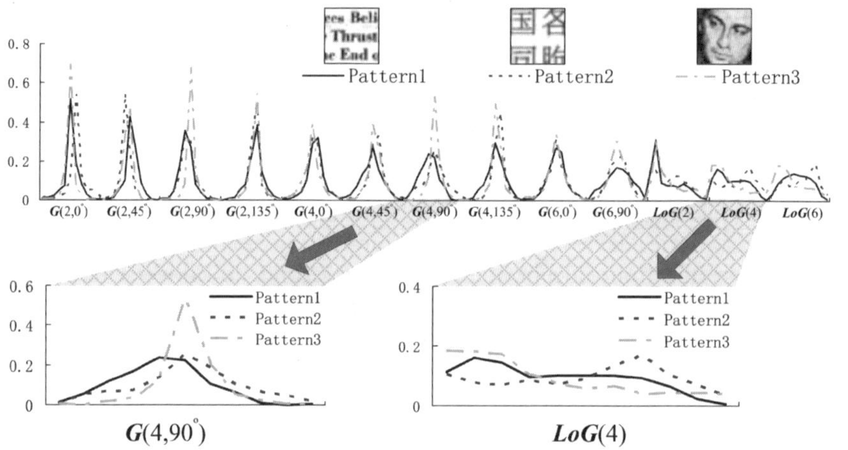

Fig. 2. GHF of different texture patterns, with the concatenated histograms of all 13 channels and the magnified histograms in two particular channels (***G***(4,90°) and ***LoG***(4))

To make the histograms extracted from different images comparable, we normalize the responses of each filtered image to the fixed range [-1, 1] before pooling histograms. In our experiment, the GHF vector H_υ for the site υ is calculated within a neighboring window of υ, where the window size we choose is 32. With 11 bins of histograms extracted from each filter channel, we construct a 143-dim Gabor histogram feature (GHF) vector for each site. Figure 3 compares the GHF vectors of different visual patterns extracted from document images.

For the second problem, we define the distance metric between two GHF vectors as their Euclidian distance, just for the convenience to perform K-means clustering.

$$D(H_{\upsilon_1}, H_{\upsilon_2}) = (\sum_i (h_{\upsilon_1}^{(i)} - h_{\upsilon_2}^{(i)})^2)^{\frac{1}{2}} \tag{3}$$

Another clustering parameter, that is, the initial class number K, is set to 4 in our experiment. This is empirically determined by observing that there are usually 4 types of contents in a document image: text, photograph, line drawing and white space. And also experiments indicate that setting K>4 will cause the homogeneous class corresponding to text contents to split into smaller classes. Therefore by setting K=4 initially we can conserve the homogeneity of text regions. As for the simple plain documents which probably contain less than 4 distinctive classes of visual patterns, we allow the clustering procedure to drop the empty classes.

After setting the distance measurement and initial state, the K-means clustering is ready to run. The clustered results are dynamic, depending on the specific contents of different documents. Therefore, we need to identify which class in the clustered results belongs to the text contents. To our empirical observation, texture features in the main body text contents usually demonstrate higher energy in the Gabor filter responses. Therefore, we calculate the following texture energy for each GHF vector as follows:

$$E_\upsilon = \sum_{i=1}^{|S|} E_\upsilon^{(i)} \tag{4}$$

Here, $E_\upsilon^{(i)}$ refers to the variance of filter responses in the ***i***th channel, which can be computed through the histogram. Then the texture energy E_k for the whole class of GHF vectors can be further estimated by counting the most frequent texture energy. By this means we can sort the K classes in descending order according to their texture energies (i.e., class 1 has the maximal texture energy). We select class 1 and class 2 as the candidate classes for text contents. In our experiments, for most tested document images, text contents occupy one of these two clustered classes.

4 Visual Saliency Detection

Compared with the top-down categorical VSC process, the VSD process undertakes a bottom-up investigation on how different a site is from its neighbors. Here we use the computational architecture proposed by Itti [18] to obtain a salient map for the input image. In [18], Itti computed saliency in three independent feature channels: the color channel, the intensity channel and the orientation channel. In our work, since the similarity of Gabor orientation features has already been investigated in the VSC process, we carry out visual saliency detection in only two feature channels: the color and the intensity channels (for gray scale image, only intensity channel is calculated).

The input image is first decomposed into one intensity and four color channels. Then multi-scale representation for each channel is constructed, using a Gaussian pyramid. The center-surround difference is calculated between different coarse scales (surrounded values) and fine scales (centered values), resulting in 12 feature maps in the color channel and 6 feature maps in the intensity channel. Finally, the color salient map, the intensity salient map and the overall salient map are calculated respectively by normalizing and combining these feature maps. Computational details can be found in [18].

5 Experimental Results

We perform several groups of experiments to test the adaptability of VSC and VSD in computing homogeneous regions and salient regions among various document images. These two kinds of information can be further utilized by other task-oriented modules to detect specific contents in document images. For example, one who is interested in extracting text lines can access the homogeneous regions in the VSC results. Another looking for titles, separating lines, edges and graphics etc., can access the salient regions in the VSD results. In the VSC process, it is obvious that with more semantic homogeneous contents categorized into the same class, the more layout segmentation can benefit from it. On the other hand, the more the salient regions are independent of the homogenous regions, the easier it is to find out the salient objects. Therefore, we pay attention to two criteria in evaluating the performance of our visual preattentive guidance computation: the region homogeneity in VSC and the complementary extent between the VSC and VSD results.

The first experiment is for complex newspaper images. Figure 3 shows the clustered results by VSC for 3 newspaper images scanned in 150 dpi. 4-class segmentation results are obtained for each sample, from which we can see that: the main body text contents in each sample occupy a major visual class stably. In the English sample, they belong to class 2 (dark gray); while in the Chinese samples, they belong to class 1 (black). It can be easily explained that when there is strong periodic texture pattern in the image (e.g., the halftone image in the English sample), text contents will not occupy the first class. Otherwise, they will occupy the first class. In figure 4, the pixels clustered as text contents are picked up separately to see the homogeneity of the clustered results particularly. As we see, the majority of text contents are successfully segmented. It should be mentioned that we have not added any spatial continuity constraints in the clustering; while the homogeneity is still satisfying, which indicate that our GHF features can really reflect visual similarity. It is interesting to see that the halftone patterns in the photographs also make them stand out as a unique visual class.

The second experiment is for simple plain document images. The experiment is repeated in both up-right and skewed samples to test the adaptability of VSC to skewness. Figure 5 shows the clustered results. Notice that they have been reduced to include only 2 classes.

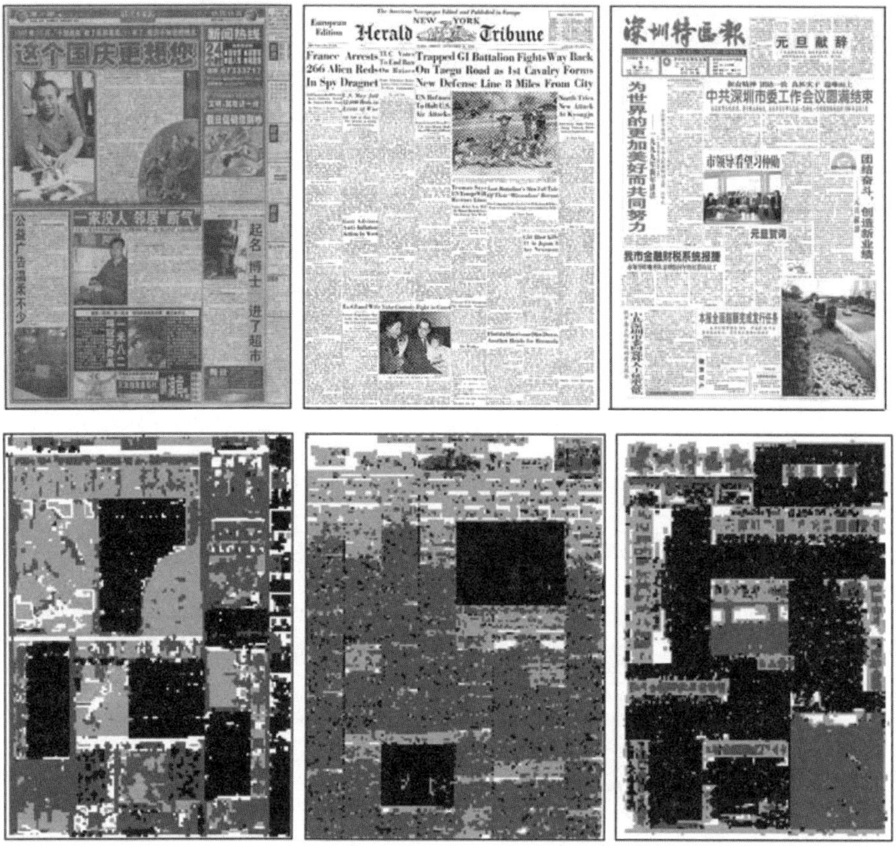

(a) (b) (c)

Fig. 3. Segmentation results in the first experiment, using K=4. The 4 pixel values: black, dark gray, light gray and white represent 4 clustered classes, sorted by their texture energy from high to low. (a) Segmentation result of a complex Chinese newspaper, with the body text occupying class 1. (b) Segmentation result of an English newspaper, with the body text occupying class 2. (c) Segmentation result of another Chinese newspaper, less complex, with the body text occupying class 1.

The third experiment compares the VSC and VSD results in the same image. Figure 6a shows the salient map calculated for a newspaper image. The gray scale values in it indicate the salient values detected in these pixels. Figure 6b shows a thresholded version of 7a. We can see that the main titles, separating lines, edges and boundaries pop out in the results. As compared with the homogenous regions shown in figure 6c (i.e., the same results in figure 5c), the VSD results are highly complementary to the VSC results and they reflect the discontinuous changes in the image.

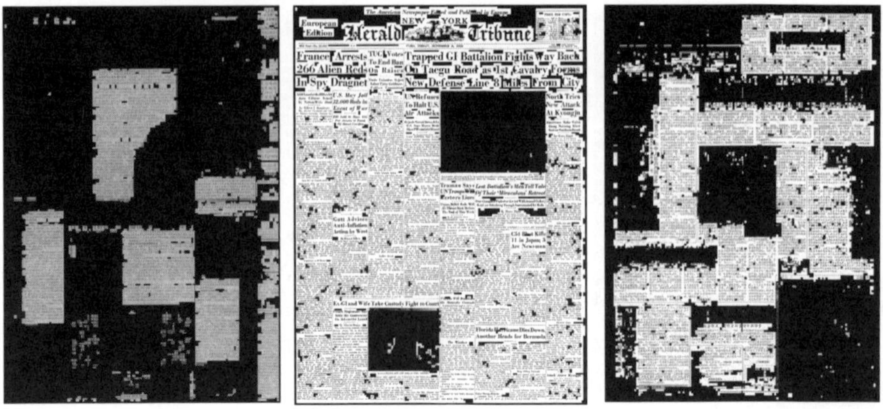

(a) (b) (c)

Fig. 4. Text contents extracted from the segmentation results in figure 4

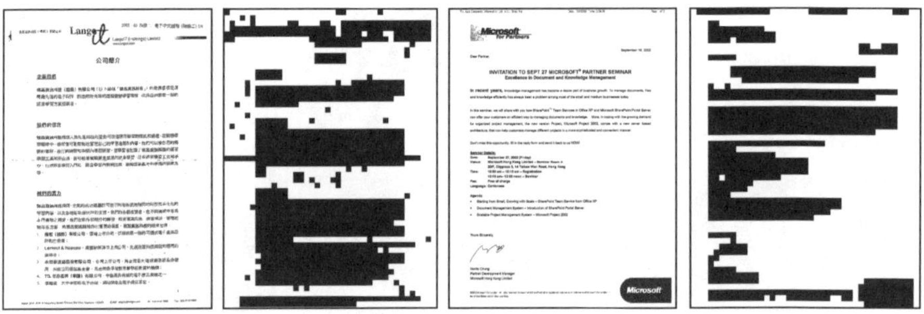

(a) (b) (c) (d)

Fig. 5. Segmentation results for simple plain documents. The algorithm automatically reduced class number K to 2 I n order to adapt the simple contents.

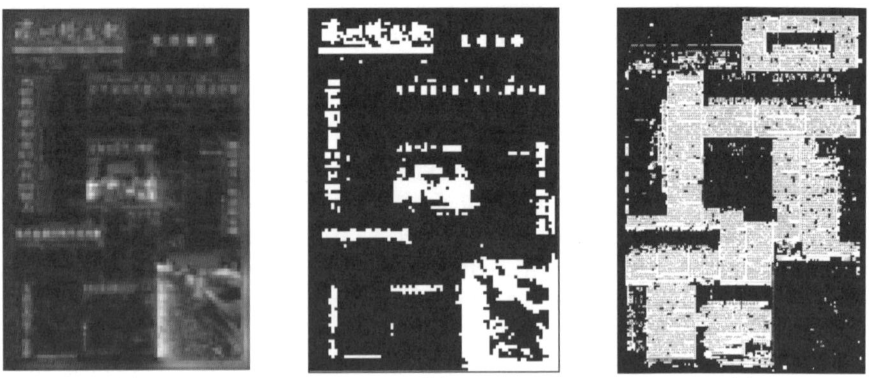

(a) (b) (c)

Fig. 6. Comparison of the VSD and VSC results. (a) salient map calculated by VSD; (b) the thresholded version of (a); (c) homogeneous text contents segmented from VSC results.

6 Conclusion and Future Work

We have demonstrated a computational method to implement preattentive visual guidance in document image analysis. Our ultimate goal is to achieve real adaptability for target segmentation in any type of document samples. The VSC computation is thus proposed to categorize similar contents in the image. And the VSD computation is introduced to simulate the detection of salient regions. Both of these two processes are proposed based on the current discovery from psychophysics experiments. Initial experiments show that the VSC process is able to cluster the image contents into visual homogenous regions, especially for the main body text contents. The clustered results are quite stable in distinctively different document samples. And the VSD results reveal the salient regions in document images, corresponding to major titles, separating lines and edges etc. Both results can be further utilized in a specific DIA task to extract and interpret different types of semantic contents. Being undertaken in a data-driven manner, these two processes both have the inherent potential to implement adaptability and the experimental results also support this fact.

Our future work will focus on two problems. The first is to develop more efficient visual similarity clustering algorithm. Since the current normalization method in VSC tends to diminish the deference between histograms, better normalization method and distance metric are needed to improve the numerical characterization of visual similarity. The second is to add more user-driven heuristic after the preattentive stage to extract task-oriented contents from the VSC and VSD results, with which the preattentive visual guidance can really benefit the adaptability of document image analysis.

Acknowledgement

This work is supported by the National Natural Science Foundation of China (project 60472002).

References

[1] Wong, K.Y., R.G. Casey, and F.M. Wahl: Document Analysis System. IBM Journal Res. Develop(1982). **26**(6): 647-656.

[2] Ittner, D.J. and H.S. Baird. Language-free layout analysis. in Proceedings of 2nd International Conference on Document Analysis and Recognition (ICDAR '93), 20-22 Oct. 1993, Tsukuba Science City, Japan, 1993//, 1993, pp. 336-40.

[3] Tang, Y.Y., S.-W. Lee, and C.Y. Suen: Automatic document processing: a survey. Pattern Recognition(1996). **29**(12): 1931-52.

[4] Nagy, G., S. Seth, and M. Viswanathan: A prototype document image analysis system for technical journals. IEEE Computer(1992). **25**(7): 10-22.

[5] Drivas, D. and A.Amin. Page Segmentation and Classification Utilizing Bottom-Up Approach. in Proceedings of the third International Conference on Document Analysis and Recognition, Aug. 14-16, 1995, pp. 610-614.

[6] Liang, J., I.T. Phillips, and R.M. Haralick: An optimization methodology for document structure extraction on Latin character documents. IEEE Trans on Pattern Analysis and Machine Intelligence(2001). **23**(7): 719-734.

[7] Jain, A.K. and S. Bhattacharjee: Text Segment Using Gabor Filters for Automatic Document Processing. Machine Vision and Applications(1992). **5**(3): 169-184.
[8] Jain, A.K. and Y. Zhong: Page Segmentation Using Texture Analysis. Pattern Recognition(1996). **29**(5): 743-770.
[9] Li, J. and R.M. Gray: Context-Based Multiscale Classification of Document Images Using Wavelet Coefficient Distributions. IEEE Trans on Image Processing(2000). **9**(9): 1604-1616.
[10] Chen, J.-L.: A simplified approach to the HMM based texture analysis and its application to document segmentation. Pattern Recognition Letters(1997). **18**(10): 993-1007.
[11] Itti, L. and K. C.: Computional Modeling of Visual Attention. Nature Reviews Neuroscience(2001). **2**(3): p194-203.
[12] Healey, C.G., K.S. Booth, and J.T. Enns: High-speed visual estimation using preattentive processing. ACM Transactions on Computer-Human Interaction (TOCHI)(1996). **3**(2): 107-135.
[13] Julesz, B.: Visual pattern discrimination. IRE Transaction of Information Theory(1962)(IT-8): 84-92.
[14] Heeger, D.J. and J.R. Bergen. Pyramid-based texture analysis/synthesis. in Computer Graphics Proceedings. SIGGRAPH 95, Los Angeles, CA, USA, 6-11 Aug. 1995, 1995, pp. p229-38.
[15] Zhu, S.C., Y.N. Wu, and D. Mumford: Minimax Entropy Principle and Its Application to Texture Modeling. Neural Computation(1997). **9**(8): 1627-1660.
[16] Treisman, A. and G. Gelade: A feature integration theory of attention. Cognitive Psychology(1980). **12**(2): 97-136.
[17] Koch C. and U. S.: Shifts in selective visual attention: towards the underlying neural circuitry. Human Neurobiology(1985). **4**(4): 219-27.
[18] Itti, L., C. Koch, and E. Niebur: A model of saliency-based visual attention for rapid scene analysis. IEEE Trans on Pattern Analysis and Machine Intelligence(1998). **20**(11): 1254-9.
[19] Liu, X. and D. Wang: Texture Classification Using Spectral Histogram. IEEE Trans on Image Processing(2003). **12**(6): 661-670.
[20] Zhu, S.C., Y.N. Wu, and D.B.Mumford: FRAME : Filters, Random fields And Maximum Entropy -- towards a unified theory for texture modeling. International Journal of Computer Vision(1998). **27**(3): 1-20.
[21] Wen, Di and Xiaoqing Ding: Visual similarity based document layout analysis. Journal of Computer Science and Technology(2006). **21**(3): 459-468.

Efficient and Robust Segmentations Based on Eikonal and Diffusion PDEs

Bertrand Peny, Gozde Unal, Greg Slabaugh, Tong Fang[1], and Christopher Alvino[2]

[1] Intelligent Vision and Reasoning
Siemens Corporate Research
Princeton NJ 08540, USA
[2] Section of Biomedical Image Analysis
Department of Radiology
University of Pennsylvania
Philadelphia PA 19104, USA

Abstract. In this paper, we present efficient and simple image segmentations based on the solution of two separate Eikonal equations, each originating from a different region. Distance functions from the interior and exterior regions are computed, and final segmentation labels are determined by a competition criterion between the distance functions. We also consider applying a diffusion partial differential equation (PDE) based method to propagate information in a manner inspired by the information propagation feature of the Eikonal equation. Experimental results are presented in a particular medical image segmentation application, and demonstrate the proposed methods.

1 Introduction

Content extraction from images usually relies on a segmentation, i.e., extraction of the borders of target structures. Accurate segmentation may be hampered by noise in the image acquisition, the complexity of the arrangement of the target objects with respect to the surrounding structures, and the computational cost of the algorithm used. In this study, a new algorithm to segment the boundary of a closed structure is developed based on ideas of propagation and diffusion of image information. Our work is motivated by anatomical structures such as lymph nodes, (see Figure 1), whose extraction from medical images, such as Magnetic Resonance (MR) images, is an important task for subsequent quantitative analysis. Clinically useful segmentations should be fast and accurate, so that quick and precise interpretation of the anatomical structures can be obtained.

Segmentation methods based on information propagation have been performed using the fast marching algorithm. For example, in Deschamps et al. [1], simultaneous propagations are performed to estimate two potentials between two points to extract a path in a vessel. The minimal paths between two points p_0 and p_1 are computed by simultaneous propagations from the two points until they meet at a common point p_2, and by back-propagating from p_2 to both p_0 and p_1, then joining the two paths. They also described an approach to build a path given only a starting point and a given path length to reach. While this approach is suitable for the extraction of tubular structures, our goal

N. Zheng, X. Jiang, and X. Lan (Eds.): IWICPAS 2006, LNCS 4153, pp. 339–348, 2006.

is different. Although we also make use of two distance maps, we do not need to extract a minimal path through a back-propagation from the point where the two fronts meet, but we seek for the result of the competition of the two fronts in reaching a given point. Similarly, Cohen et al. [2,3] used a fast marching algorithm for segmenting tubular structures like vessels, incorporating geodesic distance of the points on the propagation path to the seed point as a freezing measure. Similarly, a multiphase fast marching algorithm was utilized in [4], where all distinct regions are propagated simultaneously according to their respective velocities, which depend on posterior probability densities of each region.

There are also similarities between watershed algorithms and the fast marching algorithms. The Eikonal PDE has been used in [5] for modeling watershed segmentation that is constructed by flooding the gradient image. Different segmentation results have been obtained by changing the flooding criteria [6] such as constant height, area or volume. A form of diffusion has been used for image segmentation in [7] by a random-walker concept. This technique differs from our approach in that it was introduced in a graph theoretic framework [8], and formulated as a linear system of equations solved through conjugate gradients.

In this paper we present four methods. The first three methods compute distance functions treating image edge or image gradient information as locally slower to propagate information or as high local distance. These three methods employ the Eikonal equation and thus can be computed rapidly by the fast marching algorithm. Inspired by the same distance ideas, we also present a fourth method based on diffusion PDEs, in which edge information is propagated from the interior or exterior of the structure.

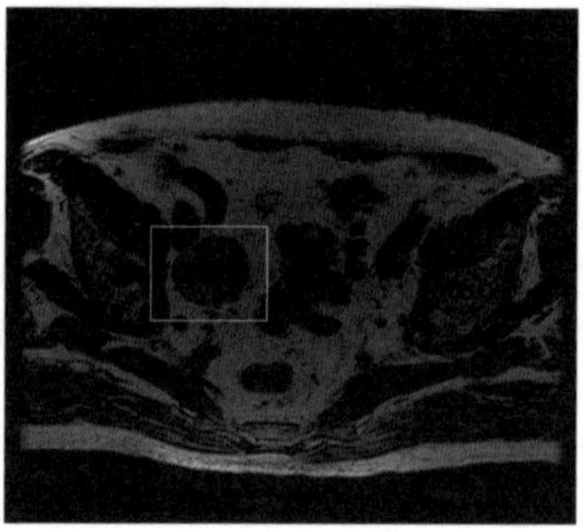

Fig. 1. Example of an MR image with a region of interest (ROI) around a lymph node

2 Segmentation by Interior/Exterior Distance Competition

The first step in the proposed segmentation method is to compute two distance functions. One distance function represents the distance of any point in the image domain to the nearest of a set of prespecified points interior to the structure and the other distance function represents the distance of any point in the image domain to the nearest of a set of prespecified points exterior to the structure. We will defer choice of the prespecified interior and exterior points until later, but for now we will state that they should respectively be clearly inside and outside the boundaries of the target structure. For instance a rectangular region of interest (ROI), completely surrounding the desired structure, whose borders are exterior points and center are interior points, can be selected. The local distance depends on the image intensity variation of the region that we want to segment. Regions that are more likely to be edges should be interpreted as regions in which distance information propagates more slowly. This idea will be implemented in several different ways. In the first, we weight the distance function directly on the binary map resulting from an edge detection on the image, for instance using a Canny edge detector. Edges in the edge map correspond to obstacles when the distance function is computed. The second method generalizes the first method, by defining the local distance as the gradient magnitude of the image. The third method combines the different weights on the distance function. The fourth method in inspired by distance propagation ideas and uses a diffusion PDE as will be explained.

The first three methods comprise a propagation of information using a weighted shortest distance, they can be implemented by solving an Eikonal PDE. To achieve fast computation of the two different distance functions, we used the fast marching algorithm. Our fourth idea requires a diffusion PDE as we will explain. The next subsections describe briefly the fast marching algorithm, how to adapt it to fit our ideas, and the diffusion method.

2.1 Method

The fast marching algorithm [9] is designed to compute the position of a propagating front with position varying speed given by the function $F > 0$. Let a function $D : \Omega \in \mathbb{R}^n \longrightarrow \mathbb{R}$ describe the arrival time of the front when it crosses each pixel (x,y), where $n = 2$ for an image function, $n = 3$ for an image volume. Fast marching solves the Eikonal equation which can be represented by

$$|\nabla D| = F, \quad D = 0 \text{ on } G$$

where G is a prespecified subset of $\mathbb{R}^n$.

If the speed function F is constant, then D represents the distance function to G. In our segmentation method the speed of the motion will be selected differently based on intensity variation as explained previously.

Our method proceeds as follows:

1. Compute the two distance functions: one for the interior by setting $G = D^i$ and the other for the exterior by setting $G = D^e$ needed in our segmentation algorithm.
2. Set up the image information propagation algorithm either through a propagation operation with fast marching or through a diffusion equation. The starting points set are the set of seeds, which we are sure that they belong to the background that surrounds the structure to segment (*Known* points). These are the boundary conditions for both the Eikonal PDE and the diffusion PDE.

   The Eikonal PDE:

   – In fast marching [9], after we label the *Known* pixels, pixels that are neighbors of the already *Known* points are labeled as *Trial*. All other image pixels are labeled as *Far* points.

- Exterior: Run the fast marching algorithm by computing the weighted L^1 distances , where the specific weights will be explained in the next subsections. The value of each pixel then corresponds to the distance to the exterior set and is denoted as D^e.
- Interior: Run the fast marching a second time for the interior set to obtain distance function D^i. The method starts this time with interior points as *Known* set.

Similarly, the diffusion PDE is solved twice with two different set of boundary conditions to obtain two distance functions D^i and D^e at its steady state solution.

3. The region interior is considered the set of points where the interior distance is less than the exterior distance, i.e., $\{(x, y) : D^i(x, y) < D^e(x, y)\}$

The different weights of the distance function as well as the diffusion are explained in the following sub-sections.

2.2 Fast Marching with Edge Map

Our first approach is to compute the distance function where edge pixels represent points where the information is propagated slowly in the shortest path between a pixel and the starting set of points, G. The Eikonal equation then transforms to:

$$|\nabla D| = (1 + \text{Edge Map})\,. \tag{1}$$

Any edge detection algorithm with binary output can be used to obtain the edge map. In our results, we use a Canny edge detector. In the fast marching algorithm the edge pixels are marked as having infinity as their initial distance and are labeled as *known*. In this way they will not be processed during the distance function computation. The first column in Figure 2 depicts the two distance functions computed by starting from both the interior and the exterior seed points.

2.3 Fast Marching with Gradient

In the second method, we treat regions with high gradient magnitude as having high local distance, and regions with low gradient magnitude as having low local distance. The Eikonal equation then takes the form:

$$|\nabla D| = (|\nabla I|) \tag{2}$$

The second column in Figure 2 depicts the two distance functions computed in this way.

2.4 Diffusion Equation

The linear heat equation on a function D is given by $\frac{dD}{dt} = \Delta D$ with initial conditions $D(x, y)|_{t=0} = D_0(x, y)$. A finite difference approximation to this equation for $n = 2$,

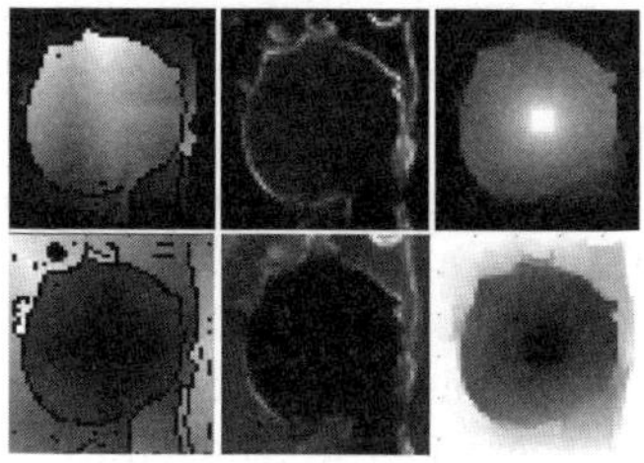

Fig. 2. Rows 1. Exterior distance; 2. Interior distance function. Columns 1. with edge map; 2. with gradient; 3. with diffusion.

that is obtained by implementing a forward Euler numerical scheme with the maximally stable time step is,

$$D(x,y) = \frac{1}{4}D(x+1,y) + \frac{1}{4}D(x-1,y) + \frac{1}{4}D(x,y-1) + \frac{1}{4}D(x,y+1)\,, \tag{3}$$

hence diffusing edge information from the boundaries towards the non-boundary regions.

Inspired by the Eikonal equation and fast marching techniques, where we propagate the information from the boundaries or the seeds of the domain Ω towards unlabeled points, diffusion equations can also be utilized for segmentation with a similar twist for creating two smooth distance functions for the interior seeds and the exterior seeds. To introduce image dependent terms to the diffusion equation, our intuition is that the diffusion takes the path of least resistance, that is the path where the one-sided image gradient in a given direction is low. The definition of the four one-sided image gradients or sub-gradients around a pixel are given by

$$I_x^-(x,y) = I(x,y) - I(x-1,y),\ I_x^+(x,y) = I(x+1,y) - I(x,y)$$
$$I_y^-(x,y) = I(x,y) - I(x,y-1),\ I_y^+(x,y) = I(x,y+1) - I(x,y)$$

We can create an image-based discrete diffusion equation by introducing the image-driven weights to the discrete Laplacian equation as follows,

$$D(x,y) = \frac{w^E}{\sum w^i}D(x+1,y) + \frac{w^W}{\sum w^i}D(x-1,y) + \frac{w^N}{\sum w^i}D(x,y-1) + \frac{w^S}{\sum w^i}D(x,y+1), \tag{4}$$

$$w^E = e^{-\beta(I_x^+)^2},\ w^W = e^{-\beta(I_x^-)^2},$$
$$w^N = e^{-\beta(I_y^-)^2},\ w^S = e^{-\beta(I_y^-)^2},\ i \in \{E,W,N,S\}.$$

Hence, using the set of seeds for the exterior region and the interior region as two distinct set of boundary conditions, we estimate the two distance functions D^e and D^i

corresponding to the exterior and interior after a set amount of diffusion time. Similar to our approach using Eikonal equation, we form the segmentation map by taking the minimum of the distance functions at each point. The last column in Figure 2 depicts the resulting distance functions estimated by the diffusion method.

This image-weighted diffusion we seek for our distance function D is similar in spirit but also quite different in the basic idea and the application from the work of Perona-Malik et al. [10] who used anisotropic diffusion for filtering images respecting image gradient directions. Using a similar weighted diffusion equation based on image gradients $\partial I/\partial t = \nabla \cdot (w(|\nabla I|)\nabla I)$, they actually solve for the image function I not the distance function D as we do.

2.5 Combined Method

In the second method explained in Section 2.3, which uses the gradient magnitude as the local distance function, we found some cases where the algorithm leaked. This is partly explained by the fact that for some interior regions, their edges are quiet weak, so the gradient is lower as expected. To prevent those leaks and increase robustness, one can combine the first two methods in Section 2.2 and 2.3. This corresponds to weight the distance function also by edge information. The method consists of first computation of the edge map as explained before to result in a binary image of the ROI. This binary image is then directly added to the gradient image by a factor α. The Eikonal equation then takes the form:

$$|\nabla D| = (|\nabla I| + \alpha * E)\,, \tag{5}$$

where E is the binary edge map. This will result in increased gradient effects where there are edges.

The algorithm described is very flexible in that it is possible to have different distance functions for the foreground and background set of points. This flexibility may help for segmentation of textured interior regions for example. One can add, to the foreground distance function, some interior intensity information, which will smooth the local gradient and decrease some texture or noise influence. We do not smooth the background distance function, because exterior region may include other structures. The idea is to compute the mean intensity of the foreground set of points, say I_{mean}. The image at each pixel p will then have a local weight of $(I\,[p] - I_{mean})^2$, which we add to the foreground Eikonal equation by a factor β:

$$\left|\nabla D^i\right| = \left(|\nabla I| + \alpha * E + \beta * (I - I_{mean})^2\right), \tag{6}$$

where E is the binary edge map and I_{mean} is the mean intensity of the foreground set of points.

3 Results and Conclusions

The Eikonal PDE-based approaches presented in this paper, as expected, are very fast. With the Eikonal PDEs (through fast marching), on a volume of interest of 60^3, the segmentation is completed in less than 0.76 seconds with the 3D algorithm, and in less than 0.03 seconds if run on single image slice, on a Pentium 4 2.4 GHz processor. With the diffusion PDE, the segmentation is completed in 1.75 seconds for a 2D implementation. Although we extended the diffusion approach to 3D as well, the computation times increased to order of 1 to 2 minutes, therefore, we have not utilized the diffusion-based approach for the 3D experiments.

Placement of interior and exterior seeds is flexible, and can be done by for instance a mouse brush. However, we opted a simple mouse drag operation on an image slice that sets exterior seeds in the form of a 2D rectangular border, then the interior seeds are automatically set to the set of pixels in the center of this rectangle. This type of 2D initialization is used in our both 2D and 3D experiments.

In Figure 3, sample segmentation results (labeled as blue contours) are presented for lymph node structures in MR images under different situations. By analyzing the results based on the edge map algorithm, in some cases the segmentation is not as precise as the other methods. The Canny edge detector propagates strong edges and discards the weak ones, and this leads to either edge noise (row 3, 4 and 5), or "holes" in the edge map (row 1). This will influence directly the distance functions and in turn the final segmentation. Still the result can be acceptable as an initialization to a more sophisticated segmentation algorithm. Those errors are reduced by our second approach that uses image gradient in the Eikonal PDE. The distances found are then smoother, and our segmentation matches the node contour better. In cases where a strong edge is situated near the node contour, the gradient method may be slightly attracted to it (rows 1 and 5), and comes from the fact that the gradient is a local intensity variation characteristic. Despite small incoherences, the results have very good quality. Finally the diffusion method performs well in strong edge neighborhoods, but easily smears the information when objects are merged, hence obtains a mid-way distance estimation (rows 1 and 3 in Fig. 3). This can be explained by the fact that the algorithm is based on a diffusion of intensity variation around pixels, so merged structures will affect the segmentation more than other structures in the neighborhood of the node. Finally our combined method optimizes the results, in difficult nodes. The edge information restrains the leak that we could see in the gradient method, for example row 3 and 5 in Fig. 3.

The results are confirmed by the statistics we found during our tests(see Table 1). We compute the mean of falsely rejected pixels (Type II error) and falsely accepted pixels (Type I error) on the resulting contours of the presented four segmentation methods compared with the manually delineated node contours. The very low value in the Type I error of the edge map method is explained by its conservative behavior due to binary edge information onto which the propagating front can get stuck. This implies that we missed part of the interior area, hence a high value for the Type II error. On the other hand the Gradient and Diffusion methods are more prone to leaks and have then a higher Type I error. Finally the combined method is a good compromise between leaking and conservative error. Of course this appreciation depends on how we want to use the segmentation and we may prefer one algorithm over another because of its evolution characteristics. We want to note that the ground truth of each node was drawn using

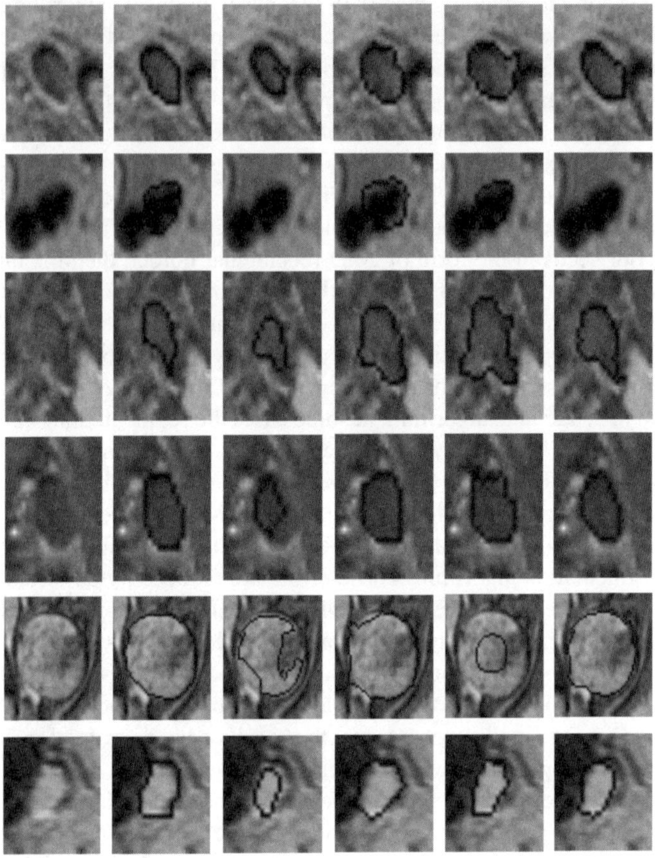

Fig. 3. Segmentation Results. Columns(a-f): a. ROI image; b. Node manually delineated; c. Edge Map Method; d. Gradient Method; e. Diffusion Method, f. Combined Method. ($\alpha = 10, \beta = 1$ in Eq.(6)).

Table 1. Error type I and II statistics over the Data Base (≈50 nodes)

	Edge Map Method	Gradient Method	Diffusion Method	Combined Method
Type I	0.015	0.247	0.256	0.081
Type II	0.453	0.115	0.189	0.257

a mouse and by our own learned interpretation from clinicians,where the boundaries should be, this may then cause some result discrepancies due to imprecisions.

Segmentation in 3D through Eikonal PDEs is easily achieved by extending the fast marching, and the gradient computations to the third dimension. Example results from two nodes are shown in Fig. 4.

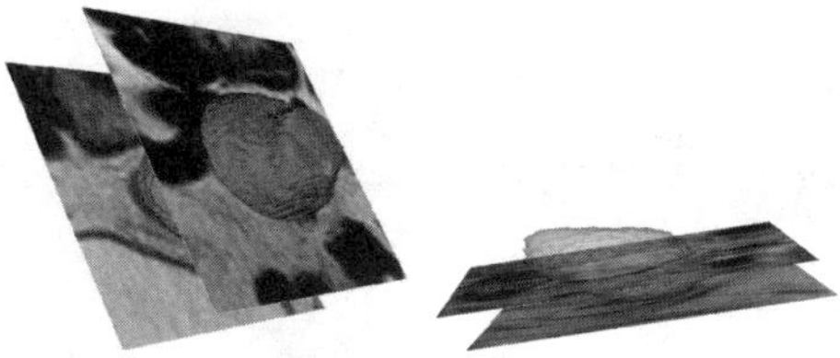

Fig. 4. 3D Segmentation of anatomic structures based on Eikonal PDEs

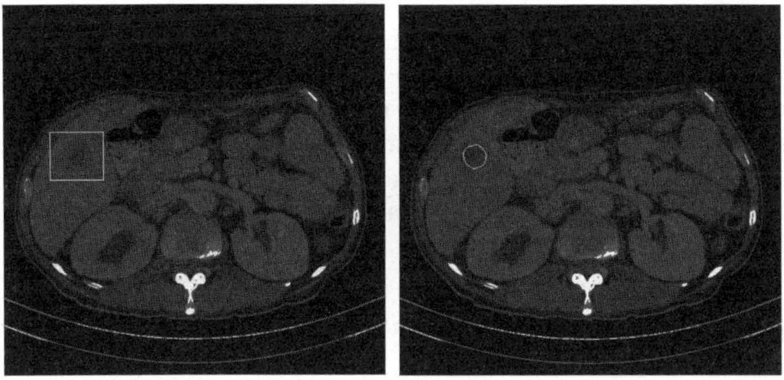

Fig. 5. A liver tumor is segmented using the Combined Algorithm on a CT volume

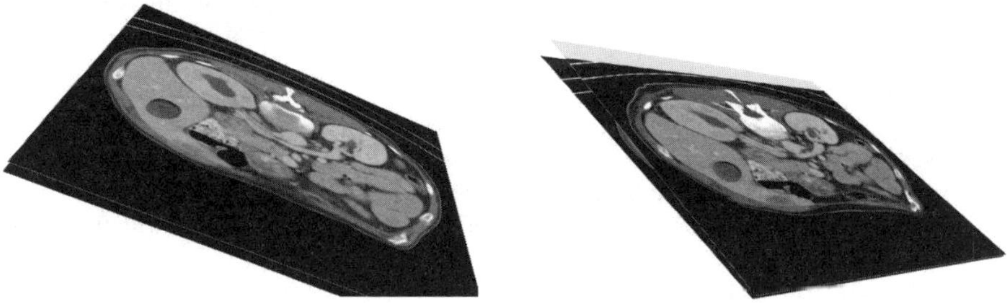

Fig. 6. 3D Segmentation results on CT sequences of Fig. 5

We perform the segmentation also on other type of images, like for example in Fig. 5 on Computed Tomography (CT) sequences to segment a tumor in the liver as shown on the right. The 3D tumor extraction results are shown in Fig. 6. The Fig. 7 is an example of a breast mass segmentation in an ultrasound image. As we can see, ultrasound images have speckle noise, that hampers segmentation, therefore we had to pre-process the image with high level of smoothing, to reduce it. The results show that our algorithm works for different types of images and may be tuned for applications other than lymph node segmentation.

In conclusion, we presented efficient and simple image segmentations based on ideas from the Eikonal and diffusion PDEs, by computing the distance functions for the

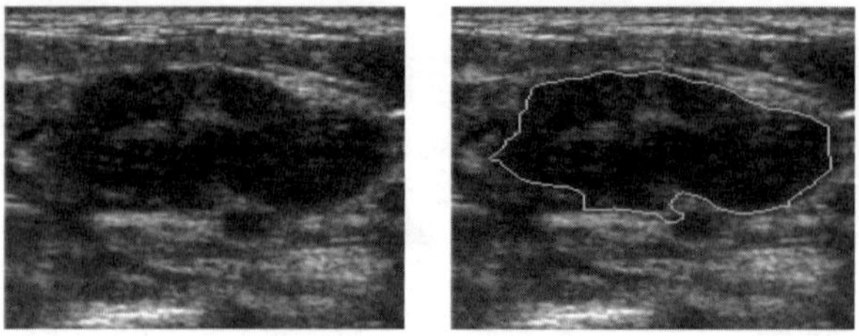

Fig. 7. A breast mass segmented using the Combined Algorithm on a Ultrasound image

exterior and interior regions, and determining the final segmentation labels by a competition criterion between the distance functions for reaching a given point. Each method has its pros and cons, according to the image characteristics, but our experiments demonstrated that among the presented methods, the combined fast marching method achieved a better speed vs. accuracy ratio, hence the best utility when compared to the other three methods.

Acknowledgements

We thank Dr. M. Harisinghani, Dr. R. Weissleder at Massachusetts General Hospital (MGH) in Boston, Dr. J. Barentsz at University Medical Center in Nijmegen, Netherlands, for clinical motivation, feedback and providing data, and Dr. R. Seethamraju for discussions, Dr. R. Krieg at Siemens Medical Solutions for support of this work.

References

1. Deschamps, T., Cohen, L.D.: Fast extraction of minimal paths in 3d images and applications to virtual endoscopy. Medical Image Analysis **5** (2001)
2. Deschamps, T., Cohen, L.D.: Fast extraction of tubular and tree 3d surfaces with front propagation methods. ICPR (2002)
3. Cohen, L.D., Kimmel, R.: Global minimum for active contour models: A minimal path approach. IJCV (1997)
4. Sifakis, E., Garcia, C., Tziritas, G.: Bayesian level sets for image segmentation. J. Vis. Commun. Im. Repres. (2001)
5. Meyer, F., Maragos, P.: Multiscale morphological segmentations based on watershed, flooding, and eikonal pde. Proc. Scale-Space (1999) 351–362
6. Sofou, A., Maragos, P.: Pde-based modeling of image segmentation using volumic flooding. ICIP (2003)
7. Grady, L., Lea, G.: Multi-label image segmentation for medical applications based on graph-theoretic electric potentials. In: ECCV, Workshop on MIA and MMBIA. (2004)
8. Boykov, Y., Jolly, M.: Interactive graph cuts for optimal boundary and region segmentation of objects in n-d images. In: ICCV. Volume 1. (2001) 105–112
9. Sethian, J.: Level Set Methods and Fast Marching Methods. CUP (1999)
10. Perona, P., Malik, J.: Scale-space and edge detection using anisotropic diffusion. IEEE Trans. Pattern Analysis, and Machine Intelligence **12**(7) (1990) 629–639

Local Orientation Estimation in Corrupted Images

Franck Michelet, Jean-Pierre Da Costa,
Pierre Baylou, and Christian Germain

LAPS – Signal & Image Team
UMR N°5131 CNRS – Bordeaux I University – ENSEIRB – ENITAB
351, Cours de la Libération – 33405 Talence Cedex – France
christian.germain@laps.u-bordeaux1.fr

Abstract. IRON is a low level operator dedicated to the estimation of single and multiple local orientations in images. Previous works have shown that IRON is more accurate and more selective than Gabor and Steerable filters, for textures corrupted with Gaussian noise. In this paper, we propose two new features. The first one is dedicated to the estimation of orientation in images damaged by impulsive noise. The second one applies when images are corrupted with an amplitude modulation, such as an inhomogeneous lighting.

Keywords: Image Processing, Orientation estimation, Anisotropy, Impulse noise, Amplitude modulation, IRON.

1 Introduction

For three decades, many works have concerned orientation estimation in images. Applications of orientation estimation concern, for example, texture characterization [4][8], anisotropic diffusion [11][13] or image segmentation [2].

Orientations have specific characteristics which have to be taken into account in the estimation process. First, orientation doesn't always exist. In case of uniform grey level images or isotropic textures, no orientation can be estimated. Besides, when orientation exists, it depends on the scale of analysis. Considering that, generally, statistical techniques can be used to derive large scale orientation from local orientation [1][7][2], we will focus on local orientation estimation.

Differential approaches [5][8] are conventional for local orientation estimation. They are based on the local computation of first or second order derivatives of all the points of the image. Nevertheless these methods fail if more than one single orientation appear at a given location. In such a case, the response of derivative operators results from a non-linear mixture of the true local orientations.

Other popular methods for orientation estimation are based on a set of oriented filters. Among them, we can quote Gabor filters [2] [3] and Steerable filters [6] [10]. Operator IRON (Isotropic and Recursive Orientation Network) is another example of an oriented operator [9]. It consists in an oriented network of parallel lines along which we compute a homogeneity feature. The output of this feature indicates the confidence in the tested orientation. For such methods, accuracy and selectivity both depend on the number of filters and on the size of their computing support. Exercised on synthetic and real images, IRON provides more accuracy, noise robustness and selectivity than Gabor or Steerable filters [9].

N. Zheng, X. Jiang, and X. Lan (Eds.): IWICPAS 2006, LNCS 4153, pp. 349 – 358, 2006.

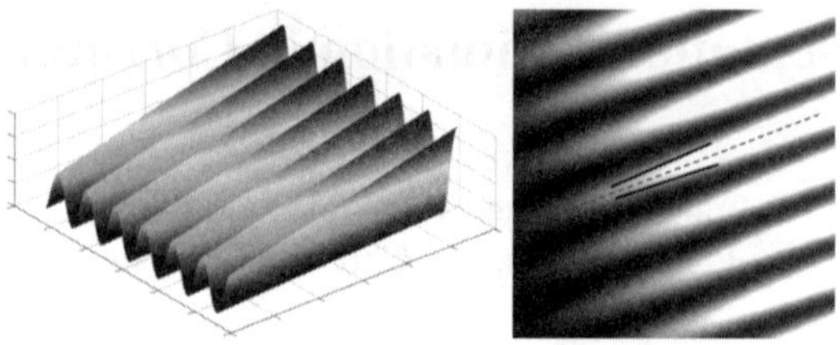

Fig. 1. Texture corrupted with amplitude modulation (profile function and grey level image). Isolevel lines orientation (solid lines), and original orientation (dashed line).

These methods are generally well suited for multiple local orientation estimation. Nevertheless, in some specific circumstances, they are unable to provide accurate and robust estimations. More particularly, we have found that when amplitude modulation occurs, orientation estimation becomes biased. Figure 1 shows a texture for which the sinusoidal profile is modulated with an affine function. This is the kind of images resulting, for example, from an inhomogeneous lighting. In this case, amplitude modulation affects the direction of isolevel curves which are not anymore equal to the perception of the orientation from the uncorrupted image. Therefore, all the classical orientation operators will provide us with an erroneous estimation.

When impulse noise occurs, classical operators also fail to estimate orientations properly. Figure 2a shows a directional texture corrupted with salt and pepper noise. Figure 2b shows the local orientation estimation in this picture, using Gabor filters. The size of the computing support is equivalent the size of the arrows. Indeed, the salt and pepper noise affects significantly the orientation estimation. Other estimators such as the Steerable Filters or Gradient masks would provide even worse estimations at the same scale.

In this paper, we propose two new homogeneity features for IRON, in order to deal with each of these problems. The first one relies on the Robust Homogeneity Function (*RHF*) instead of variance estimation, and will be effective in case of impulse noise.

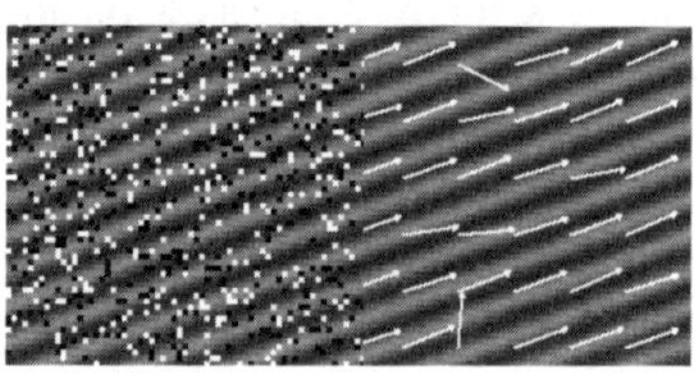

Fig. 2. Texture corrupted with salt and pepper noise and Gabor orientation estimation

The second one, based on the identification of local affine modulation parameters, solves the case of amplitude modulation.

In the second part of this paper, we shortly describe IRON, already introduced in [9]. In the third part, we propose two new homogeneity features. The first one is dedicated to images corrupted by impulse noise, and the second one to amplitude modulated directional textures. In the fourth part, we present and discuss some results.

2 The IRON Orientation Estimator

2.1 General Presentation

IRON was introduced in [9]. It is an oriented operator working in the spatial domain. Its principle is to compute a homogeneity feature along a network of parallel lines oriented θ. This feature depends on the grey levels of the pixels found on these lines.

Each network is made of *L* lines and each line consists in *p* points. The distance between each line and the distance between two consecutive points on a line are equal to the pitch of the pixel grid.

The network can be either symmetric or asymmetric. In the first case, the lines lie on both sides of the central point. The resulting orientation is estimated modulo π. In the second case, the lines lie only on one side of the central point thus providing with an orientation modulo 2π.

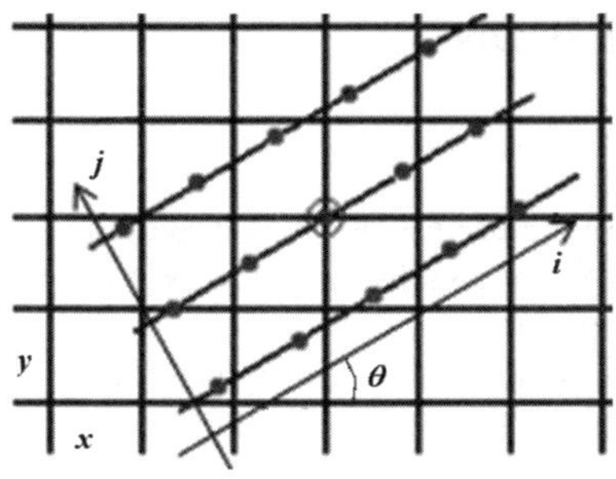

Fig. 3. IRON symmetric network of 3 lines and 5 points per line

Since the network points do not always line up on the pixel grid, the grey level values of the network points (Fig. 3) are computed using a bi-dimensional interpolation.

In [9], we have proposed an implementation based on the rotation of the image instead of the rotation of the network itself. This implementation reduces the computational cost of the interpolation stage.

2.2 Network Tuning

The parameters *L* and *p* act upon both the size and the shape of the network.

The shape of the network affects its selectivity and also its noise robustness. The size of the network depends on the scale of analysis. Increasing the number of lines allows increasing noise robustness. However, in the same time the selectivity of our operator decreases.

Another important aspect of IRON is the choice of the homogeneity feature. We have already proposed in [9] the following homogeneity feature *H*.

$$H(x,y,\theta) = \left(\varepsilon_0 + \sum_{j=1}^{L} \sum_{i=1}^{p-1} \left| v_{i,j,\theta} - v_{i+1,j,\theta} \right| \right)^{-1} \quad (1)$$

$v_{i,j,\theta}$ is the interpolated grey level on the ith point from the jth line of the network oriented θ (Fig. 3). ε_0 is a constant close to 0. It avoids the denominator to be null.

In the general case of an image corrupted with a Gaussian noise, the most appropriate function relies on variance estimation.

$$V(x,y,\theta)=\left(\varepsilon_0+\frac{1}{L(p-1)}\sum_{j=1}^{L}\sum_{i=1}^{p}\left(v_{i,j,\theta}-\frac{1}{p}\sum_{k=1}^{p}v_{k,j,\theta}\right)^2\right)^{-\frac{1}{2}} \tag{2}$$

For both features, the recursive implementation described in [9] is possible, thus reducing considerably its computational cost.

In case of more complex textures, for instance, when amplitude modulation or impulse noise occurs, other features can be defined in order to be more suited to the local configuration.

3 New Features for IRON

3.1 Robust Homogeneity Function

The classical homogeneity feature for IRON is based on variance estimation, and then it is more appropriate in case of a Gaussian noise. We propose here a new feature specifically designed to tackle impulse noise.

This new feature relies on a robust estimation of the homogeneity, using two medians instead of the two means in (**2**). It consists in computing along each line of the network "the median of the deviation from the median grey level".

For a network of *L* lines and *p* points per line, with orientation θ, we obtain the Robust Homogeneity Function *RHF*:

$$RHF(x,y,\theta)=\left(\varepsilon_0+\frac{1}{L}\sum_{j=1}^{L}\underset{i=1}{\overset{p}{M}}\left(\left|v_{i,j,\theta}-\underset{k=1}{\overset{p}{M}}\left(v_{k,j,\theta}\right)\right|\right)\right)^{-1} \tag{3}$$

where M(.) stands for the median operator and $v_{i,j,\theta}$ for the grey level of a point of the network.

Since the value of the *RHF* feature does not depend on the extreme values of the grey levels found on the network, it will be robust to a noise strongly corrupting a small number of pixels.

3.2 Affine Model Identification

We propose now a second feature for IRON. Its aim is to provide with unbiased orientation estimations when amplitude modulation affects the directional texture. Let consider a horizontal directional texture, corresponding to the following intensity model:

$$\hat{f}(i,j)=h(j).g(i) \tag{4}$$

where *h*(*j*) is a the profile function, and *g*(*i*) the modulation function.

In order to estimate the orientation $\hat{\theta}$ with IRON, we design a feature which minimizes the quadratic difference ε between the intensity $f(i,j)$ and the model:

$$\varepsilon(\theta) = \sum_{(i,j)\in V(\theta)} \left(h(j).g(i) - f(i,j)\right)^2 \tag{5}$$

$V(\theta)$ is the neighborhood used to compute IRON in the direction θ. L, the number of lines and p, and the number of points per line define the dimensions of this neighborhood.

Let us consider that the modulation is slow compared with the variation of the profile function h. Therefore, this modulation can be assumed to be locally linear and $g(i)$ can be approximated by an affine function: $g(i) = 1 + \alpha.i$.

The quadratic difference then becomes:

$$\varepsilon(\theta) = \sum_{i=1}^{p}\sum_{j=1}^{L}\left(h(j)(1+\alpha.i) - f(i,j)\right)^2 \tag{6}$$

The minimum value for ε is obtained when its derivatives, regarding h and α, are null.

$$\frac{\partial\varepsilon}{\partial h} = 2\sum_{i=1}^{p}\sum_{j=1}^{L}(1+\alpha.i).\left(h(j)(1+\alpha.i) - f(i,j)\right) = 0 \tag{7}$$

and

$$\frac{\partial\varepsilon}{\partial\alpha} = 2\sum_{i=1}^{p}\sum_{j=1}^{L} i.h(j).\left(h(j)(1+\alpha.i) - f(i,j)\right) = 0 \tag{8}$$

From these equations we obtain:

$$h(j) = \frac{\sum_{i=1}^{p} f(i,j) + \alpha\sum_{i=1}^{p} i.f(i,j)}{p + \alpha.p.(p+1) + \alpha^2\,\frac{p.(p+1).(2p+1)}{6}} \tag{9}$$

and

$$\alpha = \frac{\sum_{j=1}^{L}\sum_{i=1}^{p} h(j).i.f(i,j) - \frac{p.(p+1)}{2}\sum_{j=1}^{L} h(j)^2}{\frac{p.(p+1).(2p+1)}{6}\sum_{j=1}^{L} h(j)^2} \tag{10}$$

Let us define K_1, K_2, K_3:

$$K_1 = \sum_{j=1}^{L}\left(\sum_{i=1}^{p} f(i,j).\sum_{i=1}^{p} i.f(i,j)\right) \quad K_2 = \sum_{j=1}^{L}\left(\sum_{i=1}^{p} f(i,j)\right)^2 \quad K_3 = \sum_{j=1}^{L}\left(\sum_{i=1}^{p} i.f(i,j)\right)^2 \tag{11}$$

Introducing the following terms in (**10**), we finally obtain:

$$\begin{aligned}&\alpha^2\left(K_1(p+1)(2p+1)-3K_3(p+1)\right)\\&+\alpha\left(K_2(p+1)(2p+1)-6K_3\right)+3K_2(p+1)-6K_1=0\end{aligned} \tag{12}$$

Solving this equation allows us to determine the affine modulation function *g* and profile function *f* for each of the tested orientations. The minimum value of $\varepsilon(\theta)$ indicates the orientation for which the model fits the best with the image.

As this framework has been designed using an affine modulation model, it will apply perfectly for a texture affected by an illumination gradient (Fig. 1). We will see in the result section that it is also effective in case of a non affine modulation, while this modulation is slow regarding the amplitude variations of the profile function.

4 Results and Discussion

4.1 Impulse Noise

In order to compare the efficiency of various orientation estimators, we use synthetic textures corrupted by a salt and pepper noise. However, any kind of impulse noise could be considered as well. The profile function of the synthetic texture is a sine with period 6 pixels and θ=20° (Fig. 2). For each operator we compute the Mean Angular Deviation (*MAD*) in order to depict the effect on the noise on the orientation estimation.

$$MAD=\frac{1}{N}\sum_{(x,y)}\Delta\left(\hat{\Theta}(x,y),\Theta(x,y)\right) \tag{13}$$

where *N* is the size of the sample (i.e. the number of pixels *(x,y)* considered), $\hat{\Theta}$ stands for the estimated orientation and $\Delta(\theta_1,\theta_2)=\min\left(|\theta_1-\theta_2|,\pi-|\theta_1-\theta_2|\right),\theta\in[0,\pi[$.

We compute IRON symmetric with the RHF feature and compare the results with Gabor (quadrature) filters [2] [3] and Steerable (E4) filters [6] [10]. We test the following sizes for the computing support 11x11 and 21x21. All other parameters for Gabor and Steerable Filters are tuned in order to get the best estimations. In each case, 180 orientations are tested (angular step=1°) for 100 noise realizations, giving the following results.

Table 1. Angular error *MAD* for synthetic textures (sine profile function with period 6 pixels and θ=20°), corrupted with impulse noise

MAD (degrees)	Computing Support Size	Noisy Pixels: 5%	Noisy Pixels: 20%
IRON	11x11	0.6°	4.0°
(*RHF*)	21x21	0.0°	0.7°
Gabor	11x11	16.0°	24.0°
	21x21	0.6°	1.6°
Steerable	11x11	3.4°	0.9°
(*E4*)	21x21	14.2°	2.7°

Using the feature *RHF* with IRON gives the best estimations whatever the support size or the ratio of noisy pixels. Experiments with other textures, noises or computing support size confirm these results.

Figure 4 shows the results obtained with a real fingerprint image corrupted with impulse noise. The noisy pixel ratio is 20%. For all filters, computing support size is 15x15. This size is a fair compromise in order to obtain smooth orientation maps and to detect minutiae. All other parameters for Gabor and Steerable Filters are tuned in order to get the best estimations. 180 orientations are tested (angular step=1°).

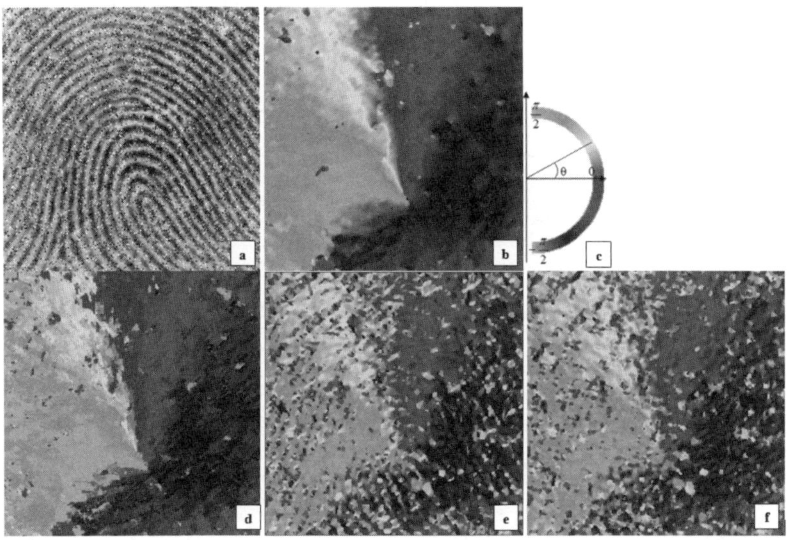

Fig. 4. a: Fingerprint image corrupted with 20% impulse noise; **b:** Orientation map without noise (IRON Variance); **c:** Color palette; **d:** Orientation map using IRON *RHF*; **e:** Orientation map using Gabor filters; **f:** Orientation map using Steerable E4 filters

Figure 4b is the reference orientation map, computed applying IRON with its original variance feature [9] to the uncorrupted version of Figure 4a. The map is smooth everywhere except around minutiae.

Figure 4d shows that the results obtained with IRON *RFH* on the corrupted image are very close to the reference map even if some errors appear.

On the opposite, Figure 4e and 4f show that Gabor and the Steerable filters are strongly affected by the impulse noise. Theses maps are very irregular and estimation error close to 90° are frequent.

4.2 Amplitude Modulation

For this experiment, we exercise IRON with affine model identification for three kinds of synthetic textures. The profile function of theses textures is a sine with period

10 pixels with various orientations. The first texture, called Tex1, is corrupted using an affine modulation with the same orientation as the texture in Fig. 1. Tex2 is corrupted using the same affine modulation but with a different orientation. Tex3 is corrupted using a non affine modulation: $g(i) = 1 + A_{\text{mod}}.\sin(2\pi.i/T_{\text{mod}})$ with $T_{\text{mod}} = 50$ pixels and $A_{\text{mod}} = 0.5$ (Fig 4a).

Table 2 shows the *MAD* values obtained with IRON, Gabor (quadrature) and Steerable Filters *E4*.

Table 2. Angular error *MAD* in case of amplitude modulation

MAD (degrees)	IRON (Affine)	Steerable (E4)	Gabor
Tex1	0.0°	1.03°	0.28°
Tex2	0.0°	1.01°	0.22°
Tex3	0.0°	1.08°	7.23°

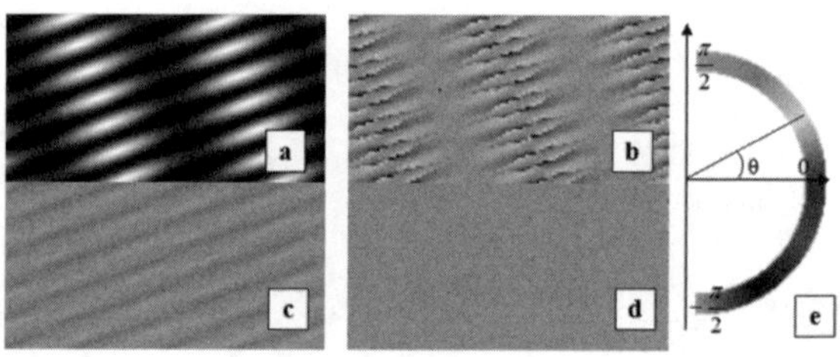

Fig. 5. a: Texture (Tex3) (non affine amplitude modulation); **b:** Gabor Filters; **c:** Steerable Filters (E4); **d:** IRON Affine; **e:** Orientation palette

Unlike Gabor and Steerable filters, our new feature appears to be insensitive to amplitude modulation, even in case of a non affine modulation (Fig. 5d).

Figure 6 shows the results obtained with an ancient engraving image corrupted with non affine amplitude modulation. The period of the modulation is 30 pixels, and its orientation is 30°. For all filters, computing support size is set to 15x15. All other parameters for Gabor and Steerable Filters are tuned in order to get the best estimations. 180 orientations are tested (angular step=1°).

Figure 6b is the reference orientation map. It is computed applying the classical IRON variance feature [9] to the uncorrupted version of figure 6a. Figure 6d depicts the results obtained with IRON Affine. As expected, the amplitude modulation does not significantly affect the corrupted image.

On an another hand, Figure 6e and 6f show that Gabor and the Steerable filters are strongly influenced by the modulation, even for the thin vertical lines.

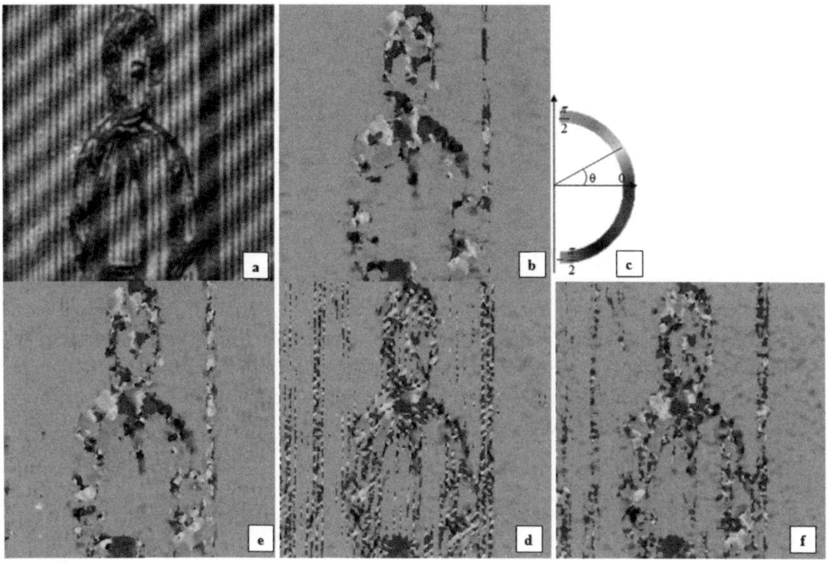

Fig. 6. a: Engraving image corrupted with amplitude modulation; **b:** Orientation map without noise (IRON Variance); **c:** Color palette; **d:** Orientation map using IRON Affine; **e:** Orientation map using Gabor filters; **f:** Orientation map using Steerable E4 filters

5 Conclusion

IRON is a general framework for single and multiple local orientation estimation. Previous works have shown that IRON is more accurate and selective than classical operators, for textures corrupted with Gaussian noise.

In this paper, we have introduced two new homogeneity features which allow us to adapt IRON when impulsive noise or amplitude modulation occurs. Exercised on both synthetic and real images, these new features show their efficiency to overcome such perturbations.

Therefore, knowing *a priori* the kind of perturbation which corrupts the image allows us to choose the appropriate feature and thus enhance the adaptability of the IRON network for single and multiple local orientation estimation.

Acknowledgements. Let us thank the FEDER InterReg IIIB (PIMHAI project) for its financial support.

References

1. Bigün, J., Bigün, T., Nilsson, K.: Recognition by symmetry derivatives and the generalized structure tensor, IEEE Transactions on PAMI, Vol. 26, no.12, (2004) 1590-1605.
2. Bigün, J., du Buf, J.H.: N-folded symmetries by complex moments in Gabor space and their application to unsupervised texture segmentation, IEEE Trans. on PAMI, Vol. 16, no. 1. (1994) 80-87.

3. Chen, J., Sato, Y., Tamura, S.: Orientation Space Filtering for Multiple Line Segmentation, Proc. of IEEE Conference on Computer Vision and Pattern Recognition, California, (1998).
4. Chetverikov, D., Hanbury, A.: Finding defects in texture using regularity and local orientation, Pattern Recognition, Vol. 35. (2002) 2165-2180.
5. Deriche, R.: Fast Algorithms for Low-Level Vision, IEEE Transactions on PAMI, Vol. 12, no.1. (1990) 78-81.
6. Freeman, W.T., Adelson, E.H.: The design and use of steerable filters, IEEE Trans. on PAMI, Vol. 13, no.9. (1991) 891-906.
7. Knutsson, H.: Representing Local Structure Using Tensors, Proceedings of Scandinavian Conference on Image Analysis, Oulu, Finland, (1989).
8. Le Pouliquen, F., Da Costa, J.P., Germain, Ch., Baylou P.: A new adaptive framework for unbiased orientation estimation, Pattern Recognition, Vol. 38. (2005) 2032-2046.
9. Michelet F., Germain Ch., Baylou P., Local Multiple Orientation Estimation: Isotropic and Recursive Oriented Network, Proc. of ICPR 2004, Cambridge, UK, (2004).
10. Perona, P.: Deformable kernels for early vision, IEEE Transactions on PAMI, Vol. 17, no.5. (1995) 488-499.
11. Perona, P., Malik, J.: Scale-space and edge detection using anisotropic diffusion, PAMI Vol. 12, no. 7. (1990) 629-639.
12. Rao, A.R.: A Taxonomy for Texture Description and Identification, Springer, (1990).
13. Terebes, R., Lavialle, O., Baylou, P., Borda, M.: Orientation driven diffusion, Acta Technica Napocensis-Electronics and Telecommunications, Cluj-Napoca, Vol 42, no.2, (2002) 20-24.

Illumination-Invariant Color Image Correction

Benedicte Bascle, Olivier Bernier, and Vincent Lemaire

France Télécom R&D Lannion, France
benedicte.bascle@francetelecom.com

Abstract. This paper presents a new statistical approach for learning automatic color image correction. The goal is to parameterize color independently of illumination and to correct color for changes of illumination. This is useful in many image processing applications, such as color image segmentation or background subtraction. The motivation for using a learning approach is to deal with changes of lighting typical of indoor environments such as home and office. The method is based on learning color invariants using a modified multi-layer perceptron (MLP). The MLP is odd-layered and the central bottleneck layer includes two neurons that estimates the color invariants and one input neuron proportional to the luminance desired in output of the MLP(luminance being strongly correlated with illumination). The advantage of the modified MLP over a classical MLP is better performance and the estimation of invariants to illumination. Results compare the approach with other color correction approaches from the literature.

1 Introduction

The apparent color of objects in images depends on the color of the light source(s) illuminating the scene. That is why changes in illumination cause apparent color changes in images. Because of this color constancy problem, image processing algorithms using color, such as color image segmentation or object recognition algorithms, tend to lack robustness to illumination changes. Such changes occur frequently in images due to shadows, switching lights on or off, and the variation of sunlight during the day. To deal with this, a color correction scheme that can compensate for illumination changes is needed.

Section 2 presents the state of the art for color correction. Section 3 details our approach, based on learning color correction using a modified MLP. The motivation for this is discussed, and the learning method is described. The approach is compared to using a classical MLP for learning color correction. Section 4 shows experimental results and comparisons.

2 Illumination Correction - State of the Art

Color in images is usually represented by a triband signal, for instance Red-Green-Blue (RGB). As discussed in the introduction, this signal is sensitive to

N. Zheng, X. Jiang, and X. Lan (Eds.): IWICPAS 2006, LNCS 4153, pp. 359–368, 2006.

changes in illumination. However, image processing techniques need to be robust to such changes. Therefore color needs to be parameterized independently of illumination. This can be done by parameterizing color with one or two parameters or by correcting the triband signal. A number of color parametrization and color correction schemes have been described in the literature.

An example of mono-band parametrization of color is hue (from hue-saturation-value, a.k.a. HSV) [GW01]. Examples of bi-band color parameterization are chrominances uv (from the YUV color space) [GW01] and the *ab* values from the CIE Lab color space [GW01]. These three color representations (H, uv or ab) are analytical and thus do not require learning. They are fast pixel-wise methods. They have a limited robustness to illumination changes.

An approach for estimating color invariants from images consists in calculating ratios of RGB components at a given pixel (R/B) or between neighboring pixels (such as $(R_{x_1}G_{x_2})/(G_{x_1}R_{x_2})$) [GS99]. This method is also pixel-wise and thus fast. These invariants are also very robust to illumination changes. However, a lot of information about the original color signal is lost, and reconstructing the original signal from these invariants is difficult.

A more sophisticated method has been proposed by [FDL04]. It estimates a mono-band invariant and is based on a physical model of image formation. It works globally on the image. In $(log(R/B), log(G/B))$ color space, an axis invariant to illuminant color is determined by entropy minimisation. The projection of colors onto a line perpendicular to the invariant axis gives corrected colors. The approach does not require learning and applies to any type of illuminant, but is relatively slow. It also requires that the image contains relatively few different colors and also includes many changes of illumination for each color.

Yet another approach explicitly estimates the color of the illuminant [FCB97]. A neural network estimated the chromaticity of the illuminant from the histogram of chromaticity of the image. The method works globally from the whole image and supposes there is only one illuminant for the entire image.

3 A Statistical Approach to Measure Color Invariants

3.1 A Modified Multi-layer Perceptron: Motivation

The motivation of this work is twofold: (1) to parameterize color compactly and independently of illumination by two invariants (2) to do it in real-time. Firstly, two parameters are needed to parameterize color with enough degrees of freedom to reconstruct a triband signal, given a luminance (or a gray level signal). Secondly, real-time processing (or more exactly video rate processing, e.g. processing 25 or 30 images per second) is also necessary for some applications. This means that methods such as [FCB97] and [FDL04] are out, since they work on the whole image. To obtain real time performance, pixel-wise processing is necessary. Hue-Saturation and uv (from YUV) and ab (from the CIE Lab color space) are three 2-parameter pixel-wise representations of color from the literature that can be calculated in real-time. However they lack robustness to illuminations changes. Mathematical and/or physical models could be used

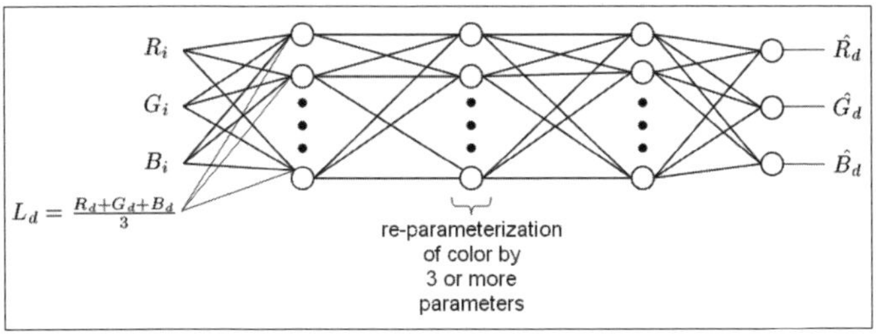

Fig. 1. A classical MLP with 4 inputs can be used to perform color correction. (R_i, G_i, B_i) is the input color. (R_d, G_d, B_d) is the desired output color, corresponding to the same color seen under a different illumination. L is the luminance of the expected output and is a direct function of the illumination. This fourth input neuron prevents the mapping to be learnt by the MLP from including one-to-many correspondences and thus makes it solvable. If the MLP contains a bottleneck layer with 3 neurons, then these perform a re-parameterization of RGB space. However the three color parameters estimated by the 3 neurons have no reason to be invariant to illumination.

to find a more robust parameterization [GS99]. They are very general, but lose information so that the original color signal is difficult to reconstruct from them. However, in practice, a limited range of illumination sources, and thus a limited range of illumination changes, are available in indoor environments. It is therefore interesting to use learning methods to find a color parameterization invariant to the "usual" illumination changes. While more restricted in their application, such parameters should also be more robust. Another interest of learning about typical illuminants in indoor environments is that it provides global a priori information about the illuminants, so the approach is not completely local (considering the fact that Land's Mondrian experiments showed that illuminant correction cannot be performed purely locally [LM71]). In practice, the lighting customarily found in home and offices comes from fluorescent lights, incandescent light bulbs and natural sunlight from windows. They tend towards the whitish and yellowish areas of the spectrum (very few bluish or reddish lights). These are the sort of illuminants that our approach will deal with.

Our learning method of choice has been neural networks and more specifically multi-layer perceptrons (or MLPs), for their ease of use and adaptability. The first architecture that comes to mind to estimate a re-parametrization of color robust to illumination changes is a odd-layered MLP with three input neurons, three output neurons, and three neurons in its bottleneck layer (plus a bias neuron of course). The 3 neurons of the bottleneck layer would reparameterize color. Or, if color reparameterization was not desired, and only color correction was aimed for, a generic MLP with 3 input neurons and 3 output neurons could be used, and the number of layers and neurons per hidden layer could be optimised. The measured (R,G,B) values corresponding to the same color viewed under two different illuminations can be given as input and ouput of the MLP to train it. However, several illumination changes are possible, and this means that the same entry could correspond to several different outputs. This is impossible for a MLP.

Therefore a classical MLP with 4 inputs needs to be used. To reflect the fact that the same input color can correspond to different output colors depending on illumination, a fourth input, the luminance desired in output, is added to the MLP. The architecture of such a MLP is shown in fig. 1 with a bottleneck layer to reparameterize color with 3 parameters. However, in such an architecture, the influence of color and illumination would be mixed in the 3 parameters. The coding of color independently of illumination is not garanteed.

To force the MLP to code color independently of illumination, the architecture of the traditional MLP is modified and a new architecture is proposed to force the network to separate color and luminance. The modified architecture is illustrated by fig. 2. The new MLP includes a compression layer with two neurons (λ, μ). During training, it learns from the inputs (R_i, G_i, B_i) and the desired outputs (R_d, G_d, B_d) to compress color into two parameters (λ, μ). However this is not a trivial compression network. The difference is that there is a fourth input, a context input, which is directly dependent on illumination, and which has its input point in the middle layer of the network (where (λ, μ) are calculated). This context input does not depend on the input (R_i, G_i, B_i) or the actual output $(\hat{R}_d, \hat{G}_d, \hat{B}_d)$ of the network, but on the desired luminance $L_d = \frac{R_d+G_d+B_d}{3}$ of the output of the network. With such an input, the network learns to reconstruct the desired output color using directly L_d as an input. Thus it learns to ignore the luminance of the input (R_i, G_i, B_i) and learns to estimate two variables (λ, μ) that are invariant to illumination, and related only to color.

The approach does not require any camera calibration or knowledge about the image.

3.2 Training the Modified Multi-layer Perceptron

As shown in fig. 2, the modified MLP includes 5 layers (this could be generalized to an odd number of layers). The input and output layers have 3 neurons each (plus an additional bias), for RGB inputs and outputs. The middle layer includes 3 neurons (two real and one virtual, excluding bias): their outputs are called λ, μ and L. The second and fourth layers have arbitrary numbers of neurons (typically between 3 and 10 in our experiments). The links between neurons are associated to weights. Neurons have sigmoid activation functions. The network includes biases and moments [Bis96].

A database of images showing the same objects under different illuminations is used to train the modified MLP. The illuminations are typical of indoor environments such as home and office: fluorescent lights, incandescent light bulbs and natural sunlight coming from windows.

A classic MLP training scheme based on backpropagation is applied, with two additional changes due to the structure of the modified MLP. As commonly done with MLPs, a pixel is randomly sampled at each iteration from the training set. Its RGB values before and after an illumination change (from real images) are used as input (R_i, G_i, B_i) and desired output (R_d, G_d, B_d) to the network. Propagation and back-propagation are then performed, with two modifications (as mentioned above). First, during propagation, the output L of the third neu-

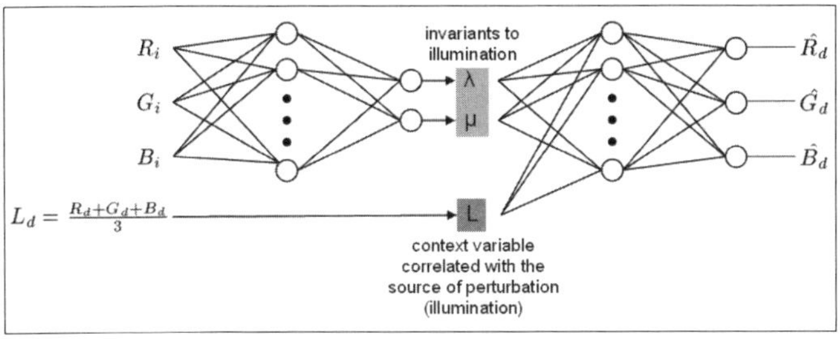

Fig. 2. A modified MLP for color correction and color invariant learning. (R_i, G_i, B_i) is the input color. (R_d, G_d, B_d) is the desired output color, corresponding to the same color seen under a different illumination. $L_d = \frac{R_d+G_d+B_d}{3}$ is the luminance of the desired output and is a direct function of the illumination. λ and μ are the color parameters invariant to illumination that the MLP is trained to estimate. $(\hat{R}_d, \hat{G}_d, \hat{B}_d)$ are the actual outputs of the network. Bias neurons are omitted from this figure.

ron of the third layer is forced to the value of the luminance corresponding to the desired output color, e.g. $L_d = (R_d + G_d + B_d)/3$. The idea is that the network is trained to do the best possible reconstruction of the RGB output (R_d, G_d, B_d) from the intermediate variables λ, μ and the imposed luminance L_d. Since L_d is a direct function of the illumination, the estimated λ and μ should be related to characteristics of color that are invariant to illumination. The second modification to training the MLP (compared to classic propagation and back-propagation) is that, during back-propagation, the error on the output L of the third neuron is not back propagated.

3.3 Use of the Modified Multi-layer Perceptron

The trained modified MLP can be used to correct color images. Each image pixel is propagated through the trained network to find the invariants λ and μ. An arbitrary luminance L is imposed on the pixel by forcing the output of the third neuron of the third layer to L. The output of the trained network then gives the corrected color. If a constant luminance $\bar{L}$ is used for all pixels in the image, an image corrected for shadows and for variations of illumination across the image and between images is obtained. The color correction can be tabulated for fast implementation.

The approach could be easily extended to a greater number of inputs and outputs than 3 or different inputs/outputs than RGB. For instance, YUV or HSV, or redundant characteristics such as RGBYUVLab could be used as inputs and outputs.

4 Image Correction Results

4.1 Experimental Conditions and Database

The network was trained using 546000 pixels. These were randomly sampled from 91 training images (6000 pixels per image), taken by 2 webcams (Philips

ToUCam Pro Camera and Logitech QuickCam Zoom). The training images are of different indoor scenes (and partial views of the outdoors through windows) under varying illuminations, from home and office environments. An example is shown in fig. 3. The variations of illuminations are caused by indoor lighting such as typically found in homes and offices (fluorescent lights and incandescent light bulbs) and natural sunlight (coming from windows). Testing was performed on other images taken by the 2 webcams used for training and by a third webcam, not used for training, a Logitech QuickCam for Notebooks Pro.

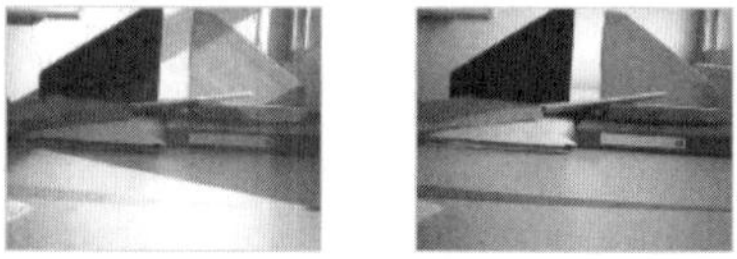

Fig. 3. Examples of images before and after an illumination change from the training database. This database includes examples of illumination changes typical of office and home environments.

In practice, using 8 neurons in the second and fourth layers of the MLP gives good performance. A gain of 1.0 was used, with a momentum factor of 0.01 and a learning rate of 0.001. Pixels that were too dark (luminance ≤ 20) or too bright / saturated (luminance ≥ 250) were not used for training.

4.2 Comparison with a "Classical" Multi-layer Perceptron

Table 1 shows that the modified MLP (fig. 2) performs better in reconstructing target images than a classic MLP (fig. 1). The reconstruction is done given the expected luminances L_d of the pixels of the desired target image.

Table 1. Mean error between reconstructed and target images for a "classical" MLP and the modified MLP presented in this article. The mean error was calculated using 748 320x240 test images (not in the training set). The error is averaged over the three color components (R,G,B).

	for a classical MLP	for the modified MLP
mean error (in pixel values, the pixel values going from 0 to 255)	10.47	5.54
relative mean error	4.11%	2.17 %

4.3 Invariant Estimation by the Modified MLP

Figure 4 shows the two invariants (λ, μ) learnt by the modified MLP and calculated on an image (see part (1) of fig 4) of unknown illumination. The two

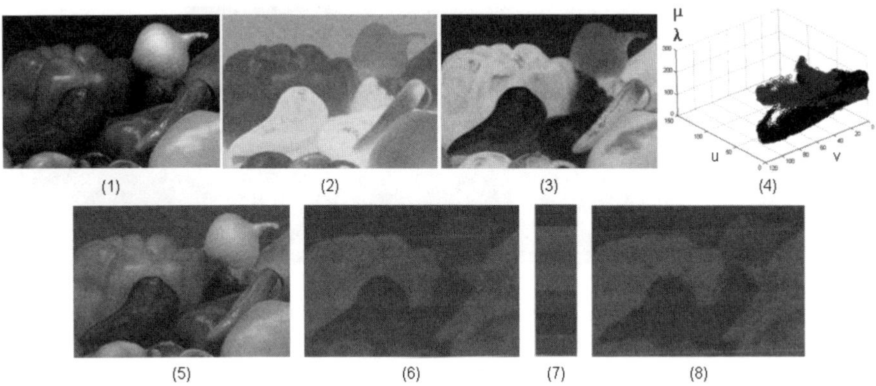

Fig. 4. Example of color correction learnt by the modified MLP. (1) is the original image (unknown illumination). (2) and (3) show the 2 invariants λ and μ estimated by the MLP from the image. (4) is the locus of the invariants in the uv chrominance space of image pixel values. (5) is the corrected image reconstructed by the modified MLP with the pixel luminance inputs set to values proportional to the pixel luminances in the original image (plus a constant). (6) is the corrected image reconstructed by the modified MLP with the pixel luminance inputs set to a constant value for all pixels. (7) shows the 7 color peaks found by mean shift [CRM00] in the corrected image shown in (6). (8) shows the resulting image segmentation.

invariants are seen in parts (2) and (3) of the figure. It can be seen that objects of similar color to the human eye have similar values of λ and μ. In addition, part (4) of fig. 4 shows the locus of the invariant values (λ, μ) in the image as a fonction of the chrominance values (u, v) (from YUV color space) of the image pixels. This plot demonstrates that the locii of the two invariants are not identical, and thus we have two invariants and not only one.

Part (6) of the figure shows the corrected image estimated by the modified MLP from the two invariants (λ, μ) and a constant luminance input over the image. Much of the influence of shading and variations of illumination across the image is removed, apart from specularities (white saturated areas) which are mapped to gray by the network. Indeed areas of similar color to the human eye in the original image (despite shading and illumination) have much more homogeneous color in the corrected image. This can be further seen by performing mean-shift based color segmentation [CRM00] on the corrected image. Seven areas of uniform color are readily identified and segmented (see part (7) and (8) of fig. 4) from the corrected image. They correspond roughly to what is expected by a human observer. This example illustrates that our modified MLP successfully learns a parameterization of color by two parameters that are invariant to illumination.

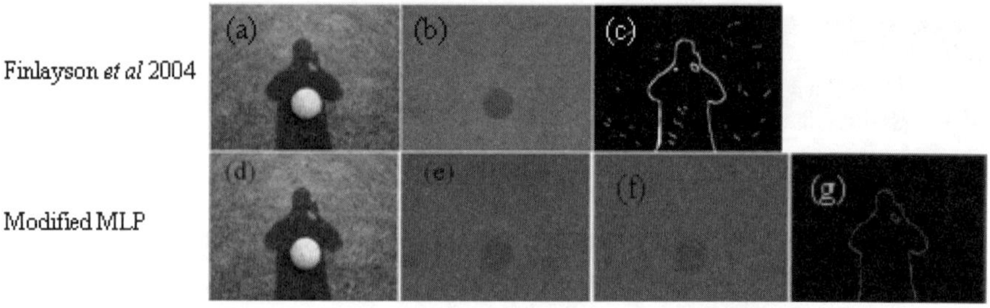

Fig. 5. Comparison of the pixel-wise color correction by the modified MLP presented in this paper and the whole-image color correction method of Finlayson *et al* [FDL04]. Application to shadow detection. Example I. (a) and (d) original image. (b) invariant image obtained using the method of [FDL04]. (c) shadow edges estimated from (b). (e) corrected image estimated using the modified MLP. (f) and (g) results of mean shift color segmentation [CRM00] from (e). (g) shadow edges estimated from (f).

4.4 Performance of a LUT Implementation of the Trained Modified MLP

Color correction by the modified MLP can be tabulated, making it one the fastest possible color correction approaches. Execution time for image correction, based on a Look-Up Table implementation of the modified MLP, is 3.75 ms for an entire 320x240 image, on a Pentium4 3GHz. Such a fast LUT implementation is possible because the approach is pixel-wise.

An HSV correction scheme could be as fast (since it could also be implemented using LUTs), but it would be less performant, as illustrated on a example by fig. 6. A color correction scheme based on [FDL04] would be of equal performance, as illustrated on examples by fig. 5. It could deal with more changes of illumination, since our approach is limited to the type of frequently found indoor lighting the modified MLP was trained for. However, working globally on the image, it could not be implemented as a LUT, and would thus be significantly slower.

4.5 Comparison with Other Color Correction Methods from the Literature

Figures 6 and 5 compare our color correction approach with an HSV-based correction (HSV being hue-saturation-value) and the color correction scheme of [FDL04] on several examples and for different applications.

Figure 6 compares our approach to HSV-based color correction and applies it to color-based background subtraction. The two first images of the first and second columns of the figure show that the color correction scheme presented in this paper is indeed robust to changes in illumination, since there is much less difference between the images after correction than before. Figure 6 also shows that the correction performed in this paper compares favorably with an

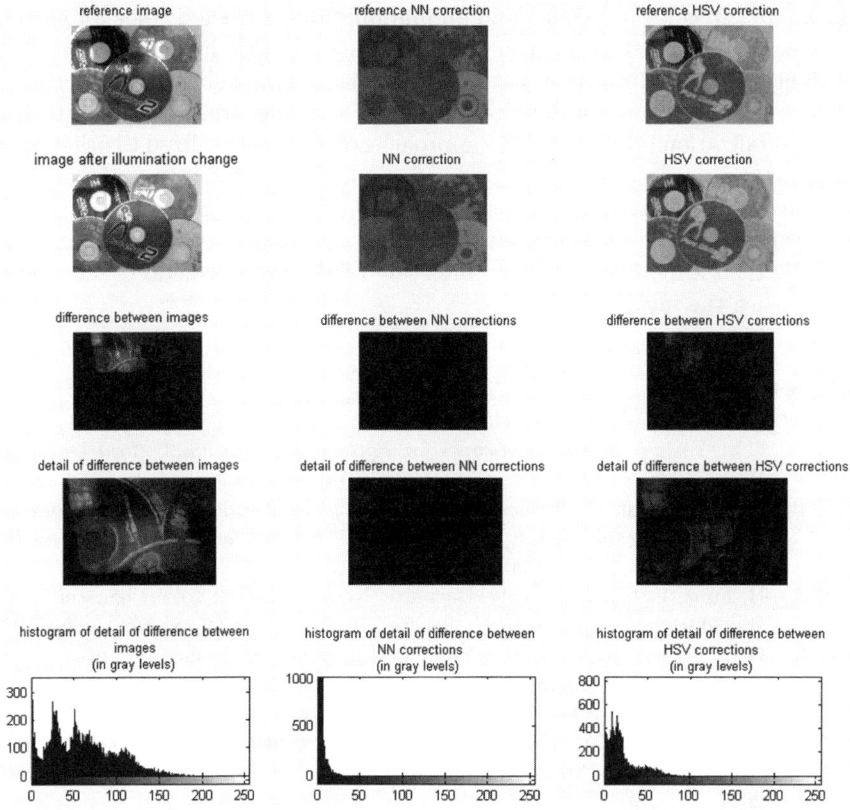

Fig. 6. Comparison of the pixel-wise color correction by the modified MLP presented in this paper and pixel-wise HSV-based color correction, HSV being the well known hue-saturation-value color space

HSV-based color correction (which consists in taking an RGB color to hue-saturation-value space, setting its value/luminance to a constant, then going back to RGB space to get the corrected color).

Figure 5 illustrates that our correction is of similar quality to that of Finlayson et al [FDL04] (briefly described in the introduction of this paper). The application of color correction is the detection of shadow contours (which can be used for shadow removal, as shown in [FDL04]). Even though it might be less robust to large light changes or unusual light changes (such as turning on a blue or red light), our method is faster, being pixel-wise.

5 Conclusion

This paper presents a new neural network-based approach to estimating image color independently of illumination. A modified multi-layer perceptron is trained to estimate two color invariants and an illumination- corrected color for each input color. It is trained for typical indoor home and office lighting (fluorescents and light bulbs) and outdoor natural light, using two webcams. Experiments with light changes and another webcam show that the training seems to have good generalization properties. The approach could be generalized to other applications where one or several invariants of a signal (here color) to a perturbation (here illumination) need to be found. If a database of signals before and after perturbation, and measurements directly correlated to the perturbation are available, then a modified MLP architecture of the type presented here can be used to learn the invariants.

References

[Bis96] C.M. Bishop. *Neural Networks for Pattern Recognition.* Oxford University Press, 1996.

[CRM00] D. Comaniciu, V. Ramesh, and P. Meer. Real-time tracking of non-rigid objects using mean shift. In *Proc. of IEEE Conf. on Comp. Vis. and Pat. Rec. (CVPR 2000)*, 2000.

[FCB97] B. Funt, V. Cardei, and K. Barnard. Neural network colour constancy and specularly reflecting surfaces. In *Proc. of AIC Color 97, Kyoto, Japan*, 1997.

[FDL04] G.D. Finlayson, M.S. Drew, and C. Lu. Intrinsic images by entropy minimization. In *Proc. 8th European Conf. on Computer Vision (ECCV'04), Prague, pp 582-595*, 2004.

[GG01] I.Y.-H. Gu and V. Gui. Colour image segmentation using adaptive mean shift filters. In *Proc. of . Int. Conference on Image Processing (ICIP'01)*, 2001.

[GS99] T. Gevers and A.W.M. Smeulders. Color based object recognition. *Pattern Recognition*, 1999.

[GW01] R.C. Gonzalez and R.E. Woods. *Digital Image Processing.* Addison-Wesley Longman Publishing Co., Inc., 2001.

[LK04] Q. Luo and T.M. Khoshgoftaar. Efficient image segmentation by mean shift clustering and MDL-guided region merging. In *Proc. of 16th IEEE Int. Conf. on Tools with Artificial Intelligence (ICTAI'04)*, 2004.

[LM71] E.H. Land and J.J. McCann. Lightness and retinex theory. *J. Opt. Soc. Am.*, 1971.

[TFA05] M.F. Tappen, W.T. Freeman, and E.H. Adelson. Recovering intrinsic images from a single image. In *IEEE Transactions on Pattern Analysis and Machine Intelligence*, 2005.

Motion Blur Identification in Noisy Images Using Feed-Forward Back Propagation Neural Network

Mohsen Ebrahimi Moghaddam[1], Mansour Jamzad[1], and Hamid Reza Mahini[2]

[1] Department of Computer Engineering Sharif University of Technology, Tehran, Iran
[2] IUST Behshahr Branch Behshahr, Iran

Abstract. Blur identification is one important part of image restoration process. Linear motion blur is one of the most common degradation functions that corrupts images. Since 1976, many researchers tried to estimate motion blur parameters and this problem is solved in noise free images but in noisy images improvement can be done when image SNR is low. In this paper we have proposed a method to estimate motion blur parameters such as direction and length using Radon transform and Feed-Forward back propagation neural network for noisy images. To design the desired neural network, we used Weierstrass approximation theorem and Steifel reference Sets. The experimental results showed algorithm precision when SNR is low and they were very satisfactory.

Keywords: Linear Motion blur, Restoration, Neural network, noisy images.

1 Introduction

The aim of image restoration is to reconstruct or estimate the uncorrupted image by using the degraded image. In this paper, we consider degradation caused by linear motion blur and additive noise. Equation (1) shows the relation between the observed image $g(x, y)$ and its uncorrupted version $f(x, y)$ [1].

$$g(x, y) = f(x, y) * h(x, y) + n(x, y) \tag{1}$$

In equation (1), h is the blurring function that convolves in original image and n is the additive noise function. According to equation (1) the aim of blur identification is to estimate h by using g. Since 1976, many researchers tried to solve this problem when the blurring function is linear motion blur and most of them tried to extend their work to noisy images [2] [3] [4][6][1].

In best of our knowledge the only method that used neural networks to estimate motion blur parameters is presented in [7]. In this paper Adaline network is used but its weak point is that it needs f to estimate h. Other methods that are based on neural networks used blind restoration methods [8][9]. In this paper we presented a method which use Radon transform to find motion direction and a Feed-Forward Back-Propagation network to find motion length. This network

N. Zheng, X. Jiang, and X. Lan (Eds.): IWICPAS 2006, LNCS 4153, pp. 369–376, 2006.

tries to model bispectrum of an image which is noise free in theory. The authors in [3] used the bispectrum of image in a different manner to find motion parameters,too. Our method works for noise free and noisy images in lower SNR. The lowest SNR that our method supports is about $20dB$ in average and in best of our knowledge it is lowest from other presented methods since now.

The rest of paper is organized as follows: In section 2 the motion blur parameters are introduced. In section 3 finding motion blur parameters in noise free and noisy images are described. In subsections of this section we described the architecture of designed neural network. Experimental results are given in section 4 and finally we present our conclusion.

2 Motion Blur Attributes

The general form of linear motion blur function is given as follows[2]:

$$h(m,n) = \begin{cases} \frac{1}{L} & if|m| \leq \frac{L}{2}\cos\phi \text{ and } n = m\,tan(\phi) \\ 0 & otherwise \end{cases} \tag{2}$$

As seen in equation (2), motion blur depends on two parameters: Motion Length (L) and Motion Direction (ϕ).

The frequency response of h is a SINC function. This implies that : "If an image is affected only by motion blur and no additive noise, then in its frequency response we can see dominant parallel dark lines (figure 1-b) that correspond to very low values (near zero) [2][6][5]".

3 Motion Blur Parameter Estimation

3.1 Motion Direction Estimation

To find motion direction, we used the parallel dark lines that appear in frequency response of degraded image as shown in figure 1-b. The motion blur direction (ϕ) is equal to the angle (θ) between any of these parallel dark lines and the vertical axis[1]. In frequency response of noisy images, these dark lines disappear but because of SINC structure of degradation function a white bound appears around frequency center (this bound also exists at frequency response of noise free image). The direction of white bound corresponds to motion blur direction. This fact is shown in figure 2. Therefore to find motion direction, in noise free images and noisy images we should find dark lines and above mentioned bound direction, respectively. Because we can assume a bound as a collection of parallel lines, we can use same algorithms for both cases. To find motion direction, Radon transform [1] is used. Following equations show using Radon transform to find motion direction.

$$k(u,v) = log(|G(u,v)|) \tag{3}$$

$$R(\rho,\theta) = \int_{-\infty}^{\infty} k(\rho\cos\theta - s\sin\theta, \rho\sin\theta + s\cos\theta)ds \tag{4}$$

In these equations $G(u, v)$ shows image frequency response and $R(\rho, \theta)$ shows Radon transform result. The highest spot of R in θ axis shows the motion direction. To find this highest spot we used cepstrum analysis as a pitch detection algorithm. Figures 3, 4 shows the result of applying Radon transform on a noise free and noisy image, respectively. As we can see in figure 4, in noisy case two peaks may exist in Radon transform result. This event occurs due to the white bound structure. The parallel lines in a bound can be extracted in two perpendicular directions along length and width of bound. Therefore to distinguish the peak that corresponds to motion direction in noisy case, the peak that is created regarding to bound length is selected. More details of using Radon transform for finding motion direction is given in our previous work [1].

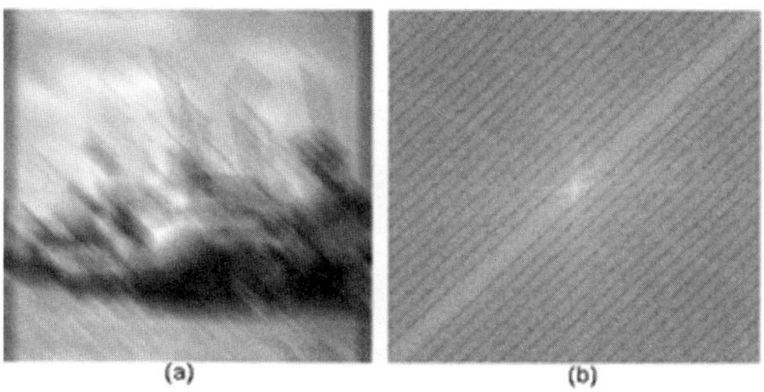

Fig. 1. (a)Boat image degraded by linear motion blur using $L = 30\,Pixel, \phi = 135°$ and no additive noise, (b) frequency response of (a)

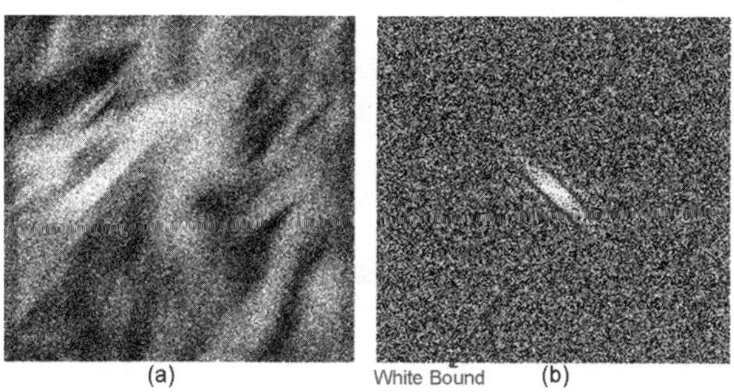

Fig. 2. (a) The image (256 × 256) of Barbara which is degraded by motion blur with parameters $L = 30$ $Pixel$ and $\phi = 45°$ and Gaussian additive noise with zero mean ($SNR = 35\,dB$). (b) its Fourier spectrum

3.2 Motion Length Estimation

After finding motion direction as described in above, we rotate image axis by motion direction. After this rotation we can consume all related functions to be

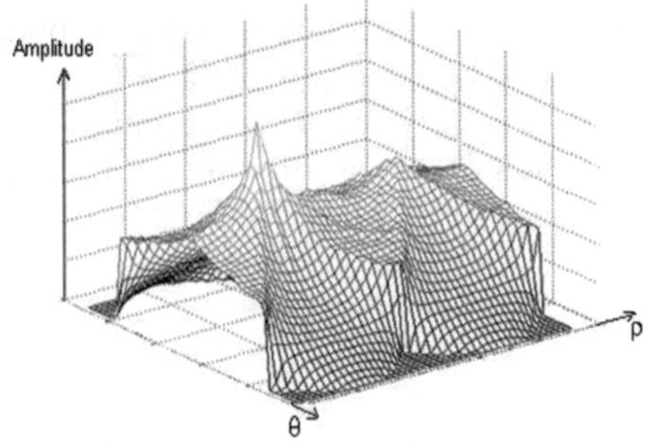

Fig. 3. Result of Radon Transform on the frequency response of a noise free image

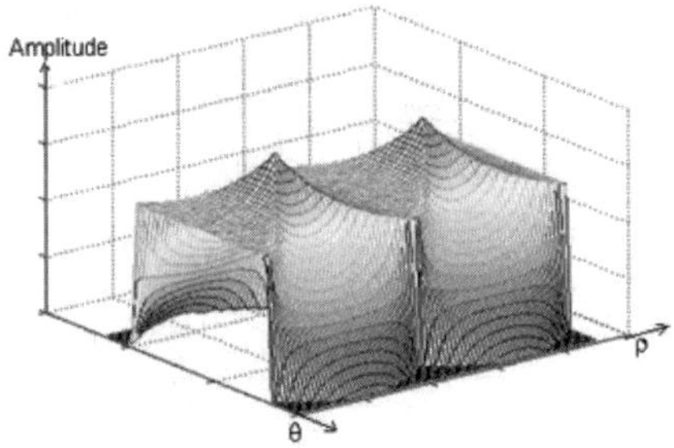

Fig. 4. Result of Radon Transform on the frequency response of a noisy image

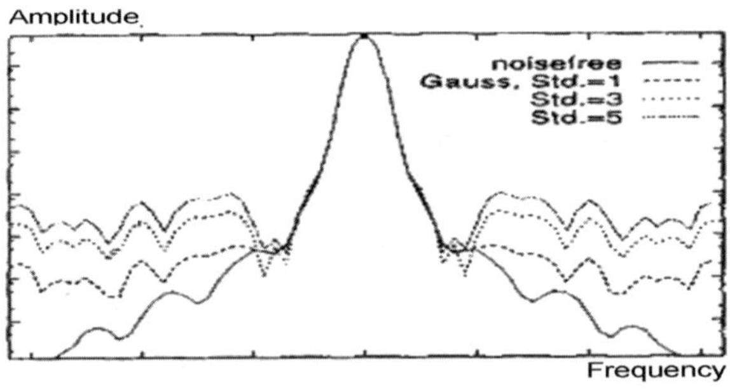

Fig. 5. Bispectrum of an image with different noise levels

in horizontal direction. To design a precise algorithm in noisy images we used the bispectrum of image which in theory is not dependent to noise. Our proposed method is different from similar works[3][6] and has higher precision and lowest SNR support. The discrete bispectrum of the ith segment of degraded image denoted by $B_i(k,l)$ is defined on $l = 0$ (central slice) in 1-D case such as follow [3]:

$$B_i(k,0) = |F_i(k)H(K) + W_i(K)|^2[F_i(0)H(0) + W_i(0)]$$

$$= |F_i(k)H(k)|^2 F_i(0)H(0) + ... + |W_i(k)|^2 W_i(0) \quad (5)$$

Where $F_i(K)$ is the Fourier transform of ith segment of original image, $H(K)$ is the Fourier transform of degradation function and $W_i(K)$ is the Fourier transform of ith segment of noise field. Each line of image is supposed to be as separate segments to calculate bispectrum of image. In theory, all terms of equation (5) except the first one should average to zero. Therefore the average of B_i on all segments does not depend on the noise. The average of bispectrum segments are define as:

$$\hat{B}(k,0) = \frac{1}{N}\sum_{i=1}^{N} |F_i(k)H(k)|^2 F_i(0)H(0) \quad (6)$$

Regarding to equation (6) we can conclude that zero places of $\hat{B}$ corresponds to zero places of H which has a SINC structure therefore some peaks and valleys created in $\hat{B}$. Figure 5 shows $\hat{B}$ of an degraded image with different noise levels. As we can see in the figure 5, the main lobe of $\hat{B}$ has the same structure and size in different noise levels. Therefore, to find the motion length we tried to model the shape of main lobe of bispectrum. Due to bispectrum properties, the lobe width is not image and noise dependent. Regarding to equation (6) we can conclude that:

$$L \propto \frac{1}{W_u} \quad (7)$$

Where W_u is central lobe width of $\hat{B}$ in a noisy image. To find motion length, we have tried to convert the equation (7) to a relation using neural networks.

3.3 Mathematical Basics

In this section we described how we can estimate the motion length based on the equation (7). The main goal in this section is to find a function $L = g(W_u)$. Based on Weierstrass approximation theorem [10], we can find a unique polynomial to model $g(W_u)$ which its error is ϵ in worst case. Regarding to these theorems, because we are sure that $g(W_u)$ exists, we try to find its coefficients. To create reference set for nonlinear interpolation we degraded some images in horizontal direction with specified motion length and we measured W_u. Because we used the specified values for motion length (L), created samples are distributed uniformly on a specified interval, But the values of measured W_u are not distributed uniformly on its interval. This indicates that we can not estimate L by using W_u in some intervals of created reference set. To overcome this problem, we tried to find a function $W_u = f(L)$ to create a complete reference set. By using $f(L)$ and by noting to Steifel reference set[11] we created a proper reference set to estimate $g(W_u)$.

To estimate a polynomial for a function, Steifel proposed the following reference set on the interval $[a, b]$:

$$x_i = \frac{b+a}{2} + \frac{b-a}{2} * \cos(\frac{\pi \times i}{n+1}) \quad i - 0..n + 1 \quad (8)$$

3.4 Neural Network Architecture

To estimate $f(L)$ and $g(W_u)$ we designed a Feed-Forward back propagation neural network. The network inputs $(x^0..x^{n-1})$ participate in computing $2^{th}..n^{th}$ coefficient of polynomial and the bias value b shows the first coefficient of it. Figures 6 and 7 show the design of this network for a polynomial of order 10. The designed network consists of two layer such that each layer has one neuron. The first layer has 9 inputs and since its transfer function is a linear transfer function, its output is :

$$O_1 = \sum_{i=1}^{9}(IW\{1,1\}_i \times x^i) + b\{1\} \tag{9}$$

In equation (9), O_1 is the output of first layer and x^i and $IW\{1,1\}_i$ are inputs (reference set) and input weights, respectively. The second layer has only one input which is connected to output of first layer which is calculated using equation (9). This layer has also an input bias. The output of second layer is calculated using following equation:

$$O_2 = LW\{2,1\} \times O_1 + b\{2\} \tag{10}$$

At first we used this network to estimate $f(L)$ by using MSE (Mean Square Error) as performance error measure, delta rule as learning rule and gradient descent back propagation as training procedure. After 71 episode MSE of result was lower than 0.0028. To estimate $L = g(W_u)$, we supposed the range of motion Length as given in [4.5, 53] and by using Steifel reference set theorem (equation (8)) the reference set was created. This reference set was used

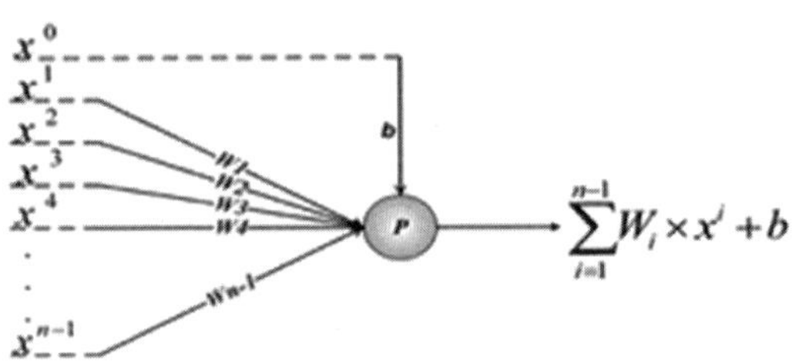

Fig. 6. Overall architecture of designed neural network

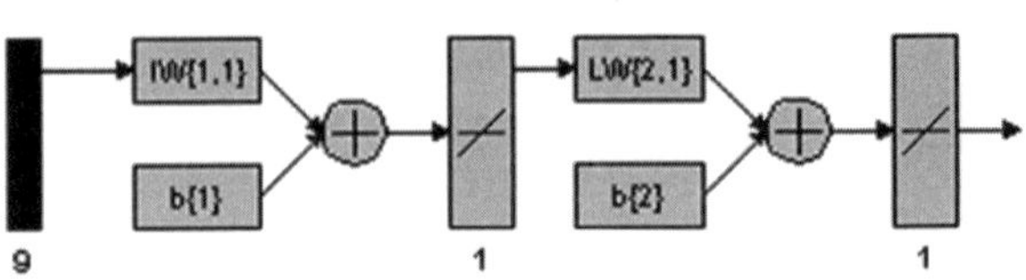

Fig. 7. Detail architecture of designed feed-forward neural network

to estimate $L = g(W_u)$ by using a network similar to network used to estimate $W_u = f(L)$. The difference between these two networks is that, in the designed network for estimating $L = g(W_u)$ we used order 14 polynomial which increased the precision. By using same learning and training method, the networks were trained. After 9636 episodes the MSE was 0.03.To find main lobe width of $\hat{B}$ cepstrum analysis was used.

4 Experimental Results

We have applied the above algorithms on more than 80 (256×256) standard images like Camera man, Lena, Barbara, Baboon,etc. These images were degraded by different orientations and lengths of motion blur ($0 \le \phi \le 180$ and $5 \le L \le 50$). Then we have added additive Gaussian noise with zero mean and different variances to these images and these images were used as our algorithm input. Table (1) show the summary of results of our algorithm. In this table the columns named "Angle Tolerance" and "Length Tolerance" show the absolute value of estimation errors respectively. The low values of the average and standard deviation of errors, show the high precision of our algorithm. Our algorithm has a robust behavior at $SNR > 20\ dB$. In lower SNR the algorithm precision decreases and sometimes it can not find motion direction. The estimated polynomial has the best performance in the range of motion length. If we increase the order of the polynomial it causes some abnormally in the curve. In comparison with related works our algorithm has better precision and supports lower SNR.

Table 1. Experimental results of our algorithm on 80 degraded standard images (256×256) with additive noise ($SNR > 20\ dB$) (using bispectrum modeling)

Cases	Angle Tolerance (Degree)	Length Tolerance (Pixel)
Best Estimate	0	0.0
Worst Estimate	2	2
Average Estimate	0.9	0.8
Standard Deviation	0.69	0.62

5 Conclusion

In this paper we presented a robust method to estimate the linear motion blur parameters. For estimating motion direction we used Radon transform which helped us to overcome the difficulties with Hough transform and similar methods to find the candidate points for line fitting. To estimate motion length in noisy images we have designed a method based on neural network with great performance. The evaluation of our method percision on more than 80 standard degraded noisy images is shown table 1. The low value of errors shows the algorithm precision. In our future work we plan to extend our work on developing noise removal methods which can preserve edges to increase the motion estimation precision.

References

1. M.Ebrahimi Moghaddam and M.Jamzad *Blur identification in noisy images using radon transform and power spectrum modeling* IEEE 12th International workshop on systems,signal and image processing(IWSSIP), Greece, Chalkida,2005.
2. Qiang Li and Yaso Yoshida *Parameter Estimation and Restoration for motion blurred Images* IEICE Trans.Fundamentals,vol E80-A , No 8 , August 1997.
3. M. M. Chang, A. M. Tekalp, and A. T. Erdem *Blur identification using the bispectrum* IEEE Trans. Acoust., Speech, Signal Processing, vol. 39, Oct. 1991.
4. M. Cannon *Blind deconvolution of spatially invariant image blurs with phase* IEEE Trans. Acoust., Speech, Signal Processing, vol. 24, pp. 58-63, Feb. 1976.
5. Ioannis M.Rekleities *Optical Flow recognition from the power spectrum of a single blurred image* ICIP 1996.
6. C.Mayntz,T.Aach,D.Kunz *Blur Identification using a spectral Inertial Tensor and Spectral zeros* ICIP 1999.
7. Wei-Guo He, Shao-Fali, Fui-Wu Hu *Blur identification using adaptive adaline network* IEEE international conference on machine learning and cybernetics, 18-21 Aug 2005,Guangzhou.
8. Cho-C-M;Don:H-S *Blur identification and image restoration using a multilayer neural network* IEEE international joint conference on Neural Networks,1991.
9. Kim-Hui Yap;Ling Guan *A recursive approach to joint image restoration and compensated blur identification* IEEE international society workshop on neural netwoks for signal processing, 11-13 Dec, 2000.
10. Todd,J *Introduction to the constructive theory of functions* California Institute of Technology, 1961.
11. Powell M.J.D. *Approximation Theory and Methods* Cambridge University Press, 1981.

Using Shear Invariant for Image Denoising in the Contourlet Domain

Jian Jia[1,2] and Licheng Jiao[1]

[1] Institute of Intelligent Information Processing, Xidian University, Xi'an, Shaanxi 710071, China
jiajianbb@126.com, lchjiao@mail.xidian.edu.cn
[2] Department of Mathematics, Northwest University, Xi'an, Shaanxi 710069, China

Abstract. A new contourlet transform based on shear invariant is proposed for image denoising. Image denoising by means of the contourlet transform(CT) introduces many visual artifacts due to the Gibbs-like phenomena. Due to the lack of transform invariance of the contourlet transform, we employ a shear technique to develop shear invariant contourlet denoising scheme (SICT). This scheme achieves enhanced estimation results for images that are corrupted with additive Gaussian noise over a wide range of noise variance. Experiments show that the proposed approach outperforms the translation invariant wavelets method and translation invariant contourlets method both visually and in terms of the PSNR values at most cases. Especially, SICT yields better visual results even has worse PSNR result than translation invariant contourlet transform.

1 Introduction

In image modeling, simple models are constructed to capture the defining characteristics of complex natural images[1]. Accurate models can enhance image processing such as compression, denoising and image retrieval. An important aspect of an efficient image transform is directionality. Having this feature, a transform would have the potential to handle 2D singularities[2]. Although the wavelet transform has been proven to be powerful in many signal and image processing applications, wavelets are not optimal in capturing the two dimensional singularities found in images. Recently, many directional image transforms have been introduced. These transforms, unlike separable transforms such as wavelets, can efficiently capture the intrinsic geometrical structures in natural images such as smooth contour edges. Candès and Donoho pioneered the Curvelet representation[3] which is shown to be optimal in a certain sense for functions in the continuous domain with curved singularities. Inspired by curvelets, Do and Vetterli developed the Contourlet representation[4] based on an efficient two dimensional nonseparable filter banks that can deal effectively with images having smooth contours.

Contourlets possess not only the main features of multiresolution and time-frequency localization, but they also show a high degree of *directionality* and

N. Zheng, X. Jiang, and X. Lan (Eds.): IWICPAS 2006, LNCS 4153, pp. 377–386, 2006.

anisotropy. The contourlet transform employs Laplacian pyramids to achieve multiresolution decomposition and directional filter banks to achieve directional decomposition. Owing to the geometric information, the contourlet transform achieves better results than discrete wavelet transform in image analysis applications[1].

Ramin Eslami and Hayder Radha develop a translation invariant (TI) scheme of a general multichannel multidimensional filter band and apply their findings to the contourlet transform to obtain a TI contourlet transform (TICT)[2]. Furthermore, they demonstrate that the TICT attains better PSNR values in most denoising experiments when compared with the TI wavelet transform (TIWT) scheme. And visually, TICT is capable of better retaining edges and textures in the denoised images.

In addition to translation invariant, an efficient image representation has to account for the geometry pervasive in natural scenes. In this paper we address a new algorithm to overcome transform variance, named the shear invariant contourlet transform (SICT), which can induce more directionality than translation invariant and produce satisfied results both visually and in terms of the PSNR values.

This paper is organized as follows. In Section 2, the construction of the contourlet transform is introduced. Then, in Section 3, translation invariant and shear invariant are described in details. Based on Bresenham algorithm, a shear invariant method for image denoising is proposed in Section 4, and the denoising results are compared with that of translation invariant contourlet and wavelets based method both visually and in terms of the PNSR. Finally, concluding remarks are given in Section 5.

2 The Contourlet Transform

Recently there has been a wide interest in image representations that efficiently handle geometric structure[5]. This comes from the recognition that wavelets essentially fail to take advantage of geometric regularity, a common feature in natural images. Minh Do and Martin Vetterli[6][7] introduced the contourlet transform as a means to fix the failure of wavelets in handling geometry, which provides sparse representation at both spatial and directional resolutions. As a new image decomposition scheme, the contourlet transform is constructed by combining two distinct and successive decomposition stages: a multiscale decomposition followed by a directional decomposition. The first stage is a Laplacian pyramid (LP) multiscale decomposition that transforms the image into one coarse version plus a set of LP bandpass images. The second stage applies appropriately 2D quincunx filtering and critical subsampling to decompose each LP detail subband into a number of wedge shaped subbands, and thus capturing directional information. Finally, the image is represented as a set of directional subbands at multiple scales. The contourlet transform is perfect reconstruction and almost critically sampled with a small redundancy factor of up 4/3 due to

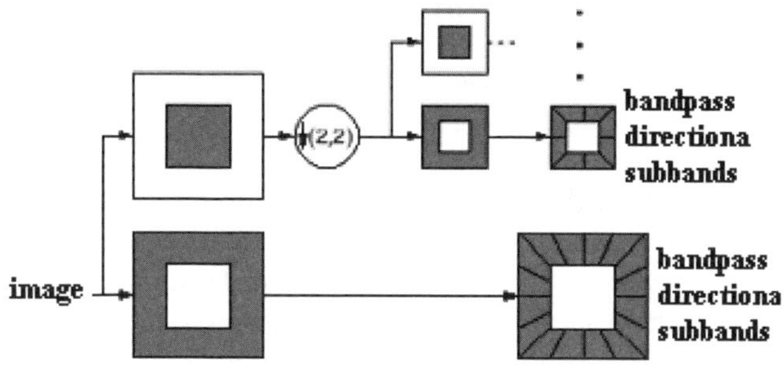

Fig. 1. A flow graph of the contourlet transform. The image is first decomposed into subbands by the Laplacian pyramid and then each detail image is analyzed by the directional filter banks

the Laplacian pyramid. Fig.1 shows a flow graph of multilevel contourlet decomposition.

When compared to the discrete wavelet transform, the contourlet transform involves basis functions that are oriented at any power of two's number of directions with flexible aspect ratios. With such richness in the choice of bases, contourlets can represent any one dimensional smooth edges with close to optimal efficiency. Various experiments clearly show that smooth edges are efficiently represented by few local coefficients in the right directional subbands, leading to better representation of fine contours. Indeed, nonlinear approximation using contourlets can achieve the optimal approximation rate for piecewise images. Fig.2 shows the subband images of test image Lena[8].

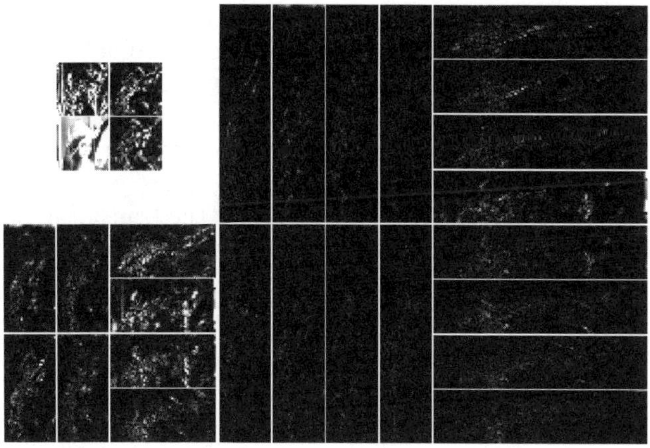

Fig. 2. An example of contourlet transform of the Lena image. Small coefficients are colored black while large coefficients are colored white. Larger rectangles correspond to finer subbands

3 Translation Invariant and Shear Invariant

The main disadvantage of the contourlet-based transforms is the occurrence of artifacts that are caused by setting some transform coefficients to zero for nonlinear approximation. Also in the context of multiscale expansions implemented with filter banks, dropping the basis requirement offers the possibility of an expansion that is translation invariant, a crucial property in a number of applications. For instance, in image denoising via thresholding in the wavelet domain, the lack of translation invariant(TI) causes pseudo-Gibbs phenomena around singularities, so does it in the contourlet domain.

Translation invariant was first introduced as a useful remedy for discrete wavelet transform(DWT). It actually provides a tight translation invariant frame which is beneficial to image denoising. Since contourlet transform is nearly critical sampled, TI was naturally adopted to boost up its denoising performances. In paper [9], R. Eslami and H. Radha introduce translation invariant in the contourlet domain using Cycle Spinning for image denoising, called TICT, TICT yields great performance than contourlet transform method.

General speaking, TI is just among a large family which follows the form:

$$\hat{f} = \frac{1}{N}(\sum_{i=1}^{N} T_i^{-1}[D[T_i(f)]]) \ . \tag{1}$$

Where f, $\hat{f}$ are the image to be and has been recovered, D is the denoising operator and T_i is an invertible change. In general speaking, the invertible change in TI is just to say translation transform.

3.1 Shear Invariant

Though TI does work, with simple translations, it wouldn't take advantage of contourlet's directionality. And, most importantly, the polyphase sampling point of a directional filter bands(DFB) has already covered the whole image grid, so translation won't help much. A new scheme that will make use of contourlet's characteristic is wanted, in this paper, we introduce shear invariant(SI) as a remedy for this problem.

Shear distorts the shape of an object such that the transforms shape appears as if the object were composed of internal layers that had been caused to slide over each other. Two common shearing transformations are those that shift coordinate x values and those that shift y values. Shear is essentially a coordinate transform:

$$S_{i,\alpha}f, i = 1,2; S_{1,\alpha} = \begin{pmatrix} 1 & \alpha \\ 0 & 1 \end{pmatrix}, S_{2,\alpha} = \begin{pmatrix} 1 & 0 \\ \alpha & 1 \end{pmatrix} \ . \tag{2}$$

An x-direction shear relative to the x axis is produced with the transformation matrix $S_{1,\alpha}$ and y-direction shear matrix is $S_{2,\alpha}$. Based on this transform, shear an image with $S_{i,\alpha}$ can introduce additional directions easily. An example can be seen in Fig.3, the shear transform for Lena image is shown with *shear factor* $\alpha = \pm 3/4$ in $S_{i,\alpha}, i = 1,2$.

Shearing presents more directions in the image, and the directional details can be maintained better after the contourlet transform. Enrichment of directions is the key advantage of SI. On the other hand, shearing will elongate the segment of special direction and thus zooms in some geometric structure, for example the horizontal line is prolonged by a factor of $\sqrt{2}$ under the shear of $S_{2,1}$, and is shifted under the shear of $S_{1,1}$. This will of course help the recovery of some specific directional information. At the same time, the shrinkage of some other structure can be compensated by other kind of shear matrix.

Fig. 3. Four direction shear transform with different value of α

3.2 The Bresenham Algorithm

For an $N \times N$ image, shear with $S_{2,\alpha}$ can be accomplished by translating the ith column with a distance of $\alpha \times i$, where i is an integer ranging from 0 to $N-1$. Interpolation is surely needed in the case of fractional translations when $|\alpha| < 1$, so it is inevitable that interpolation error would be induced. Here, the Bresenham's Line Algorithm that is invertible and high accuracy order is used for our purpose to translate the pixels in original image. Bresenham Algorithm is an accurate and efficient raster line-generating algorithm, which uses only incremental integer calculations. For instance, considered the scan-conversion process for line with positive slope less than 1.0, pixel positions along a line path are then determined by sampling at unit x intervals. Starting from the left endpoint (x_s, y_s) of a given line, we step to each successive column (x position) and plot the pixel whose scan line y value is closet to the line path. Fig.4 demonstrates the ith step in this process.

Assuming we have determined that the pixel at (x_k, y_k) is to be displayed, we next need to decide which pixel to plot in column $x_{k+1} = x_k + 1$. Our choice is the pixels at positions (x_k+1, y_k) and (x_k+1, y_k+1), it can get the right answer by the special rule. This step repeats until get the right endpoint (x_e, y_e).

As a result, for the special value of α for shear along y axis, we can computer the value of each pixel on the line from point $(0, 0)$ to point $(N-1, \alpha \times N)$, and translate each column of the image base on the pixel value and get the shearing image about shear factor α. This method is inevitable and fast, because it only operates on integer calculation.

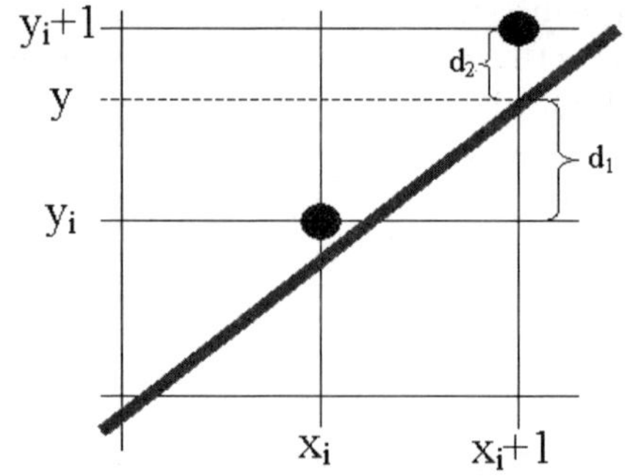

Fig. 4. Bresenham Algorithm

4 Denoising

The contourlet transform has been shown to be a better alternative choice than wavelets for image denoising. In paper [9], a cycle spinning algorithm is employed to improve the denoising performance of contourlets. Based on SI, the shear invariant contourlet transform (SICT) model is applied in denoising zero-mean additive white Gaussian noise. The SICT can be evaluate by following fomula:

$$\hat{f} = \frac{1}{N}(\sum_{i=1}^{N} S_i^{-1}[D[S_i(f)]]) \ . \tag{3}$$

Where f, $\hat{f}$ are the image to be and has been recovered, D is the contourlet transform and S_i is shear transform.

We performed a series of denoising experiments in order to test our SICT method. The paper performed a nonlinear approximation experiment in which one keeps some transform coefficients with the largest magnitudes and set the rest to zero and then reconstruct the image. Experiments are performed on two images all of size of 512×512. In particular, we examined the Wiener filter and three different types of multiresolution decomposition: TIWT, CT, TICT. The last of these has got the satisfied PSNR results. We used biorthogonal Daubechies 9/7 wavelets for comparison. The wavelet transforms and TI wavelet transform (TIWT) are implemented using Wavelab802[10]. For the LP stage of contourlets, we also used the same biorthogonal filters and applied 5 levels of decomposition. The images are contaminated by a zero-mean Gaussian noise with a standard deviation of σ , ranging from 20 to 80. Since for TI denoising, hard thresholding usually yields better results than soft thresholding, we use hard thresholding with a fixed threshold value equal to 3σ[11], so does SICT. A numerical comparison of the denoising results is given in Tables 1. One can see that the TICT approach significantly outperforms the Wiener filter, TIWT and CT approach. While in most examples, SICT gives slightly better PSNR results than the TICT and has a clearer boundary when SICT is the PSNR results of TICT's math.

Table 1. PSNR values of the denoising for different σ

	σ	Noise	Wiener	WT[1]	TIWT[2]	CT[3]	TICT[4]	SICT[5]
Lena	20	22.1029	30.2054	28.7282	30.8645	29.1384	**31.5415**	31.4524
	30	18.5779	27.9473	27.0030	28.9934	27.3083	**29.6677**	29.6542
	40	16.1042	26.1221	25.7835	27.9630	26.0215	28.3381	**28.3667**
	50	14.1424	24.5381	24.8833	26.9058	24.9406	27.3543	**27.3962**
	60	12.5674	23.1948	24.2348	26.0190	24.2137	26.5560	**26.6556**
	70	11.2390	22.0958	23.6173	25.3685	23.5297	25.9418	**26.1037**
	80	10.0742	21.0535	22.7896	24.8461	22.9321	25.3397	**25.5328**
Barbara	20	22.0977	26.2354	25.4906	27.9548	26.2708	**28.4717**	28.4004
	30	18.6013	24.7241	23.4096	25.1874	24.2674	**26.3260**	26.2814
	40	16.0771	23.4413	22.3156	24.1638	22.9531	**24.8979**	24.8719
	50	14.1566	22.3785	21.7712	23.0656	22.1341	23.8844	**23.9096**
	60	12.5780	21.4532	21.2608	22.4954	21.4699	23.1919	**23.2074**
	70	11.2285	20.5894	20.8660	22.0159	20.9387	22.6634	**22.7111**
	80	10.0600	19.7955	20.4499	21.7216	20.4327	22.2596	**22.2923**

[1]Wavelet Transform [2]TI Wavelet Transform [3]Contourlet Transform
[4]TI Contourlet Transform [5]SI Contourlet Transform

The PSNR vs. standard deviation curves for the images *Lena* and *Barbara* are provided in Fig. 5. It is clear that the TICT and SICT denoising scheme are both capable of further retaining edges and fine details when compared with others scheme. Furthermore, SICT approach yields slightly better PSNR results when compared with TICT at most cases.

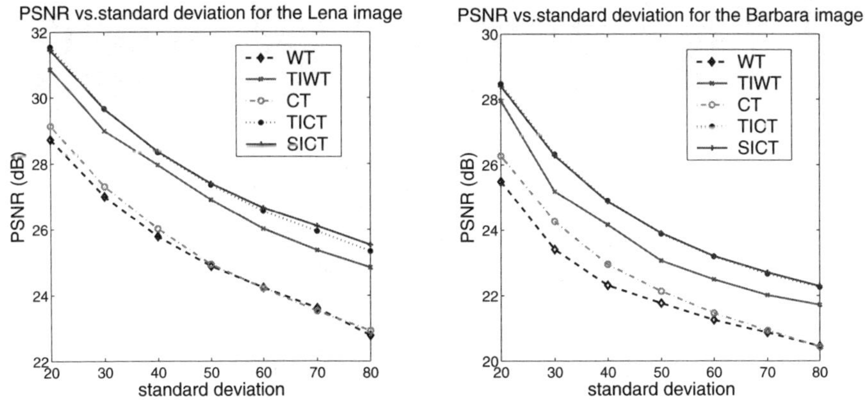

Fig. 5. PSNR vs. σ of the image denoising for the Lena and Barbara images. It should be pointed out that the curves of SICT and TICT method almost have the same path, especially in the right figure, because the PSNR value of SICT and TICT are quite similar

(a) Original image

(b) Noisy image($\sigma = 40$)

(c) Denoised Image Using Wiener Filter

(d) Denoised Image Using TIWT

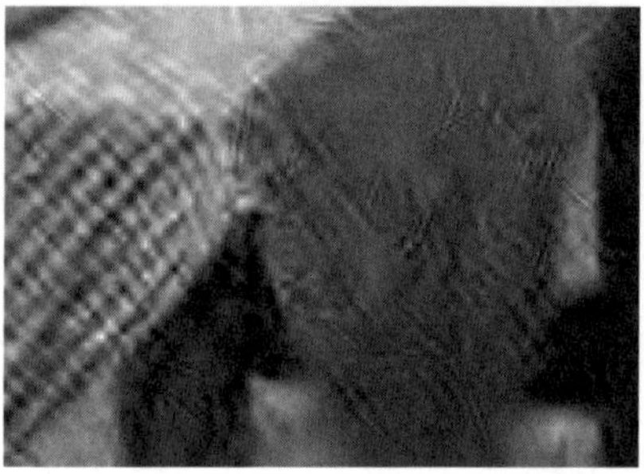

(e) Denoised Image Using CT

(f) Denoised Image Using TICT

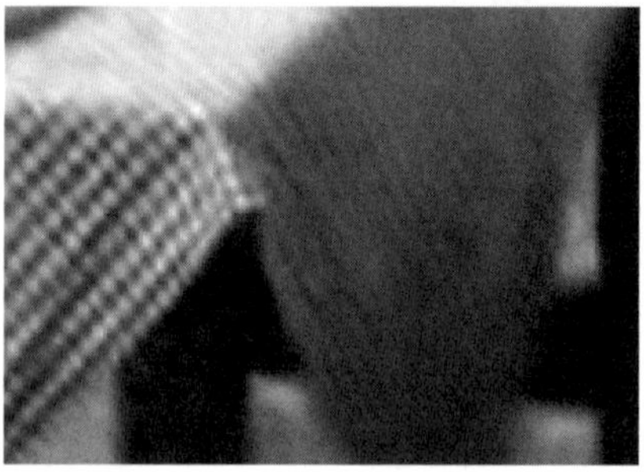

(g) Denoised Image Using SICT

Fig. 6. The original image, noisy image and denoised results of the part of Barbara image at σ=40 using different schemes(from (c) to (g)): Wiener filter, TIWT, CT, TICT, SICT

It should be pointed out that even TICT has higher PSNR result than SICT when $\sigma = 40$ for the Barbara image, TICT's artifacts of Gibbs-like phenomena is obvious than SICT's. Parts of the denoised results of the Barbara image at $\sigma = 40$ are shown in Figure 6 together with the original image and noisy image. It can be seen that the parallel lines on the tablecloth disturb each other in TICT denoising result and straight line is curved, but these texture are recovered well in SICT denoising result. So the TICT approaches produce significant visual artifacts than SICT even TICI has the better PSNR result.

5 Conclusion

Designed by Do and Vetterli, the contourlet transform provides an efficient multi scale directional representation of an image. In a contourlet decomposition, the images are first passed through a pyramid Laplacian decomposition, then the high frequency subband images from each scale are passed through directional filters with prescribed orientation resolution. Both operation above involve down-sampling in their analysis sections and therefore, they are translation variant.

According to TICT, we developed the shear invariant method in the contourlet transform, called SICT. Shearing introduces many new directions in the image, so directional details can be recovered better than TICT recur to SI in image denoising. Experiments show that SICT approach outperforms the translation invariant wavelets and translation invariant contourlets both visually and in terms of the PSNR values at most cases. Especially, SICT yields better visual results even has worse PSNR result than TICT.

References

1. Duncan D. Po, Minh N. Do: Directional multiscale modeling of images using the contourlet transform. Statistical Signal Processing, 2003 IEEE Workshop on. 28 Sept- 1 Oct. 2003 pp.262-265
2. Ramin Eslami, Hayder Radha: Image Denoising Using Translation Invariant Con tourlet Transform. Acoustics, Speech, and Signal Processing, 2005. Proceedings. (ICASSP'05). IEEE International Conference on, pp.557-560
3. E. J. Candès, D. L. Donoho (1999): Curvelets - A Surprisingly Effective Nonadaptive Representation for Objects with Edges. Curves and Surfaces, L. L. Schumaker et al. (eds), Vanderbilt University Press, Nashville, TN, 1999
4. M. N. Do, M. Vetterli: The contourlet transform: an efficient directional multiresolution image representation. IEEE Trans. on Image Pmrersing, Volume 14, Issue 12, Dec. 2005 pp.2091 - 2106
5. Arthur L. da Cunha, Minh N. Do: Bi-Orthogonal Filter Banks with Directional Vanishing Moments [image representation applications]. Acoustics, Speech, and Signal Processing, 2005. Proceedings. (ICASSP '05). IEEE International Conference on, Volume 4. 18-23 March 2005, pp.553-556
6. M. N. Do, M. Vetterli: Pyramidal directional filter banks and curvelets. Proc. of IEEE International Conference on Image Processing (ICIP), Volume 3, 7-10 Oct. 2001, pp.158-161

7. M. N. Do, M. Vetterli: Contourlets: a directional multiresolution image representation. Image Processing, 2002.Proceedings. 2002 International Conference on. Volume 1. Sept.2002 pp.357-360
8. M. N. Do: Contourlet Toolbox at *http://www.ifp.uiuc.edu/˜minhdo/software/*
9. R. Eslami, H. Radha: The Contourlet Transform for Image De-noising Using Cycle Spinning. Signals, Systems & Computers, 2003, Conference Record of the Thirty-Seventh Asilomar Conference on, Volume 2, 9-12 Nov. 2003, pp.1982 - 1986
10. D. L. Donoho: Wavelab802 at *http://www-stat.stanford.edu/˜wavelab/*
11. Stéphane Mallat: A Wavelet Tour of Signal Processing. Academic Press, 1999

Region-Based Shock-Diffusion Equation for Adaptive Image Enhancement*

Shujun Fu[1,2,**], Qiuqi Ruan[2], Wenqia Wang[1], and Jingnian Chen[3]

[1] School of Mathematics and System Sciences, Shandong University, Jinan, 250100, China
[2] Institute of Information Science, Beijing Jiaotong University, Beijing, 100044, China
[3] School of Arts and Science, Shandong University of Finance, Jinan, 250014, China
**shujunfu@163.com

Abstract. In this paper, a region-based shock-diffusion equation is presented for image denoising and edge sharpening. An image is divided into three-type different regions according to image features: edges, textures and details, and flat areas. For edges, a shock-type backward diffusion is performed in the gradient direction to the isophote line (edge), incorporating a forward diffusion in the isophote line direction; while for textures and details, a soft backward diffusion is done to enhance image features preserving a natural transition. Moreover, an isotropic diffusion is used to smooth flat areas simultaneously. Finally, a shock capturing scheme with a special limiter function is developed to speed the process with numerical stability. Experiments on real images show that this method produces better visual results of the enhanced images than some related equations.

1 Introduction

Main features and information of an image are presented in its edges, textures and local details, which are also very important to the visual quality of the image. Because of some limitations of imaging process, however, edges may not be sharp in images. In addition to noise, both small intensity difference across edge and big edge width will result in a weak and blurry edge.

Image enhancement and sharpening are important operations in image processing and computer vision. Many different methods have been put forth in the past [1]. However, major drawbacks of these methods are that they also enhance noise in image, and ringing artifacts may occur along both sides of an edge. More importantly, traditional image sharpening methods mainly increase the gray level difference across edge, while its width remains unchanged. For a wide and blurry edge, increasing simply its contrast produces only very limited effect.

In the past decades there has been a growing amount of research concerning partial differential equations in image enhancement, such as anisotropic diffusion filters [2-5] for edge preserving noise removal, and shock filters [6-9] for edge sharpening. Here

* This work is supported by the national natural science fund, China (No. 60472033), the Key Laboratory Project of Information Science & Engineering of Railway of National Ministry of Railways, China (No. TDXX0510), and the Technological Innovation Fund of Excellent Doctorial Candidate of Beijing Jiaotong University, China (No. 48007).

N. Zheng, X. Jiang, and X. Lan (Eds.): IWICPAS 2006, LNCS 4153, pp. 387 – 395, 2006.

incorporating anisotropic diffusion with shock filter, we present a region-based shock-diffusion equation to remove image noise, and to sharpen edges by reducing their width simultaneously.

An image comprises regions with different features, such as edges, textures and details, and flat areas, which should be treated differently to obtain a better result in an image processing task. In our algorithm, for edges between different objects, a shock-type backward diffusion is performed in the gradient direction to the isophote line (edge), incorporating a forward diffusion in the isophote line direction. For textures and details, shock filters with the sign function enhance image features in a binary decision process, which produce unfortunately a false piecewise constant result. To overcome this drawback, we use a hyperbolic tangent function to control softly changes of gray levels of the image. As a result, a soft shock-type backward diffusion is introduced to enhance these features while preserving a natural transition in these areas. Finally, an isotropic diffusion is used to smooth flat areas simultaneously.

After we have discussed the difficulty of the numerical implementation to this type equation, in order to solve effectively the nonlinear equation to obtain discontinuous solution with numerical instability, a shock capturing scheme is developed with a special limiter function to speed the process.

This paper is organized as follows. In section 2, some related equations are introduced for enhancing images: anisotropic diffusions and shock filters. Then, we propose a region-based shock-diffusion equation. In section 3, we implement the proposed method and test it on real images. Conclusions are presented in section 4.

2 Region-Based Shock-Diffusion Equation

2.1 Some Related Work

One of most influential work in using partial differential equations (PDEs) in image processing is the anisotropic diffusion (AD) filter, which was proposed by P. Perona and J. Malik [13] for image denoising, enhancement, sharpening, etc. Let $(x, y) \in \Omega \subset R^2$, and $t \in [0,+\infty)$, a multi-scale image $u(x, y, t): \Omega \times [0,+\infty) \to R$, is evolved according to the following equation:

$$\frac{\partial u(x,y,t)}{\partial t} = div(g(|\nabla u(x,y,t)|)\nabla u(x,y,t)),\ g(|\nabla u|) = 1/(1+(|\nabla u|/K)^2) \qquad (1)$$

where K is a gradient threshold. The scalar diffusivity $g(|\nabla u|)$, chosen as a non-increasing function, governs the behaviour of the diffusion process.

By formally developing the divergence term, (1) can be put in terms of second derivatives taken in the gradient direction ($\vec{N}$) and in the isophote line direction ($\vec{T}$):

$$\frac{\partial u}{\partial t} = (K^2(K^2 - |\nabla u|^2)/(K^2 + |\nabla u|^2)^2)u_{NN} + (K^2/(K^2 + |\nabla u|^2))u_{TT} \qquad (2)$$

where

$$u_{NN} = (u_x^2 u_{xx} + u_y^2 u_{yy} + 2u_x u_y u_{xy})/|\nabla u|^2$$
$$u_{TT} = (u_x^2 u_{yy} + u_y^2 u_{xx} - 2u_x u_y u_{xy})/|\nabla u|^2$$

$u_{\bullet}$ and $u_{\bullet\bullet}$ denote the first and the second derivatives in the corresponding directions. Performing a backward diffusion for $|\nabla u| > K$ along $\vec{N}$, this formulation can clearly interpret the edge sharpening effect by (1).

Different from the nonlinear parabolic diffusion process, L. Alvarez and L. Mazorra [7] proposed an anisotropic diffusion with shock filter (ADSF) equation by adding a hyperbolic equation, called shock Filter which was introduced by S.J. Osher and L.I. Rudin [6], for noise elimination and edge sharpening:

$$\frac{\partial u}{\partial t} = -\text{sign}(G_\sigma * u_{NN})\text{sign}(G_\sigma * u_N)|\nabla u| + cu_{TT} \tag{3}$$

where G_σ is a Gaussian function with standard deviation σ, and c is a positive constant.

A more advanced scheme was proposed by P. Kornprobst, et al. [8], which combines image coupling, restoration and enhancement (CRE) in the following equation:

$$\frac{\partial u}{\partial t} = -a_f(u-u_0)+a_r(h_\tau u_{NN}+u_{TT}) - a_e(1-h_\tau)\text{sign}(G_\sigma * u_{NN})|\nabla u| \tag{4}$$

where a_f, a_r and a_e are some constants, u_0 is the original noise image; $h_\tau = h_\tau(|G_\sigma * u_N|) = 1$, if $|G_\sigma * u_N| < \tau$, and 0 elsewhere. The first term on the right is a fidelity term to carry out a stabilization effect.

In order to reinforce robustness against noise, G. Gilboa et al. [9] generalized the real-valued diffusion to the complex domain, by incorporating the free Schrödinger equation. They utilized the imaginary part to approximate the smoothed second derivative when the complex diffusion coefficient approaches the real axis, and proposed an interesting complex diffusion process (CDP):

$$\frac{\partial u}{\partial t} = -\frac{2}{\pi}\arctan(a\text{Im}(\frac{u}{\theta}))|\nabla u| + \lambda u_{NN} + \tilde{\lambda} u_{TT} \tag{5}$$

where Im(x) is the imaginary part of a complex variable x, $\lambda = re^{i\theta}$ is a complex scalar, θ is a small angle, $\tilde{\lambda}$ is a real scalar; and a is a parameter to control the sharpness of the slope near zero.

2.2 The Region-Based Shock-Diffusion Equation

An image comprises regions with different features, such as edges, textures and details, and flat areas, which should be treated differently to obtain a better result in an image processing task. Here we divide an image into three-type regions by its smoothed gradient magnitude: big gradients (such as boundaries of different objects), medium gradients (such as textures and details) and small gradients (such as smoother segments inside different areas).

For edges between different objects, a shock-type backward diffusion is performed in the gradient direction, incorporating a forward diffusion in the isophote line. For textures and details, in equations (3) and (4), to enhance an image using the sign function sign(x) is a binary decision process, which is a hard partition without middle transition. Unfortunately, the obtained result is a false piecewise constant image in some areas producing bad visual quality (see Fig.2). We notice that the change of texture and detail is gradual in these areas. In order to approach this change, we use a hyperbolic tangent membership function th(x) to guarantee a natural smooth transition in these areas, by controlling softly changes of gray levels of the image. As a result, a soft shock-type backward diffusion is introduced to enhance these features. Finally, an isotropic diffusion is used to smooth flat areas simultaneously.

Thus, incorporating shock filter with anisotropic diffusion, we develop a region-based shock-diffusion equation (RSE) process to reduce noise, and to sharpen edges while preserving image features simultaneously:

$$\begin{cases} u_G = G_\sigma * u \\ \dfrac{\partial u}{\partial t} = c_N u_{NN} + c_T u_{TT} - w(u_N)\operatorname{sign}((u_G)_{NN})|u_N| \end{cases} \tag{6}$$

with Neumann boundary condition, where the parameters are chosen as follows according to different image regions:

	c_N	c_T	$w(u_{NN})$
$\lvert(u_G)_N\rvert > T_1$	0	$1/(1+l_1 u_{TT}^2)$	1
$T_2 < \lvert(u_G)_N\rvert \le T_1$	0	$1/(1+l_1 u_{TT}^2)$	$\lvert\mathrm{th}(l_2 u_{NN})\rvert$
else	1	1	0

where G_σ is defined in previous section, c_N and c_T are the normal and tangent flow control coefficients respectively. The tangent flow control coefficient is used to prevent excess smoothness to smaller details; l_2 is a parameter to control the gradient of the membership function th(x); T_1 and T_2 are two thresholds; l_1 and l_2 are constants.

3 Numerical Implementation and Experimental Results

3.1 A Shock Capturing Scheme

Nonlinear convection-diffusion evolution equation is a very important model in the fluid dynamics, which can be used to depict transmission processes of momentum, energy and mass of fluid. Because of its hyperbolic characteristic, the solution to the convection-diffusion equation often has discontinuity even if its initial condition is very smooth. Mathematically only weak solution can be obtained here. If a weak solution satisfies the entropic increase principle for an adiabatic irreversible system, then it is called a shock wave.

When one solves numerically a convection-diffusion equation using a difference scheme, he may find some annoying problems in numerical simulation, such as instability, over smoothing, spurious oscillation or wave shift of a scheme. The reason for above is that, despite the original equation are deduced according to some physical conversation laws, its discrete equation may deviate from these laws, which can bring about numerical dissipation, numerical dispersion and group velocity of wave packets effects in numerical solutions specially for the hyperbolic term. Therefore, the hyperbolic term must be discretized carefully so that the flow of small scale and shock waves can be captured accurately.

Besides of satisfying consistence and stability, a good numerical scheme also need to capture shock waves. One method to capture shock waves is to add artificial viscosity term to the difference scheme for controlling and limiting numerical fluctuations near shock waves. But by this method it is inconvenient to adjust free parameters for different tasks, and the resolution of shocks can also be affected. Another method is to try to stop from numerical fluctuations before them appear, which is based on the TVD (Total Variation Diminishing) and nonlinear limiters. Their main idea is to use a limiter function to control the change of the numerical solution by a nonlinear way, and the corresponding schemes satisfy the TVD condition and eliminate above disadvantage effects, which guarantee of capturing shock waves with a high resolution.

In a word, when solving numerically a nonlinear convection-diffusion equation like (6) using a difference scheme, the hyperbolic term must be discretized carefully because discontinuity solutions, numerical instability and spurious oscillation may appear. Shock capturing methods with high resolution are effective tools. For more details, we refer the reader to the book [10]. Here, we develop a speeding scheme by using a proper limiter function.

An explicit Euler method with central difference scheme is used to approximate equation (6) except the gradient term $|u_N|$. Below we detail a numerical approach to it. On the image grid, the approximate solution is to satisfy:

$$u_{ij}^n \approx u(ih, jh, n\Delta t),\ i, j, n \in Z^+ \tag{7}$$

where h and $\triangle t$ are the spatial and temporal step respectively. Let $h=1$, $\delta^+ u_{ij}^n$ and $\delta^- u_{ij}^n$ are forward and backward difference schemes of u_{ij}^n respectively. A limiter function *MS* is used to approximate the gradient term:

$$|u_N| = \sqrt{(MS(\delta_x^+ u_{ij}^n, \delta_x^- u_{ij}^n))^2 + (MS(\delta_y^+ u_{ij}^n, \delta_y^- u_{ij}^n))^2} \tag{8}$$

where

$$MS(x, y) = \begin{cases} x, & |x| < |y| \\ y, & |x| > |y| \\ x, & |x| = |y| \text{ and } xy > 0 \\ 0, & |x| = |y| \text{ and } xy \le 0 \end{cases} \tag{9}$$

The *MS* function bears fewer 0 in value than the *minmod* function does in the x-y plane (see Fig.1), which also make the scheme satisfy the numerical instability. Because the gradient term represents the transport speed of the scheme, the *MS* function makes our scheme evolve faster with a bigger transport speed than those with the *minmod* function.

In [8], other than above flux limitation technique, a fidelity term $(u - u_0)$ is used to carry out the stabilization task, and they also displayed that the SNRs of results tend towards 0 if a_f=0. However, this is not enough to eliminate overshoots, and this term also affect its performance.

3.2 The Coupled Iteration

Based on preceding discussion, when implementing iteratively equation (6), we find that the shock and diffusion forces will cancel mutually in a single formula. We split equation (6) into two formulas and propose the following coupled scheme by iterating with time steps:

$$\begin{cases} v^0 = u^0, \; u_G = G_\sigma * u^0 \\ v^{n+1} = u^n + \Delta t(-w(v^n_{NN})\mathrm{sign}((u_G)_{NN})|u_N|) \\ u^{n+1} = v^{n+1} + \Delta t(c_N v^{n+1}_{NN} + c_T v^{n+1}_{TT}) \end{cases} \tag{10}$$

where Δt is the time step, u^0 is an original image. By computing iteratively in the order of $u^0 \rightarrow v^0 \rightarrow v^1 \rightarrow u^1 \rightarrow v^2 \rightarrow u^2 \rightarrow \cdots$, we finally obtain the enhanced image after some steps.

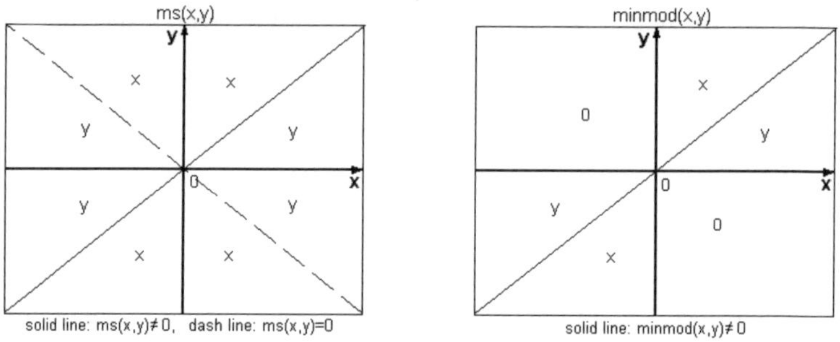

Fig. 1. The comparison of the *MS* function with the *minmod* function

3.3 Experiments

We present results obtained by using our scheme (6), and compare its performance with those of above related methods, where the parameters are selected, which allow the best results for all methods.

First, we compare performances of related methods on the blurred Cameraman image (Gaussian blur, σ=2.5) with added high level noise (SNR=14dB). In this case, weaker features are smeared by big noise in the image, which are difficult to be restored completely. In Fig.2, as it can be seen, although the AD method denoises the image well specially in the smoother segments, it produces the blurry image with unsharp edges, whose ability to sharpen edges is limited, because of its poor sharpening process with the improper diffusion coefficient along the gradient direction (see Equation (2)). Moreover, with the diffusion coefficient in inverse proportion to the image gradient magnitude along the tangent direction, it does not diffuse fully in this direction and presents rough contours.

For the ADSF and CRE methods, though they sharpen edges very well, in a binary decision process they yield the false piecewise constant images, which look unnatural with a discontinueous transition in the homogenous areas. Further, the ADSF method cannot reduce noise well only by a single directional diffusion in the smoother regions.

In Fig.2, performing a complex diffusion process, the CDP method presents a relative good result. But on edges with big gradient magnitude between different objects, because the diffusion process is weighted by the arctan(x), the sharpness of its result is

Fig. 2. Enhancement of the Cameraman by different methods (from top-left to bottom-right): a noisy blurred image, results by AD, ADSF, CRE, CDP and RSE respectively

somewhat lower than that using the sign(x). Because of its complex scalar λ, CDP does perform a complete isotropic diffusion in smoother regions, where the real part of λ is commonly not equal to $\tilde{\lambda}$ in value, and thus the result is not very satisfactory. And that, it should be pointed out that image enhancement by the complex computation is time consuming than the real one.

The best visual quality is obtained by enhancing the image using RSE, which enhances most features of the image with a natural transition in the homogenous areas, and produces pleasing sharp edges and smooth contours while denoising the image effectively (see Fig.2).

Finally, we discuss the performances of these methods in smoothing image contours on bigger gradients in the tangent direction of edges. In Fig.2, as we explain above, image contours obtained by AD are not smooth with blurry edges in the gradient direction. The results obtained using ADSF, CRE and RSE respectively all present smooth contours in the tangent direction. Because the real part of its complex scalar λ in value is not equal to zero, CDP do not perform a complete tangent diffusion, which results in its not very smooth contours.

It is also noticed that in [9], the effect of the robustness against noise by a complex diffusion was interpreted only by observations and experiments, and their theoretical justification is weak. They use the imaginary part to approach the Laplacian of the smoothed original image, which is not better choice than the smoothed second normal derivative of the image in the gradient direction. The latter can afford a more accurate directional estimation of edges in the sense of image geometry. Finally we did not find remarkable effects by the complex diffusion process in the experiments.

On the selection of parameters in our model, in order to estimate image features better and thus to obtain a more satisfactory visual quality, the standard deviation σ in Gaussian smoothing should be bigger with increasing noise's level; and, thresholds T_1 and T_2 can be adopted according to the strength of image features in the histogram of the smoothed gradient magnitude. Commonly l_1 and l_2 can be chosen as constants.

4 Conclusions

This paper deals with image enhancement for noisy blurry images. By reducing the width of edges, a region-based shock-diffusion equation is proposed to remove noise and to sharpen edges.

Our model performs a powerful process to noise blurry images, by which we not only can remove noise and sharpen edges effectively, but also can smooth image contours even in the presence of high level noise. Enhancing image features such as edges, textures and details with a natural transition in interior areas, this method produces better visual quality than some relative equations.

References

1. Castleman, K.R.: Digital Image Processing, Prentice Hall (1995).
2. Aubert, G., Kornprobst, P.: Mathematical Problems in Image Processing: Partial Differential Equations and the Calculus of Variations, vol.147 of Applied Mathematical Sciences, Springer-Verlag (2001).

3. Perona, P., Malik, J.: Scale-space and edge detection using anisotropic diffusion. IEEE Trans. Pattern Anal. Machine Intell., 12(7)(1990) 629-639.
4. Nitzberg, M., Shiota, T.: Nonlinear image filtering with edge and corner enhancement. IEEE Transactions on PAMI, 14(8)(1992) 826-833.
5. You, Y.L., Xu, W., Tannenbaum, A., Kaveh, M.: Behavioral analysis of anisotropic diffusion in image processing. IEEE Trans. on Image Processing, 5(11)(1996) 1539-1553.
6. Alvarez, L., Mazorra, L.: Signal and image restoration using shock filters and anisotropic diffusion. SIAM J. Numer. Anal., 31(2)(1994) 590-605.
7. Osher, S.J., Rudin, L.I.: Feature-oriented image enhancement using shock filters. SIAM J. Numer. Anal., 27(1990) 919-940.
8. Kornprobst, P., Deriche, R., Aubert, G.: Image coupling, restoration and enhancement via PDE's. IEEE ICIP, 2(1997) 458-461.
9. Gilboa, G., Sochen, N., Zeevi, Y.Y.: Image Enhancement and denoising by complex diffusion processes. IEEE Transactions on PAMI, 26(8)(2004) 1020-1036.
10. Liu, R.X., Shu, Q.W.: Some new methods in Computing Fluid Dynamics, Science Press of China, Beijing (2004).

A Statistical Level Set Framework for Segmentation of Left Ventricle

Gang Yu[1], Changguo Wang[2], Peng Li[1], Yalin Miao[1], and Zhengzhong Bian[1]

[1] School of Life Science and Technology, Xi'an Jiaotong University, Xi'an 710049 China
yugang@mailst.xjtu.edu.cn
[2] Nantong Vocational College, Nantong 226007, China

Abstract. A novel statistical framework for segmentation of the echocardiographic images is presented. The framework begins with pre-segmentation at a low resolution image and passes the result to the high resolution image for a fast optimal segmentation. We applied Rayleigh distribution to analyze the echocardiographic image, and introduced a posterior probability-based level set model. The model is applied for the pre-segmentation. The pre-segmentation result at the low resolution is used to initialize the front for the high resolution image with a fast scheme. At the high resolution, an efficient statistical active contour model is used to make the curve smoother and drives it closer to the real boundary. Segmentation results show that the statistical framework can extract the boundary accurately and automatically.

1 Introduction

Many heart diseases are accompanied with the change of heart shape. Automatic segmentation of echocardiographic images that helps identify early features of pathological changes plays an important role in medical diagnosis. Although various segmentation methods have been widely investigated, there are still challenges for ultrasound image segmentation because of noise and low contrast.

Early approaches for segmentation of echocardiographic images include some statistical methods[2]. However, the detection accuracy of these methods is to be validated. In the decade, many researches on ultrasound signals have proved that the intensity of ultrasound images is close to Rayleigh distribution, such as [13][14]. Some researchers began to apply the Rayleigh distribution to analyze the ultrasound images.

Recently, Sethian et al firstly introduced the level set method into geometric active contour models for numerical implementation [1]. Many level-set-based models for image segmentation were proposed in the past [4][5], because the level set method is steady and suitable for various topology changes. Chan provided an active contours model without edges[6], but it only applied the mean intensity of inner and outer curve to analyze the images, which was difficult to segment complicated images such as ultrasound ones. A geodesic model based on gradient vector flow was proposed by Nikos[7], but it costed a great deal of

N. Zheng, X. Jiang, and X. Lan (Eds.): IWICPAS 2006, LNCS 4153, pp. 396–405, 2006.

computation time and might fail in weak boundary. Other researchers developed segmentation algorithms with priori shape knowledge to detect boundaries in echocardiographic images [3]. However, the shape knowledge is usually difficult to learn. In most cases, the extensive training cost is necessary. Especially, a learned shape template can be only used to segment a specific class of images with a similar boundary shape. Recently, the shape information about the target to be segmented was combined into the active contour models, such as [9][10], which improved the segmentation result of specific shape similar to the shape template, but the shape template was difficult to describe the real medical tissues with various individuality.

This paper presents an efficient segmentation framework for echocardiographic images with Rayleigh distribution. The remainder of the paper is organized as follows. In Section 2, the proposed framework is described in detail. In Section 3, experiments are presented; and finally, conclusions are reported.

2 Statistical Segmentation Framework

The proposed segmentation framework is based on multiresolution technique, which is robust to the speckle noise in the original ultrasound images. The algorithm begins with pre-segmentation at a low resolution and passes the result to the high resolution for a fast optimal segmentation. At the low resolution, a Rayleigh distribution-based model is developed for pre-segmentation. Furthermore, a fast method passing solution from low resolution to high resolution is developed. At the high resolution, an external statistical constraint is applied to optimize the final result.

2.1 Nonlinear Scale Space

Perona and Malik showed that a scale space could be represented by a progression of images computed by the heat diffusion equation [11][12]. The heat diffusion equation for the pixel at location (x, y) of image I and time t is:

$$\frac{\partial I}{\partial t} = div(D \cdot \nabla I) \tag{1}$$

Where ∇ is the gradient operator,D is the heat diffusion coefficient. When D is defined as a constant in all locations, the diffusion equation is equal to isotropic diffusion, i.e. Gaussian smoothing. When D is a matrix, the equation is anisotropic diffusion. Perona and Malik firstly introduced nonlinear diffusion into the image processing context. The Perona-Malik(P-M) diffusion equation[12] is isotropic and nonlinear diffusion like Gaussian smoothing, but it reduces the diffusion coefficient in the edges, so it may protect the edges in the ultrasound images while removing the noise. The diffusion coefficient of P-M diffusion equation is given by

$$D = \exp(-\frac{\|\nabla I\|^2}{K^2}) \tag{2}$$

Where k is a parameter. We then build a scale space based on nonlinear diffusion pyramid to analyze the echocardiographic image by the P-M diffusion equation.

2.2 Rayleigh Distribution-Based Statistical Model

As mentioned before, the intensity distribution of the original echocardiographic image is close to Rayleigh distribution. The Rayleigh distribution is described as:

$$P(I(x)|\Omega_u) = \frac{I(x)}{\mu_u} \exp(-\frac{I(x)^2}{2\mu_u}), \mu_u > 0 \tag{3}$$

Where $I(x)$ is the intensity value of pixel x,μ_u is the Rayliegh parameter and Ω_u represents the region u in the ultrasound image. The equation (3) describes the probability density of the intensity $I(x)$ belonging to the specific Rayleigh distribution with parameter μ_u.

According to the Bayesian rule, the posterior probability can be obtained.

$$P(\Omega_u|I(x)) = \frac{P(I(x)|\Omega_u)P(\Omega_u)}{P(I(x))} \tag{4}$$

Where $P(\Omega_u)$ is the prior probability of region Ω_u . The region probability function based on the posterior probability can be defined as:

$$P_u = \prod_{x \in \Omega_u} P(\Omega_u|I(x)) \tag{5}$$

If the image has two different regions,$u = a$ or b , where a is the target to be extracted, b is the background. The segmentation procedure is to find the suitable region Ω_a and Ω_b so as to maximize the criterion $f = P_a P_b$. The maximum criterion is maximal when all the pixels including the target and background are classified accurately.

The multiplication of f can be transformed into the summation.

$$l = -\log f = -(\log P_a + \log P_b) \tag{6}$$

According to gradient descendent method, the speed function for level set can be obtained.

$$F(I_o(x)) = \log \mu_a - \log \mu_b + \frac{I_o(x)^2 - 2\mu_a}{2\mu_a} - \frac{I_o(x)^2 - 2\mu_b}{2\mu_b} + \log(p(\Omega_b)) - \log(p(\Omega_a)) \tag{7}$$

Where $\mu_u = \frac{1}{2N_u} \sum_{x \in \Omega_x} I(x)^2$. The equation (7) is the speed function of point $I_o(x)$ to be updated, which is a Rayleigh distribution-based statistical model. Obviously, the equation (7) is also a region-based model, because it only uses the inner and outer region information of the evolution curve.

Usually, the prior probability $P(\Omega_a)$ and $P(\Omega_b)$ can be obtained by a pre-segmentation algorithm such as Fuzzy C-Means. In most simple case, $P(\Omega_a)$ is approximatively equal to $P(\Omega_b)$, if the prior probability is ignored. A similar model with Rayleigh distribution was published in [13]. The model made use only of the likelihood with Rayleigh distribution, i.e. the equation (3), so the prior information about the regions to be segmented was ignored. Therefore, the model is special case of the proposed model, where $P(\Omega_a) = P(\Omega_b)$. The segmentation result of the model in [13] is demonstrated in the experiment.

According to level set method, the evolution equation for level set is defined as:

$$\frac{\partial \Phi}{\partial t} = \varepsilon(F - \lambda k)|\nabla \Phi| \tag{8}$$

Where k is the curvature of the evolution curve,Φ is the level set function, and F is given in equation (7). ε and λ are the weight parameters. The curvature item λk makes the curve length minimum when the curve converges.

In most cases, the region-based models may bring more computational cost. More importantly, the models may converge at a local minimum solution. Therefore, we choose geodesic active contour as the boundary information estimation term [4]. The pre-segmentation model is then given by:

$$\frac{\partial \Phi}{\partial t} = \alpha \times F|\nabla \Phi| + (1-\alpha)\{g(|\nabla I|)(c_1 + c_2 k) \cdot |\nabla \Phi| - (\nabla g(|\nabla I|) \cdot \overrightarrow{N}) \cdot |\nabla \Phi|\} \tag{9}$$

Where α is a weight parameter. c_1 ,c_2 are the parameters,$\overrightarrow{N}$ is the unit normal vector of the curve, k is the curvature,I is the intensity value of original image. Note that the minimum length constraint of Rayleigh model is written into the geodesic contour model. The equation (9) is the evolution equation for pre-segmentation at low resolution, which can be implemented by level set method.

2.3 Passing Solution Between the Adjacent Levels

In order to improve the segmentation performance, the pre-segmentation solution at the low resolution should be passed to the high resolution and a new evolution is performed for desirable results. Conventional methods for passing solution are high computational cost because they interpolate the obtained contour at the high resolution. In this section, we present a more efficient scheme based on mathematical morphology

Step 1. Passing all the interior points to the high resolution

If μ is a scaling factor from the low resolution L_{j+1} to the high resolution L_j, there are $\mu * \mu$ points in Level L_j, which correspond to one point at level L_{j+1}. For example, if μ is 2, for a point $u(i,j)$ at L_{j+1}, the corresponding four points are $u(2i,2j)$,$u(2j+1,2j)$,$u(2i,2j+1)$,$u(2i+1,2j+1)$ at L_j. Therefore, we can obtain all interior point locations of the evolution curve at level L_j.

Step 2. Extracting the Front

After Step 1, we obtain all interior point locations at high resolution level, seeing the left image of figure 1. We then apply morphological dilation to extract the boundary of the interior region, i.e. the front. The extraction operation is defined as:

$$ImageB = ImageA \otimes A - ImageA \tag{10}$$

The structure element A is 3*3 strong template. $ImageA$ is the mirror image at high resolution level, where let the all interior points be 1 and other points be 0. $ImageB$ is the mirror image of the extracted front. See Figure1.

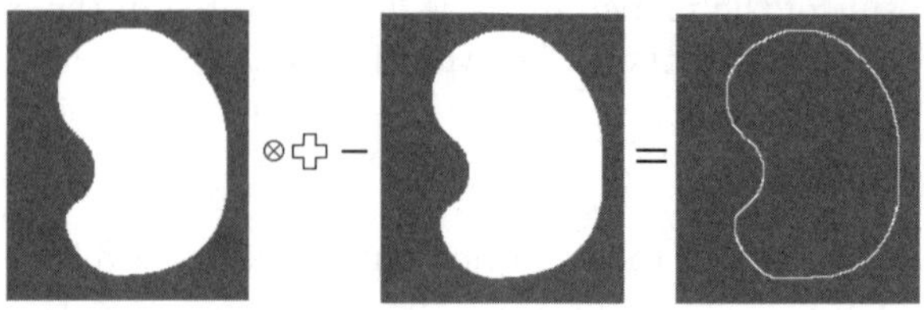

Fig. 1. Extracting the Front

Step 3. Dilation around the front
The dilation operation is defined as:

$$ImageC = ImageB \otimes B \tag{11}$$

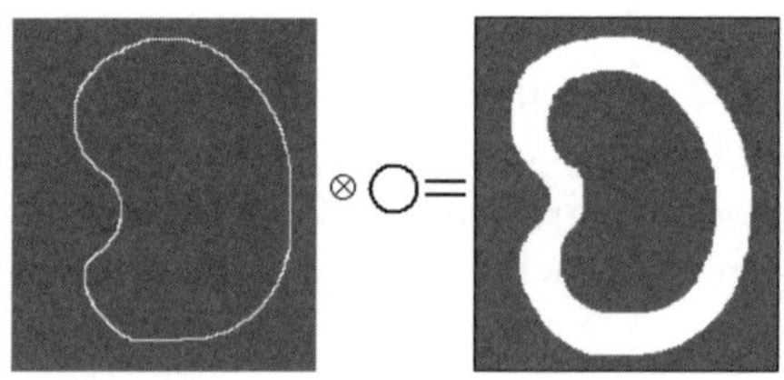

Fig. 2. Rebuilding the narrow band

Dilation operation is performed around the extracted front, whose structure element B is a disc. In our method, usual computational cost, such as fast marching algorithm, is unnecessary. Meanwhile, the reconstruction method is self-adaptive, and the radius of the disc is also the narrowband width, which can be reset during the evolution. During the dilation operation, the distance between a point in the narrow band and the center of disc should be stored in the temporary memory, which is also the new distance function value.

After Step 3, a new narrow band at the high resolution is rebuilt. It is also the initial state of a new evolution. The scheme passing solution from the low resolution to high resolution is very rapid, because the mathematical morphology operators are more efficient than conventional interpolation computation.

2.4 Local Statistical Model for Optimization

After pre-segmentation at the low resolution, the initial curve is obtained. Although the curve is close to the real boundary, the optimization segmentation is necessary for more accurate result.

Without the further constraints, the boundary-based models such as geodesic active contour are easy to leak from weak boundary. The global information-based models such as Yezzi's global model should not be applied to optimize segmentation because the global approaches are based on all the image data. They are invalid in echocardiographic images because it is very difficult to estimate the global intensity distribution in original images with a great deal of noise. The more important thing is that a pre-segmentation result has been obtained, so the global separation is unnecessary. Therefore, we develop a local model based on the statistical method. The energy function is given by:

$$E = -(\mu'_a - \mu'_b)^2 + \lambda \oint ds \tag{12}$$

Where

$$\mu'_a = \frac{1}{2N'_a} \sum_{x \in \Omega_a} I(x)^2 H(\Phi(I(x)) + r) H(-\Phi(I(x))) \tag{13}$$

$$\mu'_b = \frac{1}{2N'_b} \sum_{x \in \Omega_b} I(x)^2 H(\Phi(I(x)) + r) H(-\Phi(I(x))) \tag{14}$$

μ'_a ,μ'_b are the Rayleigh parameters of target and background region in the original image.Φ is the level set function, whose value of the points inside evolution curve is smaller than 0, and that of exterior points is bigger than 0. H is the Heaviside function. r is a positive constant, which is often defined as the width of narrowband. Accordingly, N'_a,N'_b are the pixel number inside and outside the curve in narrowband respectively. It is obvious that μ'_a ,μ'_b are also the Rayleigh parameter estimation of inside and outside curve in the narrowband, whose distance function absolute values are smaller than the constant r .$\oint ds$ is the Euclidean length of the curve, which makes the curve smoother. λ is a weight parameter. The equation (12) is a local model, which only analyzes the region, whose distance function absolute values are smaller than the constant r . The equation (12) is straightforward, where the curve should make the difference of Rayleigh distribution of the two regions inside and outside the curve as big as possible.

The Euclidean length of the curve C is given by $L = \oint ds$. It is easy to prove that the flow

$$\frac{\partial C}{\partial t} = k\vec{N} \tag{15}$$

Where k is the curvature of curve C. Accordingly, the speed function is defined as:

$$F = -\nabla E = (\mu'_a - \mu'_b) \cdot \left(\frac{I(x)^2 - 2\mu'_a}{N'_a} + \frac{I(x)^2 - 2\mu'_b}{N'_b}\right) + \lambda k \tag{16}$$

The curve evolution equation for optimization segmentation is then defined as:

$$\frac{\partial \Phi}{\partial t} = \{(\mu'_a - \mu'_b) \cdot \left(\frac{I(x)^2 - 2\mu'_a}{N'_a} + \frac{I(x)^2 - 2\mu'_b}{N'_b}\right) + \lambda k\} |\nabla \Phi| \tag{17}$$

Where Φ is level set function.

3 Experiment

We choose the sequences of echocardiographic images as experimental datasets. The final objective is to track the heart movement. We segment every image in the dataset and reconstruct the heart issue. Before reconstruction, image segmentation is performed using the proposed method in this paper.

Before the segmentation, the nonlinear diffusion pyramid is built. The parameters of Perona-Malik diffusion equation are chosen as: $t = 0.2$,$k = 0.1$, which are suitable for most images. The default iteration number is 10. After smoothing the original image, we subsample it to create the subsequent levels of the pyramid. In the following experiments, the parameters are chosen as follows. In equation 9,$\alpha = 0.6$,$c_1 = 1$,$c_2 = 0.2$ work well in most images. In the equation 17,λ is fixed to 0.4.

We provide two groups of experiments to demonstrate the performance of the proposed method, which describe the segmentation result of original ultrasound images with different slices. The original images are shown in Figure 3.1 and Figure 5.1. In the first experiment, Figure3.2 is a low resolution image obtained from the diffusion pyramid of original image. Figure 3.3 denotes the initial state of the evolution curve, which is described by a white curve. The curve is propagated under the pre-segmentation model, i.e. the equation 9, where the region-based and boundary-based information are applied for accurate segmentation. Figure 3.4 is the pre-segmentation result at a low-resolution level. Figure 4.1 magnifies the pre-segmentation result image one times. Figure 4.2 is the initial state of the curve at high resolution level. The initial solution is passed from the low resolution image Figure 3.4 by our mathematical morphology-based scheme. The curve of Figure 4.1 and Figure 4.2 is almost equivalent to each other, which proves that the solution in the low resolution is transferred to high resolution level accurately. The result demonstrates that our method has an excellent performance in terms of accuracy. Figure 4.3 is the optimized result under the local constraint of statistical model(the equation 17). Compared with the pre-segmentation result 3.4 or 4.1, it is closer to real boundary and smoother. Figure 5 and Figure 6 are the segmentation results of another slice. We also provide the pre-segmentation and optimized result respectively, which demonstrate the similar performance like the first experiment. Every computation time of the above experiments is no more than 5 seconds, where our model is implemented in the computer with CPU P4-1.6GHz and 256M memory.

The segmentation results of two conventional snake, Ning's active contour[15] and Rayleigh statistical model[13], are given by Figure 7. Figure 7.1 is the pre-segmentation result of the Ning's model in low resolution image. The intensity distribution seems to be Gaussian after a big Gaussian template is applied in the original image. However, the curve is easy to leak from the boundary, because the gradient information is too weak. Figure7.2 shows the result of Rayleigh statistical model in [13]. The curve without boundary information converges at a local minimum location and several wrong regions are labeled. It is obvious that the result of Rayleigh statistical model in [13] was sensitive to inhomogeneous

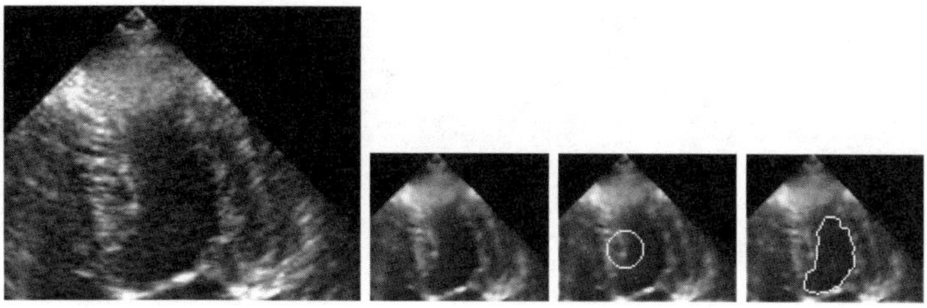

3.1 3.2 3.3 3.4

Fig. 3. original image and segmentation result at the low resolution level. 3.1 original image;3.2 low resolution image; 3.3 the initial state; 3.4 pre-segmentation result.

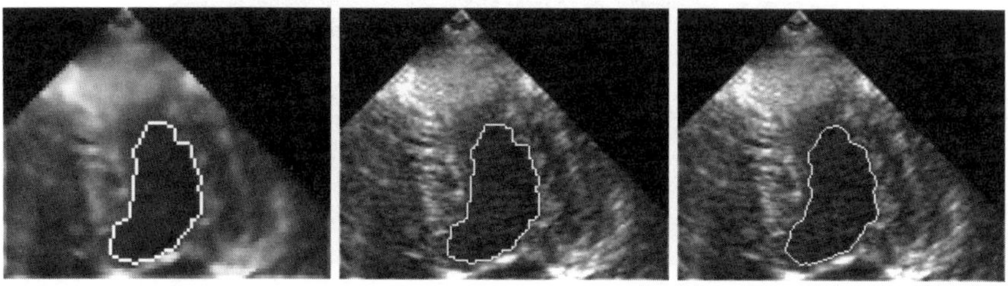

4.1 4.2 4.3

Fig. 4. the initial state and optimized result at high resolution level. The similarity of 4.1 and 4.2 shows the accuracy of our scheme for passing solutions between the adjacent levels.

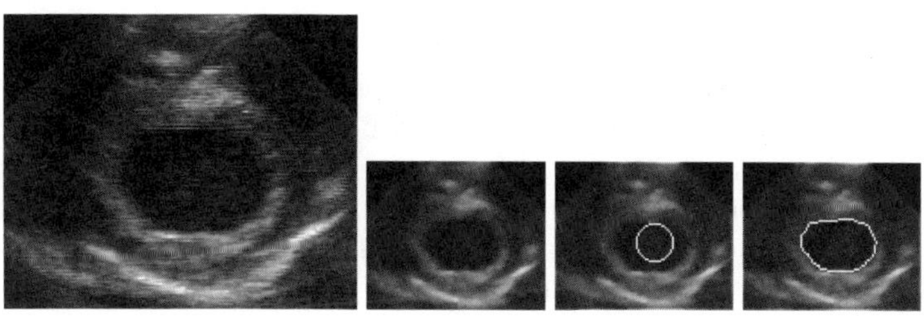

5.1 5.2 5.3 5.4

Fig. 5. original image and segmentation result at the low resolution level. 5.1 original image;5.2 low resolution image; 5.3 the initial state; 5.4 pre-segmentation result.

regions with serious noises, because the intensity of real ultrasound image is often low SNR(Signal Noise Ratio). In this case, an efficient smoothing scheme like the proposed mulitiresolution framework is necessary. Moreover, in order to describe the intensity distribution accurately, the prior information should be included.

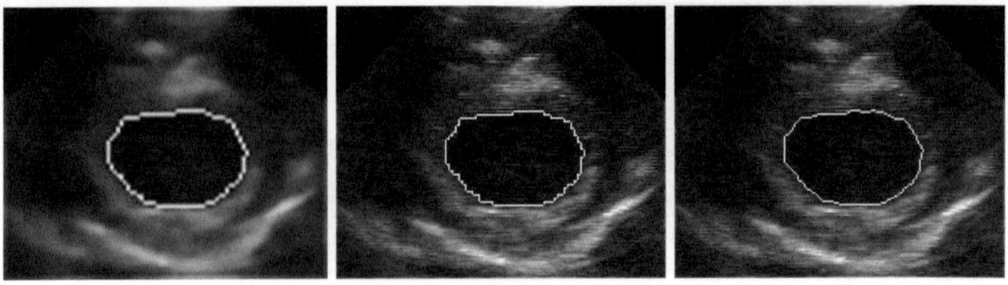

6.1 6.2 6.3

Fig. 6. the initial state and optimized result at high resolution level. 6.1 the magnified image of 5.4; 6.2 the initial state at high resolution level;6.3 the optimized result.

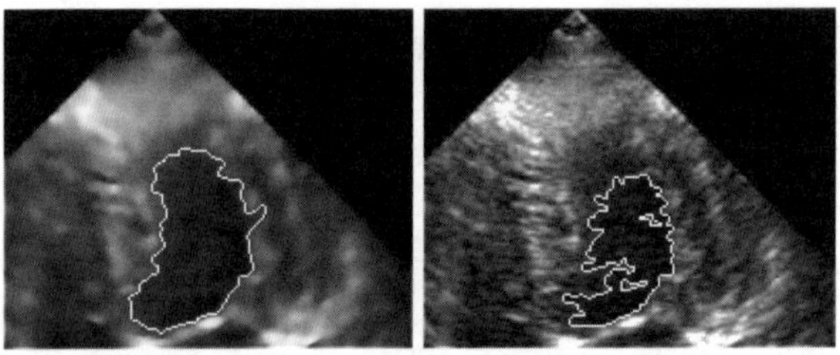

7.1 7.2

Fig. 7. The segmentation result of Ning's model and Rayleigh statistical model. 7.1 Ning's model, 7.2 Rayleigh statistical model.

4 Conclusions

In this paper, we proposed a novel statistical multiresolution framework for segmentation of left ventricle image. We applied the Rayleigh distribution to analyze the original ultrasound images, and provided a Rayleigh-based model, which describes the region information of the target to be extracted and background. The model is based on the optimization of maximal posterior probability of two partitioned regions. A pre-segmentation model integrating region- and boundary-based information function was designed to analyze the image at a low resolution level. Meanwhile, a rapid scheme passing the solution from the low resolution to high resolution was also developed. The scheme was based on mathematical morphology and did not need interpolation computation. The high performance also makes it suitable for real-time applications. Furthermore, an efficient statistical optimization method at the high resolution level was proposed, which propagates the curve towards the real boundary. The proposed optimization approach is local and rapid because the initial curve is close to desirable result. The proposed framework is implemented in a level set method and is suitable for various topologic changes. This segmentation framework was tested using a great deal of ultrasound images and the experiments showed that it is accurate.

References

1. J.A.Sechian,Level Set Methods and Fast Marching Methods. Cambridge University Press, New York(1999).
2. Xiao G., Brady M., Noble J., Zhang Y, Segmentation of Ultrasound B-mode Images with Intensity in Homogeneity Correction IEEE Transactions on Medical Imaging, Vol.21, No.1, 2002(48-57).
3. Chen Y., Thinuvenkadam S.: On the Incorporation of Shape Priors into Geometric Active Contours. IEEE Workshop on Variational and Level set Methods in Computer Vision (2001)45-152.
4. V. Caselles, R. Kimmel, G. Spairo, Geodesic Active Contours. International Journal of Computer Vision, Vol22,(1997)61-79.
5. Yezzi A., Jr., Andy T., Alan W. A Fully Global Approach to Image Segmentation via Coupled Curve Evolution Equations. Journal of Visual Communication and Image Representation 13, (2002)195-216.
6. Tony F. Chan. Active Contours without Edges. IEEE Transaction On Image Processing, Vol10, No 2, (2001)266-277.
7. Nikos P., Olivier M.G. and Visvanathan R. Gradient Vector Flow Fast Geometric Active Contours. IEEE Transactions on Pattern Analysis and Machine Intelligence, Vol26, No3, (2004)402-407.
8. Pascal M., Philippe R. and Francois G., Prederic G. Influence of the Noise Model on Level Set Active Contour Segmentation. IEEE Transactions on Pattern Analysis and Machine Intelligence, Vol.26, No.6, (2004).799-803.
9. Nikos P. A Level Set Approach for Shape-driven Segmentation and Tracking of the Left Ventricle. IEEE Transactions on medical imaging, Vol 22, No 6, (2003)773-776.
10. Zhao Z., Stephen R. A., Eam K. T. A Novel 3D Paritioned Active Shape Model for Segmentation of Brain MR Images. Part I, Medical Image Computing and Computer-Assisted Intervention, (2005)221-228.
11. S. T. Acton, A. C. Bovik, M.M. Crawford. Anisotropic diffusion pyramids for image segmentation. IEEE Conference on Image Processing, (1994)478-482.
12. P. Perona and J. Malik. Scale-space and Edge Detection using Anisotropic Diffusion. IEEE Transaction On Pattern Anal. and Mach. Intell., Vol. 12, No. 6,(1990)629-639.
13. Alessandro S., Cristiana C., Elena M., and Claudio L. Maximum Likelihood Segmentation of Ultrasound Images with Rayleigh Distribution. IEEE Transactions on Ultrasonics, Ferroelectrics, and Frequency Control, Vol. 52, No. 6, (2005)947-960.
14. Navalgund R., Sumat M. and Zhu H. Ultrasound speckle statistics variations with imaging systems impulse response. IEEE Ultrasonics Symposium, Vol.3, (1990)1435 - 1440.
15. Ning L, Weichuan Y, James S.D. Combinative Multi-scale Level Set Framework for Echocardiographic Image Segmentation. Medical Image Analysis, 7, (2004)529-537.

A Bayesian Estimation Approach to Super-Resolution Reconstruction for Face Images

Hua Huang[1], Xin Fan[2], Chun Qi[1], and Shihua Zhu[1]

[1] Xi'an jiaotong University, 710049 Xi'an, China
{huanghua, qichun, szhu}@xjtu.edu.cn
[2] Dalian Maritime University, 116026 Dalian, China
fanxin@dlmu.edu.cn

Abstract. Most previous super-resolution (SR) approaches are implemented with two individual cascade steps, image registration and image fusion, which handicaps the incorporation of the structural information of the objects of interest, e.g. human faces, into SR in a parallel way. This prior information is beneficial to either robust motion estimation or fusion with higher quality. In this paper, SR reconstruction is formulated as Bayesian state estimation of location and appearance parameters of a face model. In addition, a sequential Monte Carlo (SMC) based algorithm is proposed to achieve the probabilistic state estimation, i.e. SR reconstruction in our formulation. Image alignment and image fusion are combined into one unified framework in the proposed approach, in which the prior information from the face model is incorporated into both registration and fusion process of SR. Experiments performed on synthesized frontal face sequences show that the proposed approach gains superior performance in registration as well as reconstruction.

1 Introduction

Super-resolution (SR) refers to reconstructing a high resolution (HR) image from a series of low resolution (LR) images. In most traditional approaches, SR reconstruction is implemented with two individual cascade steps, i.e., image registration and image fusion [1]. Image registration is performed prior to the fusion step in order to compute the relative motion fields between pixels of consecutive image frames. The LR image frames are aligned by using the estimated motion fields and then fused into a HR image by some sophisticated techniques, in which additional constraints on the desired HR image are usually imposed so as to resolve the inherent illness of the inverse process of reconstruction [1,2].

Image registration is such a critical step to SR reconstruction that the accuracy of the estimated motion fields determines the quality of reconstructed HR images [3]. The Lucas-Kanade (LK) algorithm and its variants are widely used for motion estimation in SR reconstruction due to their efficiency [4]. Though the LK based algorithms with pyramid searching strategy can handle a wide range of translation, it is not robust enough to obtain accurate motion fields in many

N. Zheng, X. Jiang, and X. Lan (Eds.): IWICPAS 2006, LNCS 4153, pp. 406–415, 2006.

critical cases, e.g., non-linear motion, low quality images. The performance of motion estimation can be improved further by combining the prior information of object. These techniques may be helpful for SR reconstruction.

The second step, data fusion, essentially needs to make use of the information about the image formation process that yields the LR image sequences. Besides, the prior knowledge pertaining to the original HR image is required to regularize the ill-posed inverse process of reconstruction. Recently, recognition-based priors have been incorporated into the fusion step to substitute the smoothness priors [1,5,6,7]. However, it is supposed that accurate motion fields have been estimated prior to fusion, that is, the recognition-based priors are not incorporated into both steps of the SR reconstruction.

We observe that there exists a dilemma in the previous SR methods that the fusion of LR image frames demands accurate motion estimation. However, the lack of HR image information, leads to the difficulties in obtaining accurate motion fields. The cause of this dilemma lies in that the process of SR reconstruction is divided into two steps connected in an open-loop way. On the other hand, it is beneficial for both steps to take into account the prior information of the object. In this paper we pose SR reconstruction as Bayesian state estimation of location and appearance parameters of a face model. The face model is composed of several conditional dependent statistical models to represent facial components with geometrical constraints. Both the appearance parameters and location parameters are simultaneously estimated by a novel SMC based method within this unified Bayesian framework. The high level prior knowledge in terms of statistical models is incorporated into the both steps of SR reconstruction, which yields both robust motion estimation and high quality SR reconstruction. The textures of the facial components are generated by the estimated appearance parameters, and then laid in the estimated positions to obtain the desired HR face image.

2 Part-Based Face Model

As known, a face is such an object that presents highly structured characteristics. These characteristics can be summarized as follows: 1) a face can be composed of several components in a semantic sense, e.g., eyes, nose and mouth; 2) each component exhibits structural appearance; and 3) the locations and appearance of the components are highly constrained. We use a graphical model [8] to represent the appearance of the facial components as well as the relationships between the components.

We only consider four facial components, i.e. two eyes, nose and mouth, because these components are the key features to determine the identity of a face. Figure 1 gives the graphical structure of the proposed model. The graph is composed of four nodes and exhibits a tree structure. The nodes X_i represent the locations and appearance parameters of facial components, denoted as $\mathbf{X}_i := (\mathbf{l}_i, \mathbf{a}_i)$. Locations are given by affine parameters, i.e. translations in the image plane and scale $\mathbf{l} = (t_x, t_y, s)$, while appearance parameters for each node are determined via principal component analysis (PCA) model of each facial component, which is similar to modular eigenface [9]. The appearance of each facial component is generated by:

$$\mathbf{T}_i = \mathbf{T}_{i0} + \mathbf{\Phi}_i \mathbf{a}_i \tag{1}$$

where $\mathbf{T}_{i0}$ denotes the mean feature of the ith component and $\mathbf{\Phi}_i$ is a matrix composed of the principal eigen vectors of the covariance of the ith component.

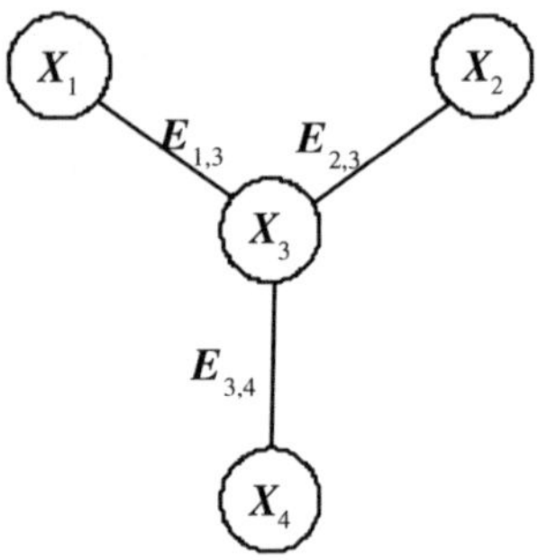

Fig. 1. The graphical structure of part-based face model

The edge set $\mathbf{E} = \bigcup \mathbf{E}_{i,j}$ in the graph indicates the conditional dependence between facial components. These dependences are related by pair wise interaction potentials $\psi(\mathbf{X}_i, \mathbf{X}_j)$:

$$\psi(\mathbf{X}_i, \mathbf{X}_j) = \psi_l(\mathbf{l}_i, \mathbf{l}_j)\psi_a(\mathbf{a}_i, \mathbf{a}_j) \tag{2}$$

where i and j are the indices of graph nodes. The tree structure in this graphical model is specified in advance for the simplicity of the learning process.

The appearance model for each facial component and the potentials in Eq. (2) are learnt from a number of example images with annotated positions and masks of facial components. Performing standard PCA on the training images of facial components can yield the appearance models. We model the potential between the positions of facial components ψ_l as a Gaussian density. The mean and variance of the Gaussian density are estimated from the annotated positions. And the potential functions ψ_a relating coefficients of appearance models are approximated by kernel density estimates [10] from the training images.

Once the trained models are available, images of any facial components can be generated by specified appearance parameters $\mathbf{a}_i$ and then these images can be set to their corresponding locations $\mathbf{l}_i$ to produce a face image. SR reconstruction of a face image becomes probabilistic estimation of the values of four nodes $\mathbf{X}_i$ from the available LR images.

3 Bayesian Formulation of SR Reconstruction

We cast the SR reconstruction of a face image as the probabilistic state estimation of N nodes $\mathbf{X}_t = (\mathbf{X}_{1t}, \cdots, \mathbf{X}_{it}, \cdots, \mathbf{X}_{Nt})$ given LR image frames $\mathbf{Y}^t = (\mathbf{Y}_1, \cdots, \mathbf{Y}_t)$ up to time t. These estimated parameters give a plausible high quality image by accumulating observed information from the LR image sequence and incorporating prior knowledge from the defined face model. The posterior probability density can be recursively updated as [11]:

$$p(\mathbf{X}_t \left| \mathbf{Y}^t \right.) \propto p(\mathbf{Y}_t \left| \mathbf{X}_t \right.) \int\limits_{\mathbf{X}_{t-1}} p(\mathbf{X}_t \left| \mathbf{X}_{t-1} \right.) p(\mathbf{X}_{t-1} \left| \mathbf{Y}^{t-1} \right.) \tag{3}$$

where the likelihood $p(\mathbf{Y}_t \left| \mathbf{X}_t \right.)$ expresses how the current state $\mathbf{X}_t$ fits the observations available at time t. We assume that a face performs the movement with slight deviation from frontal view so that facial components do not occlude each other. The likelihood can be represented as the product of the likelihood densities of facial components, that is

$$p(\mathbf{Y}_t \left| \mathbf{X}_t \right.) = \prod_i p(\mathbf{Y}_{it} \left| \mathbf{X}_{it} \right.) \tag{4}$$

The transition density $p(\mathbf{X}_t \left| \mathbf{X}_{t-1} \right.)$ gives the relationship between the face states of two consecutive time steps, t and $t-1$. Motivated by the idea of using MRF to model the constraints between components within a time step [12,13], we factorize the transition density as:

$$p(\mathbf{X}_t \left| \mathbf{X}_{t-1} \right.) \propto \prod_i p(\mathbf{X}_{it} \left| \mathbf{X}_{i(t-1)} \right.) \prod_{(i,j) \in \mathbf{E}} \psi(\mathbf{X}_{it}, \mathbf{X}_{jt}) \tag{5}$$

This factorization makes it possible to extract the interactions between nodes out of the integral over $\mathbf{X}_{t-1}$ in Eq. (3).

4 SMC Based Inference Algorithm

In a SMC method [11], the posterior density $p(\mathbf{X}_{t-1} \left| \mathbf{Y}^{t-1} \right.)$ is approximated by a set of samples $\mathbf{X}_{t-1}^k$ associated with corresponding weights w_{t-1}^k, i.e.,$\{\mathbf{X}_{t-1}^k, w_{t-1}^k\}_{k=1}^{N_s}$, where N_s is the number of samples. Then the integral in Eq. (3) is approximated as the summation of the weighted samples:

$$p(\mathbf{X}_t \left| \mathbf{Y}^t \right.) \approx p(\mathbf{Y}_t \left| \mathbf{X}_t \right.) \sum_k w_{t-1}^k p(\mathbf{X}_t \left| \mathbf{X}_{t-1}^k \right.) \tag{6}$$

We draw samples $\mathbf{X}_t^k$ from the prior transition density $p(\mathbf{X}_t \left| \mathbf{X}_{t-1}^k \right.)$, that is

$$\mathbf{X}_t^k \sim p(\mathbf{X}_t \left| \mathbf{X}_{t-1}^k \right.) \tag{7}$$

and then the associated weights w_t^k are updated as

$$w_t^k = p(\mathbf{Y}_t \left| \mathbf{X}_t^k \right.) \, w_{t-1}^k \tag{8}$$

With the samples $\mathbf{X}_t^k$ properly weighted by w_t^k , the state up to a time step t can be inferred by a MAP estimate or a mean estimate. Eqs. (7) and (8) give one iteration step of a standard SMC method. We need to devise a novel sample propagating and weight updating algorithm to accommodate the proposed graphical structure.

4.1 Sample Propagation

Substituting Eq. (5) into Eq. (6), we obtain:

$$p(\mathbf{X}_t \left| \mathbf{Y}^t \right.) \approx p(\mathbf{Y}_t \left| \mathbf{X}_t \right.) \prod_{ij \in E} \psi(\mathbf{X}_{it}, \mathbf{X}_{jt}) [\sum_k w_{t-1}^k \prod_i p(\mathbf{X}_{it} \left| \mathbf{X}_{i(t-1)}^k \right.) \tag{9}$$

This means that we can use the samples of $\prod_i p(\mathbf{X}_{it} \left| \mathbf{X}_{i(t-1)}^k \right.)$ instead of directly sampling from $p(\mathbf{X}_t \left| \mathbf{X}_{t-1}^k \right.)$ as Eq. (7) to approximate the integral over $\mathbf{X}_{t-1}$ in Eq. (refeqn3). We independently sample the transition density of each component, $p(\mathbf{X}_{it} \left| \mathbf{X}_{i(t-1)}^k \right.)$, in order to form the samples $\{\mathbf{X}_t^k\}_{k=1}^{N_s}$:

$$\mathbf{X}_t^k \sim \prod_i p(\mathbf{X}_{it} \left| \mathbf{X}_{i(t-1)}^k \right.) \tag{10}$$

For any nodes in the graph shown in Figure 1, the state vector is composed of location and appearance parameters, that is,

$$p(\mathbf{X}_{it} \left| \mathbf{X}_{i(t-1)} \right.) = p(\mathbf{l}_{it}, \mathbf{a}_{it} \left| \mathbf{l}_{i(t-1)}, \mathbf{a}_{i(t-1)} \right.) \tag{11}$$

Derived from multiplication rule, we rewrite it as

$$p(\mathbf{l}_{it}, \mathbf{a}_{it} \left| \mathbf{l}_{i(t-1)}, \mathbf{a}_{i(t-1)} \right.) = p(\mathbf{a}_{it} \left| \mathbf{l}_{it}, \mathbf{l}_{i(t-1)}, \mathbf{a}_{i(t-1)} \right.) p(\mathbf{l}_{it} \left| \mathbf{l}_{i(t-1)}, \mathbf{a}_{i(t-1)} \right.) \tag{12}$$

We assume that location $\mathbf{l}_{it}$ is determined only by the given location at the previous time step (t-1), and is independent from the appearance at (t-1), $\mathbf{a}_{i(t-1)}$, i.e.,

$$p(\mathbf{l}_{it} \left| \mathbf{l}_{i(t-1)}, \mathbf{a}_{i(t-1)} \right.) = p(\mathbf{l}_{it} \left| \mathbf{l}_{i(t-1)} \right.) \tag{13}$$

Thus, we can sample a new particle for location $\mathbf{l}_{it}^k$ from the above dynamics model as typical SMC methods do. The probability of the appearance at t given $\mathbf{l}_{it}, \mathbf{l}_{i(t-1)}$ and $\mathbf{a}_{i(t-1)}$ is assumed as a Gaussian:

$$p(\mathbf{a}_{it} \left| \mathbf{l}_{it}, \mathbf{l}_{i(t-1)}, \mathbf{a}_{i(t-1)} \right.) = N(\mathbf{a}_{i(t-1)}, \mathbf{Q}_{i(t-1)}) \tag{14}$$

where $\mathbf{Q}_{i(t-1)}$ is a diagonal matrix with the elements depending on the difference between $\mathbf{l}_{it}$ and $\mathbf{l}_{i(t-1)}$. Large movements are likely to yield great appearance variations, and thus the elements in $\mathbf{Q}_{i(t-1)}$ are rewarded with larger values. Otherwise, smaller variances will be specified. Noticing (14), we use Kalman-like updating equations to propagate appearance coefficients $\mathbf{a}_{it}$ similar to those in [14]. Starting from an initial density $\mathbf{a}_{i0} \sim N(\bar{\mathbf{a}}_{i0}, \mathbf{P}_{i0})$, the probability density of appearance is updated as:

$$\mathbf{P}_{it} = (\mathbf{\Phi}_i^T \mathbf{\Phi}_i + (\mathbf{Q}_{i(t-1)} + \mathbf{P}_{i(t-1)})^{-1})^{-1} \tag{15}$$

$$\bar{\mathbf{a}}_{it} = \mathbf{P}_{it}(\mathbf{\Phi}_i^T \mathbf{Y}_{it} + (\mathbf{Q}_{i(t-1)} + \mathbf{P}_{i(t-1)})^{-1} \bar{\mathbf{a}}_{i(t-1)}) \tag{16}$$

These updating equations circumvent sampling in the higher dimensional appearance subspace so that the proposed method can be implemented in an efficient way.

4.2 Weight Updating

Noticing Eq. (9), we can treat the constraint between nodes as an additional term to update the weights,

$$w_t^k = w_{t-1}^k p(\mathbf{Y}_t | \mathbf{X}_t^k) \prod_{ij \in E} \psi(\mathbf{X}_{it}^k, \mathbf{X}_{jt}^k) = w_{t-1}^k \prod_i p(\mathbf{Y}_{it} | \mathbf{X}_{it}) \prod_{ij \in E} \psi_l(\mathbf{l}_{it}^k, \mathbf{l}_{jt}^k) \psi_a(\mathbf{a}_{it}^k, \mathbf{a}_{jt}^k) \tag{17}$$

where $\psi_l(\mathbf{l}_{it}^k, \mathbf{l}_{jt}^k)$ and $\psi_a(\mathbf{a}_{it}^k, \mathbf{a}_{jt}^k)$ are obtained during the training stage as described above. The likelihood $p(\mathbf{Y}_{it} | \mathbf{X}_{it})$ is calculated as:

$$p(\mathbf{Y}_{it} | \mathbf{X}_{it}) \propto \exp(-\frac{1}{2} \left\| \mathbf{T}_{it}^k - \mathbf{T}_{i0} - \mathbf{\Phi}_i \mathbf{a}_{it}^k \right\|_{\Sigma}^2) \tag{18}$$

where $\mathbf{T}_{it}^k$ is the image obtained by warping the observed LR image with the affine transformation f^k, which is determined by the location samples $\mathbf{l}_{it}^k$. The distance in Eq. (18) is defined as

$$\|\mathbf{x}\|_{\Sigma}^2 = \mathbf{x}^T \Sigma^{-1} \mathbf{x} \tag{19}$$

where Σ is a diagonal matrix with the elements as the eigen values of the covariance of each component.

We perform the modified SMC iteration as Eqs. (13), (15), (16) and (17) to obtain the appearance and location parameters via given the LR images $\mathbf{Y}^t$ up to time step t. We generate patches of facial components with the estimated appearance parameters and fuse them by the estimated location parameters to yield HR face image.

5 Experimental Results

We selected 143 frontal neutral face images from AR data set [15] and flipped them horizontally to double the amount of images. All the images were manually annotated 4 points: the centers of the eyeballs, the tip of the nose, and the center of the mouth. Then PCA models of the four components were built from the extracted images of the corresponding components. We used 10 PCA coefficients to represent the appearance of each component. The interaction potentials between the coefficients were obtained by kernel density estimation from the annotated positions of facial components and corresponding appearance coefficients. Figure 2 shows the learnt interaction potential functions between the first appearance parameters of the connected facial components.

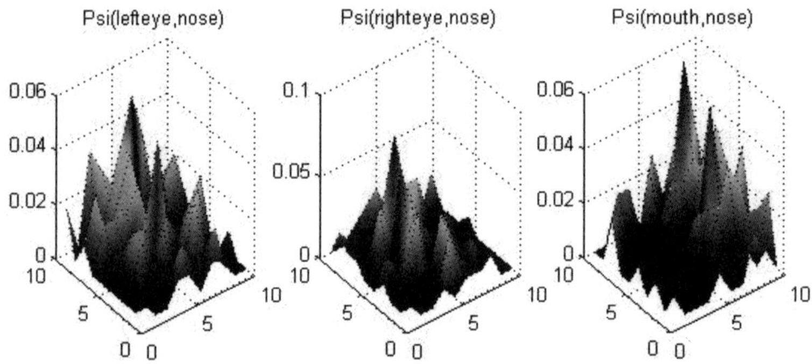

Fig. 2. The potential functions between the first appearance parameters of the facial components

The performance of the proposed approach is examined on synthetic face image sequences. We warped a HR face image into several LR images by specifying location parameters, and then corrupt the LR images by using i.i.d. Gaussian noise with various power dependent on the location parameters.

We investigate the performance of the proposed approach on alignment parameter estimation by compare with the widely used LK algorithm. Figure 3 shows the mean estimation errors obtained by the two algorithms when translational parameters vary with the scaling parameter fixed to 0.5. It can be seen that both algorithms gain accurate estimation. However, the estimation error of LK algorithm becomes higher than the proposed approach when large translation occurs, although the pyramid scheme is adopted in our implementation of LK algorithm. It is reported that LK algorithm is able to estimate large translations with the sub-pixel accuracy. But it is worth noting that the additive noise varies with movement parameters in the experiments, which breaks the brightness consistence assumption in the LK algorithm. In contrast, our approach takes the appearance variations (see Eqs. (15) and (16)) into account so that it gains superior performance. Figure 4 demonstrates the estimate errors with various scaling parameters. As the pyramid scheme cannot cope with large scale variations, LK algorithm does not work well in these cases. However, in our approach, the sampling based inference SMC algorithm that maintains multiple hypotheses can recover from non-maximal modals. Figure 4 shows that the proposed approach gives accurate estimation even when the scaling variation up to 1.8.

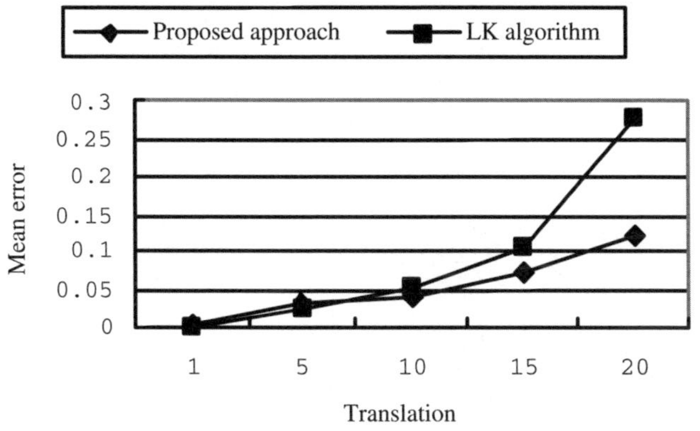

Fig. 3. The mean estimation errors obtained by the proposed approach and LK algorithm

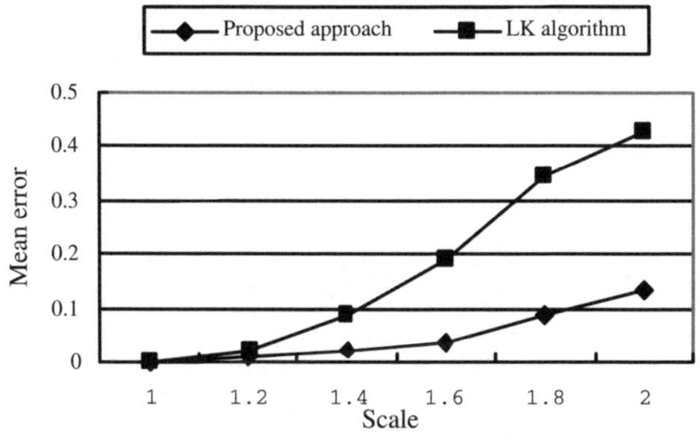

Fig. 4. The effects of scale variations on estimation accuracy

The quality of the reconstructed image by the proposed approach is evaluated subjectively. Figure 5 shows the reconstruction images when down sampling factor is set to 4. It can be shown that bi-cubic interpolation does less on details recovery. Figure 5 (c) shows the reconstructed HR images with the appearance parameters estimated by the proposed approach, where only four facial components (i.e. eyes, nose, and mouth) are considered. Thus, we only estimate the appearance parameters of these facial components and reconstruct the patches of these components. The proposed approach reconstructs HR images with superior visual quality. Because we use the PCA based models derived from the statistical characteristics of face images, the resultant images are robust to additive noise. In the experiments, we find that the reconstructed appearance is not sensitive to location parameters, especially translations, in contrast to the results of traditional two-step SR algorithms [3]. Figure 5 (d) shows that there exist distinct boundaries between facial components and inconsistent overall brightness and some trivial artifacts present. This deficiency can be amended by imposing compatible constraints among the overlapped regions of the facial components as what Freeman et al. [16] did.

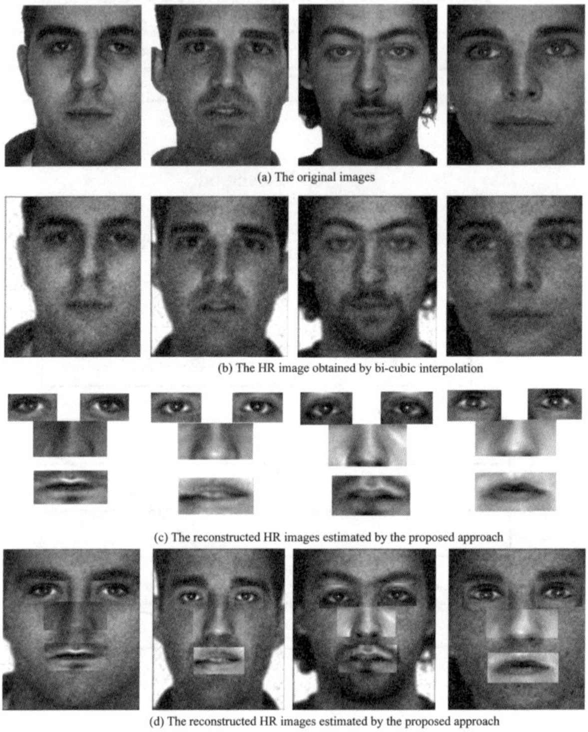

(a) The original images

(b) The HR image obtained by bi-cubic interpolation

(c) The reconstructed HR images estimated by the proposed approach

(d) The reconstructed HR images estimated by the proposed approach

Fig. 5. The results of reconstructing LR face images

6 Conclusion

In this paper, we propose a Bayesian super-resolution approach that combines image alignment and image fusion into one unified framework. The prior information of appearance and position from the face model is incorporated into both alignment and fusion processes of super-resolution, and the higher resolution images are reconstructed via an SMC based inference algorithm. Experimental results show that the proposed approach gains superior performance in the alignment as well as high quality reconstruction. The proposed approach is a primitive attempt for SR via a Bayesian estimation perspective quietly different from existing ones. It is expected that the other inference algorithm than the SMC based one can be used to get more robust and efficient estimation.

References

1. Baker, S., Kanade, T.: Limits on Super-Resolution and How to Break them. IEEE Trans. Pattern Analysis and Machine Intelligence, 9 (2002) 1167-1183.
2. Torre, D. l., Yacoob, Y., et al.: A probabilistic framework for rigid and non-rigid appearance based tracking and recognition., Inter. Conf. Face Recognition and Gesture Analysis, Grenoble, France, (2000) 491-498.
3. Robinson, D., Milanfar, P.: Fundamental Performance Limits in Image Registration. IEEE Trans. Image Processing, 6 (2004) 1185-1199.
4. Baker, S., Matthews, I.: Lucas-Kanade 20 Years On:A Unifying Framework. Inter. J. Computer Vision, 3 (2004) 221-255.
5. Capel, D. P., Zisserman, A.: Super-resolution from multiple views using learnt image models. IEEE Conf. on Computer Vision and Pattern. Recognition, (2001) 627-634.
6. Liu, C., Shum, H. Y., et al.: A two-step approach to hallucinating faces: global parametric model and local nonparametric model. in Proc. of CVPR'01, Hawaii, USA, (2001) 192-198.
7. Wang, X., Tang, X.: Hallucinating face by eigentransformation, IEEE Trans. Systems, Man and Cybernetics, Part C, 3 (2005) 425-434.
8. Jordan, M. I.: Graphical models, Statistical Science, 1 (2004) 140-155.
9. Moghaddam, B., Pentland, A.: Probabilistic Visual Learning for Object Representation IEEE Trans. Pattern Analysis and Machine Intelligence, 7 (1997) 696-710.
10. Sudderth, E. B., Ihler, A. T., et al.: Nonparametric Belief Propagation. in Proc. of CVPR'03, Madison, WI, USA, (2003) 605-612.
11. Arulampalam, S., Maskell, S., et al.: A Tutorial on Particle Filters for On-line Non-linear/Non-Gaussian Bayesian Tracking. IEEE Trans. Signal Processing, 2 (2002) 174-188.
12. Chang, C., Ansari, R., et al.:Cyclic articulated human motion tracking by sequential ancestral simulation. in Proc. of CVPR2004, Washington, DC, USA, (2004) 45-52.
13. Khan, Z., Balch, T., et al.: MCMC-Based Particle Filtering for Tracking a Variable Number of Interacting Targets. IEEE Trans. Pattern Analysis and Machine Intelligence, 11 (2005) 1805-1918.
14. Khan, Z., Balch T., et al.: A Rao-Blackwellized Particle Filter for Eigen Tracking. In: Proc. of CVPR2004, Washington, DC, USA, (2004) 980-986.
15. Martinez, A. M., Benavente R.: The AR face database. CVC Technical Report 24. 1998.
16. Freeman, W.T., Pasztor, E.C., Carmichael, O.T.: Learning Low-Level Vision. Int. J. Computer Vision, 1 (2000) 25-47.

Hierarchical Markovian Models for Hyperspectral Image Segmentation

Ali Mohammad-Djafari, Nadia Bali, and Adel Mohammadpour

Laboratoire des Signaux et Systèmes,
Unité mixte de recherche 8506 (CNRS-Supélec-UPS)
Supélec, Plateau de Moulon, 3 rue Joliot Curie, 91192 Gif-sur-Yvette, France
{djafari, bali, mohammadpour}@lss.supelec.fr
http://djafari.free.fr

Abstract. Hyperspectral images can be represented either as a set of images or as a set of spectra. Spectral classification and segmentation and data reduction are the main problems in hyperspectral image analysis. In this paper we propose a Bayesian estimation approach with an appropriate hiearchical model with hidden markovian variables which gives the possibility to jointly do data reduction, spectral classification and image segmentation. In the proposed model, the desired independent components are piecewise homogeneous images which share the same common hidden segmentation variable. Thus, the joint Bayesian estimation of this hidden variable as well as the sources and the mixing matrix of the source separation problem gives a solution for all the three problems of dimensionality reduction, spectra classification and segmentation of hyperspectral images. A few simulation results illustrate the performances of the proposed method compared to other classical methods usually used in hyperspectral image processing.

1 Introduction

Hyperspectral images data can be represented either as a set of images $x_\omega(\boldsymbol{r})$ or as a set of spectra $x_{\boldsymbol{r}}(\omega)$ where $\omega \in \Omega$ indexes the wavelength and $\boldsymbol{r} \in \mathcal{R}$ is a pixel position [1,2,3]. In both representations, the data are dependent in both spatial positions and in spectral wavelength variable. Classical methods of hyperspectral image analysis try either to classify the spectra $x_\omega(\boldsymbol{r})$ in K classes $\{a_k(\omega), k = 1, \cdots, K\}$ or to classify the images $x_\omega(\boldsymbol{r})$ in K classes $\{s_k(\boldsymbol{r}), k = 1, \cdots, K\}$, using the classical classification methods such as distance based methods (like K-means) or probabilistic methods using the mixture of Gaussian (MoG) modeling of the data. These methods thus either neglect the spatial structure of the spectra or the spectral natures of the pixels along the wavelength bands.

The dimensionality reduction problem in hyperspectral images can be written as:

$$x_{\boldsymbol{r}}(\omega) = \sum_{k=1}^{K} s_k(\boldsymbol{r})\, a_k(\omega) + \epsilon_{\boldsymbol{r}}(\omega), \tag{1}$$

N. Zheng, X. Jiang, and X. Lan (Eds.): IWICPAS 2006, LNCS 4153, pp. 416–424, 2006.

where the $a_k(\omega)$ are the K spectral source components and $s_k(\boldsymbol{r})$ are their associated images.

This relation, when discretized, can be written as follows:

$$\boldsymbol{x}(\boldsymbol{r}) = \boldsymbol{A}\boldsymbol{s}(\boldsymbol{r}) + \boldsymbol{\epsilon}(\boldsymbol{r}) \tag{2}$$

$\boldsymbol{x}(\boldsymbol{r}) = \{x_i(\boldsymbol{r}), i = 1, \cdots, M\}$ is the set of M observed images in different bands ω_i, $\boldsymbol{A}$ is the mixing matrix of dimensions (M, K) whose columns are composed of the spectra $a_k(\omega)$, $\boldsymbol{s}(\boldsymbol{r}) = \{s_k(\boldsymbol{r}), k = 1, \cdots, K\}$ is the set of K unknown components (source images) and $\boldsymbol{\epsilon}(\boldsymbol{r}) = \{\epsilon_i(\boldsymbol{r}), i = 1, \cdots, M\}$ represents the errors.

The main objective in unsupervised classification of the spectra is to find both the spectra $a_k(\omega)$ and their associated image components $s_k(\boldsymbol{r})$. This problem, written as in equation (2) is recognized as the Blind Source Separation (BSS) in signal processing community, for which, many general solutions such as Principal Components Analysis (PCA) and Independent Components Analysis (ICA) have been proposed. In general, PCA is used as a feature extraction step before applying ICA for spectral classification. However these general methods do not account for the specificity of the hyperspectral images.

Indeed, as we mentioned, neither the classical methods of spectra or images classification nor the PCA and ICA methods of BSS give satisfactory results for hyperspectral images. The reasons are that, in the first category of methods either they account for spatial or for spectral properties and not for both of them simultaneously, and PCA and ICA methods do not account for the specificity of the mixing matrix and the sources.

In this paper, we propose to use this specificity of the hyperspectral images and consider the dimensionality reduction problem as the blind sources separation (BSS) of equation (2) and use a Bayesian estimation framework with a hierarchical model for the sources with a common hidden classification variable which is modelled as a Potts-Markov field. The joint estimation of this hidden variable, the sources and the mixing matrix of the BSS problem gives a solution for all of the three problems of dimensionality reduction, spectra classification and segmentation of hyperspectral images.

2 Proposed Model and Method

We propose to consider the equation (2) written in the following vector form:

$$\underline{\boldsymbol{x}} = \boldsymbol{A}\underline{\boldsymbol{s}} + \boldsymbol{\epsilon} \tag{3}$$

where we used $\underline{\boldsymbol{x}} = \{\boldsymbol{x}(\boldsymbol{r}), \boldsymbol{r} \in \mathcal{R}\}$, $\underline{\boldsymbol{s}} = \{\boldsymbol{s}(\boldsymbol{r}), \boldsymbol{r} \in \mathcal{R}\}$ and $\underline{\boldsymbol{\epsilon}} = \{\boldsymbol{\epsilon}(\boldsymbol{r}), \boldsymbol{r} \in \mathcal{R}\}$ and we are going to account for the specificity of the hyperspectral images through a probabilistic modeling of all the unknowns, starting by assuming that the errors $\boldsymbol{\epsilon}(\boldsymbol{r})$ are centered, white, Gaussian with covariance matrix $\boldsymbol{\Sigma}_\epsilon = \text{diag}\left[\sigma^2_{\epsilon_1}, .., \sigma^2_{\epsilon_M}\right]$. This leads to

$$p(\underline{\boldsymbol{x}}|\underline{\boldsymbol{s}}, \boldsymbol{A}, \boldsymbol{\Sigma}_\epsilon) = \prod_{\boldsymbol{r}} \mathcal{N}(\boldsymbol{A}\boldsymbol{s}(\boldsymbol{r}), \boldsymbol{\Sigma}_\epsilon) \tag{4}$$

The next step is to model the sources. As we mentioned in the introduction, we want to impose to all these sources $\boldsymbol{s}(\boldsymbol{r})$ to be piecewise homogeneous and share the same common segmentation, where the pixels in each region are considered to be homogeneous and associated to a particular spectrum representing the type of the material in that region. We also want that those spectra be classified in K distinct classes, thus all the pixels in regions associated with a particular spectrum share some common statistical parameters. This can be achieved through the introduction of a discrete valued hidden variable $z(\boldsymbol{r})$ representing the labels associated to each type of material and thus assuming the following:

$$p(s_j(\boldsymbol{r})|z(\boldsymbol{r})=k) = \mathcal{N}(m_{j\,k}, \sigma^2_{j\,k}), \quad k=1,\cdots,K \tag{5}$$

with the following Potts-Markov field model

$$p(\boldsymbol{z}) \propto \exp\left[\beta \sum_{\boldsymbol{r}} \sum_{\boldsymbol{r}' \in \mathcal{V}(\boldsymbol{r})} \delta(z(\boldsymbol{r}) - z(\boldsymbol{r}'))\right] \tag{6}$$

where $\boldsymbol{z} = \{z(\boldsymbol{r}), \boldsymbol{r} \in \mathcal{R}\}$ represents the common segmentation of the sources and the data. The parameter β controls the mean size of those regions.

We may note that, assuming *a priori* that the sources are mutually independent and that pixels in each class k are independent form those of class k', we have

$$p(\underline{\boldsymbol{s}}|\boldsymbol{z}) = \sum_k \sum_{\boldsymbol{r} \in \mathcal{R}_k} \sum_j p(s_j(\boldsymbol{r})|z(\boldsymbol{r})=k) \tag{7}$$

where $\mathcal{R}_k = \{\boldsymbol{r} : z(\boldsymbol{r}) = k\}$ and $\mathcal{R} = \cup_k \mathcal{R}_k$.

To insure that each image $s_j(\boldsymbol{r})$ is only non-zero in those regions associated with the kth spectrum, we impose $K = N$ and $m_{j\,k} = 0, \forall j \neq k$ and $\sigma^2_{j\,k} = 0.001, \forall j \neq k$. We may then write

$$p(\underline{\boldsymbol{s}}|\boldsymbol{z}) = \sum_{\boldsymbol{r}} p(\boldsymbol{s}(\boldsymbol{r})|z(\boldsymbol{r})=k)) = \sum_{\boldsymbol{r}} \mathcal{N}(\boldsymbol{m}_k(\boldsymbol{r}), \boldsymbol{\Sigma}_k(\boldsymbol{r})) \tag{8}$$

where $\boldsymbol{m}_k(\boldsymbol{r})$ is a vector of size N with all elements equal to zero except the k-th element $k = z(\boldsymbol{r})$ and $\boldsymbol{\Sigma}_k(\boldsymbol{r})$ is a diagonal matrix of size $N \times N$ with all elements equal to zero except the k-th main diagonal element where $k = z(\boldsymbol{r})$.

Combining the observed data model (3) and the sources model (6) of the previous section, we obtain the following hierarchical model:

3 Bayesian Estimation Framework

Using the prior data model (4), the prior source model (5) and the prior Potts-Markov model (6) and also assigning appropriate prior probability laws $p(\boldsymbol{A})$ and $p(\underline{\boldsymbol{\theta}})$ to the hyperparameters $\underline{\boldsymbol{\theta}} = \{\boldsymbol{\theta}_\epsilon, \boldsymbol{\theta}_s\}$ where $\boldsymbol{\theta}_\epsilon = \boldsymbol{R}_\epsilon$ and $\boldsymbol{\theta}_s = \{(m_{j\,k}, \sigma^2_{j\,k})\}$, we obtain an expression for the posterior law

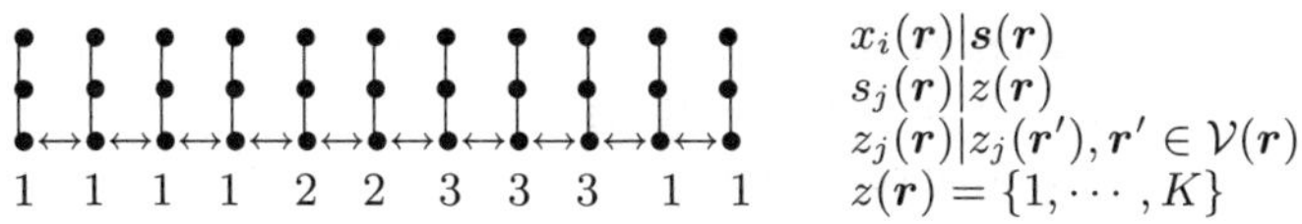

Fig. 1. Proposed hierarchical model for hyperspectral images: the sources $s_j(\boldsymbol{r})$ are hidden variables for the data $x_i(\boldsymbol{r})$ and the common classification and segmentation variable $z(\boldsymbol{r})$ is a hidden variable for the sources. In this figure the horizontal axis represents the pixel position $\boldsymbol{r}$.

$$p(\underline{\boldsymbol{s}}, \boldsymbol{z}, \boldsymbol{A}, \underline{\boldsymbol{\theta}}|\underline{\boldsymbol{x}}) \propto p(\underline{\boldsymbol{x}}|\underline{\boldsymbol{s}}, \boldsymbol{A}, \boldsymbol{\theta}_\epsilon)\, p(\underline{\boldsymbol{s}}|\boldsymbol{z}, \boldsymbol{\theta}_s)\, p(\boldsymbol{z})\, p(\boldsymbol{A})\, p(\underline{\boldsymbol{\theta}}) \tag{9}$$

In this paper, we used conjugate priors for all of them, i.e., Gaussian for the elements of $\boldsymbol{A}$, Gaussian for the means $m_{j\,k}$ and inverse Gamma for the variances $\sigma^2_{j\,k}$ as well as for the noise variances $\sigma_{\epsilon i}^{\,2}$.

When given the expression of the posterior law, we can then use it to define an estimator such as Joint Maximum A Posteriori (JMAP) or the Posterior Means (PM) for all the unknowns. The first needs optimization algorithms and the second integration methods. Both are computationally demanding. Alternate optimization is generally used for the first while the MCMC techniques are used for the second.

In this work, we propose to separate the unknowns in two sets $(\underline{\boldsymbol{s}}, \boldsymbol{z})$ and $(\boldsymbol{A}, \underline{\boldsymbol{\theta}})$ and then use the following iterative algorithm:

– Estimate $(\underline{\boldsymbol{s}}, \boldsymbol{z})$ using $p(\underline{\boldsymbol{s}}, \boldsymbol{z}|\widehat{\boldsymbol{A}}, \widehat{\underline{\boldsymbol{\theta}}}, \underline{\boldsymbol{x}})$ by

$$\widehat{\underline{\boldsymbol{s}}} \sim p(\underline{\boldsymbol{s}}|\widehat{\boldsymbol{z}}, \widehat{\boldsymbol{A}}, \widehat{\underline{\boldsymbol{\theta}}}, \underline{\boldsymbol{x}}) \qquad \text{and} \qquad \widehat{\boldsymbol{z}} \sim p(\boldsymbol{z}|\widehat{\boldsymbol{A}}, \widehat{\underline{\boldsymbol{\theta}}}, \underline{\boldsymbol{x}})$$

– Estimate $(\boldsymbol{A}, \underline{\boldsymbol{\theta}})$ using $p(\boldsymbol{A}, \underline{\boldsymbol{\theta}}|\widehat{\underline{\boldsymbol{s}}}, \widehat{\boldsymbol{z}}, \underline{\boldsymbol{x}})$ by

$$\widehat{\boldsymbol{A}} \sim p(\boldsymbol{A}|\widehat{\underline{\boldsymbol{s}}}, \widehat{\boldsymbol{z}}, \widehat{\boldsymbol{\theta}}, \underline{\boldsymbol{x}}) \qquad \text{and} \qquad \widehat{\underline{\boldsymbol{\theta}}} \sim p(\underline{\boldsymbol{\theta}}|\widehat{\underline{\boldsymbol{s}}}, \widehat{\boldsymbol{z}}, \widehat{\boldsymbol{A}}, \underline{\boldsymbol{x}})$$

In this algorithm, $\sim$ represents either *argmax* or *generate sample using* or still *compute the Mean Field Approximation (MFA)*. To implement this algorithm, we need the following expressions:

- $p(\underline{\boldsymbol{s}}|\boldsymbol{z}, \boldsymbol{A}, \underline{\boldsymbol{\theta}}, \underline{\boldsymbol{x}}) \propto p(\underline{\boldsymbol{x}}|\underline{\boldsymbol{s}}, \boldsymbol{A}, \boldsymbol{\Sigma}_\epsilon)\, p(\underline{\boldsymbol{s}}|\boldsymbol{z}, \underline{\boldsymbol{\theta}})$.

It is then easy to see that $p(\underline{\boldsymbol{s}}|\boldsymbol{z}, \boldsymbol{A}, \underline{\boldsymbol{\theta}}, \underline{\boldsymbol{x}})$ is separable in $\boldsymbol{r}$:

$$\begin{aligned} p(\underline{\boldsymbol{s}}|\boldsymbol{z}, \underline{\boldsymbol{\theta}}, \underline{\boldsymbol{x}}) &= \prod_{\boldsymbol{r}} p(\boldsymbol{s}(\boldsymbol{r})|z(\boldsymbol{r}), \boldsymbol{\theta}, \boldsymbol{x}(\boldsymbol{r})) \\ &= \prod_{\boldsymbol{r}} \mathcal{N}(\bar{\boldsymbol{s}}(\boldsymbol{r}), \boldsymbol{B}(\boldsymbol{r})) \end{aligned} \tag{10}$$

with

$$\begin{cases} \boldsymbol{B}(\boldsymbol{r}) = \left[\boldsymbol{A}^t \boldsymbol{\Sigma}_\epsilon^{-1} \boldsymbol{A} + \boldsymbol{\Sigma}_{z(\boldsymbol{r})}^{-1}\right]^{-1} \\ \bar{\boldsymbol{s}}(\boldsymbol{r}) = \boldsymbol{B}(\boldsymbol{r})[\boldsymbol{A}^t \boldsymbol{\Sigma}_\epsilon^{-1} \boldsymbol{x}(\boldsymbol{r}) + \boldsymbol{\Sigma}_{z(\boldsymbol{r})}^{-1} \boldsymbol{m}_{z(\boldsymbol{r})}] \end{cases} \tag{11}$$

In this relation $\boldsymbol{m}_{z(\boldsymbol{r})}$ is a vector of size n with all elements equal to zero except the k-th element where $k = z(\boldsymbol{r})$ and $\boldsymbol{\Sigma}_{z(\boldsymbol{r})}$ is a diagonal matrix of size $n \times n$ with all elements equal to zero except the k-th diagonal where $k = z(\boldsymbol{r})$.

- $p(\boldsymbol{z}|\boldsymbol{A}, \underline{\boldsymbol{\theta}}, \underline{\boldsymbol{x}}) \propto p(\underline{\boldsymbol{x}}|\boldsymbol{z}, \boldsymbol{A}, \underline{\boldsymbol{\theta}})\, p(\boldsymbol{z})$, where

$$p(\underline{\boldsymbol{x}}|\underline{\boldsymbol{z}}, \boldsymbol{A}, \underline{\boldsymbol{\theta}}) = \prod_{\boldsymbol{r}} p(\boldsymbol{x}(\boldsymbol{r})|z(\boldsymbol{r}), \boldsymbol{A}, \underline{\boldsymbol{\theta}}) = \prod_{\boldsymbol{r}} \mathcal{N}(\boldsymbol{A}\boldsymbol{m}_{z(\boldsymbol{r})}, \boldsymbol{A}\boldsymbol{\Sigma}_{z(\boldsymbol{r})}\boldsymbol{A}^t + \boldsymbol{\Sigma}_{\boldsymbol{\epsilon}}). \tag{12}$$

It is then easy to see that, even if $p(\underline{\boldsymbol{x}}|\underline{\boldsymbol{z}}, \boldsymbol{A}, \underline{\boldsymbol{\theta}})$ is separable in $\boldsymbol{r}$, $p(\boldsymbol{z}|\boldsymbol{A}, \underline{\boldsymbol{\theta}}, \underline{\boldsymbol{x}})$ is not and it has the same markovian structure that $p(\boldsymbol{z})$.

- $p(\boldsymbol{A}|\boldsymbol{z}, \underline{\boldsymbol{\theta}}, \underline{\boldsymbol{x}}) \propto p(\underline{\boldsymbol{x}}|\boldsymbol{z}, \boldsymbol{A}, \underline{\boldsymbol{\theta}})\, p(\boldsymbol{A})$.

It is easy to see that, with a Gaussian or uniform prior for $p(\boldsymbol{A})$ we obtain a Gaussian expression for this posterior law. Indeed, with an uniform prior, the posterior mean is equivalent to the posterior mode and equivalent to the Maximum Likelihood (ML) estimate $\widehat{\boldsymbol{A}} = \arg\max_{\boldsymbol{A}} \{p(\underline{\boldsymbol{x}}|\boldsymbol{z}, \boldsymbol{A}, \underline{\boldsymbol{\theta}})\}$ whose expression is:

$$\widehat{\boldsymbol{A}} = \left[\sum_{\boldsymbol{r}} \boldsymbol{x}(\boldsymbol{r})\bar{\boldsymbol{s}}'(\boldsymbol{r})\right] \left[\sum_{\boldsymbol{r}} \bar{\boldsymbol{s}}(\boldsymbol{r})\bar{\boldsymbol{s}}'(\boldsymbol{r}) + \boldsymbol{B}(\boldsymbol{r})\right]^{-1}$$

where $\bar{\boldsymbol{s}}(\boldsymbol{r})$ and $\boldsymbol{B}(\boldsymbol{r})$ are given by (11).

- $p(\boldsymbol{R}_\epsilon|\boldsymbol{z}, \boldsymbol{A}, \underline{\boldsymbol{\theta}}, \underline{\boldsymbol{x}}) \propto p(\underline{\boldsymbol{x}}|\boldsymbol{z}, \boldsymbol{A}, \underline{\boldsymbol{\theta}})\, p(\boldsymbol{R}_\epsilon)$.

It is also easy to show that, with an uniform prior on the logarithmic scale or an inverse gamma prior for the noise variances, the posterior is also an inverse gamma.

- $p(\underline{\boldsymbol{\theta}}|\boldsymbol{z}, \boldsymbol{A}, \underline{\boldsymbol{x}}) \propto p(\underline{\boldsymbol{x}}|\boldsymbol{z}, \boldsymbol{A}, \underline{\boldsymbol{\theta}})\, p(\underline{\boldsymbol{\theta}})$

Again here, using the conjugate priors for the means $m_{j\,k}$ and inverse gamma for the variances $\sigma^2_{j\,k}$ we can obtain easily the expressions of the posterior laws for them.

Details of the expressions of $p(\boldsymbol{A}|\boldsymbol{z}, \underline{\boldsymbol{\theta}}, \underline{\boldsymbol{x}})$, $p(\boldsymbol{R}_\epsilon|\boldsymbol{z}, \boldsymbol{A}, \underline{\boldsymbol{\theta}}, \underline{\boldsymbol{x}})$ and $p(\underline{\boldsymbol{\theta}}|\boldsymbol{z}, \boldsymbol{A}, \underline{\boldsymbol{x}})$ as well as their modes and means can be found in [4].

4 Computational Considerations and Mean Field Approximation

As we can see, the expression of the conditional posterior of the sources is separable in $\boldsymbol{r}$ but this is not the case for the conditional posterior of the hidden variable $z(\boldsymbol{r})$. So, even if it is possible to generate samples from this posterior using a Gibbs sampling scheme, the cost of the computation is very high for real applications. The Mean Field Approximation (MFA) then becomes a natural tool for obtaining approximate solutions with lower computational cost.

The mean field approximation is a general method for approximating the expectation of a Markov random variable. The idea consists in, when considering a pixel, to neglect the fluctuation of its neighbor pixels by fixing them to their mean values [5,6]. Another interpretation of the MFA is to approximate a non separable

$$\begin{aligned} p(\boldsymbol{z}) &\propto \exp\left[\beta \sum_{\boldsymbol{r}} \sum_{\boldsymbol{r}'} \delta(z(\boldsymbol{r}) - z(\boldsymbol{r}'))\right] \\ &\propto \prod_{\boldsymbol{r}} p(z(\boldsymbol{r})|z(\boldsymbol{r}'), \boldsymbol{r}' \in \mathcal{V}(\boldsymbol{r})) \end{aligned}$$

with the following separable one:

$$q(\boldsymbol{z}) \propto \prod_{\boldsymbol{r}} q(z(\boldsymbol{r})|\bar{z}(\boldsymbol{r}'), \boldsymbol{r}' \in \mathcal{V}(\boldsymbol{r}))$$

where $\bar{z}(\boldsymbol{r}')$ is the expected value of $z(\boldsymbol{r}')$ computed using $q(\boldsymbol{z})$. This approximate separable expression is obtained in such a way to minimize the Kullback-Leibler divergence measure $KL(p, q)$ for a given class of separable distributions $q \in \boldsymbol{Q}$.

Using now this approximation in the expression of the conditional posterior law $p(\boldsymbol{z}|\boldsymbol{A}, \underline{\boldsymbol{\theta}}, \underline{\boldsymbol{x}})$ gives the separable MFA

$$q(\boldsymbol{z}|\boldsymbol{A}, \underline{\boldsymbol{\theta}}, \underline{\boldsymbol{x}}) = \prod_{\boldsymbol{r}} q(z(\boldsymbol{r})|\bar{z}(\boldsymbol{r}'), \boldsymbol{r}' \in \mathcal{V}(\boldsymbol{r}), \boldsymbol{A}, \boldsymbol{\theta}, \boldsymbol{x}(\boldsymbol{r}))$$

where $q(z(\boldsymbol{r})|\bar{z}(\boldsymbol{r}'), \boldsymbol{r}' \in \mathcal{V}(\boldsymbol{r}), \boldsymbol{A}, \boldsymbol{\theta}, \boldsymbol{x}(\boldsymbol{r})) = p(\boldsymbol{x}(\boldsymbol{r})|z(\boldsymbol{r}), \boldsymbol{A}, \boldsymbol{\theta})\, q(z(\boldsymbol{r})|\bar{z}(\boldsymbol{r}'), \boldsymbol{r}' \in \mathcal{V}(\boldsymbol{r}))$

and $\bar{z}(\boldsymbol{r})$ can be computed by

$$\bar{z}(\boldsymbol{r}) = \frac{\sum_{z(\boldsymbol{r})} z(\boldsymbol{r})\, q(z(\boldsymbol{r})|\bar{z}(\boldsymbol{r}'), \boldsymbol{r}' \in \mathcal{V}(\boldsymbol{r}), \boldsymbol{A}, \boldsymbol{\theta}, \boldsymbol{x}(\boldsymbol{r}))}{\sum_{z(\boldsymbol{r})} q(z(\boldsymbol{r})|\bar{z}(\boldsymbol{r}'), \boldsymbol{r}' \in \mathcal{V}(\boldsymbol{r}), \boldsymbol{A}, \boldsymbol{\theta}, \boldsymbol{x}(\boldsymbol{r}))}$$

5 Simulation Results

The main objectives of these simulations are: first to show that the proposed algorithm gives the desired results, and second to compare its relative performances with respect to some classical methods. For this purpose, first we generated some simulated data according to the data generatin model, i.e.; starting by generating $z(\boldsymbol{r})$, then the sources $\boldsymbol{s}(\boldsymbol{r})$, then using some given spectral signatures obtained from real materials, construct the mixing matrix $\boldsymbol{A}$ and finally generate data $\boldsymbol{x}(\boldsymbol{r})$. Fig. 2 shows two examples of such data generated with the following parameters: **case 1:** $M = 32, N = 4, K = 4$ and SNR=20 dB and **case 2:** $M = 32, N = 8, K = 8$ and SNR=20 dB.

Fig. 3 shows a comparison of the results obtained by two classical spectral and image classification methods using the classical K-means with the results obtained by the proposed method on these two simulated data sets.

We are applying these methods on other dataset with ground truth and will report on this in the final camera ready paper of the conference.

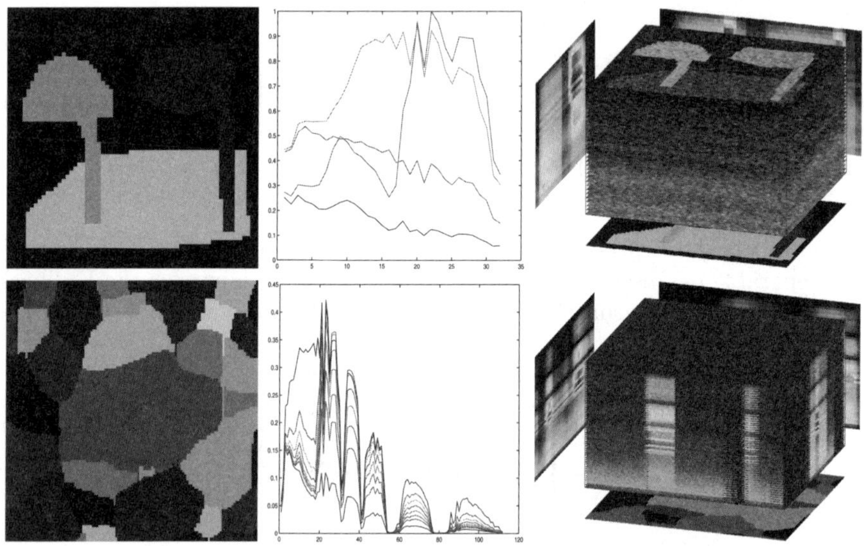

a b c

Fig. 2. Examples of data generating process: a) $z(\boldsymbol{r})$ b) spectral signatures used to construct the mixing matrix $\boldsymbol{A}$ and c) M simulated images. Upper row: $M = 32$, $K = 4$ and image sizes (64x64), Lower row: $M = 56$, $K = 8$ and image sizes (128x128).

6 Conclusion

Classical methods of data reduction in hyperspectral imaging use classification methods either to classify the spectra or to classify the images in K classes where K is, in general, much less than the number of spectra or the number of observed images. However, these methods neglect either the spatial organization of the spectra or the spectral property of the pixels along the spectral bands. In this paper, we considered the dimensionality reduction problem in hyperspectral images as a source separation and presented a Bayesian estimation approach with an appropriate hierarchical prior model for the observations and sources which accounts for both spectral and spatial structure of the data, and thus, gives the possibility to jointly do dimensionality reduction, classification of spectra and segmentation of the images.

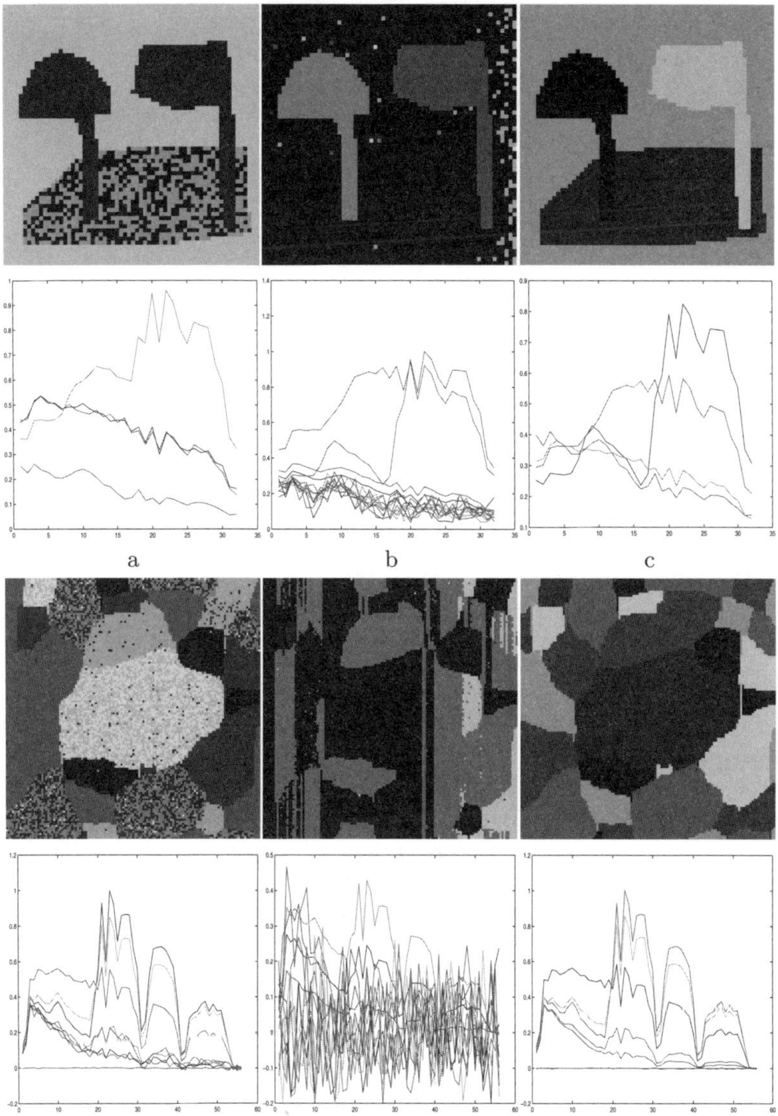

Fig. 3. Dimensionality reduction by different methods: a) Spectral classification using K-means, b) Image classification using K-means, c) Proposed method. Upper row shows estimated $z(\boldsymbol{r})$ and lower row the estimated spectra. These results have to be compared to the original $z(\boldsymbol{r})$ and spectra in previous figure.

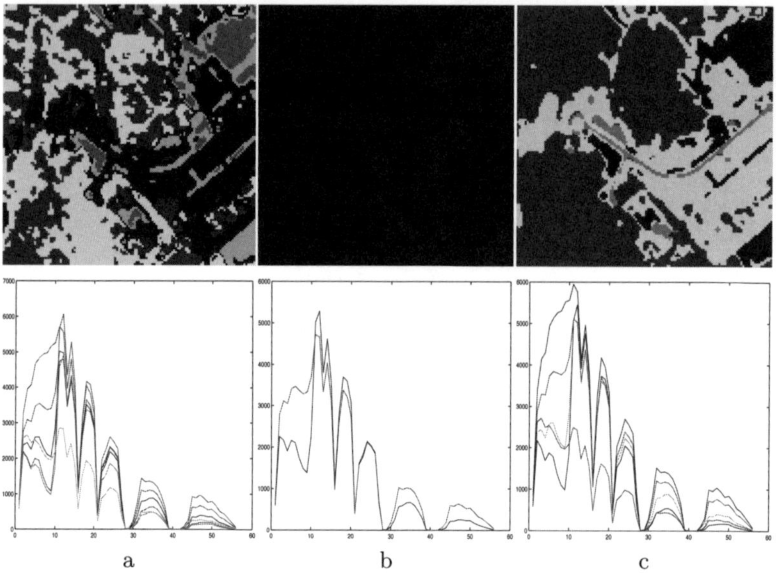

Fig. 4. Real data: a) Spectral classification using K-means, b) Image classification using K-means, c) Proposed method. Upper row shows estimated $z(\boldsymbol{r})$ and lower row the estimated spectra

References

1. K. Sasaki, S. Kawata, and S. Minami, "Component analysis of spatial and spectral patterns in multispectral images. I. basics," *Journal of the Optical Society of America. A*, vol. 4, no. 11, pp. 2101–2106, 1987.
2. L. Parra, C. Spence, A. Ziehe, K.-R. Mueller, and P. Sajda, "Unmixing hyperspectral data," in *Advances in Neural Information Processing Systems 13, (NIPS'2000)*. 2000, pp. 848–854, MIT Press.
3. Nadia Bali and Ali Mohammad-Djafari, "Mean Field Approximation for BSS of images with compound hierarchical Gauss-Markov-Potts model," in *MaxEnt05,San Jos CA,US*. Aug. 2005, American Institute of Physics (AIP).
4. Hichem Snoussi and Ali Mohammad-Djafari, "Fast joint separation and segmentation of mixed images," *Journal of Electronic Imaging*, vol. 13, no. 2, pp. 349–361, Apr. 2004.
5. J. Zhang, "The mean field theory in EM procedures for blind Markov random field image restoration," *IEEE Trans. Image Processing*, vol. 2, no. 1, pp. 27–40, Jan. 1993.
6. D. Landgrebe, "Hyperspectral image data analysis," *IEEE Trans. Signal Processing*, vol. 19, pp. 17–28, 2002.

Adaptive Geometry Compression Based on 4-Point Interpolatory Subdivision Schemes

Hui Zhang[1], Jun-Hai Yong[1], and Jean-Claude Paul[1,2]

[1] School of Software, Tsinghua University, Beijing 100084, P.R. China
huizhang@tsinghua.edu.cn,
http://cgcad.thss.tsinghua.edu.cn/~zh/
[2] CNRS, France

Abstract. We propose an adaptive geometry compression method based on 4-point interpolatory subdivision schemes. It can work on digital curves of arbitrary dimensions. With the geometry compression method, a digital curve is adaptively compressed into several segments with different compression levels. Each segment is a 4-point subdivision curve with a subdivision step. In the meantime, we provide high-speed 4-point interpolatory subdivision curve generation methods for efficiently decompressing the compressed data. In the decompression methods, we consider both the open curve case and the closed curve case. For an arbitrary positive integer k, formulae of the number of the resultant control points of an open or closed 4-point subdivision curve after k subdivision steps are provided. The time complexity of the new approaches are $O(n)$, where n is the number of the points in the given digital curve. Examples are provided as well to illustrate the efficiency of the proposed approaches.

Keywords: geometry compression, subdivision scheme, 4-point subdivision, interpolatory subdivision, high-speed curve generation.

1 Introduction

It is a common practice to compress data before they are archived. With ubiquitous applications of computers and network, gigantic amount of data are continuously generated. In the meantime, the increasing demand for communication and data exchange over network beats the limitation of the network band. Data compression becomes more and more important and receives more and more attentions [7, et al]. While data compression has a long history and has achieved a high level of sophistication, some new tools are eager to be discovered to fill the gap between the requirement and the ability of data compression. Geometry compression is relatively new, and becomes a hot topic in a short time after it appeared [6,7,9,10,11,12,13, et al]. Wavelet transforms [7, et al], multiresolution [6, et al] and various trees [13, et al] are frequently used in geometry compression.

Almost all geometry compression methods focus on how to compress three-dimensional meshes. In this paper, we will propose a new geometry compression method based on 4-point interpolatory subdivision schemes. With our new

N. Zheng, X. Jiang, and X. Lan (Eds.): IWICPAS 2006, LNCS 4153, pp. 425–434, 2006.

method, a digital curve of an arbitrary dimension is compressed into one or several subdivision curve segments. The advantages of our method are at least as follows.

- It is able to work on a digital curve of an arbitrary dimension. And any sequence of data can be considered as a digital curve of a certain dimension.
- The set of the inner control points of the resultant subdivision curves is exactly a subset of the points of the compressed curve.
- It is possible to simplify the pattern recognition of some digital curves into the pattern recognition of the subdivision curve segments after data compression. The inner control points of the resultant subdivision curves may be considered as the key points of the given digital curves, since they can be used to reproduce the given digital curves after data decompression.

Our work gives contributions to the area about subdivision curves and surfaces as well. The first subdivision scheme for generating subdivision curves was proposed by Chaikin [2] in 1974. The 4-point interpolatory subdivision [4] appeared in 1987. Recently, research on subdivision schemes for generating curves and surfaces becomes popular in graphical modeling [3,9, et al], animation [14, et al] and CAD/CAM [8, et al] because of their stability in numerical computation and simplicity in coding. Much work on subdivision surfaces is carried out in several important topics such as Boolean operations [1], mesh editing [14], and adaptive tessellation [9]. And a lot of work [5, et al] has been carried out on the 4-point subdivision schemes as well. In this paper, we will provide approaches for the high-speed 4-point interpolatory subdivision curve generation to speed up the data decompression.

The remaining part of the paper is arranged as follows. A brief review of the 4-point interpolatory subdivision curve is given in Section 2. A data compression method is provided in Section 3. The high-speed generation approaches are provided in Section 4 for the open 4-point interpolatory subdivision curve and the closed 4-point interpolatory subdivision curve, respectively, to speed up the data decompression. Section 5 uses some examples to illustrate the efficiency of the proposed approaches. Some concluding remarks are given in the last section.

2 4-Point Interpolatory Subdivision Schemes

In this section, we briefly go through the 4-point interpolatory subdivision schemes given by [4]. Initially, a set of points $\mathbf{M}_0 = \{\mathbf{P}_{0,0}, \mathbf{P}_{1,0}, \cdots, \mathbf{P}_{n_0-1,0}\}$ is given, where $\mathbf{P}_{i,0}(i = 0, 1, \cdots, n_0 - 1)$ are points, and n_0 is the number of the points. The subdivision is preformed in a recursive procedure. At each subdivision step, some points before the subdivision are inherited, and some new points are inserted into the point set such that the number of the points usually becomes larger and larger. Let $\mathbf{M}_k = \{\mathbf{P}_{0,k}, \mathbf{P}_{1,k}, \cdots, \mathbf{P}_{n_k-1,k}\}$ be the resultant point set after the kth $(k = 0, 1, 2, \cdots)$ subdivision step, where n_k is the number of the points in $\mathbf{M}_k$. All points $\mathbf{P}_{i,k}$ in $\mathbf{M}_k$ are called control points as well.

The 4-point interpolatory subdivision curves can be classified into categories: the open case or the close case. At the kth subdivision step, the points inherited from $\mathbf{M}_{k-1}$ are $\mathbf{P}_{i,k-1}$, where $i = 1, 2, \cdots, (n_{k-1} - 2)$ for the open case, and $i = 0, 1, \cdots, (n_{k-1} - 1)$ for the close case. The point $\mathbf{P}_{j,k}$ to be inserted between $\mathbf{P}_{i,k-1}$ and $\mathbf{P}_{i+1,k-1}$ at the kth subdivision step is

$$\mathbf{P}_{j,k} = (w + 0.5)(\mathbf{P}_{i,k-1} + \mathbf{P}_{i+1,k-1}) - w(\mathbf{P}_{i-1,k-1} + \mathbf{P}_{i+2,k-1}), \tag{1}$$

for each $i = 1, 2, \cdots, (n_{k-1} - 3)$ under the open case, and

$$\begin{aligned} \mathbf{P}_{j,k} = (w + 0.5)&(\mathbf{P}_{(i\%n_{k-1}),k-1} + \mathbf{P}_{((i+1)\%n_{k-1}),k-1}) \\ &-w(\mathbf{P}_{((i-1)\%n_{k-1}),k-1} + \mathbf{P}_{((i+2)\%n_{k-1}),k-1}), \end{aligned} \tag{2}$$

for each $i = 0, 1, \cdots, (n_{k-1} - 1)$ under the close case, where the weight w is a given real number. Usually, the value of w is suggested to be $\frac{1}{16}$. In Equation (2), the modulus symbol (%) is used such that each subscription is in the set $\{0, 1, \cdots, n_{k-1} - 1\}$. Note that from $\mathbf{M}_{k-1}$ to $\mathbf{M}_k$, the points $\mathbf{P}_{0,k-1}$ and $\mathbf{P}_{n_{k-1}-1,k-1}$ are discarded for the open case after the subdivision, which is called the shrink property of an open 4-point interpolatory subdivision curve. When $k \to \infty$, the point set $\mathbf{M}_\infty$ becomes a limit subdivision curve. $\mathbf{M}_\infty$ is an open curve under the open case, and a closed curve under the close case.

3 Data Compression

In this section, we propose a geometry compression method for digital curves based on the above schemes. Here, a digital curve is an open polygonal curve or a closed polygonal curve (i.e. a polygon), represented by n vertices $\{\mathbf{P}_0, \mathbf{P}_1, \cdots, \mathbf{P}_{n-1}\}$. The principle of the geometry compression is, as shown in Figure 1(a),

- that for the open case, we do not need to store $\mathbf{P}_i$ which satisfy

$$\|\mathbf{P}_i - [(w + 0.5)(\mathbf{P}_{i-1} + \mathbf{P}_{i+1}) - w(\mathbf{P}_{i-3} + \mathbf{P}_{i+3})]\|_2 \le e, \tag{3}$$

  where $i = 3, 4, \cdots, (n - 4)$, and e is the given error tolerance;
- and that for the close case, we do not need to store $\mathbf{P}_i$ which satisfy

$$\left\|\mathbf{P}_i - \left[(w + 0.5)(\mathbf{P}_{(i-1)\%n} + \mathbf{P}_{(i+1)\%n}) - w(\mathbf{P}_{(i-3)\%n} + \mathbf{P}_{(i+3)\%n})\right]\right\|_2 \le e, \tag{4}$$

  where $i = 1, 3, 5, \cdots$, $i \le (n - 1)$, and e is the given error tolerance.

The points satisfying Equations (3) and (4) are called the removable points, which can be reproduced by the 4-point interpolatory subdivision schemes.

If the given digital curve is a closed curve with an even number of the vertices and each odd vertex $\mathbf{P}_i$, where $i = 1, 3, \cdots, (n - 1)$, is a removable point the digital curve can be compressed into a closed subdivision curve with the control points $\{\mathbf{P}_0, \mathbf{P}_2, \cdots, \mathbf{P}_{n-2}\}$. Thus, the compression ratio is $2 : 1$. And the procedure can be recursively carried out, so the compression ratio can be higher than $2 : 1$. Otherwise, we compress the digital curve in the same way as the open case.

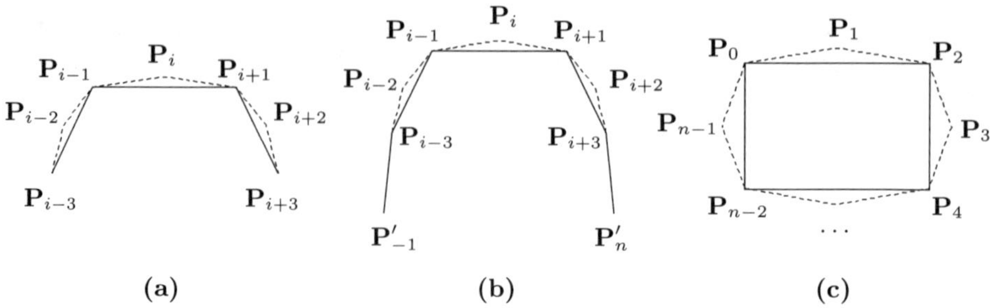

Fig. 1. Principle of geometry compression: **(a)** mask of a removable point, **(b)** boundary case, and **(c)** close case

If the given digital curve is an open curve and $\{\mathbf{P}_a, \mathbf{P}_{a+2}, \cdots, \mathbf{P}_b\}$ are removable points, then the points $\{\mathbf{P}_{a-3}, \mathbf{P}_{a-2}, \cdots, \mathbf{P}_{b+2}, \mathbf{P}_{b+3}\}$ can be compressed into $\{\mathbf{P}'_{-1}\mathbf{P}_{a-3}, \mathbf{P}_{a-1}, \cdots, \mathbf{P}_{b+1}, \mathbf{P}_{b+3}, \mathbf{P}'_n\}$, where

$$\mathbf{P}'_{-1} = \frac{(w+0.5)(\mathbf{P}_{a-3}+\mathbf{P}_{a-1}) - \mathbf{P}_{a-2}}{w} - \mathbf{P}_{a+1} \tag{5}$$

and

$$\mathbf{P}'_{n} = \frac{(w+0.5)(\mathbf{P}_{b+3}+\mathbf{P}_{b+1}) - \mathbf{P}_{b+2}}{w} - \mathbf{P}_{b-1} \tag{6}$$

are two auxiliary points. Because of the shrink property, we need two auxiliary points $\mathbf{P}'_{-1}$ and $\mathbf{P}'_n$ to keep $\mathbf{P}_{a-3}$ and $\mathbf{P}_{b+3}$ after one subdivision step, Under this case, the compression ratio is $[(b-a)+7] : \frac{(b-a)+12}{2}$. For example, as shown in Figure 1(b), when $a = b = i$, the compression ratio is $7 : 6$. Thus, the algorithms for the open case and the close case are as follows.

Algorithm 1. Geometry compression for the open case.
Input: the point set $\{\mathbf{P}_0, \mathbf{P}_1, \cdots, \mathbf{P}_{n-1}\}$, the error tolerance e, the weight w, and the current subdivision step k (with an initial value $k = 0$).
Output: a set of compressed data set $\mathbf{S}$ (with an empty initial value $\mathbf{S} = \mathbf{\Phi}$).

1. if $(n \leq 7)$ // note: the number of the vertices is too small for the compression.
   let $\mathbf{M}$ be an open subdivision curve with $\{\mathbf{P}_0, \mathbf{P}_1, \cdots, \mathbf{P}_{n-1}\}$ and the subdivision step k; insert $\mathbf{M}$ into $\mathbf{S}$, and **output** $\mathbf{S}$; go to Step 7;
2. let $a = 0$;
   for $(i = 3; i \leq (n-4); i += 2)$
   if ($\mathbf{P}_i$ is a removable point according to Equation (3))
   let $a = i$, and go to Step 3;
3. if (a is zero) // note: no points could be compressed.
   let $\mathbf{M}$ be an open subdivision curve with $\{\mathbf{P}_0, \mathbf{P}_1, \cdots, \mathbf{P}_{n-1}\}$ and the subdivision step k; insert $\mathbf{M}$ into $\mathbf{S}$, **output** $\mathbf{S}$, and go to Step 7;

else if ($a > 3$)
let $\mathbf{M}$ be an open subdivision curve with $\{\mathbf{P}_0, \mathbf{P}_1, \cdots, \mathbf{P}_{a-3}\}$ and the subdivision step k; insert $\mathbf{M}$ into $\mathbf{S}$;

4. let $b = a$;
for ($i = a + 2; i \leq (n - 4); i+ = 2$)
if ($\mathbf{P}_i$ is not a removable point according to Equation (3))
go to Step 5;
else let $b = i$;
5. call Algorithm 1 with the input $\{\mathbf{P}'_{-1}\mathbf{P}_{a-3}, \mathbf{P}_{a-1}, \cdots, \mathbf{P}_{b+1}, \mathbf{P}_{b+3}, \mathbf{P}'_n\}$, e, w and $(k+1)$, where $\mathbf{P}'_{-1}$ and $\mathbf{P}'_n$ are calculated according to Equations (5) and (6), and obtain the set $\mathbf{S}_1$; insert all elements of $\mathbf{S}_1$ into $\mathbf{S}$;
6. if ($b < (n - 4)$)
call Algorithm 1 with the input $\{\mathbf{P}_{b+3}, \mathbf{P}_{b+4}, \cdots, \mathbf{P}_{n-1}\}$, e, w and k, and obtain the set $\mathbf{S}_2$; insert all elements of $\mathbf{S}_2$ into $\mathbf{S}$;
output $\mathbf{S}$;
7. **End** of Algorithm 1.

Algorithm 2. Geometry compression for the close case.
Input: the point set $\{\mathbf{P}_0, \mathbf{P}_1, \cdots, \mathbf{P}_{n-1}\}$, the error tolerance e, the weight w, and the current subdivision step k (with an initial value $k = 0$).
Output: a set of compressed data set $\mathbf{S}$ (with an empty initial value $\mathbf{S} = \mathbf{\Phi}$).

1. if ($n < 6$) // note: the number of the vertices is too small for the compression.
let $\mathbf{M}$ be a closed subdivision curve with $\{\mathbf{P}_0, \mathbf{P}_1, \cdots, \mathbf{P}_{n-1}\}$ and the subdivision step k; insert $\mathbf{M}$ into $\mathbf{S}$, **output** $\mathbf{S}$, and go to Step 4;
2. if (n is odd)
call Algorithm 1 with the input $\{\mathbf{P}_0, \mathbf{P}_1, \cdots, \mathbf{P}_{n-1}\}$, e, w and k, and obtain the set $\mathbf{S}$; **output** $\mathbf{S}$, and go to Step 4;
3. if (all points $\mathbf{P}_i$ (where $i = 1, 3, \cdots, (n-1)$) are removable points)
call Algorithm 2 with the input $\{\mathbf{P}_0, \mathbf{P}_2, \cdots, \mathbf{P}_{n-2}\}$, e, w and $(k+1)$, and obtain the set $\mathbf{S}$; **output** $\mathbf{S}$;
else
call Algorithm 1 with the input $\{\mathbf{P}_0, \mathbf{P}_1, \cdots, \mathbf{P}_{n-1}\}$, e, w and k, and obtain the set $\mathbf{S}$; **output** $\mathbf{S}$;
4. **End** of Algorithm 2.

In Algorithms 1 and 2, we only check whether the points in the given point set are removable points at most twice, and we do not check whether any auxiliary point produced by Equation (5) or (6) is a removable point. Therefore, although Algorithms 1 and 2 contain loops and recursive procedures, the time complexity of both Algorithms 1 and 2 is $O(n)$.

4 Data Decompression

With the method introduced in Section 3, a digital curve is compressed into some subdivision curve segments. Hence, the problem here is how to obtain the points in $\mathbf{M}_k$, which is the point set after k subdivision steps are carried out from the initial control point set $\mathbf{M}_0$. According to the method in Section 2, in order to obtain $\mathbf{M}_k$, we need to calculate all the control points in $\mathbf{M}_1, \mathbf{M}_2, \cdots, \mathbf{M}_{k-1}$. Unfortunately, we do not need $\mathbf{M}_1, \mathbf{M}_2, \cdots, \mathbf{M}_{k-1}$ at all, but only $\mathbf{M}_k$. Thus, we need extra memory to store those unnecessary points, and experience shows that the time cost in this way increases sharply with respect to the subdivision step k. In this section, we will provide the high-speed generation approaches. One is for the open subdivision curve, and the other one is for the closed curve.

4.1 Open Curve Generation

In this subsection, we only consider the open 4-point subdivision curve. First, we need to obtain the value of n_k, which is the number of points in $\mathbf{M}_k$, such that we could allocate memory to store the coordinates of the points in $\mathbf{M}_k$ before computing the coordinates. According to Section 2, from $\mathbf{M}_{k-1}$ to $\mathbf{M}_k$, all the points except for the first and the last points in $\mathbf{M}_{k-1}$ are inherited, and the number of new points inserted into $\mathbf{M}_k$ is 3 less than the number of the points in $\mathbf{M}_{k-1}$. Thus, we obtain n_k with respect to n_{k-1} in Lemma 1.

Lemma 1. *If $n_0 \geq 5$, the number of the points in $\mathbf{M}_k$ is $n_k = (n_{k-1} - 2) + (n_{k-1} - 3) = 2n_{k-1} - 5$, for $k = 1, 2, \cdots$.*

According to Algorithms 1 and 2, no subdivision is necessary to be performed on a set of points which number is less than 5. Therefore, we do not consider the case when $n_0 < 5$. Recursively apply the above lemma, and we obtain n_k with respect to n_0 in Theorem 1.

Theorem 1. *If $n_0 \geq 5$, the number of the points in $\mathbf{M}_k$ is $n_k = 2k(n_0 - 5) + 5$, for $k = 0, 1, 2, \cdots$.*

The remaining part of the subsection will provide the method for calculating the coordinates of the points in $\mathbf{M}_k$. It is based on the following important theorem. The theorem can be proved by the mathematical induction method according to Section 2.

Theorem 2. *For $k = 0, 1, 2, \cdots$, we have $\mathbf{P}_{i \times 2^k + 2, k} = \mathbf{P}_{i+2,0}$, where $i = 0, 1, 2, \cdots$, and $i \times 2^k + 2 < n_k$.*

Thus, according to Theorem 2 and Equation (1), we have the following algorithm for calculating the coordinates of the points in $\mathbf{M}_k$.

Algorithm 3. Calculating coordinates of points in $\mathbf{M}_k$ for the open case.
Input: $\mathbf{M}_0$ and the weight w with the assumption that $n_0 \geq 5$.
Output: $\mathbf{M}_k$.

1. calculate n_k according to Theorem 1;
2. allocate memory for $\mathbf{M}_k$ to store the coordinates of n_k points in $\mathbf{M}_k$;
3. for $(i = 0, i_0 = 2, i_k = 2; i_k < n_k; i++, i_0++, i_k+ = 2^k)$
   $\mathbf{P}_{i_k,k} = \mathbf{P}_{i_0,0}$ according to Theorem 2;
4. $\mathbf{P}_{0,k} = \mathbf{P}_{0,0}$; $\mathbf{P}_{1,k} = \mathbf{P}_{1,0}$; $\mathbf{P}_{n_k-1,k} = \mathbf{P}_{n_0-1,0}$; $\mathbf{P}_{n_k-2,k} = \mathbf{P}_{n_0-2,0}$;
5. for $(i = k; i >= 1; i--)$
   $\mathbf{P} = (w + 0.5)(\mathbf{P}_{1,k} + \mathbf{P}_{2,k}) - w(\mathbf{P}_{0,k} + \mathbf{P}_{2^i+2,k})$;
   $\mathbf{P}_{2^{i-1}+2,k} = (w + 0.5)(\mathbf{P}_{2,k} + \mathbf{P}_{2^i+2,k}) - w(\mathbf{P}_{1,k} + \mathbf{P}_{2^{i+1}+2,k})$;
   $\mathbf{P}_{0,k} = \mathbf{P}_{1,k}$; $\mathbf{P}_{1,k} = \mathbf{P}$;
   for $(j = 2^i + 2^{i-1} + 2, m = 2; j < n_k - 3 - 2^{i-1}; j+ = 2^i, m+ = 2^i)$
   $\mathbf{P}_{j,k} = (w + 0.5)(\mathbf{P}_{2^i+m,k} + \mathbf{P}_{2^{i+1}+m,k}) - w(\mathbf{P}_{m,k} + \mathbf{P}_{3\times2^i+m,k})$;
   $\mathbf{P} = (w + 0.5)(\mathbf{P}_{n_k-2,k} + \mathbf{P}_{n_k-3,k}) - w(\mathbf{P}_{n_k-1,k} + \mathbf{P}_{n_k-3-2^i,k})$;
   $\mathbf{P}_{n_k-3-2^{i-1},k} = (w + 0.5)(\mathbf{P}_{n_k-3,k} + \mathbf{P}_{n_k-3-2^i,k}) - w(\mathbf{P}_{n_k-2,k} + \mathbf{P}_{n_k-3-2^{i+1},k})$;
   $\mathbf{P}_{n_k-1,k} = \mathbf{P}_{n_k-2,k}$; $\mathbf{P}_{n_k-2,k} = \mathbf{P}$;
6. **End** of Algorithm 3.

In Algorithm 3, we assume that $n_0 \geq 5$, so we have $n_k \geq 5$. In the algorithm, any point in $\mathbf{M}_k$, except for $\mathbf{P}_{0,k}$, $\mathbf{P}_{1,k}$, $\mathbf{P}_{n_k-1,k}$ and $\mathbf{P}_{n_k-2,k}$, are calculated only once. Therefore, the time complexity of Algorithm 3 is $O(n_k)$, which is the lowest bound of calculating all points in $\mathbf{M}_k$.

4.2 Closed Curve Generation

This subsection focuses on the approach for the high-speed generation of the closed subdivision curve. According to Section 2, from $\mathbf{M}_{k-1}$ to $\mathbf{M}_k$, all the points in $\mathbf{M}_{k-1}$ are inherited, and the number of new points inserted into $\mathbf{M}_k$ is equal to n_{k-1}. Thus, we obtain the conclusions in Lemma 2 and Theorem 3.

Lemma 2. *The number of the points in* $\mathbf{M}_k$ *is* $n_k = 2n_{k-1}$, *for* $k = 1, 2, \cdots$.

Theorem 3. *The number of the points in* $\mathbf{M}_k$ *is* $n_k = n_0 \times 2^k$, *for* $k = 0, 1, \cdots$.

To calculate the coordinates of the points in $\mathbf{M}_k$, one important conclusion is drawn in Theorem 4.

Theorem 4. *For* $k = 0, 1, 2, \cdots$, *we have* $\mathbf{P}_{i\times2^k,k} = \mathbf{P}_{i,0}$, *where* $i = 0, 1, 2, \cdots$, *and* $i \times 2^k < n_k$.

Thus, according to Theorem 4 and Equation (2) in Section 2 for calculating new points, we obtain the following algorithm. Similar to Algorithm 3, the time complexity of the following algorithm is $O(n_k)$.

Algorithm 4. Calculating coordinates of points in $\mathbf{M}_k$ for the close case.
Input: $\mathbf{M}_0$ and the weight w.
Output: $\mathbf{M}_k$.

1. calculate n_k according to Theorem 3;
2. allocate memory for $\mathbf{M}_k$ to store the coordinates of n_k points in $\mathbf{M}_k$;
3. for $(i = 0, i_k = 0; i_k < n_k; i++, i_k+ = 2^k)$
   $\mathbf{P}_{i_k,k} = \mathbf{P}_{i,0}$ according to Theorem 4;
4. for $(i = k; i >= 1; i--)$
   for $(j = 2^{i-1}, m = -2^i; j \le n_k - 2^{i-1}; j+ = 2^i, m+ = 2^i)$
   $\mathbf{P}_{j,k} = (w+0.5)(\mathbf{P}_{(2^i+m)\%n_k,k} + \mathbf{P}_{(2^{i+1}+m)\%n_k,k}) - w(\mathbf{P}_{m\%n_k,k} + \mathbf{P}_{(3\times 2^i+m)\%n_k,k})$;
5. **End** of Algorithm 4.

5 Examples

Experiment has been carried out on a lot of examples. Three examples are shown in Figures 2 and 3. The first example is a digital curve, which is the contour curve of a horse as shown in Figure 2. The original curve as shown in Figure 2(a) contains 5413 points. It is compressed into 11 subdivision curve segments, which total number of the control points are 178. The ratio of the numbers of points is $5413 : 178 \approx 30 : 1$. We alternate the red solid lines and blue dashed lines to identify different subdivision curve segments. Due to the shrink property of the 4-point interpolatory subdivision curves, some auxiliary points, which are out of the contour curve of the horse, are necessary as shown in Figure 2(b). In these examples in this section, the error tolerance is 0.007, and $w = \frac{1}{16}$. In Example 1, we consider the original digital curve as an open curve. The closed curve case is shown in Figure 3(d). The blue solid curve is the original digital curve, which contains 672 points. After the data compression, it becomes a closed subdivision curve with 21 control points. The ratio of the numbers of points is $672 : 21 = 32 : 1$.

Two examples as shown in Figures 3 are used to illustrate the efficiency of the data decompression algorithms. The polygonal curves or the polygons formed by $\mathbf{M}_0$ are dashed in those two figures, and the solid curves are the results after several iterate subdivision steps. The numbers of the control points in $\mathbf{M}_0$ of Examples 2 and 3 are 14 and 21, respectively. Table 1 gives the time cost of

(a) (b)

Fig. 2. Example 1: **(a)** before data compression, and **(b)** after data compression

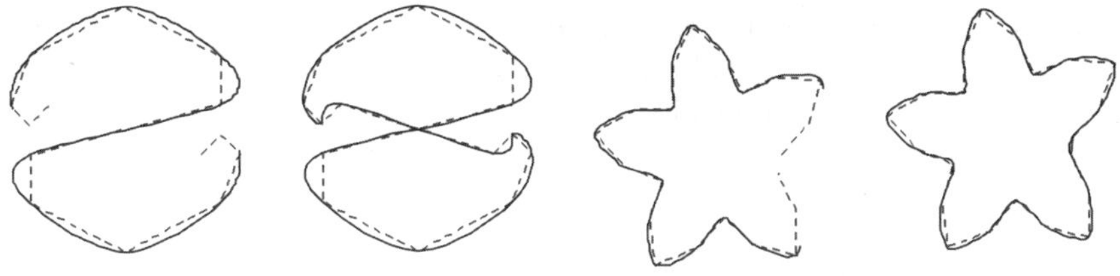

Fig. 3. Open case **(a)** and close case **(b)** of Example 2; open case **(c)** and close case **(d)** of Example 3

Table 1. Performance of approaches

	Example 2				Example 3			
k	T_{no}(s)	T_{fo}(s)	T_{nc}(s)	T_{fc}(s)	T_{no}(s)	T_{fo}(s)	T_{nc}(s)	T_{fc}(s)
3	0.00026	0.00022	0.00030	0.00025	0.00040	0.00035	0.00045	0.00037
4	0.00046	0.00037	0.00063	0.00049	0.00089	0.00067	0.0011	0.00077
5	0.0011	0.00069	0.0019	0.00096	0.0020	0.00012	0.0030	0.00015
6	0.0027	0.0013	0.0040	0.0019	0.0053	0.0023	0.0071	0.0029
7	0.0064	0.0026	0.012	0.0045	0.015	0.0050	0.023	0.0069
8	0.019	0.0053	0.038	0.0084	0.050	0.010	0.081	0.013
9	0.061	0.011	0.14	0.016	0.18	0.020	0.30	0.026
10	0.23	0.023	0.52	0.036	0.67	0.043	1.24	0.054
11	0.88	0.047	2.47	0.073	3.25	0.080	5.96	0.11
12	4.33	0.090	11.5	0.14	14.8	0.16	25.9	0.21

the approaches on Examples 2 and 3. In the table, k represents for the iterate subdivision steps. T_{no} and T_{nc} represent for the time cost with the method given by [4] on the open curves and the closed curves, respectively. T_{fo} and T_{fc} represent for the time cost by Algorithm 3 on the open curves and Algorithm 4 on the closed curves, respectively. All the data are calculated on a personal computer with 2.0 GHz CPU and 512M memory. The programming language is C++. As shown in Table 1, the new approaches are much faster than the traditional method in [4].

6 Conclusions

This paper provides an adaptive geometry compression method based on 4-point interpolatory subdivision schemes. It can work on digital curves of arbitrary dimensions, for example, d dimensions if the points are all of $d-$dimensions. The examples shown in Figures 2 and 3(d) show that the data compression ratios could be about 30 : 1. For decompressing the compressed data, this paper as well provides high-speed 4-point interpolatory subdivision curve generation methods such that decompression could be performed efficiently. As shown in the examples, the new approaches are able to reduce the time cost sharply. The high-speed 4-point interpolatory subdivision curve generation methods not only take advantages to data decompression, but also give great benefit to the real-time display and interaction of 4-point subdivision curves.

Acknowledgements

The research was supported by Chinese 973 Program(2002CB312100), and the National Science Foundation of China (60403047, 60533070). The second author was supported by the project sponsored by a Foundation for the Author of National Excellent Doctoral Dissertation of PR China (200342), and a Program for New Century Excellent Talents in University(NCET-04-0088).

References

1. H Biermann, D Kristjansson, and D Zorin. Approximate Boolean operations on free-form solids. In *Proceedings of SIGGRAPH*, pages 185–194, 2001.
2. G Chaikin. An algorithm for high-speed curve generation. *Computer Graphics and Image Processing*, 3:346–349, 1974.
3. F Cheng and J-H Yong. Subdivsion depth computaion for Catmull-Clark subdivsion surfaces. *Computer-Aided Design and Applications*, 3(1-4):to appear, 2006.
4. N Dyn, D Levin, and JA Gregory. A 4-point interpolatory subdivision scheme for curve design. *Computer Aided Geometric Design*, 4(4):257–268, 1987.
5. MF Hassan, IP Ivrissimitzis, NA Dodgson, and MA Sabin. An interpolating 4-point C^2 ternary stationary subdivision scheme. *Computer Aided Geometric Design*, 19(1):1–18, 2002.
6. A Khodakovsky, P Schroder, and W Sweldens. Progressive geometry compression. In *Proceedings of SIGGRAPH*, pages 271–278, 2000.
7. Z Ma, N Wang, G Wang, and S Dong. Multi-stream progressive geometry compression. *Journal of Computer-Aided Design & Computer Graphics*, 18(2):200–207, 2006.
8. J Stam. Exact evaluation of Catmull-Clark subdivision surfaces at arbitrary parameter values. In *Proceedings of SIGGRAPH*, pages 395–404, 1998.
9. J-H Yong and F Cheng. Adaptive subdivision of Catmull-Clark subdivision surfaces. *Computer-Aided Design and Applications*, 2(1-4):253–261, 2005.
10. J-H Yong, S-M Hu, and J-G Sun. Degree reduction of uniform B-spline curves. *Chinese Journal of Computers*, 23(5):537–540, 2000.
11. J-H Yong, S-M Hu, and J-G Sun. CIM algorithm for approximating three-dimensional polygonal curves. *Journal of Computer Science and Technology*, 16(6):552–559, 2001.
12. J-H Yong, S-M Hu, J-G Sun, and X-Y Tan. Degree reduction of B-spline curves. *Computer Aided Geometric Design*, 18(2):117–127, 2001.
13. J Zhang and CB Owen. Octree-based animated geometry compression. In *Data Compression Conference*, pages 508–517, 2004.
14. D Zorin and P Schröder. Interactive multi-resolution mesh editing. In *Proceedings of SIGGRAPH*, pages 259–268, 1997.

Parametrization Construction of Integer Wavelet Transforms for Embedded Image Coding*

Zaide Liu and Nanning Zheng

Institute of Artificial Intelligence & Robotics, Xi'an Jiaotong University, Xi'an 710049, China
zdliu@aiar.xjtu.edu.cn (Zaide Liu)

Abstract. The Integer Wavelet Transform (IWT) has proved particularly successful in the area of embedded lossy-to-lossless image coding. One of the possible methods to realize the IWT is the lifting scheme. Here we construct a new class of IWTs parameterized simply by one free parameter, which are obtained by introducing a free variable to the lifting based factorization of a Deslauriers-Dubuc interpolating filter. The exact one-parameter expressions for this class of IWTs are deduced and different IWT can be easily obtained by adjusting the free parameter. In particular, several IWTs with binary coefficients are constructed. Extensive experiments show, as compared with some state-of-the-art IWTs, that our transforms have more superior compression performance for both lossless and lossy image coding, and yet require only comparable computational complexity. Besides, a quantization method suitable for IWT is also discussed in this paper.

Keywords: Integer Wavelet Transform (IWT); Lossy-to-lossless image coding; Lifting scheme; Compression performance; Computational complexity; Quantization.

1 Introduction

The Discrete Wavelet Transform (DWT) has been applied extensively to digital signal and image processing, especially digital image transform coding. However, it has an insufferable drawback, i.e., the wavelet coefficients are real numbers, and in this case efficient lossless image coding is not possible with it. With the introduction of the Integer Wavelet Transform (IWT), there has been a growing interest in it for embedded image coding application [1,2,3,4,5,6,7]. Such transforms are invertible in finite-precision arithmetic, map integers to integers, and approximate to their conventional counterparts (i.e., nonreversible DWT) from which they are derived [3,4]. Due largely to these properties, transforms of this type are extremely useful for compression systems requiring efficient handling of lossless coding, minimal memory usage, or low computational complexity.

* This work was supported by the National Natural Science Foundation of China under Grant 60021302 and the National Natural Science Foundation of China under Grant 60405004.

N. Zheng, X. Jiang, and X. Lan (Eds.): IWICPAS 2006, LNCS 4153, pp. 435–445, 2006.

Furthermore, these transforms are particularly attractive for supporting functionalities such as progressive lossy-to-lossless recovery of images [2,5,7]. The symmetric extension, as a solution to the boundary problem of finite-length signals during the transform, is also well explored [6].

Using IWT instead of DWT, most DWT-based codecs can be used for lossless image coding without any modification, and yield very good performance [7,8]. They often produce an embedded bitstream, that is, the quality of the reconstructed image increases as more encoded bits become available to the decoder. The decoding can be stopped at any point of the bitstream.

One of the methods to realize the IWT is the Lifting Scheme (LS) [9,10], which allows an efficient implementation of the DWT. Since Perfect Reconstruction (PR) is ensured by the structure of the LS itself, the IWT can be realized by a basic modification to the lifting based DWT, i.e., result in each lifting step is rounded to the nearest integer [1]. The IWT family constructed here is also based on this LS framework. It begins with the lifting based factorization of a Deslauriers-Dubuc interpolating filter [11]. After factorization, a free variable is introduced and the one-parameter expressions for this class of IWTs are deduced. This parameter presents us a free choice to construct different IWT, and it can be assigned any real number. We then construct several IWTs with their lifting filters all having binary (dyadic-fraction) coefficients, and compare them with some state-of-the-art transforms on the basis of their computational complexity, lossy compression performance, and lossless compression performance. The evaluation results show that our transforms give people new choices to build systems with improved compression performance. We also discuss a quantization method suitable for IWT, which is similar to that used in [5].

2 Construction of the Integer Wavelet Transforms

2.1 Lifting Scheme for Integer Wavelet Transform

The LS is a possible implementation of the DWT. Its structure guarantees that the scheme is reversible, regardless of the filters used. Figure 1 depicts the lifting based forward wavelet decomposition (The reconstruction algorithm is a simple reverse procedure). The input signal $s^{(l-1)}$ (The superscript 'l' is used to denote the current level of the DWT) is split into two signals corresponding to evenly and oddly indexed samples. Then the even signal is convolved with the lifting filter $P_i(z)$ and the result is subtracted from the odd one. This action is called a *dual lifting step* or *prediction step*. The predicted odd signal is then convolved with the lifting filter $U_i(z)$ and added to the even one. We call it a *prime lifting step* or *update step*. Eventually, after, say, M pairs of prediction and update steps, the even samples will become the low-pass coefficients $s^{(l)}$, while the odd samples become the high-pass coefficients $d^{(l)}$, up to a scaling factor K. Again, the low-pass coefficients $s^{(l)}$ is regarded as input signal to implement the next level of wavelet decomposition.

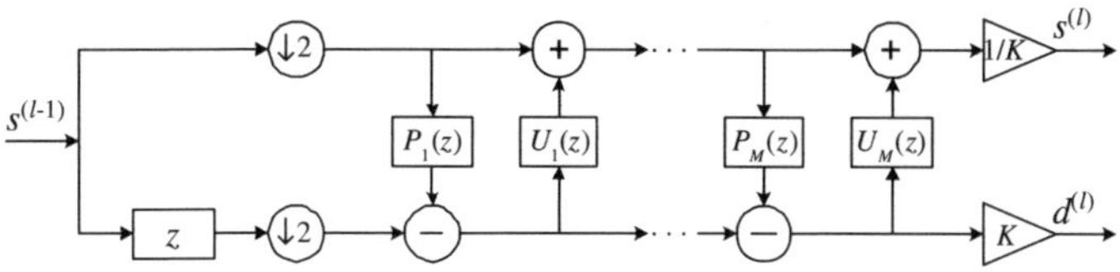

Fig. 1. The lifting based forward wavelet transform: First splitting the signal, then alternating prediction and update steps, and finally a scaling

Without loss of generality, it will be assumed that the LS starts with a prediction step and is composed of an even number of steps. It is sufficient to set $P_1(z)$ or $U_M(z)$ to be 0 to take into account all other cases.

To realize the IWT, one can round the result in each lifting step to the nearest integer [1]. This kind of operation is nonlinear, however, the structure of LS ensures that PR property is still preserved. Here, there arises one problem that how to deal with the scaling factor K because of dividing one integer by it is nonreversible. Two solutions to this issue are available: If K is close to 1, we can omit the scaling step. Otherwise, it has been shown in [10], with at most three extra lifting steps, K can always be set to 1. If we denote the rounding operation as *Round*(), the lifting based forward IWT can be shown as Fig. 2. Also, the inverse transform can be trivially deduced by a simple reverse procedure.

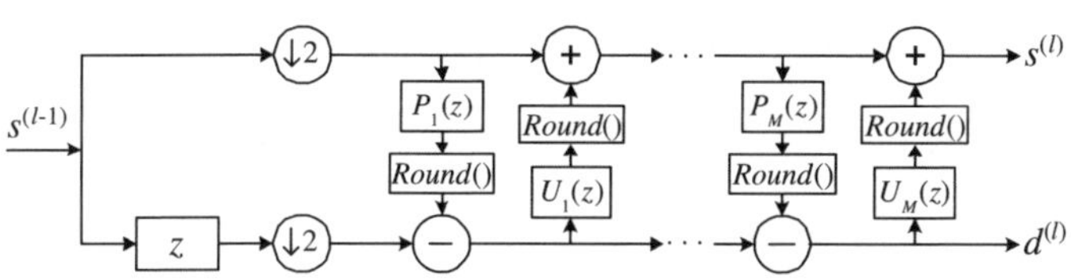

Fig. 2. Forward IWT based on the lifting scheme. Each lifting step is followed by a rounding to the nearest integer operation

2.2 Parametrization Construction of the IWTs

Our new IWT family is also based on the LS framework. It begins with the well-known Deslauriers-Dubuc interpolating filter with 4 Vanishing Moments (VMs) [11], which is given by

$$H(z) = 2^{-5}(-z^3 + 9z + 16 + 9z^{-1} - z^{-3}) \ . \tag{1}$$

We use it as the synthesis low-pass filter. Obviously, by letting the analysis low-pass filter $\tilde{H}(z) = 1$, and the associated high-pass filters satisfy

$$G(z) = z^{-1}\tilde{H}(-z^{-1}), \quad \tilde{G}(z) = z^{-1}H(-z^{-1}) \ , \tag{2}$$

we can find a trivial Biorthogonal Wavelet Filter Bank (BWFB) permitting PR condition.[1]

Using the Euclidean algorithm presented in [10], the analysis polyphase matrix $\tilde{\boldsymbol{P}}(z)$ for this BWFB is factored into

$$\tilde{\boldsymbol{P}}(z) = \begin{bmatrix} \tilde{H}_e(z) & \tilde{G}_e(z) \\ \tilde{H}_o(z) & \tilde{G}_o(z) \end{bmatrix} = \begin{bmatrix} 1 & \frac{-9(1+z^{-1})+(z+z^{-2})}{16} \\ 0 & 1 \end{bmatrix} , \tag{3}$$

where $\tilde{H}_e(z^2) = (\tilde{H}(z) + \tilde{H}(-z))/2$ and $\tilde{H}_o(z^2) = z(\tilde{H}(z) - \tilde{H}(-z))/2$; $\tilde{G}_e(z^2)$ and $\tilde{G}_o(z^2)$ are similarly defined.

To improve $\tilde{H}(z)$, we introduce a new lifting filter having the linear phase

$$U(z) = \alpha(1 + z) + \beta\left(z^{-1} + z^2\right) , \tag{4}$$

and append it into (3). Then the new analysis polyphase matrix $\tilde{\boldsymbol{P}}_{new}(z)$ is turned into

$$\tilde{\boldsymbol{P}}_{new}(z) = \begin{bmatrix} 1 & \frac{-9(1+z^{-1})+(z+z^{-2})}{16} \\ 0 & 1 \end{bmatrix} \begin{bmatrix} 1 & 0 \\ U(z) & 1 \end{bmatrix} . \tag{5}$$

Now we should find the relationship between parameters α and β. It is easy to obtain the new analysis low-pass filter $\tilde{H}_{new}(z)$ using (5), which is given by

$$\begin{aligned} \tilde{H}_{new}(z) = {} & \tfrac{8-9\alpha+\beta}{8} + \alpha\left(z + z^{-1}\right) - \tfrac{8\alpha+9\beta}{16}\left(z^2 + z^{-2}\right) \\ & + \beta\left(z^3 + z^{-3}\right) + \tfrac{\alpha-9\beta}{16}\left(z^4 + z^{-4}\right) + \tfrac{\beta}{16}\left(z^6 + z^{-6}\right) . \end{aligned} \tag{6}$$

$\tilde{H}_{new}(z)$ must satisfy the low-pass and high-pass conditions

$$\tilde{H}_{new}(1) = 1, \quad \tilde{H}_{new}(-1) = 0 , \tag{7}$$

and after simple manipulation, we can achieve

$$\beta = \frac{1}{4} - \alpha . \tag{8}$$

Substituting (8) into (6), we can obtain the final expression for $\tilde{H}_{new}(z)$

$$\begin{aligned} \tilde{H}_{new}(z) = {} & \tfrac{33-40\alpha}{32} + \alpha\left(z + z^{-1}\right) + \tfrac{4\alpha-9}{64}\left(z^2 + z^{-2}\right) \\ & + \tfrac{1-4\alpha}{4}\left(z^3 + z^{-3}\right) + \tfrac{40\alpha-9}{64}\left(z^4 + z^{-4}\right) + \tfrac{1-4\alpha}{64}\left(z^6 + z^{-6}\right) . \end{aligned} \tag{9}$$

According to (5), the filter $\tilde{G}(z)$ is invariable, this implies that filter $H(z)$ is also changeless, i.e., (1). The associated high-pass filters can be obtained with (2).

[1] In practical application, it should handle the normalizing factor $\sqrt{2}$, which can be ignored in the implementation of the DWT by scaling the analysis low-pass filter and the synthesis low-pass filter by factors of $1/\sqrt{2}$ and $\sqrt{2}$, respectively, or vice versa, so that perfect reconstruction is maintained.

In (5), substituting (8) into the lifting filter $U(z)$, we obtain

$$\tilde{\boldsymbol{P}}_{new}(z) = \begin{bmatrix} 1 & \frac{-9(1+z^{-1})+(z+z^{-2})}{16} \\ 0 & 1 \end{bmatrix} \begin{bmatrix} 1 & 0 \\ \frac{4\alpha(1+z)+(1-4\alpha)(z^{-1}+z^2)}{4} & 1 \end{bmatrix} . \qquad (10)$$

If we denote the input signal $s^{(l-1)}[n]$ is split into two signals $s_0^{(l)}[n]$ and $d_0^{(l)}[n]$, the above matrix factorization can generate a new class of IWTs parameterized by the free parameter α, which are shown as (for convenience of exposition, the superscript 'l' is omitted)

$$\begin{cases} d[n] = d_0[n] - \lfloor \frac{1}{16}(9(s_0[n]+s_0[n+1]) - (s_0[n-1]+s_0[n+2])) + \frac{1}{2} \rfloor \\ s[n] = s_0[n] + \lfloor \frac{1}{4}(4\alpha(d[n-1]+d[n]) + (1-4\alpha)(d[n-2]+d[n+1])) + \frac{1}{2} \rfloor \end{cases} . \qquad (11)$$

Here, $\lfloor t \rfloor$ indicates the largest integer not exceeding t.

Now we can see that a new class of 13/7 BWFBs and their associated IWTs parameterized simply by the free parameter α are constructed. We employ the notation $(\tilde{N}, N)$ to indicate that the analysis and synthesis wavelets have $\tilde{N}$ and N VMs, respectively, then in this case, it has VMs (4, 2).

Remark 1. About the construction technique, we also point out that

- The construction technique never yields a particular BWFB (or IWT) that somehow could not be found using other techniques before. The significance of this technique is that it generates closed-form parametrization expression for a new class of 13/7 BWFBs (or IWTs). Using the expressions, one can construct an infinite number of IWTs with simple lifting filter coefficients and desired properties.
- This construction technique can be generalized to other case, for example, by using the Deslauriers-Dubuc interpolating filter with 2 VMs, one can construct a new class of 9/3 IWTs parameterized by one free parameter.

3 Examples and Quantization

3.1 Examples

In (11), we can assign arbitrary real number to the free parameter α to obtain different IWT, however, for the purpose of decreasing computational complexity, the dyadic fractions are preferable. Here we give 5 transforms with their lifting filters all having binary coefficients. To make a through comparison, 3 state-of-the-art IWTs known to be effective for image coding are also presented. They are listed in Table 1.

3.2 Quantization

The transforms under evaluation are 1-D in nature, 2-D images are handled by transforming the rows and columns in succession. Although it is possible to

Table 1. Integer wavelet transforms under evaluation

Name	α	CG[a]	VMs	Description
13/7-A	3/8	8.798	(4, 2)	——
13/7-B	5/16	9.414	(4, 2)	——
13/7-C	9/32	9.359	(4, 4)	equation (4.5) in [1]
13/7-D	17/64	9.240	(4, 2)	——
9/7-M[b]	1/4	9.066	(4, 2)	equation (4.2) in [1]
5/11	—	9.039	(4, 2)	equation (4.6) in [1]
9/3	—	9.153	(2, 4)	equation (4.3) in [1]
5/3	—	9.092	(2, 2)	equation (4.1) in [1], recommended in JPEG2000 [7]

[a] "CG" denotes the coding gain (in dB) of the corresponding nonreversible DWT. It is computed using the method presented in [13], and a first-order Markov model with correlation factor $\rho = 0.95$ is assumed as the input. The DWT decomposition level is 5.

[b] 13/7-C and 9/7-M wavelets were, respectively, also known as the improved Donoho wavelets having VMs (4, 4) and (4, 2) [9].

utilize these transforms without quantization, for example, in JPEG 2000 standard [7], it should be noted that these transforms are not orthonormal. Thus, the transformed image subband coefficients need to be scaled (quantized) appropriately to ensure optimum rate-distortion performance. We use a method similar to that described in [5] to compute the scaling factor (the reciprocal of the quantization step) of every subband. This consists of the following three stages: For each subband, first the scaling factor of the corresponding nonreversible DWT is computed using the method presented in [12]; Because the obtained scaling factors are usually floating point numbers, and cannot be used on the integer subband coefficients, they then be normalized so that the minimum scaling factor is 1.0; finally, all the normalized scaling factors are rounded to the nearest power of two. The last stage make the multiplication operation become an upward shift of the image bitplanes. In our experiment, a 5-level IWT is applied and 16 subbands are generated, the normalized scaling factors are given in Table 2. The values in the table were obtained by normalizing all the scaling factors such that the scaling factor of *HH* subband of the finest level is 1.0 (See [7] to obtain the details about the naming rule for subbands).

4 Performance Analysis

Now we investigate the performance of the transforms under evaluation for image compression. Comparisons of their computational complexity as well as the lossless and lossy image compression performance are made.

4.1 Computational Complexity

All of the transforms under evaluation are calculated using only fixed-point arithmetic; particularly, only integer addition/subtraction, and multiplication

Table 2. Normalized scaling factors for the IWTs under evaluation for a 5-level 2-D wavelet decomposition

	IWTs							
Subbands	13/7-A	13/7-B	13/7-C	13/7-D	9/7-M	5/11	9/3	5/3
LL_5	38.024	39.501	39.138	38.685	38.066	31.183	30.172	29.696
$HL_5(LH_5)$	20.295	20.655	20.673	20.639	20.575	16.900	15.573	15.773
HH_5	10.832	10.800	10.920	11.011	11.121	9.160	8.038	8.378
$HL_4(LH_4)$	10.149	10.329	10.338	10.321	10.289	8.492	7.838	7.934
HH_4	5.417	5.401	5.461	5.507	5.562	4.620	4.066	4.234
$HL_3(LH_3)$	5.083	5.173	5.178	5.169	5.152	4.328	4.020	4.062
HH_3	2.718	2.710	2.739	2.762	2.789	2.388	2.127	2.207
$HL_2(LH_2)$	2.597	2.644	2.645	2.639	2.629	2.319	2.205	2.215
HH_2	1.417	1.413	1.427	1.437	1.450	1.345	1.251	1.283
$HL_1(LH_1)$	1.560	1.590	1.583	1.574	1.561	1.465	1.456	1.445
HH_1	1.0	1.0	1.0	1.0	1.0	1.0	1.0	1.0

operations are required. Since all lifting filter coefficients are dyadic fractions, the division operations can be implemented as bit shifts, this means that $\lfloor x/2^N \rfloor$ is equivalent to the arithmetic right shift of x by N bits. We use the number of addition, multiplication, and shift operations of computing one sample pair $(s[n], d[n])$ as the comparison unit. Since the forward transform has the same computational complexity as that of the inverse transform, we only consider the former. The comparison results are listed in Table 3.

Table 3. Computational complexity. Note, the results of the last three transforms are concluded from [1]

Transform	13/7-A	13/7-B	13/7-C	13/7-D	9/7-M	5/11	9/3	5/3
Addition	10	10	10	10	8	10	8	6
Multiplication	2	2	3	2	1	0	2	0
Shift	2	2	2	2	2	3	2	2
Total	14	14	15	14	11	13	12	8

From Table 3, we can see that the 5/3 transform requires the least computation, followed by the 9/7-M, 5/11, and 9/3 transforms as a group, and then the others as a group. Particularly, the 5/3, and 5/11 transforms are truly multiplierless (i.e., their underlying lifting filters all have coefficients that are strictly powers of two).

4.2 Compression Performance

Extensive experiments were performed to compare the performance of the IWTs under evaluation for image compression. For the purpose of fair and consistent comparisons, except for the type of transform, other experiment conditions are same: A 5-level transform is applied to the source images to generate a wavelet subband decomposition consisting of 16 subbands; and the symmetric extension is used at the image edges during transforms. The subbands are quantized using the method described in Sect. 3.2, and then encoded with one of the best DWT-based image codecs, called "Set Partitioning in Hierarchical Trees (SPIHT)",[2] as proposed by Said and Pearlman [8].

The experiment is performed using a large number of images. Due to the limitation of space, we have selected two standard grayscale images, namely, Lena and Barbara as representatives. Lena is chosen because of its predominantly "smooth" background which is typical of natural images, while Barbara is selected for its high frequency or texture regions in the tablecloth, trousers, and the scarf. Both lossy and lossless compression were considered here.

Lossless Compression Performance. In the lossless case, compression performance was measured in terms of the final bit rate (in bpp). Table 4 shows the final bit rates of the test images for the various transforms under evaluation. For each image, the best result has been highlighted, whereas the worst result has been highlighted and shown in italics type. Clearly, no single transform performs best for both images. For Lena, the 13/7-C, 13/7-D, 13/7-B, 9/7-M, and 5/11 transforms perform best, on the contrary, the 9/3, 5/3, and 13/7-A transforms are inferior. For Barbara, the 13/7-B, 13/7-C, and 13/7-D transforms perform best, followed by the 5/11, 9/7-M, and 13/7-A transforms as a group, and then the 9/3 and 5/3 transforms perform worst. Obviously, the 13/7-B and 13/7-C transforms are preferable for both images.

Table 4. Lossless compression results (in bpp)

	IWTs							
Image	13/7-A	13/7-B	13/7-C	13/7-D	9/7-M	5/11	9/3	5/3
Lena	4.4240	4.3904	**4.3861**	4.3880	4.3911	4.3912	***4.4359***	4.4240
Barbara	4.8918	**4.8443**	4.8553	4.8655	4.8728	4.8709	4.9505	***4.9656***

Objective Lossy Compression Performance. Both images are compressed in a lossy manner at five compression ratios (i.e., 128:1, 64:1, 32:1, 16:1, and 8:1) using the transforms under evaluation. The image quality was then measured using the well-known PSNR metric (in dB). The test results are given in Table 5. For each test image and compression ratio pair, the best result and worst result are shown in the same manner as that used in Table 4.

As can be seen, for Lena, at high compression ratios (i.e., 32:1 or greater), the 13/7-B, 13/7-C, and 13/7-D transforms perform best in approximately that order, followed by the 9/3, 5/11, and 9/7-M transforms as a group, and the

[2] The "SPIHT" codec used here is rebuilt based on the "Qccpack" software packet by J. E. Fowler, which is downloaded from the website: http://qccpack.sourceforge.net.

Table 5. Lossy compression results for Lena and Barbara images (in dB)

	Lena Compression ratios					Barbara Compression ratios				
Transforms	128:1	64:1	32:1	16:1	8:1	128:1	64:1	32:1	16:1	8:1
13/7-A	27.67	30.33	***32.93***	35.79	***38.44***	22.68	24.34	26.85	30.49	35.19
13/7-B	**27.96**	**30.63**	**33.20**	36.08	38.79	**22.97**	**24.56**	**27.19**	**31.07**	**35.65**
13/7-C	27.94	30.61	33.19	36.06	38.76	22.92	24.40	26.97	30.91	35.55
13/7-D	27.91	30.54	33.13	35.96	38.65	22.90	24.30	26.83	30.74	35.30
9/7-M	27.82	30.39	32.98	***35.76***	38.50	22.77	24.11	26.62	30.49	35.16
5/11	27.70	30.46	33.19	**36.15**	38.86	***22.65***	***23.78***	26.36	30.42	35.53
9/3	27.84	30.46	33.16	36.14	38.93	22.86	23.99	26.50	30.33	35.22
5/3	***27.66***	***30.29***	32.96	36.05	**38.99**	22.75	23.81	***26.20***	***30.01***	***34.97***

5/3 and 13/7-A transforms fare the worst. As the compression ratio decreases, the 5/11, 5/3, and 9/3 transforms perform best, whereas the 9/7-M and 13/7-A transforms fare the worst; although the 13/7 transforms (except for 13/7-A) are inferior to the 5/11, 5/3, and 9/3 transforms, the differences among them are small, and can be neglected in practice. For Barbara, generally, the 13/7-B and 13/7-C transforms perform best, followed by 13/7-D, 13/7-A, and 9/7-M transforms as g group, whereas the 5/3, 5/11, and 9/3 transforms are the worst. Clearly, the 13/7-B and 13/7-C perform best for both images.

Surprisingly, the 5/3 transform cannot result in the expected results, the reason is that with the introduction of the quantization, the rate-distortion performance of the IWT is very similar to that of the real transform (DWT), however the 5/3 real transform has lower coding gain (see Table 1).

Subjective Lossy Compression Performance. For lossy image compression, from above analysis, we can see that the transforms under evaluation can be divided into three groups in the descending order of the compression performance. The 13/7-B and 13/7-C transforms are regarded as a group, followed by the 13/7-D, 9/3, and 9/7-M transforms as a group, and lastly the 13/7-A, 5/11, and 5/3 transforms as a group. From each group we select one representative, respectively, i.e., 13/7-B, 9/7-M, and 5/3 transforms, to evaluate their subjective compression performance, particularly, the potential of preserving edges and textures. Since the human eye often cannot distinguish a low compression ratio lossy reconstruction of an image from the original, the subjective testing was done at compression ratio of 32:1. Figure 3 shows the reconstructed Barbara image for three representatives. To make the differences evident and also the limitation of space, we only give part of the image. It is observed that the image quality corresponds well with the objective measure of PSNR. Clearly, the 13/7-B transform preserves more textures in the tablecloth and trousers than 9/7-M and 5/3 transforms.

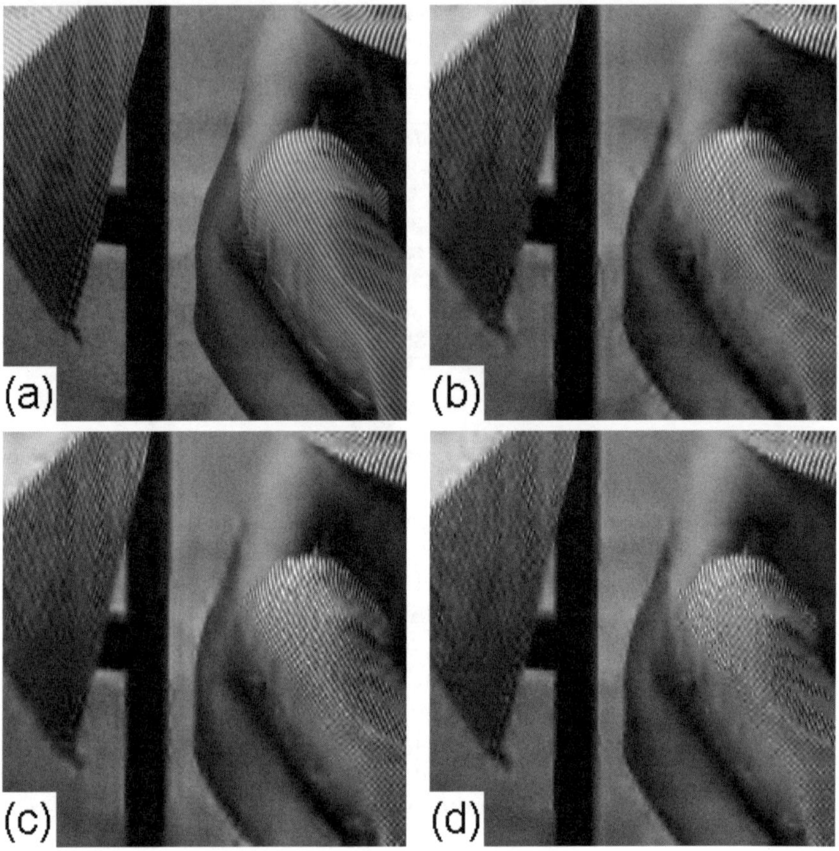

Fig. 3. Part of the reconstructed Barbara image at compression ratio of 32:1. (a) Original image, (b) 13/7-B transform, (c) 9/7-M transform, (d) 5/3 transform

5 Conclusion

We have constructed a new class of 13/7 integer wavelet transforms (IWTs) parameterized simply by one free parameter, this class of transforms are obtained by appending a free variable to the lifting based factorization of a Deslauriers-Dubuc interpolating filter. The free parameter presents people a choice to construct different IWT. By assigning dyadic fractions to the free parameter, we constructed 5 IWTs, i.e., 13/7-A, 13/7-B, 13/7-C, 13/7-D, and 9/7-M transforms, with their lifting filters all having binary coefficients. Comparisons between these transforms and 3 state-of-the-art IWTs, i.e., 5/11, 9/3, and 5/3 transforms, which are suitable for image coding, are made on the basis of their computational complexity, lossy compression performance, and lossless compression performance. The results show that 13/7-B and 13/7-C transforms have more superior compression performance to other transforms under evaluation for both lossless and lossy image coding, and yet require only comparable computational complexity. These new transforms give us new choices to build systems with improved compression performance. Besides, a quantization method for the IWT is discussed, and the experiment results show that it is very effective to improve the compression performance.

The transforms constructed here also have drawbacks, for example, their computational complexity is higher than 5/3 transform, so constructing new IWT with higher compression performance and computational complexity comparable to that of 5/3 transform is expected in the next stage of our research.

References

1. A.R. Calderbank, I. Daubechies, W. Sweldens, B.L. Yeo, Wavelet transforms that map integers to integers. Appl. Comput. Harmon. Anal. 5 (1998) 332–369.
2. A. Said, W.A. Pearlman, An image multiresolution representation for lossless and lossy compression. IEEE Trans. Image Proc. 5 (1996) 1303–1310.
3. J. Reichel, G. Menegaz, M.J. Nadenau, M. Kunt, Integer wavelet transform for embedded lossy to lossless image compression. IEEE Trans. Image Proc. 10 (2001) 383–392.
4. M.D. Adams, F. Kossentini, Reversible integer-to-integer wavelet transforms for image compression: Performance evaluation and analysis. IEEE Trans. Image Proc. 9 (2000) 1010–1024.
5. A. Bilgin, P.J. Sementilli, Fang Sheng, M.W. Marcellin, Scalable image coding using reversible integer wavelet transforms. IEEE Trans. Image Proc. 9 (2000) 1972–1977.
6. M.D. Adams, R.K. Ward, Symmetric-extension-compatible reversible integer-to-integer wavelet transforms. IEEE Trans. Signal Proc. 51 (2003) 2624–2636.
7. ISO/IEC 15444-1 (2nd edition), Information technology—JPEG 2000 image coding system: core coding system, 2004.
8. A. Said, W.A. Pearlman, A new, fast, efficient image codec based on set partitioning in hierarchical trees. IEEE Trans. Circuits Syst. Video Tech. 6 (1996) 243–250.
9. W. Sweldens, The lifting scheme: a custom-design construction of biorthogonal wavelets. Appl. Comput. Harmon. Anal. 3 (1996) 186–200.
10. I. Daubechies, W. Sweldens, Factoring wavelet transforms into lifting steps. J. Fourier Anal. Appl. 4 (3) (1998) 245–267.
11. G. Deslauriers, S. Dubuc, Symmetric iterative interpolation processes, Constructive Approx. 5 (1989) 49–68.
12. J.W. Woods, T. Naveen, A filter based bit allocation scheme for subband compression of HDTV. IEEE Trans. Image Proc. 1 (1992) 436–440.
13. J. Katto and Y. Yasuda, Performance evaluation of subband coding and optimization. Proc. of the SPIE Symposium on Visual Commu. and Image Proc. 1605 (1991) 95–106.

Reinforcement Learning with Raw Image Pixels as Input State

Damien Ernst[1], Raphaël Marée, and Louis Wehenkel

Department of Electrical Engineering and Computer Science
Institut Montefiore - University of Liège
Sart-Tilman B28 - B4000 Liège - Belgium
[1] Postdoctoral Researcher FNRS
{ernst, maree, lwh}@montefiore.ulg.ac.be

Abstract. We report in this paper some positive simulation results obtained when image pixels are directly used as input state of a reinforcement learning algorithm. The reinforcement learning algorithm chosen to carry out the simulation is a batch-mode algorithm known as fitted Q iteration.

1 Introduction

Reinforcement learning (RL) is learning what to do, how to map states to actions, from the information acquired from interaction with a system. In its classical setting, the reinforcement learning agent wants to maximize a long term reward signal and the information acquired from interaction with the system is a set of samples, where each sample is composed of four elements: a state, the action taken while being in this state, the instantaneous reward observed and the successor state.

In many real-life problems, such as robot navigation ones, the state is made of visual percept. Up to now, the standard approach for dealing with visual percept in the reinforcement learning context is to extract from the images some relevant features and use them, rather than the raw image pixels, as input state for the RL algorithm (see e.g. [3]). The main advantage of this approach is that it leads to a reduction of the input space for the RL algorithm which eases the problem of generalization to unseen situations. Its main drawback is that the feature extraction phase needs to be adapted to problem specifics.

Recently, several research papers have shown that in the image classification framework, it was possible to obtain some excellent results by applying directly state-of-the-art supervised learning algorithms (e.g. tree-based ensemble methods, SVMs) on the image pixels (see e.g. [5]). Also, recent developments in reinforcement learning have led to some new algorithms which allow to take full advantage, in the reinforcement learning context, of the generalization performances of any supervised learning algorithm [1,4]. We may therefore wonder whether using one of these new RL algorithms directly with the raw image pixels

N. Zheng, X. Jiang, and X. Lan (Eds.): IWICPAS 2006, LNCS 4153, pp. 446–454, 2006.

as input state, without any feature extraction, could lead to some good performances. In a first attempt to answer this question, we carried out simulations and report in this paper our preliminary findings.

The next section of this paper is largely borrowed from [1] and introduces, in the deterministic case, the fitted Q iteration algorithm used in our simulations. Afterwards, we describe the test problem and discuss the results obtained in various settings. And, finally, we conclude.

2 Learning from a Set of Samples

2.1 Problem Formulation

Let us consider a system having a deterministic *discrete-time dynamics* described by:

$$x_{t+1} = f(x_t, u_t) \quad t = 0, 1, \ldots \tag{1}$$

where for all t, the state x_t is an element of the state space X, the action u_t is an element of the action space U.

To the transition from t to $t+1$ is associated an instantaneous *reward signal* $r_t = r(x_t, u_t)$ where $r(x, u)$ is the reward function bounded by some constant B_r.

Let $\mu(\cdot) : X \to U$ denote a stationary control policy and J^μ denote the return obtained over an infinite time horizon when the system is controlled using this policy (i.e. when $u_t = \mu(x_t), \forall t$). For a given initial condition $x_0 = x$, J^μ is defined as follows:

$$J^\mu(x) = \lim_{N\to\infty} \sum_{t=0}^{N-1} \gamma^t r(x_t, \mu(x_t)) \tag{2}$$

where γ is a discount factor ($0 \le \gamma < 1$) that weighs short-term rewards more than long-term ones. Our objective is to find an optimal stationary policy μ^*, i.e. a stationary policy that maximizes J^μ for all x.

Reinforcement learning techniques do not assume that the system dynamics and the cost function are given in analytical (or even algorithmic) form. The sole information they assume available about the system dynamics and the cost function is the one that can be gathered from the observation of system trajectories. Reinforcement learning techniques compute from this an *approximation* $\hat{\pi}^*_{c,T}$ of a T-stage optimal (closed-loop) policy since, except for very special conditions, the exact optimal policy can not be decided from such a limited amount of information.

The *fitted Q iteration* algorithm on which we focus in this paper, actually relies on a slightly weaker assumption, namely that a set of one step system transitions is given, each one providing the knowledge of a new sample of information (x_t, u_t, c_t, x_{t+1}) that we name four-tuple. We denote by $\mathcal{F}$ the set $\{(x^l_t, u^l_t, c^l_t, x^l_{t+1})\}_{l=1}^{\#\mathcal{F}}$ of available four-tuples.

2.2 Dynamic Programming Results

The sequence of Q_N-functions defined on $X \times U$

$$Q_N(x,u) = r(x,u) + \gamma \max_{u' \in U} Q_{N-1}(f(x,u),u') \forall N > 0$$

with $Q_0(x,u) \equiv 0$ converges, in infinity norm, to the Q-function, defined as the (unique) solution of the Bellman equation:

$$Q(x,u) = r(x,u) + \gamma \max_{u' \in U} Q(f(x,u),u') \tag{3}$$

A policy μ^* that satisfies

$$\mu^*(x) = \arg\max_{u \in U} Q(x,u) \tag{4}$$

is an optimal stationary policy.

Let us denote by μ_N^* the stationary policy

$$\mu_N^*(x) = \arg\max_{u \in U} Q_N(x,u) \quad . \tag{5}$$

The following bound on the suboptimality of μ_N^* holds:

$$\|J^{\mu^*} - J^{\mu_N^*}\|_\infty \leq \frac{2\gamma^N B_r}{(1-\gamma)^2} \quad . \tag{6}$$

2.3 Fitted Q Iteration

The fitted Q iteration algorithm computes from the set of four-tuples $\mathcal{F}$ the functions $\hat{Q}_1$, $\hat{Q}_2$, ..., $\hat{Q}_N$, approximations of the functions Q_1, Q_2, ..., Q_N defined by Eqn (3), by solving a sequence of standard supervised learning regression problems. The policy

$$\hat{\mu}_N^*(x) = \arg\max_{u \in U} \hat{Q}_N(x,u) \tag{7}$$

is taken as approximation of the optimal stationary policy. The training sample for the kth problem ($k \geq 1$) of the sequence is

$$((x_t^l, u_t^l), r_t^l + \gamma \max_{u \in U} \hat{Q}_{k-1}(x_{t+1}^l, u)), l = 1, \ldots, \#\mathcal{F} \tag{8}$$

with $\hat{Q}_0(x,u) = 0$ everywhere. The supervised learning regression algorithm produces from this training sample the function $\hat{Q}_k$ that is used to determine the next training sample and from there, the next function of the sequence.

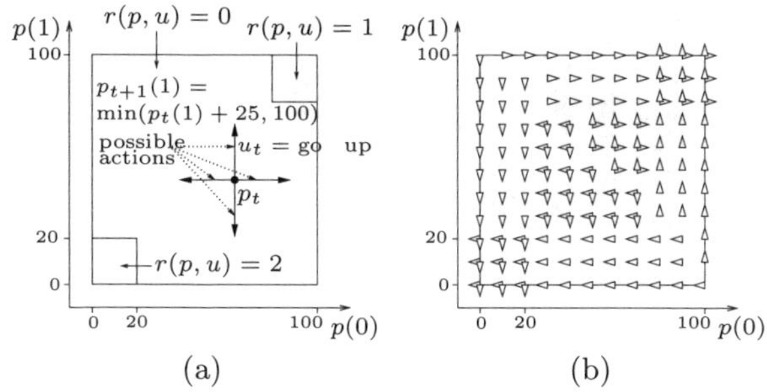

Fig. 1. Figure (a) gives information for the position dynamics and the reward function for the agent navigation problem. Figure (b) plots the optimal policy $\mu^*(p)$ for the values of $p \in \{0, 10, \ldots, 100\} \times \{0, 10, \ldots, 100\}$. Orientation of the triangle for a position p gives information about the optimal action(s) $\mu^*(p)$.

3 Simulation Results

3.1 The Test Problem

Experiments are carried out on the navigation problem whose main characteristics are illustrated on Figure 1a. An agent navigates in a square and the reward he gets is function of his position in the square. He can at each instant t either decide to go up, down, left of right ($U = \{up, down, left, right\}$). We denote by p the position of the agent. The horizontal (vertical) position of the agent $p(0)$ ($p(1)$) can vary between 0 and 100 with a step of 1. The set of possible positions is $P = \{0, 1, 2, \ldots, 100\} \times \{0, 1, 2, \ldots, 100\}$. When the agent decides at time t to go in a specific direction, he moves 25 steps at once in this direction, unless he is stopped before by the square boundary.

The reward signal r_t observed by the agent is always zero, except if the agent is at time t in the upper right part of the square and the lower left part of the square where reward signals of 1 and 2 are observed, respectively ($B_r = 2$). The decay factor γ is equal to 0.5. The optimal policy, plotted on Figure 1b drives the agent to one of these corners. Even if larger reward signals are observed the lower left corner, the optimal policy does not necessarily drive the system to this corner. Indeed, due to the discount factor γ that weighs short-term reward signal more than long-term ones, it may be preferable to observe smaller reward signals but sooner.

Our goal is to study the performances of the fitted Q iteration algorithm when the input state for the RL algorithm is not the position p but well a visual percept. In this context, we represent on top of the navigation square a *navigation image*, and we have supposed that when being at position p, the agent has access to the visual percept $pixels(p)$ which is a vector of pixel values that encodes the image region surrounding its position p (Figure 2). The matrix giving the grey levels of the 100 tiles of Figure 2 is given in 5.

In our study, we have partionned the 100×100 navigation image into one hundred 10×10 subimages that we name *tiles*. For every tile, we have selected a

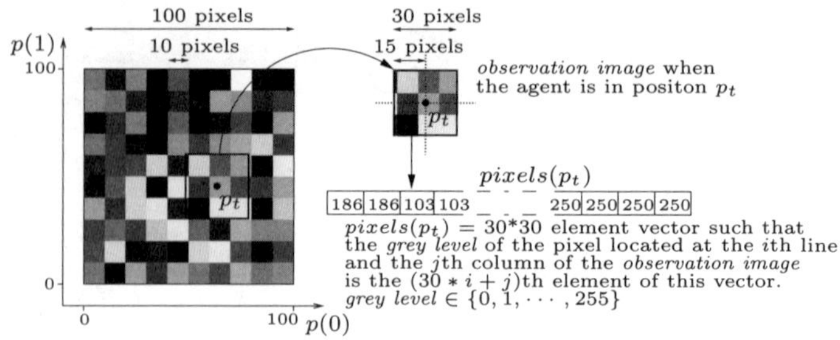

Fig. 2. Visual percept *pixels*(p_t) for the agent when being position p_t. Pixels of the 30×30 *observation image* which are not contained in the 100×100 *navigation image*, which happens when $p_t(i) < 15$ and/or $p_t(i) > 85$, are assumed to be black pixels (*grey level*=0).

grey level at random in $\{0, 1, \ldots, 255\}$ and set all its pixels to this grey level. After having generated the image, we have checked whether two different positions p were indeed leading to different vectors of pixel values $pixels(p)$. This check has been done in order to make sure that considering $pixels(p)$ rather than p as input state does not lead to a partially observable system.

3.2 Four-Tuples Generation

To generate the four-tuples we consider one step episodes with the initial position for each episode being chosen at random among the $101 * 101$ possible positions p and the action being chosen at random among U. More precisely, to generate a set $\mathcal{F}$ with n elements, we repeat n times the sequence of instructions:

1. draw p_0 at random in P and u at random in U;
2. observe r_0 and p_1;
3. add $(pixels(p_0), u_0, r_0, pixels(p_1))$ to $\mathcal{F}$.

3.3 Fitted Q Iteration Algorithm

Within the fitted Q iteration algorithm, we have used in our simulations a regression tree based ensemble method called Extra-Trees [2].[1] To apply this algorithm at each iteration, the training sample defined by Eqn (8) is split into four subsamples according to the four possible values of u, and $\hat{Q}_k(x, u)$ for each value of u is obtained by calling the Extra-Trees algorithm on the corresponding subsample. The number of iterations N of the fitted Q iteration algorithm is chosen equal to 10, leading to an upper bound of 0.015625 in Eqn (6) which is tight enough for our purpose, since $J^{\mu^*}(x) \in [0.25, 4]$. The policy $\hat{\mu}^*_{10}(x) = \arg\max_u \hat{Q}_{10}(x, u)$ is taken as approximation of the optimal stationary policy.

[1] The Extra-Trees algorithm has three parameters M (the number of trees that are built to define the ensemble model), $n_{\min}$ (the minimum number of samples of non-terminal nodes) and K (the number of cut-directions explored to split a node). They

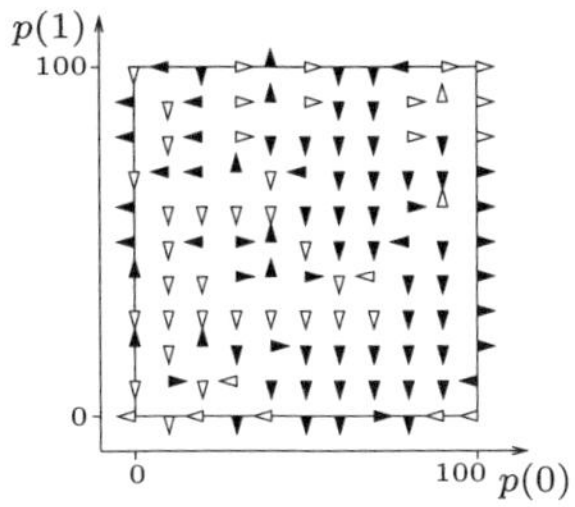

(a) $\hat{\mu}^*_{10}$, 500 four-tuples

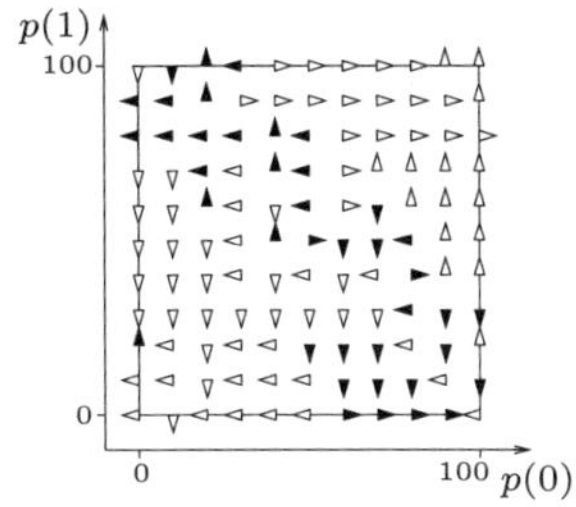

(b) $\hat{\mu}^*_{10}$, 2000 four-tuples

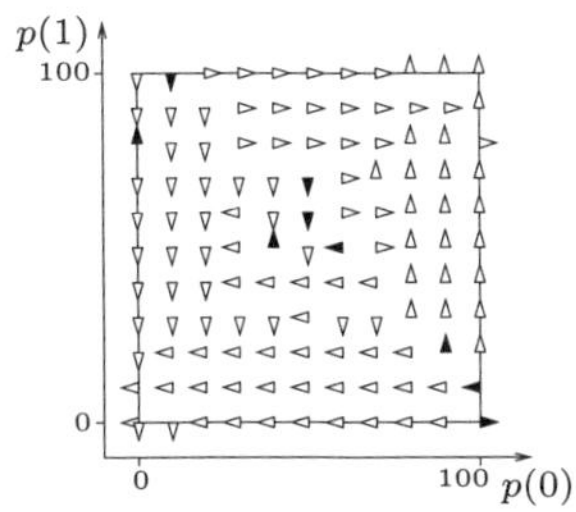

(c) $\hat{\mu}^*_{10}$, 8000 four-tuples

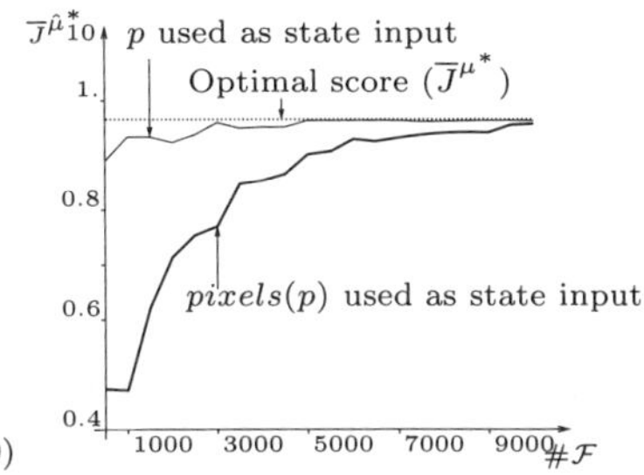

(d) score versus nb four-tuples

Fig. 3. Figures (a-c) plot the policy $\hat{\mu}^*_{10}$ computed for increasing values of $\#\mathcal{F}$. The orientation of the triangles indicate the value of $\hat{\mu}^*_{10}(pixels(p))$; white triangles indicate that it coincides with an optimal action. Figure (d) plots the score of the policies: the horizontal line indicates the score of the optimal policy, the darker curve (with smaller scores) corresponds to the case of pixel based learning with growing number of four-tuples, while the lighter curve provides the scores obtained with the same samples when the position p is used as state representation.

3.4 Results

Figures 3a-c show how the policies $\hat{\mu}^*_{10}$ change when increasing the size of the set of four-tuples. In particular, Figure 3c shows that with 8000 four-tuples, the policy almost completely coincides with the optimal policy μ^* of Figure 1b. To further assess the speed of convergence of the algorithm, we have plotted on Figure 3d the score[2] of policies obtained in different conditions. We observe that with respect to the compact state representation in terms of positions, the use of the pixel based representation slows down but does not prevent convergence. Indeed, with $\#\mathcal{F} = 10,000$ the score of the pixel based policy has almost converged to the optimal one, which is a fairly small sample size if we compare it to the dimensionality of the input space of 900. This suggests that the fitted Q iteration algorithm coupled with Extra-Trees is able to cope with a low-level

have been set to $M = 50$, $n_{\min} = 2$ (yielding fully developed trees) and $K = 900$ (equal to the dimensionality of the input space).

[2] The score of a policy is defined here as the average value over all possible initial states of the return obtained over an infinite time horizon when the system follows this policy.

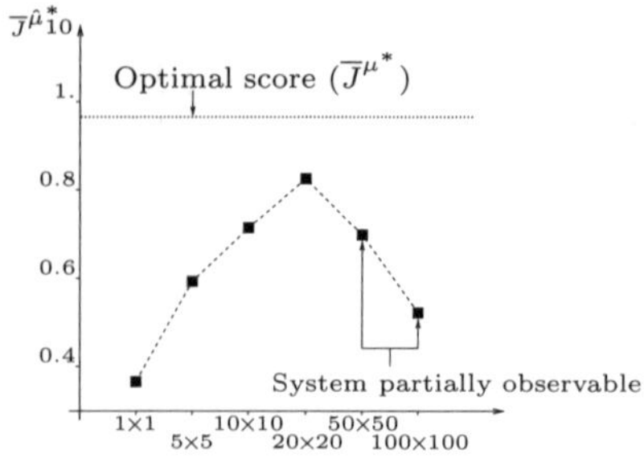

Fig. 4. Evolution of the score with the size of the constant grey level tiles. $\#\mathcal{F} = 2000$.

representation where information is scattered in a rather complex way over a large number of input variables.

To illustrate the influence of the navigation image characteristics on the results, we carried out an experiment where we have changed the size of the constant grey level tiles while keeping constant the size of the observation images. The results, depicted on Figure 4, show that the score first increases, reaches a maximum, and decreases afterwards.

To explain these results, we first notice that the Extra-Trees method works by inferring from a sample $\mathcal{TS} = ((i^l, o^l), l = 1, \dots, \#\mathcal{TS})$ a kernel $K(i, i')$, from which an approximation of the output o associated with an input i is computed by $\hat{o}(i) = \sum_{(i^l,o^l)} K(i, i^l) o^l$. The value of $K(i, i^l)$ thus determines the importance of the output o^l in the prediction, and for our concern the main property of the Extra-Trees kernel is that it takes larger values if the vectors i and i^l have many components which are close to each other, i.e. if there exists many values of $j \in \{1, 2, \cdots, \text{size of vector } i\}$ such that $i[j]$ is close from $i^l[j]$ [2]. Next, we note from Figure 3d that when the algorithm is applied to a training set of size 2000 with positions as inputs (i.e. $\mathcal{TS}_p = ((p^l, o^l), l = 1, \dots, \#\mathcal{TS}_p))$ it provides close to optimal scores. With this input representation, elements (p^l, o^l) such that p^l is geometrically close to p tend to lead to a high value of $K(p, p^l)$ and one may therefore reasonably suppose that when using pixel vectors as inputs, good results will be obtained only if the resulting kernel $K(pixels(p), pixels(p^l))$ is strongly enough correlated with the geometrical distance between p and p^l, which means that the closer two positions the more similar the corresponding vectors of pixel values should be.

With this we can explain the influence of the size of the tiles on the score in the following way. Let p^l be a position such that its 30×30 observation image is fully contained in the square. Then, when the navigation image is composed of randomly chosen 1×1 tiles, for a position $p \neq p^l$ there is no reason that the value of $K(pixels(p), pixels(p^l))$ should depend on the geometrical distance between p and p^l. In other words, the kernel derived in these conditions will take essentially only two values, namely $K(pixels(p), pixels(p^l)) = 1$ if $p = p^l$ and $K(pixels(p), pixels(p^l)) \approx 1/\#\mathcal{TS}$ otherwise. Thus, the output predicted at a position far enough from the square boundary will essentially be the average output of the training set, except for positions contained in the training sample.

When the tiles become larger, the dependence of the amount of similar pixels of two observation images on their geometrical distance increases, which leads to a more appropriate approximation architecture and better policies. However, when the tiles size becomes too large the sensitivity of the pixel based kernel with respect to the geometrical distance eventually decreases. In particular, the loss of observability above a certain tiles size translates into a dead-band within which the kernel remains constant, which implies suboptimality of the inferred policy, even in asymptotic conditions.

4 Conclusions

We have applied in this paper a reinforcement learning algorithm known as fitted Q iteration to a problem of navigation from visual percepts. The algorithm uses directly as state input the raw pixel values. The simulation results show that in spite of the fact that in these conditions the information is spread in a rather complex way over a large number of low-level input variables, the reinforcement learning algorithm was nevertheless able to converge relatively fast to near optimal navigation policies. We have also highlighted the strong dependence of the learning quality on the characteristics of the images the agent gets as input states, and in particular on the relation between distances in the high-dimensional pixel-based representation space and geometrical distances related to the physics of the navigation problem.

5 Image Description

We provide hereafter the 10×10 matrix giving the grey levels of the 100 tiles of Figure 2:

$$
\begin{bmatrix}
164 & 55 & 175 & 6 & 132 & 27 & 35 & 255 & 47 & 11 \\
169 & 155 & 87 & 5 & 77 & 39 & 197 & 179 & 82 & 111 \\
5 & 92 & 176 & 10 & 148 & 37 & 57 & 119 & 32 & 193 \\
156 & 110 & 54 & 38 & 186 & 103 & 190 & 212 & 241 & 108 \\
65 & 103 & 125 & 239 & 73 & 235 & 128 & 199 & 3 & 247 \\
42 & 129 & 233 & 3 & 250 & 101 & 196 & 119 & 108 & 192 \\
199 & 91 & 240 & 254 & 71 & 2 & 250 & 250 & 36 & 227 \\
109 & 150 & 111 & 224 & 244 & 152 & 57 & 205 & 173 & 174 \\
124 & 242 & 42 & 62 & 0 & 234 & 252 & 127 & 28 & 114 \\
163 & 7 & 198 & 92 & 192 & 163 & 115 & 208 & 160 & 168
\end{bmatrix}
$$

References

1. D. Ernst, P. Geurts, and L. Wehenkel. Tree-based batch mode reinforcement learning. *Journal of Machine Learning Research*, 6:503–556, April 2005.
2. P. Geurts, D. Ernst, and L. Wehenkel. Extremely randomized trees. *Machine Learning*, 36(1):3–42, 2006.

3. S. Jodogne and S. Piater. Interactive learning of mappings from visual percepts to actions. In L. De Raedt and S. Wrobel, editors, *Proceedings of the 22nd International Conference on Machine Learning*, pages 393–400, August 2005.
4. M. Lagoudakis and R. Parr. Reinforcement learning as classification: leveraging modern classifiers. In T. Faucett and N. Mishra, editors, *Proceedings of 20th International Conference on Machine Learning*, pages 424–431, 2003.
5. R. Marée, P. Geurts, J. Piater, and L. Wehenkel. Random subwindows for robust image classification. In C. Schmid, S. Soatto, and C. Tomasi, editors, *Proceedings of the IEEE International Conference on Computer Vision and Pattern Recognition*, volume 1, pages 34–40. IEEE, June 2005.

New Region of Interest Medical Image Coding for JPEG2000: Compensation-Based Partial Bitplane Alternating Shift

Li-bao Zhang[1] and Xian-zhong Han[2]

[1] College of Information Science and Technology,
Beijing Normal University,
Beijing 100875, China
libaozhang@163.com

[2] College of Information Science and Technology,
Agricultural University of Hebei,
Hebei 071001, China
hxz0312@126.com

Abstract. Regions of Interest (ROI) image coding enables the regions important to medical diagnosis to be encoded and transmitted at higher quality than the other regions. In the paper, a new ROI coding method called Compensation-based Partial Bitplane Alternating Shift (CPBA-Shift) is described. The proposed method divides all bitplanes of ROI and background (BG) coefficients into two portions-Alternating Shift Portion (ASP) and Compensation Shift Portion (CSP). In ASP, partial the most significant bitplanes of ROI and BG coefficients are shifted by bitplane-by-bitplane. In CSP, the least significant bitplanes of ROI and BG coefficients are scaled using compensation scheme according to the compression quality in ROI and BG. Simulation experiments show that the new method, in addition to alleviating the drawbacks of both ROI coding methods in JPEG2000, can support arbitrarily shaped multiple ROI coding with different degrees of interest without coding the shapes information.

Keywords: medical image, image coding, region of interest, JPEG2000, bitplane shift.

1 Introduction

The medical image compression is necessary because they produce prohibitive amounts of data. For example, the CT or MRI image, which produce human body pictures in digital form. Additionally, the wireless transmission of medical images and wireless medical diagnosis also need the efficient and high quality medical image compression methods. Many current compression schemes provide a very high compression rate but with considerable loss of quality. On the other hand, in some areas in medicine, it may be sufficient to maintain high image quality only in the Region of Interest (ROI) or in diagnostically important regions. Based on these facts, ROI coding for medical images is proposed [1], [2].

N. Zheng, X. Jiang, and X. Lan (Eds.): IWICPAS 2006, LNCS 4153, pp. 455–464, 2006.

The functionality of ROI coding is significant in medical applications where certain parts of the image are of higher importance than others. In such a case, these ROIs need to be encoded at higher quality than the background (BG). During the transmission of the image, these regions need to be transmitted first or at a higher priority, as for example in the case of progressive transmission. ROI coding is based on wavelet transforms and lifting scheme. More recently, two basic coding strategies are presented in the literatures-ROI coding based on zerotree or zero-block scheme [1], [2] and ROI coding based on EBCOT [3], [4]. Because the latter can realize spatial scalability and reduces coding complexity, it has been researched and applied widely for medical image compression. The most important ROI coding methods based on EBCOT are Maxshift method and the general scaling-based method, which are recommended by the JPEG2000 standard [3], [4].

Although these ROI coding methods in JPEG2000 are efficient, they have some disadvantages for the medical image compression. For example, in the general scaling based method, all shape information of ROI must be encoded and transmitted, which rapidly increases the complexity of encoder implementations and decreases the overall coding efficiency [5]. In Maxshift method, the scaling value of the ROI coefficients is constant. This means in all the subbands, where the ROI/BG distinction is applied, no information about the non-ROI coefficients can be received until every detail of the ROI coefficients has been fully decoded, even if the detail is imperceptible random noise or unnecessary information [6], [7].

In this paper, we present a efficient ROI coding method for medical image called Compensation-based Partial Bitplane Alternating Shift (CPBAShift). The new method takes advantage of the flexibility of bitplane scaling scheme and divides all bitplanes of ROI and BG coefficients into two portions-Alternating Shift Portion (ASP) and Compensation Shift Portion (CSP). For different portions, different shift strategies are implemented. The CPBAShift method not only enables the flexible adjustment of compression quality between ROI and BG, but also alleviates the drawbacks of both ROI coding methods in JPEG2000. Additionally, the proposed method can support arbitrarily shaped multiple ROI coding with different degrees of interest without coding the ROI shapes.

This paper is organized as follows. In Section 2, ROI coding methods in JPEG2000 and their disadvantages are reviewed. In Section 3, the CPBAShift method for single ROI coding is presented, while the multiple ROI coding based on the presented method is given in Section 4. In Section 5, experimental results for CT and MRI medical images are shown. Finally, the conclusions are drawn in Section 6.

2 ROI Coding in JPEG2000 and Their Disadvantages

JPEG2000 defines two kinds of ROI coding methods: Maxshift method and the general scaling base method. They can be completed by bitplanes scaling of ROI coefficients, which includes four-step process: ROI mask generation, scaling value selection, coefficients of ROI or BG shift, and bitplane entropy coding. The main purpose of ROI mask is to determine the set of wavelet coefficients that belong to the ROI and BG. When an image is coded with one ROI, it should be possible to reconstruct the entire ROI at a higher bit rates than BG portion [4].

2.1 The General Scaling Based Method

The general scaling based method is recommended by part 2 of the JPEG2000 standard. In the method, regions of interest can have better quality than the rest at any decoding bit-rate. In other words, this implies a non-uniform distribution of the quality inside the image. The general scaling-based method can support a bitplane scaling with the arbitrary value, so allows fine control on the relative importance between ROI and BG [3].

However, the general scaling based method has two major drawbacks. First, it needs to encode and transmit the shape information of the ROIs. This rapidly increases the algorithm complexity. Second, if arbitrary ROI sharps are desired, the shape coding will consume a large number of bits, which significantly decreases the overall coding efficiency [4].

2.2 Maxshift Method

We know that both the general based scaling method and Maxshift method take full advantage of the bitplane scaling scheme, but "max-shift" technology must scale all bitplanes of ROI coefficients up over the maximum bitplane of all BG coefficients or scale all bitplanes of BG coefficients down below the minimum bitplane of all ROI coefficients. So Maxshift method is a particular case of the general scaling-based method when the scaling value is so large that there is no overlapping between BG and ROI bitplanes, i.e., so the scaling value, s, must satisfy (1):

$$s \geqslant max\left(M_b\right); \tag{1}$$

The $max(M_b)$ is the largest number of magnitude bitplanes for all BG coefficients. All significant bits associated with the ROI after scaling will be in higher bitplanes than all the significant bits associated with the background. Therefore, ROI shape is implicit for the decoder in this method, and arbitrarily shaped ROI coding can be supported. Based on the above advantages, JPEG2000 coding standard recommends Maxshift method in part 1 as the core ROI coding algorithm [7].

Fig. 1 shows the comparison of scaling scheme between the general scaling based method and Maxshift method. The upper diagram shows the bitplane distribution based on the general scaling based method and the scaling value is 6. The lower diagram depicts the scaling strategy of Maxshift method and the scaling value is 11.

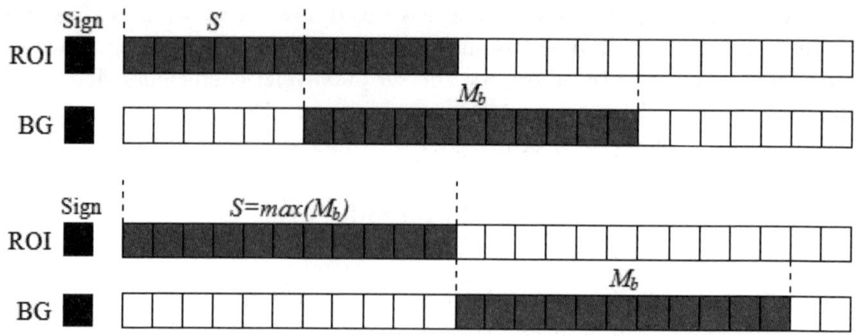

Fig. 1. Comparison of scaling scheme between the general scaling based method and Maxshift method

2.3 The Disadvantages of ROI Coding Methods in JPEG2000

For the general scaling based method, there are two main drawbacks. First, it needs to encode and transmit the shape information of the ROIs. This rapidly increases the complexity of encoder and decoder. Second, if arbitrary ROI sharps are desired, the shape coding will consume a large number of bits, which significantly decreases the overall coding efficiency.

Maxshift method can solve above these problems efficiently, but it has three limitations. First, it does not have the flexibility for an arbitrary scaling value to define the relative importance of the ROI and the BG wavelet coefficients as in the general scaling-based method. Second, this method requires decoding of all ROI coefficients before accessing bitplanes of the background and uses large shifting values that significantly increase the number of total bitplanes to encode. Finally, when there are multiple ROIs in the same image, any ROI cannot have its own scaling value and therefore different priority during encoding and transmission of the image.

Because of the limitations of two standard ROI coding algorithms, A improved Maxshift method was proposed in [6] with low scaling values. It is implemented by removing all the overlapping bitplanes between ROI and BG coefficients, which relatively modified the quantization steps of coefficients. However, the method brought the reduction of final ROI and BG qualities. A bitplane-by-bitplane shift (BbBShift) method was proposed in [7] by shifting these bitplanes on a bitplane-by-bitplane basis instead of shifting them all at once in Maxshift method. Although it supports arbitrarily shaped ROI coding without coding shapes, it is difficult for the BbBShift method to code multiple ROIs with different priority during encoding and transmission.

3 New ROI Coding Scheme Using CPBAShift Method

The proposed CPBAShift method, which combines the advantages of bitplane-by-bitplane shift scheme and the maximum shift technique, can encode ROI image efficiently. It divides all original bitplanes of ROI and BG coefficients into two portions-ASP and CSP. For different portions, different shift strategies are implemented. In ASP, partial the most significant bitplanes of ROI and BG coefficients are shifted by bitplane-by-bitplane. In CSP, the general and least significant bitplanes of ROI and BG coefficients are scaled using compensation scheme according to the compression quality in ROI and BG.

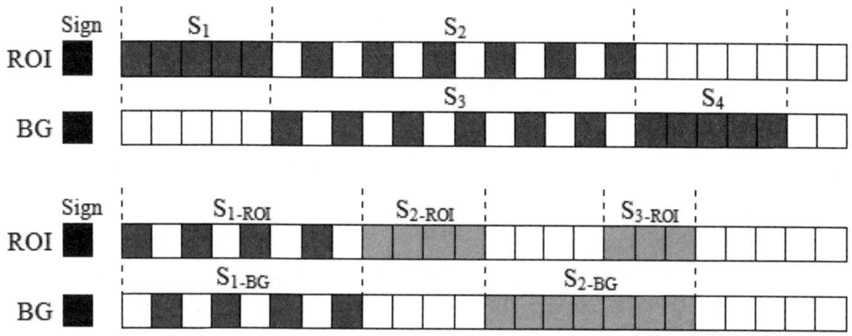

Fig. 2. Comparison of scaling scheme between CPBAShift method and BbBShift method

Fig. 2 shows the comparison of scaling scheme between CPBAShift method and BbBShift method. The upper diagram gives the bitplane scaling model based on BbBShift method and the number of bitplanes by alternating scaling is 6. The lower diagram depicts the scaling strategy of CPBAShift method. According to Fig. 2, we can define these bitplanes of ROI and BG in ASP or CSP using a series of symbols as follows:

1. S_{1-ROI} is the number of the most significant ROI bitplanes.
2. S_{1-BG} is the number of the most significant BG bitplanes.
3. S_{2-ROI} is the number of the general significant ROI bitplanes.
4. S_{2-BG} is the number of the least significant BG bitplanes.
5. S_{3-ROI} is the number of the least significant ROI bitplanes.

Definition 1. *The symbol b is defined as a bitplane belonged to the ROI or the BG before the bitplanes are shifted.*

Definition 2. *The bottom bitplane of original image before shifted is defined as bitplane 1, the next to bottom as bitplane 2, and so on.*

At the encoder, the basic encoding steps are given as follows:

Step 1. For any bitplane $b \in ROI$;
1. If $0 < b \leqslant S_{3-ROI}$ then no shift b;
2. If $S_{3-ROI} < b \leqslant S_{2-ROI} + S_{3-ROI}$ then shift b up to bitplane $b + S_{2-BG} - S_{3-ROI}$;

3. If $b > S_{2-ROI} + S_{3-ROI}$ then shift b up to bitplane $2(b - S_{3-ROI}) - S_{2-ROI} + S_{2-BG}$.

Step 2. For any bitplane $b \in BG$;

1. If $0 < b \leqslant S_{2-BG}$ then no shift b;
2. If $b > S_{2-BG}$ then shift b up to bitplane $2b + S_{2-ROI} - S_{2-BG} - 1$;

At the decoder, for any given bitplane of non-zero wavelet coefficient, the first step is to complete the arithmetic decoding. The second step is to identify whether it is a bitplane of the ROI coefficient or the BG coefficient. Third step is to shift all bitplanes of ROI and BG down to the original positions. the basic encoding steps are given as follows:

1. If $0 < b \leqslant S_{2-BG}$ then $b \in ROI$ or $b \in BG$, no shift b and decoding directly;
2. If $S_{2-BG} < b \leqslant S_{2-BG} + S_{2-ROI}$ then $b \in ROI$, shift b down to bitplane $b + S_{3-ROI} - S_{2-BG}$;
3. If $b = S_{2-ROI} + S_{2-BG} + 2i, i = 1, 2, \cdots, S_{1-ROI}$ then $b \in ROI$, shift b down to bitplane $(b + S_{2-ROI} - S_{2-BG})/2 + S_{3-ROI}$;
4. If $b = S_{2-ROI} + S_{2-BG} + 2i - 1, i = 1, 2, \cdots, S_{1-BG}$ then $b \in BG$, shift bitplane b down to $(b - S_{2-ROI} + S_{2-BG} + 1)/2$.

At the encoder, S_{2-ROI}, S_{3-ROI} and S_{2-BG} must satisfy (2):

$$S_{2-BG} = S_{2-ROI} + S_{3-ROI}; \tag{2}$$

At the decoder, if the wavelet coefficient's most significant bitplane belongs to bitplanes of ROI, then it must be is an ROI coefficient. Otherwise, it is a BG coefficient. The bitplanes are then shifted back to their original levels by the decoding algorithm.

4 Multiple ROI Coding Based on CPBAShift Method

In JPEG2000, both the Maxshift method and the general scaling based method can support the multiple ROI coding. However, the drawback of Maxshift is that the bitplanes of all ROIs must be scaled with the same values, which does not have the flexibility to allow for an arbitrary scaling value to define the relative importance of the ROIs and BG wavelet coefficients, and cannot code ROIs according to different degrees of interest. Additionally, in Maxshift method, all bitplanes of the BG coefficients cannot be decoded until the all bitplanes of all ROIs are decoded.

The general scaling based method can offer the multiple ROIs coding with different degrees of interest, but it needs to encode the shape information of ROIs. This shape information significantly increases the complexity of encoder/decoder when the number of the ROIs increases. Additionally, it is not convenient for the general scaling based method to deal with different wavelet subbands according to different degrees of interest, which is very important to code and transmit for objectors.

The proposed CPBAShift method not only can support arbitrary ROIs shape with-out shape coding, but also allows arbitrary scaling value between the ROIs and BG, which enables the flexible adjustment of compression quality in ROIs and BG ac-cording to different degrees of interest. The encoding and decoding algorithm for multiple ROIs are similar to that for single ROI in CPBAShift method. Fig. 3 presents the basic scaling scheme of CPBAShift method in multiple ROI coding.

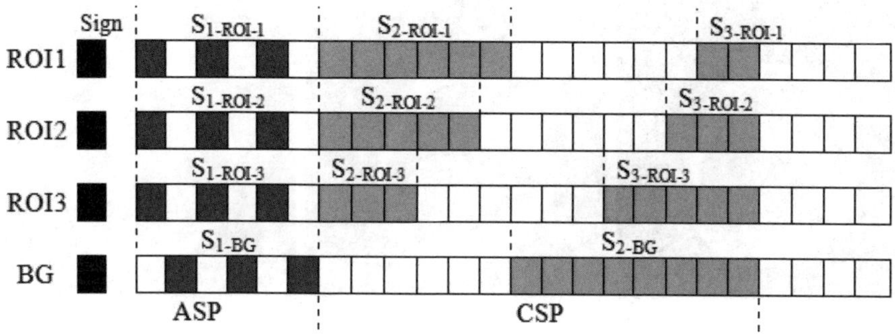

Fig. 3. The basic scaling scheme of CPBAShift method in multiple ROI coding

Although CPBAShift method can code multiple ROIs efficiently using the alternating and compensating scheme, two points must be satisfied during bit-plane scaling. First, if the degree of interest of every ROI is different, $S_{2-ROI-i}$ and $S_{3-ROI-i}$ will is various. However, the scaling values from $S_{3-ROI-i}$ to $S_{2-ROI-i}$ must is constant and equal to $max(S_{2-ROI-i})$. Second, $S_{1-ROI-i}$ must is equal to S_{1-BG}:

$$S_{1-BG} = S_{1-ROI-i} = c(i = 1, 2, \cdots); \tag{3}$$

According to the scaling rules for multiple ROI coding, at low bit rates, these most important bitplanes of ROIs and BG will be encoded and transmitted firstly. At mediate bit rates, these ROIs will obtain different coding qualities based on different degrees of interest by adjusting the values of S_{2-ROI}. At high bit rates, both ROIs and BG can be coded with high quality and difference between them is not very noticeable.

5 ROI Coding Results for Medical Images

Fig. 4 shows the comparison of single ROI coding results between CPBAShift method and Maxshift method at 0.5bpp for 512 × 512 CT image. the left shows the original CT image. The mediate is the reconstructed CT image using

Maxshift method and the right gives the reconstructed CT image using CP-BAShift method. We adopt (5, 3) integer wavelet and select an arbitrarily shaped ROI covering 11.66% of the whole image.

Fig. 5 presents two reconstructed 512 × 512 MRI images based on multiple ROI coding with two arbitrary shaped ROIs. The left picture is the compression result using Maxshift method, but the right picture is the coding result using CPBAShift method. The decoding rate is 1.0bpp and ROI-1 covering about 5.63% of the whole image and ROI-2 covering about 3.95%. We still adopt (5, 3) integer wavelet filters.

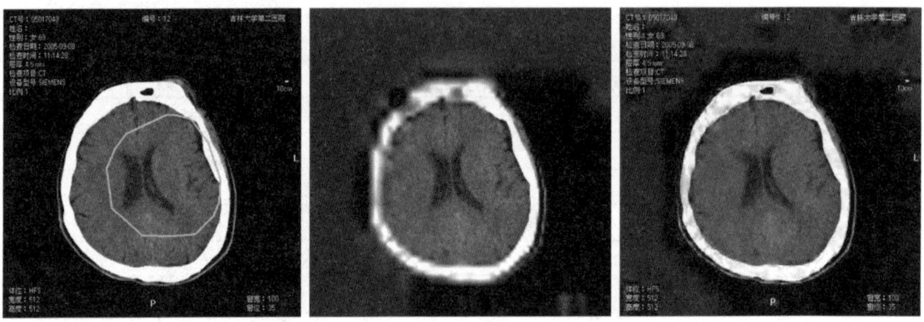

Fig. 4. Comparison of single ROI coding between Maxshift method (mediate) and CPBAShift (right) at 0.5bpp for 512 × 512 CT image

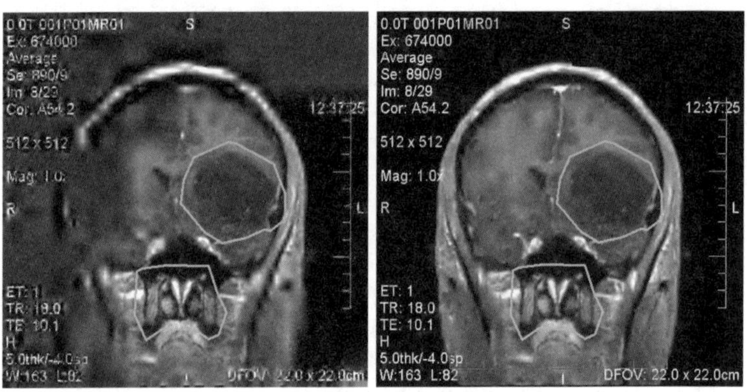

Fig. 5. Comparison of multiple ROI coding between Maxshift method (left) and CP-BAShift (right) at 1.0bpp for 512 × 512 MRI image

In Fig. 6, we give two reconstructed 512 × 512 CT images with two arbitrary shaped ROIs. The left picture is the compression result using Maxshift method,. The right picture is the coding result using CPBAShift method. The decoding rate is 0.5bpp and ROI-1 covering about 4.18% of the whole image and ROI-2 covering about 3.18%.

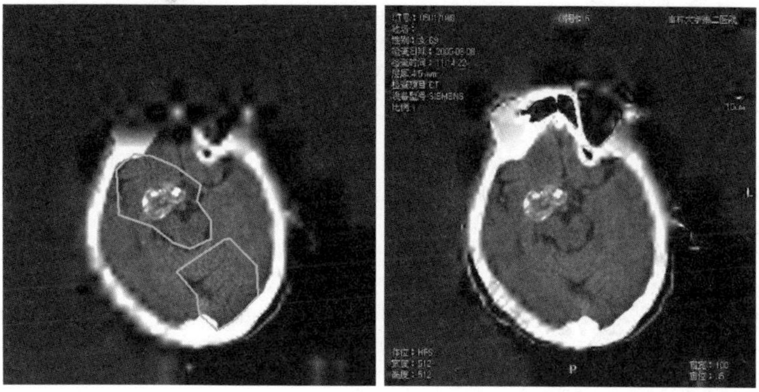

Fig. 6. Comparison of multiple ROI coding between Maxshift method (left) and CP-BAShift (right) at 0.5bpp for CT image

6 Conclusions

In this paper, we describe a new ROI coding method so-called CPBAShift. The new algorithm can not only complete single and multiple ROI coding efficiently, but also has more flexible strategy of bitplane scaling, its primary advantages are presented as follows:

First, the new method can support arbitrary shaped ROI coding without coding the shape information, which ensures the low complexity in real-world applications. Second, the whole scaling values of all bitplanes are fewer than Maxshift method, which decreases the risk of bitstream overflow. Third, the proposed method can control flexibly the quality between the ROIs and BG by adjusting scaling values of ROI or BG. Finally, the new method can support multiple ROI coding with different degrees of interest. In a word, we expect this idea is valuable for future research in medical image coding based on ROI.

Acknowledgments. The authors would like to express their gratitude to the anonymous reviewers for their useful comments and thank all of the participants in the subjective testing for their time and effort. This paper is supported in part by the Natural Science Foundation of Beijng (No. 4062020), and the Youth Teacher Foundation of Beijng Normal University.

References

1. Penedo, M., Pearlman, W.A., Tahoces, P.G., Souto, M., Vidal, J.J.: Region-Based Wavelet Coding Methods for Digital Mammography. IEEE Transation on Medical Imaging, Vol. 22, No. 10, (2003) 1288–1296
2. Ueno, I., Pearlman, W.A.: Region of Interest Coding in Volumetric Images with Shape-Adaptive Wavelet Transform. SPIE/IS&T Electronic Imaging 2003, Vol. 5022, Proceedings of SPIE, (2003) 1048–1055

3. ISO/IEC, ISO/IEC 15444-1: Information technology JPEG 2000 image coding system-Part 1: Core coding system. http://www.jpeg.org(2004)
4. Christopoulos, C., Askelf, J., Larsson, M.: Efficient methods for encoding regions of interest in the upcoming JPEG 2000 still image coding standard. IEEE Signal Processing Letters, Vol. 7, No. 9, (2000) 247-249
5. Skodras, A., Christopoulos, C.A., Ebrahimi, T.: The JPEG 2000 still image compression standard. IEEE Signal Processing Magazine, Vol. 12, No. 9, (2001) 36-58
6. Grosbois, R., Cruz, D.S., Ebrahimi, T.: New approach to JPEG 2000 compliant region of interest coding. Proceeding of SPIE, the 46th Annual Meeting, Applications of Digital Image Processing, San Diego, Vol. XXIV, CA, August, (2001).
7. Wang, Z., Bovik, A.C.: Bitplane-by-Bitplane shift-a suggestion for JPEG 2000 region of interest image coding. IEEE Signal Processing Letters, Vol, 9, No. 5, (2002) 321-324.
8. Li-bao, Z.: A New Region of Interest Image Coding for Narrowband Network: Partial Bit-plane Alternating Shift. Lecture Notes in Computer Science, Vol. 3779. Springer-Verlag, Berlin Heidelberg New York (2005) 425-432

A New Wavelet Lifting Scheme for Image Compression Applications

Guoan Yang and Shugang Guo

Institute of Artificial Intelligence and Robotics of Xi'an Jiaotong University
No.28 West Xianning Road, 710049, Xi'an, China
{Guoan, Yang}gayang@aiar.xjtu.edu.cn
http://www.aiar.xjtu.edu.cn
{Shugang, Guo}sgguo@aiar.xjtu.edu.cn

Abstract. A new lifting scheme of 7/5 biorthogonal wavelet filter banks (BWFB) which include BT 7/5 filter banks of Brislawn and Treiber for image compression applications is presented in this paper. The functional relations between all coefficients of the 7/5 BWFB and their lifting parameters with respect to a one free lifting parameter are derived. Moreover, all coefficients of 7/5 BWFB and their lifting parameters are rational numbers, compared to CDF 9/7 filter banks of Cohen, Daubechies and Feauveau with irrational coefficients in JPEG2000 standard, 7/5 BWFB not only have advantage of easy computation but also are very suitable for VLSI hardware implementation. Finally, two 7/5 BWFB namely 7/5 BWFB-1 and 7/5 BWFB-2 are proposed. The experimental results show that the peak signal-to-noise ratio (PSNR) of the reconstructed images using 7/5 BWFB-1 and 7/5 BWFB-2 is 0.1dB less than CDF 9/7 filter banks but is higher 1.2dB than LT 5/3 filter banks of LeGall and Tabatabai within compression ratio 100:1. Therefore, the 7/5 BWFB-1 and 7/5 BWFB-2 are the ideal replacement of CDF 9/7 filter banks in the JPEG2000 standard for image compression applications.

1 Introduction

The design of the wavelet filter and the algorithm of compression coding are two most important factors in JPEG2000 image compression systems [1]. Since CDF 9/7 filter banks [2] developed by Cohen, Daubechies and Feauveau have linear phase and excellent image compression performance, they have been applied most widely in the image compression applications. However, there is a common complaint about CDF 9/7 filter banks by some researchers that their coefficients are irrational number and thus requires a floating-point implementation. This will not only increase the computational complexity but also bring a great disadvantage to VLSI hardware implementation. The purpose of our study is to find a new wavelet filter banks with rational coefficients whose the image compression performances are close to CDF 9/7 filter banks and better than LT 5/3 filter banks of LeGall and Tabatabai. Sweldens et al have presented the lifting scheme [3][4] in 1996 that is called as the second generation wavelet,

N. Zheng, X. Jiang, and X. Lan (Eds.): IWICPAS 2006, LNCS 4153, pp. 465–474, 2006.

and is an entirely spatial construction of wavelet. The lifting scheme for fast wavelet transform has many characteristics that are suitable for the VLSI hardware implementation. For example, the lifting scheme doesn't refer to the Fourier transformation, which leads to a speedup of 2 times faster than the Mallat algorithm based on convolution; it allows for an in-place implementation of the fast wavelet transform, this means the wavelet transform can be calculated without allocating auxiliary memory; all operations within one lifting step can be done entirely in parallel while the only sequential part is the order of the lifting operations; it is particularly easy to build nonlinear wavelet transform, a typical example is a wavelet transform that maps integers to integers, such transform is important for hardware implementation and lossless image coding; it allows for adaptive wavelet transforms, this means one can start the analysis of a function from the coarsest levels and then build the finer levels by refining only in the areas of interest; the multiresolution analysis for classical wavelet transform is inherited.

This paper constructs a class of biorthogonal 7/5 wavelet filter banks (BWFB), and also presents a kind of structure and implementation of the 7/5 BWFB for the lifting scheme of fast wavelet transform. In addition, it is found that when the lifting parameter for the 7/5 BWFB is 0.05 and 0.08, the performance for image compression turns out to be better than other situations, we named them as 7/5 BWFB-1 and 7/5 BWFB-2 in this paper that are recommended in JPEG2000 standard part 2. [5]-[7]. Finally, in order to verify the image compression performances of 7/5 BWFB-1 and 7/5 BWFB-2, we have developed the system of the image compression that supports the 7/5 BWFB-1 and 7/5 BWFB-2 as well as the CDF 9/7 and LT 5/3 filter banks.

The present paper is organized as follows. In section 2, the lifting scheme using Euclidean algorithm on two channel filter banks is introduced. In section 3, lifting implementation for fast wavelet transform using 7/5 BWFB is carried out. Section 4 provides both 7/5 BWFB-1 and 7/5 BWFB-2 for JPEG2000 image compression coding, and experimental results are discussed. Finally, in section 5, we conclude the paper.

2 The Lifting Scheme for 7/5 BWFB

2.1 Two Channel Filter Banks for 7/5 BWFB

We consider a two channel filter banks as shown in Fig.1, suppose a symmetric 7/5 BWFB, and $\{H_0(z), G_0(z)\}$ denotes low pass filters and $\{H_1(z), G_1(z)\}$ denotes high pass filters for analysis and synthesis stage respectively.

The low pass filters of 7/5 BWFB are given by

$$\begin{cases} H_0(z) = h_0 + h_1(z + z^{-1}) + h_2(z^2 + z^{-2}) + h_3(z^3 + z^{-3})) \\ G_0(z) = g_0 + g_1(z + x^{-1}) + g_2(z^2 + z^{-2}) \end{cases} \tag{1}$$

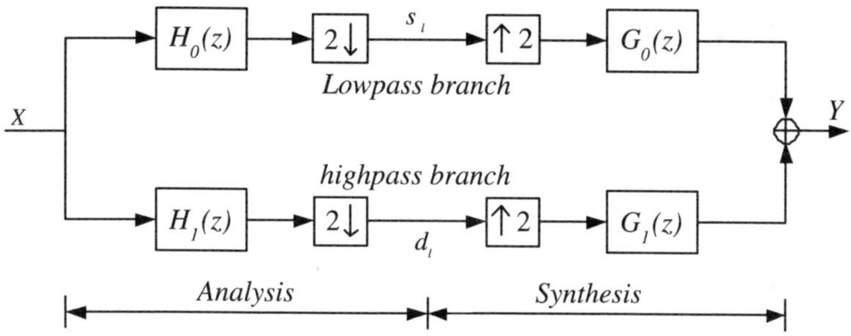

Fig. 1. Two channel filter banks

The polyphase representation of the lowpass analysis filter $H_0(z)$ and the lowpass synthesis filter $G_0(z)$ for 7/5 BWFB are given by

$$\begin{cases} H_{0e}(z) = h_0 + h_2(z + z^{-1}) \\ H_{0o}(z) = h_1(z + 1) + h_3(z^2 + z^{-1}) \end{cases} \tag{2}$$

$$\begin{cases} G_{0e}(z) = g_0 + g_2(z + z^{-1}) \\ G_{0o}(z) = g_1(z + 1) \end{cases} \tag{3}$$

Where $H_{0e}(z)$ and G_{0e} contains the even coefficients, and H_{0o} and G_{0o} contains the odd coefficients. Thus we can build the decomposition based on the Euclidean algorithm [8] with a focus on applying it to wavelet filtering.

2.2 Lifting Scheme of 7/5 BWFB

Here take two Laurent polynomials $a(z)$ and $b(z)$ with the restricts that $a(z)$ and $b(z) \neq 0$ with $|a(z)| \geq |b(z)|$. Then there always exist a Laurent polynomial $q(z)$ (i.e. quotient) with $|q(z)| = |a(z)| - |b(z)|$, and a Laurent polynomial $r(z)$ (i.e. remainder) with $|r(z)| < |b(z)|$ to make the equation reasonable. We denote this as: $q(z) = a(z)/b(z)$ and $r(z) = a(z)\%b(z)$. First let $a_0(z) = H_{0e}(z)$ and $b_0(z) = H_{0o}(z)$, then iterate the following steps starting from $i = 0$

$$\begin{cases} a_{i+1}(z) = b_i(z) \\ b_{i+1}(z) = a_i(z)\%b_i(z) \end{cases} \tag{4}$$

Note that in case $|H_{0o}(z)| > |H_{0e}(z)|$, the first quotient $q_1(z)$ is zero. We thus obtain the Euclidean decomposition as follows

$$Step1 \quad \begin{cases} a_1(z) = b_0(z) = H_{0o} = h_1(z + 1) + h_3(z^2 + z^{-1}) \\ b_1(z) = a_0(z)\%b_0(z) = H_{0e}(z) = h_0 + h_2(z + z^{-1}) \\ q_1(z) = 0 \end{cases} \tag{5}$$

$$Step2 \quad \begin{cases} a_2(z) = b_1(z) = H_{0e} = h_0 + h_2(z + z^{-1}) \\ b_2(z) = a_1(z)\%b_1(z) = s_2(1 + z) \\ q_2(z) = t_2(1 + z) \end{cases} \tag{6}$$

$$Step3 \quad \begin{cases} a_3(z) = b_2(z) = s_2(1+z) \\ b_3(z) = a_2(z)\%b_2(z) = s_3 \\ q_3(z) = t_3(1+z^{-1}) \end{cases} \tag{7}$$

$$Step4 \quad \begin{cases} a_4(z) = b_3(z) = s_3 \\ b_4(z) = a_3(z)\%b_3(z) = s_4 = 0 \\ q_4(z) = t_4(1+z) \end{cases} \tag{8}$$

In the equations above, s_i is the lifting parameter and t_i is the dual lifting parameter, which are as follows

$$\begin{cases} s_1 = 0, \quad t_1 = 0 \\ s_2 = h_1 - h_3 - h_0 h_3/h_2, \quad t_2 = h_3/h_2 \\ s_3 = h_0 - 2h_2, \quad t_3 = h_2^2/[h_1 h_2 - (h_0 + h_2)h_3] \\ s_4 = 0, \quad t_4 = [(h_1 - h_3)h_2 - h_0 h_3]/[(h_0 - 2h_2)h_2] \end{cases} \tag{9}$$

3 Implementation of Lifting Scheme for 7/5 BWFB

Using the method described above, this section will provides the implementation of lifting scheme for 7/5 BWFB. Here the factorization of filter pair $\{H_{0e}, H_{0o}\}$ are as follows

$$\begin{bmatrix} H_{0e}(z) \\ H_{0o}(z) \end{bmatrix} = \begin{bmatrix} 1 & 0 \\ q_2(z) & 1 \end{bmatrix} \begin{bmatrix} 1 & q_3(z) \\ 0 & 1 \end{bmatrix} \begin{bmatrix} 1 & 0 \\ q_4(z) & 1 \end{bmatrix} \begin{bmatrix} s_3 \\ 0 \end{bmatrix} \tag{10}$$

Set $\alpha = t_2$, $\beta = t_3$, $\gamma = t_4$, $K = s_3$, so the polyphase matrix for the 7/5 BWFB can be expressed as

$$\begin{aligned} \tilde{P}(z) &= \begin{bmatrix} h_0 + h_2(z + z^{-1}) & g_1(1 + z^{-1}) \\ h_1(z+1) + h_3(z^2 + z^{-1}) & -g_0 - g_2(z + z^{-1}) \end{bmatrix} \\ &= \begin{bmatrix} 1 & 0 \\ q_2(z) & 1 \end{bmatrix} \begin{bmatrix} 1 & q_3(z) \\ 0 & 1 \end{bmatrix} \begin{bmatrix} 1 & 0 \\ q_4(z) & 1 \end{bmatrix} \begin{bmatrix} K & 0 \\ 0 & 1/K \end{bmatrix} \\ &= \begin{bmatrix} 1 & 0 \\ \alpha(1+z) & 1 \end{bmatrix} \begin{bmatrix} 1 & \beta(1+z^{-1}) \\ 0 & 1 \end{bmatrix} \begin{bmatrix} 1 & 0 \\ \gamma(1+z) & 1 \end{bmatrix} \begin{bmatrix} K & 0 \\ 0 & 1/K \end{bmatrix} \end{aligned} \tag{11}$$

So we have

$$\begin{cases} h_0 = (1 + 2\beta\gamma)K \\ h_1 = [\alpha(1 + \beta\gamma) + \gamma(1 + 2\alpha\beta)]K \\ h_2 = \beta\gamma K \\ h_3 = \alpha\beta\gamma K \\ g_0 = (1 + 2\alpha\beta)/(2K) \\ g_1 = -\beta/(2k) \\ g_2 = \alpha\beta/(2k) \end{cases} \tag{12}$$

We start with a sequence $x = \{x_j | j \in \mathbb{Z}\}$ and denote the result of applying the lowpass filter $H_0(z)$ and downsampling as a $s = \{s_j | j \in \mathbb{Z}\}$, and sequence

$s^{(i)}$ and $d^{(i)}$ are used to denotes the intermediate values computed during lifting. Then Lazy wavelet are given by

$$s_i^{(0)} = x_{2i}, \quad d_i^{(0)} = x_{2i+1}$$

Finally, the factorization leads to the following implementation of the forward transform

$$\begin{aligned} s_l^{(1)} &= s_l^{(0)} + \alpha(d_l^{(0)} + d_{l-1}^{(0)}) \\ d_l^{(1)} &= d_l^{(0)} + \beta(s_l^{(1)} + s_{l+1}^{(1)}) \\ s_l^{(2)} &= s_l^{(1)} + \gamma(d_l^{(1)} + d_{l-1}^{(1)}) \\ s_l &= K s_l^{(2)} \\ d_l &= d_l^{(1)}/K \end{aligned}$$

The implementation of the inverse transform are as follows

$$\begin{aligned} s_l^{(2)} &= s_l/K \\ d_l^{(1)} &= K d_l \\ s_l^{(1)} &= s_l^{(2)} - \gamma(d_l^{(1)} + d_{l-1}^{(1)}) \\ d_l^{(0)} &= d_l^{(1)} - \beta(s_l^{(1)} + s_{l+1}^{(1)}) \\ s_l^{(0)} &= s_l^{(1)} - \alpha(d_l^{(0)} + d_{l-1}^{(0)}) \end{aligned}$$

The lifting structure of the 7/5 BWFB is shown in Fig.2.

From Equation (12) and normalization condition for the 7/5 BWFB we can get

$$\beta = -1/[2(1+2\alpha)], \quad \gamma = (1-4\alpha^2)/4, \quad K = 1/(1+2\alpha) \tag{13}$$

Equation (13) shows that β, γ, K can be all expressed by a free parameter α. We consider now using the algorithm of approximation and Hölder regularity [9][10] to find a compactly supported 7/5 BWFB which will satisfy the perfect reconstruction (PR) condition. In the 7/5 category this leaves a single unused degree of freedom $\alpha = 0.05$ and $\alpha - 0.08$ that have an excellent image compression performances than other situations, and they are defined as 7/5 BWFB-1 and 7/5 BWFB-2. The structure of 7/5 BWFB for lifting scheme is plotted as in Fig.2. The coefficients of 7/5 BWFB-1 and 7/5 BWFB-2 and corresponding lifting parameters are shown in Table.1-Table.4.

4 Experiment and Discussion

In order to verify the performances of image compression for 7/5 BWFB-1 and 7/5 BWFB-2, we have developed a new image compression system based on JPEG2000 standard, it not only supports both CDF 9/7 filter and LT 5/3 filter banks but also supports both 7/5 BWFB-1 and 7/5 BWFB-2 through improves Jasper1.701.0 version in JPEG2000 standard. In addition, a great deal

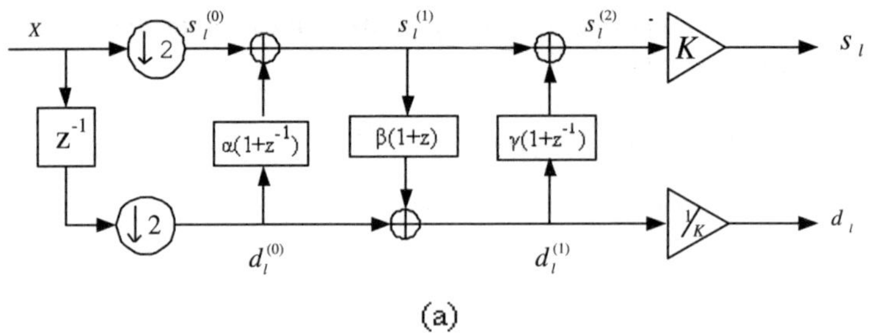

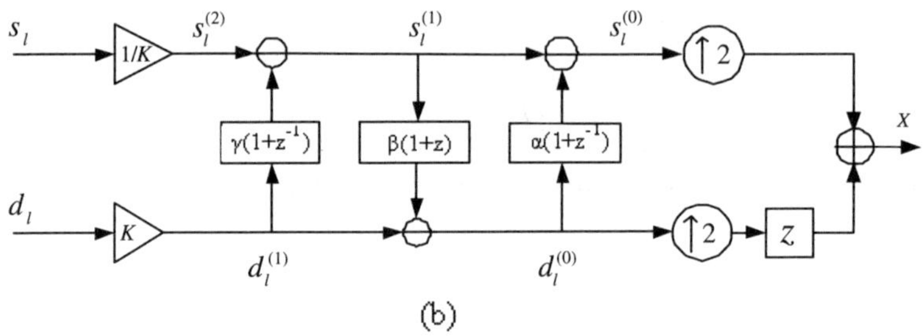

Fig. 2. The structure of 7/5 BWFB for lifting scheme (a) the decomposition (b) the reconstruction

Table 1. The coefficients of the 7/5 BWFB-1

n	$h_i(analysis)$	$g_i(synthsis)$
0	31/44	21/40
±1	449/1760	1/4
±2	-9/88	-1/80
±3	-9/1760	

Table 2. The lifting parameters of the 7/5 BWFB-1

parameters	values
α	1/20
β	-5/11
γ	99/400
K	11/10

of gray bitmaps in standard test image library were tested using 5 levels of wavelet decomposition and scalar quantization and EBCOT coding algorithm [11][12]. The objective coding results with PSNR in dB for standard 512×512 pixel and 8bits depth Peppers.bmp, Lena.bmp, Goldhill.bmp, Baboon.bmp and Women.bmp testing images were tabulated in Table.5-Table.9. The differences

Table 3. The coefficients of the 7/5 BWFB-2

n	$h_i(analysis)$	$g_i(synthsis)$
0	79/116	27/50
±1	373/1450	1/4
±2	-21/232	-1/50
±3	-21/2900	

Table 4. The lifting parameters of the 7/5 BWFB-2

parameters	values
α	2/25
β	-175/406
γ	609/2500
K	29/25

of PSNR values for the reconstructed image between 7/5 BWFB-1 and CDF 9/7 filter banks were represented as Δ_{1D}, similarly, the differences between 7/5 BWFB-2 and CDF 9/7 filter banks were represented as Δ_{2D}, the differences between 7/5 BWFB-1 and LT 5/3 filter banks were represented as Δ_{1L}, the differences between 7/5 BWFB-2 and LT 5/3 filter banks were represented as Δ_{2L}. It is easy to find from table.5-Table.9 that the performances of the image compression for 7/5 BWFB-1 and 7/5 BWFB-2 are very close to CDF 9/7 filter banks and also is much better than LT 5/3 filter banks. Moreover, we compared PSNR values of reconstructed image using different filters in Fig.3, and the abscissa denotes compression ratio which is integral power for 2, the ordinate denotes PSNR values of the reconstructed image. It is illustrated that PSNR values of the reconstructed image using 7/5 BWFB-1 is only 0.1dB less than the CDF 9/7 filter banks, but 1.2dB higher than the LT 5/3 filter banks about testing image Woman.bmp in Fig.3. However, when the compression ratio (C.R.) is greater than 100:1, the compression performances using 7/5 BWFB-1 is 0.01dB less than the LT 5/3 filter banks. The subjective comparisons of the

Table 5. PSNR evaluation for the Peppers.bmp in dB

C.R.	CDF 9/7	LT 5/3	7/5 BWFB-1	7/5 BWFB-2	Δ_{1D}	Δ_{2D}	Δ_{1L}	Δ_{2L}
4:1	43.1083	41.3481	42.6307	42.7673	-0.4476	-0.3410	+1.2826	+1.4192
8:1	38.2030	37.5476	37.9269	37.9936	-0.2761	-0.2094	+0.3793	+0.4460
16:1	35.7832	35.2654	35.4361	35.4170	-0.3471	-0.3662	+0.1707	+0.1516
32:1	33.4908	33.0552	33.0767	33.0125	-0.4141	-0.4783	+0.0215	-0.0427
64:1	30.7161	30.3354	30.3600	30.2256	-0.3561	-0.4905	+0.0246	-0.1098
100:1	28.4688	28.2567	28.0892	28.1015	-0.3796	-0.3673	-0.1675	-0.1552
128:1	27.5009	27.2342	27.2028	27.1584	-0.2981	-0.3425	-0.0314	-0.0758

Table 6. PSNR evaluation for the Lena.bmp in dB

C.R.	CDF 9/7	LT 5/3	7/5 BWFB-1	7/5 BWFB-2	Δ_{1D}	Δ_{2D}	Δ_{1L}	Δ_{2L}
4:1	42.9495	41.1995	42.3858	42.4764	-0.5637	-0.4731	+1.1863	+1.2769
8:1	38.0703	37.3410	37.6658	37.6953	-0.4045	-0.3750	+0.3248	+0.3543
16:1	35.1721	34.4984	34.6425	34.6254	-0.5296	-0.5467	+0.1441	+0.1270
32:1	32.3538	31.7087	31.7193	31.7408	-0.6345	-0.6130	+0.0106	+0.0321
64:1	29.5526	28.9618	29.0785	29.0370	-0.4741	-0.5156	+0.1167	+0.0752
100:1	27.7308	27.2636	27.2375	27.2836	-0.4933	-0.4472	-0.0261	+0.0200
128:1	26.8370	26.4218	26.5133	26.4455	-0.3237	-0.3915	+0.0915	+0.0237

Table 7. PSNR evaluation for the Goldhill.bmp in dB

C.R.	CDF 9/7	LT 5/3	7/5 BWFB-1	7/5 BWFB-2	Δ_{1D}	Δ_{2D}	Δ_{1L}	Δ_{2L}
4:1	39.5641	38.6910	39.0016	39.1366	-0.5625	-0.4275	+0.3106	+0.4456
8:1	35.0873	34.5923	34.8390	34.9030	-0.2483	-0.1843	+0.2467	+0.3107
16:1	32.3438	31.9067	32.0199	32.0405	-0.3239	-0.3033	+0.1132	+0.1338
32:1	30.0213	29.6347	29.7234	29.8100	-0.2979	-0.2113	+0.0887	+0.1753
64:1	28.1324	27.8516	27.8709	27.9310	-0.2615	-0.2014	+0.0193	+0.0794
100:1	26.9970	26.5792	26.7023	26.7312	-0.2947	-0.2658	+0.1231	+0.1520
128:1	26.3435	26.1060	26.1177	26.0853	-0.2258	-0.2582	+0.0117	-0.0477

Table 8. PSNR evaluation for the Baboon.bmp in dB

C.R.	CDF 9/7	LT 5/3	7/5 BWFB-1	7/5 BWFB-2	Δ_{1D}	Δ_{2D}	Δ_{1L}	Δ_{2L}
4:1	34.8018	34.1268	34.2124	34.2179	-0.5894	-0.5839	+0.0856	+0.0911
8:1	29.0705	28.6222	28.4054	28.4574	-0.6651	-0.6131	-0.2168	-0.1648
16:1	25.5388	25.0646	25.1061	25.2201	-0.4327	-0.3187	+0.0415	+0.1555
32:1	23.1835	22.8077	22.8375	22.8973	-0.3460	-0.2862	+0.0298	+0.0896
64:1	21.6200	21.3188	21.2840	21.3689	-0.3360	-0.2511	-0.0348	+0.0501
100:1	20.8802	20.6963	20.7797	20.8718	-0.1005	-0.0084	+0.0834	+0.1755
128:1	20.6537	20.4250	20.5121	20.5506	-0.1416	-0.1031	+0.0871	+0.1256

reconstructed image were demonstrated in Fig.4 at compression ratio 16:1 with the testing image Women.bmp. The compression performances using the 7/5 BWFB-1 and 7/5 BWFB-2 are almost identical with CDF 9/7 filter banks.

We can see easily from this paper that compression performances using the CDF 9/7 filter banks are always better than 7/5 BWFB-1, 7/5 BWFB-2 and LT 5/3 filter banks when compression ratios is less than 100:1, 0.1-0.6dB higher than 7/5 BWFB-1 and 7/5 BWFB-2, and 0.5-1.4dB higher than LT 5/3 filter banks. When compression ratio are 100:1 and over, the compression performance using LT 5/3 filter banks are little better than 7/5 BWFB-1 and 7/5 BWFB-2 by about 0.05-0.1 dB. In addition, when testing image includes much information for low frequency such as Woman.bmp bitmap, PSNR values of reconstructed

Table 9. PSNR evaluation for the Women.bmp in dB

C.R.	CDF 9/7	LT 5/3	7/5 BWFB-1	7/5 BWFB-2	Δ_{1D}	Δ_{2D}	Δ_{1L}	Δ_{2L}
4:1	45.8728	44.4178	45.4255	45.5494	-0.4473	-0.3234	+1.0077	+1.1316
8:1	39.1503	38.1474	38.7211	38.8229	-0.4292	-0.3274	+0.5737	+0.6755
16:1	34.5551	33.9244	34.1463	34.2185	-0.4088	-0.3366	+0.2219	+0.2941
32:1	31.4530	31.0521	31.2834	31.3065	-0.1696	-0.1465	+0.2313	+0.2544
64:1	29.5272	29.1728	29.2553	29.2425	-0.2719	-0.2847	+0.0825	+0.0697
100:1	28.2210	27.9241	27.9271	27.8405	-0.2939	-0.3805	+0.0030	-0.0836
128:1	27.3979	27.2418	27.1850	27.1185	-0.2129	-0.2794	-0.7391	-0.1233

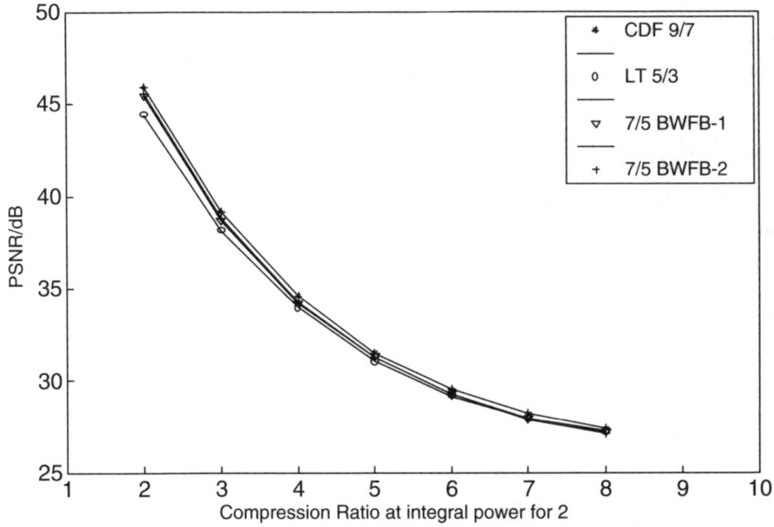

Fig. 3. The objective comparison of compression performance using different filter

(a) (b) (c) (d) (e)

Fig. 4. The compression performance comparison using different filter (a) original image (b) CDF 9/7 filter banks (c) LT 5/3 filter banks (d) 7/5 BWFB-1 (e) 7/5 BWFB-2 image reduce slowly with the increase of the compression ratio because loss for low frequency is very little. However, when testing image includes many information for high frequency, for example Babbon.bmp bitmap, PSNR values for reconstructed image reduce quickly with the increase of the compression ratio because loss for high frequency is very much.

5 Conclusions

The lifting scheme and implementation structure of 7/5 BWFB-1 and 7/5 BWFB-2 are derived in detail. In addition, the 7/5 BWFB-1 and 7/5 BWFB-2 with rational coefficients whose performances of image compression are highly close to CDF 9/7 filter banks have been obtained. Finally, we can concluded that the image compression performances using 7/5 BWFB-1 and 7/5 BWFB-2 based on JPEG2000 standard will be better than CDF 9/7 filter banks in terms of computational complexity and VLSI hardware implementation.

Acknowledgements

This work is supported by the national science foundation of China (No.60021302, No.60405004).

References

1. ISO/ IEC 15444-1, ITU-T RT800,2003, JPEG2000 image coding system, part 1.
2. Cohen, A, Daubechies, I, Feauveau, J.C, Biorthogonal bases of compactly supported wavelets, Commun Pure Appl Math,Vol.45, (1992) 485-560
3. Sweldens, W, The lifting scheme: a custom-design construction of biorthogonal wavelets, Applied and computational Harmonic Analysis, Vol. 3, (1996) 186-200
4. Sweldens, W, The lifting scheme: A construction of second generation wavelets, SIAM J Math Anal, Vol.29, No.2, (1997) 511-546
5. ISO/ IEC, 15444-2, ITU-TR T800, 2004, JPEG2000 image coding system, part 2.
6. Guoan Yang, Nanning Zheng, et al, Research on cluster of 7/5-tap wavelet filters and their image compression performances, Journal of Xi'an Jiaotong University, Vol.39, No.6, (2005) 628-632
7. Guoan Yang, Nanning Zheng,et al, Extensible JPEG2000 image compression systems, IEEE ICIT2005 conference proceeding, December 14-17, HongKong, (2005)1376-1380
8. Daubechies, I, Sweldens, W, Factoring wavelet transforms into lifting steps, Fourier analysis and applications,Vol.4, No.3, (1998) 247-269
9. Antonini, M, Barlaud, M, Mathieu, P, Daubechchies, I, Image coding using wavelet transform, IEEE Trans on Image processing, Vol.1, No.2, (1992) 205-220
10. Unser, M, Blu, T, Mathematical properties of the JPEG2000 wavelet filters, IEEE Trans on Image processing, Vol.12,No.9, (2003) 1080-1090
11. Bilgin, A, Sementilli, P.J, Sheng, F, et al, Scalable image coding using reversible integer wavelet transforms, IEEE Trans on Image Processing, Vol.9, No.11, (2000) 1972-1977
12. Taubman, D, High performance scalable image compression with EBCOT, IEEE Trans on Image processing, Vol.9, No.7, (2000) 1158-1170

BTF Modelling Using BRDF Texels

J. Filip and M. Haindl

Dept. of Pattern Recognition, Institute of Information Theory and Automation,
Academy of Sciences of the Czech Republic, Prague, Czech Republic
{filipj, haindl} @utia.cas.cz

Abstract. The highest fidelity representations of realistic real-world materials currently used comprise Bidirectional Texture Functions (BTF). The BTF is a six dimensional function depending on view and illumination directions as well as on planar texture coordinates. The huge size of such measurements, typically in the form of thousands of images covering all possible combinations of illumination and viewing angles, has prohibited their practical exploitation and obviously some compression and modelling method of these enormous BTF data spaces is inevitable. The proposed approach combines BTF spatial clustering with cluster index modelling by means of an efficient Markov random field model. This method allows to generate seamless cluster index of arbitrary size to cover large virtual 3D objects surfaces. The method represents original BTF data using a set of local spatially dependent Bidirectional Reflectance Distribution Function (BRDF) values which are combined according to synthesised cluster index and illumination / viewing directions. BTF data compression using this method is about 1 : 100 and their synthesis is very fast.

1 Introduction

Recent progress in graphics hardware computational power finally enables fast and visually realistic rendering of virtual reality models that until recently was impossible. Such realistic models require, among others, natural looking textures covering virtual objects of rendered scene. Applications of these advanced texture models in virtual reality systems now allow photo-realistic material appearance approximation for such complex tasks as visual safety simulations or interior design in automotive/airspace industry or architecture.

For the aim of such advanced applications a smooth textures lit by reflectance models alternatively combined with bump-mapping are not able to offer correct and realistic reproduction of material appearance. This is caused due to inherited complexity of many materials whose rough structure produces such visual effects as self-shadowing, masking, inter-reflection or subsurface scattering. The one way to capture these material's attributes is using much more complex representation of a rough or 3D texture called Bidirectional Texture Function (BTF). BTF is a six dimensional function depending on view and illumination directions as well as on planar texture coordinates as illustrated in Fig.1. This function is typically acquired in the form of several thousands images covering varying light and camera directions. However, a huge size of measured BTF data prevents

N. Zheng, X. Jiang, and X. Lan (Eds.): IWICPAS 2006, LNCS 4153, pp. 475–484, 2006.

their usage in any useful application so introduction of some fast compression and modelling method for BTF data is inevitable.

The majority of results in the BTF area deal mainly with compression. They are based either on eigen-analysis of BTF data space [1,2,3,4] or on applications of pixel-wise reflectance models [5,6,7,8]. Although these methods can provide reasonable compression ratios ($\frac{1}{20} - \frac{1}{200}$) and visual quality, their main drawback is that they do not allow arbitrary size BTF synthesis, i.e. the texture enlargement.

To solve this problem additional BTF enlargement methods are necessary. Unfortunately there are not many BTF enlargement approaches available. A majority of the available methods are based either on simple texture repetition with edge blending or on more or less sophisticated image tiling methods [9,10,11,12] and they can be adapted also for BTF synthesis, e.g., [13].

Finally a group of probabilistic BTF models was recently proposed [14], [15]. These methods allow unlimited texture enlargement, BTF texture restoration, huge BTF space compression and even modelling of previously unseen BTF data. They are based on rough BTF segmentation in a space of illumination and viewing directions. The individual clusters representatives are BTF images closest to cluster centers, which are combined with estimated range-map in bump-mapping filter for required illumination and viewing angles. Although these methods reach huge impressive compression ratios they sometimes compromise visual quality for certain materials. In this paper we present a novel BTF model enabling

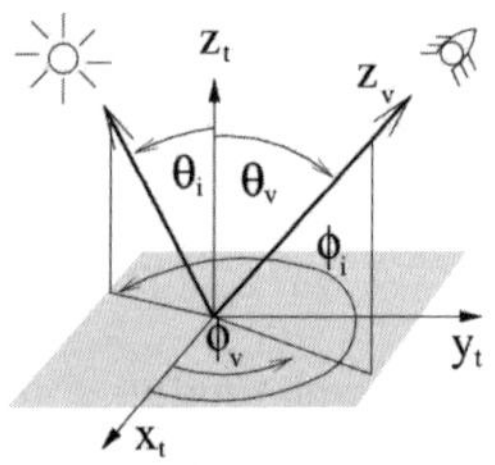

Fig. 1. Relationship between illumination and viewing angles within texture coordinate system

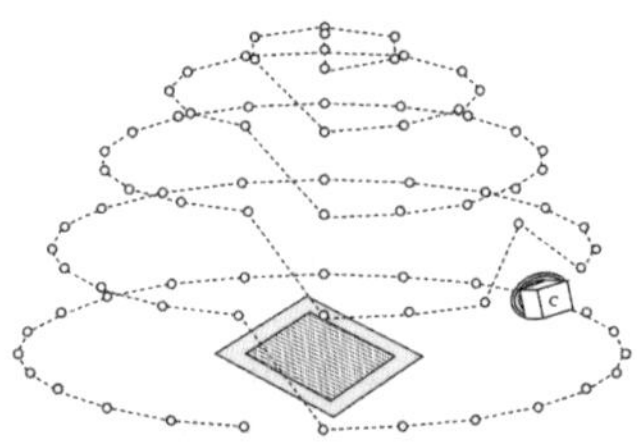

Fig. 2. Illumination directions ($i = 1 \dots 81$) in used BTF data. Viewing directions ($v = 1 \dots 81$) are the same.

seamless enlargement of BTF data. The overall scheme of the proposed model is illustrated in Fig.3. The method starts with normal-map estimation of the underlying material surface using photometric stereo. The estimated normal-map $\mathbf{N}$ is enlarged to the required size using probabilistic MRF model. In the following step the original BTF data are clustered in the spatial planar space. The results are cluster representatives $\mathbf{C}$ and cluster index $\mathbf{I}$, which is used for new cluster index $\mathbf{I}_S$ generation up to the size of synthesised normal-map $\mathbf{N}_S$. This enlargement exploits matching between estimated $\mathbf{N}$ and synthesised $\mathbf{N}_S$ normal-maps and BRDFs at neighbouring spatial locations.

This paper is organised as follows. The spatial BTF data segmentation is described in Section 2, the surface geometry estimation (normal-map) is described

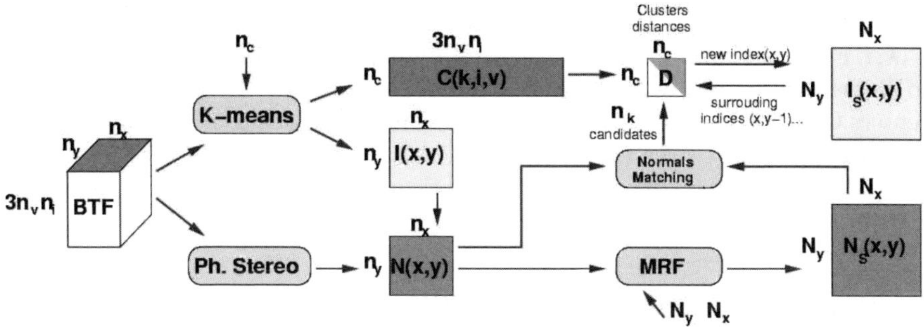

Fig. 3. The overall scheme of the proposed BTF enlargement method

in Section 3. The surface geometry synthesis using MRF model is subject of Section 4, while the final BTF data enlargement step is described in Section 5. Following sections show results of the proposed model, discuss its properties and conclude the paper.

2 BTF Space Segmentation

BTF data employed in this study were measured at the Bonn University [16]. We used BTFs of two different types of lacquered wood. Each dataset comprises 81 viewing positions n_v and 81 illumination positions n_i (see Fig.2) resulting into 6551 images with resolution (rectified measurements) 800×800. To decrease computational demands of the following BTF clustering step an image tiling approach was applied. The method [12] finds sub-optimal paths in original data to cut required set of contactable BTF tiles. In our experiments only one BTF tile per material was used.

The input to our algorithm is such a seamless BTF tile in the form of $n_i\, n_v$ illumination/view dependent images of size $n_x \times n_y$. A vector of BTF values for a fixed planar position will be called local BRDF and denoted as BRDF in scope of this paper. In the first preprocessing step all BTF images were converted to CIE Lab perceptually uniform colour space and only data from luminance channel L was used in data vector. The following K-means clustering was performed in the $n_x \times n_y$ planar space corresponding to individual pixels of BTF. Each pixel represents BRDF of surface geometry at a planar location (x, y). The clustering distance function is:

$$d(x, y, i, v, k) = \sum_{v=1}^{n_v} \sum_{i=1}^{n_i} |\mathbf{B}(i, v, x, y) - \mathbf{C}(k, i, v)| \cos \theta_v \ , \tag{1}$$

where $\mathbf{B}(i, v, x, y)$ is the corresponding BTF value, $\mathbf{C}(k, i, v)$ are cluster centers and $i = 1 \ldots n_i$ and $v = 1 \ldots n_v$ are illumination and viewing directions of the original BTF data (see Fig.2), respectively. The view elevation angle cosine accommodates the shortening of surface emitting area. The clustering results in the index array $\mathbf{I}(x,y) \in 1 \ldots n_c$ and the set of n_c cluster representatives $\mathbf{C}(k,i,v)$ of the size $n_c \times 3n_i n_v$ corresponding to the closest colour BRDFs to cluster centers. Note that the individual colour BRDFs representing cluster centers $\mathbf{C}$ correspond to representative set of material locations bearing the most distinct appearance over the BTF tile. Results of the proposed BTF clustering ($n_c = 256$) mapped on 3D object in comparison with original BTF data mapping are shown in the first two rows of Fig.6.

3 Surface Geometry From BTF

In order to find smooth spatial representation of the cluster index $\mathbf{I}$ for a further enlargement by means of MRF model we used normal-map describing a geometry of the original material surface. For this purpose the standard photometric stereo technique [17] was applied. This approach is advantageous since the BTF data comprises number of images with fixed viewpoint and variety of defined illumination source directions. As we have much more than three different light positions we used overdetermined photometric stereo. All directions to light sources are ordered in rows of matrix $\mathbf{L}$ and corresponding pixel intensity for different illumination directions are ordered to the vector $\mathbf{E}(x,y)$. Then surface normal-map $\mathbf{N}$ of BTF tile at each pixel was computed by means of the least-squares fitting

$$\mathbf{N}(x,y) = \frac{(\mathbf{L}^T\mathbf{L})^{-1}\mathbf{L}^T\mathbf{E}(x,y)}{||(\mathbf{L}^T\mathbf{L})^{-1}\mathbf{L}^T\mathbf{E}(x,y)||} \quad . \tag{2}$$

Alternative approach using range-scanner is costly and does not allow satisfactory measurement of textile materials due to laser beam scattering in material structure.

4 Probabilistic Normal-Map Modelling

The smooth texture model based on MRF 3D causal auto-regressive (CAR) model [18,19] was applied to normal-map modelling. The overall scheme of the 3D CAR MRF model is depicted in Fig.4. As an input of the model was image of size $N \times M = 512 \times 512$ generated by repetition of the seamless normal-map tile estimated in the previous step.

4.1 Spatial Factorisation

Input tiled normal-map $\bar{Y}_\bullet$ (the notation $\bullet$ has the meaning of all possible values of the corresponding index) is decomposed into a multi-resolution grid and each resolution data are independently modelled by their dedicated CAR models. Each one generates a single spatial frequency band of the normal-map. An analysed normal-map is decomposed into multiple resolutions factors using Laplacian pyramid and the intermediary Gaussian pyramid $\ddot{Y}_\bullet^{(k)}$ which is a

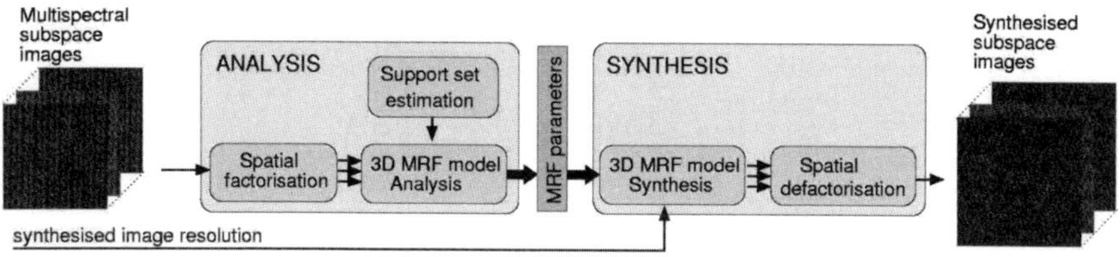

Fig. 4. The overall 3D CAR smooth model scheme

sequence of images in which each one is a low-pass down-sampled version of its predecessor. The Gaussian pyramid for a reduction factor n is

$$\ddot{Y}_r^{(k)} = \downarrow_r^n (\ddot{Y}_{\bullet,i}^{(k-1)} \otimes w) \quad k = 1, 2, \dots \ , \tag{3}$$

where $\ddot{Y}_\bullet^{(0)} = \bar{Y}_\bullet$, $\downarrow^n$ denotes down-sampling with reduction factor n and $\otimes$ is the convolution operation. The convolution mask based on weighting function (FIR generating kernel) w is assumed to execute separability, normalisation, symmetry and equal contribution constrains. The FIR equation is then $\ddot{Y}_r^{(k)} = \sum_{i,j=-l}^{l} \hat{w}_i \hat{w}_j \ddot{Y}_{2r+(i,j)}^{(k-1)}$. The Laplacian pyramid $\dot{Y}_r^{(k)}$ contains band-pass components and provides a good approximation to the Laplacian of the Gaussian kernel. It can be constructed by differencing single Gaussian pyramid layers:

$$\dot{Y}_r^{(k)} = \ddot{Y}_r^{(k)} - \uparrow_r^n (\ddot{Y}_\bullet^{(k+1)}) \qquad k = 0, 1, \dots \ , \tag{4}$$

where $\uparrow^n$ is the up-sampling with an expanding factor n.

4.2 3D Causal Auto-Regressive Model

Multi-spectral normal-map was in the previous step decomposed into a multi-resolution grid and each resolution data is modelled independently by independent Gaussian noise driven 3D CAR MRF model that enable simultaneous modelling of all resolution factors.

Let the normal map Y is indexed on a finite rectangular three-dimensional $N \times M \times 3$ underlying lattice I, where $N \times M$ is the image size. Let us denote a simplified multi-index r to having two components $r = \{r_1, r_2, r_3\}$. The first component is a row index, the second one is a column index and the third is a normal vector index, respectively. I_r specifies shape of the contextual neighbourhood (CN) around the actual index $r = \{r_1, r_2, r_3\}$. Causality is fulfilled when all data obtained from CN are known (not missing pixels).

From this causal CN the data are arranged in a vector $X_r = [Y_{r-s}^T : \forall \{s\} \in I_r^c]^T$.

The (CAR) random field is a family of random variables with a joint probability density on the set of all possible realisations Y of the $M \times N \times 3$ lattice I, subject to the following condition:

$$p(Y \mid \Theta, \Sigma^{-1}) = (2\pi)^{-\frac{3(MN-1)}{2}} |\Sigma^{-1}|^{\frac{(MN-1)}{2}} \exp\left\{ -\frac{1}{2} tr \left\{ \Sigma^{-1} \begin{pmatrix} -I \\ \Theta^T \end{pmatrix}^T \tilde{V}_{MN-1} \begin{pmatrix} -I \\ \Theta^T \end{pmatrix} \right\} \right\} \ , \tag{5}$$

where I is identity matrix, Θ is parameter matrix, Σ is covariance matrix of Gaussian white noise and

$$\tilde{V}_{r-1} = \begin{pmatrix} \tilde{V}_{YY(r-1)} & \tilde{V}_{XY(r-1)}^T \\ \tilde{V}_{XY(r-1)} & \tilde{V}_{XX(r-1)} \end{pmatrix} \ . \tag{6}$$

The used notion is $\tilde{V}_{AB(r-1)} = \sum_{k=1}^{r-1} A_k B_k^T$.

Simplified notation r, $r-1, \ldots$ denotes the multi-channel process position in I, i.e., $r = \{r_1, r_2, r_3\}$, $r-1$ is the location immediately preceding $\{r_1, r_2, r_3\}$, etc. A direction of movement on the underlying image sub-lattice is common rows scanning. The data from model history obtained during adaptation are denoted as $Y^{(r-1)}$.

The 3D CAR model can be expressed as a stationary causal uncorrelated noise driven 3D autoregressive process:

$$Y_r = \Theta X_r + e_r \ , \tag{7}$$

where $\Theta = [A_1, \ldots, A_\eta]$ is the $3 \times 3\eta$ parameter matrix and $\eta = card(I_r^c)$, I_r^c is a causal CN, e_r is a Gaussian white noise vector with zero mean and a constant but unknown covariance matrix Σ.

4.3 Parameter Estimation

There are two matrices, the parameterer matrix $\hat{\Theta}_r$ and the noise covariance matrix $\hat{\Sigma}_r$, to estimate / update in each step, i.e., CN shift on image lattice. Owing to the model causality and the normal-Wishart parameter prior single CAR model parameters (8),(9) can be estimated analytically [19]. The parameter matrix estimate is

$$\hat{\Theta}_{r-1}^T = V_{XX(r-1)}^{-1} V_{XY(r-1)} \ , \tag{8}$$

while the covariance matrix estimate is

$$\hat{\Sigma}_{r-1} = \frac{\lambda_{(r-1)}}{\beta(r)} \ , \tag{9}$$

where $\lambda_{(r)} = V_{YY(r)} - V_{XY(r)}^T V_{XX(r)}^{-1} V_{XY(r)}$, $V_{AB(r-1)} = \tilde{V}_{AB(r-1)} + V_{AB(0)}$ and matrices $V_{AB(0)}$ are the corresponding matrices from the normal-Wishart parameter prior. The estimates (8),(9) can be also evaluated recursively if necessary. Where the $\beta(r) = \beta(0) + r - 1$ represents number of model movements on image plane ($\beta(0) > 1$).

4.4 Normal-Map Synthesis

The CAR model synthesis is very simple and the Markov random field can be directly generated from the model equation (7) with respect to CN data vector X_r and the estimated parameter matrix $\hat{\Theta}_r$ using a multivariate Gaussian white-noise generator. The fine-resolution normal-map is obtained from the pyramid collapse procedure, which is inverse process to the spatial factorisation (3),(4) described in Section 4.1. The comparison of synthesised normal-maps $\mathbf{N}_S$ with their originals $\mathbf{N}$ is illustrated in the first row of Fig.5.

Fig. 5. The first row: Estimated normal tiles (small) and their synthesised counterparts (large) for *wood01* (left) and *wood01* (right). The second row: clustered BTF tiles for $\theta_i = 15^o, \phi_i = 180^o, \theta_v = 0^o, \phi_v = 0^o$ (small) and corresponding BTF images synthesised using enlarged cluster index $\mathbf{I}_S$ (large).

5 New Cluster Index Synthesis

New cluster index $\mathbf{I}_S$ is obtained by row-wise scanning of synthesised normal-map $\mathbf{N}_S$. For each normal in the $\mathbf{N}_S$ the n_k closest normals from normal-map $\mathbf{N}$ of original BTF tile is determined with respect to the Euclidean metric between two unite vectors. However, this approach alone is unsatisfactory because it allows ambiguous normals assignment owing to the material surface. For instance, a normal vector pointing straight upwards can represent either a peak or a valley on the surface. Thus, if a new index is created only based on normal matching the resulted enlarged BTF images are very noisy, while the synthesised structure of normal-map is considerably suppressed. To improve a spatial continuity of generated new cluster index we used information of surface height, occlusion and masking of surface points which is hidden in colour BRDFs of individual stored clusters $\mathbf{C}$. Individual cluster indices corresponding to candidate normal k from $\mathbf{N}$ are obtained from the same (x, y) location from $\mathbf{I}$ as is the spatial location of the normal k. From obtained n_k normal candidates from the original index $\mathbf{I}$ the optimal one k^* is chosen that minimise distance D between the candidate's BRDF and the BRDFs of its surrounding pixels at the locations $(x, y-1)$ and $(x-1, y)$ from the causal neighbourhood in $\mathbf{I}_S$ (10)

$$k^* = \arg \min_{k=1\ldots n_c} (\mathbf{D}(\mathbf{I}(x_k, y_k), \mathbf{I}_S(x, y-1)) + \mathbf{D}(\mathbf{I}(x_k, y_k), \mathbf{I}_S(x-1, y))) \ . \quad (10)$$

To speed up this process a mutual distances between each couple of n_c clusters is precomputed (11) and stored in a form of matrix $\mathbf{D}$ of size $n_c \times n_c$

$$\mathbf{D}(a,b) = \sum_{v=1}^{n_v} \sum_{i=1}^{n_i} |\mathbf{C}(a,i,v) - \mathbf{C}(b,i,v)| \cos\theta_v \ . \tag{11}$$

The (x_{k^*}, y_{k^*}) position in new index $\mathbf{I}_S$ is obtained by means of $\mathbf{I}_S(x,y) = \mathbf{I}(x_{k^*}, y_{k^*})$ using the clusters indices from original index $\mathbf{I}$. Proposed matching scheme incorporates such effects as masking and occlusions and together with normals matching enable reliable and perceptually correct spatial ordering of individual clusters in new enlarged index $\mathbf{I}_S$. Additionally, this ordering enforces continuity constraint by placement of the similar BRDFs into neighbouring positions in generated cluster index $\mathbf{I}_S$.

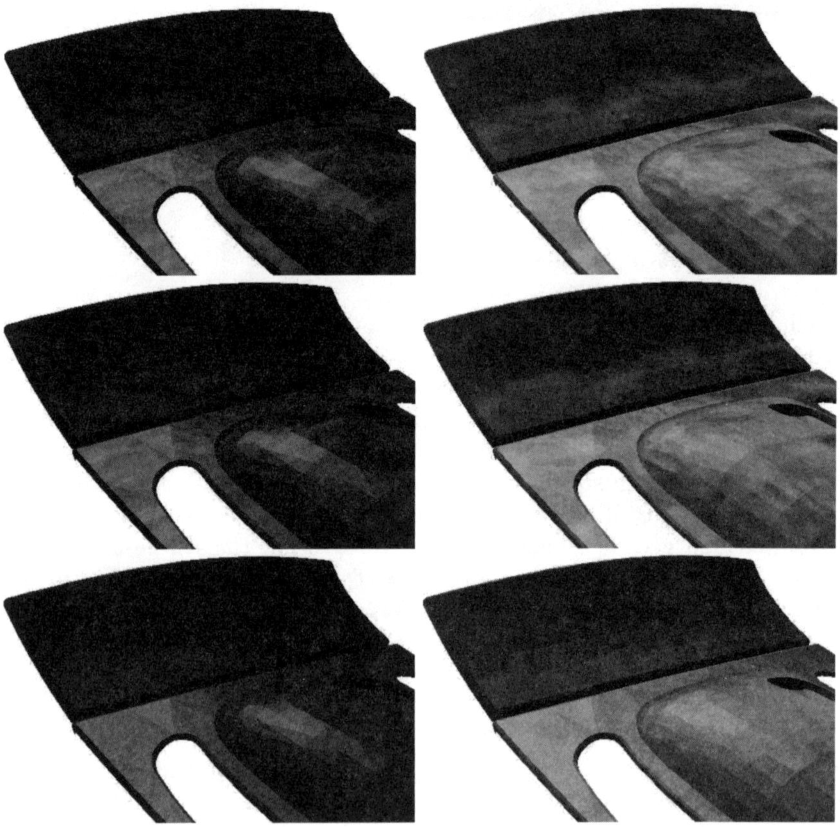

Fig. 6. Results of the proposed BTF data enlargement method mapped on 3D object (third row) in comparison with one original BTF tile mapping (first row) and its segmentation into $n_c = 256$ clusters (second row) for two kinds of lacquered wood.

For BTF rendering from the proposed model the cluster representatives $\mathbf{C}$ and synthesised cluster index $\mathbf{I}_S$ have to be stored enabling compression ratio approximately $\frac{1}{100}$ (for $n_c = 256$). The required BTF value is obtained as

$$BTF(x, y, i, v) = \mathbf{C}(\mathbf{I}_S(x, y), i, v) \ .$$

An example of BTF images synthesised from the model for both tested materials compared with original BTF tiles is shown in the second row of Fig.5.

6 Results

The proposed method was applied to BTF enlargement of two different types of smooth lacquered wood. The original BTF tile of *wood01* have size 122×125 and for *wood02* it is 137×142. The size of synthesised normal-maps and subsequently index arrays was for both the materials 300×300. Example of single planar BTF image enlarged by the proposed method is shown in the second row of Fig.5. Comparison of the enlarged BTF data mapped on 3D object with original BTF tile mapping is shown in Fig.6. The interpolation for arbitrary (non-measured) illumination and viewing angles was performed by means of barycentric coordinates [20]. The time demands of the analytical part of the proposed method are not too important since the BTF segmentation, normal-map estimation and synthesis and finally estimated and synthesised normals matching are offline tasks. The most time-consuming part of the method is BTF tile clustering that takes approximately one hour when using $n_c = 256$ clusters for BTF tile of *wood02*, while the remaining analytical steps are much faster, depending on the size of original and required normal-map. For BTF tile of *wood02* and required new cluster index $\mathbf{I}_S$ size 512×512 it takes several seconds only. All experiments were performed on PC Athlon 1.9GHz, 2GB RAM. A compression ratio of the proposed method for 256 clusters is approximately $\frac{1}{100}$.

7 Summary and Conclusions

This paper proposes new technique for seamless BTF data enlargement. The method strictly separates analytical offline part from the fast possibly real-time synthesis part of the modelling process. The BTF clustering allows to trade-off compression ration and visual quality. The method shows the best performance for spatially random i.e. non-regular types of BTFs such as the tested lacquered wood or leather, etc. The method enables fast seamless BTF data enlargement to arbitrary size with minimal additional storage requirements since the number of clusters is fixed.

Acknowledgements

This research was supported by the EC project no. FP6-507752 MUSCLE and partially by the grants no. A2075302, 1ET400750407, of the Grant Agency of the Academy of Sciences CR, and MSMT project no. 1M0572.

References

1. Koudelka, M., Magda, S., Belhumeur, P., Kriegman, D.: Acquisition, compression, and synthesis of bidirectional texture functions. In: Proceedings of the 3rd International Workshop on texture analysis and synthesis (Texture 2003). (2003) 47–52
2. Vasilescu, M., Terzopoulos, D.: TensorTextures: Multilinear image-based rendering. ACM SIGGRAPH 2004, ACM Press **23**(3) (2004) 336–342
3. Sattler, M., Sarlette, R., Klein, R.: Efficient and realistic visualization of cloth. In: Eurographics Symposium on Rendering 2003. (2003)
4. Müller, G., Meseth, J., Klein, R.: Compression and real-time rendering of measured BTFs using local PCA. In: Vision, Modeling and Visualisation 2003. (2003)
5. McAllister, D.K., Lastra, A., Heidrich, W.: Efficient rendering of spatial bidirectional reflectance distribution functions. Graphics Hardware (2002) 77–88
6. Malzbender, T., Gelb, D., Wolters, H.: Polynomial texture maps. In: ACM SIGGRAPH 2001, ACM Press, Eurographics Association, Switzerland (2001) 519–528
7. Meseth, J., Müller, G., Klein, R.: Preserving realism in real-time rendering of bidirectional texture functions. In: OpenSG Symposium 2003, Eurographics Association, Switzerland (2003) 89–96
8. Filip, J., Haindl, M.: Efficient image based bidirectional texture function model. In Chantler, M., Drbohlav, O., eds.: Texture 2005: Proceedings of 4th Internatinal Workshop on Texture Analysis and Synthesis, Edinburgh, Heriot-Watt University (2005) 7–12
9. Efros, A.A., Freeman, W.T.: Image quilting for texture synthesis and transfer. In Fiume, E., ed.: ACM SIGGRAPH 2001, ACM Press. (2001) 341–346
10. Cohen, M., Shade, J., Hiller, S., Deussen, O.: Wang tiles for image and texture generation. In: ACM SIGGRAPH 2003, ACM Press. Volume 22., New York, NY, USA (2003) 287–294
11. Kwatra, V., Schödl, A., Essa, I., Bobick, A.: Graphcut textures: image and video synthesis using graph cuts. ACM SIGGRAPH 2003, ACM Press **22**(2) (2003) 277–286
12. Somol, P., Haindl, M.: Novel path search algorithm for image stitching and advanced texture tiling. In: Proceedings of 13-th International Conference in Central Europe on Computer Graphics, Visualization and Computer Vision, WSCG05. (2005)
13. Dong, J., Chantler, M.: Comparison of five 3D surface texture synthesis methods. In: Proceedings of the 3rd International Workshop on texture analysis and synthesis (Texture 2003). (2003) 47–52
14. Haindl, M., Filip, J.: A fast probabilistic bidirectional texture function model. In: Proceedings of International Conference on Image Analysis and Recognition. (Lecture Notes in Computer Science. 3212). Volume 2., Berlin Heidenberg, Springer-Verlag (2004) 298–305
15. Haindl, M., Filip, J., Arnold, M.: BTF image space utmost compression and modelling method. In: Proceedings of 17th International Conference on Pattern Recognition. Volume 3., IEEE Computer Society Press (2004) 194–198
16. Database, B.U.B. |URL: http://btf.cs.uni-bonn.de/— (2003)
17. Woodham, R.: Analysing images of curved surface. Artificial Intelligence **17**(5) (1981) 117–140
18. Haindl, M.: Texture synthesis. CWI Quarterly **4**(4) (1991) 305–331
19. Haindl, M., Šimberová, S.: A Multispectral Image Line Reconstruction Method. In: Theory & Applications of Image Analysis. World Scientific Publishing Co., Singapore (1992) 306–315
20. Coxeter, H.S.M.: Introduction to Geometry. New York: Wiley (1969)

Texture Classification Via Stationary-Wavelet Based Contourlet Transform

Ying Hu, Biao Hou, Shuang Wang, and Licheng Jiao

Institute of Intelligent Information Processing and National Key Lab for Radar Signal Processing, PO Box 224, Xidian University, 710071 Xi'an, China
freely-611@163.com

Abstract. A directional multiresolution approach was proposed for texture analysis and classification based on a modified contourlet transform named the stationary wavelet-based contourlet transform (SWBCT). In the phase for extracting features after the decomposition, energy measures, Hu moments and co-occurrence matrices were calculated respectively. The progressive texture classification algorithm had better performance compared with several other methods using wavelet, stationary wavelet, brushlet, contourlet and Gabor filters. Moreover, in the case that there are only small scale samples for training, our method can also obtain a satisfactory result.

1 Introduction

The analysis of texture in images plays an important role in image processing. A great deal of research on how to analyze texture efficiently has been done during the past decades. Early work about texture analysis is based on the second-order statistics of textures. However, a common weakness shared by these methods is that they primarily focus on the coupling between image pixels on a single scale, while methods based on multiresolution analysis often outperform them and have received more and more attention [1]. So far, the most popular spatial-frequency technique in texture analysis is wavelet [2], [3] and Gabor filters [4], [5].

As we all know, direction is a vital feature of texture. However, separable 2D wavelet transform has limited directions which are horizontal, vertical, or diagonal. Although it can provide an optimal representation for one-dimensional piecewise smooth signals, it fails in the geometry of image edges. Therefore, several new Multiscale Geometric Analysis (MGA) systems have been proposed, such as brushlet [6], [7], [8] and contourlet [9], [10]. In this paper, we present a modified contourlet transform based on stationary-wavelet, which keeps the merits of contourlet and has much finer directional decomposition. We apply it to the classification of the Brodatz texture images and show its efficiency in extracting features of texture images.

The rest of the paper is organized as follows. First, contourlet and WBCT are explained briefly in Section 2. The construction of SWBCT we proposed is elucidated in Section 3. And Section 4 describes several methods for feature extraction of SWBCT coefficients. Section 5 illustrates the simulation and numerical results. Finally, the conclusions are drawn in Section 6.

N. Zheng, X. Jiang, and X. Lan (Eds.): IWICPAS 2006, LNCS 4153, pp. 485–494, 2006.

2 Contourlet and WBCT

2.1 Contourlet

Contourlet transform, which is one of the new MGA tools and is proposed by M.N. Do and Martin Vetterli in 2002, can efficiently represent contours and textures in images. It is based on a local, directional, and multiresolution expansion.

Curvelet frame is a multiscale, directional transform for detecting smooth contours. However, curvelet, introduced in the continuous domain firstly, is fit for rotation calculation and two-dimensional frequency partition based on pole coordinate, which makes it easy to implement in continuous domain but difficult in discrete. On the contrary, contourlet is proposed directly in discrete domain and has a double filter bank structure by combining LP and DFB for obtaining sparse expansions for typical images having smooth contours.

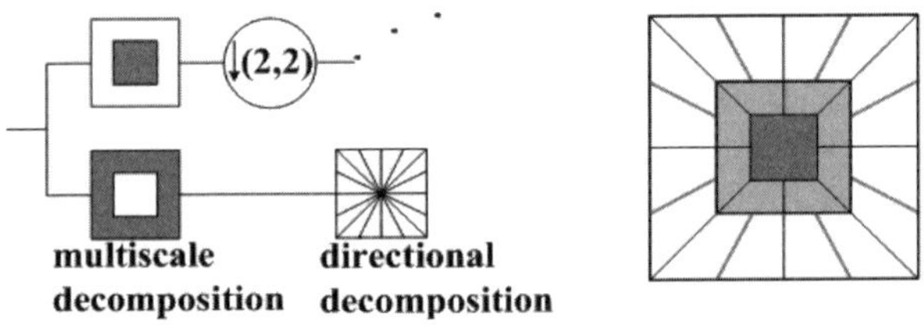

Fig. 1. The construction of contourlet

2.2 Wavelet-Based Contourlet Transform (WBCT)

Some approaches have been proposed based on contourlet. One of them is CRISP-contourlet [11] which is out of redundancy and uses a non-separable filter bank. Another is WBCT [12] which has a structure similar to that of contourlet. Wavelet is used to implement the multiscale decomposition, and then the DFB is applied to each highpass subband for the angular decomposition (Fig.2). Since wavelet filters are not perfect in splitting the frequency space to the lowpass and highpass components, fully decomposed DFB is used on each band [12].

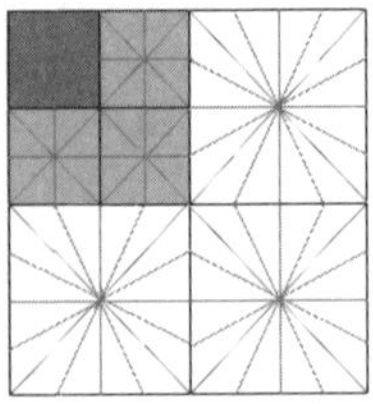

Fig. 2. A schematic plot of WBCT using 2 wavelet levels with 4, 8 directional subbands

3 Stationary-Wavelet Based Contourlet Transform

When WBCT is applied to texture analysis, the classification accuracy declines rapidly with increasing levels, which can be seen clearly from the results of experiments later. The reason is that when the levels increase, the subbands will narrow. If the subband is too small, the local features will change greatly with different samples which actually belong to the same class. Thus the features extracted are unstable. That's why the classification accuracy of many transforms, such as wavelet, brushlet, WBCT, descends when the levels increase to a certain degree. The subbands of WBCT are much smaller than those of wavelet and contourlet. Thus in the case of small number of levels, WBCT has high accuracy. But in the case of large number of levels, its accuracy drops faster than that of wavelet.

Redundant information is useful in image processing, such as edge detection, denoising, and image reconstruction. Considering that stationary wavelet has a high redundancy, it has superiority over wavelet in texture analysis. Hence, we introduce stationary wavelet to overcome the disadvantages of WBCT. Stationary wavelet does not carry out subsampling operation after every filtering. Instead, it implements the expansion of filters by inserting zero in every two coefficients of both highpass filter and lowpass filter. For example, the jth highpass and lowpass filters are as follows:

$$h_k^{(j)} = \begin{cases} h_{k/2^j}, k = 2^j m & m \in \mathbb{Z} \\ 0 & \text{else} \end{cases}, g_k^{(j)} = \begin{cases} g_{k/2^j}, k = 2^j m & m \in \mathbb{Z} \\ 0 & \text{else} \end{cases}. \quad (1)$$

The steps of our algorithm are as follows: first, carry out stationary wavelet transform to images. Next, apply DFB to three highpass subbands, LH, HL, and HH, and obtain 3×2^n directional subbands. Then iterate these steps for lowpass subband until satisfy the decomposition levels. The construction of SWBCT is shown in Fig.3. Due to the redundancy of stationary wavelet, the highpass

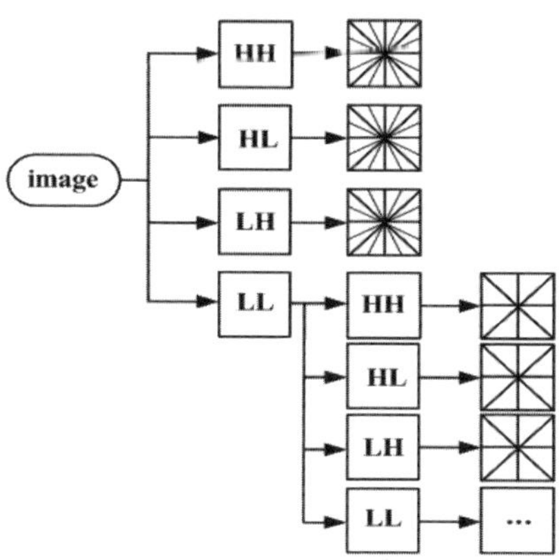

Fig. 3. A schematic plot of SWBCT

subbands obtained by multiscale decomposition have the same size with the original image. Thus when DFB is used to highpass subbands, it will not happen that the decomposition subbands narrow with the increasing levels. So, higher accuracy can be gotten. The following experiments also show that our method is effective in texture analysis.

4 Texture Classification Based on SWBCT

4.1 Feature Extraction Based on SWBCT

At present, among the spatial-frequency techniques for the texture feature extraction, energy measures of the wavelet subbands have been known as effective features and widely used. Hu invariant moments, as well as statistics of co-occurrence matrices of the subbands, can also be features. In this paper, we compare these three methods through experiments, and demonstrate that energy measures of subbands shows better in the texture classification for SWBCT.

Energy Measures. The method Energy Measure has been used widely. Both [1] and [8] adopt this method. We apply SWBCT to the classification of texture images. In the feature extraction stage, our strategy is to take the energy measures of all the subbands including one lowpass band and every directional subband in each level. The dimension is determined by levels and directions in each level. Different energy measures can be defined as the texture features. In our experiment, the Norm1 Energy Measure is used

$$E = \frac{1}{N} \sum_{K=1}^{N} |C_K| \ . \tag{2}$$

Co-occurrence Matrices. The method in [13] is that first, SWBCT is used, followed by calculating co-occurrence matrices from all the subbands, then contrast, entropy, angular second moment, and inverse different moment are computed via the co-occurrence matrices. We also adopt this method in this paper.

Hu Moments. The quantized Hu invariant moment vectors are used [7]. To begin with, SWBCT is applied to the texture images. Then we derive seven Hu moments respectively from all the subbands that we got previously. The seven Hu moments are denoted as

$$M_1 = (\mu_{20} + \mu_{02}), \tag{3}$$

$$M_2 = (\mu_{20} - \mu_{02})^2 + 4\mu_{11}^2, \tag{4}$$

$$M_3 = (\mu_{30} - 3\mu_{12})^2 + (3\mu_{21} - \mu_{03})^2, \tag{5}$$

$$M_4 = (\mu_{30} + \mu_{12})^2 + (\mu_{21} + \mu_{03})^2, \tag{6}$$

$$M_5 = (\mu_{30} - 3\mu_{12})(\mu_{30} + \mu_{12})[(\mu_{30} + \mu_{12})^2 - 3(\mu_{21} + \mu_{03})^2] + (3\mu_{21} - \mu_{03})(\mu_{21} + \mu_{03})[3(\mu_{30} + \mu_{12})^2 - (\mu_{21} + \mu_{03})^2], \quad (7)$$

$$M_6 = (\mu_{20} - \mu_{02})[(\mu_{30} + \mu_{12})^2 - (\mu_{21} + \mu_{03})^2] + 4\mu_{11}(\mu_{30} + \mu_{12})(\mu_{21} + \mu_{03}), \quad (8)$$

$$M_7 = (3\mu_{21} - \mu_{03})(\mu_{30} + \mu_{12})[(\mu_{30} + \mu_{12})^2 - 3(\mu_{21} + \mu_{03}^2)] + (\mu_{30} - 3\mu_{12})(\mu_{21} + \mu_{03})[3(\mu_{30} + \mu_{12})^2 - (\mu_{21} + \mu_{03})^2], \quad (9)$$

where $\mu_{pq} = \frac{1}{NM} \sum_1^N \sum_1^M f(x,y)(x-\bar{x})^p (y-\bar{y})^q, \bar{x} = m_{10}/m_{00}$, and $\bar{y} = m_{01}/m_{00}$.

4.2 Texture Classification Based on SWBCT

The whole classification system in this paper is shown in Fig.4. In the stage of feature extraction following decomposition, for comparison, three methods above are used respectively. Considering the effectiveness of our method itself, the simple classifier KNN is used. We also use wavelet, stationary wavelet, contourlet, WBCT, brushlet and Gabor filters to perform the same experiments for the comparison with SWBCT.

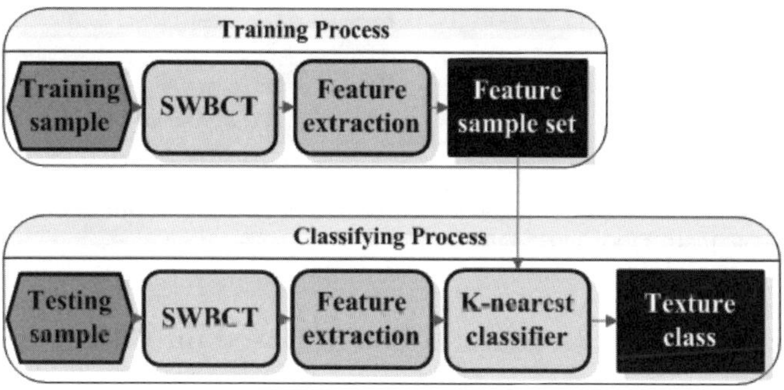

Fig. 4. Texture classifying system

5 Experiments

All experiments here adopt both wavelet and stationary wavelet with the 'db4' filters and decomposition levels from 1 to 5. For contourlet, WBCT and SWBCT, in the DFB stage we use the 'pkva' filters [9], and in the multiscale decomposition stage, the '9-7' filters for contourlet while the 'db4' filters for WBCT and SWBCT. With regard to the DFB, When decomposition levels from 1 to 5 are used respectively, the numbers of directional decomposition from the coarsest scale to the finest are 8 for 1 level, 4,8 for 2 levels, 4,4,8 for 3 levels, 4,4,8,8 for 4 levels, 4,4,8,8,16 for 5 levels. For comparison, Gabor filters are also used. Jain and Farrokhnia [5] suggested a dyadic Gabor filter bank. 5 radial frequencies (for images of size **128 × 128**) and 4 directions are suggested [5]. In this paper, the discrete radial center frequencies $2\sqrt{2}$,$4\sqrt{2}$,$8\sqrt{2}$,$16\sqrt{2}$,$32\sqrt{2}$ cycles/image-width and directions 0°,45°,90°,135° are used, so a total of 20 filters can be gotten.

The set of test data in our experiments is constituted under the Brodatz album. Brodatz album consists of 112 natural textures, each of which has been stored as a 640×640 image. Given that some of the textures in the album are not homogeneous (Fig.5), to some extent, the existing of these textures hardly has anything to do with the comparison between different algorithms [8], so they are removed in our experiment. There are 34 inhomogeneous textures removed. Accordingly we get a test data set of 78 textures, which includes some visual similar texture images. Each texture selected is divided into 25 non-overlapping sub-samples of size 128×128, 10 for training and 15 for test. Thus, the whole training data set has 780 samples and the whole test data set has 1950 ones. In our experiments, 10 training samples for each class are selected stochastically, and 15 samples left as testing ones. An average of results is calculated by running the program many times. The 34 textures removed in our experiment are listed as follows: D005, D007 D013, D030, D031, D036, D038, D040, D042, D043, D044, D045, D054, D058, D059, D061, D063, D069, D079, D080, D088, D089, D090, D091, D094, D096, D097, D098, D099, D100, D103, D106, D108, D110.

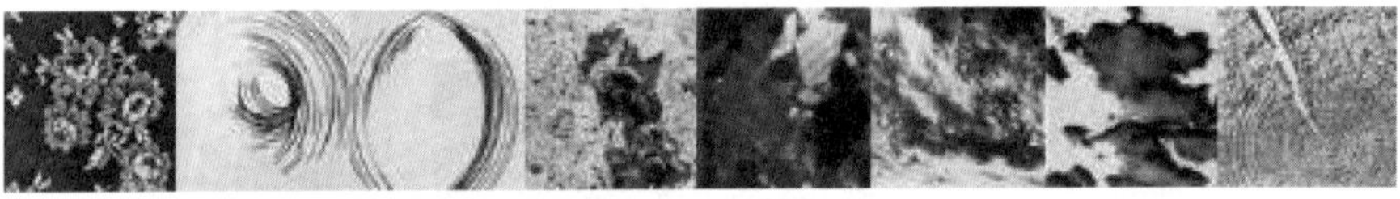

Fig. 5. Eight examples of inhomogeneous textures in Brodatz album; left to right: D42, D43, D44, D58, D59, D90, D91, D97

5.1 Classification of Brodatz Textures Based on Energy Measures

This experiment is carried out to test the performance of energy measures of SWBCT for texture classification. The Norm1 energy measures are calculated, and K in KNN is 1, 3, 5 respectively. The results are shown in Table 1. L in tables means the decomposition level.

From Table 1, when the level is three, most methods here achieve their best accuracy and among the best results of all methods, SWBCT produces the best one. It's clear that texture features can be extracted effectively by SWBCT. From Table 2, we can conclude that the performance of the popular Gabor filters is inferior to SWBCT and even not superior to wavelet, although Gabor filters are the preferred filter in several works [4], [5], [14]. The poor performance of the Gabor filter which has optimal joint resolution in the spatial and the frequency domains indicates that optimal joint resolution is not the ultimate goal [15].

Table 1. Classification accuracy of Brodatz textures with energy measures

		L=1	L=2	L=3	L=4	L=5
K=1	Wavelet	0.8782	0.9420	0.9487	0.9410	0.9200
	Stationary wavelet	0.8813	0.9415	0.9649	0.9728	0.9610
	Brushlet	0.5695	0.8582	0.9577	0.9521	0.9400
	Contourlet	0.8729	0.9523	0.9612	0.9651	0.9719
	WBCT	0.9032	0.9567	0.9584	0.9468	0.9037
	SWBCT	0.9579	0.9711	0.9786	0.9730	0.9723
K=2	Wavelet	0.8051	0.8924	0.9220	0.9058	0.8849
	Stationary wavelet	0.8155	0.9085	0.9372	0.9471	0.9429
	Brushlet	0.3875	0.7810	0.9359	0.9367	0.8945
	Contourlet	0.8494	0.9258	0.9405	0.9548	0.9547
	WBCT	0.8675	0.9271	0.9317	0.9212	0.8666
	SWBCT	0.9248	0.9470	0.9588	0.9564	0.9499
K=3	Wavelet	0.7687	0.8651	0.9035	0.8885	0.8706
	Stationary wavelet	0.7786	0.8863	0.9265	0.9398	0.9324
	Brushlet	0.3765	0.7600	0.9196	0.9188	0.8818
	Contourlet	0.8341	0.9073	0.9283	0.9490	0.9463
	WBCT	0.8553	0.9049	0.9205	0.9167	0.8605
	SWBCT	0.9121	0.9323	0.9429	0.9437	0.9370

Table 2. Classification accuracy using dyadic Gabor filter bank with energy measures

	$K = 1$	$K = 3$	$K = 5$
Dyadic Gabor filter bank	0.9171	0.8624	0.8120

5.2 Classification in the Case of Small Scale Training Samples

This experiment is carried out for testing the performance of our method in the case of small scale training samples. Learning from the conclusion in 5.1, 3 decomposition levels are used for all methods. The other parameters in this experiment are the same with those in 5.1. Here, we figure out the classification accuracy curves in Fig.6. The level axis gives the number of training samples and the vertical one gives the classification accuracy with $K = 1$.

Even in the case of small scale training samples, our method can still get high classification accuracy. With the number of training samples increasing from 1 to 24, SWBCT almost gets the best results all the time, and has a notable predominance with small scale training samples. When there are only 2 samples of each class for training, the accuracy of SWBCT exceeds 90% and it reaches 95% when 4 for training, while the other methods' accuracy is much lower. It's of great significance to have high accuracy in the case of small scale samples in some applications of image processing, especially for SAR, of which we can hardly afford enough samples for training.

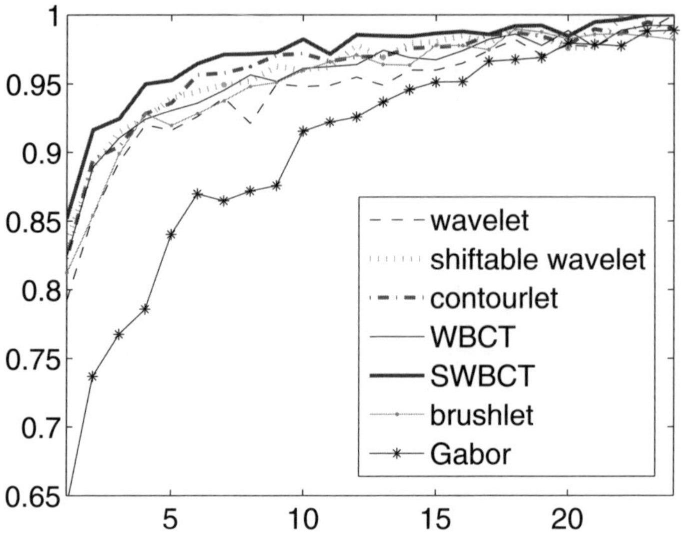

Fig. 6. The classification accuracy curves with increasing training samples

5.3 Classification Based on Hu Moments and Co-occurrence Matrices

In order to find the effects of different methods for extracting features of subband coefficients on classification accuracy, Hu moments and co-occurrence matrices are used respectively. 10 training samples for each class are selected stochastically and an average of results is calculated by running the program many times. K in KNN equals 1. L means the decomposition level.

From Table 3 and 4, we find the method based on Hu moments is better than the one based on co-occurrence matrices but not performs as well as energy measures. The method based on SWBCT can still has a better result than the other ones. It must be pointed out that an accuracy of 99.7% is received in paper [13], for there are only 10 textures in its experiments rather than 78 here.

From Table 5, we can find that when Hu moments and co-occurrence matrices are used, Gabor filters have better performance than wavelet. Especially, in the case of co-occurrence matrices, Gabor filters get the best result compared with

Table 3. Classification accuracy with Hu moments

	$L = 1$	$L = 2$	$L = 3$	$L = 4$	$L = 5$
Wavelet	0.8615	0.9116	0.9348	0.9271	0.8499
Stationary wavelet	0.8782	0.9174	0.9488	0.9509	0.9531
Brushlet	0.5308	0.7944	0.9365	0.9311	0.8679
Contourlet	0.9191	0.9415	0.9475	0.9336	0.9620
WBCT	0.9130	0.9164	0.9321	0.9167	0.8393
SWBCT	0.9463	0.9650	0.9723	0.9691	0.9713

Table 4. Classification accuracy with co-occurrence matrices

	$L=1$	$L=2$	$L=3$	$L=4$	$L=5$
Wavelet	0.8121	0.8347	0.7835	0.7531	0.7507
Stationary wavelet	0.8001	0.8473	0.8665	0.8844	0.8823
Brushlet	0.7820	0.7757	0.7897	0.6759	0.5470
Contourlet	0.7747	0.8336	0.8147	0.8307	0.7909
WBCT	0.6723	0.7061	0.7041	0.6263	0.6528
SWBCT	0.7769	0.8118	0.8686	0.8783	0.9237

Table 5. Classification accuracy using dyadic Gabor filter bank with Hu moments and co-occurrence matrices

	Hu moments	Co-occurrence matrices
Dyadic Gabor filter bank	0.9373	0.9325

the other transforms in this paper, but it's not as good as that of wavelet with energy measures. So it can be concluded that for Gabor filters, Hu moments may be the best choice, while energy measures for the other transforms in this paper.

6 Conclusion

In this paper, we proposed a new multiscale and multidirectional transform for texture analysis. The results of the experiments above show our method gets the highest classification accuracy. Even in the case of small scale training samples, it can still have accuracy over 90%. In the meantime, we can draw the conclusion that when wavelet, stationary wavelet, brushlet, contourlet, and SWBCT are used for texture classification, energy measures of subbands outperform Hu moments and co-occurrence matrices, and have less time for training and testing.

SWBCT inherits almost all the advantages of contourlet, multiresolution, multidirectional and anisotropy, and has much finer directional decomposition while overcoming the disadvantages of WBCT. When it refers to texture classification, SWBCT outperforms those widely used methods based on wavelet and contourlet, and can go further in mining the texture features than WBCT.

Acknowledgments

This work is partially supported by the National Natural Science Foundation of China under Grant 60472084 and the Major State Basic Research Development Sub-program of China under Grant 2001CB309403.

References

1. Chang, T., Kuo, C.C.J: Texture analysis and classification with tree-structured wavelet transform. IEEE Trans. on Image Processing. 2 (1993) 429–441
2. Gross, M.H., Koch, R., Lippert, L., Dreger, A.: Multiscale image texture analysis in wavelet spaces. Proc. IEEE ICIP. Austin, Texas, USA 3 (1994) 412–416
3. Unser, M.: Texture classification and segmentation using wavelet frames. IEEE Trans. on Image Processing. 4 (1995) 1549–1560
4. Bovik A.C., Clark M., Geisler W.S.: Multichannel texture analysis using localized spatial filters. IEEE Trans. on PAMI. 12 (1990) 55–73
5. Jain A.K., Farrokhnia F.: Unsupervised texture segmentation using Gabor filters. Pattern Recognition. 24 (1991) 1167–1186
6. Meyer, F.G., Coifman, R.R.: Brushlets: a tool for directional image analysis and image compression. Applied and Computational Harmonic Analysis. 5 (1997) 147–187
7. Biao Hou: Ridgelet and directional information detection: theory and applications. Ph.D. Xidian University. (2003)
8. Shan Tan, Xiangrong Zhang, Licheng Jiao: A brushlet-based feature set applied to texture classification. Springer-Verlag, Berlin Heidelberg. 3314 (2004) 1175–1180
9. Do, M.N., Vetterli, M.: Contourlets: a directional multiresolution image representation. Proc. of IEEE ICIP. Rochester, NY 1 (2002) 357–360
10. Licheng Jiao, Shan Tan: Development and prospect of image multiscale geometric analysis. Acta Electronica Sinica. 31 (2003) 43–50
11. Lu, Y., Do, M.N.: CRISP-contourlets: a critically sampled directional multiresolution image representation. Proc. of SPIE conference on Wavelet Applications in Signal and Image Processing X. San Diego, USA. 5207 (2003) 655–665
12. Ramin Eslami, Hayder Radha: Wavelet-based contourlet transform and its application to image coding. ICIP. Singapore 5 (2004) 3189–3192
13. Thyagarajan, K.S., Nguyen, T., Persons, C.E.: A maximum likelihood approach to texture classification using wavelet transform. International Conference on Image Processing (ICIP), IEEE Computer Society. Austin, Texas, USA. 2 (1994) 640–644
14. S.E. Grigorescu, N. Petkov, and P. Kruizinga: Comparison of texture features based on Gabor filters. IEEE Trans. on Image Processing. 11 (2002) 1160–1167
15. Randen T., John Håkon Husøy: Filtering for texture classification: a comparative study. IEEE Trans. on Pattern Analysis and Machine Intelligence. 21 (1999) 291–310

Automatic Color-Texture Image Segmentation by Using Active Contours

Mohand Saïd Allili and Djemel Ziou

Sherbrooke University, Faculty of Science,
Department of Computer Science,
Sherbrooke, J1K 2R1, Quebec, Canada
{MS.Allili, D.Ziou}@Usherbrooke.ca
Tel.: 1(819) 821 8000 ext. 3247/2859
Fax: 1(819) 821 8200

Abstract. In this paper, we propose a novel method for unsupervised color-texture segmentation. The approach aims at combining color and texture features and active contours to build a fully automatic segmentation algorithm. By fully automatic, we mean the steps of region initialization and calculation of the number of regions are performed automatically by the algorithm. Furthermore, the approach combines boundary and region information for accurate region boundary localization. We validate the approach by examples of synthetic and natural color-texture image segmentation.

Keywords: Color, texture, boundary, active contours, automatic segmentation.

1 Introduction

Image segmentation has been, and still is, the subject of active research in computer vision and image analysis. In most of past works, the emphasis was put to develop algorithms based either on color [13,15] or texture features [8,9,11]. However, there is a limited number of works that attempted to consider both features together to build a unified segmentation framework. The benefice of combining color and texture features has been shown in the past for distinguishing between regions having the same color but different textures and vice-versa [2,6,12]. Also, there has been a very few attempts to combine region and boundary information while taking color and texture properties into account. On the other hand, texture-based segmentation techniques require a prior learning step about the type of textures to be segmented, which makes the methods not fully automatic.

In [12,15], an active contours approach was proposed to segment texture images where the contours are driven by a combination of texture and color features. However, the results were shown only for bimodal image segmentation and the region initialization is performed manually. A major issue comes when extending these methods to an arbitrary number of regions where the complexity

N. Zheng, X. Jiang, and X. Lan (Eds.): IWICPAS 2006, LNCS 4153, pp. 495–504, 2006.

of the algorithms increases and the segmentation is prone to converge to undesirable local minima [2,14]. In [4], the authors proposed an automatic segmentation into blobs having the same color. However, since no texture information is used, the approach may over-segment images with different texture. Recently, we proposed in [2] an approach based on active contours for automatic segmentation of images with arbitrary number of regions. The approach combines region and boundary information for segmentation and proved to be less sensible to over-segmentation than in [4]. However, it relies on color image information to discriminate between different regions which may still fail to differentiate between different textures having the same color.

In the present work, we propose an automatic method for color-texture segmentation based on active contours model. The segmentation is steered by the combination of region and boundary information. The region information is based on mixture modeling of the combined color and texture features, while the boundary information is modeled by using the polarity information. The algorithm is based on a novel region initialization method that we have proposed recently in [2]. Moreover, we use the level set formalism for the implementation of the contour evolution. We show on real world examples the performance of the proposed method in achieving a fully automatic segmentation of color-texture images with an arbitrary number of regions.

This paper is organized as follows: In section (2), we present the proposed model for automatic segmentation. In section (3) some experimental results are shown, followed by general conclusions and future work.

2 Description of the Segmentation Model

2.1 Region Initialization

To initialize correctly the region contours, we proceed by the method that we have proposed recently in [2]. The method is composed of two steps. The first step aims at capturing the region kernels by using homogeneous seeds. The second step consists of calculating the number of regions and grouping the seeds to form the initial regions.

To capture the region kernels in the first step, we perform a smoothing on the image by using an adaptive scale. This aims at diminishing color fluctuations in texture areas while preserving the region boundaries. To detect if a pixel lies on a texture, we calculate the polarity of the neighborhood of the pixel. Let $\boldsymbol{v}(v_x, v_y)$ be the color gradient vector as proposed in [2]. A structure matrix S for the pixel $\mathbf{x} = (x, y)$ is defined by:

$$\mathcal{S} = G_\sigma * (\boldsymbol{v}^T \boldsymbol{v}) = G_\sigma * \begin{pmatrix} v_x \cdot v_x & v_x \cdot v_y \\ v_y \cdot v_x & v_y \cdot v_y \end{pmatrix} \quad (1)$$

where v^T denotes the transpose of the vector v. G_σ is a Gaussian kernel with a scale σ that smoothes each element of the matrix S by the convolution operation $*$. Assume now that ν_1 and ν_2 are the eigenvalues of $\mathcal{S}$, where $\nu_1 > \nu_2$. When

$\nu_1 \gg \nu_2$, the neighborhood of the pixel $W(\mathbf{x})$ has a dominant orientation in the direction of the eigenvector that corresponds to ν_1. This constitutes an index of the presence of a real region boundary. Let us denote the normalized vector in this direction by $\boldsymbol{\eta}$. The polarity $P(\mathbf{x})$ that measures the extent at which the color gradient vectors in the neighborhood of $\mathbf{x}$ are oriented in the same direction, is given by:

$$P(\mathbf{x}) = \sum_{(p,q)\in W(\mathbf{x})} G_\sigma * \langle \boldsymbol{v}(p,q), \boldsymbol{\eta} \rangle \quad (2)$$

where $\langle\rangle$ denotes the vector scalar product. The smoothing scale for the pixel neighborhood $W(\mathbf{x})$ is chosen by looking at the behavior of $P(\mathbf{x})$ to changing σ. In a typical image region, homogeneous in color or texture, an edge will hold the polarity near 1 for all the scale values; whereas, the polarity vanishes on a texture by increasing the scale (see fig. (1) for illustration). By varying the scale σ from 1 to 6, we choose the smoothing scale beyond which the polarity does not vary more than a fixed threshold. In fig. (2), we show the polarity output

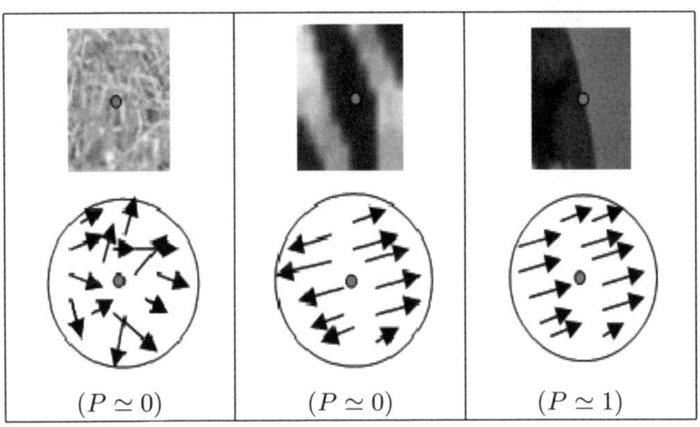

Fig. 1. Different values of the polarity of a pixel represented by the green point in different images containing texture

(rightmost image) calculated for texture image (left image). We show also the gradient response for the image (middle image). Note that to visualize the gradient response and polarity images, we changed the dynamic of their grey levels. Clearly, the polarity permits for capturing more accurately the real boundaries of the texture object. Finally in fig. (3), an example of region initialization is shown where the images contain texture regions. Seeds are initialized where the value of the polarity vanishes. Remark that no seeds were initialized on the real region boundaries, allowing to capture only the region kernels. Note that at this stage of the algorithm, the seeds are not classified yet to regions.

The second step of the region initialization algorithm consists of grouping the seeds into regions. Here, we use a combination of color and texture features to

Fig. 2. An example of pixel polarity calculation. Fig. (a) represents the original image, fig. (b) represents the gradient response for the image and fig. (c) represents the polarity image.

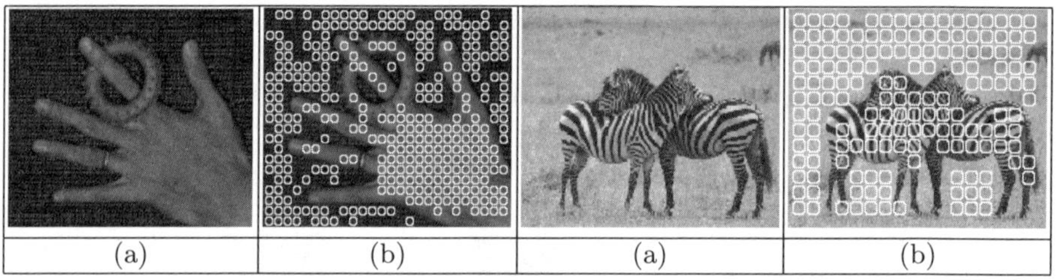

Fig. 3. Examples of region contours initialization by using homogeneous seeds. Fig. (a) represents the original image and (b) the result of region initialization.

calculate a mixture of pdfs that models the distribution of these features. For color features, CIE-$L^*a^*b^*$ color space has been chosen for its uniformity. For texture features, for each pixel neighborhood, a correlogram [7] is calculated. An element of the correlogram matrix $C^{d,\theta}(c_i;c_j)$ should give the probability that given a pixel $\mathbf{x}_1$ of color c_i, a pixel $\mathbf{x}_2$ at distance d and orientation θ from $\mathbf{x}_1$ is of color c_j. We calculate the correlogram for 4 orientations $(d,0)$, $(d,\frac{\pi}{4})$, $(d,\frac{\pi}{2})$ and $(d,\frac{3\pi}{4})$. Let D, be the total number of displacements. We derive from each correlogram three typical characteristics that are namely: *Inverse Difference Moment (IDM)*, *Energy (E)* and *Correlation (C)*. E and C measure respectively the homogeneity of the texture while *IDM* measures the coarseness of the texture. The formulation of these characteristics is given by:

$$E = \frac{1}{D}\sum_{c_i,c_j}\sum_{d,\theta}(C^{d,\theta}(c_i;c_j))^2 \tag{3}$$

$$IDM = \sum_{c_i,c_j}\sum_{d,\theta}\frac{1}{D(1-\|c_i-c_j\|^2)}C^{d,\theta}(c_i;c_j) \tag{4}$$

$$C = \sum_{c_i,c_j}\sum_{d,\theta}\frac{(c_i-\mu_i)(c_j-\mu_j)}{D|\Sigma_i||\Sigma_j|}C^{d,\theta}(c_i;c_j) \tag{5}$$

where $\mu_i = \sum_{c_j} c_i C^{d,\theta}(c_i;c_j)$ and $\Sigma_i = \sum_{c_j}(c_i-\mu_i)^T(c_i-\mu_i)C^{d,\theta}(c_i;c_j)$. The first sum of the above equations is made over the color entries of the correlogram matrix. The second sum averages the features over all the considered displacements. Note here that for simplicity, we used only one neighborhood size for each pixel neighborhood to calculate the correlogram matrix.

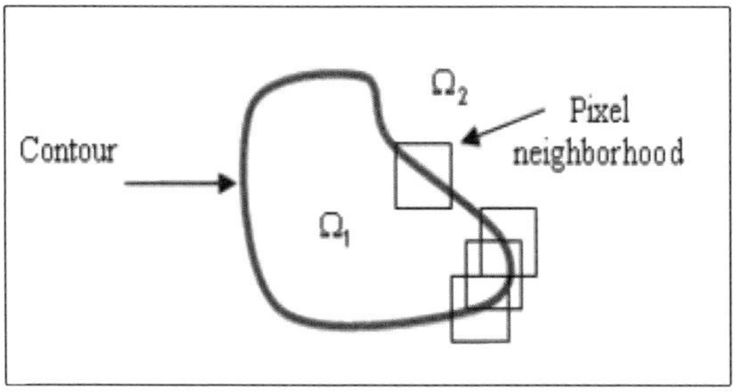

Fig. 4. Representation of the neighborhood used to calculate the correlogram matrix

2.2 Fitting a Mixture Model to Regions

To model the distribution of the features, we use a mixture of General Gaussian distributions (GGD) as in [2]. The formalism GGD yielded a good compromise between fitting the image data while not over-fitting the real number of components in the mixture [2,3]. In the following, we give the formalism of GGD. Let $U = (u_1, \ldots, u_n)$ be the combined color-texture features vector; the probability of the vector according to the mixture is given by:

$$p(U/\theta_k) = \prod_{i=1}^{n} \left(\frac{\varrho_{ki}}{2\sigma_{ki}} \cdot \exp\left(-\psi_{ki} \left| \frac{u_i - \mu_{ki}}{\sigma_{ki}} \right|^{\lambda_{ki}} \right) \right) \quad (6)$$

where the coefficients ϱ and ψ are given by: $\varrho_{ki} = \frac{\lambda_{ki}\sqrt{\frac{\Gamma(3/\lambda_{ki})}{\Gamma(1/\lambda_{ki})}}}{\Gamma(1/\lambda_{ki})}$ and $\psi_{ki} = \left[\frac{\Gamma(3/\lambda_{ki})}{\Gamma(1/\lambda_{ki})}\right]^{\frac{\lambda_{ki}}{2}}$. We denote by $\Gamma(u)$ the gamma function that is defined by the integral: $\Gamma(m) = \int_0^\infty z^{m-1}e^m dz$, where m and z are real variables. In function (6), μ_{ki} and σ_{ki} are the pdf location and standard deviation in the ith dimension of the feature vector U. In the same dimension, the parameter $\lambda_{ki} \geq 1$ controls the tails of the distribution for being peaked or flat. Having M regions, a mixture of M GGDs is calculated for the seeds data by using the Maximum Likelihood Estimation [2]. In order to estimate automatically the number of components of the mixture, we use the AIC information-theory criterion [1] that is given by the following formula:

$$AIC = -log(L(\Theta)) + 2\xi \quad (7)$$

Where $log(L(\Theta))$ is the log-likelihood given the data. The log-likelihood reflects the overall fit of the mixture model (smaller values indicate worse fit). Thus, the first term of the AIC decreases with the number of mixture components. ξ is the number of estimated parameters included in the model. The second term of the AIC penalizes over-fitting the number of components in the mixture.

In a final step for region initialization, we group the seeds into regions by maximizing for each seed the membership probability of its features vectors, given by following function:

$$argmax_k \left(\prod_{l=1}^{N} (\pi_k p(U_l/\theta_k)) \right) \tag{8}$$

where N is the number of pixels contained in each seed. $\pi_{k \in \{1,...,M\}}$, designates the *a priori* probability of the kth mixture component. Fig. (5) shows the result of seed grouping. The first image shows the homogeneous seed initialization. The second image shows the seeds after being grouped into regions.

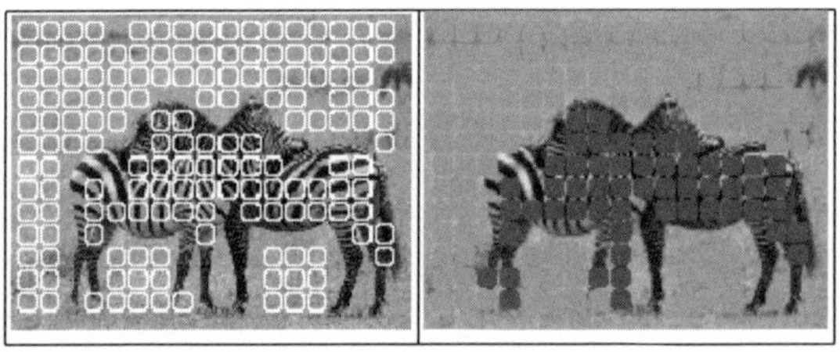

Fig. 5. Example of grouping the seeds into regions

2.3 Adaptive Color-Texture Segmentation

In the following, we use the notation Ω_k and $\partial\Omega_k$ to designate respectively a region and its boundaries. The objective of the segmentation is to create a partition of the image composed of M regions $P = \{\Omega_1, ..., \Omega_M\}$, where $\bigcup_{i=1}^{M} \Omega_k = \Omega$ and the formed regions are considered to be homogeneous with respect to color and texture characteristics variation. We formulate the segmentation by using a variational model as we have proposed recently in [2]. In the model, the parameters of the mixture of pdfs modelling the region information are calculated adaptively to segmentation. The objective function underlying the model is formulated by the following energy functional:

$$E(\partial\Omega_{k\in\{1,...,M\}}, \Theta) = \sum_{k=1}^{M} \Bigg[\alpha \oint_{\partial\Omega_k} g(P(s))ds + \beta \iint_{\Omega_k} -log\left(p(\theta_k/U(\mathbf{x}))\right) d\mathbf{x} \Bigg] \tag{9}$$

where Θ designates the mixture parameters that include the parameters of each pdf of the mixture θ_k and the mixing parameters $\pi_{k\in\{1,...,M\}}$. The boundary information is added in the first term of the functional (9) by using the formalism of GAC [5]. Here g is a strictly decreasing function of the absolute value of the polarity P, which is given by $g(P(\mathbf{x})) = \frac{1}{|P(\mathbf{X})|+\varepsilon}$ with ε is a constant parameter. In this term s represents the arc-length parameter. The second term of the functional (9) represents the region information. This term aims to minimize the Bayes error classification of the pixels in each region [2].

To minimize the energy according to the region contours, we calculate the Euler-Lagrange equations. After introducing the level set formalism for the contours [10], we obtain the following motion equation for each region contour:

$$\frac{d\Phi_k}{dt} = (\alpha V_b(\Phi_k) - \beta V_r(\Phi_k)) |\nabla\Phi_k| \tag{10}$$

where

$$V_b(\Phi_k) = g(P(\Phi_k))\kappa + \nabla g(P(\Phi_k)) \cdot \frac{\nabla\Phi_k}{|\nabla\Phi_k|} \tag{11}$$

$$V_r(\Phi_k) = log\,(\pi_k \cdot p(U(\Phi_k)/\theta_k)) - log\,(\pi_h \cdot p(U(\Phi_k)/\theta_h)) \tag{12}$$

where $\Phi_k : \Re^2 \rightarrow \Re$ is a level set function and the contour $\partial\Omega_k$ is represented by its zero level set. The symbol κ stands for the curvature of the zero level set. The term V_b represents the boundary velocity that regularizes the curve and aligns it with the region boundaries. Meanwhile, the term V_r represents the region velocity. In the interior of a region, the boundary term vanishes and the contour is driven only by the region information. Here, in the objective of having the best classification of pixels, the region term is made as a competition for a given pixel between the current region Ω_k and the region $\Omega_h \neq \Omega_k$ that has the maximum posterior probability for the pixel feature vector.

3 Experiments

The experiments that we have conducted consists of the segmentation of synthetic and natural images containing texture regions. For all the segmentations, the size of the seeds in region initialization is fixed to (7×7) pixels and the inter-seed distance is 3 pixels. Note that we used the approach that we have proposed in [2] to minimize the energy functional (9). This involves a minimization according to the region contours and another minimization according to the mixture parameters. Moreover, for all the segmentation examples we set $\alpha = \beta = 0.5$. We put $\varepsilon = 0.5$ in the function g of the boundary term of the functional (9). Note also that to reduce the computation time, the steps of polarity and texture features calculation for each pixel in a segmented image is performed in an off-line process.

To illustrate the advantage of combining color and texture features, we show on fig. (6) the segmentation of mosaic images composed by 4 regions each. These images have the following property: each region has the same color as its horizontal/vertical neighboring region, while the vertical/horizontal neighboring region has the same texture. Clearly separating texture and texture features yielded incorrect segmentations while combining them resulted in good segmentations. To measure the performance of our method, we show on fig. (7) two examples of images segmented by using our method and the Blobworld method [4]. Clearly, our method suffers less from over-segmentation where the capturing of region kernels initially excluded the pixels of the boundaries, which avoided the creation of small regions that over-segment the images in these parts as Blobworld does. The evolution of the region kernels by the combination region and boundary information permits for capturing the real boundaries of the salient objects.

In fig. (8), we show the segmentation of images with different number of regions. The first row of the figure shows three segmentations mosaic of Brodatz textures. The second and third rows of the figure show the segmentation of examples of natural images. The salient regions (with homogeneous color and texture) have been successfully retrieved in both synthetic and natural images by the algorithm, which proves the performance of the approach. We emphasize on the fact that all the segmentations have been performed in a fully automatic fashion, which is an important factor for segmenting automatically large collections of natural images for the purpose of content-based image retrieval for instance. This point constitutes one of the key contributions of the present work. Finally, for computation time, the algorithm is relatively fast comparing to the state of the art. Excluding the time spent for computing the boundary (polarity) and texture features, the algorithm took few seconds to segment the most of the images shown in the present section.

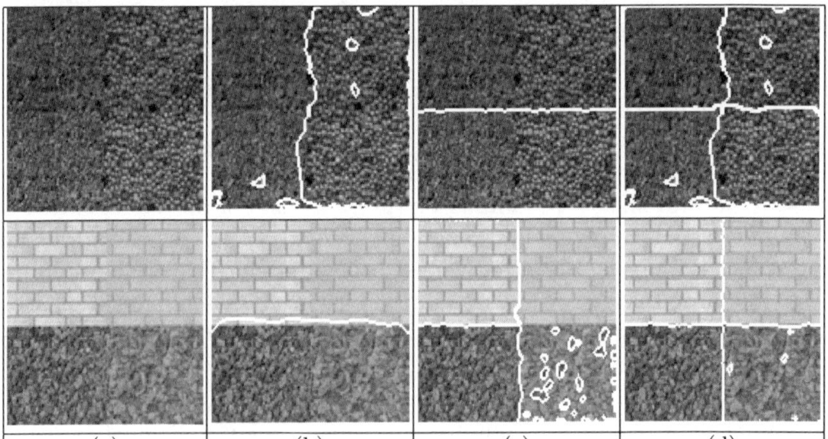

(a) (b) (c) (d)

Fig. 6. Fig(a) represents the original image. Fig(b) represents a segmentation by using only texture features. Fig(c) represents a segmentation by using only color features. Fig(c) represents a segmentation by using a combination of texture and color features.

Fig. 7. Examples showing the performance of our method: (a) shows the original images, (b) shows a smoothed version of the images by using an adaptive scale, (c) shows the segmentation of the images by using the Blobworld method and (d) shows the segmentation by using our method

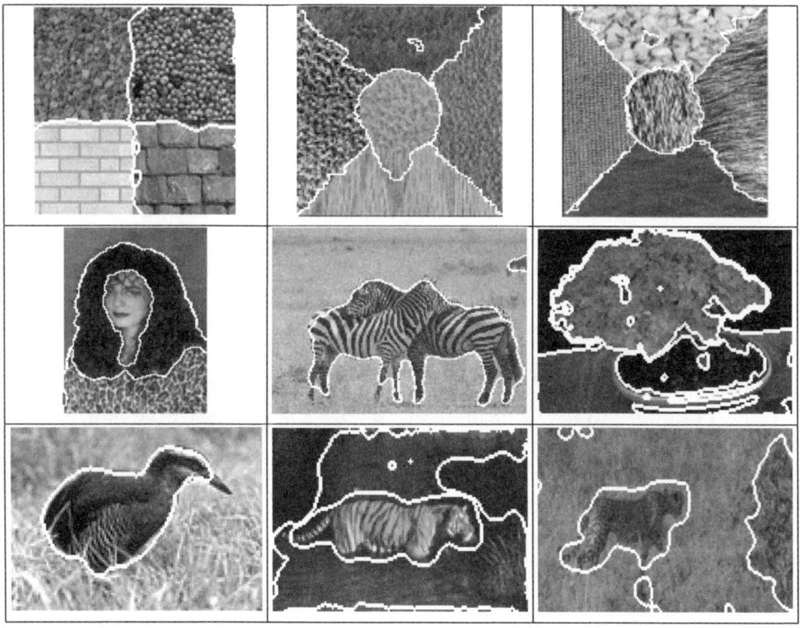

Fig. 8. Examples of color-texture image segmentation by using the proposed approach

4 Conclusions

In the presented approach, we proposed a new framework for unsupervised color-texture segmentation by using active contours. The method takes advantage of boundary and region information sources to perform a segmentation of color texture images with an arbitrary number of regions. Moreover, the method operates in a fully automatic fashion, which makes a contribution in the state of the art of the domain and motivates its application to the purpose of segmenting image collections in the future.

Acknowledgments

We thank the Natural Sciences and Engineering Research Council (NSERC Canada) for supporting the completion of the present work.

References

1. H. Akaike. A New Look at the Statistical Model Identification. *IEEE Trans. on Automatic Control*, 19:716-723, 1974.
2. M. S. Allili and D. Ziou. An Automatic Segmentation Combining Mixture Analysis and Adaptive Region Information: A Level Set Approach. *In proceedings of IEEE CRV*, 73-80, 2005.
3. M.S. Allili, N. Bouguila and D. Ziou. Generalized Gaussian Mixture and MML, *Technical Report.*
4. C. Carson, S. Belongie, H. Greenspan and J. Malik. Blobworld: Image Segmentation Using Expectation-Maximization and Its Application to Image Querying. *IEEE Trans. on PAMI*, 24(8):1026-1038, 2002.
5. V. Caselles, R. Kimmel, and G. Shapiro. Geodesic Active Contours. *IJCV*, 22:61-79, 1997.
6. J. Freixenet, X. Munoz, J. Marti, and X. Llado. Colour Texture Segmentation by Region-Boundary Cooperation. *In proceedings of ECCV*, 1:250–261, 2004.
7. J. Huang, S. R. Kumar, M. Mitra, W.-J. Zhu, and R. Zabih. Image Indexing Using Color Correlograms. *In proceedings of IEEE CVPR*, 762-768, 1997.
8. A. Jain and F. Farrokhnia. Unsupervised Texture Segmentation by Using Gabor Filters. *Pattern Recognition*, 24:1167-1186, 1991.
9. S. Liapis, E. Sifakis, and G. Tziritas. Colour and Texture Segmentation Using Wavelet Frame Analysis, Deterministic Relaxation and Fast Marching Algorithms. *JVCIR*, 15(1):1-26, 2004.
10. S. Osher and J. Sethian. Fronts Propagating with Curvature-dependant Speed: Algorithms Based on Hammilton-Jacobi Formulations. *Journal of Computational Physics*, 22:12-49, 1988.
11. N. Paragios and R. Deriche. Geodesic Active Regions and Level Set Methods for Supervised Texture Segmentation. *IJCV*, pages 223–247, 2002.
12. M. Rousson, T. Brox, and R. Deriche. Active Unsupervised Texture Segmentation on a Diffusion Based Feature Space. *In proceedings of IEEE CVPR*, 2:699-704, 2003.
13. E. Sifakis, C. Garcia, and G. Tziritas. Bayesian Level Sets for Image Segmentation. *JVCIR*, 13:44-64, 2002.
14. A. Yezzi and A. Tsai and A. Willsky. A Fully Global Approach to Image Segmentation Via Couples Curve Evolution Equations. *JVCIR*, 13:195-216, 2002.
15. S. Zhu and A. Yuille. Region competition: Unifying Snakes, Region Growing and Bayes/MDL for Multiband Image Segmentation. *IEEE Trans. PAMI*, 18:884-900, 1996.

Author Index

Lecture Notes in Computer Science

For information about Vols. 1–4027

please contact your bookseller or Springer

Vol. 4153: N. Zheng, X. Jiang, X. Lan (Eds.), Advances in Machine Vision, Image Processing, and Pattern Analysis. XIII, 506 pages. 2006.

Vol. 4146: J.C. Rajapakse, L. Wong, R. Acharya (Eds.), Pattern Recognition in Bioinformatics. XIV, 186 pages. 2006. (Sublibrary LNBI).

Vol. 4144: T. Ball, R.B. Jones (Eds.), Computer Aided Verification. XV, 564 pages. 2006.

Vol. 4139: T. Salakoski, F. Ginter, S. Pyysalo, T. Pahikkala, Advances in Natural Language Processing. XVI, 771 pages. 2006. (Sublibrary LNAI).

Vol. 4138: X. Cheng, W. Li, T. Znati (Eds.), Wireless Algorithms, Systems, and Applications. XVI, 709 pages. 2006.

Vol. 4137: C. Baier, H. Hermanns (Eds.), CONCUR 2006 – Concurrency Theory. XIII, 525 pages. 2006.

Vol. 4133: J. Gratch, M. Young, R. Aylett, D. Ballin, P. Olivier (Eds.), Intelligent Virtual Agents. XIV, 472 pages. 2006. (Sublibrary LNAI).

Vol. 4130: U. Furbach, N. Shankar (Eds.), Automated Reasoning. XV, 680 pages. 2006. (Sublibrary LNAI).

Vol. 4129: D. McGookin, S. Brewster (Eds.), Haptic and Audio Interaction Design. XII, 167 pages. 2006.

Vol. 4127: E. Damiani, P. Liu (Eds.), Data and Applications Security XX. X, 319 pages. 2006.

Vol. 4121: A. Biere, C.P. Gomes (Eds.), Theory and Applications of Satisfiability Testing - SAT 2006. XII, 438 pages. 2006.

Vol. 4117: C. Dwork (Ed.), Advances in Cryptology - Crypto 2006. XIII, 621 pages. 2006.

Vol. 4115: D.-S. Huang, K. Li, G.W. Irwin (Eds.), Computational Intelligence and Bioinformatics, Part III. XXI, 803 pages. 2006. (Sublibrary LNBI).

Vol. 4114: D.-S. Huang, K. Li, G.W. Irwin (Eds.), Computational Intelligence, Part II. XXVII, 1337 pages. 2006. (Sublibrary LNAI).

Vol. 4113: D.-S. Huang, K. Li, G.W. Irwin (Eds.), Intelligent Computing, Part I. XXVII, 1331 pages. 2006.

Vol. 4112: D.Z. Chen, D. T. Lee (Eds.), Computing and Combinatorics. XIV, 528 pages. 2006.

Vol. 4111: F.S. de Boer, M.M. Bonsangue, S. Graf, W.-P. de Roever (Eds.), Formal Methods for Components and Objects. VIII, 447 pages. 2006.

Vol. 4109: D.-Y. Yeung, J.T. Kwok, A. Fred, F. Roli, D. de Ridder (Eds.), Structural, Syntactic, and Statistical Pattern Recognition. XXI, 939 pages. 2006.

Vol. 4108: J.M. Borwein, W.M. Farmer (Eds.), Mathematical Knowledge Management. VIII, 295 pages. 2006. (Sublibrary LNAI).

Vol. 4106: T.R. Roth-Berghofer, M.H. Göker, H. A. Güvenir (Eds.), Advances in Case-Based Reasoning. XIV, 566 pages. 2006. (Sublibrary LNAI).

Vol. 4104: T. Kunz, S.S. Ravi (Eds.), Ad-Hoc, Mobile, and Wireless Networks. XII, 474 pages. 2006.

Vol. 4099: Q. Yang, G. Webb (Eds.), PRICAI 2006: Trends in Artificial Intelligence. XXVIII, 1263 pages. 2006. (Sublibrary LNAI).

Vol. 4098: F. Pfenning (Ed.), Term Rewriting and Applications. XIII, 415 pages. 2006.

Vol. 4097: X. Zhou, O. Sokolsky, L. Yan, E.-S. Jung, Z. Shao, Y. Mu, D.C. Lee, D. Kim, Y.-S. Jeong, C.-Z. Xu (Eds.), Emerging Directions in Embedded and Ubiquitous Computing. XXVII, 1034 pages. 2006.

Vol. 4096: E. Sha, S.-K. Han, C.-Z. Xu, M.H. Kim, L.T. Yang, B. Xiao (Eds.), Embedded and Ubiquitous Computing. XXIV, 1170 pages. 2006.

Vol. 4094: O. H. Ibarra, H.-C. Yen (Eds.), Implementation and Application of Automata. XIII, 291 pages. 2006.

Vol. 4093: X. Li, O.R. Zaïane, Z. Li (Eds.), Advanced Data Mining and Applications. XXI, 1110 pages. 2006. (Sublibrary LNAI).

Vol. 4092: J. Lang, F. Lin, J. Wang (Eds.), Knowledge Science, Engineering and Management. XV, 664 pages. 2006. (Sublibrary LNAI).

Vol. 4091: G.-Z. Yang, T. Jiang, D. Shen, L. Gu, J. Yang (Eds.), Medical Imaging and Augmented Reality. XIII, 399 pages. 2006.

Vol. 4090: S. Spaccapietra, K. Aberer, P. Cudré-Mauroux (Eds.), Journal on Data Semantics VI. XI, 211 pages. 2006.

Vol. 4088: Z.-Z. Shi, R. Sadananda (Eds.), Agent Computing and Multi-Agent Systems. XVII, 827 pages. 2006. (Sublibrary LNAI).

Vol. 4085: J. Misra, T. Nipkow, E. Sekerinski (Eds.), FM 2006: Formal Methods. XV, 620 pages. 2006.

Vol. 4079: S. Etalle, M. Truszczyński (Eds.), Logic Programming. XIV, 474 pages. 2006.

Vol. 4077: M.-S. Kim, K. Shimada (Eds.), Advances in Geometric Modeling and Processing. XVI, 696 pages. 2006.

Vol. 4076: F. Hess, S. Pauli, M. Pohst (Eds.), Algorithmic Number Theory. X, 599 pages. 2006.

Vol. 4075: U. Leser, F. Naumann, B. Eckman (Eds.), Data Integration in the Life Sciences. XI, 298 pages. 2006. (Sublibrary LNBI).

Vol. 4074: M. Burmester, A. Yasinsac (Eds.), Secure Mobile Ad-hoc Networks and Sensors. X, 193 pages. 2006.

Vol. 4073: A. Butz, B. Fisher, A. Krüger, P. Olivier (Eds.), Smart Graphics. XI, 263 pages. 2006.

Vol. 4072: M. Harders, G. Székely (Eds.), Biomedical Simulation. XI, 216 pages. 2006.

Vol. 4071: H. Sundaram, M. Naphade, J.R. Smith, Y. Rui (Eds.), Image and Video Retrieval. XII, 547 pages. 2006.

Vol. 4070: C. Priami, X. Hu, Y. Pan, T.Y. Lin (Eds.), Transactions on Computational Systems Biology V. IX, 129 pages. 2006. (Sublibrary LNBI).

Vol. 4069: F.J. Perales, R.B. Fisher (Eds.), Articulated Motion and Deformable Objects. XV, 526 pages. 2006.

Vol. 4068: H. Schärfe, P. Hitzler, P. Øhrstrøm (Eds.), Conceptual Structures: Inspiration and Application. XI, 455 pages. 2006. (Sublibrary LNAI).

Vol. 4067: D. Thomas (Ed.), ECOOP 2006 – Object-Oriented Programming. XIV, 527 pages. 2006.

Vol. 4066: A. Rensink, J. Warmer (Eds.), Model Driven Architecture – Foundations and Applications. XII, 392 pages. 2006.

Vol. 4065: P. Perner (Ed.), Advances in Data Mining. XI, 592 pages. 2006. (Sublibrary LNAI).

Vol. 4064: R. Büschkes, P. Laskov (Eds.), Detection of Intrusions and Malware & Vulnerability Assessment. X, 195 pages. 2006.

Vol. 4063: I. Gorton, G.T. Heineman, I. Crnkovic, H.W. Schmidt, J.A. Stafford, C.A. Szyperski, K. Wallnau (Eds.), Component-Based Software Engineering. XI, 394 pages. 2006.

Vol. 4062: G. Wang, J.F. Peters, A. Skowron, Y. Yao (Eds.), Rough Sets and Knowledge Technology. XX, 810 pages. 2006. (Sublibrary LNAI).

Vol. 4061: K. Miesenberger, J. Klaus, W. Zagler, A. Karshmer (Eds.), Computers Helping People with Special Needs. XXIX, 1356 pages. 2006.

Vol. 4060: K. Futatsugi, J.-P. Jouannaud, J. Meseguer (Eds.), Algebra, Meaning, and Computation. XXXVIII, 643 pages. 2006.

Vol. 4059: L. Arge, R. Freivalds (Eds.), Algorithm Theory – SWAT 2006. XII, 436 pages. 2006.

Vol. 4058: L.M. Batten, R. Safavi-Naini (Eds.), Information Security and Privacy. XII, 446 pages. 2006.

Vol. 4057: J.P.W. Pluim, B. Likar, F.A. Gerritsen (Eds.), Biomedical Image Registration. XII, 324 pages. 2006.

Vol. 4056: P. Flocchini, L. Gąsieniec (Eds.), Structural Information and Communication Complexity. X, 357 pages. 2006.

Vol. 4055: J. Lee, J. Shim, S.-g. Lee, C. Bussler, S. Shim (Eds.), Data Engineering Issues in E-Commerce and Services. IX, 290 pages. 2006.

Vol. 4054: A. Horváth, M. Telek (Eds.), Formal Methods and Stochastic Models for Performance Evaluation. VIII, 239 pages. 2006.

Vol. 4053: M. Ikeda, K.D. Ashley, T.-W. Chan (Eds.), Intelligent Tutoring Systems. XXVI, 821 pages. 2006.

Vol. 4052: M. Bugliesi, B. Preneel, V. Sassone, I. Wegener (Eds.), Automata, Languages and Programming, Part II. XXIV, 603 pages. 2006.

Vol. 4051: M. Bugliesi, B. Preneel, V. Sassone, I. Wegener (Eds.), Automata, Languages and Programming, Part I. XXIII, 729 pages. 2006.

Vol. 4049: S. Parsons, N. Maudet, P. Moraitis, I. Rahwan (Eds.), Argumentation in Multi-Agent Systems. XIV, 313 pages. 2006. (Sublibrary LNAI).

Vol. 4048: L. Goble, J.-J.C.. Meyer (Eds.), Deontic Logic and Artificial Normative Systems. X, 273 pages. 2006. (Sublibrary LNAI).

Vol. 4047: M. Robshaw (Ed.), Fast Software Encryption. XI, 434 pages. 2006.

Vol. 4046: S.M. Astley, M. Brady, C. Rose, R. Zwiggelaar (Eds.), Digital Mammography. XVI, 654 pages. 2006.

Vol. 4045: D. Barker-Plummer, R. Cox, N. Swoboda (Eds.), Diagrammatic Representation and Inference. XII, 301 pages. 2006. (Sublibrary LNAI).

Vol. 4044: P. Abrahamsson, M. Marchesi, G. Succi (Eds.), Extreme Programming and Agile Processes in Software Engineering. XII, 230 pages. 2006.

Vol. 4043: A.S. Atzeni, A. Lioy (Eds.), Public Key Infrastructure. XI, 261 pages. 2006.

Vol. 4042: D. Bell, J. Hong (Eds.), Flexible and Efficient Information Handling. XVI, 296 pages. 2006.

Vol. 4041: S.-W. Cheng, C.K. Poon (Eds.), Algorithmic Aspects in Information and Management. XI, 395 pages. 2006.

Vol. 4040: R. Reulke, U. Eckardt, B. Flach, U. Knauer, K. Polthier (Eds.), Combinatorial Image Analysis. XII, 482 pages. 2006.

Vol. 4039: M. Morisio (Ed.), Reuse of Off-the-Shelf Components. XIII, 444 pages. 2006.

Vol. 4038: P. Ciancarini, H. Wiklicky (Eds.), Coordination Models and Languages. VIII, 299 pages. 2006.

Vol. 4037: R. Gorrieri, H. Wehrheim (Eds.), Formal Methods for Open Object-Based Distributed Systems. XVII, 474 pages. 2006.

Vol. 4036: O. H. Ibarra, Z. Dang (Eds.), Developments in Language Theory. XII, 456 pages. 2006.

Vol. 4035: T. Nishita, Q. Peng, H.-P. Seidel (Eds.), Advances in Computer Graphics. XX, 771 pages. 2006.

Vol. 4034: J. Münch, M. Vierimaa (Eds.), Product-Focused Software Process Improvement. XVII, 474 pages. 2006.

Vol. 4033: B. Stiller, P. Reichl, B. Tuffin (Eds.), Performability Has its Price. X, 103 pages. 2006.

Vol. 4032: O. Etzion, T. Kuflik, A. Motro (Eds.), Next Generation Information Technologies and Systems. XIII, 365 pages. 2006.

Vol. 4031: M. Ali, R. Dapoigny (Eds.), Advances in Applied Artificial Intelligence. XXIII, 1353 pages. 2006. (Sublibrary LNAI).

Vol. 4029: L. Rutkowski, R. Tadeusiewicz, L.A. Zadeh, J.M. Zurada (Eds.), Artificial Intelligence and Soft Computing – ICAISC 2006. XXI, 1235 pages. 2006. (Sublibrary LNAI).

Vol. 4028: J. Kohlas, B. Meyer, A. Schiper (Eds.), Dependable Systems: Software, Computing, Networks. XII, 295 pages. 2006.